Germanic Heritage Languages in North America

Studies in Language Variation (SILV)

ISSN 1872-9592

The series aims to include empirical studies of linguistic variation as well as its description, explanation and interpretation in structural, social and cognitive terms. The series will cover any relevant subdiscipline: sociolinguistics, contact linguistics, dialectology, historical linguistics, anthropology/anthropological linguistics. The emphasis will be on linguistic aspects and on the interaction between linguistic and extralinguistic aspects — not on extralinguistic aspects (including language ideology, policy etc.) as such.

For an overview of all books published in this series, please see *http://benjamins.com/catalog/silv*

Editors

Peter Auer
Universität Freiburg

Frans Hinskens
Meertens Instituut &
Vrije Universiteit,
Amsterdam

Paul Kerswill
University of York

Editorial Board

Jannis K. Androutsopoulos
University of Hamburg

Arto Anttila
Stanford University

Gaetano Berruto
Università di Torino

Paul Boersma
University of Amsterdam

Jenny Cheshire
University of London

Gerard Docherty
Newcastle University

Penny Eckert
Stanford University

William Foley
University of Sydney

Peter Gilles
University of Luxembourg

Barbara Horvath
University of Sydney

Brian Joseph
The Ohio State University

Johannes Kabatek
Eberhard Karls Universität
Tübingen

Juhani Klemola
University of Tampere

Miklós Kontra
Károli Gáspár University of the
Reformed Church in Hungary

Bernard Laks
CNRS-Université Paris X Nanterre

Maria-Rosa Lloret
Universitat de Barcelona

K. K. Luke
Nanyang Technological
University, Singapore

Rajend Mesthrie
University of Cape Town

Pieter Muysken
Radboud University Nijmegen

Marc van Oostendorp
Meertens Institute & Leiden
University

Sali Tagliamonte
University of Toronto

Johan Taeldeman
University of Gent

Øystein Vangsnes
University of Tromsø

Juan Villena Ponsoda
Universidad de Málaga

Volume 18

Germanic Heritage Languages in North America
Acquisition, attrition and change
Edited by Janne Bondi Johannessen and Joseph C. Salmons

Germanic Heritage Languages in North America

Acquisition, attrition and change

Edited by

Janne Bondi Johannessen
University of Oslo

Joseph C. Salmons
University of Wisconsin

John Benjamins Publishing Company
Amsterdam / Philadelphia

∞™ The paper used in this publication meets the minimum requirements of
the American National Standard for Information Sciences – Permanence
of Paper for Printed Library Materials, ANSI Z39.48-1984.

DOI 10.1075/silv.18

Cataloging-in-Publication Data available from Library of Congress:
LCCN 2015020903 (PRINT) / 2015025427 (E-BOOK)

ISBN 978 90 272 3498 8 (HB)
ISBN 978 90 272 6819 8 (E-BOOK)

© 2015 – John Benjamins B.V.
No part of this book may be reproduced in any form, by print, photoprint, microfilm, or any other means, without written permission from the publisher.

The e-book edition of this book is made available under a CC BY-NC-ND 4.0 license.
http://creativecommons.org/licenses/by-nc-nd/4.0

John Benjamins Publishing Co. · https://benjamins.com

Table of contents

The study of Germanic heritage languages in the Americas   1
   Janne Bondi Johannessen and Joseph Salmons

Part I. Acquisition and attrition

Word order variation in Norwegian possessive constructions:
Bilingual acquisition and attrition   21
   Marit Westergaard and Merete Anderssen

Attrition in an American Norwegian heritage language speaker   46
   Janne Bondi Johannessen

Reexamining Icelandic as a heritage language in North America   72
   Birna Arnbjörnsdóttir

Part II. Phonetic and phonological change

Heritage language obstruent phonetics and phonology:
American Norwegian and Norwegian-American English   97
   Brent Allen and Joseph Salmons

The history of front rounded vowels in New Braunfels German   117
   Marc Pierce, Hans C. Boas and Karen Roesch

Part III. (Morpho-)syntactic and pragmatic change

Functional convergence and extension in contact: Syntactic
and semantic attributes of the progressive aspect in Pennsylvania Dutch   135
   Joshua R. Brown and Michael Putnam

Hybrid verb forms in American Norwegian and the analysis
of the syntactic relation between the verb and its tense   161
   Tor A. Åfarli

Discourse markers in the narratives of New York Hasidim:
More V2 attrition   178
   Zelda Kahan Newman

Part IV. Lexical change

Maintaining a multilingual repertoire: Lexical change
in American Norwegian 201
Lucas Annear and Kristin Speth

How synagogues became *shuls*: The boomerang effect
in Yiddish-influenced English, 1895–2010 217
Sarah Bunin Benor

Phonological non-integration of lexical borrowings
in Wisconsin West Frisian 234
Todd Ehresmann and Joshua Bousquette

Borrowing modal elements into American Norwegian:
The case of *suppose(d)* 256
Kristin Melum Eide and Arnstein Hjelde

Part V. Variation and real-time change

Changes in a Norwegian dialect in America 283
Arnstein Hjelde

On two myths of the Norwegian language in America:
Is it old-fashioned? Is it approaching the written Bokmål standard? 299
Janne Bondi Johannessen and Signe Laake

Coon Valley Norwegians meet Norwegians from Norway: Language,
culture and identity among heritage language speakers in the U.S. 323
Anne Golden and Elizabeth Lanza

Variation and change in American Swedish 359
Ida Larsson, Sofia Tingsell and Maia Andréasson

On the decrease of language norms in a disintegrating language 389
Caroline Smits and Jaap van Marle

Index of languages and dialects 407

Index of names 409

Index of subjects 415

The study of Germanic heritage languages in the Americas

Janne Bondi Johannessen and Joseph Salmons
University of Oslo / University of Wisconsin–Madison

1. Introduction*

This volume grows from recent collaboration among a group of scholars working on Germanic immigrant languages spoken in North America, initially faculty and students working on German dialects and Norwegian, and steadily expanding since to cover the family more broadly. More structured cooperation began with a small workshop at the University of Wisconsin–Madison in 2010 and continued with larger workshops sponsored in turn by the University of Oslo, Pennsylvania State University, University of Iceland, and University of California, Los Angeles.[1] The volume you're reading is the first group publication in English (though see Johannessen and Salmons 2012 for a collection of papers on and written in Norwegian), and several others are in preparation. Most of the papers included in this volume have grown from the ongoing set of international workshops just sketched. These were started by the co-editors, led initially by the first co-editor, a trajectory reflected in the relatively heavy representation of work on Norwegian. A number of the chapters have been developed specifically from these networks and ongoing dialogues about heritage languages.

This introduction has three simple aims, namely to provide for this volume: (1) the scholarly context, in terms of traditional work on Germanic immigrant languages in North America, (2) an overview of how we see the contributions cohering around the themes in our subtitle, and (3) some basic, brief background on the languages under discussion.

---

*   The work was partly supported by the Research Council of Norway through its Centres of Excellence funding scheme, project number 223265, and through its funding of the project NorAmDiaSyn, project number 218878, under the BILATGRUNN/FRIHUM scheme.

1.   Programs from the four workshops held to date are available here: http://tekstlab.uio.no/WILA5/index.html

DOI 10.1075/silv.18.001int
© 2015 John Benjamins Publishing Company

2. Immigrant languages and heritage languages

Work on immigrant languages in North America, Germanic and otherwise, has a long and rich history, including work by important figures in the broader field of linguistics, including Einar Haugen, Max and Uriel Weinreich and more recently Joshua Fishman. The figures just named, widely cited to this day, played tremendous roles in understanding both the effect of language contact in such bilingual settings and the way languages have been maintained or populations have shifted to English. But aside from the work of a few such giants, until recently research on immigrant languages in North America has overwhelmingly been very local, often focused on identifying dialect patterns and possible 'base dialects' or cataloguing examples of contact. Today, the context has been transformed, thanks to strong connections to synchronic linguistic theory (notably Putnam 2011 for German varieties), as well as to language contact studies, sociolinguistics and historical linguistics (see the references to virtually any chapter in this book).

In the aftermath of immigration, new generations often speak "heritage languages," a recent notion that Rothman (2009: 159) defines this way: "A language qualifies as a heritage language if it is a language spoken at home or otherwise readily available to young children, and crucially this language is not a dominant language of the larger (national) society." Under this and similar definitions, the immigrant languages we treat here are clearly 'heritage languages.' Heritage languages have only recently become a major topic of interest among linguists (as noted by Polinsky and Kagan 2007), explored for their implications for linguistic theory, especially in terms of acquisition, attrition and change. Still, the current wave of work is new enough that little comparative research has been undertaken. In that regard in particular, we hope to advance both more traditional work on immigrant languages and the still emerging 'heritage language' linguistics.

3. Acquisition, attrition and change

This book presents a wide range of new empirical findings about heritage languages, focused on varieties of Germanic languages spoken in the North American context. Theoretically, the volume coheres by a focus on the critical issues that underlie the notion of 'heritage language': acquisition, attrition and change. Specifically, much research on heritage languages has debated the role of 'incomplete acquisition' versus 'attrition,' within the broader context of the psycholinguistics and sociolinguistics of bilingualism, along with the effects of language contact (see Grosjean 2008, Montrul 2008, Polinsky and Kagan 2007, Rothman 2009).

The basic idea behind this volume is twofold. First we provide theoretically-informed discussion of heritage language processes across a range of subfields – traditional 'modules' of grammar, plus sociolinguistic and historical and contact settings. Second, we provide relatively broad coverage of Germanic languages in North America in a variety of different settings. Theoretically, the volume includes a wide variety of frameworks and approaches, spanning synchronic and diachronic studies, acoustic phonetics, corpus-oriented work, and language-contact theoretic work. Papers cover a variety of subfields, including phonetics-phonology, morphology and syntax, the lexicon, and sociolinguistics. Empirically, chapters cover a broad range of Germanic varieties spoken in North America: Dutch, German, Pennsylvania Dutch, Icelandic, Norwegian, Swedish, Yiddish, and West Frisian, along with attention to varieties of English spoken by heritage speakers and communities after language shift.

Despite some notable exceptions, as already hinted at above, a major shortcoming of traditional work on heritage languages is that work on a given community has been done all too often in isolation from related work on other languages and sometimes with little regard for goals beyond documenting a local variety. This volume collects work that moves past precisely these two boundaries. We have worked to provide close coordination, sharing of drafts and open discussion to build on the foundation created by the workshops. We trust that this has helped create a more comparative perspective built by specialists in each relevant language and creating a more cohesive volume than is typical for edited volumes.

We will forgo here the usual summaries of each chapter, instead providing a brief discussion of how they address the themes in our subtitle (i.e., acquisition, attrition and change). To the last first, every contribution to the volume deals pretty directly with linguistic change over time.

The two chapters by Westergaard and Anderssen and by Johannessen both see attrition in the context of acquisition, while Arnbjörnsdóttir focuses more singularly on the attrition and change perspective. **Westergaard and Anderssen** directly address acquisition – comparing child language acquisition patterns with patterns of use found in American Norwegian and with an eye to attrition as well. The data are discussed in terms of general concepts such as frequency and complexity, and the authors suggest that while complexity is more important in acquisition, high frequency of a construction protects against attrition. **Johannessen**'s case study of attrition in one speaker of American Norwegian compares the degree of apparent attrition with the steps of acquisition. **Arnbjörnsdóttir** takes stock of a language long understudied as an immigrant language, but to which tremendous attention is now being devoted. Her main ambition is to identify different patterns of attrition and change in American and European Icelandic.

The phonetics and phonology papers show two very different ways of approaching this field: Allen and Salmons use acoustic measurements, while Pierce et al. base their findings on descriptions and impressionistic interpretations of recordings, i.e., without acoustic analysis. **Allen and Salmons** document phonetic realizations of obstruents in English and Norwegian acoustically, thus also documenting a change that has occurred in the English language of the Norwegian heritage areas. **Pierce et al.** study the loss of rounding in front vowels in New Braunfels German and find that multiple factors brought about this change, all motivations widely accepted in historical linguistics.

The change in the morphosyntax of three different heritage languages is described differently in three papers. Brown and Putnam as well as Åfarli look to the principled grammatical system for explanations, while Kahan Newman assumes a pure borrowing approach. **Brown and Putnam** study an extension of the progressive aspect in Pennsylvania Dutch (also known as Pennsylvania German) which has gone beyond the range of the progressive in English. They use this change to document that convergence in language contact is not a simple one-to-one mapping between languages. **Åfarli** proposes a theoretical account for the fact that although English words are borrowed into American Norwegian, they are usually adapted to Norwegian grammar; they do not bring with them English morphosyntax. **Kahan Newman** finds changes in the syntax of Hassidic New York Yiddish to the effect that these varieties use less subject-verb inversion than expected. She attributes this to a movement towards the English word order norm.

Vocabulary change is assumed to be constrained by the human cognitive capacity in both Annear and Speth's chapter and in Eide and Hjelde's chapter, while Benor looks at changes in the vocabulary from the point of view of ethnic identity. Ehresmann and Bousquette, like Benor, argue that social factors account for their vocabulary findings. **Annear and Speth** examine the vocabulary of American Norwegian and discover that lexical convergence tends toward overlap in phonemic shape as well as semantics, reducing the cognitive load of the speakers. **Benor** studies changes in Yiddish-influenced English among American Jews. It turns out that there is not an ever smaller Yiddish substrate in English, but a boomerang effect, where some loanwords are increasing in use among American Jews. This is explained sociolinguistically, by speakers embracing their identity. **Ehresmann and Bousquette** focus on West Frisian in Wisconsin, and particularly on the frequency and linguistic integration of loanwords. The number of loanwords was relatively low in their corpus, and they were not well integrated. The authors argue that the social context of controlled bilingualism, as well as a multiple-lexicon coordinate bilingualism model, account for their findings. **Eide and Hjelde** describe the borrowing of a modal verb from English into Norwegian as typical of borrowings in contact situations, where modal expressions are often borrowed. The way it has been borrowed points toward convergence.

The final chapters treat variation and real-time change, where all but Lanza and Golden study their respective heritage languages in a comparative, chronological perspective. **Hjelde** deals with the development of phonology, morphology and vocabulary among American Norwegians in a small area of Wisconsin originally populated by immigrants with different Norwegian dialect backgrounds. He shows that the language of the youngest generation seems to have developed towards a common form, i.e., a koiné. **Johannessen and Laake** focus on vocabulary, morphology and syntax, asking whether American Norwegian is old-fashioned and whether it has changed toward a written standard. They compare their findings with the language found in a European Nordic dialect corpus and a written language corpus, and find that both questions must be answered negatively. **Lanza and Golden** focus on identity construction in the presentation and positioning of self in social experiences related to migration, language learning and use and literacy among elderly third generation speakers of American Norwegian. **Larsson, Tingsell** and **Andréasson** investigate American Swedish and find that particularly in the vocabulary, there has been development towards a koiné. Many speakers nonetheless have features otherwise connected to second language acquisition, which they attribute to language acquisition rather than attrition. **Smits and van Marle** look for possible differences between American Dutch and Standard Dutch, using data from acceptability tests and recorded conversations. What they found was a reduced form of Dutch and speakers who were uncertain about the norms. Their spontaneous speech was closer to the standard than their grammar evaluations, possibly due to self-imposed restrictions when they were speaking.

4. Background on Germanic immigrant languages in North America

Because so much current work on Germanic immigrant languages, and heritage languages in the broader sense, has been insular (if that pun can be forgiven), we provide a simple comparative sketch here, some basic information on the languages treated in the present book, to set up the individual discussions that follow. The languages investigated in the volume come from both branches of Germanic spoken today, West Germanic – represented here by German, Pennsylvania Dutch, Yiddish, West Frisian, and Dutch – and North Germanic – represented by Norwegian, Swedish, and Icelandic.

First, consider some basic numbers reported by the US Census and the American Community Survey on languages spoken in the US (and we consciously restrict this discussion to the US for simplicity). The decennial census of the United States has long included questions about language use, though which languages were tallied and how they were defined vary widely by decade. For instance, no clear distinction is made in many cases between German and Pennsylvania Dutch, though the 2000 US Census did make the distinction. 'Frisian' was surely reported mostly by people who speak or spoke West Frisian, the indigenous language of the northern Netherlands, but there are also North Frisian (with great dialectal diversity) and East Frisian, not mutually intelligible with West Frisian. Moreover, the Census questions asked vary significantly, even aside from sampling (where language questions applied to foreign-born or the whole population, for instance). In 1910 and 1920, people were asked whether they could speak English and if they could not, the language spoken was reported for those over 10 years of age. This is tremendously valuable for tracking monolingualism (see Wilkerson and Salmons 2008 and 2012 for Germans in Wisconsin), though less so for tracking use in bilingual households. Waggoner (1981) lays out the basics for later years, with the 1940 question phrased in terms of the "language spoken in earliest childhood" while the 1970 question was "What language, other than English, was spoken in this person's home when he was a child?" (Waggoner 1981: 487). That change in the relevant question is no doubt connected with the large jump in the 1970 numbers in Table 1. Keeping in mind the sometimes severe limits of census data (on which see especially Veltman 1983), they provide a first look at how widespread Germanic immigrant languages have been. The three tables below give snapshots from the Census and the most recent information from the American Community Survey (http://www.census.gov/hhes/socdemo/language/ and related links on that site).

Table 1. Reported numbers of speakers over time (Census, data drawn from Fishman 1991:47).

Mother tongue	1940	1960 (est.)	1970	% Change 1940–70
Norwegian	81,160	–	204,822	152.37
Swedish	33,660	17,000	113,119	236.06
Danish	9,100	6,000	29,089	219.66
Dutch	65,800	74,000	102,777	56.20
German	518,780	383,000	1,460,130	181.45
Yiddish	52,980	39,000	170,174	221.20

Table 2. 2000 US Census, home language.

English only	215,423,555
German	1,382,615
Pennsylvania Dutch	83,720
Yiddish	178,945
Dutch	150,485
Afrikaans	16,010
Frisian	920
Luxembourgian	830
Swedish	67,655
Danish	33,395
Norwegian	55,465
Icelandic	5,660
Faroese	70

Table 3. American Community Survey 2011.

Population 5 years and over	
Spoke only English at home	230,947,071
German	1,083,637
Yiddish	160,968
Other West Germanic	290,461
Scandinavian languages	135,025

Even allowing for inaccuracies and inconsistencies across the surveys, these numbers reflect a highly dynamic situation. In part, these numbers will reflect the shift to English in long-settled immigrant communities, like many of those discussed in this volume, balanced against the arrivals of new immigrants.

Second, we supplement those numbers with an outline of some salient issues about each language:

- Period of immigration, size of migrant population
- Dialectal variation, koiné formation
- Institutional support and role of standard
- Basic community demographics, age of youngest speakers / robustness of transmission; language shift.[2]

These brief sections are simply arranged alphabetically.

4.1 Dutch[3]

Dutch immigration to North America came in two waves. The first, the First Immigration, relates to the founding of New Netherlands in the early 17th century. Dutch immigrants settled in the territory now part of New York and New Jersey. Dutch continued to be spoken in these areas for 300 years. However, all present-day Dutch-American communities are in the Midwest and date to the 19th century, the Second Immigration. The most important early Dutch settlements are Pella in Iowa, the Holland area in Michigan and the Waupun-Alto area in Wisconsin. All stem from the late 1840s. Nearly all were orthodox Calvinists. In the case of Iowa and Michigan, the Dutch settlers travelled to the US under the leadership of a minister. At the same time, a group of Roman Catholic immigrants went to Wisconsin, where they settled in the Little Chute area. They travelled under the leadership of a priest. According to Swierenga (2000), between 1835 and 1880 75,000–100,000 Dutch migrated to the US. The majority of the Protestants who went to Iowa came from the western parts of the Netherlands, while those who went to Michigan came from the eastern areas. The Roman Catholic immigrants came from the southern parts of the Netherlands. In the smaller settlements in Michigan and Wisconsin, the original dialects (eastern in the former case, eastern and southern in the latter) have been largely maintained for

---

2. The sections on German and Norwegian were written by the authors of this introduction while information and prose for the others were contributed by the following authors and then integrated into the paper by the editors: Jaap Van Marle on Dutch, Birna Arnbjörnsdóttir on Icelandic, Mike Putnam and Josh Brown on Pennsylvania Dutch, Ida Larsson on Swedish, Joshua Bousquette and Todd Ehresmann on West Frisian, Sarah Benor with assistance from Zelda Kahan Newman on Yiddish.

3. For a recent overview, see Krabbendam (2009).

a considerable period of time. In other cases, particularly in 'mixed' settlement areas including other immigrant groups, Dutch was given up more quickly.

Around the turn of the 20th century, a mixed 'Yankee Dutch' developed as a group code of the acculturating Dutch in American big cities such as Grand Rapids. In this mixed code, Dutch sounds and grammar were retained, whereas its word stock came to be heavily influenced by English. In Iowa, Dutch-Americans switched to the spoken standard language gradually developing in the Netherlands in the second half of the 19th century – a trend also found in the other Dutch settlements, if more sporadically.

The Dutch language was intimately linked to the Dutch Calvinist tradition. As a consequence, many immigrants felt a deep love for their native language and quite a few of the early immigrants refused to learn English. Also, in some churches Dutch was maintained relatively long and it was taught in many schools. In addition, there were many newspapers and other types of publications in Dutch. However, in the course of the 20th century, Dutch developed more and more into an informal, exclusively spoken in-group language. At present, only a handful of speakers are left, all in their eighties.

4.2 German[4]

German speakers may have been coming to North America since at least the Jamestown settlement in the early 17th century. Leaving aside the communities that came to speak Pennsylvania Dutch (on which see below), though, the roots of contemporary German-speaking communities typically go back to the 1830s or later, with some groups arriving after World War II. German speakers of course continue to come to the US and sometimes settle in established German communities. German speakers were the largest non-English speaking immigrant population among the Germanic languages; millions came, mostly before a German nation state was established in 1871. Particularly large populations settled across the entire Midwest, across the Great Plains and in Texas, but significant pockets exist or existed in the northeast and parts of the South. Essentially every dialect area is represented – just in Wisconsin, Swiss dialects, Rhenish and Low German dialects are still spoken, reaching from the southwestern part of German-speaking Europe through the west and on to the northeastern corner.

In various communities, koinés (in the sense of Kerswill 2002 or Kerswill and Trudgill 2005) began to form, and often reached significant degrees of leveling, though Nützel (2009) provides one striking example of a community where virtually

---

4. This immigrant group is too large and diverse to give a reasonable sketch. Indeed, many of the 'German' varieties spoken are not mutually intelligible with the standard language called 'German' and many speakers came from areas far from contemporary Germany, especially eastern Europe. See Gilbert (1971) and Salmons (1993) for some basics on the bigger picture, along with the myriad individual studies cited throughout this book.

no leveling took place in over a century and a half. The role of the standard likewise varied, from a full range of institutional support including German-medium schooling, so that standard-like German was learned and used, to settings where the standard was overwhelmingly absent. More uniform is the pattern of shift, where communities (aside from religious groups like Pennsylvania Dutch-speaking Old Order Anabaptists [again, see below] or Hutterites) have reached their last generation of native speakers, who are typically older than 60. A burgeoning literature seeks to understand language shift here in terms of a 'verticalization' model, i.e., a shift of control over local institutions to non-local powers (Frey 2013, Lucht manuscript, Salmons 2002, 2005a, 2005b, others).

4.3 Icelandic

The history of the Icelandic settlement in North America is somewhat unique in that the original immigrants came to the new world with the intention of forming a 'New Iceland'. 15,000 Icelanders (out of about 70,000 inhabitants at the time) are thought to have settled in the United States and Canada from 1873 to 1914 (Kristjánsson 1983). Icelanders settled mainly in the Canadian Interlake region north of Winnipeg in Manitoba and around Wynyard in Northern Saskatchewan, and in Pembina County in North Dakota in the United States, and more recently, on the West Coast of Canada and the United States.

The variety of Icelandic spoken in the Icelandic settlements of North America has few speakers under 60. The number of heritage speakers of Icelandic is not known, but according to the Canadian Census from 1986 14,470 persons in Canada as a whole claimed Icelandic ethnic origins and of those, 6,980 lived in Manitoba. Of the 6,980 in Manitoba, 305 claimed that Icelandic was their first language and 800 said that they had grown up with English and Icelandic as home languages. In 1986 there is a dramatic decline in numbers from previous censuses and in the Canadian census from 2006, only a little over 2000 individuals claimed that they spoke (North American) Icelandic.[5]

During the first decade in Canada the Icelandic settlers had their own government, laws, schools and newspapers. Many second and third generation North American Icelanders could read and write Icelandic. Travel to and from Iceland was almost non-existent from 1914 until 1975, when regular excursion flights began between Winnipeg and Iceland. Despite the physical isolation, the 'New Icelanders' kept abreast of current events in Iceland through their Icelandic newspapers and extensive letter writing. Yet the Icelanders had social mobility and from very early on had representatives in education, politics, business and medicine. Bilingualism and biculturalism were encouraged and this served North American Icelanders well.

---

5. http://www76.statcan.gc.ca/stcsr/query.html?style=emp&andqt=Icelandic&andcharset=iso-8859-1&andqm=1

The survival of the language is interesting as there has been no continuation of immigration after 1914 until recently, and thus not a constant influx of new immigrants to sustain the language. The North American Icelandic of those who learned the language 'at their mother's knee' shows signs of influence from English in the lexicon, phonology, morphology and syntax as well as signs of attrition (Arnbjörnsdóttir 2006).

Recently, a new comprehensive multidisciplinary research project on North American Icelandic was launched with funding from the Icelandic Centre for Research. Its goal is to examine North American Icelandic as a heritage language from linguistic and cultural perspectives.

4.4 Norwegian

The first Norwegians arrived in New York in 1825, but it was not until some decades later that the number of immigrants really rose. By 1930, 810,000 had arrived in the US and 40,000 in Canada. No country except Ireland had a higher rate of emigration. Einar Haugen (1953: 29) writes that the 1800s was a century of huge population growth in Norway, and the number of immigrants equaled the 1800 population. Many immigrants came from agricultural and backgrounds, and chose the Midwest as their new homeland: Illinois, Iowa, Wisconsin, Minnesota and the Dakotas. New arrivals typically started with very little, and their first shelter was often reported to be a "lowly sod hut or the ramshackle log cabin" (Haugen 1953: 30). Even with this harsh start, Norwegians quickly built institutions that were important to them. They organized and built churches, hospitals, old peoples' homes, and established Luther College (Decorah, Iowa) as early as in 1861, and St. Olaf College (Northfield, Minnesota) in 1875. There were Norwegian-language schools, and newspapers, such as *Decorah-Posten* and *Nordisk Tidende*.

All dialect groups were represented in the immigrant population, but they tended to engage in chain migration and settle together. According to Haugen (1953: 340), the first immigrants were from the Norwegian west coast county Rogaland, and later groups followed as news of prospects in America arrived. In 1850 large numbers came from the Norwegian east country and valley regions. Those from the east and the west had little contact with each other. Recent publications (Johannessen and Laake 2012, and forthcoming) show that mainly these eastern varieties are spoken today. It may even be true to say that a koiné has emerged, based on east Norwegian dialects. In 2010 a project supported by the Research Council of Norway was formed, with the documentation of the American Norwegian language as one of its goals. It turned out to be very difficult to find speakers with dialects from the Norwegian west coast area after 2010. Descendants of immigrants who settled before 1920 who speak Norwegian, are typically older than 70.

4.5 Pennsylvania Dutch

The Pennsylvania Dutch community traces its origins to central Europeans who immigrated to pre-Revolutionary America. By the end of the seventeenth century, William Penn and his fellow Quakers had founded their 'Holy Experiment' of Pennsylvania in the New World and welcomed their first group of German and Dutch immigrants (Mennonites). The group settled just outside of Philadelphia in Germantown and proclaimed Francis Daniel Pastorius its leader. Pastorius and Penn worked together to welcome new immigrants to cultivate the area. Thus began a 'great migration' to Pennsylvania, stretching from 1683 to 1775 (Louden 1988: 72). Estimates are that 81,000 immigrants settled the historic Pennsylvania Dutch region (Wokeck 1999). With them, the immigrants brought their own dialects, from which developed what is today known as Pennsylvania Dutch. Most scholars define Pennsylvania Dutch as a language which most closely resembles the varieties of the eastern Palatinate, but with some influence from Alemannic, other German dialects, and English (Haldeman 1870: 80, Buffington 1939: 276). There are three distinct groups of Pennsylvania Dutch: (1) nonsectarians, members of the Lutheran, Reformed, Schwenkfelder and related Protestant denominations, (2) sectarians, members of one of the Anabaptist groups, either Amish or Mennonite, and (3) the Moravians, often described as being somewhere (religiously and socially) between the sectarians and nonsectarians. Most research, following Huffines (1980), separates Pennsylvania Dutch speakers into sectarians and nonsectarians due to the linguistic and marked sociocultural differences.

Today, there are nearly 300,000 native speakers of Pennsylvania Dutch, almost all Old Order Amish (270,000) and Team Mennonites, as nearly all Old Orders speak Pennsylvania Dutch as their first language and learn English upon entering school. For an immigrant population to maintain a heritage language for centuries on foreign soil especially in the US is extraordinarily unusual, and the number of speakers is growing today thanks to population growth in these communities. Socioreligious isolation (e.g., Kloss 1966) played an important role in the maintenance of Pennsylvania Dutch for the earlier generations, but an increase in urbanization and integration into societal fabric of the nonsectarians led to incipient language shift. Today, most nonsectarian speakers are elderly, heavily attrited native speakers. The prominent connection between Pennsylvania Dutch and ethnoreligious identity remains the primary reason for its survival into the twenty-first century (Johnson-Weiner 1998, Louden 2006). For most of its history, Pennsylvania Dutch has been almost exclusively an oral language, however efforts to standardize its orthography and structure exist and are primarily geared toward language revival on the part of remaining nonsectarian speakers of the dialect (Frey 1985, Beam et al. 2004).

4.6 Swedish

The first wave of emigration from Sweden took place in the 1840s, and the rate of emigration rose after crop failures at the end of the 1860s. By 1930, when the period of mass migration came to an end, more than a million Swedes had left. Most Swedish emigrants settled in the Midwest, with the largest concentration in Minnesota and Illinois. Although the majority came from rural areas, around a fourth came from towns, and around a third of them settled in American cities like Chicago (Beijbom 1971:11). The Swedish language was preserved longer in rural settlements with a high density of Swedish speakers. This is where we find most heritage speakers today, with most now over 70.

All Swedish dialect areas were represented among the emigrants, and there is clear evidence of dialect leveling and koiné formation among the first and second generation American-Swedes. Standard Swedish has had some influence, particularly through the written language and churches. Religious organizations established hospitals and colleges like Augustana in Illinois, and Gustavus Adolphus in Minnesota, and published both religious literature and journals in Swedish. The shift to English starts in the 1920s, and, in the public domain, it is more or less complete by the end of World War II. The Augustana Book Concern published 90 titles in Swedish between 1891–1895, with editions of over 300,000. The numbers drop from 1921 onwards, and after 1937 books and journals are published in English, with few exceptions. In 1921, 85% of the sermons in the Augustana Synod were held in Swedish, but from the middle of the 1930s, English can be considered the dominant language of Augustana (Hasselmo 1974:57–58). Other organizations experienced parallel developments. For people with a Swedish heritage born after World War II, Swedish is generally a foreign language, and it is taught as such at some of the colleges.

4.7 West Frisian

The history of West Frisian immigration to the United States is closely tied to that of Dutch, its political and linguistic neighbor. Both share a history of relatively low out-migration compared to many other European groups, especially for a region with such relatively high population density: while there were roughly 80,000 Dutch in the United States when the nation was formed, overseas emigration of combined Dutch and Frisians between 1820 and 1920 totaled 272,882 individuals (Van Hinte and Swieringa 1985). Separating the West Frisian records from the Dutch proves difficult, though the best available data suggest that emigration from Friesland was much higher per capita than the national average (Galema 1996:59).

Frisian settlement was highly concentrated. Major rural communities were founded in Randolph, Friesland and La Crosse, Wisconsin, and Orange City and Pella, Iowa, and elsewhere. In 1900 these communities included between 127 and 533 first- and second-generation Frisians (Galema 1996:126–127). Even though such raw numbers are low, local concentrations constituted a majority of the municipality (Bousquette and Ehresmann 2010: 260). Frisian emigration to Wisconsin took place relatively late and was short-lived. It peaked around 1880–1910 and then experienced a resurgence following World War II. Some of the Frisians who came over are still alive. In the first half of the 20th century, Frisian was the majority language in Columbia County, WI, with 15% of the population of Friesland, WI, reporting in the 1910 census as monolingual Frisian speakers; extrapolation of the data finds that over 55% of the community was likely proficient in West Frisian (Bousquette and Ehresmann 2010: 262). Today, there are less than two dozen living speakers in and around Friesland, WI.

A bi- or multi-lingual situation was defined by a separation of language domains, with Frisian as the language of everyday informal interaction, English as the language of school instruction, and Dutch and English as church languages. This situation mirrors the bilingual situation of the European Frisians before emigration, where Dutch was the language of school instruction. With immigration, English supplanted Dutch in church and school. Galema suggests that this may have occurred in the first generation of US-born Frisians (1996: 198). The last Dutch sermon was given in the 1990s. Turning to print media, a number of Dutch newspapers were printed in Michigan and Iowa. Frisian was exclusively a spoken variety.

4.8 Yiddish

Millions of Jews in Central and Eastern Europe spoke Yiddish, and a large percentage of them immigrated to the United States between 1880 and 1920. While the majority settled in New York, especially on the Lower East Side of Manhattan, there were also pockets of Yiddish speakers elsewhere. After World War II, many Yiddish-speaking survivors of the Nazi Holocaust, including many Hasidim and other Haredim (strictly Orthodox Jews), settled in the New York area.

The vast majority of descendants of the first wave of immigration (which ranged from secular to Orthodox) shifted to English within a few generations (Fishman 1981). The same is true for most of the non-Hasidic Yiddish speakers who immigrated after World War II. But many descendants of Hasidic immigrants have maintained Yiddish as a primary language of communication, especially among men (Isaacs 1999, Fader 2009), no doubt because they tend to live in insular communities and eschew elements of secular society. Due to high birth rates and communal retention, the number of Yiddish-speaking Hasidim has increased rapidly in the past few decades (Barrière 2013).

Among non-Hasidic Jews, the majority of Yiddish speakers today are elderly Holocaust survivors, and only a few dozen families have transmitted Yiddish to subsequent generations. In addition, Yiddish is still a language of instruction in some non-Hasidic Haredi yeshivas (religious educational institutions for boys and young men). Although over 150,000 people in the United States speak Yiddish today (Shin and Kominsky 2010: 6–7), there is a discourse of language endangerment among non-Hasidic Yiddish enthusiasts (Avineri 2012).

Eastern Yiddish (in contrast with the obsolete Western Yiddish, which was spoken in Germany and the Netherlands) is divided into three major dialects: Northeastern (considered the standard), Central, and Southeastern (Katz 1988, Jacobs 2005). These dialects differ mostly at the level of phonology along with some morphosyntactic distinctions. Yiddish speakers who immigrated between 1880 and 1920 spoke various dialects, and most Hasidim speak Central Yiddish (except Lubavitch Hasidim, who speak Northeastern Yiddish), with a large lexical component from Hebrew and Aramaic.

Today, among non-Hasidic Jews, there are several organizations dedicated to Yiddish, including Yugntruf, Yiddish Farm, League for Yiddish, Yiddishkayt LA, and Workmen's Circle. Some of these groups deal with Yiddish as a postvernacular language (Shandler 2006, Avineri 2012), while others focus on transmitting Yiddish as a vernacular. The YIVO Institute for Jewish Research – founded in Vilna in 1925 and based in New York since 1940 – has played a major role in the standardization of the language through research and publications.

5. Concluding remarks

Since we began this project, the Workshops on Immigrant Languages in the Americas have become a regular event, with planning presently underway for the 2015 event, to be held at Uppsala University, Sweden. Two further volumes are in planning as well, one each from the third and fourth workshops. When we put together the first little workshop in Madison, we had a hope that it would grow into a network of scholars, but no inkling that it would lead to a regular conference and to a string of volumes. We're excited to see where things go from here.

Finally, we are grateful to many people for making this volume possible, including the editors of the series, the organizers of the previous workshops, and participants. Alyson Sewell has provided invaluable editorial assistance in the last stages of the project. We owe special thanks to all those who reviewed papers so carefully, leading to significant improvements in both style and content and better integration with our overarching themes. The papers have each been reviewed by at least two external reviewers as well as by the present editors. Expert reviewing is of course essential in order to ensure high quality, and we are very grateful to the following linguists for their invaluable comments, in addition to many of the contributors to the volume who helped out as well: Suzanne Aalberse, Karin Aijmer, Gisle Andersen, Kate Burridge, Kersti Börjars, Nanna Haug Hilton, Eric Hoekstra, Rob Howell, Gisela Håkanson, Pavel Iosad, Neil Jacobs, Kristín Jóhannsdóttir, Jóhannes Gísli Jónsson, Merel C. J. Keijzser, Terje Lohndal, B. Venkat Mani, and Alyson Sewell. Some of the papers have been adapted from Norwegian after publication of earlier versions in the

Norwegian Linguistics Journal issue mentioned at the beginning of this chapter; those were reviewed by these scholars who also deserve special thanks: Hans-Olav Enger, Pål Kristian Eriksen, Jan Terje Faarlund, Nina Gram Garmann, Madeleine Halmøy, Kristian Emil Kristoffersen, Björn Lundquist, Helge Lødrup, Klaus Johan Myrvoll, Curt Rice, Andreas Sveen, Kjell Johan Sæbø, Arne Torp, Camilla Wide. All remaining errors should be chalked up to the editors.

References

Arnbjörnsdóttir, Birna. 2006. *North American Icelandic: The Life of a Language*. Winnipeg: University of Manitoba Press.

Avineri, Netta. 2012. *Heritage Language Socialization Practices in Secular Yiddish Educational Contexts: The Creation of a Metalinguistic Community*. Los Angeles, CA: University of California Los Angeles dissertation.

Barrière, Isabelle. 2013. "Lecture on Contemporary Hasidic Yiddish." Presented at the *YIVO*, October.

Beam, C. Richard, et al. 2004. *The Comprehensive Pennsylvania Dutch Dictionary*. Millersville, PA: Center for Pennsylvania German Studies.

Beijbom, Ulf. 1971. *Swedes in Chicago. A Demographic and Social Study of the 1846–1880 Emigration*. Diss. Studia Historica Upsaliensia/Chicago Historical Society. Läromedelsförlagen.

Bousquette, Joshua and Todd Ehresmann. 2010. "West Frisian in Wisconsin: A Historical Profile of Immigrant Language Use in Randolph Township." *It Beaken* 72(1): 247–278.

Buffington, Albert F. 1939. "Pennsylvania German: Its Relation to Other German Dialects." *American Speech* 14: 276–286. DOI: 10.2307/451627

Fader, Ayala. 2009. *Mitzvah Girls: Bringing Up the Next Generation of Hasidic Jews in Brooklyn*. Princeton, NJ: Princeton University Press.

Fishman, Joshua A. (ed). 1981. *Never Say Die: A Thousand Years of Yiddish in Jewish Life and Letters*. The Hague: Mouton. DOI: 10.1515/9783110820805

Fishman, Joshua A. 1991. *Reversing Language Shift*. Clevedon, UK: Multilingual Matters.

Frey, Benjamin. 2013. *Toward a General Theory of Language Shift: A Case Study in Wisconsin German and North Carolina Cherokee*. Madison, WI: University of Wisconsin-Madison dissertation.

Frey, J. William. 1985. *A Simple Grammar of Pennsylvania Dutch*. Lancaster, PA: Brookshire.

Galema, Annemieke. 1996. *Frisians to America 1880–1914: With the Baggage of the Fatherland*. Groningen: REGIO-Projekt Uitgevers.

Gilbert, Glenn G. (ed). 1971. *The German Language in America*. Austin, TX: University of Texas Press.

Grosjean, François. 2008. *Studying Bilinguals*. Oxford: Oxford University Press.

Haldeman, Samuel Stehman. 1870. *Pennsylvania Dutch: A Dialect of South German with an Infusion of English*. London: Trübner & Co.

Hasselmo, Nils. 1974. *Amerikasvenska. En bok om språkutvecklingen i Svensk-Amerika*. (Skrifter utg. av Svenska språknämnden 51). Lund: Esselte.

Haugen, Einar. 1953. *The Norwegian Language in America: A Study in Bilingual Behavior*. 2nd Edition. Bloomington, IN: Indiana University Press.

Huffines, Marion Lois. 1980. "Pennsylvania German: Maintenance and Shift." *International Journal of the Sociology of Language* 25: 43–57.

Isaacs, Miriam. 1999. "Haredi, Haymish and Frim: Yiddish Vitality and Language Choice in a Transnational, Multilingual Community." *International Journal of the Sociology of Language* 138: 9–30.

Jacobs, Neil. 2005. *Yiddish: A Linguistic Introduction*. Cambridge: Cambridge University Press.

Johannessen, Janne Bondi and Joseph Salmons (eds). 2012. *Norsk i Amerika*. Special issue of the *Norsk Lingvistisk Tidsskrift [Norwegian Linguistics Journal]* 2.

Johannessen, Janne Bondi and Signe Laake. 2012. "Østnorsk som norsk fellesdialekt i Midtvesten." *Norsk Lingvistisk Tidsskrift [Norwegian Linguistics Journal]* 30(2): 365–380.

Johannessen, Janne Bondi and Signe Laake. Forthcoming. "Eastern Norwegian as a Common Norwegian Dialect in the American Midwest." *Journal of Language Contact*.

Johnson-Weiner, Karen. 1998. "Community Identity and Language Change in North American Anabaptist Communities." *Journal of Sociolinguistics* 2(3): 375–394. DOI: 10.1111/1467-9481.00051

Katz, Dovid (ed). 1988. *Dialects of the Yiddish Language*. (Winter Studies in Yiddish, vol. 2: Papers from the Second Annual Oxford Winter Symposium in Yiddish Language and Literature, 14–16 December 1986). Oxford: Pergamon Press.

Kerswill, Paul. 2002. "Koineization and Accommodation." In *The Handbook of Language Variation and Change*, ed. by J. K. Chambers, Peter Trudgill and Natalie Schilling-Estes, 669–702. Oxford: Blackwell.

Kerswill, Paul and Peter Trudgill. 2005. "The Birth of New Dialects." In *Dialect Change: Convergence and Divergence in European Languages*, ed. by Peter Auer, Frans Hinskens and Paul Kerswill, 196–220. Cambridge: Cambridge University Press. DOI: 10.1017/CBO9780511486623.009

Kloss, Heinz. 1966. "German-American Language Maintenance Efforts." In *Language Loyalty in the United States: The Maintenance and Perpetuation of Non-English Mother Tongues by American Ethnic and Religious Groups*, ed. by Joshua Fishman, 206–252. Hague: Mouton.

Krabbendam, Hans. 2009. *Freedom on the Horizon: Dutch Immigration to America, 1840–1940*. Grand Rapids, MI: Eerdmans.

Kristjánsson, Júníus. 1983. *Vesturfaraskrá, 1870–1914: A Record of Emigrants from Iceland to America 1870–1914*. Reykjavík: Institute of History, University of Iceland.

Louden, Mark L. 1988. *Bilingualism and Syntactic Change in Pennsylvania German*. Ithaca, NY: Cornell University dissertation.

Louden, Mark L. 2006. "Pennsylvania German in the Twenty-First Century." In *Sprachinselwelten – The World of Language Islands*, ed. by Nina Berend and Elisabeth Knipf-Komlósi, 89–107. Frankfurt: Peter Lang.

Lucht, Felecia. Manuscript. *Life after Language Death: The Effects of Community Change on the History and Future of German in Southeastern Wisconsin*. Wayne State University.

Montrul, Silvia. 2008. *Incomplete Acquisition in Bilingualism: Re-examining the Age Factor*. Amsterdam: John Benjamins. DOI: 10.1075/sibil.39

Nützel, Daniel. 2009. *The East Franconian Dialect of Haysville, Indiana: A Study in Language Death / Die ostfränkische Mundart von Haysville, Indiana: Eine Untersuchung mit ausgewählten morphologischen und syntaktischen Phänomenen*. (Regensburger Dialektforum, vol. 15). Regensburg: Edition Vulpes.

Polinsky, Maria and Olga Kagan. 2007. "Heritage Languages in the 'Wild' and in the Classroom." *Language and Linguistics Compass* 1: 368–395. DOI: 10.1111/j.1749-818X.2007.00022.x

Putnam, Michael T. (ed). 2011. *Studies on German-Language Islands*. Amsterdam: Benjamins. DOI: 10.1075/slcs.123

Rothman, Jason. 2009. "Understanding the Nature and Outcomes of Early Bilingualism: Romance Languages as Heritage Languages." *The International Journal of Bilingualism* 13: 155–163. DOI: 10.1177/1367006909339814

Salmons, Joseph (ed). 1993. *The German Language in America: 1683–1991*. Madison: Max Kade Institute.

Salmons, Joseph. 2002. "The Shift from German to English, World War I, and the German-Language Press in Wisconsin." In *Menschen zwischen zwei Welten: Auswanderung, Ansiedlung, Akkulturation*, ed. by W. G. Rödel and Helmut Schmahl, 179–193. Trier: Wissenschaftlicher Verlag Trier.

Salmons, Joseph. 2005a. "Community, Region and Language Shift in German-Speaking Wisconsin." In *Regionalism in the Age of Globalism, vol. 1: Concepts of Regionalism*, ed. by Lothar Hönnighausen, Marc Frey, James Peacock, and Niklaus Steiner, 129–138. Madison, WI: Center for the Study of Upper Midwestern Cultures.

Salmons, Joseph. 2005b. "The Role of Community and Regional Structure in Language Shift." In *Regionalism in the Age of Globalism, vol. 2: Forms of Regionalism*, ed. by Lothar Hönnighausen, Anke Ortlepp, James Peacock, Niklaus Steiner, and Carrie Matthews (consulting editor), 133–144. Madison, WI: Center for the Study of Upper Midwestern Cultures.

Shandler, Jeffrey. 2006. *Adventures in Yiddishland: Postvernacular Language and Culture*. Berkeley: University of California Press.

Shin, Hyon B. and Robert A. Kominski. 2010. *Language Use in the United States: 2007*. American Community Survey Reports. U.S. Census Bureau. http://www.census.gov/hhes/socdemo/language/data/acs/ACS-12.pdf.

StatCan. www.statcan.gc.cahttp://www76.statcan.gc.ca/stcsr/query.html?style=empandqt=Icelandicandcharset=iso-8859-1andqm=1). Retrieved November 21, 2013.

Swierenga, Robert P. 2000. *Faith and Family: Dutch Immigration and Settlement in the United States, 1820–1920*. New York, London: Holmes and Meier.

Van Hinte, Jacob and Robert P. Swierenga. 1985. *Netherlanders in America: A Study of Emigration and Settlement in the Nineteenth and Twentieth Centuries in the United States of America*. Grand Rapids, MI: Baker Book House.

Van Marle, Jaap. 2001. "The Acculturation of Dutch Immigrants in the USA: A Linguist's view." In *The Dutch Adapting in North America*, ed. by Richard Harms, 18–26. Grand Rapids, Michigan: Calvin College.

Veltman, Calvin. 1983. *Language Shift in the United States*. Berlin: Walter de Gruyter. DOI: 10.1515/9783110824001

Waggoner, Dorothy. 1981. "Statistics on Language Use." In *Language in the USA*, ed. by Charles A. Ferguson and Shirley Brice Heath, 486–515. Cambridge, UK: Cambridge University Press.

Wilkerson, Miranda and Joseph Salmons. 2008. "'Good Old Immigrants of Yesteryear' Who Didn't Learn English: Germans in Wisconsin." *American Speech* 83(3): 259–283. DOI: 10.1215/00031283-2008-020

Wilkerson, Miranda and Joseph Salmons. 2012. "Linguistic Marginalities: Becoming American Without Learning English." *Journal of Transnational American Studies* 4(2). acgcc_jtas_7115. http://www.escholarship.org/uc/item/5vn092kk.

Wokeck, Marianne S. 1999. *Trade in Strangers: The Beginnings of Mass Migration to North America*. University Park, PA: Pennsylvania State University Press.

PART I

Acquisition and attrition

Word order variation in Norwegian possessive constructions
Bilingual acquisition and attrition

Marit Westergaard and Merete Anderssen
UiT The Arctic University of Norway

In Norwegian possessive constructions, the possessive may either precede or follow the noun. Monolingual children initially show a preference for the prenominal possessive construction, although it is much less frequent than the postnominal one in the adult language. A likely explanation is that postnominal possessives are structurally more complex. In this paper, we examine this word order variation in two bilingual populations, Norwegian-English children growing up in Norway and adult Norwegian heritage speakers in the USA. We expected both groups to exhibit a stronger preference for prenominal possessives than the monolingual children due to influence from English. However, we only find this in the bilingual children. One possible explanation is that, while complexity plays a major role in acquisition, high frequency protects against language attrition.

Keywords: Norwegian, Norwegian-English bilinguals, language acquisition, attrition, heritage speakers, possessives, word order, definiteness, frequency, complexity

1. Introduction

Norwegian possessives may be either pre- or postnominal; the two word orders are illustrated in (1)–(2). Postnominal possessives have to co-occur with a noun in the definite form, while this is not possible with prenominal possessives, which must appear with a bare noun.

(1) *min bil* **min bilen*
 my car my car.DEF
 'My car'

(2) bilen   min   *bil min
 car.DEF my   car my
 'My car'

In this paper, we discuss this word order variation and investigate how these structures are acquired by Norwegian-English bilingual children, that is, in a context in which Norwegian is acquired simultaneously with a language that only permits one of the two word orders. We compare these findings with data from monolingual Norwegian children investigated in Anderssen and Westergaard (2010), henceforth referred to as A&W. We also consider how this variation affects the language of bilingual adults in a situation where the second language (English) is extremely dominant, which is the situation for the descendants of Norwegian immigrants in the USA.

According to A&W, monolingual Norwegian children show a preference for prenominal possessive structures at an early stage of the acquisition process, despite the fact that the postnominal possessive is considerably more frequent in child-directed speech, as well as in the adult language generally. As the postnominal possessive is also more complex than the prenominal one (morphologically and syntactically), A&W suggest that complexity has a larger impact on the acquisition process than frequency.

In the present study, we show that bilingual children, like monolinguals, produce predominantly prenominal possessives at an early stage of development. In addition, this preference seems to be stronger and to last longer in the bilingual children. This is in sharp contrast to the Norwegian heritage speakers. Given the strong predominance of English in the linguistic environment of these speakers, we expected the postnominal possessive to be vulnerable to language attrition. Surprisingly, this is not the case.

The paper consists of eight sections. In the next section, we provide a brief overview of the syntactic structure, interpretation and frequency of the two word orders in (1)–(2), and in Section 3 we describe the findings from previous research on first language acquisition of Norwegian. Based on these findings, we make predictions for the present study in Section 4. In Section 5, we describe the data from the bilingual children and provide an overview of the results. Section 6 provides equivalent data from the heritage speakers. In Section 7, we discuss the results of the study in light of three questions related to differences between language acquisition and language attrition. The final section provides a brief summary.

2. Pre- and postnominal possessives: Syntactic structure, interpretation and frequency

As mentioned above, A&W argue that postnominal possessive structures are more complex than prenominal ones. In this section, we start by providing a brief overview of the theoretical assumptions behind this description of these structures. We then consider the interpretation of pre- and postnominal possessives. Finally, we provide an overview of how often the two word orders are used by adult speakers, showing that the postnominal possessive is considerably more frequent than the prenominal one.

2.1 Syntactic structure

The syntactic structure of these two word orders has represented a challenge within theoretical linguistics. One problem has been to come up with an analysis that can derive both pre- and postnominal structures in a manner that explains why the latter has to occur with the suffixal article. There exist a considerable number of studies on Scandinavian DP-structure, and many of these also provide an account of possessive structures; while there still is no generally agreed-upon analysis, some aspects tend to be shared by most accounts. Let us consider some of these.

First, Scandinavian DPs are assumed to have two syntactic positions for determiners. One of these is located higher than attributive adjectives while the other is located lower down in the structure (Taraldsen 1990).[1] The main argument for this assumption is so-called double definiteness, as in *den lille gutten* 'the little boy.DEF' (cf. Vangsnes 1999, Julien 2005, Anderssen 2006). The suffixal article is consequently also assumed to be associated with the lowest of these two positions (Julien 2005, Anderssen 2006). Possessives are taken to be base-generated higher in the structure than the base position of the noun, but lower than the suffixal article. Based on these arguments, the following basic order can be assumed in the DP:

(3) DETERMINER – ADJECTIVE – DETERMINER (suffix) – **POSSESSIVE** – NOUN

Given this structure, the prenominal possessive reflects the basic word order in DPs (4), while the postnominal possessive is derived by moving the noun across the possessive to merge with the determiner (5).

(4)   *min*   *bil*
                      my   car
       (DET- suff)   POSS – NOUN

(5) *bilen*   *min*   ~~*bil*~~
     car.DEF   my   car
     NOUN+DET   POSS   NOUN

Based on this analysis, A&W argue that the structure in (5) is structurally more complex than the one in (4).[2] To produce a prenominal possessive, children can use the

---

1. As this discussion regards basic word order, the higher determiner will always be to the left of the one lower down in the structure, and adjectives will consequently be located to the right of the free determiner and to the left of the suffixal article.

2. Given the assumptions that have been made here about Norwegian DP-structure, it could be argued that the possessive also has to move in some contexts. For example, this seems to be required when the prenominal possessive co-occurs with an attributive adjective (such as in *min grønne bil* 'my green car'). That is, one possible interpretation of these data is that the possessive always has to move to a high position in the DP-structure, also when there is no adjective present. This would challenge the assumption that prenominal possessives are less complex than postnominal ones, as both would be the result of syntactic movement. Irrespective of how these structures

basic word order, while to produce a postnominal structure, the noun has to move past the possessive. Postnominal possessives are also morphologically more complex in that they have to occur with a noun marked for definiteness. Furthermore, postnominal possessive pronouns go against the general word order pattern of (free) determiners in Norwegian, which are typically prenominal.[3] Lødrup (2012: 191–196) also argues that the prenominal word order is the unmarked one, partly because it is sometimes the only possible option. For example, this is the only possible word order in cases when the noun cannot co-occur with the suffixal article (e.g., *mitt Norge* 'my Norway' vs. *Norge mitt 'Norway my'). Similarly, prenominal structures are used in many fixed expressions (e.g., *på min måte* 'in my way' vs. *på måten min 'in way.DEF my').

2.2 The interpretation of pre- and postnominal possessives

Pre- and postnominal possessives are used in different contexts. According to standard Norwegian grammar, e.g., Faarlund et al. (1997: 265), prenominal possessives are emphatic or contrastive, while postnominal possessives have a parenthetical possessive interpretation. This is also reflected in the prosodic structure of the elements involved. In prenominal possessives the possessive pronoun is the most prominent element (*MIN bil* 'my car'), while in postnominal structures, it is the noun that is the most prominent element (*BILEN min* 'car.DEF my'). Lødrup (2011, 2012) captures this difference in terms of information structure and the relationship between strong and weak pronouns. He follows Cardinaletti and Starke's (1999) categorization of pronouns as weak or strong and argues that postnominal possessives are weak, while prenominal possessives are strong. Weak pronouns are typically used with topical information, while strong ones are used with focal information, at least in the spoken language (Lødrup 2012: 197). Furthermore, he shows that while postnominal (topical) possessive pronouns may be contrastive (6a), topical prenominal possessives are in general unacceptable, consider (6b) (both from Lødrup 2012: 197):

(6) a. De stjal **bilen**   HANS.
       they stole car.DEF his
       'They stole HIS boat.'
    b. Ola reparerte **båten**   sin /??sin båt.
       Ola repaired boat.DEF his/   his boat
       'Ola repaired his boat.'

---

are analysed, however, this does not represent a problem for our data, as the Tromsø dialect generally does not allow attribution adjectives with prenominal possessives (see A&W 2010: 2580), except in abstract expressions such as *min største drøm* 'my biggest dream'. Furthermore, the fact remains that prenominal possessive structures can be produced without involving syntactic movement in unmodified cases, while this is never possible with postnominal possessives.

3. We thank an anonymous reviewer for this observation.

This is not the case in written Norwegian, where prenominal possessive structures can also be used with topical possessive pronouns. This is most likely also true of more formal varieties of spoken Norwegian.[4] In the Tromsø dialect, however, prenominal possessives are primarily used with contrastive focus.

A&W (2010: 2580–2581) illustrate the difference between the interpretation of pre- and postnominal possessive structures with authentic examples from a corpus of spontaneous speech, such as (7), where a mother is talking about her daughter:

(7) a. *ja den derre* **jabba** *hennes, den går i ett sett.*
yes that there mouth.DEF her it goes in one set
'Yes, that mouth of hers, it moves non-stop.'
b. *æ hørte* **hennes stemme** *over alle de andre når æ kom....*
I heard her voice over all the others when I came
'I could hear HER voice above all the others when I came (to pick her up).'

In (7a), the mother is referring to her daughter's mouth in a non-contrastive way. The possessive relationship is already known and obvious, and consequently, a postnominal possessive is used. In the second sentence, where the woman is contrasting her daughter's voice with those of the other children, the possessive is focused and emphatic, and hence the prenominal possessive is used.

2.3 The distribution of pre- and postnominal possessives

We have seen that pre- and postnominal possessive structures are used in different contexts, depending on whether the possessive is topical or focal. This difference is also reflected by the fact that the two structures are used with very different frequencies. A&W (2010: 2581) investigated the relative frequency of the two word orders in the data of eight adults in a large child language corpus consisting of almost 73,000 adult utterances (Anderssen 2006), and found that postnominal structures are used at 75% (851/1135), while prenominal possessives only represent 25% (284/1135) of the total number of possessives. Based on the observed distribution, A&W concluded that children acquiring Norwegian (and specifically the Tromsø dialect) are exposed to many more postnominal than prenominal possessives. To ensure that this frequency did not only apply to child-directed speech, we also investigated the proportion of pre- and postnominal possessive structures in *Norsk Talespråkskorpus* (NoTa, the Norwegian Spoken Corpus), which consists of recordings of 166 adult speakers from Oslo. The results of this count confirmed the findings from child-directed speech, as this investigation revealed that prenominal possessives make up 27% (700/2583) of all possessive structures, while postnominal ones represent 73% (1883/2583). As we have

---

4. We use the terms *variety* rather than *dialect* here because we are assuming that topical prenominal possessives are primarily used in higher registers/styles. We return to this point in the next section.

argued that postnominal possessives are more complex due to syntactic movement of the noun past the possessive, we have a (relatively unusual) situation where the most frequent structure is also the most complex one. We now consider which possessive structure monolingual Norwegian children prefer.

3. Possessive structures and monolingual acquisition

As mentioned in the introduction, A&W's goal was to test the relative impact of frequency and complexity, which is a central question within language acquisition research. Furthermore, it is a question that typically distinguishes generative and constructivist theories. Norwegian possessive structures are well suited for this kind of study, due to the fact that these structures allow two word orders, where one, POSS-N, is both less complex and less frequent than the other, N-POSS. Accordingly, we would expect POSS-N to be acquired *before* N-POSS if complexity is the more important factor in language acquisition, but *after* it if frequency plays a more important role. To test this, the distribution of pre- and postnominal possessives was investigated in spontaneous production data of three monolingual children growing up in Tromsø. These child language data come from the Anderssen corpus mentioned in 2.3 above, which consists of almost 47,000 child utterances.

Table 1 (based on Table 9 in A&W 2010: 2582) provides an overview of the distribution of pre- and postnominal possessives in the corpus data of the three monolingual Norwegian children.

Table 1. Number/total and percentage of postnominal possessives (N-POSS) in Norwegian child data.

Child	Period 1 (1;8–2;0)	Period 2 (2,0–2;4)	Period 3 (2;4–2;8)	Period 4 (2;8–3;0)
Ina	0/0 (0%)	8/12 (67%)	37/43 (86%)	84/135 (62)
Ann	0/2 (0%)	10/19 (53%)	27/34 (79%)	20/30 (67%)
Ole	0/5 (0%)	6/14 (43%)	23/31 (74%)	43/105 (41%)
Total	0/7 (0%)	24/45 (53%)	87/108 (81%)	147/270 (54%)

The results reveal that the children have a clear preference for prenominal possessives early on in development. Prenominal possessives are attested in the data of all three children before postnominal ones; that is, before the children reach the age of two, only prenominal possessives are attested in their production. Examples of early prenominal possessives are provided in (8)–(10) (A&W 2010: 2582).

(8) min seng.   (Ann, 1;11.0)
     my bed
     'My bed.'

(9) han er **min mann**. (Ole, 1;10.22)
　　he is my man
　　'It is my man.'

(10) det er **min kjole**. (Ina, 2;1.23)
　　 it is my dress
　　 'It is my dress.'

After the children's second birthday, the first postnominal possessives appear, and between the ages of two (2;0) and two years and four months (2;4), these make up approximately 50%, which is still considerably less than in the adult data (75%). Examples of early postnominal structures are provided in (11)–(13) (A&W 2010: 2582).

(11) sola　　di. (Ann, 2;0.17)
　　 sun.DEF your
　　 'Your sun.'

(12) han være i **skufla**　di. (Ole, 2;0.10)
　　 he be　in shovel.DEF your
　　 '(He (should) be in your shovel.'

(13) nei no dætt ned mannen på **foten**　min. (Ina, 2;1.29)
　　 no now falls down man.DEF on foot.DEF my
　　 'Oh, now the man is falling down on my foot.'

Only when they are between the age of 2;4 and 2;8 do the children use the postnominal possessive as frequently as the adult speakers. At this stage, the children use this word order 81% of the time.[5]

A&W also show that the early predominance of prenominal possessives cannot only be due to a greater propensity on the part of the children to want to put focus on the possessor, even though this may be a contributing factor. The children clearly also use the prenominal possessive in a non-target-consistent way; that is, in situations that are not contrastive. Examples of this are provided in (14) and (15) (A&W 2010: 2583–2584). In both these dialogues, the adult speakers are using postnominal possessives, while the children are using prenominal ones.

(14) Ole: 　her dætt av hjulan.
　　　　　here fall off wheels.DEF
　　　　　'Look, the wheels are falling off.'
　　 Adult: dætt hjulan　　 demmes av?
　　　　　 fall wheels.DEF their　 off
　　　　　 'Are their wheels falling off?'

---

5. The proportion of postnominal possessives decreases again in the fourth period as the recordings from this period contain many more contrastive contexts, cf. A&W 2010: 2584–2585.

	Ole:	ja, **demmes hjula** dætt av.	
		yes their wheels fall off	
		'Yes, their wheels are falling off.'	(Ole, 2;2)
(15)	Adult:	ja eg ser det kjem opp igjennom sugerøret.	
		yes I see it comes up through straw.DEF	
		'Yes, I can see it coming up through the straw.'	
	Ina:	i **min munn.**	
		into my mouth	
		'Into my mouth.'	
	Adult:	ja og opp i munnen din.	
		yes and up into mouth.DEF your	
		'Yes, and up into your mouth.'	(Ina, 2;9)

A&W claim that, on its own, frequency can neither predict the order of acquisition nor the types of errors that children produce. If frequency were the most important factor, we would expect the children to prefer the postnominal possessive. Instead, the least frequent but also least complex word order seems to be acquired first, and according to A&W, this suggests that complexity has a stronger impact on language acquisition, in that less complex structures are acquired before more complex ones.

Other studies of the acquisition of Norwegian have shown that children have an early command of word order variation that is dependent on fine syntactic distinctions or information structure, e.g., Westergaard (2009) on variation between V2 and non-V2 in North Norwegian dialects. In cases where there is a (slight) delay in the acquisition of this variation and the children prefer one of the two word orders, this has been explained with reference to complexity or a principle of economy rather than frequency, e.g., Westergaard and Bentzen (2007) on word order in subordinate clauses and Anderssen, Bentzen, Rodina and Westergaard (2010) on subject and object shift.

4. Hypotheses

So far we have assumed that the postnominal possessive structure is syntactically more complex than the prenominal one due to the movement of the noun past the possessive. We have also shown that the prenominal structure seems to be preferred at an early stage of acquisition by monolingual Norwegian children, even though it is considerably less frequent in the input. Because of this, it is likely that the postnominal possessive structure will be even more vulnerable in bilingual situations, where the other language only has prenominal structures. Consequently, we propose the following hypotheses for bilingual Norwegian-English contexts:

A. The preference for the prenominal possessive construction should be both stronger and last longer in bilingual Norwegian-English children than in monolingual Norwegian children.

B. The postnominal possessive construction should be less frequent in the language of bilingual Norwegian-English adults, where English is the dominant language, than in that of monolingual Norwegian adults.

5. Bilingual acquisition

5.1 Informants and data collection

To test hypothesis A, we have investigated the acquisition of possessive structures in spontaneous production data from two Norwegian-English bilingual children growing up in Tromsø. The two children, Emma and Sunniva, both live in homes in which one of the parents is a native speaker of English; Emma's mother is American and Sunniva's father is British. In both families, English is the home language and is used by both parents when speaking to the child and each other. Norwegian is used everywhere else in society; both children have attended nursery from the age of one and are consequently regularly exposed to Norwegian.

Seven Norwegian recordings were made of both children, but the data collection was quite different in the two cases, which makes it difficult to make direct comparisons. Sunniva was recorded for approximately one year (age: 1;8.8–2;7.24), while Emma was recorded much more intensively in the course of a three-month period (2;7.10–2;10.9). Unfortunately, there are relatively few examples of possessive structures produced by the two children, and as a result, our findings have to be interpreted with some caution.

5.2 Results – overview

Table 2 provides an overview of the distribution of pre- and postnominal possessives in the production of the two Norwegian-English children. Despite the very low number of relevant occurrences, the children's files have been divided into four periods, as was done for the monolingual data in A&W. Data from both children are available in only one of these periods, Period 3.

Table 2. Number/total and percentage of postnominal possessives in bilingual Norwegian-English child data.

Child	Period 1 (1;8–2;0)	Period 2 (2,0–2;4)	Period 3 (2;4–2;8)	Period 4 (2;8–3;0)
Sunniva	4/15 (27%)	2/2 (100%)	1/3 (33%)	NO DATA
Emma	NO DATA	NO DATA	3/10 (30%)	21/25 (84%)
Total	4/15 (27%)	2/2 (100%)	4/13 (31%)	21/25 (84%)

As we can see in Table 2, the development of the bilingual children resembles that of the monolinguals in the sense that they also seem to prefer the prenominal possessive structure at an early stage of development. The data are also different in some ways.

The first of these differences might not be directly relevant, but should nevertheless be commented on: Unlike the monolingual children, Sunniva produces both pre- and postnominal possessives in Period 1 (cf. (16) and (17)), though the latter clearly represent the minority (4/15). It is difficult to explain this difference, other than by referring to individual differences and coincidence: Sunniva seems to be an unusually precocious talker compared to other children. However, despite the fact that she is very advanced for her age linguistically, she seems to acquire target-like use of postnominal possessives somewhat later than the monolingual peers discussed in A&W.

(16) nei, ikke **min kjole**. (Sun, 1;8.8)
 no   not my   dress
 'No, not my dress.'

(17) **baby** min.
 baby my
 'My baby' Target: *babyen min*

The second difference between the bilingual and the monolingual children is that the bilingual children seem to exhibit an even stronger preference for prenominal possessives than the monolinguals, as predicted by Hypothesis A. As illustrated in Table 2, postnominal possessives represent 33.3% (10/30) in Periods 1–3.[6] This proportion is lower than what is reported in A&W for for the monolinguals at the same age, where the average percentage for the first three periods is 69.4% (111/160), cf. Table 1. Thus, the predominance of prenominal possessives may last somewhat longer in the bilingual children's production. This suggests that the development of the bilinguals is slightly delayed compared to the monolingual children. This observation is also compatible with Hypothesis A. Due to the limited data on which this study is based, any conclusions drawn about these results need to be made with caution. However, the results indicate that our hypothesis is confirmed: The bilingual children may have both a stronger and a longer lasting preference for prenominal possessives. If so, it is likely that simultaneous exposure to English possessives enhances the prenominal possessive in Norwegian and causes a stronger dominance of this word order. Thus, frequency does seem to have an impact on the acquisition process, but only indirectly, by prolonging a stage during which one word order is preferred due to its lower complexity. A similar argument has been used to explain the difference in the acquisition of subject and object shift in Norwegian monolinguals (Anderssen et al. 2010).

---

6. Obviously, this is not true of the second period, when only two possessives are produced, both of which are postnominal. Most likely this is a coincidence.

5.3 Similarities between mono- and bilinguals: The overuse of prenominal possessives

We have seen that there are both similarities and differences between mono- and bilingual children with respect to the acquisition of possessive structures. In this connection, it is relevant to ask whether the bilingual children also use prenominal possessives in situations in which postnominal structures would be more appropriate. In Section 2.2 we reported that pre- and postnominal possessives do not have the same interpretation. In postnominal possessives, possessive pronouns are usually topical and make up part of the background of the utterance, while in prenominal possessives, they are focal and the possessive relationship is foregrounded, often contrastively (Faarlund et al. 1997, A&W, Lødrup 2012). In Section 3, we showed that monolingual children struggle with this distinction at an early stage and use prenominal possessives in situations in which the possessive relationship is part of the background of the utterance (topical information). Not surprisingly, the bilingual children also appear to overuse prenominal possessives this way, as illustrated in the following examples.

(18) *den er ikke i min veska.* (Sun, 1;10.16)
   it   is not in my   handbag
   'It is not in my handbag.'

(19) *den tog har æ fått   mi mamma.* (Emm, 2;7.10)
   that train have I received my mummy
   'My mummy gave me that train.'

Accordingly, we can conclude that the preference for prenominal possessives found in the data of the bilingual children cannot be due to a tendency for them to want to foreground the possessive relationship. In this respect mono- and bilingual children behave in a similar way.

5.4 Differences between mono- and bilinguals: Definiteness marking and postnominal possessives

So far, we have seen that both the monolingual and the bilingual children use prenominal possessive structures more than adults, and that some of these structures are pragmatically inappropriate. One striking difference between these two groups relates to definiteness marking. In Section 2.1, we showed that prenominal possessives must be accompanied by nouns in the bare form, while postnominal ones co-occur with definite nouns. The monolingual children rarely make any mistakes with regard to definiteness marking in the two word orders. This is especially true of postnominal possessives, with which the three children Ina, Ann and Ole use bare nouns only 6.7% (10/150), 3.5% (2/57) and 1.4% (1/72) respectively. In prenominal possessive structures, the proportion of non-target-consistent production is slightly higher: Ina, Ann and Ole have definiteness marking on the noun in these structures 11.4% (9/79), 7.1% (2/28) and 4.8% (4/83). The bilingual children, on the other hand, seem to have relatively little trouble with null definiteness marking on prenominal possessives. There is only one example of a prenominal possessive occurring with a noun in the definite form in Emma's data (cf. (20)), representing 9.1% (1/11). Sunniva produces one structure that could be interpreted as containing a definiteness error (cf. (21)), but it is uncertain whether the *-a* ending should be interpreted as a definiteness marker here.[7] It is a possible interpretation based on the fact that in the same file, Sunniva says *xx putte kjola* (put dress.DEF) in what appears to be a definite context. If Example (21) is included, this represents 7.7% (1/13) of Sunniva's prenominal possessives.

(20) æ vil ha < stor ku> [///] **min kua** der oppi. (Emm, 2;8.7)
 I will have big cow my cow.DEF there up-in
 'I want to have my cow in there.'

(21) *min kjola.* (Sun, 1;8.8)
 my dress.DEF?
 'My dress.'

Thus, the bilingual children appear to fall within the variation observed in the data of the monolingual children with respect to definiteness marking on prenominal possessives. All children make between 4.8% and 11.4% errors. In the postnominal possessive structures produced by the bilinguals, however, 32.3% of all the lack the definite suffix. For Emma, these structures represent 33.3% (8/24) and for Sunniva 28.6% (2/7). Examples are provided in (22)–(24) (cf. also (17) above).

(22) og han tok [?] ikke med **kylling min**. (Emm, 2;8.20)
 and he took not with chicken my
 'And he didn't bring my chicken.'

(23) sånn som æ bruke på **finger mi**. (Emm 2;9.11)
 like that I use on finger my
 'Like the type I use on my finger.'

(24) *Noddy min.* (Sun, 1;9.22)
 Noddy my
 'My Noddy.'

Again, the limited data available makes it necessary to draw our conclusions with caution. However, the bilingual children could possibly be distinguished from the monolinguals not only by exhibiting a stronger and more persistent preference for

---

7. *Kjole* 'dress' is a masculine noun in the Tromsø dialect, and the definite form should consequently be *kjole-n* 'dress-the.' The use of *-a* here might be an (unsuccessful) attempt at definiteness marking.

prenominal possessives; they also have somewhat more trouble with definiteness marking on postnominal possessives.[8]

5.5 Intermediate summary

In this section, we have shown that Norwegian-English bilingual children are similar to monolingual children in the sense that both groups show a preference for prenominal possessives. Like monolinguals, bilinguals use prenominal possessives in contexts in which an adult would have used postnominal ones. The goal of the study was to test whether the preference for prenominal possessives would be stronger and more persistent in the bilingual children due to influence from English. The (admittedly very limited) data indicate that this could be the case. The fact that English only has a prenominal possessive construction seems to have the effect that it further enhances the prenominal possessive in Norwegian. Furthermore, it was found that the bilingual children have certain problems with definiteness marking in postnominal possessive structures, which suggests that they do not only prefer the least complex structure (the prenominal one), but also disprefer postnominal structures, possibly because they require definiteness marking.

6. Heritage speakers

6.1 Informants

In order to test our Hypothesis B, that the prenominal possessive construction would be preferred also by bilingual Norwegian-English adults, we have studied a selection of Norwegian-Americans in the USA, more specifically informants that were interviewed in connection with the NorAmDiaSyn fieldwork in Wisconsin and Minnesota in September 2010. The selection consists of 37 speakers, 10 women and 27 men, from the following locations: Blair (4), Spring Grove (8), Harmony (5), Decorah (2), Westby (9), Mabel (2), and Coon Valley (7).[9]

---

[8]. It is unlikely that the problems that the two bilingual children have with definiteness marking in postnominal possessives is due to a general problem related to the suffixal article. For example, in the two first files (1;8.8 and 1;9.22), Sunniva produces 38 nouns in the definite form (with the suffixal article), and only three ungrammatical bare nouns (7.3%). This is very low for her age. She uses definiteness marking in more than 90% of appropriate cases. Emma, on the other hand, sometimes replaces the definite suffix with the demonstrative determiner *den*, and says *den hest* 'the horse' instead of *hest-en* 'horse-the' (cf. Anderssen and Bentzen 2013). However, such examples are rare in Emma's data as well.

[9]. In this article we use a coding for the informants that only shows gender and location.

The informants are roughly 70 to 90 years of age and mainly third generation immigrants who grew up speaking Norwegian at home with their parents and grandparents. Most of them did not learn English until they started school around the age of six, and they may therefore be characterized as successive bilinguals. The home language was Norwegian, but they generally had little opportunity to use Norwegian in the community, and English has thus been the dominant language for these speakers throughout their adult lives. They have not passed on the language to their own children, and they rarely speak Norwegian today, mainly due to the very limited number of possible conversation partners. Furthermore, most of these speakers have never learned to read and write Norwegian.

Most of our informants are descendants of immigrants who came from rural areas in Eastern Norway. This means that they generally speak rural East Norwegian dialects, which are different from standard Norwegian and most urban dialects in that they allow postnominal possessor constructions with an indefinite form of the noun if this is a kinship term, as illustrated in (25), cf. Julien (2005). However, it is important to point out that not all kinship terms allow indefinite nouns in this context, cf. (26). This is relevant, as kinship terms are quite frequent in the production data of the heritage speakers.

(25) *far   min, mor   mi, sønn min, bestemor   mi*
     father my   mother my   son my   grandmother my

(26) **kjerring mi *kone mi *søskenbarn mitt*
     woman   my   wife my   cousin   my

6.2 Results – overview

Four of the 37 informants do not produce possessive constructions at all. The remaining 33 speakers produce 453 examples altogether, and Table 3 provides an overview of the word orders used.

Table 3. Word order in possessive constructions, 33 heritage speakers.

Construction	N	%
N_{def}-POSS	153	33.8%
N_{indef}-POSS	209	46.1%
POSS-N	90	19.9%
POSS-N-POSS	1	0.2%
Total	453	100%

The most striking result is that the word order N-POSS is very robust in these data. Even though only 153 examples (33.8%) are of the type N_{def}-POSS, i.e., postnominal possessives with a definite noun, there are additionally 209 examples (46.1%) of the type N_{indef}-POSS, i.e., nouns without the definiteness suffix. This means that postnominal possessives are attested as much as 79.9%, which is actually somewhat higher than the percentages found in the corpora of adult speakers from Tromsø and Oslo (cf. Section 2). We thus do not have any evidence that the postnominal possessor construction is vulnerable in heritage Norwegian. In fact, the prenominal possessor construction, which was expected to be more frequent in these data, according to our Hypothesis B, only makes up 19.9%. There is additionally one example with both a prenominal and a postnominal possessor, and as shown in (27) this is a mixed-language DP where the prenominal possessor is English and the postnominal one is Norwegian.

(27) Og son min, **my gamlaste son min**, han like ... (8M Spring Grove)
and son my my oldest son my he likes ...
'And my son, my oldest son, he likes ...'

Furthermore, the relatively complex nominal morphology with respect to gender and number is generally also in place in the data from the heritage speakers, as shown by the examples in (29)–(31):

(28) *farmen min* (1M Blair)
farm.DEF my.MASC.SG
'My farm.'

(29) *kjerringa mi*
wife.DEF my.FEM.SG
'My wife.'

(30) *maskineriet mitt*
machinery.DEF my.NEUT.SG
'My machinery.'

(31) *unga mine*
kids.DEF my.PL
'My kids.'

6.3 Possessive constructions with a postnominal possessive

As shown in the previous section, the postnominal possessive construction is clearly intact in the grammar of these bilingual speakers. On closer inspection, the postnominal possessors are not only robust, but also productive, as this construction is also used when the informants use loanwords from English, illustrated in (32)–(33). There are also occasional examples in the data where the noun is Norwegian and the possessive is English, but the word order is nevertheless N-POSS, as in (34).

(32) schoolhouse'n din (3M Spring Grove)
school.house.DEF your
'Your schoolhouse.'

(33) family'n hennes (5M Spring Grove)
family.DEF her
'Her family.'

(34) bestemor   mi, familien   her   (1M Spring Grove)
     grandmother my family.DEF her
     'My grandmother, her family …'

The most frequent possessive construction in these data is the postnominal possessive without the definite suffix on the noun, i.e., N_{indef}-POSS. This construction makes up almost half of all the possessives in the data, 46.1%. As mentioned above, these are grammatical when the noun is a very frequent kinship term. Such nouns are often used in this material, and some typical examples are given in (35).

(35) dotter   mi, sønn hass,   mor   våres, bæssfar   min   (1M Blair)
     daughter my, son   his, mother our,   grandfather my

Some of these examples, 14.4% (30/209), are ungrammatical, however, illustrated in (36)–(37). In Section 7 we discuss some possible accounts of these examples in the data.

(36) *søskenbarn vårt, *onkel vårres   (4M Coon Valley)
     cousin   our,   uncle our

(37) *forelder dems   (1M Decorah)
     parents their

6.4 Possessive constructions with prenominal possessives

According to Hypothesis B, the prenominal possessive constructions should be more frequent in the data of the Norwegian-Americans than in the Norwegian corpora, but as we saw in Table 3, this is not the case. In fact, the prenominal possessive is somewhat less frequent than in the Norwegian corpus material discussed in Section 2. A closer investigation of these constructions in the data of the heritage speakers reveals that most of these POSS-N constructions (73.3%, 66/90) are found in the data of only three informants, who produce almost exclusively prenominal possessives. This is illustrated in Table 4, and (38) provides an example.

Table 4. Informants producing mainly POSS-N.

Informant	N	%
1F Harmony	17/28	60.7%
3M Westby	28/29	96.6%
6M Spring Grove	21/21	100%

(38) **Min bestmor,**   je kan itte husse   at jeg hørde henne si
     My grandmother, I can not remember that I heard her   say
     'My grandmother, I can't remember hearing her say

     ett engelsk ord.
     one English word
     a single English word.'

The remaining examples of prenominal possessive constructions (24/90) are produced by as many as 16 informants, which means that most of the speakers produce only one or two examples, and that as many as 14 speakers do not produce a single example of POSS-N. Furthermore, most of these prenominal possessive constructions are of the type that may not appear with postnominal possessors, such as the fixed expressions in (39) or (40), the latter in fact being a direct translation of an English expression and ungrammatical in Norwegian.

(39) i mi tid (*i tida mi)
    in my time

(40) *alt mitt liv
    all my life

6.5 Some questions

Given these results, it is natural to ask some further questions about the data: First, is there a difference between the three informants who use almost exclusively prenominal possessives compared to the majority of speakers who virtually only produce postnominal ones? Second, is there anything in the conversations with these three speakers which indicates that they had a bigger challenge than the others when speaking Norwegian, i.e., are the conversations more demanding in that the speakers have to use nouns that are more infrequent compared to the nouns appearing in the conversations with the other informants? Furthermore, is there any indication in the data that these Norwegian-American speakers master the pragmatic distinction between the two word orders? Alternatively, could it be that they are in fact doing the opposite of the bilingual children, i.e., that they have a preference for the postnominal possessive construction and use it also in contrastive contexts where the prenominal possessor would be more natural? This would open up an interesting issue from the point of view of the regression hypothesis discussed by Johannessen (this volume). This hypothesis predicts that structures that are acquired late should be lost early, while structures that are acquired early should be lost late in language attrition. Johannessen studies determiners and verb placement in an attrited speaker of heritage Norwegian and finds some support for the regression hypothesis, while our results point in the opposite direction.

Unfortunately it is impossible to answer the last question due to limitations in the data. First, it is difficult to identify clearly contrastive contexts in these conversations. Second, in oral speech it is always possible to use prosody to express contrast by adding stress on the possessor, as in (41), cf. Lødrup (2012). It is therefore unclear whether the Norwegian-American informants are any different from the adults in the two Norwegian corpora in the sense that they overuse the postnominal possessor construction.

(41) bilen   MIN
    car.DEF MY
    'MY car.'

Furthermore, there are simply not enough informants producing both word orders and it is therefore impossible to investigate whether they make any distinction between the two. In fact, there is only one speaker who produces a considerable number of examples of both word orders (1F Harmony, cf. Table 4), and an investigation of her data shows that her word order choice seems to be relatively random and does not seem to be determined by whether the possessive is contrastive or not, cf. Examples (42)–(43). Furthermore, there is no indication that this variation is due to different registers or stylistic levels (cf. Section 2).

(42) **Min mor** arbeide for ho når **min mor** var ung. (1F Harmony)
my mother worked for her when my mother was young
'My mother worked for her when she was young.'

(43) Ja, men *far* **min** arbeide med stein, med meisel ... (1F Harmony)
yes, but father my worked with stone, with chisel ...
'Yes, but my father worked with stone, with a chisel ...'

With respect to the second question, it turns out that the type of noun used in the conversations with the three speakers who predominantly produce prenominal possessive constructions does not differ from the noun types used in the conversations with the other speakers. All the informants mainly speak about their families and what it was like growing up as a Norwegian-American in the Midwest, and the nouns that are typically used are generally kinship terms, such as *mor* 'mother,' *far* 'father,' *bror* 'brother,' *sister* (loanword, Norwegian: *søster*), or other high-frequency everyday words, e.g., *farm* 'farm,' *krøtter* 'cattle,' etc.

Finally, we consider the first question, i.e., whether there could be a difference in the background of the three informants using predominantly prenominal possessives compared to the other 30 speakers. It is not easy to find such a distinction, as these three do not seem to differ in any obvious way from the others with respect to family situation and immigrant history. It could of course be that these three have a somewhat weaker competence in Norwegian and therefore more transfer from English. However, listening to the recordings, one is not immediately struck by any difference in proficiency. And according to the background questionnaires of these three speakers, it turns out that they in fact have a very active and conscious relationship to Norway and the language. All three read Norwegian books (regularly or occasionally), which, by comparison with the others, is relatively unusual. Only four of the other 30 claim to have any reading knowledge of Norwegian, and with the exception of an old cartoon magazine (*Han Ola og han Per*), which is mentioned by a number of the informants, they hardly ever read any Norwegian at all.[10]

---

10. *Han Ola og han Per* is a cartoon created by Peter Julius Rosendahl from Spring Grove, Minnesota. This was first published in the Norwegian newspaper *Decorah-Posten* between 1918 and 1935.

One would normally expect that literacy in a language would protect against language attrition. In this case, however, we might interpret this in the following way: These three informants are no longer first language speakers of Norwegian. The reason why they know as much Norwegian as they do is that they are actively re-learning Norwegian as adults. If this is the case, then these three could be considered to be second language learners of Norwegian. Overuse of the POSS-N construction could then be characterized as a feature of the acquisition of Norwegian (as a first or a second language), and not as a sign of attrition.

The question is whether there is any support for such an interpretation of the data, beyond the fact that these three informants read Norwegian. It is again not easy to find evidence, but it is striking that two of these three informants make certain mistakes in other parts of the language that are unusual in the production of the majority of Norwegian-American speakers. This is shown in Examples (44)–(45): Word order (non-V2) and present instead of past tense in (44), and in (45) incorrect irregular past tense form, use of the indefinite article with a profession and the definite suffix on the noun in a prenominal possessive.

(44) *Og så min tippelderfar*   *han kommer i 1864.*   (1F Harmony)
and so my great-grandfather he comes in 1864
'And then my great grandfather came in 1864.'
Target: *Og så kom min tippoldefar i 1864.*

(45) *Så jeg lørte det til mine studentene*   (6M Spring Grove)
so I taught it to my students.DEF
'So I taught it to my students'

når jeg var en lærer...
when I was a teacher ...
'when I was a teacher ...'
Target: *Så jeg lærte det til mine studenter (studentene mine) da jeg var lærer...*

A further explanation for why these three informants have a predominance of prenominal possessives in their production could also be related to the fact that they read Norwegian. As mentioned above, it is reasonable to assume that literacy protects against language attrition, but this requires that there is overlap between the spoken and the written language. This is generally the case in Norwegian, but the possessive constructions actually constitute an exception. Recall from Section 2 that the prenominal possessive is focused, while the possessor is normally topical in the postnominal possessive construction. This is the case in most Norwegian dialects, and topical prenominal possessives are generally odd or unacceptable in the spoken language (Lødrup 2012). But the most frequently used written standard (*bokmål*) is very different from this. According to Lødrup (2012: 191, footnote 2), a search in the Oslo corpus of written Norwegian shows that only 22% of all possessives in texts from newspapers and magazines were postnominal (out of a total of 43,449). In fictional texts this word order made up 47% (out of a total of 12,884). These percentages are in strong contrast with the proportions we attested in the spoken language: 73% in NoTa and 75% in the Tromsø corpus. Because of these differences, it is conceivable that being literate in Norwegian is not necessarily an advantage with respect to the acquisition or maintenance of word order variation in possessive constructions. In fact, it seems relatively unlikely that it would be possible to learn the pragmatic difference between the two word orders (in the spoken language) from the written language alone. Thus, reading Norwegian is obviously a good solution for people who wish to learn or maintain their Norwegian in situations where they have few conversation partners. But with respect to the two word orders in possessive constructions and the pragmatic distinction between them, considerable exposure to written Norwegian may in fact turn out to be a disadvantage.

7. Discussion

In this section we discuss more general issues related to bilingualism and the word order in Norwegian possessive constructions:

1. If our assumption about the three informants in Section 6 is correct (i.e., that they should be considered second language learners), why is it the case that the postnominal possessive construction is vulnerable in acquisition, but not in attrition?
2. Does the fact that the difference between the two word orders is partly pragmatic play an important role?
3. Why is definiteness morphology vulnerable in both bilingual situations, but not (to the same extent) in first language acquisition?

In Section 2 we argued that the postnominal possessive construction is morphologically and syntactically more complex than the prenominal one, as it involves movement of the noun across the possessive in order to merge with the definiteness suffix. We also showed that this is more frequent in the spoken language. We can therefore answer the first question by referring to these factors. As shown in many studies of both first and second language acquisition, syntactic complexity is an important factor, which often causes a certain delay in the acquisition process. In A&W we also showed that monolingual Norwegian children are slightly delayed in the production of the postnominal possessive construction.

It is therefore not surprising that this construction is acquired late also in a bilingual situation. But why do we not see the same vulnerability in the production of the bilingual Norwegian-Americans? A likely explanation is that, once a construction has been acquired, its complexity is somehow lost. The construction has simply been automatized in the grammar of the speaker of the language, and using it no longer involves any extra effort or cost in the speech situation, compared to the less complex construction. Frequency presumably also plays a role here: A highly frequent construction will continually be strengthened in the speaker's grammar, and this input should therefore protect this construction against attrition.

However, it needs to be investigated whether the difference between the bilingual children and the heritage speakers could not simply be related to dialect differences. According to Larsson et al. (this volume), early Swedish settlements saw the development of a standard American Swedish based on features from the different dialects, as well as features from English. As Johannessen and Laake (this volume) point out, such a standard may not have developed in American Norwegian due to the higher status of dialects in Norway (see also Hjelde this volume). A high proportion of Norwegian heritage speakers in the US descend from the rural eastern part of Norway, and they thus grew up hearing rural Eastern dialects, while the bilingual children studied here live in Tromsø and are mainly exposed to Northern dialects. Both word orders are found in the Tromsø dialect today (cf. the adults in the acquisition corpus), but it is unclear whether the prenominal possessive exists at all in the Norwegian dialects spoken in the USA. For obvious reasons we do not know what these dialects were like approximately 150 years ago when the first generation of Norwegians emigrated, but it is possible to investigate present-day Eastern dialects in the Nordic Dialect Corpus (Johannessen et al. 2009). Thus, we have studied the files of speakers from Oppland county, and our findings show that 76.2% (172/252) of the possessives in this material are postnominal, 57 of which (22.6%) are kinship terms appearing without a definite suffix. This means that 23.8% (60/252) of the possessives are prenominal, which corresponds exactly to the findings in the Tromsø and NoTa corpora. Furthermore, the prenominal possessives are typically used in contrastive contexts, as shown in (46). These findings indicate that it is unlikely that dialect differences are responsible for the high frequency of postnominal possessives in the production of the heritage speakers.

(46) ... *og gjorde det samme som han gjorde* (Brekkom01um)
     and did the same as he did
     '... and I would do the same as he did

     med sin traktor med min trå -traktor.
     with his tractor with my pedal-tractor
     with his tractor with my pedal tractor.'

A further possible explanation for the lack of prenominal possessives in the production of the Norwegian-Americans could simply be that the interview situations and the topics of the conversations make it more natural to use postnominal possessives, i.e., that there are few contrastive contexts. If so, there would be no difference in the I-language grammars of the heritage speakers compared to adult speakers in Norway. However, given that the interviews in NoTa and the Nordic Dialect Corpus are similar to the interviews carried out in the NorAmDiaSyn project, this is not a particularly likely explanation either.

    Finally, we would like to suggest that frequency in fact plays an important role here, in the following way: As discussed above, we may assume that for constructions that are already acquired, complexity is no longer an important factor. The language of an adult may instead be more influenced by frequency. Just as the postnominal possessive may be protected against language attrition by its high frequency, the correspondingly low frequency of the prenominal possessive may cause *this* construction to be vulnerable. We can thus turn the question around and ask if it could be that it is the prenominal possessive that is vulnerable in the language of the heritage speakers, due to its low frequency. The data show that the majority of the speakers do not produce this construction at all. In our view this is an interesting hypothesis, which should be investigated in further research on acquisition and attrition.

We now turn to the question whether the pragmatic difference between the two word orders plays a role for the results of our investigation. It has recently been argued that constructions involving the interface between syntax and pragmatics are especially vulnerable in bilingual acquisition and attrition. This is referred to as the Interface Hypothesis (e.g., Sorace 2011), which, among other things, has been used to account for the vulnerability of null subjects, e.g., in the Italian produced by English-Italian bilinguals, both children and adults. The choice between a pronominal and a null subject in Italian is dependent on whether the speaker wishes to mark a topic shift, which means that this involves the syntax-pragmatics interface. Brown and Putnam (this volume) also refer to the permeability of the semantic and discourse-pragmatic levels of the grammar in their discussion of a change in Pennsylvania Dutch involving an extension of the progressive aspect to certain stative verbs. For the possessives in Norwegian, we may argue that the choice between the two word orders is dependent on the interpretive difference between them (contrastive or neutral), and this distinction should also be vulnerable according to the Interface Hypothesis. In our acquisition material we have also shown that the bilingual children (just like the monolinguals) do not seem to have understood the contrastive interpretation of the prenominal possessive, in that they use it also in non-contrastive contexts, cf. Examples (18)–(19) in Section 5. For the Norwegian-Americans, on the other hand, the data material is too limited, as also mentioned in Section 6: Hardly any of the informants produce both word orders to an extent that makes it is possible to investigate whether there is an interpretive distinction between them. None of the examples stand out as pragmatically odd. Contrastive contexts are rare in the data, and as mentioned above, a contrastive interpretation may also be expressed by stress on the postnominal possessive, which means that word order is less important.

Finally, we discuss the vulnerability of definiteness morphology in bilingual situations, which we saw examples of in Sections 5 and 6 (*baby min* 'baby my,' target: *babyen min*; *søskenbarn vårt* 'cousin our,' target: *søskenbarnet vårt*), where the definite suffix is missing. Bilingual acquisition thus seems to be different from monolingual acquisition, where morphology does not seem to pose any particular problems, cf. Wexler's (1999: 43) claim that small children are "little inflection machines." Anderssen (2006, 2010) also shows that the definite suffix is acquired very early by monolingual Norwegian children, which has also been found in Swedish first language acquisition (cf. Bohnacker 2004). In the grammars of the heritage speakers, morphology is generally not vulnerable, according to Johannessen and Laake (this volume), with the possible exception of the loss of dative case. The possessives may be another exception, as there seems to be a distinction between syntax and morphology in this context: while the N-POSS word order is both robust and productive, definiteness morphology is somewhat more vulnerable. In our view there could be two different explanations of this: First, what we see in the data could be an internal overgeneralization in Norwegian, i.e., from the frequent kinship terms (which typically appear without definiteness in the relevant dialects) to other kinds of nouns. This explanation is of course only relevant for the heritage speaker data, as the bilingual children are growing up in Tromsø and are therefore mainly exposed to a dialect where the lack of definiteness with kinship terms is uncommon. Second, omission of definiteness may be caused by interference from English, where the definite article is never included in possessive constructions, e.g., *the my car. It should be noted that these explanations in principle do not exclude each other.

8. Conclusion

We have discussed the word order variation in Norwegian possessive constructions (POSS-N or N-POSS) in two bilingual populations, bilingual Norwegian-English children growing up in Norway (Tromsø) and a group of Norwegian-Americans who have English as their dominant language. Given previous research on monolingual Norwegian children, our hypothesis was that the word order with a postnominal possessive would be vulnerable in these bilingual contexts, despite the fact that it is considerably more frequent than the prenominal possessor construction in spontaneous speech: This construction is morphologically and syntactically more complex (requires definiteness marking on the noun as well as movement of the noun across the possessor to merge with the definiteness suffix) and it is somewhat delayed in the production of monolingual children. Furthermore, we expected that the prenominal possessor construction would be reinforced by the speakers' exposure to English. Our investigation shows that the bilingual children produce a higher proportion of the prenominal possessor construction at an early stage, and that this tendency seems to last longer than in the monolingual data. In the data of the Norwegian-American heritage speakers, the picture is completely different: The postnominal possessive construction is both robust and productive; it is even more frequent than in the corpora of Norwegian adults and it is also used with English loanwords. We therefore conclude that our hypothesis is partly confirmed. Our interpretation of this is that linguistic complexity is an important factor in the acquisition process (mono- or bilingual), while high frequency may protect against language attrition.

References

Anderssen, Merete. 2006. *The Acquisition of Compositional Definiteness in Norwegian*. Tromsø, Norway: University of Tromsø dissertation.
Anderssen, Merete. 2010. "Tidlig tilegnelse av bestemt artikkel i norsk. [Early acquisition of the definite article in Norwegian]." *Norsk Lingvistisk Tidsskrift* [Norwegian Linguistics Journal] 28(2): 153–172.
Anderssen, Merete and Marit Westergaard. 2010. "Frequency and Economy in the Acquisition of Variable Word Order." *Lingua* 120(11): 2569–2588. DOI: 10.1016/j.lingua.2010.06.006
Anderssen, Merete, Kristine Bentzen, Yulia Rodina and Marit Westergaard. 2010. "The Acquisition of Apparent Optionality: Word Order in Subject and Object Shift Constructions in Norwegian." In *Variation in the Input: Studies in the Acquisition of Word Order* (Studies in Theoretical Psycholinguistics 39), ed. by Merete Anderssen, Kristine Bentzen and Marit Westergaard, 241–270. Dordrecht: Springer.
Anderssen, Merete and Kristine Bentzen. 2013. "Cross-Linguistic Influence Outside the Syntax-Pragmatics Interface: A Case Study of the Acquisition of Definiteness." *Studia Linguistica* 67(1): 82–100. DOI: 10.1111/stul.12011
Bohnacker, Ute. 2004. "Nominal Phrases." In *The Acquisition of Swedish Grammar*, ed. by Gunlög Josefsson, Christer Platzack and Gisela Håkansson, 195–260. Amsterdam: John Benjamins. DOI: 10.1075/lald.33.08boh
Brown, Joshua R. and Michael Putnam. This volume. "Functional Convergence and Extension in Contact: Syntactic and Semantic Attributes of the Progressive Aspect in Pennsylvania Dutch."
Cardinaletti, Anna and Michal Starke. 1999. "The Typology of Structural Deficiency: A Case Study of the Three Classes of Pronouns." In *Clitics in the Languages of Europe*, ed. by Henk van Riemsdijk, 145–233. Berlin: Mouton de Gruyter.
Faarlund, Jan Terje, Svein Lie and Kjell Ivar Vannebo. 1997. *Norsk referansegrammatikk* [Norwegian reference grammar]. Oslo: Universitetsforlaget.
Hjelde, Arnstein. This volume. "Changes in a Norwegian Dialect in America."
Johannessen, Janne Bondi, Joel Priestley, Kristin Hagen, Tor Anders Åfarli and Øystein Alexander Vangsnes. 2009. "The Nordic Dialect Corpus – An Advanced Research Tool." In *Proceedings of the 17th Nordic Conference of Computational Linguistics NODALIDA 2009*. NEALT Proceedings Series 4, ed. by Kristiina Jokinen and Eckhard Bick, 73–80. Tartu: Tartu University Library (electronic publication).
Johannessen, Janne Bondi and Signe Laake. This volume. "On Two Myths of the Norwegian Language in America: Is it Old-Fashioned? Is it Approaching the Written *Bokmål* Standard?"
Johannessen, Janne Bondi. This volume. "Attrition in an American Norwegian Heritage Language Speaker."
Julien, Marit. 2005. *Nominal Phrases from a Scandinavian Perspective* (Linguistics Today 87). Amsterdam: John Benjamins. DOI: 10.1075/la.87
Larsson, Ida, Sofia Tingsell and Maia Andréasson. This volume. "Variation and Change in American Swedish."
Lødrup, Helge. 2012. "Forholdet mellom prenominale og postnominale possessive uttrykk. [The relationship between prenominal and postnominal possessive expressions]." In *Grammatikk, bruk og norm* [Grammar, Use and Norm], ed. by Hans-Olav Enger, Jan Terje Faarlund and Kjell Ivar Vannebo, 189–203. Oslo: Novus.

Lødrup, Helge. 2011. "Norwegian Possessive Pronouns: Phrases, Words or Suffixes?" In *Proceedings of the LFG11 Conference*, ed. by Miriam Butt and Tracy Holloway King, 383–403. Stanford: CSLI Publications.

Norsk talespråkskorpus [NoTa corpus]– the Oslo part, The Text Lab, ILN, University of Oslo. http://www.tekstlab.uio.no/nota/oslo/index.html

Sorace, Antonella. 2011. "Pinning Down the Concept of 'Interface' in Bilingualism." *Linguistic Approaches to Bilingualism* 1(1): 1–33. DOI: 10.1075/lab.1.1.01sor

Taraldsen, Knut Tarald. 1990. "D-Projections and N-Projections in Norwegian." In *Grammar in Progress*, ed. by Joan Mascaró and Marina Nespor, 419–431. Dordrecht: Foris. DOI: 10.1515/9783110867848.419

Vangsnes, Øystein Alexander. 1999. *The Identification of Functional Architecture*. Bergen, Norway: University of Bergen dissertation.

Westergaard, Marit. 2009. *The Acquisition of Word Order: Micro-Cues, Information Structure and Economy* (Linguistik Aktuell/Linguistics Today 145), Amsterdam: John Benjamins. DOI: 10.1075/la.145

Westergaard, Marit and Kristine Bentzen. 2007. "The (Non-)Effect of Input Frequency on the Acquisition of Word Order in Norwegian Embedded Clauses." In *Frequency Effects in Language Acquisition: Defining the Limits of Frequency as an Explanatory Concept* (Studies on Language Acquisition), ed. by Insa Gülzow and Natalia Gagarina, 271–306. Berlin/New York: Mouton de Gruyter. DOI: 10.1515/9783110977905.271

Wexler, Kenneth. 1999. "Very Early Parameter Setting and the Unique Checking Constraint: A New Explanation of the Optional Infinitive Stage." In *Language Acquisition: Knowledge Representation and Processing* (Special issue of *Lingua*), ed. by Antonella Sorace, Caroline Heycock and Richard Shillock, 23–79. Amsterdam: Elsevier.

Attrition in an American Norwegian heritage language speaker

Janne Bondi Johannessen
University of Oslo

This paper investigates the language of one person: an elderly bilingual lady who speaks Heritage Norwegian in addition to English. Her heritage language production reveals language that is different both from what we know of Heritage Norwegian from other sources and from European Norwegian, and which is taken to be the result of language attrition. Her language is therefore well-suited for studying the regression hypothesis (Jakobson 1941), i.e., whether what is learnt first is retained longest, and whether what is learnt last is lost first. After having established the order of acquisition, her morphological and syntactic production is investigated. The paper examines the noun-phrase-related categories of definiteness suffix, indefinite determiner, compositional definiteness and pronouns, as well as clause-related structures: verb second (V2) word order with topicalization of two kinds of adverbials, V2 with negation, and target V3 in subordinate clauses. The main result is that the regression hypothesis is supported but more for clause-related categories than noun-phrase-related ones. One specific finding is that V2 occurs in place of light, simple preposed adverbials, but not with heavy, complex ones.

Keywords: Norwegian, attrition, acquisition, regression hypothesis, verb second, noun phrase grammar

1. Introduction[1]

Heritage language is often different from the original mother language. Questions concerning what factors cause what kind of effects have resulted in much research in recent years. Concepts such as incomplete acquisition and attrition have been central

---

1. I am grateful for constructive comments from two anonymous reviewers, as well as from Arnstein Hjelde, Joseph Salmons and Per Erik Solberg. I would also like to thank the participants at the Second Workshop on Immigrant Languages in America, Fefor, Norway, 2011, for

(see for example Larsson and Johannessen 2015a, b, Montrul 2008, Montrul et al. 2008, Polinsky 2008, 2011, Putnam and Sánchez 2013, Rothman 2009).

The present paper focuses on language attrition caused, it is assumed, by many years of absence of exposure to and use of the heritage language. Schmid and Köpke (2008) define attrition thus: "The term first language (L1) attrition refers to a change in the native language system of the bilingual who is acquiring and using a second language (L2). This change may lead to a variety of phenomena within the L1 system, among which are interferences from the L2 on all levels (phonetics, lexicon, morphosyntax, pragmatics), a simplification or impoverishment of the L1, or insecurity on the part of the speaker, manifested by frequent hesitations, self-repair or hedging strategies." Although it will not be the main focus of this paper, it is pointed out that the attrition effects that are studied here cannot be direct translations or influences from English.

The data presented in this study should not, then, be seen as examples of incomplete acquisition, but as language loss in an individual. An alternative question is whether language loss in an individual follows the reverse path of the acquisition process. This idea is called the regression hypothesis, expressed by Roman Jakobson (1941) and investigated by, amongst others, Renate Born (2003) and Merel Keijzer (2007, 2010). The basic claim is that language loss is the mirror image of acquisition. What is learnt early is lost late, while what is learnt late is lost early.

As pointed out by Keijzer, most research on the regression hypothesis has compared the language of young children with that of aphasics. Since the latter group may also have other cognitive problems it is not ideal for this purpose (Keijzer 2010: 10). Further, while acquisition is gradual, language loss as a result of aphasia is sudden. Also, while acquisition involves the language system, aphasia typically affects only part of it. In addition, some researchers have focused on the regression hypothesis with L2 learners. Keijzer focuses on L1 speakers: Dutch speakers who had immigrated to English-speaking Canada after the age of 15 and whose mean age was 66.4, and whose mean length of stay was 43.5 years.

In this paper the regression hypothesis is tested with respect to a heritage speaker, a different kind of informant from the informant types tested in the research reported by Keijzer (2010). This speaker is ideal for testing, since she shows attrition effects in several aspects of her language production. The paper examines the noun-phrase-related categories of definiteness suffix, indefinite determiner, compositional definiteness and pronouns, as well as clause-related structures: verb second (V2) word order with topicalization, V2 with negation, and target V3 in subordinate clauses.

---

valuable feedback. (http://www.hf.uio.no/iln/english/about/organization/text-laboratory/news-events/events/2011/feforseminar-norskiamerika.html).

The work was partly supported by the Research Council of Norway through its Centres of Excellence funding scheme, project number 223265, and through its funding of the project NorAmDiaSyn, project number 218878, under the BILATGRUNN/FRIHUM scheme.

Section 2 presents the general data and methodology, while Section 3 gives an overview of the relevant features of Norwegian and the age in which they are acquired. In Section 4 the attrition data are presented, and in Section 5 the acquisition and the attrition data are seen relative to each other, while the paper is concluded in Section 6.

2. Data and methodology

2.1 Informant and linguistic evidence

The person whose language is investigated in this paper had not spoken Norwegian for a long time. Daisy, 89.5 years old at the time of the recording in 2010, was born in 1920 in Chicago, had more than 12 years of education, and used to work in a telephone company. Her parents were both Norwegian, born in Østfold and Sunnfjord (East and West Norway, respectively), and had immigrated in 1907 and 1909 as teenagers. Norwegian was spoken alongside English in her childhood home.[2] Her late husband did not speak Norwegian, and neither did her children. However, her father had lived with her until he died 15 years previously, when Daisy was 75 years old. They spoke Norwegian together, and she had not spoken Norwegian since. Daisy had been to Norway on 5–6 short trips.

It was her sons that contacted us when they saw our advertisement where we tried to get in touch with Norwegian-speaking Americans. Daisy, who lived alone in her beautiful house, was charming, attentive, humorous and intelligent. In every way, she came across as being cognitively on top of things. The effects of old age on language have been debated in the literature. Burke and Shafto (2008: 374) mention such factors as general resource deficits (e.g., processing speed, efficiency of inhibition, working memory capacity), and transmission deficits. However, such factors were not visible in Daisy's English language production, which makes it less likely that they would be disturbing her Norwegian language.

However, linguistically, when speaking Norwegian rather than English, she clearly had difficulty. She spoke with long pauses and searched for words. Sometimes she switched to English when she was stuck in the attempt to express something in Norwegian. Importantly, for the purposes of this paper, her Norwegian grammar was clearly different from that of European Norwegians, and of the other fluent heritage American Norwegians we have met. Methodologically, one might argue that we do not know whether her Norwegian language has ever been different. There are no recordings of her speaking Norwegian from ten, twenty, thirty or more years ago. But based on the facts about her childhood linguistic situation and the fact that other American

---

[2] When her maternal grandmother came from Norway to live with them, Daisy was 7. They spoke only Norwegian together. Daisy's Norwegian is definitely the dialect of her mother and maternal grandmother, originating in the town of Moss, Østfold.

Norwegians who still use the language, speak more fluently than her, it will be assumed here that she is an attrited speaker of a heritage language, rather than a person who has never learnt heritage Norwegian properly. The fluency of her intonation, including the realization of the East Norwegian toneme differences, supports this assumption. The extent to which her grammar deviates from the norm must therefore be due to lack of use.

This paper draws data from a recorded conversation with Daisy lasting 30–40 minutes with altogether 6000 words. It consists of an interviewer asking questions that are partly motivated by the need for background information (on family and immigration history) and partly by the need for as much speech as possible, in a friendly and relaxed atmosphere. The conversation is now part of the growing Corpus of American Norwegian Speech (Johannessen 2015).[3] This corpus consists of recordings with transcriptions that are linked to each other. It has a web interface with advanced search possibilities, both with respect to individual suffixes, words and phrases, and to morphosyntactic categories.

During fieldwork in 2010–2012 in the American Midwest the present author met more than a hundred American Norwegian language heritage speakers. They had in common that they had grown up in a family of descendants of Norwegian immigrants arriving in the US before 1920. Many did not know English before they started school, and they were all part of a larger Norwegian community. Most of these speakers were fluent, with only a few features distinguishing their language from Norwegian as it is spoken in Scandinavia. The specific American Norwegian features are especially phonological (for earlier work on American Norwegian phonology, see Hjelde 1992) and lexical (see Johannessen and Laake 2011, forthcoming, and this volume). These speakers, therefore, can be seen as a control group for Daisy, given that it can be argued that Heritage Norwegian is standardized into one single language or dialect (see Johannessen and Laake forthcoming), and that we already know about an array of linguistic features in Heritage Norwegian (see Johannessen and Laake 2011 and this volume, Annear and Speth, Hjelde and Eide, Hjelde, as well as Westergaard and Anderssen, all in this volume).

2.2 Methodology and background material

The main purpose of this paper is to test the regression hypothesis using Daisy as a test case. The paper will investigate whether what she has kept and what she has lost (compared with standard Heritage Norwegian and European Norwegian) can be seen as a scale that reflects the order of acquisition. In order to compare with acquisition, a short overview of what is known about the age of acquisition of some of the main linguistic features in Norwegian is given here. It is based on different works on Norwegian, but also on Swedish – a language so close to Norwegian that the order of acquisition will

---

3. Available at http://www.tekstlab.uio.no/nota/NorAmDiaSyn/english/index.html.

be the same. Swedish is included since the knowledge of acquisition of Norwegian is limited. A problem is that the studies on acquisition are very different methodologically, so that it is difficult to set up a trajectory of all the features and categories. Below follows a brief description of the sources used in this paper to ascertain the steps of acquisition.

Anderssen (2007) uses recordings of three Norwegian children at the age 1;8.20–3;3.18. This study is used for pronouns and compositional definiteness in the present paper. Only one Norwegian child (1;8.20–3;4) is described in Anderssen (2010), used here for definiteness. Some of these data have also been used by Westergaard and Anderssen (this volume). Bentzen's (2004) study is also based on the recordings of only one child, a bilingual Norwegian American child at the age 2;7.10–2;10.9. This study has been used here for the investigation of word order. The data in Kristoffersen and Simonsen (2012) is on the complete opposite end of the scale, being based on what 6500 parents report about their children's achievements on an online web-form. Their study follows the pattern of CDI (MacArthur-Bates communicative development inventories), see Kristoffersen et al. (2012) for the basic methodology.[4] For each category (for example the present tense suffix) Kristoffersen and Simonsen (2012) present a table of all the reported answers for this category; the answers belong to one of three grades: "not yet," "sometimes" or "often," and with percentages summarized for each monthly age. In the present paper the age that corresponds to the "often" category for more than 50 percent of the children is used as the general age of acquisition for that feature. Their data is used here for the definiteness category, along with Anderssen (2006, 2010). Waldman (2008) uses a corpus of spontaneous speech of six monolingual Swedish children recorded over six years (0;10–7;0). This work is used here for word order in main and subordinate clauses. Westergaard (2005) studies the recordings of three Norwegian children (the same as those of Anderssen 2007) at the ages 1;8.20–3;3.18. Her study is used here for word order together with Waldman (2008) and Wikström (2008). The latter investigates a corpus of the spontaneous speech of one Swedish child 1;1.10–2;10.8.

There are thus vast differences with respect to the amount of data that the literature has employed when assessing the age of acquisition of linguistic phenomena; from one subject to 6500. The way the data has been collected also differs a lot, from

---

4. The method of using parents' reports of course faces certain problems. Kristoffersen and Simonsen (2012: 25, fn. 4) do not regard it as a problem that dialects differ, while the web form contains only written standard forms. However, when it comes to the grammatical part of their investigation, such problems should not be dismissed. For example, the form asks for present tense suffix by saying (translated from Norwegian): *After some time, children add an -r and say sover (sleeps), spiser etc., like we adults do. Does your child do this?* (Kristoffersen and Simonsen 2012: 165). In many parts of Norway the present tense form is not formed by adding an -r to the stem, but instead a different inflectional paradigm is used (known as "strong" inflection), like *søv* 'sleeps' (vs. standard *sover*). In most parts of Norway the present tense is also expressed without -r, as in *huksa* or *huse* (both meaning 'remember').

careful studies of spontaneous speech to lay people's reports on web forms. It is difficult to know whether this has any consequences for the comparisons that will be made in this chapter, but the present author thinks it is worth the attempt, and then later research may confirm or refute the ages of acquisition that have been assumed in this paper. However, where more sources have been available, attempts have been made to compare them and choose the appropriate age. In the next section the studies will be investigated in order to establish at which age which linguistic phenomenon is acquired.

3. Norwegian language and the order of acquisition

In this section those parts of the Norwegian language that are necessary to understand the attrition data are presented. For each feature the age in which this feature is expected to have been learnt is assessed on the basis of the studies reported in Section 2.

3.1 The noun phrase and its categories

The grammar of Norwegian noun phrases is best illustrated by some examples.

(1) a. en   gammel   hest
       an.SG.M   old.SG.INDEF.M   horse. SG.INDEF
       'an old horse'
    b. et   gammelt   hus
       a.SG.N   old.SG.INDEF.N   house.SG.INDEF
       'an old house'

(2) a. den   gamle   hest-en
       the.SG.M   old.SG.DEF   horse.SG.DEF.M
       'the old horse'
    b. det   gamle   hus-et[5]
       the.SG.M   old.SG.DEF   house.SG.DEF.N
       'the old house'

(1a,b) show that an indefinite noun phrase with a preposed adjective has a preposed indefinite determiner. In addition there is gender agreement determined by the noun between the determiner, the adjective and the noun. The adjective is also inflected for number and definiteness, and if singular, the adjective is also inflected for gender.

The examples in (2) show that there is also agreement in the definite form. Importantly, the noun has a definiteness suffix even when the determiner is also

---

5. The final -t in *det* and *hus-et* is not pronounced in spoken language.

definite, and the adjective is inflected for definiteness.[6] This is known as compositional definiteness. The adjective has the same form whatever the gender when the noun phrase is definite, while the determiner also shows gender and number distinctions. For more information on the noun phrase, see for example Julien (2005) and Faarlund et al. (1997).

3.1.1 The acquisition of the definiteness suffix

Definiteness in the noun is realized as a suffix (as in *hesten, huset* in (1)), whereas the indefinite form is realized as a bare stem and a preposed determiner. Anderssen (2010), discussing the role of metric structure on the acquisition process, shows that the definiteness suffix is acquired much earlier, viz. a whole year, than the indefinite determiner. She shows that the suffix appears in 63.3% of the contexts in which it would be expected to occur already at age 1;8.20, and that as many as 90.6% of the contexts have the suffix at age 2;3.12 (Anderssen 2010: 157),[7] a result confirmed by Kristoffersen and Simonsen (2012: 109) in their study, with exactly the same age: 2;3. The definiteness suffix is also acquired very early in Swedish (see Anderssen 2006, 2007, 2010 for references).

3.1.2 The acquisition of the indefinite preposed determiner

The indefinite determiner (*en, et* in (1)) is acquired a lot later that the definiteness suffix. Looking at Anderssen's data, the indefinite determiner is actually not properly acquired even when her research period ends. The child is at this point 3;3.18, and uses the indefinite determiner in 70% of the expected contexts.

3.1.3 The acquisition of compositional definiteness

Noun phrases in Norwegian that contain a modifier (such as an adjective) need a definite preposed determiner in addition to the suffix. This is exemplified by *den ... hesten*, and *det ... huset* in Examples (1) and (2). In unmodified noun phrases, the definiteness suffix carries both uniqueness and specificity features (cf. Julien 2005), while in modified noun phrases, the definiteness suffix expresses specificity and the preposed definite determiner expresses uniqueness. We have seen that the definiteness suffix is acquired very early, while the indefinite determiner is late. Anderssen (2007) has investigated the acquisition of the definite preposed determiner. It appears that the prenominal definite determiner "is omitted for a very long time" (Anderssen 2007: 264).

---

6. Norwegian also allows definite noun phrases without a definiteness suffix on the noun. This can occur in a formal, bookish style, but will be considered ungrammatical here since our informant never enters into this mode of formality or plays with different registers.

7. Those that might want to look at Anderssen's data more thoroughly should be aware that Anderssen (2010: 157) actually gives the file-number as age reference, so the actual age when this file was recorded had to be looked up in Anderssen (2006: 12). I have referred to the second age period here: her files 6–10, which have been recorded from age 2;1.0 to 2;3.12.

Her child informant (who is the same as for the other two phenomena mentioned) still at age 3;3.18 only produced the target compositional definiteness in 18.2% of the cases. This must also mean that the uniqueness feature is acquired late.

3.1.4 The acquisition of pronouns

Anderssen (2007) estimates that pronouns are acquired later than the definiteness suffix. This means that both the person category and the uniqueness category are acquired late (Anderssen 2007: 267). Anderssen (2007: 266) shows that her informant Ina reaches the adult ratio of pronouns: nouns (taken by Anderssen to be 45%) at age 2;7.8. She reaches half the amount of that already at age 1;11.22, but it is not until age 2;6.19 that she reaches 75% of the ratio. This is more than three months after comparable numbers for the definiteness suffix.

3.2 Clauses and sentences

In Norwegian, declarative main clauses are V2, i.e., the verb must be in the second position in the sentence, whatever phrase fills the first position. Thus, if a sentence has a topicalized object, the verb must still be in the second position, and the subject has to move, unlike English. This is exemplified in (3):

(3) a. *Mari kjøpte bøker i dag*
      Mari bought books today
      'Mari bought books today.'
   b. *Bøker kjøpte Mari i dag*
      books bought Mari today
      'Books, Mari bought today.'
   c. **Bøker Mari kjøpte i dag*
      books Mari bought today
      'Books, Mari bought today.'

Negation is expressed as an adverb following the finite verb:

(4) a. *Mari kjøpte ikke bøker*
      Mari bought not books
      'Mari didn't buy books.'
   b. **Mari ikke kjøpte bøker*
      Mari not bought books
      'Mari didn't buy books.'

In subordinate clauses the standard language does not have V2; instead the verb will be in the third position (V3) if there is also an adverb in the clause, see (5). There are some exceptions to this generalisation both generally in Norwegian and in some dialects, depending on matrix predicate and adverb, respectively (see Julien 2007, 2008, 2009 and Bentzen 2007). The present investigation avoids such cases.

(5) a. *Jeg spurte om Mari ikke kjøpte bøker i dag*
 I   asked if   Mari not bought books today
 'I asked if Mari did not buy books today.'
 b. **Jeg spurte om Mari kjøpte   ikke bøker i dag*
 I   asked if   Mari bought not books today
 'I asked if Mari did not buy books today.'

3.2.1   The acquisition of V2 with topicalization

Westergaard (2005) shows that by age 2;4 children produce more than 90% of the target word order, i.e., V2, for topicalization constructions of the type (3b). Her study is supported by Bentzen (2004), who looks at the acquisition of verb movement in bilingual first language acquisition. She compares the language production of a child aged 2;7.10–2;10.9. This child overgeneralizes Norwegian word order, as 23.7% of the English non-subject-initial sentences are pronounced with V2 (Bentzen 2004: 163), while only 3.4% of her topicalized Norwegian sentences have the English word order, V3 (Bentzen 2004: 166). We can conclude from her study that V2 is in place for Norwegian by this age.

Westergaard (2005) also refers to a study of Swedish (Platzack 1996: 376), which has found that V2 starts at age 1;9 and is completed a year later. Waldmann (2008: 158–164) shows that three of the four Swedish children he studies have acquired V2 order with topicalization and other non-subject initial elements already before the age 2;0.16. V2 is thus acquired early.

3.2.2   V2 with negation

Westergaard (2005) has also looked at V2 with respect to negation. She found that the target order with finite verbs in main clauses, X-FinV-Neg, was acquired by age 2;2.12. One child had the target order for 88.5% of all examples; another had 92.9%. The very early acquisition of this order is supported for Swedish by Waldmann (2008: 146–154). His study of four children shows that three of them have the target word order with both finite and infinite verb w.r.t. negation in more than 95% of the utterances from the time that they start using negation with verbs. This varies between the age of 1;10.04 and 2;7.04.

3.2.3   Target V3 in subordinate clauses

Westergaard (2005: 168–174) only looked at children under the age of 3, which made it difficult to study the word order in embedded clauses, since these are known to be acquired late. However, she did find 29 embedded clauses with negation, so these should in principle say something about the word order. Unfortunately, in half of the cases, the negation followed the subjunction directly, thereby rendering it impossible to see whether there was V2 or V3 order. However, there were more examples of clear violations of the target subordinate V3 order (subjunction-Adv-FinV) all the way up to the age of 3;0.0 than of the target V3. One example is:[8]

(6) *Det er ho mamma som har også tegna
    it is she mommie who has also drawn
    'It's mommie who has also drawn.'

These violations show that embedded word order in Norwegian is acquired relatively late. Waldmann's (2008: 221–240) Swedish data show the same; he finds that the main acquisition of the target V3 embedded order takes place between the ages 2;9 and 3;3. Table 1 summarizes the findings in order of ascending age:

Table 1. Linguistic structures and categories and their age of acquisition.

Language construction	Age	Research reference
V2 word order with negation	2;2.12	Westergaard (2005: 140), Waldmann (2008: 146–154)
Definiteness suffix	2;3.12	Anderssen (2006: 12; 2010: 28, 153–172), Kristoffersen and Simonsen (2012: 109)
Pronouns	After 2;3.12	Anderssen (2007: 267)
V2 word order with topicalization	2;4	Westergaard (2005: 231). Also: Bentzen (2004), Platzack (1996), Waldmann (2008: 158–164), Wikström (2008: 98–104)
Indefinite determiner	3;3.18	Anderssen (2006: 12; 2010: 28, 153–172)
Compositional definiteness	After 3;3.18	Anderssen (2007: 264)
Target V3 order in subordinate clauses	After 3;0.0	Westergaard (2005: 168–174), Waldmann (2008: 221–240)

4. Results of the investigation of Daisy's American Norwegian

4.1 Results regarding the noun phrase

4.1.1 *The definiteness suffix*
In this subsection, we will only address noun phrases that consist of a single noun (possibly with some postmodification), but not premodified noun phrases that require agreement and definiteness. These are discussed in Section 4.1.3. The Norwegian system is illustrated in Example (1) (*hest-en, hus-et*).

---

8. In the rest of the paper, the asterisk is used to indicate that the utterance deviates from the target standard language (adult language and non-attrited language).

Our informant Daisy does use the definiteness suffix, but not in a stable manner. Some of her nouns are given below. In (7) her nouns are correctly marked, but in (8) we see many examples of a missing definiteness suffix. Enough linguistic context is included there to show that the noun should have been marked for definiteness:

(7) Definiteness suffix in accordance with target:
    a. *i krigen*
        in war.DEF
    b. *på rivern*
        on river.DEF
    c. *den kanten av byen*
        that part.DEF of town.DEF

(8) Definiteness suffix missing:
    a. **gikk fra telefonkompani neri Texas*
        went from telephone.company down.in Texas
            (expected: *telefonkompaniet*)
    b. **bestefar var fra fjell*
        grandad was from mountain
            (expected: *fjellet*)
    c. **mange har vondt i fot*
        many have pain in foot
            (expected: *foten*)
    d. **en kirke som var i nabolag*
        a church that was in neighbourhood
            (expected: *nabolaget*)
    e. **slutten av parade*
        end.DEF of parade
            (expected: *paraden*)
    f. **jeg gikk i baderom i skip*
        I went to bathroom in ship
            (expected: *baderommet, skipet*)

It should be noted that whenever the definiteness suffix is missing, it is not due to direct influence from English, since English, while it has no definiteness suffix, uses a preposed determiner as exemplified in (9) (compare with Daisy's (8f)):

(9) I went to *the bathroom* in *the ship*.

To quantify Daisy's command of the definiteness suffixes of unmodified noun phrases, the Corpus of American Norwegian Speech has been employed counting the number of common nouns occurring with the prepositions *fra* 'from', *til* 'to' and *på* 'on', since preposition phrases often require definiteness. Only those that require definiteness have been counted. Daisy has two nouns with *fra* in the relevant category; one definite and one indefinite. She has seven relevant nouns with *til*, four definite ones.

With *på* she has 13 relevant nouns, nine that are definite. Summarizing these, we find 22 relevant nouns, of which 14 are definite in accordance with the target, yielding 63 percent. (Gender has not been a focus in the count.) It is safe to say that Daisy does not have a full grip of the use of the definiteness suffix.

4.1.2 The indefinite determiner

There are some cases of missing indefinite determiners in Daisy that shows that she does not have a full mastery of the indefinite determiner. A few examples where she has used the indefinite determiner in accordance with the target are shown in (10); examples with missing indefinite determiners are shown in (11).

(10) a. *Så mannen   min og jeg fikk en apartment*
       so husband.DEF my and I   got an apartment
       '… so my husband and I got an apartment.'
   b. *Så var det en kirke   som var i   nabolaget*
       so was it a church that was in neighbourhood.DEF
       'Then there was a church that was in the neigbourhood.'
   c. *Det er en fisk jeg vil ikke ha   i hus*
       that is a fish I   will not have in house
       'That is a fish I don't want to have in my house.'
   d. *Han arbeider på et hotell*
       he works   at a hotel
       'He works at a hotel.'

(11) a. **Jeg jobbet   på telefonkompani*
       I   worked   at telephone.company
       'I worked at a telephone company.'
                  (expected: *et telefonkompani*)
   b. **Det er bare par   av oss som gjør det*
       it is only couple of us who do   it
       'There are only a couple of us that do it.'
                  (expected: *et par*)
   c. **Det er hvit   bygning som er på banen*
       it is white building that is on field.DEF
       'It's a white building that's on the field.'
                  (expected: *en hvit bygning*)

Although Daisy has a few examples that lack an indefinite determiner, there are not many. On the other hand, the recording abounds with target uses of the indefinite determiner. There are 27 occurrences of the common gender article *en* 'a' followed by a singular noun in the Corpus of American Norwegian Speech, all used in accordance with the target, i.e., 100%. A search for indefinite nouns directly following verbs, excluding names and name-like words like *mor* 'mother,' yielded 33 relevant cases, 21 of which are target uses, i.e., 63%.

4.1.3 Compositional definiteness

Compositional definiteness was illustrated in (2). It is a very complex construction given that a phrase containing an adjective requires a preposed definite determiner, a definiteness suffix on the adjective and a definiteness suffix on the noun. In addition, the determiner and the suffix must agree in number, gender and definiteness. Our informant Daisy clearly has some problems with compositional definiteness.

(12) a. Lacks determiner: *den*
**andre   kanten*
other.DEF edge.DEF.SG.M
b. Lacks determiner: *det*
**norske   flagget*
Norwegian.DEF flag.DEF.SG.N
c. Lacks suffix: *bygningen*
**den   store   building*
the.DEF.SG.M big.DEF building.SG
d. Lacks suffix: *året*
**det   samme   år*
the.DEF.SG.N same.DEF year.SG
e. Lacks suffix: *nabolagene*
**disse   nabolag*
these.DEF.PL neighbourhoods.PL
f. Lacks suffix: *barna*
**de   to   barn*
the.DEF.PL two children.PL
g. Lacks suffix: *recorderne*
**de   gamle   recorder*
the.DEF.PL old.DEF records.PL
h. Wrong gender+lacks suffix: *kirken*
**det   gamle   kirke*
the.DEF.SG.N old.DEF church.SG
i. Wrong gender+lacks suffix: *gangen*
**det   første   gang*
the.DEF.SG.N first.DEF time.SG
j. Lacks two suffixes: *første, gangen*
**de   først   par   ganger*
the.DEF.PL først.INDEF couple times.INDEF.PL

Compositional definiteness is clearly a problem for Daisy. There are hardly any well-formed examples of such noun phrases in the recordings. It is worth noting that noun phrases containing compositional definiteness are very different from English noun phrases, as exemplified in (13):

(13) a. the first time
b. the first times

English noun phrases have no number or gender inflection on the preposed definite determiner or any inflection on the adjective. They have no definiteness suffix; only a plural suffix, which is the same for most nouns.

Daisy's compositional noun phrases are not like the English ones, since most of the time, only one feature is missing; most often the definiteness suffix. She keeps most of the inflection; i.e., agreement marking with respect to definiteness marking on the adjective, and various inflections of the preposed determiner.

Her use of noun phrases with the masculine and neuter singular determiner as well as the plural determiner has also been checked, using the Corpus of American Norwegian Speech (searching for either *den* 'the.M.SG,' *det* 'the.N.SG,' or *de* 'the.PL' followed by an adjective followed by a noun). There were eight of these altogether, and they all lacked one or more suffixes, thus supporting the general findings above.

4.1.4   Pronouns

Daisy's use of personal pronouns is fine:

(14) a. *Ho var hjelp*
      she was help
      'She was a help.'

   b. *Hun hadde familie her*
      she had family here
      'She had family here.'

   c. *Han var fra Flekke i Sunnfjord*
      he was from Flekke in Sunnfjord
      'He was from Flekke in Sunnfjord.'

   d. *Han gikk opp til Minneapolis*
      he went up to Minneapolis
      'He went up to Minneapolis.'

   e. *Da fløtte dem til Flekke*
      then moved they to Flekke
      'Then they moved to Flekke.'

In the corpus of American Norwegian Speech, Daisy uses the third person feminine pronoun *hun* (and its variant *ho*) 'she' 47 times, all, i.e., 100%, in accordance with the target.[9] The other pronouns are also used in a target-like manner.

---

[9] It should be mentioned that in many Norwegian dialects the personal pronouns *han* 'he' and *hun* 'she' are also used with inanimate masculine and feminine gender nouns. This is not the case in Moss, however, which is the town from where Daisy's language clearly originates.

4.2 Clauses and sentences

4.2.1 *V2 word order with topicalization*

In describing Daisy's word order pattern, it can be useful to present them by type, after what syntactic category is preposed. Let us first make the assumption that in order to have a fully working V2 system for all categories, we should expect V2 with simple SVA word order. However, Daisy does some somewhat surprising things. With sentences containing adverbs, we find them intervening before the verb, causing V3 word order, which is not grammatical in declarative main clauses in Norwegian.

(15) a. *Hennes familie også var norsk
       her   family also was Norwegian
       'Her family was also Norwegian.'
                          (expected: *var også*)
   b. *Vi alle sammen spiste torsk
       we all together ate   cod
       'All of us had cod.'
                          (expected: *spiste alle sammen*)
   c. *Vi bestandig hadde fisk
       we always   had   fish
       'We always had fish.'
                          (expected: *hadde bestandig*)
   d. *Vi alle sammen spiser lefse
       we all together eat   lefse
       'All of us eat lefse.'
                          (expected: *spiser alle sammen*)

With sentence-initial subjects we find, then, that Daisy produces V3 if the adverb is *også* 'also,' *bestandig* 'always' or a quantifier like *alle sammen* 'all, everybody.' We shall see in Section 4.2.2 that if the adverb is *ikke* 'not,' the standard V2 word order is used.

There is one example of a topicalized subordinate subject noun phrase. It does not trigger V2:

(16) *Alle sammen jeg trur gikk på kirke   i Voss
      all together I think went on church in Voss
      'I think everybody went to church in Voss.'
                          (expected: *trur jeg*)

Let us turn to preposed preposition phrases. We first present some that have ungrammatical word order. Given what we have just seen, it is not surprising that we find V3 here, with the order PP+subject+verb.

(17) a. *I skolen vi snakte bare engelsk
        in school we talked only English
        'At school we only spoke English.'
                          (expected: *snakte vi*)

b. *I Norge <u>dem ville</u> aldri møte
   in Norway they would never meet
   'In Norway, they would never meet.'
   (expected: *ville dem*)

In (18), however, we find some target-like seemingly PP-initial sentences.

(18) a. *I Humboldt Park står en vi kaller det*
   in Humboldt Park stands one we call it
   'In Humboldt Park, there is a, we call it,
   statue of Leif Eriksson
   statue of Leif Eiriksson
   statue of Leif Eiriksson.'
   b. *I depression så måtte dem stenge*
   in depression then must they close
   'In the depression they had to close.'
   c. *Etter krigen så kom han tilbake*
   after war then came he back
   'After the war he came back.'

It is debatable whether the sentence in (18) should be interpreted as a sign that Daisy sometimes has V2 with PP-initial sentences. (18a) is PP-initial and has V2, but it could be that this is due to the subject being too long and heavy to move to the second position, where Daisy has put her subjects in (17). The left dislocation nature of the PPs in (18b, c) means that these clauses are not PP-initial, but light-adverb-initial.

We now turn from preposed PP adverbials to preposed adverbial clauses. Daisy never has the verb in the standard second position in these cases:

(19) a. *Når jeg kom tilbake, <u>jeg kunne</u> ikke gå bak*
   when I came back I could not walk behind
   'When I came back, I couldn't walk behind.'
   (expected: *kunne jeg*)
   b. *Hvis det hadde vært oss, <u>vi ville</u> ha...,*
   if it had been us we would have
   'If it had been us, we would have...'
   (expected: *ville vi*)
   c. *Når alle norskene kom isammen, <u>dem bestandig snakte</u> norsk*
   when all Norwegians came together they always spoke Norwegian
   'When all the Norwegians met, they always spoke Norwegian.'
   (expected: *snakte dem bestandig*)
   d. *Når du går oppe i Wisconsin, <u>du finner</u> mange plasser*
   when you walk up in Wisconsin you find many places
   'When you go up to Wisconsin, you find many places.'
   (expected: *finner du*)

(19) e. *Når vi kom ut i Nordsjøen, vi gikk   bak og
       when we came out in North.Sea we walked back and
       'When we came out in the North Sea we went back and
       frem i sengene
       forth in beds
       forth in our beds.'
                    (expected: gikk vi)
   f. *Når vi gikk   ner   for 17.mai-parade, vi gikk   der
      when we walked down for 17.May parade we walked there
      'When we went down for the 17. May parade, we walked there.'
                    (expected: gikk vi)
   g. *Etter krigen kom, så mannen min og jeg fikk en apartment
      after war   came so husband my and I got an apartment
      'After the war had started, my husband and I got an apartment.'
                    (expected: fikk mannen min og jeg)

The last example, (19g), actually contains a left dislocated clause, with a light adverb inserted in the proper topic position. Unlike in (18b,c) above it does not make V2 more accessible this time.

Having seen that light adverbs may have an effect on the choice between V2 and V3 pattern, we now look at some of Daisy's sentences that have preposed light adverbs.

(20) a. Da fløtte   dem til Flekke
       then moved they to Flekke
       'Then they moved to Flekke.'
   b. Så var det en kirke   som var i nabolaget
      then was it a church that was in neighbourhood
      'Then there was a church that was in the neighbourhood.'
   c. Da skjærte jeg
      then cut   I
      'Then I cut.'

In the Corpus of American Norwegian Speech, Daisy has 14 target occurrences of the adverb *da* 'then' followed by a finite verb (V2), and one non-target followed by a pronoun (V3). This gives her 92% target V2 word order with light adverbs.

Preposed noun phrases functioning as adverbials have V2 order, as in (21). However, notice that (21a) has a left dislocated adverbial with a light adverb in the proper topic position.

(21) a. Lørdag og søndag så   har han fri
       Saturday and Sunday then has he   off
       'Saturdays and Sundays, he is off.'
   b. En gang imellom   var det fra   øst
      one time inbetween was it   from East
      'Sometimes it was from the East.'

Finally, a preposed adverbial question phrase consisting of one question word is included. Question phrases in many dialects do not trigger V2, yielding exactly the word order we see in (22).

(22) *Åssen de sier..,
     how they say
     'How do they say…?'
                    (standard dialect: *sier de*)

Johannessen and Laake (2011, this volume) have shown that many Norwegian Americans have this question word order as part of their heritage variety, just as in the locations their ancestors come from. It is clear that Daisy does not speak those dialects, but her father is from Sunnfjord, an area that does have this word order. It is in principle possible that she has this feature from him (or other people she has known), although she does not have other dialect features from that dialect, so we should be careful to judge it as an attrited feature here.

A search of the Corpus of American Norwegian Speech yielded 16 cases of sentence-initial subordinate clauses by Daisy. Only four of them have a verb in the target second position, after the clause, i.e., 25%. However, there are 92% clauses with fronted light adverbs that do have target word-order. This means that Daisy's grammar distinguishes between the kinds of syntactic categories in the adverbials that are preposed, adverbs versus adverbial clauses.

4.2.2   V2 with negation

In (23) we see some examples with a sentence-initial subject and the negation adverb placed according to the target order: after the verb. (23d) shows that Daisy also masters object shift, i.e., that a light pronominal object can occur preposed to the negative adverb.

(23) a. *Jeg er ikke sikkert*
        I   am not certain
        'I'm not certain.'
     b. *Vi snakket ikke i sammen*
        we talked   not together
        'We didn't speak together.'
     c. *Jeg husker   ikke nå   hva det var*
        I   remember not now what it was
        'I don't remember now what it was.'
     d. *Jeg sier det ikke riktig*
        I   say it not right
        'I don't say it right.'

Daisy's recording in the Corpus of American Norwegian Speech contains 78 occurrences of *ikke*. They all follow a finite verb or a light shifted object, i.e., 100% target use. Note that the number depends somewhat on what is included in the count. Here the count includes all the target occurrences in all clauses. In 4.2.3, we will see that subordinate clauses often have the non-target verb-adverb word order. Such occurrences have not been subtracted from the target results in this section. It can be concluded that Daisy has full mastery of the word order with negation in main clauses, which is surprising given the ungrammatical examples with the other adverbs in 4.2.1. We should also notice that this word order is not in any way like English, which has do-support with lexical verbs, like *snakke* 'talk', *huske* 'remember', and *si* 'say' (cf. (23b, c, d)).

4.2.3 Target V3 in subordinate clauses

Section 3.2 described the general pattern of subordinate clauses in European Norwegian, which is V3 in the case that there is an adverb in the clause. Daisy's subordinate clauses in (24) show that she does not normally have the target word order ((24f) is an exception to her general pattern).

(24) a. *Når du <u>skal ikke</u> forstå, da begynner du å lære
when you shall not understand then begin you to learn
'When you are not meant to understand then you begin to learn.'
(expected: *ikke skal*)

b. *Jeg studerte noe ganger hvorfor dem <u>lærte ikke</u>
I wondered some times why they learnt not
'I wondered sometimes why they didnt learn.'
(expected: *ikke lærte*)

c. *Det er en norsk mat som jeg <u>har aldri</u> likt
it is a Norwegian food that I have never liked
'That is a kind of Norwegian food that I have never liked.'
(expected: *aldri har*)

d. *Det er en fisk jeg <u>vil ikke</u> ha i hus!
that is a fish I will never have in house
'That is a kind of fish that I will never have in my house.'
(expected: *ikke vil*)

e. *Jeg trur hun <u>arbeider nå</u> for Macys
I think she works now for Macys
'I think she works for Macy's now.'
(expected: *nå arbeider*)

f. det er et par koner [...]som still snakker norsk
it is a couple women who still speak Norwegian
'There are a few women that still speak Norwegian.'

We notice first that the structure in the sentences in (24) is not English. English has *do*-support with negated lexical verbs, something which cannot be said of Daisy's Norwegian sentences, as illustrated in (24b), which has the lexical verb *lære* 'learn' with negation. Larsson and Johannessen (2015a, b) discuss such structures and conclude that they do not represent English word order or a generalized V2 word order. Instead, they assume that what is at stake is incomplete acquisition of syntactic features. This can be supported by the fact that such constructions are learned very late. In her case she probably never learned them properly.

In the Corpus of American Norwegian Speech there are six hits for sentences with a subjunction and an adverb in the subordinate clause (it is more difficult to search for sentences without subjunctions, so that was not done). Out of these, only one has the target order, somewhat surprisingly with an English adverb: *still*, (24f). The other five have the non-target V2 order, similar to the examples shown in (24a–e). This means that only 17% target have the word order.

However, importantly, V3 word order is one in which European Norwegian and Heritage Norwegian seem to differ, see Taranrød (2011) and Larsson and Johannessen (2015a, b). The latter argue that the V-Adv order found in many Heritage Norwegian speakers is best explained as a result of incomplete acquisition, i.e., that it has probably never been learnt, and hence cannot be lost. While Daisy's subordinate clauses fit with the general pattern, they should not be seen as a sign of attrition.

5. Daisy's results relative to the acquisition data

5.1 Noun-phrase related categories

Starting with the noun phrase and its categories, we have seen that there is a hierarchy in acquisition in which the definiteness suffix is learnt first, followed by pronouns, then indefinite determiners, and finally compositional definiteness, as depicted in Table 2.

There is thus a hierarchy that we can compare with Daisy's language. The definiteness suffix is missing in several of Daisy's utterances. She does use it, but in no way in every target context. On the other hand, she does not use it wrongly, for example in a context where the indefinite determiner would have been more appropriate. We saw that her indefinite determiners are mostly in place, although there are some examples of missing determiners. Pronouns, however, present no problems, and the discourse seems fluent in the choice of pronoun and lexical noun phrase. We insert these categories into Table 2 in order of how well the categories are mastered by Daisy.

Table 2. The hierarchies of acquisition of categories and structures related to the noun phrase.[10]

Noun-phrase-related acquisition	Age	Daisy's noun-phrase-related production	Numbers
Definiteness suffix	2;3.12	Pronouns	100%
Pronouns	After 2;3.12	Indefinite determiners	63%
Indefinite determiners	3;3.18	Definiteness suffix	63%
Compositional definiteness	After 3;3.18	Compositional definiteness	0%

Table 2 shows that there is no one-to-one correspondence between acquisition and well-formed production. If the regression hypothesis worked blindly, Daisy's most perfect categories would coincide with those that were acquired earliest. There is a discrepancy between the early acquisition of the definiteness suffix, and Daisy's poor production of it in the right target contexts. However, it could depend on what is counted. Here it is missing definiteness suffixes in target contexts that have been the focus of attention. On the other hand, the focus could instead have been the phonological expression of the suffixes, in either non-target or target positions. So given the methodological problem with this category (and the same with indefinite determiners), it is hard to conclude for these categories. However, compositional definiteness is different. It seems always to fail at least once in each noun phrase in Daisy's recordings. It is also the category that is acquired last. This gives some support for the regression hypothesis.

5.2 Clause-related categories

The syntactic problem structures that have been investigated are related to verb and adverb word order. We saw in Section 3.2 that target V2 with negation is acquired early, while word order with other topicalized elements are learnt a bit later. What is clearly much harder is target V3 in subordinate clauses, which is learnt beyond 3 years of age. These are inserted as a new column in Table 3.

Looking at Daisy's production, first, she does not have V2 in declarative clauses with adverbs, i.e., target SVA, (15). We then looked at topicalized clauses with a fronted PP. These are not produced according to the target. (17) showed two relatively simple sentences, both of which were V3. There were three PP-initial clauses with V2, (18). However, the first one had such a long and heavy subject that it could not have been moved further towards the front of the clause. The PPs of the other two were actually not sentence-initial, but left dislocated, followed by a light adverb each. The

---

10. Tables 2 and 3 are formatted differently than Table 1, in that they have no horizontal lines across the whole table. This is because the two columns in each of the table are independent of each other. The left-hand side shows the general order of acquistion according to the literature, and the right-hand side shows Daisy's production in terms of success towards the target. Ideally, both colums of each table should have the grammatical categories in the same order, if her production mirrored exactly the order of acquisition.

sentences in (20) show that Daisy nearly always (92% of the occurrences with topicalized *da* 'then') has V2 after light adverbs, something that is also supported further in yet another example of left dislocation followed by a light adverb. The seemingly PP-initial V2 sentences have the target word order, but it can be concluded that this is due to reasons other than the fact that there might be a PP in the topic position. The sentences that contain preposed clauses, like those in (19), have V2 in only 25% of the cases. Daisy has no discrepancies from the target, however, with respect to negation. Her negated sentences, like those in (23), have V2 word order. With respect to V2, it can be concluded that Daisy masters this word order for simple clauses, both those that have a light adverb in the topic position and those that are negated. There are approximately 60 negated main clauses by Daisy, all with a target word order. She does not master V2 with PP topics or with clausal topics. Daisy's target V3 sentences nearly all have non-target V-Adv order (but see Section 3.2.3 and below). The results are compared with the age of acquisition for each type in Table 3. However, children do not use complicated structures like preposed adverbial clauses at the time that they learn V2 with topicalization, so this cell is left blank here.

Table 3. The hierarchies of acquisition and production of clause-related structures.

Clause-related structures	Age	Daisy's clause-related production	Percent
V2 word order with negation	2;2.12	V2 word order with negation	100%
V2 word order with topicalized light adverbs	2;4	V2 word order with topicalized light adverbs	92%
V2 word order with topicalized subordinate clauses		V2 word order with topicalized subordinate clauses	25%
Target V3 order in subordinate clauses	After 3;0.0	Target V3 order in subordinate clauses	17%

When it comes to clause-related structures there is a total correlation between the acquisition hierarchy and Daisy's production hierarchy. Larsson and Johannessen (2015a, b) discuss similar problems with target V3 subordinate word order in American Norwegians that are otherwise fluent speakers. We argue there that this is due to incomplete acquisition of the last step in the syntactic development of the speakers. If those fluent speakers fell victim to incomplete acquisition, there is no reason to assume that this is not also the case for Daisy. In that case, we should not count the failure of target V3 in subordinate clauses as attrition, and we should not compare it directly to the acquisition stage.[11] However, notice that in any case, the fact that target V3 is acquired very late in the child is a kind of support for the incomplete

---

11. Notice that attrition and incomplete acquisition are not the same, although some scholars (such as Putnam and Sánchez 2013) suggest that they are interrelated. The present author follows the same ideas as those in Larsson and Johannessen (2015a, b), where, if something is incompletely acquired, it is not learnt properly, which can be seen in non-consistency in language production. If, on the other hand, a linguistic feature of a speaker is attrited, it has existed and been used consistently by that speaker, but is subsequently lost.

acquisition hypothesis; other things in the environment may cause the child not to learn the last steps within a development. Our conclusion here, though, does not hinge on the target V3 pattern, since we have also looked at V2, where there does indeed seem to be a mirror-image correlation between the order of acquisition and attrition.

6. Conclusion

This paper has tested the regression hypothesis on the language of a Norwegian language heritage speaker, Daisy, whose language, it is argued, is attrited. Daisy's language has been studied with respect to four noun-phrase-related categories and four clause-related categories. While Daisy's production of some categories is almost identical to European Norwegian and Heritage, the production of other categories is clearly very different. Two categories that show no attrition effects are those of pronouns and of V2 word order with negation.

The eight categories have been investigated with the aim of finding when they are acquired and in which order, consulting relevant literature. If the non-affected categories are those that are learnt first, and the attrited categories are those that are learnt last, there is a mirror-effect between the orders of acquisition and attrition, and the regression hypothesis is supported.

My findings are not totally clear, but the general picture supports the regression hypothesis. The noun phrase-related categories definiteness suffix and indefinite determiner are somewhat problematic in how they should be counted. These two categories therefore cannot be decisive for the conclusion. Pronouns, on the other hand, are assumed to be acquired early, and are also fully in place for Daisy. Compositional definiteness is assumed by the acquisition literature to be learnt very late, and this is also a category where Daisy's language differs a lot from the target.

Amongst the clause-related categories, all appear to have mirror-image correlation between acquisition and attrition. V2 word order with negation is acquired very early, and is also in place in Daisy's language. V2 with topicalization of adverbials, which is supposed to be learnt at a later stage, also is less like the target in Daisy's speech. She distinguishes between sentences whose initial adverbial is a light adverb and those whose adverbial contains a heavy phrase, for example a preposition phrase or an adverbial subordinate clause. The fourth clause-relevant category studied here is target V3 in subordinate clauses. This is a category that is learnt very late, and is also one in which Daisy produces extremely few target-like examples. Larsson and Johannessen (2015a, b) have analyzed this type as it has been produced by other, fluent Norwegian Americans, as incomplete acquisition. It should therefore not be regarded here as attrition. The main conclusion of the present paper is, all the same, that it is possible to see the relationship between acquisition and attrition data as support for the regression hypothesis.

Finally, a note of comparison should be made to the study of Keijzer (2010). She looks closely at two noun-phrase-related morphological features (plural suffix and diminutive suffix). While she finds some mirror-image correlations when performing an elicitation test, her free speech recordings, which are most comparable to the study conducted here, shows hardly any non-target results. She does, however, refer to a more comprehensive study where more morphological and also syntactic categories were tested (Keijzer 2007). There, negation behaved similarly for her two groups, learners and emigrants, while V2 did not (Keijzer 2010: 15). These results are interesting when compared with the clause- related ones here: Negation is straightforward for both groups, while target V2 should be divided into several categories depending on what syntactic category sits in the topic position. Clearly more research is needed on this.

References

Anderssen, Merete. 2006. *The Acquisition of Compositional Definiteness in Norwegian*. Tromsø, Norway: University of Tromsø dissertation.
Anderssen, Merete. 2007. "The Acquisition of Compositional Definiteness in Norwegian." *Nordlyd* 34(3): 252–275.
Anderssen, Merete. 2010. "Tidlig tilegnelse av bestemt artikkel i norsk. [Early acquisition of the definite article in Norwegian]." *Norsk Lingvistisk Tidsskrift* [Norwegian Linguistics Journal] 28(2): 153–172.
Annear, Lucas and Kristin Speth. This volume. "Maintaining a Multilingual Repertoire: Lexical Change in American Norwegian."
Bentzen, Kristine. 2004. "Cues and Economy in the Acquisition of Verb Movement." *Nordlyd* 32(1): 156–175.
Bentzen, Kristine. 2007. *Order and Structure in Embedded Clauses in Northern Norwegian*. Tromsø, Norway: University of Tromsø dissertation.
Born, Renate. 2003. "Regression, Convergence, Internal Development: The Loss of the Dative Case in German-American Dialects." In *German Language Varieties Worldwide: Internal and External Perspectives*, ed. by William D. Keel and Klaus J. Mattheier, 151–164. Frankfurt am Main: Lang.
Burke, Deborah M. and Meredith A. Shafto. 2008. "Language and Aging." In *The Handbook of Aging and Cognition*, ed. by Fergus I. M. Craik and Timothy A. Salthouse, 373–443. New York: Psychology Press.
Corpus of American Norwegian Speech: http://tekstlab.uio.no/glossa/html/?corpus=amerikanorsk.
Eide, Kristin and Arnstein Hjelde. This volume. "Borrowing Modal Elements into American Norwegian: The Case of *suppose(d)*."
Faarlund, Jan Terje, Svein Lie and Kjell Ivar Vannebo. 1997. *Norsk referansegrammatikk* [Norwegian reference grammar]. Oslo: Universitetsforlaget.
Hjelde, Arnstein. This volume. "Changes in a Norwegian Dialect in America."
Hjelde, Arnstein. 1992. *Trøndsk talemål i Amerika*. Trondheim: Tapir.

Jakobson, Roman. 1941. *Kindersprache. Aphasie und allgemeine Lautgesetze*. Uppsala: Almqvist.
Johannessen, Janne Bondi. 2015. The Corpus of American Norwegian Speech (CANS). In Béata Megyesi (ed.): *Proceedings of the 20th Nordic Conference of Computational Linguistics, NODALIDA 2015*, May 11–13, 2015, Vilnius, Lithuania. NEALT Proceedings Series 23. http://www.ep.liu.se/ecp_article/index.en.aspx?issue=109;article=040
Johannessen, Janne Bondi and Signe Laake. 2011. "Den amerikansk-norske dialekten i Midtvesten." In *Studier i dialektologi och sociolingvistik. Föredrag vid Nionde nordiska dialektologkonferensen i Uppsala 18–20 augusti 2010. Acta Academiae Regiae Gustavi Adolphi 116*, ed. by Lars-Erik Edlund, Lennart Elmevik and Maj Reinhammar, 177–186. Uppsala: Kungl. Gustav Adolfs Akademien för svensk folkkultur.
Johannessen, Janne Bondi and Signe Laake. Forthcoming. "Eastern Norwegian as a Common Norwegian Dialect in the American Midwest." *Journal of Language Contact*.
Johannessen, Janne Bondi and Signe Laake. This volume. "On two Myths of the Norwegian Language in America: Is it Old-Fashioned? Is it Approaching the Written Bokmål Standard?"
Julien, Marit. 2005. *Nominal Phrases from a Scandinavian Perspective*. Amsterdam: John Benjamins Publishing Company. DOI: 10.1075/la.87
Julien, Marit. 2007. "Embedded V2 in Norwegian and Swedish." *Working Papers in Scandinavian Syntax* 80.
Julien, Marit. 2008. "Så vanleg at det kan ikkje avfeiast: om V2 i innføydde setningar." In *Språk i Oslo. Ny forskning omkring talespråk*, ed. by Janne Bondi Johannessen and Kristin Hagen, 159–171. Oslo: Novus Forlag.
Julien, Marit. 2009. "The force of the argument." *Working Papers in Scandinavian Syntax* 84:225–232.
Keijzser, Merel. 2007. *Last in First Out? An Investigation of the Regression Hypothesis in Dutch Emigrants in Anglophone Canada*. Utrecht: LOT publications.
Keijzser, Merel. 2010. "The Regression Hypothesis as a Framework for First Language Acquisition." *Bilingualism: Language and Cognition* 13(1): 9–18. DOI: 10.1017/S1366728909990356
Kristoffersen, Kristian E., Hanne Gram Simonsen, Dorthe Bleses, Sonja Wehberg, Rune Nørgård Jørgensen, Eli Anne Eiesland, and Laila Y. Henriksen. 2012. "The Use of the Internet in Collecting CDI Data – An Example from Norway." *Journal of Child Language* 40(3): 567–585. DOI: 10.1017/S0305000912000153
Kristoffersen, Kristian Emil and Hanne Gram Simonsen. 2012. *Tidlig språkutvikling hos norske barn. MacArthur-Bates foreldrerapport for kommunikativ utvikling*. Oslo: Novus forlag.
Larsson, Ida and Janne Bondi Johannessen. 2015a. "Embedded Word Order in Heritage Scandinavian." In *New trends in Nordic and General Linguistics (Linguae et Litterae series)*, ed. by Martin Hilpert, Jan-Ola Östman, Christine Mertzlufft, Michael Riessler, and Janet Duke. Berlin: De Gruyter Mouton, 239–266.
Larsson, Ida and Johannessen, Janne Bondi. 2015b. Incomplete Acquisition and Verb Placement in Heritage Scandinavian. In Page, Richard S; Putnam, Michael T. (eds.): *Moribund Germanic Heritage Languages in North America: Theoretical Perspectives and Empirical Findings*. Brill Academic Publishers.
Montrul, Silvina A. 2008. *Incomplete Acquisition in Bilingualism: Re-examining the Age Factor*. Amsterdam: John Benjamins Publishing Company. DOI: 10.1075/sibil.39
Montrul, Silvina, Rebecca Foote and Silvia Perpiñán. 2008. "Gender Agreement in Adult Second Language Learners and Spanish Heritage Speakers: The Effects of Age and Context of Acquisition." *Language Learning* 58: 503–553. DOI: 10.1111/j.1467-9922.2008.00449.x

Platzack, Christer. 1996. "The Initial Hypothesis of Syntax: A Minimalist Perspective on Language Acquisition and Attrition." In *Generative Perspectives on Language Acquisition: Empirical Findings, Theoretical Considerations, Crosslinguistic Comparisons*, ed. by Harald Clahsen, 369–414. Amsterdam: John Benjamins. DOI: 10.1075/lald.14.15pla

Polinsky, Maria. 2008. "Gender Under Incomplete Acquisition: Heritage Speakers' Knowledge of Noun Categorization." *Heritage Language Journal* 6(1): 40–71.

Polinsky, Maria. 2011. "Reanalysis in Adult Heritage Language: New Evidence in Support of Attrition." *Studies in Second Language Acquisition* 33: 305–328. DOI: 10.1017/S027226311000077X

Putnam, Michael and Liliana Sánchez. 2013. "What's So Incomplete About Incomplete Acquisition? – A Prolegomenon to Modeling Heritage Language Grammars." *Linguistic Approaches to Bilingualism* 3(4): 478–508. DOI: 10.1075/lab.3.4.04put

Rothman, Jason. 2009. "Understanding the Nature and Outcomes of Early Bilingualism: Romance Languages as Heritage Languages." *International Journal of Bilingualism* 13(2): 155–163. DOI: 10.1177/1367006909339814

Schmid, Monika S. and Barbara Köpke. 2008. "L1 Attrition and the Mental Lexicon." In *The Bilingual Mental Lexicon: Interdisciplinary Approaches*, ed. by Aneta Pavlenko, 209–238. Clevedon: Multilingual Matters.

Second Workshop on Immigrant Languages in America, Fefor, Norway, 2011: http://www.hf.uio.no/iln/english/about/organization/text-laboratory/news-events/events/2011/feforseminar-norskiamerika.html.

Taranrød, Beate. 2011. *Leddstillingen i relativsetninger i amerikansknorsk*. Oslo, Norway: University of Oslo MA Thesis.

Waldmann, Christian. 2008. *Input och output. Ordföljd i svenska barns huvudsatser och bisatser*. Lund, Sweden: Lund University dissertation.

Westergaard, Marit. 2005. *The Development of Word Order in Norwegian Child Language: The Interaction of Input and Economy Principles in the Acquisition of V2*. Tromsø, Norway: University of Tromsø dissertation.

Westergaard, Marit and Merete Anderssen. This volume. "Word Order Variation in Norwegian Possessive Constructions: Bilingual Acquisition and Attrition."

Wikström, Åsa. 2008. *Den finita satsen i små barns språk. Nordlund 28. Småskrifter från Nordiska språk*. Lund: Lund University.

Reexamining Icelandic as a heritage language in North America

Birna Arnbjörnsdóttir
University of Iceland

This chapter presents a general description of North American Icelandic (NA Icelandic), a heritage language spoken by a few hundred speakers in language conclaves on the Northern Plains of the United States and Canada. The description is mainly based on studies of the development of Icelandic as a heritage language in intense contact with English in North America (Arnbjörnsdóttir 2006). Generalizations about features of the NA Icelandic lexicon, morphosyntax and phonology are presented in an effort to lay the groundwork for the next stage of NA Icelandic heritage linguistics. Finally, a possible future research agenda for NA Icelandic is outlined that is in line with the recent discussion about the importance of heritage languages for our understanding of the acquisition and loss of language (Benmamoun et al. 2010).

Keywords: North American Icelandic, heritage languages, general description, language attrition, language acquisition, multilingualism, language contact

1. Introduction

Prompted by a recent paradigm shift in heritage language research, this chapter will present available corpora and previous general descriptions of North American Icelandic (NA Icelandic), a heritage language spoken by a few hundred speakers in language conclaves on the Northern Plains of the United States and Canada. The goal is to compile available resources and outline a possible research agenda for NA Icelandic that is in line with the recent discussion on the importance of heritage languages for our understanding of the acquisition and loss of language. A definition of a heritage speaker as presented by Polinsky (2008) is adopted here:

> ... a heritage speaker of language A is an individual who grew up speaking (or only hearing) A as his/her first language but for whom A has been replaced by another language as dominant and primary. (Polinsky 2008: 40)

As Polinsky (2008) points out, an important characteristic of heritage speakers is that they are not a homogeneous group (see also Arnbjörnsdóttir 2006), nor have they had formal instruction in the heritage language. This last point is important as a renewed interest in Icelandic as a heritage language has encouraged many Canadians and Americans of Icelandic descent to study the language as a second language. This had led to proficiency in a variety that is closer to Icelandic as it is spoken in Iceland and is therefore outside the scope of studies of heritage languages.

Over twenty-five years ago when this author first encountered NA Icelandic, immigrant languages were studied from the standpoint of variation and the effect of the interaction of language and society on language development (Arnbjörnsdóttir 2006). Those first studies were descriptive and examined immigrant languages as derivatives of the languages as they were spoken in the "old country." The goal of previous linguistic studies of NA Icelandic was to illustrate the developments of Icelandic as a heritage language, with a narrowing functional range and disintergrating social networks (Milroy 1987), in intense contact with English in North America, and compare to the development of modern Icelandic as a fully fledged national language in Iceland (Arnbjörnsdóttir 2006).

Recent developments in heritage language linguistics have altered views about how their study can contribute to an understanding of the development of bilingual grammars and the role of input in the language acquisition process, in addition to what they can tell us about language variation and attrition. In addition to several chapters in the present volume, especially Westergaard and Andersson and Johannessen, see Putnam and Sánchez 2013, Putnam and Arnbjörnsdóttir 2015, Polinsky 2011, Benmamoun et al. 2010, Kim et al. 2009, Montrul 2008). This paradigm shift has rekindled interest in investigating NA Icelandic, especially now that the numbers of speakers are dwindling. With fewer speakers, the opportunity to fortify existing naturalistic corpora with specifically elicited data diminishes. North American Icelandic lends itself well to the study of features associated with heritage languages. It is spoken by a population that learned it as a first language until about age 5 or 6 when formal schooling began and English was introduced. Initial acquisition may have been fortified by early literacy in the L1 Icelandic as many consultants claim to have been able to read Icelandic before starting to learn English. NA Icelandic is also important for the study of heritage languages because immigration to the Icelandic conclaves stopped almost completely after about 40 years in 1914. That means that the language developed for over 60 years as a heritage language with minimal influence from Icelandic in Iceland. Icelandic is an interesting addition to the heritage language flora in different ways. Unlike Swedish and Norwegian, Icelandic has modest geographic variation. It is spoken by a tight knit community of speakers with a cultural and linguistic purism streak. Icelandic also has a rich morphology the development of which is interesting to study in contact with English.

The goal of this paper is to lay the groundwork for the next stage of NA Icelandic heritage linguistics. First the historical background of North American Icelandic and its speakers is outlined. This is followed by an overview of available corpora and previous descriptive studies. Generalizations about features of the NA Icelandic lexicon, morpho-syntax and phonology are presented in the fourth section. These generalizations were chosen because of their perceived relevance to the current (and future) theoretical discussion within heritage language linguistics. The discussion is heavily influenced by Benmamoun, Montrul and Polinsky's white paper on heritage linguistics (2010). In the final section some suggestions for further research will be presented.

2. Background: Icelandic emigration to North America

North American Icelandic is spoken by descendants of emigrants from Iceland who settled in the Midwestern regions of the United States and Canada. Emigration from Iceland to North America began in the 1870s and ended (almost entirely) in 1914. Almost fifteen thousand Icelanders are documented to have emigrated between 1874 and 1914 (Kristjánsson 1983). From the end of immigration in 1914 up until 1975 there was limited communication between Iceland and the Icelandic immigrants in North America with the exception of the exchange of letters (Arnbjörnsdóttir 2006).

Icelanders settled in many areas of Manitoba and Saskatchewan, but mainly in Winnipeg and in the Interlake on the shores of Lake Winnipeg in Manitoba in Canada and in North Dakota in the United States. Many of the immigrants settled initially in "New Iceland," a tract of land on the shores of Lake Winnipeg that was reserved for Icelanders alone. "New Iceland" was a self-governing language enclave for almost a decade with its own government and written laws in Icelandic. Later some of the settlers moved on to North Dakota and to other areas of North America. Today, speakers of Icelandic as a heritage language may be found in and around the original settlements but also as far as the West Coast of the US and Canada (Bessason 1967, Arnbjörnsdóttir 2006).

The number of Icelandic heritage speakers is not known. According to the Census of 1931 there were 19,382 persons who claimed Icelandic ancestry in all of Canada. Of the 82% of those who listed Icelandic as their primary language, 73% were born in North America. By 1961 the numbers of people of Icelandic descent had risen to 30,623 in Canada and 8,669 in the US. In 1986, 14,470 persons in Canada as a whole claimed Icelandic ethnic origins and of those, 6,980 lived in Manitoba. Of the 6,980, 305 claimed that Icelandic was their first language and 800 said that they had grown up with English and Icelandic as home languages (Arnbjörnsdóttir 2006). The 2001 Census for the whole of Canada did not have a category for Icelandic ethnic origin, but the numbers in Manitoba alone had risen to 25,735 (up from 6,980 in 1986) for those who had Icelandic ancestry on one side and 4,785 who claimed to be of Icelandic background on both sides. This rise in numbers of Icelandic ancestry is most likely an indication of the increased interest that third and fourth generation immigrants have in their origins. In the census from 2001 there were not enough speakers of Icelandic to warrant a separate category and the numbers are therefore unavailable. It is an indication of how few speakers are left, though, that some of the categories for other heritage languages had as few as 70 speakers (www.statcan.ca) (Arnbjörnsdóttir 2006).

Many scholars have commented on the longevity or long survival of North American Icelandic especially given the number of emigrants (fewer than 15,000) and the fact that immigration went down to a trickle after 1914. There was not the kind of renewal that is known from other immigrant groups (Bessason 1984, Haugen 1956). People of the third and fourth generations from immigration still spoke the language in 1986, when the author collected linguistic data in the "settlements." The speech of the informants seemed fluent or, at least at the time, the lack of fluency, or a "slow speech rate" (Polinsky 2008), did not seem to be a noticeable factor warranting further examination.

Icelanders settled in rural communities where they were the dominant group, had their own governance and published papers and books in Icelandic. They also continued traditions of literary practice such as teaching children to read Icelandic prior to formal education. The Icelandic immigrants kept up the tradition of home schooling but established English schools immediately upon arrival. Bilingualism was encouraged (Arnbjörnsdóttir 2006).

Icelandic was used almost exclusively by the early immigrants and many informants claimed to have been able to read Icelandic prior to the start of formal schooling. These informants do not therefore fit neatly into Benmamoun et al.'s (2010: 15) view that lack of literacy is a common characteristic of heritage speakers. Crucially though, these heritage speakers' language acquisition may have been fortified by early literacy, even though they were not all comfortable reading Icelandic as adults (Arnbjörnsdóttir 2006). Icelandic has survived in these communities beyond the three-generation paradigm. Icelandic in North America diverged enough from Icelandic to be considered by Bessason (1984) a variety in its own right.

NA Icelandic consists of several regional subvarieties, familylects and idiolects. That is, different settlements may have developed separate dialectal features as suggested by many of the consultants, but so did families and even individuals. Subvarieties are thus made up of familylects and idiolects, both in the traditional sense as having the general idiosyncratic characteristics of individual speakers, and also reflecting the different ranges of embeddedness of English influences into the grammar of Icelandic that vary vastly from speaker to speaker (Stefánsson 1903, Bessason 1967, 1984, Arnbjörnsdóttir 2006).

After the initial decades of isolation, the linguistic situation in the Icelandic settlements in North America over more than a 130 year period constitutes a high contact situation, where NA Icelandic is a heritage language whose speakers have shifted their loyalties towards the dominant language, English.

Variation in the speech of adult bilinguals in heritage situations is social as well as grammatical. The contexts for language use become limited to friends, relatives, acquaintances, i.e., the most informal registers. When one of the languages is almost entirely relegated to the most informal speech situations, there is an added probability that language use, and therefore input, becomes variable making perception, and thus acquisition, more difficult. Changes that are characteristic of the most relaxed register, or most informal speech, become prevalent. This is the case for NA Icelandic. Children who initially grow up speaking Icelandic go to school and bring home English, the younger siblings follow, and soon the children have a life in common that is outside the realm of the language of the parents. While the parents (i.e., those who learned English) were Icelandic-dominant bilinguals, the children, in most cases, become English-dominant. As the children's center of existence moves outside the home, English takes over, even in the most intimate speech situations. Formerly tightly knit social networks begin to disintegrate, new people move in who do not speak Icelandic, and children and grandchildren move on. English becomes the medium for transactions outside the family and with younger persons. Opportunities for language production diminish and along with that metalinguistic awareness in the heritage language and comprehension of the language exceeds the ability to produce the language (Putnam and Sánchez 2013). The level of metalinguistic awareness and unfamiliarity in speaking the language with non-intimates may affect consultants' performance as much as their general proficiency in the language and should be a consideration in research methodology (Benmamoun et al. 2010: 16).

Linguistic purism runs deep in Icelandic culture and found its way to the NA Icelandic settlements in the form of loyalty to the old language by many, as exemplified by the frequent newspaper articles deploring the condition of Icelandic in the "colony." Many NA Icelanders were avid readers of newspapers, books and poetry as seen in the prolific publishing of Icelandic texts by NA Icelanders (Arnbjörnsdóttir 2006). Some of the consultants from the 1986 corpora mentioned that they themselves did not speak 'proper' Icelandic, often followed by a suggestion that they knew people who did. Comments like the following were quite common: *"hann pabbi talaði ósköp fallega íslensku"* 'my father spoke beautiful Icelandic' and *"amma kunni að tala rétta íslensku"* 'my grandmother knew how to speak correct Icelandic' and even *"börnin tala íslensku en eru nógu gáfuð til að tala hana ekki fyrir framan aðra"* 'the children speak Icelandic but they are smart enough not to speak it in front of others.' Others commented that their way of speaking was not the same as in Iceland but that it worked for them (Arnbjörnsdóttir 2006). The author had an opportunity to take part in two social occasions in 1986 in Mountain – the centennial anniversary of the first Icelandic church in North Dakota, and an "Icelandic" picnic. Very little Icelandic was spoken on either of these occasions except in groups were one or more guests from Iceland were present. One informant remarked that the only time she could think of when Icelandic was used outside the home these days was at the funeral of a prominent "Icelander" out of reverence for the deceased.

Results of an informal survey of attitudes towards Icelandic by Icelandic Americans in North Dakota in 1986 provide a good picture of the use of Icelandic in North Dakota. Out of fifty people surveyed, thirty-two said they had spoken Icelandic exclusively to their parents and grandparents and most often to their siblings as preschool aged children. As adults, the same individuals speak Icelandic mostly to their siblings and not exclusively so. Most participants in the survey were able to read and write Icelandic as children. Those surveyed who always spoke Icelandic as youngsters, ranged in age from forty-five to eighty-six at the time they were surveyed in 1986. Only three speakers were under sixty-five (Arnbjörnsdóttir 1990). North American Icelandic is spoken by bilinguals who, in 1986, used it almost entirely in the most familiar and intimate situations at home and with family and friends. They use English on all other occasions. The consultants seemed to be able to speak with some fluency, mostly with a natural speech rate. This differs from Polinsky's heritage language informants, whose language was characterized by slow speech rates (Polinsky 2008).

3. Previous linguistic research and available resources

North American Icelandic is a threatened heritage language with very few speakers left. Early studies focused on describing NA Icelandic, especially the NA Icelandic lexicon, and three main corpora have been collected that contain examples of NA Icelandic speech. Two of those were collected for ethnographic purposes with a focus on linguistic and cultural adaptations to a new way of life in a new environment. One corpus, collected by the author, focused on examining linguistic and social variation in NA Icelandic.

3.1 Early studies

The first reference to special characteristics of North American Icelandic speech in the linguistic literature is Vilhjálmur Stefánsson's article (1903) on English loanwords (nouns) in the variety of Icelandic spoken in North Dakota. At the time, Vilhjálmur estimates that there are about three thousand speakers of Icelandic in North Dakota. The purpose of his description is to shed light on how gender is assigned to new loanwords in the NA Icelandic lexicon along with reflections about their pronunciation. He provides a list of 467 nouns, 176 of which have been assigned neuter (sometimes words ending in -l, -ll; 137 masculine (e.g., English words ending in -r, -er); and 44 feminine. A further 110 words could have two or three genders depending on the speaker (Stefánsson 1903: 362). Stefánsson (1903) points out that there is "no uniformity of pronunciation" among loanwords in the speech of Icelandic immigrants living in North Dakota (355). He also mentions the variation in the degree of "mixing" amongst individuals in the settlement (Stefánsson 1903: 355). Some speakers might borrow heavily from English while many "use scarcely one of the words" in his list. It is therefore difficult to determine the degree of integration of the words on his list into NA Icelandic. It is not clear whether any of the words on his list come from spontaneous code switching, but the same variation in assimilation of loanwords in the speech of different individuals seems to be true today.

The bulk of what is known about the NA Icelandic lexicon comes from Haraldur Bessason's (1967) important article on borrowings in NA Icelandic based on interviews he conducted in the early sixties. Bessason's examination of the NA Icelandic lexicon appeared in the journal *Scandiavian Studies* in February 1967. The study is based on thirty interviews Bessason conducted with NA Icelanders in 1963 and 1964. This is a decade prior to renewed interactions between Iceland and the heritage speakers in Manitoba. His consultants were 10 speakers from the Geysir district and 20 from Winnipeg. The conversations were casual and taped and excerpted on a card index. Five of the consultants were born in Iceland and came to Canada at an early age. Fifteen were second generation and ten were third generation Canadians in 1963–4 (born between 1917 and 1932).

Haraldur presents an analysis of lexical developments in NA Icelandic adopting a categorical system created by Haugen (1956). The categories were pure loanwords such as *beisment* (basement) and *address* (address); loanblends such as *drugbúð* (drugstore) and *sprústré* (spruce tree) and also loan shifts that include words which "have the appearance of an Icelandic word or phrase even though they occur in a new context" (Bessason 1967: 122). Examples of these are *blakkborð* (black board) and *kar* (car). Bessason (1967) concludes that nouns are the largest category of words borrowed into NA Icelandic followed by verbs and adjectives. He suggests that pure loan nouns are "brought into harmony with the largest declension types of the Icelandic grammar" (129). There is one exception to this; NA Icelandic proper nouns such as family names and place names have become Anglicized and are not declined according to Icelandic morphological rules. Names retain their English characteristics in otherwise Icelandic speech parts. This is the case for the twenty-five or so Icelandic place names approved for Manitoba by the Canadian Board of Place Names (Bessason 1967: 137). Names like *Arborg, Baldur, Gimli, Mikley,* and *Lundar* are found on Manitoba maps and pronounced according to English phonetic rules. In his article, Haraldur Bessason discussed the adaptation of Icelandic names and naming customs into English from a patronymic system ending in -son and -daughter to a family name system. Adoption of family names was not random. Bessason divides them into two main groups, one group containing names derived from the person's place of origin, the other involving Anglicizing the Icelandic last name.

Haraldur Bessason presents a list of 360 loan words, 47% of which have neuter gender, 29% have masculine gender and 20% are feminine. Only 4% show variation in gender. This list is compiled some 64 years after Vilhjálmur´s taxonomy of loan words and it suggests that their use has stabilized.

Very little is known about how second language learners learn grammatical gender and closer inspection of how loan words received gender in NA Icelandic could provide important insight into the universal characteristics of how and why adults seem to be consistent in assigning the same words to the same grammatical categories. This data warrants further examination in light of more recent studies of gender assignment by heritage speakers of Russian and Norwegian (Polinsky 2011, Hjelde 1996).

Before moving on to the structure of NA Icelandic, a few final words about the NA Icelandic lexicon are in order and its relevance to current issues in heritage linguistics. As described by Bessason (1967) and Sigurðsson (1984), the lexicon of North

American Icelandic reflects a changing culture, a changing way of life in the new world demographically and diachronically. NA Icelandic has numerous lexical additions; both borrowings and neologisms mostly in semantic fields related to geography, technology, education, farming and fishing as the settlers shifted from a costal culture to an inland culture, from mixed farming and fishing to agriculture and lake fishing, from home schooling to formal education. Needless to say almost all of the loanwords come from English as seen above.

Polinsky (2008) reports a correlation between lexical knowledge and extent of morphosyntactic attrition in heritage speakers of Russian. Benmanoun et al. (2010: 28) cites Hulsen's lexical retrieval studies that examined to what extent Dutch heritage speakers in Australia were able to retrieve nouns in two types of tasks; a picture-naming and a picture-matching task. The Dutch speakers were able to perform the picture-matching task (comprehension) but had difficulty performing the picture-naming task (production). This did not seem to be a factor in the picture-naming task that was part of the author's data collection on naturalistic speech in NA Icelandic in 1986 (Arnbjörnsdóttir 2006). It would be specifically interesting to examine the role of early heritage language literacy on retrieval and production ability.

An area of heritage language studies that has not received much attention is the role of multi-word borrowings or chunks in code switching and in general language proficiency and use. Several English phrases and speech conventions from English have been borrowed into NA Icelandic, translated, adapted and are used with some frequency. It would be interesting to revisit the English words and expressions that are found in NA Icelandic and have also found their way into modern Icelandic from English. Some of the NA Icelandic data dates from the late sixties and early seventies and the author's own data from the late eighties. In 2006 when the 1986 study became a book (Arnbjörnsdóttir 2006), a reanalysis was necessary for many of the words and phrases in the NA Icelandic data, as they had over the course of 30–40 years become part of modern Icelandic. Again a word of caution: It is very difficult to determine which words are the results of code switching and which are "legitimate" words in the NA Icelandic lexicon. The fact that more than one speaker uses the words could still merely be an indication that speakers are likely to transfer certain types of words and expressions from English to Icelandic. That, in and of itself, would be an interesting area of further study as it would shed light on the language use of bilinguals and when and how they switch from one language to another.

3.2 Available NA Icelandic corpora

Three corpora with naturalistic North American Icelandic speech are available for further linguistic study. Hallfreður Örn Eiríksson collected about 60 hours of interviews with about 90 informants in 1972–1973 (Eiríksson 1974). The informants were from Manitoba, North Dakota and British Columbia and the goal was to collect stories and poetry about life in the Icelandic "settlements" in North America for ethnographic purposes. The corpus includes about 60 hours of data including naturalistic conversation, reading and poetry (www.arnastofnun.is).

Gísli Sigurðsson (1984) collected interviews with twenty informants from Winnipeg and from Gimli, Riverton and Árborg in "New Iceland" in 1981–1982. He collaborated with Haraldur Bessason on the data collection and they developed a guiding questionnaire focusing mainly on work related topics and daily life in the informants' youth. The goal was to gather linguistic and ethnographic data on how Icelandic had been adapted to realities in the New World: new methods of lake fishing, agriculture, the lumber industry, food and anything related to human existence. Gísli made an effort to elicit natural speech. These interviews are now available orthographically transcribed and in digital form at *Stofnun Árna Magnússonar í íslenskum fræðum* in Reykjavík (www.arnastofnun.is). In his language analysis, Gísli focuses on lexical change and used Haraldur Bessason's categorization system from 1967. Gísli divides the categories into (1) loan shifts, (2) loan words, but adds an important category, (3) which includes various characteristics "that cannot be traced to the influence of English" (Sigurðsson 1984).

The third corpus of NA Icelandic was collected by the author as a part of a variation study of NA Icelandic phonology. The author conducted interviews in 1986 with 50 consultants from Winnipeg, "New Iceland" in the Interlake area of Manitoba, around Wynyard in Saskatchewan and from North Dakota in The United States. Interviews with thirty-eight of the informants from North Dakota and New Iceland provide the empirical basis of a book published in 2006 (Arnbjörnsdóttir 2006). The consultants were heritage speakers, men and women in age ranging from 30 to 83 years who had acquired the language at home as children. They had not received formal instruction in Icelandic, but many were able to read Icelandic as children prior to the onset of formal education in an English medium school. Many were third and fourth generation immigrants. Data were collected through three types of interview strategies. The first part of each interview was a general conversation (from 20 minutes up to several hours for group interviews). The topics of the conversations were usually the experiences of the informants' ancestors when they came to the new world in an effort to elicit a register where the least amount of attention would be given to speech (Labov 1972). Second, informants were asked, individually, to perform a picture identification task, naming objects or actions illustrated in twenty-six pictures. None of the consultants seemed to have difficulty with this task. Finally, some of the consultant read short passages (Arnbjörnsdóttir 2006: 80–82). This corpus is being incorporated into the IcelandicSpeech Corpus,[1] *ÍsTal, Íslenskur talmálsbanki* (https://notendur.hi.is/~eirikur/istal/) for further study and analysis. The general description of the grammar of North American Icelandic presented in the next section is mainly based on the author's study.

---

1. This work is funded by The Vigdís Finnbogadóttir Research Fund and The University of Iceland Research Fund.

The main emphasis of the 1986 study is on examining the linguistic and social variables affecting apparent vowel mergers in NA Icelandic. Based on the data collected the author also presents a short overview of other grammatical features that characterize North American Icelandic as it was spoken in 1986. These include other aspects of phonetics and phonology (consonant clusters and especially the vowel system), examples from syntax (e.g., case assignment, word order, agreement, use of the subjunctive) and morphological changes. However, much of the data collected still remains to be systematically analyzed.

It is a challenging task at best to collect the appropriate data for the study of heritage languages and identify the methodology best suited for the investigation at hand (Polinsky 2008). No data is available where specific grammatical structures of NA Icelandic have been elicited. The naturalistic corpora described here contain linguistic production by Icelandic heritage speakers with different levels of fluency that may be performance based, i.e., due to a lack of facility with using the language in formal situations, with non-intimates. However, the fact that emigration ended in 1914 and the relative fluency of the remaining speakers in the corpora minimize difficulties in identifying who actually is a heritage speaker, a problem pointed out by Benmamoun et al. (2010:20). Efforts are currently under way to elicit data specifically for the purpose of examining some of the linguistic features described below.

4. Another glance at North American Icelandic as a heritage language[2]

Below, some grammatical features of North American Icelandic are presented. This is not an exhaustive description and the features included were chosen primarily because they are consistently found in the speech of a cross-section of its speakers and because of their perceived relevance to the current discussion in heritage linguistics. We begin with a note on morphology.

4.1 Morphology

Morphological changes received a great deal of attention in early descriptive studies of immigrant language attrition. The studies reported collapse of oblique cases, regularizations of verb paradigms and loss of tense distinctions (Arnbjörnsdóttir 2006, Karttunen 1977, Lambert and Freed 1982). The vulnerability of morphology to attrition (or incomplete acquisition) is also a prevailing view in the current heritage literature (see discussion in Benmamoun et al. 2010) especially in languages with rich morphological systems. Bar-Shalom and Zaretsky (2008) claim that this is a "hallmark" of heritage languages (281), more so in case markings in nominal than verbal morphology (Benmamoun et al. 2010:31). The reasons for this are not clear.

---

2. The title is borrowed partially from a subtitle in Benmamoun et al. (2010).

Benmamoun et al. (2010) suggest that inflectional morphology is extra-syntactic and thus heritage speakers reflect either a reduced ability to perform post syntactic operations or some confusion in the mechanism of case licencing (39).

North American Icelandic shows surprisingly little attrition in its morphology, and although variation is found in the overt marking of case, there are no speakers who display a consistent loss of these distinctions. The case system of North American Icelandic does not differ in major respects from that of Icelandic in Iceland. Nominal case is assigned either by prepositions or by verbs in Icelandic. There are a few characteristics of case assignment that warrant further scrutiny. These will be presented briefly below.

The most consistent characteristic in NA Icelandic morphology is that, unlike in Icelandic in Iceland, proper names of people and places are always in the nominative case regardless of the preposition that precedes them. In case assignment by prepositions in general there appears to be an interplay of transfer of English meaning onto the NA Icelandic form, a collapse of two or more prepositions into one, and other phenomena that warrant further study. The NA Icelandic preposition *fyrir* functions in many cases like the English 'for' and includes the meaning of Icelandic *í* in some cases as in *ég lenti á spítala fyrir tvær nætur*, 'I was in the hospital for two nights.' The Icelandic *fyrir* can have the same meaning as 'for' as in *...búið að gera nýjar blæjur fyrir gluggunum* DAT [....búið að gera ný gluggatjöld fyrir gluggana ACC] '...had made new curtains for the windows' (Arnbjörnsdóttir 2006). Although there are some changes apparent in this category, the influence of semantic transfer should not be ignored and awaits further study.

Icelandic nouns are difficult to categorize according to inflectional patterns, as there is no general consensus on the number of declension patterns for Icelandic. Nouns in Icelandic have four cases: nominative, accusative, dative and genitive, and three grammatical genders: masculine, feminine and neuter. In the NA Icelandic data there was some variability in overt marking of case, both by prepositions and by verbs, although this was neither regular nor consistent upon preliminary analysis.

Some examples of regularization of paradigms are found in NA Icelandic verbal morphology. Verbs in Icelandic are divided into two main classes according to the conjugation patterns they follow. There are twenty-four conjugation classes in all, but for our purposes a description of the weak and strong classes suffices. Weak verbs are those whose past tense is formed by adding a suffix that consists of *ð, t* or *d* + vowel – four classes in all. Examples: *kalla* INF *-kallaði* PST, *heyra* INF *-heyrði* PST and *telja* INF *-taldi* PST where the root vowel must also be changed. The strong verb classes have irregular conjugation paradigms and consist of much fewer verbs than the weak class. The strong conjugation paradigms are characterized by the various vowel changes in the verb roots. Note that the term regular and irregular classes are purposely avoided in this context, as they do not neatly apply to verb conjugation classes in Icelandic. Icelandic verbs can have regular endings, but also vowel alternations in the stems (Arnbjörnsdóttir 2006).

In the NA Icelandic data the majority of borrowed verbs seem to be conjugated according to the most common verb class exemplified by *kalla-kallaði*. In addition, strong verbs are conjugated as weak verbs, weak verbs are re-categorized and strong verb paradigms are simplified. None of these were extensive in the data but need further study. A few examples where a strong verb is conjugated as a weak verb are included here for illustration. The first line has examples from North American Icelandic and the second example is from European Icelandic.

(1) *maður sem <u>hlaðaði</u>* PST *því* (NAI)
 [*maður sem <u>hlóð</u>* PST *því*] (EI)
 'A man who <u>loaded</u> it'

(2) *hann <u>kveðaði</u>* PST (NAI)
 [*hann <u>kvað</u>* PST] (EI)
 'he <u>recited</u>'

(3) *þau <u>hlaupuðu</u>* PST *framhjá* (NAI)
 [*þau <u>hlupu</u>* PST *framhjá*] (EI)
 'they <u>ran</u> past'

(4) *það voru menn sem <u>bjóu</u>* PST *þetta til* (NAI)
 [*það voru menn sem <u>bjuggu</u>* PST *þetta til*] (EI)
 'there were men who <u>made</u> this'

(5) *ég <u>róaði</u>* PST *yfir vatnið* (NAI)
 [*ég <u>réri</u>* PST *yfir vatnið*] (EI)
 'I <u>rowed</u> across the lake'

There are a few examples of loss of umlaut i.e., verbs which have alternations between (a)–(ö), (a)–(ɛ). Notice if this were merely a case of phonetic change i.e., unrounding of front rounded /ö/, the sound would become /ɛ/ as in **kvertuðu* /kvɛʀtyðy/. This is not the case. The forms in the following examples have the underlying sound /a/ in all forms in the paradigm:

(6) *þeir <u>kvartuðu</u>* PST *undan því* (NAI)
 [*þeir <u>kvörtuðu</u>* PST *undan því*] (EI)
 'they <u>complained</u> about it'

(7) *stúlkurnar sem þær voru að leika sér við <u>talaði</u>* PST *ekkert nema íslensku* (NAI)
 [*stúlkurnar sem þær voru að leika sér við <u>töluðu</u>* PST *ekkert nema íslensku*] (EI)
 'The girls that they were playing with <u>spoke</u> only Icelandic'

(8) *þeir <u>kalluðu</u>* PST *mig Gallann* (NAI)
 [*þeir <u>kölluðu</u> mig* PST *Gallann*] (EI)
 'They <u>called</u> me 'the Gall''

A prominent modification in NA Icelandic morphology is in the case assignment by a category of verbs called impersonal verbs with subjects in oblique cases (quirky subjects). These will be discussed in the next section.

4.2 Impersonal verbs

Impersonal verbs assign oblique cases (accusative, dative or genitive) to their subjects (often referred to as quirky subjects). Impersonal verbs do not agree in person and number with their subjects and are always in the 3rd person. Impersonal verbs in Icelandic can be subdivided according to their thematic roles into accusative subjects (about 175) and dative subjects (about 300) (Jónsson 1997–1998). There are also a handful of genitive subjects that will not be discussed here.

Verbs like *langa* 'want/long for,' *vanta* 'need,' and *gruna* 'suspect' have accusative case. Others carry dative case such as *þykja* 'seem to be/believe to be,' *finna* 'perceive/feel,' *vera illa við/vera vel við* 'like/dislike,' and *sýnast* 'to appear.'

The change in impersonal verbs with quirky subjects in North American Icelandic seems to be caused by three processes interacting: The first one is a preference for dative subjects where accusative subjects would have been 'appropriate'. This process is found in all varieties of Icelandic in Iceland. There are two processes likely caused by transfer from English. The first is a shift which causes a recategorization of impersonal verbs as personal verbs that now receive nominative case. The second is the relexification of several verbs into one, *vanta*, the cognate of English 'want' which has become a personal verb with nominative case in North American Icelandic (Arnbjörnsdóttir 2006). These two processes are referred to as nominative preference below.[3]

The extent of dative preference and nominative preference in impersonal verbs in the speech of the emigrants to North America is not known, nor the extent of its use in Iceland at the time of the emigrations although its existence is documented in the 19th century (Viðarsson 2009). Below are some examples of dative preference.

In the examples below the verb *langa* has retained its meaning in NA Icelandic and should retain the accusative subject as in *hana langar í köku*, but the subjects have dative case which is in line with the phenomenon found in European Icelandic (EI).

(9) <u>Henni</u> DAT *langaði* (NAI)
 [<u>Hana</u> ACC *langaði*] (EI)
 '<u>She</u> wanted'

(10) <u>Mér</u> DAT *langar til að tefla* (NAI)
 [<u>Mig</u> ACC *langar til að tefla*] (EI)
 '<u>I</u> want to play chess'

The following examples of dative preference are not found in Icelandic in Iceland. Here the verb *langa* has been collapsed into *vanta* in NA Icelandic.

(11) *Svo vantaði <u>henni</u>* DAT *náttúrulega að vita hvað það væri* (NAI)
 [*Svo langaði <u>hana</u>* ACC *náttúrulega að vita hvað það væri*] (EI)
 'Of course <u>she</u> wanted to know what it was'

---

3. This is also called dative substitution and nominative substitution.

(12) ...*þeim* DAT *vantaði að vera þar sem var nógu mikill viður* (NAI)
[*þeir* NOM *þurftu að vera* (*vildu vera?*) *þar sem var nógu mikill viður*] (EI)
'...they needed to be where there was enough wood'

In the following examples from NA Icelandic the verbs have become regular personal verbs and assign nominative case to their subjects. In the first example, the subject is in plural nominative and the verb agrees. In Icelandic in Iceland the subject is in the dative case:

(13) ...*þeir* NOM PL *voru* PST PL *illa við úlfana* (NAI)
[...*þeim* DAT PL *var* PST SG *illa við úlfana*] (EI)
'...they did not like the wolves'

(14) ...*pabbi* NOM *var nú alltaf illa við það* (NAI)
[...*pabba* DAT *var nú alltaf illa við það*] (EI)
'...dad never liked that'

(15) ... *ég* NOM *var alltaf illa við fisk* (NAI)
[... *mér* DAT *var illa við fisk*] (EI)
'I always disliked fish'

All of the subjects below are experiencer subjects and do not fall into the category of subjects associated with nominative preference above. The phrases *að vera vel við* 'to like' or *að vera illa við* 'to dislike' have dative experiencer subjects in Icelandic. In this case one would expect few deviations given the tendency to use dative above, but the preferred case is nominative and the subject and verb also agree in number as in personal verbs.

The verb *þykja* 'seem to be/believe to be' also has a dative subject in Icelandic in Iceland but in the examples from NA Icelandic the preference for nominative subject is clear. This is seen in the sentence below that has a coordinated/conjoined subject yet the verb retains the singular form where one might expect a plural form consistent with personal verbs.

(16) ... *mamma og pabbi* NOM *þótti voða gaman* (NAI)
[... *mömmu og pabba* DAT *þótti voða gaman*] (EI)
'... mom and dad liked it'

(17) ... *unga fólkið* NOM *þótti þetta erfitt* (NAI)
[...*unga fólkinu* DAT *þótti þetta erfitt*] (EI)
'...the young people thought it was difficult'

The North American Icelandic verb *vanta* 'need' has almost entirely been given the function of its English cognate 'want' and is used as such to cover the meaning of Icelandic verbs like the impersonal *vanta* and *skorta* (both with accusative subjects), and regular personal verbs like *þurfa*, *þarfnast* and *vilja* (all with nominative subjects). The meaning of these verbs has been collapsed into the meaning of English 'want' and relexified into the personal verb *vanta* in NA Icelandic.

(18) *Ég* NOM *mundi ekki vanta að vera* ... . (NAI)
    [*ég* NOM *mundi ekki vilja vera*] (EI)
    'I would not want to be'

(19) *Maður gerði það sem maður* NOM *vantaði* (NAI)
    [*maður gerði það sem maður* NOM *vildi*] (EI)
    'One just did what one wanted'

In the sentences above, the verb 'want' overtly represented by *vanta* in NA Icelandic has the semantic function or meaning of *vilja* in Icelandic in Iceland. *Vilja* is a regular verb with a nominative subject.

The results reported here support an overall thesis that speakers might try to reconcile the cognitive and grammatical function in case assignment. However, the results also suggest a more complex process wherein three factors interact. Two of these processes are possibly the result of transfer from the dominant language: one due to relexification and subsequent recategorization of impersonal verbs as personal, the other due to meaning shift and recategorization as impersonal verbs become personal. The third process is the dative preference found also in Icelandic in Iceland and may be a simplification process that reduces the number of variables available to the speakers in case assignment of impersonal verbs. The next obvious step is to place the data described above into the theoretical context of the nature and development of impersonal verbs in general and into their role in the development of heritage language grammars in particular. This process also suggests that developmental processes may be more complex than simple surface features may suggest.

4.3 Anaphoric binding

Heritage speakers seem to have general difficulty in establishing syntactic dependencies at a distance. This includes anaphoric binding relations (Kim et al. 2009, 2010, Polinsky 2006). Benmamoun et al. (2010: 36) call for more data on binding in more heritage languages. Long distance anaphoric binding seems to have almost disappeared from NA Icelandic as seen in the examples below. Obligatory anaphoric binding between an antecedent and anaphor that reside in the same tensed clause is found both in Icelandic and in English. On the other hand, long-distance binding between an anaphor and its antecendent exists in Icelandic across clause and sentence boundaries. This is not found in English. The general consensus is that the presence of subjunctive mood is required for long-distance binding to occur in Icelandic. So any loss of subjunctive mood could have repercussions for anaphoric binding in Icelandic. While clause bound anaphora is intact in NA Icelandic, no examples of long distance binding were found in the data. The first example contains clause bound reflexives, which pose no problem for the NA Icelandic consultants:

(20) *Hún hafði börnin í kringum sig*
    'She had the children around 'herself"

(21) *Maður gerði vel að halda í sér bara lífinu*
 'One did well to keep oneself alive'

In the instances where long distance binding could have occurred in NA Icelandic, consultants did not produce the forms and show an obvious uncertainty through pauses and hesitations as in the examples below from Sigurðsson (1984) and Arnbjörnsdóttir (2006):

(22) *Þeir$_i$ voru vanir við þetta frá þeirra$_i$ (sínum) heimalöndum*
 They were used to it from selfs' (ANPH) home countries
 'They were used to it from their home countries'

(23) *Hann$_i$ segir alltaf að mamma hafi verið svo vond við ... mig$_i$ (sig$_i$)*
 He$_i$ says always that mom was very mean to self$_i$ (ANPH)
 'He$_i$ always says that mom was so mean to him$_i$.'

The following example is still clausebound, but it seems that the further away from the antecedent, the more difficulty the speaker has in producing the reflexive form.

(24) *Hann$_i$ bjó hjá ömmu sína$_i$ og afa og langafa*
 He$_i$ lived with self's$_i$ grandmother and grandfather
 'He lived with his grandmother and grandfather

 ... <u>hans$_i$</u> *(sínum)*
 ... and his$_i$ great grandfather
 ...and his great grandfather'

These examples were found in naturalistic data that were not elicited for the purpose of examining anaphora. Anaphoric binding in NA Icelandic is further explored in Putnam and Arnbjörnsdóttir (2015), and also currently in an extensive data collection effort to elicit specific linguistic data on binding in NA Icelandic.

4.4 Subjunctive

Montrul (2008) defines an individual's grammar as incomplete when it fails to reach age-appropriate linguistic levels of proficiency as compared with the grammar of monolingual or fluent bilingual speakers of the same age, cognitive development, and social group. She introduces a study on the acquisition of the subjunctive in Spanish referencing Blake (1983), whose subjects did not show categorical knowledge of Spanish subjunctive until after age 10. Heritage speakers who receive less input at an earlier age and no schooling in the language never fully acquire all the uses and semantic nuances of the subjunctive in Spanish, as reported in many studies (see Benmamoun et al. 2010: 45). This is reminiscent of Jakobson's (1968) regression hypothesis, which states that the process of language attrition is the reverse of language acquisition or language learning process. Structures acquired late in childhood would thus be the first to disappear in attrition (see the chapters in this volume by

Johannessen and by Westergaard and Anderssen), or alternatively, late acquired features may not reach the level of fluency required for retention into adulthood supporting a notion of incomplete maintenance rather than incomplete acquisition (Putnam and Sánchez 2013).

The NA Icelandic data revealed some loss of subjunctive but sometimes only in the overt marking of subjunctive. Speakers would sometimes substitute the Icelandic subjunctive forms with the word *mundi*, possibly transferring English 'would' (a form also found in Icelandic in Iceland). The example below shows this (subjunctive forms in Icelandic are in the second line):

(25) ... *ég mundi ekki vanta að vera* (NAI)
 [... *ég vildi* SUBJV *ekki vera*] (EI)
 'I would not want to be'

In most cases the subjunctive mood is replaced by verbs in indicative mood as in the examples below.

(26) *Þeir vildu nú ekki trúa mér að ég kom* IND *frá Kanada* (NAI)
 [*Þeir vildu nú ekki trúa mér að ég kæmi* SUBJV *frá Kanada*] (EI)
 'They would not believe me that I came from Canada'

(27) *Ég hélt að það var* IND *miklu kaldara* (NAI)
 [*Ég hélt að það væri* SUBJV *miklu kaldara*] (EI)
 'I thought it was much colder'

For some consultants the loss of subjunctive is very clear as even in a sentence from a reading passage that said 'hefði' SUBJV, the NA Icelandic reader read 'hafði' IND.

(28) *Sumir sögðu að hann hafði* IND PST *átt að keppa* (NAI)
 [*Sumir sögðu að hann hefði* SUBJV *átt að keppa*] (EI)
 'Some said that he should have competed'

Preparations are already under way to examine when Icelandic children acquire subjunctive in order to compare with the development of subjunctive in Icelandic as a heritage language.

4.5 Syntax

According to the heritage language literature, syntactic knowledge is resilient under reduced input conditions (see also Johannessen, this volume). This is true of the NA Icelandic data. However, a prominent change in the syntax of NA Icelandic is in the position of the finite verb, especially verb-second (V2). V2-languages require the finite verb to be no further to the right in the clause than in second position, following a clause-initial phrase. Placement of verbs in Germanic languages varies from one language to another. In particular, English separates itself from other Germanic languages in that it has a very restricted V2 rule. In English, the finite verb remains in situ in the verb phrase (VP) while auxiliaries appear outside the VP (Eyþórsson 1997–1998). Håkansson (1995) reports that her Swedish heritage speakers have native-speaker control of the V2 phenomenon. The Icelandic heritage speakers seem to have varied control of V2, especially in sentences with sentential adverbs, sometimes referred to as "verb-third" (V3). V3-order (where the finite verb follows a sentential adverb) is possible in most types of embedded clauses in Icelandic, but it is severely restricted and heavily marked (Angantýsson 2007). This may explain the variability in the NA Icelandic data. The NA Icelandic examples below contain adverbs that could be categorized as sentential adverbs. In these examples finite verbs are in third position. The first two examples involve main clauses, where the placement of these adverbs is not possible in Icelandic. The third example, however, involving the adverb *fyrst* in an embedded clause, would be possible in Icelandic.

(29) Dolly stundum talar íslensku (NAI)
 [Dolly talar stundum íslensku] (EI)
 'Dolly sometimes speaks Icelandic'

(30) ... við aldrei notuðum... (NAI)
 [... við notuðum aldrei...] (EI)
 '... we never used ...'

(31) Hún var fjórtán ára þegar hún fyrst kom frá Kanada (NAI)
 [Hún var fjórtán ára þegar hún kom fyrst frá Kanada] (EI)
 'She was fourteen when she first came from Canada'

The issue of verb placement (including V2) is being explored in an ongoing project where further data is being elicited specifically to examine the nature of this word order phenomenon in NA Icelandic and its importance to acquisition and attrition.

4.6 Phonetics and phonology

The pronunciation of heritage speakers remains an understudied area of heritage linguistics (Benmamoun et al. 2010: 28). The NA Icelandic speakers all spoke with some level of an English accent. Clearly though, the accent differed from the accents of those who have learned Icelandic as a second language. Phonetic and phonological change is a matter of theoretical debate on what constitutes bilingual proficiency as opposed to second language proficiency.

The study reported here examined the social and linguistic constraints which affected the occurence or non-occurrence of one specific feature of NA Icelandic phonology undergoing change, namely *Flámæli*. *Flámæli* 'skewed speech' refers to the apparent mergers of two sets of front vowels, on the one hand /ɪ/ and /ɛ/, and on the other hand their rounded counterparts /ʏ/ and /ö/ so they become homophonous. See examples below.

(32) Loss of distinction between /ɪ/ and /ɛ/
viður 'wood' and *veður* 'weather'

(33) Loss of distinction between /ʏ/ and /ö/
flugur 'flies' and *flögur* 'chips'

Flámæli was considered undesirable language. *Flámæli*, previously a pronounced feature of speech in three geographical areas of Iceland, was stigmatized and through official efforts around the middle of the previous century was almost eradicated from modern Icelandic speech.

These efforts took place around the middle of the last century or about sixty years after the first emigrants left Icelandic in 1873. It is safe to assume that at least some of the emigrants had *flámæli*. The author has argued that in fact the majority of the emigrants did **not** have *flámæli* (Arnbjörnsdóttir 2006). Yet, in NA Icelandic, *flámæli* has developed and spread unchecked by the preservation forces that reversed its spread in Icelandic in Iceland. There is ample evidence to suggest that once in North America, the linguistic conditions as Icelandic became a heritage language were created that caused the vowel mergers to accelerate. The results of the variation study show that the vowel mergers are confined to long vowels, and the younger the informant, the more likely he/she is to have this feature in their speech, women are more likely than men to have *flámæli* and informants in North Dakota are more likely than informants in "New Iceland" to merge the vowels.

Teasing apart the role of input and the effect of intense language contact, but also recognizing the sociolinguistic conditions that frame heritage speakers' language use and may affect structural developments is challenging, but the sociolinguistic conditions cannot be ignored in the development of explanatory theories of bilingual language acquisition and use.

5. Conclusions

In conclusion I would like to summarize why the NA Icelandic data and the preliminary analysis presented here should be of interest to heritage language linguists. First the NA Icelandic consultants are unquestionably heritage language speakers. As Polinsky (2008) has pointed out, one of the challenges inherent in the study of heritage languages is to identify consultants who are actual heritage speakers who have not had formal instruction in the language making them similar to second language learners or even L1 speakers. Because immigration to North America from Iceland ceased in 1914, there was little fortification of the developing language in the new world (letter writing is an exception to this). These are excellent conditions for heritage language development.

Secondly, NA Icelandic is a new language in the pool of languages available for further study. Some corpora exist and efforts are under way to gather more data that addresses specific structural features of interest to heritage linguists, but also to linguists interested both in property theories and in transition theories of language.

Many of the structural characteristics of NA Icelandic are of interest and are being examined in other heritage languages. The available naturalistic data is important for a reanalysis given a new research paradigm, but the corpora need to be strengthened with elicited data that is collected to address specific grammatical characteristics. Some of the identified characteristics of NA Icelandic are a marked tendency toward phonological neutralization, lexical restriction, simplification and regularization of morphology (Benmamoun et al. 2010), changes in V2 (Håkanson 1995), attrition in the subjunctive (Montrul 2008), changes in the use of anaphora (Kim et al. 2009, Putnam and Arnbjörnsdóttir 2015) and issues related to gender assignment (Polinsky 2011).

Important questions remain unanswered about how reduced input affects language acquisition and regression. It seems relevant that features of morpho-syntax such as subjunctive, long distance binding and V2 in Icelandic as a heritage language may illuminate how features acquired late in the acquisition process may attrite first. Is this due to incomplete acquisition or incomplete maintenance because they are not a characteristic of the caretaker speech the child is exposed to in early childhood (see also Johannessen, this volume, for similar questions)? Or are they caused by attrition of a grammatical system that at some point was "complete" but simplified due to language shift? Or are the features a result of transfer from the dominant language? These questions pose challenges for research methodology in this emerging research field.

Lastly, the description presented above is based on existing naturalistic data. Hopefully it has laid the groundwork for directions in further data collection, especially what type of additional elicited data is needed in order to illuminate specific features of the structure of NA Icelandic phonology and morpho-syntax. New data may also illuminate the role of age and amount and nature of input in language acquisition and regression across the lifespan of bilingual heritage speakers.

References

Angantýsson, Ásgrímur. 2007. "Verb-Third in Embedded Clauses in Icelandic." *Studia Linguistica* 61(3): 237–260. DOI: 10.1111/j.1467-9582.2007.00134.x

Arnbjörnsdóttir, Birna. 1990. "Use of Icelandic Among Bilinguals in North Dakota." Unpublished surveys.

Arnbjörnsdóttir, Birna. 2006. *North American Icelandic: The Life of a Language*. Winnipeg: University of Manitoba Press.

Bar-Shalom, Eva and Elena Zaretsky. 2008. "Selective Attrition in Russian-English Bilingual Children: Preservation of Grammatical Aspect." *International Journal of Bilingualism* 12: 281–302. DOI: 10.1177/1367006908098572

Benmamoun, Elabbas, Silvina Montrul and Maria Polinsky. 2010. "White Paper: Prolegomena to Heritage Linguistics." Harvard University.

Bessason, Haraldur. 1967. "A Few Specimens of North American Icelandic." *Scandinavian Studies* 9(1): 115–147.

Bessason, Haraldur. 1984. "Íslenskan er lífseigari en nokkurt annað Þjóðarbrotsmál í Kanada." *Interview in Morgunnblaðið, February* 12: 64–65.

Blake, Robert. 1983. "Mood Selection Among Spanish Speaking Children, Ages 4 to 12." *The Bilingual Review* 0: 21–32

Eiríksson, Hallfreður Ö. 1974. *Interviews with Canadian Icelanders.* Unpublished manuscript. University of Manitoba.

Eyþórsson, Þórhallur. 1997–1998. "Uppruni sagnfærslu í germönskum málum." *Íslenskt mál* 19–20: 133–180.

Håkansson, Gisela. 1995. "Syntax and Morphology in Language Attrition. A Study of Five Bilingual, Expatriate Swedes." *International Journal of Applied Linguistics* 5: 153–171. DOI: 10.1111/j.1473-4192.1995.tb00078.x

Haugen, Einar. 1956. *Bilingualism in the Americas: A Bibliography and Research Guide.* (Publications of the American Dialect Society 26). Tuscaloosa, AL: University of Alabama Press.

Hjelde, Arnstein. 1996. "The Gender of English Nouns Used in American Norwegian." In *Language Contact Across the North Atlantic*, ed. by P. S. Ureland and I. Clarkson, 297–312. Tübingen: Max Niemeyer Verlag.

Jakobson, Roman. 1968. *Child Language. Aphasia and Phonological Universals.* The Hague: Mouton. DOI: 10.1515/9783111353562

Johannessen, Janne Bondi. This volume. "Attrition in an American Norwegian heritage language speaker."

Jónsson, Jóhannes Gísli. 1997–1998. "Sagnir með aukafallsfrumlagi." *Íslenskt mál* 19–20: 11–43.

Karttunen, Frances. 1977. "Finnish in America: A Case Study in Monogenerational Language Change." In *The Social Dimensions of Language Change*, ed. by Ben Blount and Mary Sanches, 173–184. New York: Academic Press. DOI: 10.1016/B978-0-12-107450-0.50016-4

Kim, Ji Hye, Silvina Montrul and James Yoon. 2009. "Binding Interpretation of Anaphors in Korean Heritage Speakers." *Language Acquisition* 16(1): 3–35. DOI: 10.1080/10489220802575293

Kim, Ji Hye, Silvina Montrul and James Yoon. 2010. "Dominant Language Influence in Acquisition and Attrition of Binding: Interpretation of the Korean Reflexive *caki*." *Bilingualism: Language and Cognition* 13: 73–84. DOI: 10.1017/S136672890999037X

Kristjánsson, Júníus. 1983. *Vesturfaraskrá, 1870–1914: A Record of Emigrants from Iceland to America 1870–1914.* Reykjavík: University of Iceland.

Labov, William. 1972. *Sociolinguistic Patterns.* Philadelphia: University of Pennsylvania Press.

Lambert, Richard and Barbara Freed. 1982. *Loss of Language Skills.* Rowley, MA: Newbury House.

Milroy, Leslie. 1987. *Observing and Analyzing Natural Language: A Critical Account of Sociolinguistic Method.* Oxford: Basil Blackwell.

Montrul, Silvina. 2008. *Incomplete Acquisition in Bilingualism: Re-examining the Age Factor.* Amsterdam: John Benjamins. DOI: 10.1075/sibil.39

Polinsky, Maria. 2006. "Incomplete Acquisition: American Russian." *Journal of Slavic Linguistics* 14: 191–262.

Polinsky, Maria. 2008. "Gender Under Incomplete Acquisition: Heritage Speakers' Knowledge of Noun Categorization." *Heritage Language Journal* 6(1): 1–33.

Polinsky, Maria. 2011. "Reanalysis in Adult Heritage Language." *Studies in Second Language Acquisition* 33: 305–328. DOI: 10.1017/S027226311000077X

Putnam, Michael and Birna Arnbjörnsdóttir. 2015. "Anaphoric Binding in North American Icelandic." In *Moribund Germanic Heritage Languages in North America. Theoretical Perspectives and Empirical Findings*, ed. by B. Richard Page and Michael T. Putnam, 203–223. Leiden: Brill.

Putnam, Michael and Liliana Sánchez. 2013. "What's So Incomplete about Incomplete Acquisition? – A Prolegomenon to Modeling Heritage Language Grammars." *Linguistic Approaches to Bilingualism* 3(4): 478–508. DOI: 10.1075/lab.3.4.04put

Sigurðsson, Gísli. 1984. *Viðtöl við Vestur-Íslendinga*. Unpublished interviews. University of Manitoba.

Stefánsson, Vilhjálmur. 1903. "English Loan-Nouns Used in the Icelandic Colony of North Dakota." *Dialect Notes* 2: 354–362.

Viðarsson, Heimir Freyr. 2009. "Tilbrigði í fallmörkun aukafallsfrumlags – Þágufallshneigð í forníslensku." *Íslenskt mál* 31: 15–66.

Westergaard, Marit and Merete Anderssen. This volume. "Word order variation in Norwegian possessive constructions: Bilingual acquisition and attrition."

PART II

Phonetic and phonological change

Heritage language obstruent phonetics and phonology
American Norwegian and Norwegian-American English

Brent Allen and Joseph Salmons
University of Wisconsin–Madison

This chapter explores the acoustics and phonology of speech sounds produced by Norwegian heritage speakers in the Upper Midwest in Norwegian and to a lesser extent in English. The study reports work on acoustic differences in obstruents spoken by heritage speakers whose L1 and L2 are both 'aspiration' languages, namely Norwegian and American English, but which differ phonologically in other ways. Our focus falls in particular on laryngeal features, that is, the realization of the distinction between 'voiced' and 'voiceless' or 'lenis' and 'fortis' consonants, along with the closely related issue of durational contrasts in Norwegian. Building on Allen and Salmons (2012), we argue that the Norwegian and English spoken by Norwegian-American bilinguals will each show influence from the other language, but asymmetrically.

Keywords: laryngeal phonetics, laryngeal phonology, aspiration, sonorant devoicing, passive voicing, duration

1. Introduction[1]

This chapter deals with speech sounds produced by Norwegian speakers in the Upper Midwest in Norwegian and, to a lesser extent, English. Our focus falls on laryngeal features, the distinction between 'voiced' and 'voiceless' or 'lenis' and 'fortis' consonants,

---

[1]. This paper is an expansion and development of material first presented in Allen and Salmons (2012). We are grateful to Janne Bondi Johannessen and colleagues for inspiring us to undertake this work, as well as to Luke Annear and Kristin Speth for sharing their field recordings with us. An initial version of this paper was presented at the Second Workshop on Immigrant Languages, Fefor, September 2011. We thank the following for comments and suggestions on this project: The audience at the Fefor workshop, Curt Rice and Nina Gram Garmann, as well as Arnstein

along with the closely related issue of durational contrasts in Norwegian. Norwegian and English spoken by Norwegian-American bilinguals both show influence from the other language, but asymmetrically.

A first basic goal here is simply descriptive. We know much about English phonetics and phonology generally, but far less about Upper Midwestern English. We know less yet about some relevant areas of Norwegian. Some work has been done on the phonetics and phonology of American Norwegian, but no instrumental analysis until Allen and Salmons (2012). Our second, broader goal is to look at heritage speaker sound patterns and realizations in terms of van Coetsem's theory of borrowing and imposition, situated in phonetic and phonological theory and language change.

This paper is hardly the first study of Norwegian in the Upper Midwest, or English as spoken by Norwegian Americans there. Before the papers in the present volume, Simley (1930) examines Norwegian and English as they were spoken in Minnesota. Haugen (1953) is an exhaustive study of Norwegian dialects across America in addition to being a classic text on language contact and sociolinguistics, a tradition continued by many papers in Johannessen and Salmons (2012) and in other work especially by Hjelde (e.g., 1992). Moen (1988, 1991, 2001) investigates in particular the English of Norwegian Americans in terms of both pronunciation and syntax. However, these studies are largely descriptive and impressionistic in nature. The present paper differs from previous work in presenting, as far as we are aware, the first acoustic study of the speech of Norwegian Americans (aside from Allen and Salmons 2012).

In the rest of this paper, we present theoretical background in §2, first in terms of language-contact theory and then phonetics and phonology. We give information on the speakers in §3. The heart of the paper then presents phonetic data for our speakers: §4 treats one claimed phonological difference between Norwegian and English, namely that Norwegian lacks the pattern of 'sonorant devoicing.' In line with Allen (2011), we show that the phonetics of European Norwegian aligns more closely with English than the literature would suggest. That is, analysis of the hearth language shows that we should not have expected differences. §5 examines intervocalic voicing. In both languages we expect partial voicing of lenis obstruents, save for the absence of /z/ in Norwegian. This is particularly important as the absence of [z] is widely reported to be characteristic of Norwegian-influenced English in the Upper Midwest. Our speakers show English-like realizations of English /z/. §6 treats the realization of final laryngeal contrasts. Here, the evidence suggests that heritage speakers' English shows subtle influence from Norwegian. Conclusions are provided in §7.

Hjelde, Luke Annear, Greg Iverson, Janne Bondi Johannessen, Signe Laake, Tom Purnell, Eric Raimy, Alyson Sewell and Kristin Speth. The feedback from these colleagues has greatly helped our thinking on this topic but the usual disclaimers apply.

2. Theoretical background

We first introduce the framework we adopt for understanding contact between English and Norwegian in the American setting and then the phonological perspective we adopt here.

2.1 Language contact

We adopt the model of borrowing and imposition first developed by van Coetsem (1988, 2000), since developed by Howell (1993), Winford (2005) and others. At the heart of this theory is an asymmetry between the effects of an L1 on an L2 and vice versa in a situation of language contact involving adult learners. Coarsely reckoned, with our speakers, people who learned Norwegian first and English only later, we expect borrowings into Norwegian, which may be more or less integrated into the sound system, but impositions from Norwegian onto English in phonetics and phonology. A Norwegian heritage speaker would be expected, then, to borrow lexical material like *store, tavern, lake* from English. At the same time, in speaking English as a second language, they may fail to produce segments that are contrastive in English but absent in Norwegian, so that the interdental fricatives /θ, ð/ are produced as [t, d] and /z/ as [s]. In other cases, speakers may not produce allophones, like the English 'light' (alveolar) /l/ versus 'dark' (velarized) [ɫ], where many varieties of Norwegian have only the alveolar variant and, mainly in Eastern and Trøndelag Norwegian, the so-called *tjukk* 'thick' (retroflex) /ɭ/. Or they may produce a different form of a sound that is readily interpreted by English speakers, such as having a dental rather than alveolar place of articulation for /t, d, n/. In fact, such effects are reported for American English spoken by Norwegian-English bilinguals. Simley (1930: 470) finds, for instance, widespread fortis realization of /z, ʒ/ as [s, ʃ] as well as 'stopping' of interdental fricatives, so that *thing* can be pronounced [tʰɪŋ]. Since then, Haugen (1953: 47) and Moen (1991: 104–105) have found similar patterns.

In terms of imposition, work on second language phonology has long shown clear effects of a traditionally-learned L2 on an L1, as detailed by Eckman and Iverson (forthcoming). These effects include changes to the laryngeal system of the L1, both allophonic and phonemic. For instance, recent work on Dutch speakers who are advanced learners of English shows that they develop longer Voice Onset Time (VOT) in Dutch than other native speakers (Simon 2011). Beyond such phonetic effects, the rise of a word-initial laryngeal distinction in English /v/ ≠ /f/ has been tied to influence from Norman French speakers by some scholars, though Minkova (2011) shows the complexities of that case. With regard to borrowing, we see more complexity than the basic model predicts, though in ways consistent with van Coetsem's thinking. Haugen (1953: 394) notes about English loans into American Norwegian: "The loan is ... subject to continual interference from the model in the other language, a process which will here be called *reborrowing*." He exemplifies this with data including the following (with his original transcription):

Table 1. Examples of Haugen's 'reborrowing.'

	tavern	crackers	lake
Older	taˋvan	kræk'is	le'k
Younger	tæ'vərn	kræ'kərs	lei'k

That is, a lexical item and its basic meaning are borrowed early, while later generations of speakers, at home in both languages, may produce them with English-like phonetics and phonology.

2.2 English and Norwegian laryngeal phonetics and phonology

We adopt here the view now known as 'laryngeal realism' (Iverson and Salmons 1995 et seq., and a view so named by Honeybone 2005), namely that the distinction often called one of 'voicing' and spelled typically with *t* vs. *d* and *s* vs. *z* in the Roman alphabet in fact corresponds to two different phonological systems, [voice] and [spread glottis] languages, or Glottal Width versus Glottal Tension languages (Avery and Idsardi 2001). Languages like Dutch, French and Polish on the one hand have essentially unaspirated *p, t, k* but heavily voiced *b, d, g*. We treat the phonological feature [voice] as active in these languages. In such languages, it is voicing rather than voicelessness which tends to spread. Languages like English, German and Somali, on the other hand, have heavily aspirated *p, t, k* at least in stressed positions and show limited voicing on *b, d, g*. In these languages, voicelessness rather than voicing tends to spread. We treat the phonological features [spread glottis] as active in these languages. An important consequence of this analysis is that laryngeal features appear to be privative. That is, there is only one active feature in each system and it may spread, while the absent feature is truly absent and cannot spread.

Much work on second language acquisition and language contact to date has contrasted, if without benefit of laryngeal realist thinking, [voice] and [spread glottis] languages, like Flege (1987), Piske et al. (2001), and much other work on Romance languages and English, Simon (2011) on Dutch and English, or Nagy and Kochetov's (2011) work on English and a variety of other languages, especially Slavic. These comparisons are extremely valuable because they have provided a secure starting point in terms of maximally different phonological and phonetic systems. Norwegian and English, however, are in our view both [spread glottis] languages, albeit with significant differences in terms of phonological contrasts and their phonetic implementation.

Differences between the systems include inventory differences like these: (1) English contrasts /s/ ≠ /z/, while Norwegian has only /s/, and (2) Norwegian possesses geminate consonants while English does not. Another reported difference involves a phonological process. English, like most [spread glottis] languages, shows sonorant devoicing in obstruent-sonorant clusters in stressed positions. Norwegian is reported to lack this process with /s/ (Kristoffersen 2000).

Other, relatively minor differences may be attributable to the implementation of contrasts. Both languages have final laryngeal contrasts, unlike their cousins Dutch and German, but English is reported to implement the contrast more by lengthening a preceding vowel, while Norwegian is reported to have less lengthening and more actual glottal pulsing (see, for example, Chen 1970 and Ringen and Van Dommelen 2013).

Finally, we provide data on an issue of phonetic implementation. Under a privative analysis in a [spread glottis] system, the contrast is typically carried by the fortis character of sounds like *p, t, k, s*, not by glottal pulsing on *b, d, g* and *z*. In such a system, the latter are free to pulse in voicing-friendly contexts, as an enhancement of the contrast. That is, in the environment between robustly voiced sounds like vowels, these laryngeally-unspecified segments are susceptible to glottal pulsing. While both labials in *bob* are usually pronounced with little glottal pulsing in English, the same obstruent in *Abba* is typically heavily voiced. This process, known as 'passive voicing,' may exist in Norwegian depending on the patterns of phonetic implementation the language possesses.

Let us turn now to our speakers and then to data and findings on the issues mentioned above, namely sonorant devoicing, medial voicing, and final laryngeal distinctions.

3. Speakers and community

Our data are drawn from interviews with three heritage speakers conducted by Luke Annear and Kristin Speth in 2010. All three were living in Minnesota at the time of the interview but all have ancestry in different dialect regions of Norway:

1. Mandal area, Vest-Agder, southernmost area of West Norwegian
2. Singsås, Trøndelag Norwegian
3. Nesna, Nordland, near Mo-i-Rana, North Norwegian

Our first speaker, a female, was born in 1924 in New York, not the Midwest. Her parents came from the Mandal area in Vest-Agder county at the southern tip of Norway and left Norway in 1907 (mother) and 1910 (father). She lived in California briefly as an adult before moving to Minneapolis, and has since lived in various places in Illinois, Wisconsin, and Minnesota, and currently resides in Burnsville, MN. The second speaker, also female, was born in 1929 in Hendricks, MN, and has lived there all her life. Her grandparents came from Singsås and Digre in South Trøndelag county, though we do not know exactly when they left Norway. The third speaker is male, born in 1937 in Tracy, MN, and has lived in Minneapolis for most of his adult life, but lived in Oslo for two years as an adult. His grandparents came from Nesna in Nordland county and left Norway in 1893. We therefore have a set of speakers with considerably different backgrounds in terms of dialect and life experience. The idea here is not to start from a particularly representative sample, but to survey the kinds of patterns we may find within a single small community of speakers, and the diversity in our speakers aids that.

After a century in the Upper Midwest, there may be considerable realignment of dialect patterns, as suggested by Johannessen (p.c., also Hjelde, this volume). In that case, so-called base dialect patterns may be less important than the later development of compromise forms in North America. This would parallel patterns well attested in German in the same region (Nützel and Salmons 2011, many others). At any rate, we are not aware of dialect differences on the issues at hand, though we'll say more about this below. Only one major known dialect pattern, lenition of /p, t, k/ in some areas, appears in the speech of our Burnsville consultant, a typical feature of the Mandal dialect.

Following the traditions of sociophonetics rather than laboratory phonetics, we draw our data from conversational settings, in this case made with non-native interviewers from the same region of the U.S. who learned Norwegian at the university.

Our data comes from heritage speakers. Rothman (2009: 159) defines a heritage language this way (with related views found through the present volume):

> A language qualifies as a heritage language if it is a language spoken at home or otherwise readily available to young children, and crucially this language is not a dominant language of the larger (national) society. Like the acquisition of a primary language in monolingual situations and the acquisition of two or more languages in situations of societal bilingualism/multilingualism, the heritage language is acquired on the basis of an interaction with naturalistic input and whatever in-born linguistic mechanisms are at play in any instance of child language acquisition. Differently, however, there is the possibility that quantitative and qualitative differences in heritage language input and the influence of the societal majority language, and difference in literacy and formal education can result in what on the surface seems to be arrested development of the heritage language or attrition in adult bilingual knowledge.

That is, the situations of heritage speakers may not conform fully to usual patterns of acquisition, but we are not concerned with exactly what the sources of those differences might be, e.g., in attrition or incomplete acquisition, but rather with the contact effects in this setting. Heritage speakers may or may not have relatively comparable control of the two languages, but even if they do, with reference to van Coetsem above, their bilingualism is strikingly asymmetrical and the situation anything but 'stable.'

4. The problem of description: Sonorant devoicing

The definitive work on Norwegian phonology is Kristoffersen's *Phonology of Norwegian*, where he notes (2000: 10):

> Not much has been published in English, German or French that covers substantial portions of Norwegian phonology. ... Also when we turn to what is published in Norwegian, the account will by no means be impressive.

Aside from a few often controversial issues like retroflexion, this remains as true now as when Kristoffersen wrote. Aside from retroflexion and some work on vowels, there is less on Norwegian phonetics. We begin with a pattern identified as a difference between English and Norwegian. English has pervasive devoicing of sonorant consonants after fortis obstruents. For instance, in word-initial clusters, a sonorant following an initial fortis obstruent largely lacks glottal pulsing, illustrated here with the lateral after an obstruent:

(1) Sonorant devoicing in English
    play [pl̥]
    clay [kl̥]
    slay [sl̥]

Kristoffersen posits a more limited rule for Norwegian: "sequences where a non-nasal sonorant (including /ʋ/) follows a voiceless stop or /f/" exhibit full or partial sonorant devoicing (2000: 75). He further reports that "devoicing does not take place after /s/" (2000: 81), in forms such as: *slå* /slo/ [ʃloː] 'to beat,' and *svi* /svi/ [sʋiː] 'to burn' (2000: 76). In contrast, Popperwell's impressionistic description of Norwegian pronunciation describes "partial devoicing" of /n/, including after /s/ (1963: 50) but asserts that /l/ "tends to devoice after p, k, f," without any indication of devoicing of the lateral after /s/ (1963: 52). Phonologically, Kristoffersen argues, the absence of an /s/ ≠ /z/ contrast in Norwegian leaves /s/ laryngeally unspecified, so that it does not trigger sonorant devoicing.

This description suggests a potentially fruitful area of phonological comparison. To secure the phonetic underpinning and allow more precise comparison, Allen (2011) analyzed a set of obstruent-sonorant onsets from a broad range of Norwegian dialects, drawing data from the Nordic Dialect Corpus (see Johannessen et al. 2009). The range of dialects surveyed was intended to see how widespread and how variable sonorant devoicing might be across major Norwegian areas. The key results, reproduced below, show the same amount of sonorant devoicing after /s/ as elsewhere.[2]

---

2. Beckman and Ringen (2009) come to similar conclusions on different grounds.

Table 2. Percent glottal pulsing in sonorants in word-initial fortis obstruent-sonorant clusters.

	Hammerfest	Skaugdalen	Fredrikstad	Lyngdal	Stryn
pr	34.34	29.89	51.55	17.12	46.61
pl	35.87	72.19	80.51	27.37	55.19
tr	17.02	39.97	59.40	8.11	34.65
kr	34.90	47.64	49.09	12.91	51.09
kl	32.98	59.61	76.03	19.77	50.81
kn	29.74	40.89	40.46	46.69	60.78
sl	28.19	49.57	40.30	30.46	45.03
sn	34.79	42.11	56.13	47.51	50.60

Earlier work on related problems in American English (Purnell et al. 2005) has used greater than 50% glottal pulsing as a guide to considering a segment phonetically 'voiced.' In this dataset, some speakers (Hammerfest, Lyngdal) show consistently less than 50% pulsing while the most heavily voicing speakers are mostly around 50%, but none show consistently higher rates of pulsing. Allen (2011) concludes, as we do here, that Norwegian /s/ is indeed specified for [spread glottis]. As argued at length by Allen (2011), this undermines Kristoffersen's analysis of Norwegian phonology, which accepts the basics of laryngeal realism, but not privativity. Based on Allen's data (and see his paper for much more detail), Norwegian appears to be a well-behaved [spread glottis] language.

This analysis is supported by the following data from our heritage speakers, which shows approximately the same amount of sonorant devoicing after voiceless obstruents for both English and Norwegian as seen in Allen's results above.[3]

Table 3. Speaker from Findlay: English and Norwegian percent glottal pulsing.

English		Norwegian	
Token	%Pulsing	Token	%Pulsing
pleasure	47.85	klokkar	65.06
sledge	62.99	pliktet	51.03
slips	49.00	slepp	53.92
Average	53.28	**Average**	56.67

---

3. Results were only available for the speakers from Findlay and Hendricks. The recording for the speaker from Burnesville contained low-level static that made it difficult to make reliable measurements.

Table 4. Speaker from Hendricks: English and Norwegian percent glottal pulsing. Numbered tokens (e.g., 'slag1', 'slag2', etc.) indicate that there were multiple tokens in the recording and they were numbered in the order they occurred, though it was not always the case that each token was usable (e.g., 'snakka2', 'snakka6', etc.).

English		Norwegian	
Token	%Pulsing	Token	%Pulsing
Christmas	49.19	klasse	72.88
closer	8.39	slag1	55.09
(Eau) Claire	78.46	slag2	33.91
		slag3	100.00
		slag4	64.15
		slag5	37.33
		slekt	39.89
		slik	75.93
		snakka2	47.37
		snakka6	29.91
		snakka10	30.70
Average	45.35	Average	53.38

We notice here quite a bit of variability in percent glottal pulsing between tokens, but the average for both speakers, for both English and Norwegian, is consistently around 50%. We stress, however, that in nearly every case there is at least some, and in most cases quite a bit, of sonorant devoicing, which is an indication of aspiration after the stops and a spread configuration of the glottis for all fortis obstruents. The large amount of variation is likely due to the nature of the recordings, which contain free conversation rather than controlled experiments and wordlists.

In some tokens, though, there is no sonorant devoicing for good reasons. We see quite often, in both Allen (2011) and in the American Norwegian data, the presence of schwa epenthesis before flapped /r/ and retroflex flapped /l/. We have not included tokens exhibiting schwa epenthesis in our discussion, but Endresen (1989) explains that this is a common feature in Norwegian because of what he terms *open overgang* (open transition), contrasting with *tett overgang* (tight transition) in English, referring to the amount of articulatory overlap in consonant clusters. We mention this here only in passing since some tokens may have a wider transition without necessarily showing schwa epenthesis, but the reader should be aware of this feature of Norwegian.[4]

The major point is this: Something discussed in the best available literature as a difference between the languages turns out, on systematic investigation, to be illusory, at least in the data presented to date. It would have been quite easy to declare the Norwegian-American patterns the result of American English influence on American Norwegian, save for a study of closely comparable forms available thanks to the Nordic Dialect Corpus.

---

4. See Bradley (2002, 2007) for discussion of schwa epenthesis in word-final clusters in Norwegian.

5. Medial voicing: An under-investigated area

In light of the last section, an obvious area to pursue is the phonetic realization of lenis obstruents in Norwegian. If Norwegian /s/ were unspecified laryngeally, it should first and foremost show passive voicing effects in intervocalic position, as does the laryngeally unspecified /z/ in English. Even if European Norwegian fails to evince these patterns – as we would expect based on the preceding section – this would be a place where American Norwegian-English might show different patterns, directly or indirectly connected to English.

This is also an area for which we have some acoustic data from a relevant variety of Norwegian. Van Dommelen and Ringen (2007) provide a study of intervocalic stops in Trøndelag Norwegian. The key findings are reproduced in Figures 1 and 2, for consonant duration in the first instance and glottal pulsing in the second.

Closure durations of intervocalic stops

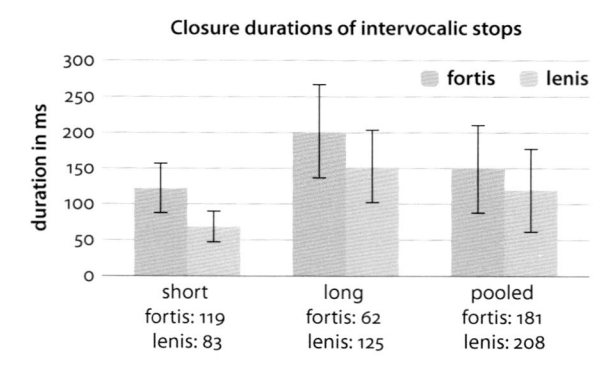

	short	long	pooled
fortis	119	62	181
lenis	83	125	208

Figure 1. Closure durations of intervocalic fortis and lenis stops. Short consonants are preceded by long vowels; long consonants are preceded by short vowels. Means and standard deviations in ms. Numbers of each type of token are noted below each category. (Data from Van Dommelen and Ringen 2007)

Percent voicing in intervocalic lenis stops

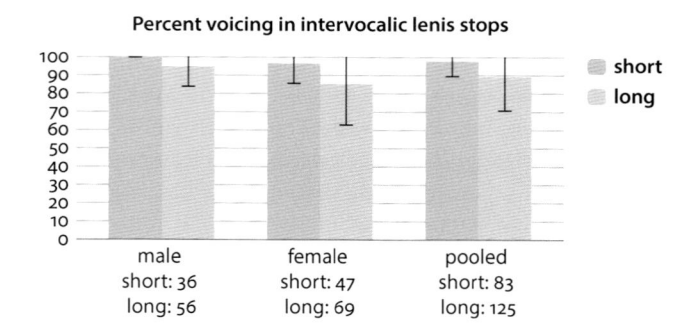

	male	female	pooled
short	36	47	83
long	56	69	125

Figure 2. Amount of voicing in % in intervocalic lenis stops. Short consonants are preceded by long vowels; long consonants are preceded by short vowels. Numbers of each type of token are noted below each category. (Data from Van Dommelen and Ringen 2007)

In short, fortis stops are much longer than lenis, and lenis show considerable voicing, that is, they have passive voicing, possible because they are not specified for [spread glottis] which would prohibit phonetic voicing.

Comparing first lenis and fortis closure duration (measured from the offset of discernible formant structure in the spectrogram to the burst release after closure) in American Norwegian with Van Dommelen and Ringen's results, we see that fortis obstruents are longer than their lenis counterparts, and that singleton /s/ is about as long as fortis geminates at just over 120 ms (Figure 3).

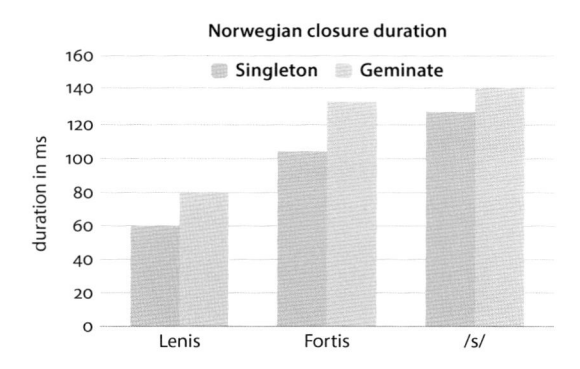

Figure 3. American Norwegian: mean medial obstruent closure duration in ms.

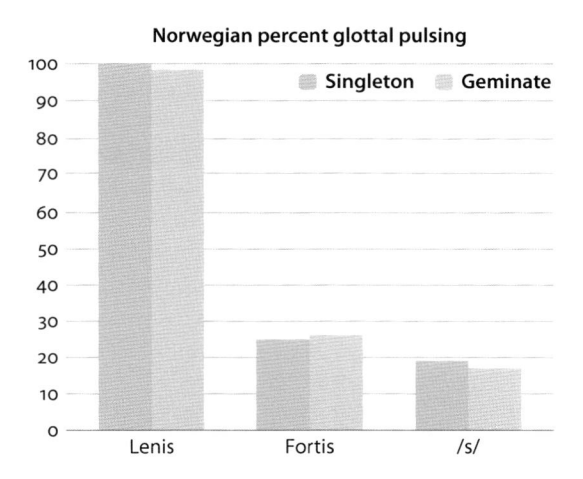

Figure 4. American Norwegian: mean medial obstruent percent glottal pulsing.

However, the results in Figure 4 indicate that medial /s/ shows relatively little voicing, around 20% or less, which is even less than the fortis geminates. This suggests that /s/ is not subject to passive voicing and is specified for [spread glottis] in American Norwegian.

As far as the English of our speakers is concerned, evidence from earlier speakers in Norwegian American communities indicates that Norwegian imposition on English played a clear role here. As noted in §2, in a study of English spoken by Norwegian Americans in Crookston, Minnesota (in the northwestern part of the state), Simley (1930: 470) found very widespread fortis realization of /z, ʒ/ as [s, ʃ], a finding echoed clearly by Haugen (1953: 47). Indeed, Simley points to this as the most consistent impact of Norwegian on the English pronunciation of her subjects: 95 of 115 American-born school students of Norwegian heritage showed the feature, including in final position.

From our contemporary speakers, the patterns are somewhat different. First of all, we see that /s/ is generally longer than /z/, which suggests that there is still some distinction being made between the two.

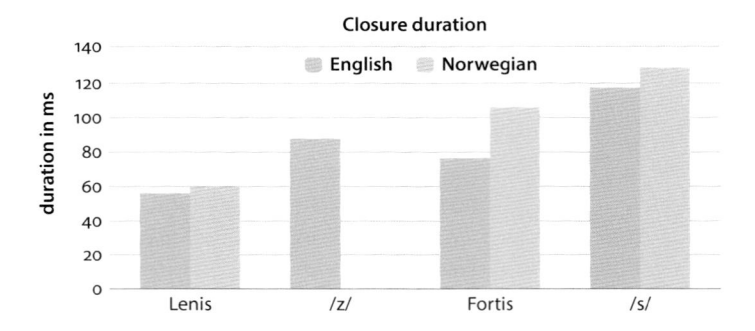

Figure 5. Mean medial obstruent closure duration in ms for all speakers.

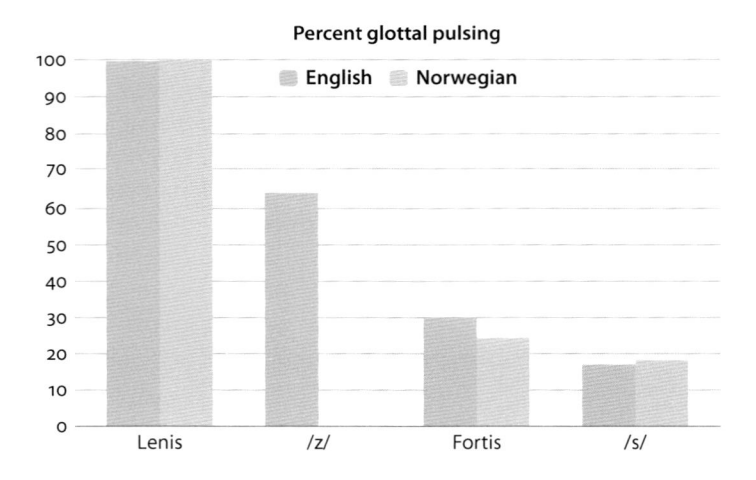

Figure 6. Medial consonants: mean percent glottal pulsing for all speakers.

The difference between /s/ and /z/ is even more pronounced in terms of percent glottal pulsing. In Figure 6, we see that /z/ is approximately 60% percent voiced whereas /s/ is closer to 20%. This means that if /z/ is around 85 ms long, only about 20–30 ms will be voiceless. The inverse would be true for /s/, with about 20–30 ms being voiced. This suggests that the fortis realization of /z/ may no longer be a feature of Norwegian-American English speech, and that a more native-like pattern has emerged with a clear laryngeal distinction between /z/ and /s/. Even though /z/ is longer in duration than the fortis stops in our speakers' English, the fortis stops nevertheless have a much lower percent glottal pulsing.

This raises phonological questions that we will not pursue here about the nature of phonological contrast, but we note two scenarios in passing. One way of explaining this situation would be to argue that the fortis stops (as well as /s/) are specified for [spread glottis] and are therefore resistant to passive voicing, which /z/ is not because it is unspecified. Another possibility is that we have an instantiation of Vaux's Law (Vaux 1998), namely that a laryngeally unspecified fricative acquires specification for [spread glottis] as a phonetic enhancement.

The prominence of this feature raises the question of whether there is more at play than simple phonological specification. There appears to be. First, note that /s/ appears in the above figures to be the longest obstruent in Norwegian. Fintoft (1961) in fact indicates that /s/ is the longest of Norwegian stops, fricatives, nasals, and liquids. Stevens et al. (1992: 2979), moreover, write the following about how listeners perceive fricative voicing:

> Listeners base their voicing judgments of intervocalic fricatives on an assessment of the time interval in the fricative during which there is no glottal vibration. This time interval must exceed about 60 ms if the fricative is to be judged as voiceless.

In other words, based on this, a speaker could produce a Norwegian or Norwegian-like /s/ and even with voicing through half of it, it could be perceived as voiceless.

We see that /s/ is not subject to passive voicing in the Norwegian or in the English of our heritage speakers. This suggests that /s/ is specified for [spread glottis] in both languages. This raises the question of whether the [spread glottis] specification was inherited from Norwegian or borrowed from English. As noted previously, if Norwegian /s/ is laryngeally unspecified, we might expect to see passive voicing as we do for the laryngeally unspecified /z/ in English. However, there is no evidence that Norwegian /s/ has ever behaved like English /z/ in the speech of Norwegian immigrants. In fact, the opposite is reported; both Simley and Haugen found that the English /z/ of (at least the earlier) Norwegian immigrants behaved more like Norwegian /s/. Based on the findings presented above and in §3, the most plausible explanation for this is that the [spread glottis] specification was inherited in their Norwegian and then imposed on their English, and that later heritage speakers have learned to make the distinction in English.

6. Final laryngeal distinctions

Turning finally to the phonetics and phonology of final laryngeal distinctions, English generally and Upper Midwestern English in particular show striking patterns we do not expect to see shared with Norwegian. First, while languages in general show longer vowel duration before a voiced or lenis coda consonant than before a fortis or voiceless one, English is widely reported to show this to a much greater extent than many other languages. The figure below, reproduced from Chen (1970: 138) shows this for a variety of languages, including, it happens, Norwegian (with data drawn from Fintoft 1961). In the Upper Midwest, a stream of research (especially Purnell et al. 2005) has shown that some parts of the region appear to be undergoing a neutralization of the distinction. Those areas, typically in eastern Wisconsin and heavily settled by German-speaking immigrants, are becoming much more distinct in this regard from the southwestern part of the state where, in addition to significant German settlement, there was always a large Old Stock American or Yankee presence and, in many areas, significant Norwegian immigration.

Vowel duration before voiceless and voiced consonants

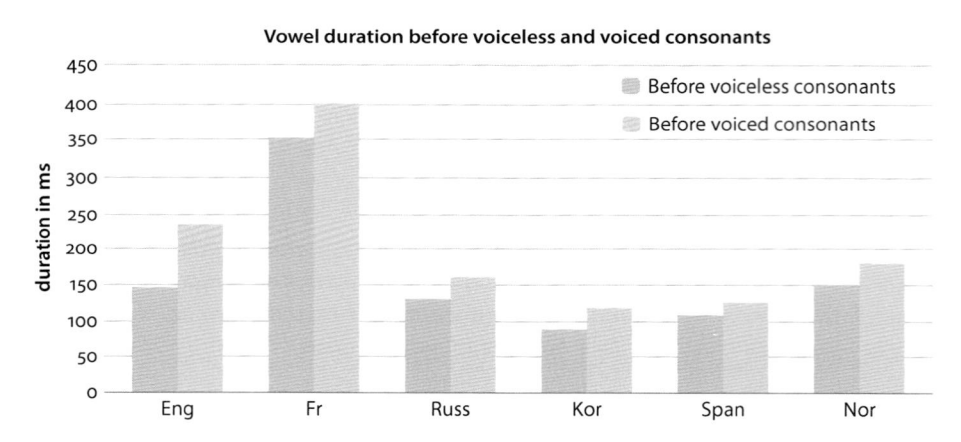

Figure 7. Vowel duration before voiceless and voiced consonants (Chen 1970: 138).

The values in Figure 7, presented with additional data in Table 5, show that English is somewhat unusual cross-linguistically in that the ratio of vowel length before lenis and fortis stops is much greater than in the other languages reported on, suggesting that vowel length plays a greater role in marking laryngeal distinctions in English.

Table 5. Additional figures for vowel length from Chen (1970: 138–139).

	Vowel duration in ms			
	Before voiceless consonants	Before voiced consonants	Mean difference	Ratio
English	146	238	92	0.61
French	354	407	53	0.87
Russian	131	160	29	0.82
Korean	91	119	28	0.78
Spanish	109	127	18	0.86
Norwegian	148	181	33	0.82

If we compare these numbers with the data from our heritage speakers, we see that the difference in vowel length before lenis and fortis stops in both their English and Norwegian look very similar to Chen's results in Figure 7 and Table 5, the main difference being a shorter duration in general:

Vowel duration before voiceless and voiced consonants

[Bar chart showing duration in ms for Eng (Chen), Nor (Chen), Eng (Heritage), and Nor (Heritage), comparing before voiceless consonants and before voiced consonants]

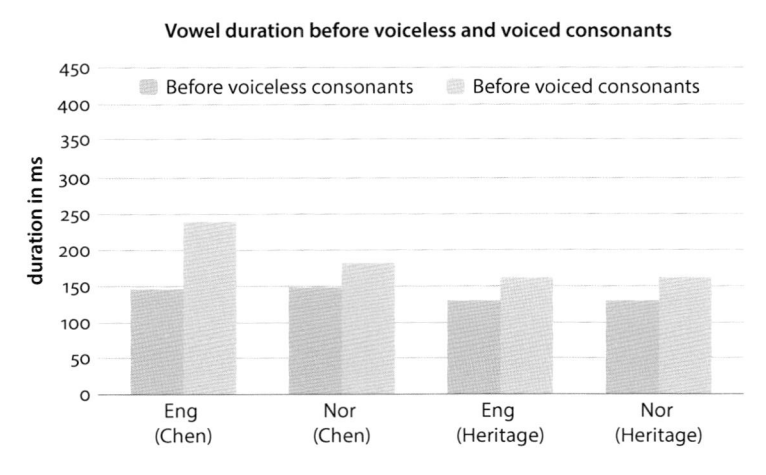

Figure 8. Vowel duration before voiceless and voiced consonants; Chen's (1970) results compared with our heritage Norwegian speakers.

Table 6 shows that while our heritage speakers may have shorter durations than Chen reports for both English and Norwegian in his study, the mean differences and vowel duration ratios are very similar to Norwegian:

Table 6. Chen's and heritage speakers' results compared.

		Vowel duration in ms			
		Before fortis stops	Before lenis stops	Mean difference	Ratio
Chen (1970)	English	146	238	92	0.61
	Norwegian	148	181	33	0.82
Heritage speakers	English	128.72	160.84	32	0.80
	Norwegian	129.19	161.25	32	0.80

This suggests that heritage Norwegian speakers in the Upper Midwest have retained a Norwegian-like method of marking final laryngeal distinctions, relying less on vowel length than is otherwise reported for English.[5]

---

5. Chen (1970) cites several other studies that include relevant data from English, namely Peterson and Lehiste (1960), Zimmerman and Sapon (1958), and House and Fairbanks (1953), all of whom report results similar to his.

Figure 9 reveals that final lenis stops are heavily voiced, which suggests that instead of using vowel length to distinguish between final lenis and fortis stops, which tends to be the pattern in American English, these speakers make the distinction between lenis and fortis by actively voicing final lenis stops rather than lengthening the vowel.

Percent glottal pulsing

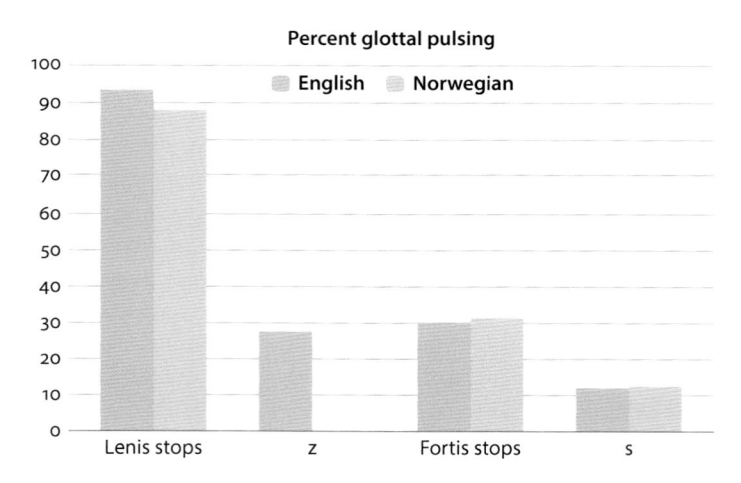

(bar chart showing English and Norwegian values for Lenis stops, z, Fortis stops, and s)

Figure 9. Percent glottal pulsing of word-final consonants in both English and Norwegian.

When comparing the vowel duration ratio data in Table 6 with Chen's results for English and Norwegian, we see that the English of the Norwegian Americans is more in line with Chen's results for Norwegian. If the heritage speakers are relying less on vowel duration to mark laryngeal distinctions in finals, we would expect to see them making this distinction in some other way, and in fact the results for percent glottal pulsing in Figure 9 suggest that they rely more heavily on laryngeal activity, i.e., voicing of lenis stops, than vowel duration. In terms of Keyser and Stevens (2006), this is seen as a phonetic enhancement of final laryngeal distinctions. In the case of at least much of American English, the phonetic enhancement is an increase in the duration of a vowel preceding a final lenis obstruent, whereas for the Norwegian Americans in the Upper Midwest, the phonetic enhancement appears to be the active voicing of a final lenis obstruent.

7. Summary and conclusions

This paper has provided an initial foray into a new area in several regards, but a number of patterns emerge. Even where we cannot directly map the productions of heritage speakers to those of European Norwegian speakers or, to a lesser extent, to American English speakers in the Upper Midwest, we have provided some descriptive baseline for future comparison.

First, while previous research led us to expect differences in patterns of sonorant devoicing between the two languages, specifically with regard to /s/-sonorant clusters, investigation of a set of European Norwegian dialects indicates none. We take this as a reminder of the need for careful verification of the empirical basis of heritage language research, an issue well known in other settings, such as German-American linguistics.

Second, with regard to passive voicing of obstruents in medial, especially intervocalic position, our evidence suggests that Norwegian /s/ in the Upper Midwest behaves like a phonologically or phonetically marked /s/, that is, not a lenis segment susceptible to passive voicing.

Third, in English, our bilingual speakers no longer show clear evidence of what was once a very prominent, perhaps the most prominent feature of a Norwegian-American accent: realization of /z/ as [s]. This classic feature has receded at least for these speakers.

Fourth, there are subtle differences in the ways that final laryngeal distinctions are realized in Norwegian American English as opposed to values reported for monolingual Americans. This suggests some influence from Norwegian in the phonetic implementation of laryngeal phonology. Such phonetic patterns can easily be exploited sociolinguistically and if these features persist into monolingual English in Norwegian American communities, they would provide evidence for substratal effects beyond the bilingual generation. This would parallel the findings of Purnell et al. (2005, also Annear et al. 2011) on German influences on the English of eastern Wisconsin.

Overall, Heritage Norwegian, in fact, looks largely like its parent language and its contact language. The speech of the bilinguals reported here shows full command of the phonetics and phonology of both languages on the issues investigated, with obvious adjustments for regional variation in both languages. Evidence of influence or 'seepage' between the languages is relatively modest, in sharp contrast particularly to the heavily Norwegian-colored English reported for earlier generations in the region.

References

Allen, Brent. 2011. "Laryngeal Phonology in Norwegian: Sonorant Devoicing." Manuscript. University of Wisconsin – Madison.

Allen, Brent and Joseph Salmons. 2012. "Obstruenters fonetikk og fonologi i amerikanorsk og norskamerikansk engelsk." *Norsk Lingvistisk Tidsskrift* [Norwegian Linguistics Journal] 30: 149–169.

Annear, L., E. Clare, A. Groh, T. C. Purnell, E. Raimy, M. Simonsen and J. C. Salmons. 2011. *Why do English speakers neutralize VOICING finally?* Paper presented at *New Ways of Analyzing Variation (NWAV)*, Georgetown University, Washington, DC.

Avery, Peter and William Idsardi. 2001. "Laryngeal Dimensions, Completion and Enhancement." In *Distinctive Feature Theory*, ed. by T. Alan Hall, 41–70. Berlin: Mouton de Gruyter.

Beckman, Jill and Catherine Ringen. 2009. "A Typological Investigation of Evidence for [sg] in Fricatives." Paper Presented at the *Manchester Phonology Meeting*.

Bradley, Travis G. 2002. "Gestural Timing and Derived Environment Effects in Norwegian Clusters." In *WCCFL 21 Proceedings*, ed. by Line Mikkelsen and Christopher Potts, 43–56. Somerville: Cascadilla Press.

Bradley, Travis G. 2007. "Morphological Derived-Environment Effects in Gestural Coordination: A Case Study of Norwegian Clusters." *Lingua* 117: 950–985. DOI: 10.1016/j.lingua.2006.05.004

Chen, Matthew. 1970. "Vowel Length Variation as a Function of the Voicing of Consonant Environment." *Phonetica* 22: 129–159. DOI: 10.1159/000259312

Eckman, Fred R. and Gregory K. Iverson. Forthcoming. "Second Language Acquisition and Phonological Change." In *The Oxford Handbook of Historical Phonology*, ed. by Patrick Honeybone and Joseph Salmons. Oxford: Oxford University Press.

Endresen, Rolf Theil. 1989. *Fonetikk: Ei elementær innføring*. Oslo: Universitetsforlaget.

Fintoft, Knut. 1961. "The Duration of Some Norwegian Speech Sounds." *Phonetica* 7: 19–39. DOI: 10.1159/000258096

Flege, James E. 1987. "The Production of 'New' and 'Similar' Phones in a Foreign Language: Evidence for the Effect of Equivalence Classification." *Journal of Phonetics* 15: 47–65.

Haugen, Einar. 1953. *The Norwegian Language in America* (2 vols.). Madison: University of Pennsylvania Press.

Hjelde, Arnstein. 1992. *Trøndsk talemål i Amerika*. Trondheim: Tapir.

Hjelde, Arnstein. This volume. "Changes in a Norwegian Dialect in America."

Honeybone, Patrick. 2005. "Sharing Makes us Stronger: Process Inhibition and Segmental Structure." In *Headhood, Elements, Specification and Contrastivity*, ed. by Philip Carr, Jacques Durand and Colin Ewen, 167–192. Amsterdam: Benjamins. DOI: 10.1075/cilt.259.12hon

House, Arthur S. and Grant Fairbanks. 1953. "The Influence of Consonant Environment Upon the Secondary Acoustical Characteristics of Vowels." *Journal of the Acoustical Society of America* 25: 105–113. DOI: 10.1121/1.1906982

Howell, Robert B. 1993. "German Immigration and the Development of Regional Variants of American English: Using Contact Theory to Discover Our Roots." In *The German Language in America*, ed. by Joseph Salmons, 190–212. Madison: Max Kade Institute.

Iverson, Gregory and Joseph Salmons. 1995. "Aspiration and Laryngeal Representation in Germanic." *Phonology* 12: 369–396. DOI: 10.1017/S0952675700002566

Iverson, Gregory and Joseph Salmons. 1999. "Glottal Spreading Bias in Germanic." *Linguistische Berichte* 178: 135–151.

Iverson, Gregory and Joseph Salmons. 2003a. "Laryngeal Enhancement in Early Germanic." *Phonology* 20: 43–74. DOI: 10.1017/S0952675703004469

Iverson, Gregory and Joseph Salmons. 2003b. "Legacy Specification in the Laryngeal Phonology of Dutch." *Journal of Germanic Linguistics* 15(2): 1–26. DOI: 10.1017/S1470542703000242

Iverson, Gregory and Joseph Salmons. 2006. "On the Typology of Final Laryngeal Neutralization: Evolutionary Phonology and Laryngeal Realism." *Theoretical Linguistics* 32: 205–216. DOI: 10.1515/TL.2006.014

Iverson, Gregory and Joseph Salmons. 2007. "Domains and Directionality in the Evolution of German Final Fortition." *Phonology* 24: 121–145. DOI: 10.1017/S0952675707001133

Iverson, Gregory and Joseph Salmons. 2008. "Germanic Aspiration: Phonetic Enhancement and Language Contact." *Sprachwissenschaft* 33(3): 257–278.

Iverson, Gregory and Joseph Salmons. 2011. "Final Devoicing and Final Laryngeal Neutralization." In *Companion to Phonology* Volume 3, ed. by Marc van Oostendorp, Colin Ewen, Beth Hume and Keren Rice, 1622–1643. Oxford: Wiley-Blackwell.

Johannessen, Janne Bondi, Joel Priestley, Kristin Hagen, Tor Anders Åfarli and Øystein Alexander Vangsnes. 2009. "The Nordic Dialect Corpus — An Advanced Research Tool." In *Proceedings of the 17th Nordic Conference of Computational Linguistics NODALIDA 2009, NEALT Proceedings Series*, Volume 4, ed. by Kristiina Jokinen and Eckhard Bick, online at http://beta.visl.sdu.dk/~eckhard/nodalida/paper_26.pdf.

Johannessen, Janne Bondi and Joseph Salmons (eds). 2012. *Norsk i Amerika*. Special issue of the *Norsk Lingvistisk Tidsskrift / Norwegian Linguistics Journal 2*.

Keyser, Samuel Jay and Kenneth Stevens. 2006. "Enhancement and Overlap in the Speech Chain." *Language* 82: 33–63. DOI: 10.1353/lan.2006.0051

Kristoffersen, Gjert. 2000. *The Phonology of Norwegian*. New York: Oxford University Press.

Minkova, Donka. 2011. "Phonemically Contrastive Fricatives in Old English?" *English Language and Linguistics* 15: 31–59. DOI: 10.1017/S1360674310000274

Moen, Per. 1988. "The English Pronunciation of Norwegian-Americans in Four Midwestern States." *American Studies in Scandinavia* 20: 105–121.

Moen, Per. 1991. "The Influence of a Norwegian Substratum on the Pronunciation of Norwegian-Americans in the Upper Midwest." In *Norsk språk i Amerika – Norwegian Language in America*, ed. by Botolv Helleland, 97–115. Olso: Novus.

Moen, Per. 2001. "The English of Norwegian Americans in the Upper Midwest with Special Reference to the Substratum Effect on Syntax and Idioms." In *Global Eurolinguistics: European Languages in North America – Migration, Maintenance and Death*, ed. by Sture Ureland, 243–264. Tübingen: Niemeyer.

Nagy, Naomi and Alexei Kochetov. 2011. "VOT Across the Generations: A Cross-Linguistic Study of Contact-Induced Change." Paper presented at the *6th International Conference on Language Variation in Europe (ICLaVE 6)*, Freiburg, Germany, June 29. http://individual.utoronto.ca/ngn/research/abstracts/ICLaVe2011_abstract_NagyKochetov.htm

Nützel, Daniel and Joseph Salmons. 2011. "Language Contact and New Dialect Formation: Evidence from German in North America." *Language and Linguistics Compass* 5: 705–717. DOI: 10.1111/j.1749-818X.2011.00308.x

Peterson, G.E. and Ilse Lehiste. 1960. "Duration of Syllable Nuclei in English." *Journal of the Acoustical Society of America* 32: 693–703. DOI: 10.1121/1.1908183

Piske, Thorsten, Ian R.A. MacKay and James E. Flege. 2001. "Factors Affecting Degree of Foreign Accent in an L2: A Review." *Journal of Phonetics* 29: 191–215. DOI: 10.1006/jpho.2001.0134

Popperwell, R.G. 1963. *The Pronunciation of Norwegian*. Cambridge: Cambridge University Press.

Purnell, Thomas, Joseph Salmons, Dilara Tepeli and Jennifer Mercer. 2005. "Structured Heterogeneity and Change in Laryngeal Phonetics: Upper Midwestern Final Obstruents." *Journal of English Linguistics* 33(4): 307–338. DOI: 10.1177/0075424205285637

Ringen, Catherine and Wim A. Van Dommelen. 2013. "Quantity and laryngeal contrasts in Norwegian." *Journal of Phonetics* 41: 479–490.

Rothman, Jason. 2009. "Understanding the Nature and Outcomes of Early Bilingualism: Romance Languages as Heritage Languages." *The International Journal of Bilingualism* 13(2): 155–163. DOI: 10.1177/1367006909339814

Simley, Anne. 1930. "A Study of Norwegian Dialect in Minnesota." *American Speech* 5: 469–474. DOI: 10.2307/452337

Simon, Ellen. 2011. "Laryngeal Stop Systems in Contact: Connecting Present-Day Acquisition Findings and Historical Contact Hypotheses." *Diachronica* 28: 225–254. DOI: 10.1075/dia.28.2.03sim

Stevens, Kenneth N., Sheila E. Blumenstein, Laura Glicksman, Martha Burton, and Kathleen Kurowski. 1992. "Acoustic and Perceptual Characteristics of Voicing in Fricatives and Fricative Clusters." *Journal of the Acoustic Society of America* 91: 2979–3000. DOI: 10.1121/1.402933

Van Coetsem, Frans. 1988. *Loan Phonology and the Two Transfer Types in Language Contact.* Dordrecht: Foris.

Van Coetsem, Frans. 2000. *A General and Unified Theory of the Transmission Process in Language Contact.* Heidelberg: Winter.

Van Dommelen, Wim A. and Catherine Ringen. 2007. "Intervocalic Fortis and Lenis Stops in a Norwegian Dialect." *Proceedings Fonetik 2007, Stockholm, May 30-June 1, 2007. Speech, Music and Hearing, Quarterly Progress and Status Report, TMH-QPSR* 50: 5–8.

Vaux, Bert. 1998. "The Laryngeal Specifications of Fricatives." *Linguistic Inquiry* 29: 497–511. DOI: 10.1162/002438998553833

Winford, Donald. 2005. "Contact-Induced Changes: Classification and Processes. *Diachronica* 22: 373–427. DOI: 10.1075/dia.22.2.05win

Zimmerman, Samuel A. and Stanley M. Sapon. 1958. "Note on Vowel Duration Seen Crosslinguistically." *Journal of the Acoustical Society of America* 30: 152–153. DOI: 10.1121/1.1909521

The history of front rounded vowels in New Braunfels German

Marc Pierce*, Hans C. Boas* and Karen Roesch**
*The University of Texas at Austin / **Indiana University – Purdue University Indianapolis

While earlier studies of New Braunfels German (NBG), a dialect of Texas German (TxG), e.g., Eikel (1954, 1966b) and Gilbert (1972), report the existence of front rounded vowels to various degrees, they are almost completely absent from present-day NBG (Boas 2009). This paper describes the history of such vowels in NBG and assesses possible causes of their loss. We first sketch the history of German in Texas, in order to set the stage for the following discussion. We then review the status of front rounded vowels in NBG, as reported by three landmark studies of TxG, namely Eikel (1954), Gilbert (1972), and Boas (2009), and then discuss motivations for their loss. We argue that five major factors drove this loss: (1) the original donor dialects of NBG, (2) the markedness of front rounded vowels, (3) contact with English, (4) limited exposure to Standard German, and (5) the changing linguistic and social contexts of NBG.

Keywords: sound change, Texas German, phonology, front rounded vowels, markedness, language contact

1. Introduction[1]

In his study of New Braunfels German (NBG), a dialect of Texas German (TxG)[2] spoken in New Braunfels, Texas, a city of approximately 65,000 located about 35 miles northeast of San Antonio, Eikel (1954) reports that words like *Bücher* 'books' and *zwölf*

---

1. An earlier version of this paper was presented at the 20th International Conference on Historical Linguistics (Osaka, Japan, August 2011). We thank the conference participants for their input and are especially indebted to two anonymous referees, Paul Kerswill, and Joe Salmons for a number of valuable comments.

2. A precise definition of the term "Texas German" is somewhat elusive. Here we use it to refer to a set of varieties of German spoken in Texas descended from the dialects of German brought to Texas in the 19th century.

DOI 10.1075/silv.18.05pie
© 2015 John Benjamins Publishing Company

'twelve' contain front rounded vowels. These vowels are almost completely absent in NBG today; none of the 52 speakers of NBG interviewed for Boas (2009) used a front rounded vowel in *Haarbürste* 'hairbrush,' for instance. In this paper, which builds on Boas (2009), we describe the history of front rounded vowels in this dialect and assess possible causes of their loss, focusing on developments since the 1940s, when the data discussed in Eikel (1954, 1966b) was collected. We connect this change to five major factors: (1) the original donor dialects of NBG; (2) the markedness of front rounded vowels; (3) contact with English; (4) limited exposure to standard German; and (5) the changing linguistic and social contexts of NBG. We begin with some brief remarks on the history of German in Texas, in order to outline the social and historical contexts of our analysis. We then describe the status of front rounded vowels in NBG as described in three major works on TxG, Eikel (1954, 1966b), Gilbert (1972), and Boas (2009), before discussing possible motivations for their changing status.

The first large wave of German settlers to Texas arrived in the early 1840s, and large-scale immigration continued for a number of decades thereafter. By 1860 there were nearly 20,000 German-born immigrants, mostly from northern and central Germany, living in Texas, and approximately 30,000 Texas Germans, including the American-born children of immigrants (Jordan 1975: 54). Although German immigration to Texas eventually slackened, the number of Texas Germans continued to increase: by 1940 there were approximately 159,000 Texas Germans (Kloss 1977).

For the first several decades of German settlement in Texas, the Texas Germans were relatively isolated from non-German speakers, thanks to a number of political and/or social factors (e.g., the abolitionist tendencies of many Texas Germans, which would have set them apart from many of their neighbors in a slave state like Texas).[3] This isolation, coupled with serious attempts at language maintenance, allowed for the general retention of TxG. There were numerous German-language church services, newspapers and other periodicals, schools, and social organizations (ranging from choirs to shooting clubs). This situation has since changed dramatically, due to factors like English-only laws; anti-German sentiment; the development of the American interstate highway system in the 1950s, which made the once-isolated TxG communities much more accessible, making it easier for non-German speakers to visit or live in previously monolingual German communities, and for German-speakers to accept employment in more urban areas; and the increasing tendency for speakers of TxG to marry partners who could not speak TxG.

These developments had devastating consequences for TxG. Institutional support for German was largely abandoned; German-language newspapers and periodicals stopped publishing altogether or switched to English as the language of publication; some German-language schools closed and German instruction was dropped in others; and German-speaking churches replaced German-language services with English-language ones. Speakers of English moved in increasing numbers to the traditional

---

3. Immigrant letters, like those collected in works like Brister (2008), indicate that connections to German-speaking Europe remained strong.

German enclaves, and generally refused to assimilate linguistically to their new neighbors by learning German, while younger Texas Germans left the traditional German-speaking areas for employment or education, and began to speak primarily English. Today only an estimated 6000–8000 Texas Germans, primarily in their sixties or older, still speak TxG fluently (Boas 2009), and English has become the primary language for most Texas Germans in all domains.

2. Previous research

We rely on three large-scale studies of TxG: first, the pioneering work of Fred Eikel (e.g., Eikel 1954 and 1966a, b), which is based on data collected in the 1930s and 1940s;[4] second, Glenn Gilbert (1972), whose fieldwork in the 1960s led to the publication of the massive *Linguistic Atlas of Texas German*; and third, the Texas German Dialect Project (TGDP; www.tgdp.org), directed by Hans C. Boas,[5] which has been underway since 2001. We focus on these three studies for two major reasons: (1) they are the largest-scale studies of TxG available, and (2) they provide us with a rich pool of real-time data to draw on.[6]

We begin with Eikel (1954, 1966b).[7] Eikel (1954: 26) includes the front rounded vowels, each of which in his view has long and short allophones, in his table of NBG phonemes. About the high front rounded vowels, Eikel (1954: 28) writes, "NBG /y:/ is a long, high-front, rounded, open vowel ...," while "NBG /y/ is a short, high-front, rounded, open vowel, as in S[tandard] G[erman]," and he transcribes words like *Bücher* 'books' and *Rüben* 'beets,' with the long allophone and words like *Schlüssel* 'key' and *fünfzig* 'fifty' with the short allophone. As for the mid front rounded vowels, Eikel (1954: 29) states, "NBG /ø:/ is a long mid-front, rounded, open vowel, as in sG," and that "NBG /ø/ is a short, mid-front, open, rounded vowel," and he transcribes words like *schön* 'beautiful' and *Öl* 'oil' with the long allophone and words like *zwölf* 'twelve'

---

4. Other contemporary studies, e.g., Clardy (1954), generally reinforce the description of NBG presented in Eikel (1954, 1966b). For this reason, and because Eikel (1954, 1966b) is a considerably better-known study, we focus on Eikel's work here.

5. See Boas et al. (2010) for details on the design of the TGDP and the resulting Texas German Dialect Archive (TGDA).

6. In the case of the TGDP, for instance, TGDP members have re-recorded Eikel's (1954) and Gilbert's (1972) word and sentence lists and resampled the Gilbert data (i.e., collected data using the same questionnaire), which facilitates comparison. In fact, the TGDP team has to date interviewed two speakers who were also interviewed by Fred Eikel.

7. The relationship between these two works is a bit unclear; Eikel (1966b) is based on the same data as Eikel (1954), and in fact cites many of the same forms. We rely largely on Eikel (1954), but also refer readers to Eikel (1966b), which is readily available via JSTOR (in contrast to Eikel 1954, which is considerably more difficult to obtain).

and *gehört* 'hear (past participle)' with the short allophone.⁸ Eikel's data indicates that front rounded vowels were a well-established part of the phonemic system of NBG in the 1940s.⁹

At the same time, it is also clear that a generational unrounding of originally front rounded vowels was already underway in NBG at the time of Eikel's fieldwork. Eikel (1954: 28) writes, in his discussion of /y:/:

> Of the oldest generation of speakers of NBG two round this vowel distinctly and consistently, two show occasions of unrounding, and two do not round at all. Of the twelve informants of the second generation, one rounds consistently, all the others fluctuate, showing more instances of unrounding than rounding. All six informants of the third generation show no signs of rounding. Here /y:/ is completely replaced by /i:/.

He reports the same unrounding process for /y/ and the mid front rounded vowels.¹⁰
Examples of words with front rounded vowels in Eikel's data are given in (1).¹¹

(1) Front rounded vowels in Eikel (1954)
   a. /y:/: *Bücher* 'books' [by:çɐʁ], *Rüben* 'beets' [ry:bən], *Bühne* 'stage' [by:nə], *Gemüse* 'vegetable' [gəmy:zə], *Hühnchen* 'chicken' [hy:nçən], *Überzüge* 'coatings' [y:bərtsy:jə]

---

8. Note that Eikel transcribes all four of these vowels as tense vowels, as opposed to most current scholars, who would presumably transcribe the short allophones as lax vowels, i.e., [ʏ] and [œ], respectively. Gilbert (1972) follows the same practice, writing that "[s]ince tense vowels in Texas German ... are at the same time long and raised and non-tense vowels are both non-long and lowered ..., the symbol [:] will be sufficient to distinguish tense, long, raised vowels from their non-tense, non-long, and lowered counterparts" (Gilbert 1972: 6). In addition, Eikel's terminology is not always entirely clear; by "open" he presumably means the feature that more current practice would describe as "tense," and his hyphenated terms "high-front" and "mid-front" would be written as "high front" and "mid front" today. Moreover, the vowel chart he provides (Eikel 1954: 26) omits the term "open."

9. Clardy (1954: 53) draws a similar conclusion: three of her six informants have, in her view, "all the front rounded vowels as phonemes."

10. Clardy (1954) also notes this process: her oldest informant has front rounded vowels in all contexts where they appear in standard German, while her next age group is somewhat less consistent in their use of front rounded vowels, and her youngest informant does not have front rounded vowels. See Boas (2009: 107) for discussion.

11. We have modified Eikel's transcriptions slightly in accordance with more current practices. For instance, he transcribes *Bücher* 'books' as [by:çəR] and describes [R] as "a weak post-velar fricative" (Eikel 1954: 37). We have, however, retained his transcription of all four front rounded vowels as tense. Moreover, Eikel's examples indicate that his informants spoke a version of Texas German that was very close to the standard language. To the best of our knowledge, his examples are indeed representative of the NBG speech community of his time, although at this remove it is impossible to determine this with complete confidence.

b. /y/: *Küste* 'coast' [kystə], *Brücke* 'bridge' [brykə], *Schlüssel* 'key' [ʃlysəl], *Nüsse* 'nuts' [nysə], *Frühstück* 'breakfast' [fry:ʃtyk], *fünfzig* 'fifty' [fynftsiç]

c. /ø:/: *schön* 'pretty' [ʃø:n], *bös* 'evil, angry' [bø:s], *Vögel* 'birds' [fø:jəl], *Öl* 'oil' [ø:l], *Brötchen* 'roll' [brø:tçən], *gewöhnlich* 'usual' [gəvø:nliç]

d. /ø/: *zwölf* 'twelve' [tsvølf], *möchte* 'would like' [møçtə], *könnte* 'could' [køntə], *gehört* 'heard' (p.p.) [gəhøʁt]

The next work to consider is Gilbert (1972). Gilbert's first mention of front rounded vowels in TxG comes as part of a summary of linguistic differences between TxG and Standard German. He writes, "[f]or many speakers, all front vowels are non-round" (Gilbert 1972: 3), indicating that the process of unrounding mentioned in Eikel (1954, 1966b) and Clardy (1954) had been completed for some speakers. The maps collected in Gilbert (1972) paint a similar picture. There are five maps for words that contain front rounded vowels in standard German (map 17, *the door/ die Tür*; map 18, *two daughters/ zwei Töchter*; map 19, *sweet potatoes/ Bataten, Süßkartoffeln*; map 20, *two cooking pots/ zwei Kochtöpfe*; and map 21, *a hairbrush/ eine Haarbürste*), and we might therefore expect to find front rounded vowels in these words in TxG.

As these maps all yield the same general results, here we only consider the maps for *die Tür* and *zwei Töchter* (i.e., one form each containing a high front rounded vowel and a mid front rounded vowel). For *die Tür*, all of Gilbert's New Braunfels informants use a high front long unrounded vowel, i.e., [i:]. As for *zwei Töchter*, Gilbert's informants use the rounded variant much more consistently than they did for the high front vowel. In New Braunfels, although one speaker does retain a mid front rounded vowel, other speakers normally unround the vowel to [e:]. The data from Gilbert (1972) is summarized in (2).[12]

(2) Front rounded vowels in Gilbert (1972)
  a. Map 17 (*the door/ die Tür*): all of Gilbert's NBG speakers use [i:] in this word (i.e., [ti:r]).[13]
  b. Map 18 (*two daughters / zwei Töchter*): in New Braunfels, one speaker does retain a mid front rounded vowel, but other speakers normally unround the vowel to [e:]

---

12. Front rounded vowels had not been lost in these words in all dialects of TxG, and there is also some inconsistency among speakers, as shown by the maps in Gilbert (1972). In Fayetteville (approximately 110 miles northeast of New Braunfels), for instance, there is variation between [y:], [ɛ] and [o:] (and note the differences in vowel length). Also of interest here is that other speakers of TxG (e.g., some in Kendall County, approximately 50 miles west of New Braunfels) backed /ø:/ to [o:], suggesting that vowel frontness was more important for speakers of NBG and vowel rounding was more important to those speakers in Kendall County.

13. Although the lenition of [t] to [d] is a widespread process in TxG, as indicated by maps 8–12 in Gilbert (1972), neither Gilbert (1972) nor Boas (2009) report it for NBG. See also Allen and Salmons (this volume) on obstruents in English and Norwegian.

The most recent treatment of front rounded vowels in NBG is Boas (2009), who notes that front rounded vowels have been almost completely eliminated. Here we again only examine the two forms we considered above when discussing Gilbert (1972), namely *die Tür* and *zwei Töchter*. For *die Tür*, 49 of Boas' 52 New Braunfels-area informants (98%) produced a high front unrounded vowel, i.e., [i:], while one informant produced the high front rounded vowel [y:], and two did not provide any answer.[14] As for *zwei Töchter*, 3 of his 52 informants (6%) produced [ø], 27 (55%) produced [e], 19 (39%) produced [o], and 3 produced *Schwestern* 'sisters' instead of *Töchter*.

In addition to resampling the Gilbert data (fn. 6), Boas and his team also conducted more open-ended interviews with the informants. A search of this data conducted in August 2011 produced much the same results (i.e., the widespread loss of front rounded vowels), albeit with a few twists. There are nine instances of *Tür*, none of which contain a front rounded vowel (all the informants produced *Tier* in this context).[15] There are also seven instances of *Töchter*, none of which contain a front rounded vowel (there are three instances of *Techter* and two each of *Tochter* and *Tochtern*). However, some words do have front rounded vowels: there are nine instances of *Gemüse* in the open-ended data (four with a front rounded vowel, four with a front unrounded vowel, i.e., *Gemiese*, and one with a back rounded vowel, i.e., *Gemuse*). In addition, there are 46 instances of *zwölf*, eleven (24%) of which have a front rounded vowel, while the remaining 35 have a front unrounded vowel (i.e., *zwelf*). These open-ended interviews are more relaxed than the interviews resampling the Gilbert data, indicating that speakers are presumably not as aware of their speech as they are during the questionnaire portion of the interviews and consequently produce more natural speech. The presence of front rounded vowels in the open-ended interview data therefore suggests that front rounded vowels are still part of the phoneme inventory of NBG, albeit for only a handful of speakers. In (3) we summarize the findings of Boas (2009) with regard to front rounded vowels.

(3) Front rounded vowels in Boas (2009)
    a. In the resampled Gilbert data
       die Tür: 49 of 52 informants (98%) produced [i:], one informant produced [y:], and two did not provide any answer.
       zwei Töchter: 3 of 52 informants (6%) produced [ø], 27 (55%) produced [e], 19 (39%) produced [o], and 3 produced *Schwestern* 'sisters' instead of *Töchter*.

---

14. Unfortunately, not all of Boas' informants were able to remember all the words he was interested in all of the time, presumably due to fading fluency in TxG, age, or general cognitive factors. See also Larsson et al. (this volume) on the question of language attrition vs. second language acquisition in American Swedish.

15. The unrounding process has produced a number of lexical mergers, e.g. between *Tür* 'door' and *Tier* 'animal'.

b. In the more open-ended interview data:
   Tür: 9 instances (no front rounded vowels)
   Töchter: 7 instances (no front rounded vowels)
   Gemüse: 9 instances (4 front rounded vowels)
   zwölf: 46 instances (11 front rounded vowels)

3. The current analysis

As noted in the introduction, we view the treatment of these front rounded vowels in NBG as the result of several factors, both language-internal and language-external. We begin by looking at a language-internal factor, namely the original donor dialects of NBG (cf. the analysis developed in Boas 2009). Although standard German has front rounded vowels, many of the German dialects do not, as indicated by some of the maps in works like Wiesinger (1970), König (1978), and the Digital Wenker Atlas (*Deutscher Sprachatlas* 1927–1956). Schirmunski (1962) discusses the development of these vowels in the German dialects in some detail, pointing out for instance that Middle High German [ø] has been unrounded in some dialects (e.g., Hessian, Alsatian, and Mosel Franconian), diphthongized in others (e.g., North Bavarian and Swabian), shifted to [y] in Ripuarian, and retained only in East Franconian and some of the Swiss German dialects (Schirmunski 1962: 238). In other words, there is a widespread absence of front rounded vowels from the German dialects, complemented by their presence in a few pockets. The implication of this distribution for the status of front rounded vowels in NBG is clear: if the donor dialects of German out of which NBG was formed did not contain front rounded vowels, then there would be no reason for NBG itself to contain such vowels. This possibility is also acknowledged by Gilbert (1972: 1, fn 5), who notes that "[m]any, though not all, of the features listed as characteristic of Texas German may be recognized as belonging to certain nonstandard varieties of German that are or were spoken in the Old World."[16]

Ultimately, however, this solution proves problematic, for at least two major reasons. First, as Boas (2009) notes, it is difficult, if not impossible, to identify the exact donor dialects of NBG, as the necessary demographic information is not available. In light of this, we are unable to point to any specific donor dialect without front rounded vowels as the source of NBG words lacking front rounded vowels that do have such vowels in standard German (or to a specific donor dialect with front rounded vowels as the source of NBG words with front rounded vowels, for that matter). Second, the

---

16. Salmons (2012: 240, fn. 4) makes a similar point, writing that "[t]hat so many German dialects spoken in the United States and Canada have unrounding is not, for the most part, due to influence from English, as many laypeople believe, but rather the pattern can be traced back to original dialects with unrounding that were imported to the Western Hemisphere. Low German dialects, for instance, did not unround and they have often retained front rounded vowels in diaspora."

data collected by Eikel (1954, 1966b) and Clardy (1954) on NBG indicates that front rounded vowels were indeed present at earlier stages of NBG in greater quantities than they are now. Therefore, even if the original donor dialects were the cause of some of the missing front rounded vowels at earlier stages of NBG, we contend that this factor alone cannot fully account for the current NBG situation, or for the presence of these vowels in some dialects of TxG versus their absence in others.

Beyond this, we point to the special status of front rounded vowels in the world's languages. Such vowels are cross-linguistically very rare – of the 562 languages surveyed by Maddieson (2013), only 37 (6.6%) exhibit such vowels. In addition, such vowels are lost reasonably often, as they have been in the history of English (compare, for instance, OE *mys* [my:s] with Modern English *mice*, or OE *goes* [gø:s] with Modern English *geese*). These two factors indicate that the front rounded vowels are the most marked of the vowels, and it is therefore not surprising that they are among the first vowels to be eliminated in NBG. This is in the spirit, if perhaps not precisely the letter, of the "Diachronic Maxim" of Vennemann (1988:2), which holds that "[l]inguistic change on a given parameter does not affect a language structure as long as there exist structures in the language system that are less preferred in terms of the relevant preference law." That is, the most marked forms will be eliminated first – exactly what we see in the vowel system of NBG. This also allows us to account for a seemingly casual observation made by Eikel (1954:28), who noted that "individual speakers are consistent: if a speaker unrounds /y/, he invariably also unrounds /ø/." This statement suggests to us that /ø/ is more marked than /y/ – a claim borne out by the observation in Maddieson (2013) that of the 37 languages in his sample that do contain front rounded vowels, 8 of them have only high front rounded vowels, while 6 have only mid front rounded vowels. Although we do not want to draw any firm conclusions based on such a small sample of data, we do find these indications suggestive, and attribute the loss of at least some front rounded vowels to the markedness of these sounds.

Three language-external factors must also be considered, beginning with influence from English. The exact role of English in changes in TxG remains debatable (and that debate cannot be resolved here).[17] In some areas, its influence is clear, e.g., in the lexicon, as there are a number of English loanwords in TxG (Boas and Pierce 2011). In other areas, its influence is less clear. Eikel (1949), for instance, attributes the general loss of the dative case and its replacement by the accusative case in NBG to contact with English. Eikel (1949:281) does admit that language-internal factors (specifically the original donor dialects of NBG) could have caused this change,[18] but calls contact with English "much more important" than any possible language-internal

---

17. See also studies like Brown and Putnam (this volume) on the limitations of an approach relying on contact with English, as well as Annear and Speth (this volume) on phonemic overlap and lexical convergence in American Norwegian.

18. If the cause of the NBG situation is the original donor dialects of NBG, then it is more accurate not to describe this as language change, of course.

factors.[19] Boas (2009), on the other hand, offers an account of these changes that takes both language-internal (e.g., the original donor dialects of NBG and the process of new dialect formation (Trudgill 2004)) and language-external factors (e.g., language contact) into consideration.

In the case of front rounded vowels in NBG, at first blush, interference from English could be seen as the main cause of the change. After all, as just noted, English generally lacks front rounded vowels,[20] and since there are no monolingual speakers of NBG, they could simply be eliminating a phonemic contrast from one of their languages under the influence of the other. Under this view, the continuing loss of front rounded vowels from Eikel (1954) to Gilbert (1972) to Boas (2009) would be traced to the increasing contact between NBG speakers and English speakers, and the resulting increasing influence of English on NBG from the 1940s to the 1960s to the present day.

On the other hand, if this were the case, we would expect to find the same widespread loss of front rounded vowels in other dialects of TxG, given that there are no monolingual speakers of any dialect of TxG and that speakers of all dialects of TxG have had increasing contact with English speakers since the 1940s. This is not actually what we find, as at least one dialect of TxG exhibits more front rounded vowels than NBG. Specifically, Texas Alsatian, a dialect of TxG spoken mainly in and around the city of Castroville (approximately 60 miles southwest of New Braunfels), recently described and analyzed in Roesch (2012), shows front rounded vowels to a greater extent than NBG.[21] Gilbert (1972) identifies eight participants as speakers of Texas Alsatian, and two of his maps lend insight into these speakers' use of front rounded vowels. Map 102, for 'cabbage' (Standard German *Kohl*), indicates that all eight of these speakers have a front rounded vowel in this word, as their responses were [kry:t], [gry:t], or [syrgrut] (cf. Standard German *Kraut*).[22] Map 19, for 'sweet potatoes' (Standard German *Bataten* or *Süßkartoffeln*) shows that five of these eight speakers have a front rounded vowel in this word, while the other three speakers do not.[23] These maps therefore show that Texas Alsatian as spoken in the 1960s had front rounded vowels as part of its phonology.

---

19. Eikel (1949: 281) also calls the dative case "an überflüssiger Luxus," which lends insight into his views on the causes of language change.

20. Some dialects of English are developing front rounded vowels (Maddieson 2013), but in American English this is a socially restricted development (Salmons 2004) and presumably plays no role in the NBG situation.

21. The source of these front rounded vowels is difficult to pinpoint, since some dialects of European Alsatian lack front rounded vowels (Philipp and Bothorel-Witz 1989), and we leave this issue aside here.

22. We have modified Gilbert's transcription slightly in accordance with more current practice.

23. As there is a great deal of phonetic variation in response to this lexical item, we do not give phonetic transcriptions here.

Consider the same words in present day Texas Alsatian. For 'cabbage,' 22 of Roesch's 27 informants retained [y] in this word, while 1 unrounded it to [i], one was unable to recall the word, and three were not polled on this particular term. As for 'sweet potatoes,' 17 of Roesch's informants retained a front rounded vowel in this word; one unrounded it to [i], albeit not the same informant who showed unrounding in the 'cabbage' word; four produced [patʰa:dəs], presumably due to interference from English *potatoes*; two produced forms influenced by standard German *Kartoffel* 'potato'; two did not know the word; and one was not polled. In (4) we summarize Roesch's results for these two words.

(4) Front rounded vowels in Texas Alsatian
    a. 'cabbage':   22 informants retain [y] in this word
                              1 unrounded it to [i]
                              1 was unable to recall the word
                              3 were not polled on this word
    b. 'sweet potatoes': 17 informants retain [y] in this word
                              1 unrounded it to [i]
                              4 produced [patʰa:dəs]
                              2 produced forms influenced by standard
                                  German *Kartoffel* 'potato'
                              2 did not know the word
                              1 was not polled

While we do not intend to ignore or minimize the (possible) influence of English, in light of this retention of front rounded vowels in Texas Alsatian, even though it is subject to the same conditions as NBG, and given that other factors are certainly at play here, we see contact with English as a factor reinforcing these ongoing changes, and not as the sole (or even the main) cause of the changes themselves.

Another language-external factor to consider here is the role of Standard German. This factor also must be treated with caution, as the role of standard German in Texas, its effects on the development of TxG, and the question of just how close TxG is to the standard language all remain controversial.[24] Two main viewpoints on the status of Standard German in Texas can be found in the relevant scholarly literature, which can be exemplified by Salmons and Lucht (2006) on the one hand and Boas (2009) on the other. Salmons and Lucht (2006) contend that standard German played an important role in Texas, stating that "rank-and-file German speakers, beginning with their arrival in Texas, had remarkable exposure to written and spoken Standard German

---

24. To take up just the last of these questions, various (and conflicting) assessments of the closeness of TxG to Standard German can be found in the literature, e.g., Wilson (1977: 57) claims that TxG "is essentially good standard German," while Gilbert (1965: 102) writes that TxG "deviates in certain characteristic ways from Contemporary Standard German…. Nevertheless it is sufficiently intelligible to the speaker of Standard German to be classed as a colonial variety of the standard language and not as a separate entity."

even far into the twentieth century" (Salmons and Lucht 2006: 167), and muster a sizable body of evidence in support of this claim (e.g., the use of standard German in TxG churches and the existence of numerous Standard German-language periodicals). Boas (2009: 51), however, while conceding that Salmons and Lucht's "observations regarding the important role of standard German in the schools, newspapers, and churches are certainly correct," contends that "the use of standard German in Texas is overestimated." Boas (2009) grounds his arguments mainly in the length of the standardization process, what he sees as the more minimal role played by Standard German in the development of TxG, and the relative lack of exposure of most speakers of TxG to standard German (agricultural pursuits kept many TxG children from extensive school attendance, for example, which limited their exposure to the standard language).

Two separate issues are involved here, namely the role of standard German in the formation of TxG and the impact of the standard language on NBG during the time period addressed in this paper (beginning with Eikel's collection of TxG data in the 1930s and 1940s and continuing to the present day). To the first of these: we do not want to overemphasize the role of the standard language in the formation of TxG pronunciation here. Since German pronunciation was not standardized until around 1900 (Salmons 2012) and was thus not standardized at the beginning stages of the emergence of TxG, there simply was no standard German pronunciation available for speakers of TxG to model their own (TxG) pronunciation on. In light of this absence, it would not be surprising to find less influence from the standard language on TxG pronunciation than on other areas of the grammar (e.g. the case system or word order).[25]

The role of standard German in Texas during and following the time period in which Eikel collected his data is of more relevance here. Over the course of this time period, although some opportunities for access to the standard language remained,[26] exposure to standard German decreased considerably for speakers of TxG in general and for speakers of NBG in particular, as illustrated by some of the developments mentioned in the introduction, e.g., that German was no longer taught in the schools[27] and that German-language church services were gradually abandoned. The implications for our proposal are straightforward: in our view, extensive exposure to

---

25. We also point out that Salmons and Lucht (2006) do not address pronunciation in their article, beyond citing the statement from Wilson (1960: 86) that "ministers preach in S[tandard] G[erman] with a very good pronunciation."

26. In the case of church services, for instance, some German-language services were retained, especially on holidays like Good Friday and Christmas (Nicolini 2004), and as of 2010 at least one church still offered a German-language service on 'fifth Sundays' (Roesch 2012). Cf. also the statement from Wilson (1960: 86) cited in the preceding footnote. German was also still taught in some Texas schools.

27. German instruction in the schools in New Braunfels ceased in 1942 (Eikel 1966a: 14).

the standard language with its front rounded vowels would presumably have reinforced the presence of front rounded vowels in NBG. Conversely, limited exposure to Standard German would presumably have reinforced any lack or loss of front rounded vowels in NBG. We therefore contend that the more limited exposure to the standard language since the 1940s typical of most NBG speakers is an additional factor contributing to the loss of front rounded vowels in NBG.

Compare here Salmons (1983: 191), who notes the number of recent immigrants from German-speaking areas to Texas, and concludes that "[o]nly further research can clarify the exact role of these immigrants and the other contacts with contemporary Germany, but important cultural and linguistic contact with Germany must be noted as a factor in TxG language maintenance. Texas Germans have not existed for a century and a half isolated from the rest of the German-speaking world." Although this stance generally remains as valid today as it was in 1983, and we would underscore the role of contact with other German speakers as a possible factor in this area, we also note that these contacts can sometimes complicate matters, as when a class on Texas Alsatian had to be abandoned in 2006 because the two teachers, one of whom was a Texas Alsatian and the other a European Alsatian, could not agree on which version of Alsatian should be taught in the class (Roesch 2012: 28–29).

In line with some of the literature on language death, we also point to a final possible causal factor of vowel unrounding, namely the changing linguistic and social contexts of NBG (Boas 2009). When Eikel's data was collected, NBG was still in a state of language maintenance, although language shift was underway, and the NBG of Eikel's time consequently retained marked linguistic phenomena (like front rounded vowels) to a considerable extent. When Gilbert's data was collected, NBG was also still in a state of language maintenance, but its position was much weaker than it had been twenty years previously (in the 1960s there were approximately 70,000 speakers of TxG, as opposed to over 150,000 speakers in the 1940s). The NBG data collected in Gilbert (1972) therefore shows fewer marked linguistic phenomena like front rounded vowels. By now, the situation has changed radically, and NBG is critically endangered and in fact dying (as noted above).

Nettle and Romaine (2000: 53) point out that gradual language death of the type NBG is undergoing can have profound linguistic consequences: "[w]hen a dying language declines gradually over a period of generations, it … is not used for all the functions and purposes it was previously. Like a limb not used, it atrophies."[28] In the specific case of NBG, as its linguistic and social contexts changed, NBG speakers simply stopped using the language in various situations, meaning that speakers' fluency declined substantially.[29] As their fluency declined, NBG speakers tended to abandon

---

28. See also Trudgill (2011) on the linguistic consequences of language death.

29. At times, this atrophy has some surprising results; for example, one TxG speaker from Doss (about 110 miles from New Braunfels) interviewed by Boas seemed to understand all of Boas' questions, but struggled to respond to them, until Boas happened to ask the informant

marked linguistic structures like front rounded vowels in favor of less marked, more English-like structures, as reflected by the considerably greater presence of such vowels in the Eikel data than in the Boas/TGDP data.

4. Conclusion

In sum, then, we trace the decrease of front rounded vowels in NBG from Eikel (1954) to Boas (2009) to the interaction of several factors. First, some NBG words that lack front rounded vowels where standard German has them are not really examples of sound change, as NBG never had front rounded vowels in these words, due to a lack of front rounded vowels in the original donor dialects of NBG. Second, front rounded vowels are highly marked, as reflected by the rarity of such sounds in the world's languages and by their tendency to be lost. Their loss in NBG therefore fits well with the second of these conditions. Third, contact with English reinforced these two ongoing causal factors, presumably increasingly so as English came to play a more dominant role in TxG society; and, on a related note, a relative dearth of exposure to standard German meant that the use of standard German could not really reinforce the use of front rounded vowels in NBG. Finally, the changing social context of NBG, i.e., from a state of language maintenance to a state of language shift, and the accompanying decline in fluency in NBG among speakers, also caused unrounding, as NBG entered what we might label a state of "linguistic meltdown,"[30] en route to what we see as its inevitable death.

References

Allen, Brent, and Joseph C. Salmons. This Volume. "Heritage Language Obstruent Phonetics and Phonology: American Norwegian and Norwegian-American English."
Annear, Lucas and Kristin Speth. This Volume. "Maintaining a Multilingual Repertoire: Lexical Change in American Norwegian."
Boas, Hans C. 2009. *The Life and Death of Texas German*. Durham: Duke University Press.

---

about an upcoming hunting trip. It turned out that the informant could speak very fluently and knowledgeably about hunting in TxG, as he had often gone hunting with family members when he was younger and had always spoken TxG on those trips. This informant therefore shows considerable atrophy of his TxG abilities, with the exception of the one area where he seems to have used TxG the most (Boas and Pierce 2011: 145).

30. This kind of "meltdown" in TxG has so far mostly been investigated with regard to the lexicon and the morphosyntax (e.g., an increased variability in relative pronouns), largely in as yet unpublished studies. We plan to investigate its phonological effects in future work.

Boas, Hans C., Marc Pierce, Hunter Weilbacher, Karen Roesch, and Guido Halder. 2010. "The Texas German Dialect Archive: A Multimedia Resource for Research, Teaching, and Outreach." *Journal of Germanic Linguistics* 22: 277–296. DOI: 10.1017/S1470542710000036

Boas, Hans C. and Marc Pierce. 2011. "Recent Lexical Borrowings in Texas German." In *Studies on German-Language Islands*, ed. by Michael T. Putnam, 129–150. Amsterdam: Benjamins. DOI: 10.1075/slcs.123.06bao

Brister, Louis E. (ed. and translator). 2008. *John Charles Beales's Rio Grande Colony. Letters by Eduard Ludecus, a German Colonist, to Friends in Germany in 1833–1834, Recounting his Journey, Trials, and Observations in Early Texas*. Denton, TX: Texas State Historical Association.

Brown, Joshua R. and Michael T. Putnam. This Volume. "Functional Convergence and Extension in Contact: Syntactic and Semantic Attributes of the Progressive Aspect in Pennsylvania Dutch."

Clardy, Catherine. 1954. *A Description and Analysis of the German Language Spoken in New Braunfels, Texas*. Austin, TX: University of Texas at Austin MA thesis.

Deutscher Sprachatlas. 1927–1956. Reduced black-and-white version of maps from the unpublished *Sprachatlas des Deutschen Reichs*, by Georg Wenker, Emil Maurmann, and Ferdinand Wrede, ed. by Ferdinand Wrede, Walther Mitzka, and Bernhard Martin. Marburg: Elwert. Original hand-drawn color maps available at <http://www.diwa.info/main.asp>.

Eikel, Fred Jr. 1949. "The Use of Cases in New Braunfels German." *American Speech* 24: 278–281. DOI: 10.2307/453049

Eikel, Fred Jr. 1954. *The New Braunfels German Dialect*. Baltimore, MD: Johns Hopkins University dissertation.

Eikel, Fred Jr. 1966a. "New Braunfels German, Part I." *American Speech* 41: 5–16. DOI: 10.2307/453239

Eikel, Fred Jr. 1966b. "New Braunfels German, Part II." *American Speech* 41: 254–260. DOI: 10.2307/453499

Gilbert, Glenn. 1965. "English Loanwords in the German of Fredericksburg, Texas." *American Speech* 40: 102–112. DOI: 10.2307/453716

Gilbert, Glenn. 1972. *Linguistic Atlas of Texas German*. Austin, TX: University of Texas Press.

Jordan, Terry G. 1975. *German Seed in Texas Soil: Immigrant Farmers in Nineteenth-Century Texas*. Austin: University of Texas Press.

Kloss, Heinz. 1977. *The American Bilingual Tradition*. Rowley, MA: Newbury House.

König, Werner. 1978. *DTV-Atlas zur deutschen Sprache*. München: DTV.

Larsson, Ida, Sofia Tingsell and Maia Andréasson. This Volume. "Variation and Change in American Swedish."

Maddieson, Ian. 2013. "Front Rounded Vowels." In *The World Atlas of Language Structures Online, chapter 11*, ed. by Matthew S. Dryer and Martin Haspelmath. Munich: Max Planck Digital Library. Available online at <http://wals.info/chapter/11>. Accessed on November 19, 2013.

Nettle, Daniel and Suzanne Romaine. 2000. *Vanishing Voices. The Extinction of the World's Languages*. Oxford: Oxford University Press.

Nicolini, Marcus. 2004. *Deutsch in Texas*. Münster: LIT-Verlag.

Philipp, Marthe and Arlette Bothorel-Witz. 1989. "Low Alemannic." In *The Dialects of Modern German*, ed. by Charles Russ, 313–335. Stanford, CA: Stanford University Press.

Roesch, Karen A. 2012. *Language Maintenance and Language Death. The Decline of Texas Alsatian*. Amsterdam: John Benjamins. DOI: 10.1075/clu.6

Salmons, Joseph C. 1983. "Issues in Texas German Language Maintenance and Shift." *Monatshefte* 75: 187–196.
Salmons, Joseph C. 2004. "How (Non-)Indo-European is the Germanic Lexicon? And What Does That Mean?" In *Etymologie, Entlehnungen und Entwicklungen: Festschrift für Jorma Koivulehto zum 70. Geburtstag*, ed. by Irma Hyvärinen, Petri Kallio and Jarmo Korhonen, 311–321. Helsinki: Société Néophilologique.
Salmons, Joseph C. 2012. *A History of German: What the Past Reveals about Today's Language*. Oxford: Oxford University Press.
Salmons, Joseph C. and Felecia Lucht. 2006. "Standard German in Texas." In *Studies in Contact Linguistics: Essays in Honor of Glenn G. Gilbert*, ed. by Linda L. Thornburg and Janet M. Fuller, 167–188. New York: Peter Lang.
Schirmunski, Viktor M. 1962. *Deutsche Mundartkunde. Vergleichende Laut- und Formenlehre der deutschen Mundarten*. Translated and edited by Wolfgang Fleischer. Berlin: Akademie Verlag.
Trudgill, Peter. 2004. *New-Dialect Formation: The Inevitability of Colonial Englishes*. Oxford: Oxford University Press.
Trudgill, Peter. 2011. *Sociolinguistic Typology. Social Determinants of Linguistic Complexity*. Oxford: Oxford University Press.
Vennemann, Theo. 1988. *Preference Laws for Syllable Structure*. Berlin: de Gruyter.
Wiesinger, Peter. 1970. *Phonetisch-phonologische Untersuchungen zur Vokalentwicklung in den deutschen Dialekten*. Berlin: de Gruyter.
Wilson, Joseph B. 1960. "The Texas German of Lee and Fayette Counties." *Rice University Studies* 47: 83–98.
Wilson, Joseph B. 1977. "The German Language in Central Texas Today." *Rice University Studies* 63: 47–58.

PART III

(Morpho-)syntactic and pragmatic change

Functional convergence and extension in contact
Syntactic and semantic attributes of the progressive aspect in Pennsylvania Dutch

Joshua R. Brown and Michael Putnam
University of Wisconsin–Eau Claire / Penn State University

This paper investigates the extension of the progressive aspect in contemporary Pennsylvania Dutch. The scope of convergence in contact varieties is a debated subject in theoretical linguistics; the most recent and promising research finds that convergence in contact is not a simple one-to-one mapping, nor an opportunity for any structural anomaly to present. Previous studies concluded that Pennsylvania Dutch had matched and gone beyond English semantic constraints for the progressive aspect. The extent of the progressive in Pennsylvania Dutch has not been systematically documented. To account for these findings, we propose, as most recently suggested by Putnam and Sánchez (2013), an analysis of feature reconfiguration, with the result of progressive aspect appearing with different aspectual classes of verbs (most notably, with certain types of statives).

Keywords: aspect, convergence, feature reconfiguration, hyperextension, Pennsylvania Dutch, semantics, syntax

1. Introduction[1]

In this paper, we discuss some peculiarities of progressive aspect in Pennsylvania Dutch (hereafter, PD). Previous research by Huffines (1986), Louden (1988), Burridge (1992), and Fuller (1996) (all contra Reed 1947) demonstrate that the incorporation of

---

[1]. The authors' names appear in alphabetical order and represent an equal contribution on their respective parts. We would like to thank Barbara Bullock and Jacqueline Toribio who commented on a very early version of this paper and the participants of the Second Workshop on Immigrant Languages in America for their comments and suggestions. In particular, we would like to thank Janne Bondi Johannessen, Paul Kerswill, Mark Louden, Joe Salmons, and Marit

elements of English progressive aspect in PD allows stative predicates to appear with progressive aspect (which is ungrammatical in standard English):

(1) *Ich bin am wotte fer sell.*
    I   am on want for that
    Intended: 'I am wanting that.' (Burridge 1992: 212)

(2) *Ich bin am Sache besser versteh.*
    I   am on things better understand
    Intended: 'I'm understanding things better.' (Burridge 1992: 212)

These previous studies only provide a surface understanding of the issues surrounding the evolution of progressive aspect in PD. As we show in this paper, many fundamental aspects of the (morpho)syntactic representation of progressive aspect in PD are under-researched and, as a result, poorly understood. Our primary objectives in this paper are the following:

a. To contextualize how this development in PD connects with other research in contact linguistic literature concerning semantic-discourse properties of language;
b. To demonstrate how the particular syntactic structures and semantic description of progressive aspect represent an ideal interface platform for such changes to take place; and
c. To show that PD relies on Aktionsart-related information in determining which structures to employ in forming progressive aspect.

In particular, we focus on the extension of progressive aspect to Aktionsart-classes of predicates that do not entail duration in events (i.e., verbal classes of aspectual classification that are [– stages] in Rothstein's (2004) system, to be defined and discussed in §2); namely, achievement and stative predicates. Many cursory treatments of Aktionsart-classes claim that a common battery test for a stative predicate is its inability to exhibit a progressive form (ex. English **I am knowing the answer*). Following recent work by Maienborn (2003, 2005) and Rothmayr (2009) building on earlier proposals by Carlson (1977), Taylor (1977), and Dowty (1979/1991), we argue here that 'statives' do not represent a homogeneous class of predicates as commonly assumed in the literature. The fact that statives do not form a natural class of predicates is paramount to our analysis of progressive aspect in PD, especially with regard to the forms that appear in PD that are not possible in English. In §4, we provide a theoretical analysis along the lines proposed by Putnam and Sánchez (2013) arguing for the

---

Westergaard for their feedback. Outside of the conference participants, we would also like to thank John Beavers, Dave Embick, Volker Gast, John Hale, Nick Henry, Diego Krivochen, Sylvia Reed Schreiner, Ralf Vogel, the graduate seminar in Sociolinguistics (University of Wisconsin-Madison, Fall 2012) and two anonymous reviewers for insightful comments, which undoubtedly improved our arguments here. Thanks are also due to Don Vosburg for his statistical assistance and to Hyoun-A Joo for proofreading the final version of this manuscript. The usual disclaimers apply.

re-assembly of functional features (e.g., tense, aspect, and mood (among others)) as the culprit for some of these attested progressive forms in PD.

From a theoretical perspective, our research confirms previous findings by Silva-Corvalán (1994/2000, 1993), Toribio (2004), and Sánchez (2003, 2004), who suggest that one of the most permeable aspects of grammar can be found at the semantic and discourse-pragmatic level (cf. Sánchez' Functional Convergence Hypothesis).[2] The results from our pilot research show that PD speakers have distinct structures for stative and achievement predicates – with the stative progressive present being similar to the structure used for marking progressive aspect with activity and accomplishment √roots (i.e., [+ stages]). For this study, we collected grammaticality judgments from 8 PD-speakers (4 from Big Valley, Pennsylvania and 4 from Holmes County, Ohio) with a focus on progressive aspect in all Aktionsart-classes. Our data in this study demonstrate clearly that the range of stative events that can appear with the progressive in PD is much more extensive than in English. In our analysis, we put forward the hypothesis that extension of progressive aspect marking on certain sub-classes of stative predicates in PD that are absent in English are the result of the reorganizing and re-assembly of functional features onto syntactic structures.[3]

This paper has the following structure: In §2, we provide a brief overview of progressive aspect in English. In particular, we focus on progressive aspect in achievement and stative predicates. Adopting arguments and data primarily from Rothstein (2004), we show how progressive aspect in achievement predicates is not identical to progressive aspect in non-telic, durative (i.e., [+ stages]) predicates such as activities. Secondly, we show that stative predicates do not form a homogeneous group. §3 elaborates on formal semantic and syntactic properties of progressive aspect in English. In §4, we discuss progressive aspect in German, dialectal German, and PD, showing how the latter is both related to continental varieties of German and how it clearly contrasts with them. Our theoretical analysis of the PD data can be found in §5, where we demonstrate that the differences between English and PD with respect to progressive aspect appearing with stative predicates can be easily and efficiently modeled in a system where the relexification/reassembly of functional features leads to the emergence of these different (and often unique) forms of progressive aspect. We illustrate that the extension of progressive aspect into stative predicates is not uncommon in contact situations in §6, where we discuss examples from World Englishes that exhibit patterns similar (and, in some cases, identical) to what we find in PD. §7 concludes this paper and discusses remaining questions and puzzles.

---

2. Sánchez (2003: 150) defines convergence as "the common specification for equivalent functional features for two languages spoken by the bilingual in a language contact situation, takes place only when the languages have partially similar matrices of features associated with the same functional category. Frequent activation of the two matrices triggers convergence in features."

3. See e.g., Howell (1993) for an influential discussion of the role of lexical semantics in language contact.

2. Progressive aspect – an overview

In this section we undertake a brief introduction to progressive aspect, along the way defining a binary-featural distinction of Vendler's (1957, 1967) classification of verbs used by Rothstein (2004). Consider the following examples from Rothstein (2004: 11; (14)):

(3) a. *John is believing in the afterlife/loving Mary. (state)
 b. *Mary is recognizing John/losing her pen. (achievement)
 c. Mary is running/walking. (activity)
 d. John is reading a book. (accomplishment)

As noted, states and (traditionally) achievements do not appear in the progressive (although there are clear counterexamples, see below). In general, a sentence in the progressive asserts that an eventuality of a particular kind is 'in progress' or 'currently taking place.' According to this simple definition of progressive aspect, it is relatively clear for activities and accomplishments that this is taking place; i.e., in Example (3c) Mary is in the middle of a running activity, and in Example (3d) John is in the middle of reading a book. For states and achievements on the other hand, there does not appear to be any natural sentence where the eventualities are progressing or continuing. Based on this observation, Landman (1992) "argues that the meaning of a progressive sentence is that a stage of the eventuality given by the verb occurred, or is in the process of occurring, where *e* is a stage of e 'if *e* develops into e'" (Rothstein 2004: 12).

Together with telicity [± telic], Rothstein (2004: 12) establishes the following binary feature sets to distinguish the four (traditional) verb classes:[4]

(4) a. States [− telic, − stages]
 b. Activities [− telic, + stages]
 c. Achievements [+ telic, − stages]
 d. Accomplishments [+ telic, + stages]

Based on the preliminary examples laid out in (3) above and the binary featural distribution of eventualities established in (4), predicates that are specified as [− stages] (i.e., states and achievements) should not appear with progressive aspect. As we discuss below, this assumption is easily falsifiable. There are, however, clear semantic

---

4. As pointed out by Smith (1991) and others, there is another class of eventualities, called SEMELFACTIVES (e.g., *kick the door, wink, cough, sneeze*, etc.). Smith argues that these events are "conceptualized as instantaneous" (1991: 29) (i.e., are punctual), but unlike achievements, are atelic [− telic] since they can be modified by durative temporal phrases (i.e., for α minutes) and do not instantiate a change of state. Rothstein (2004: Chapter 8) takes on the task of defining how to classify SEMELFACTIVES in her binary feature system. Since this has little bearing on the data discussed and analyzed here, we direct the reader to Rothstein and references *inter alia* for further discussion.

differences between [− stages]-predicates and [+ stages]-predicates when it comes to their meaning in combination with progressive aspect, differences that play a fundamental role in our analysis of PD extensions of progressive aspect.

2.1 Achievements in the progressive

Although classified as [− stages], some – but crucially not all – achievements can occur in the progressive. Consider the following examples (Rothstein 2004: 36; (1)–(2)):

(5) a. #Jane is reaching the summit of the mountain.[5]
   b. #Mary is spotting her friend at the party.
   c. Susan was arriving at the station when she heard that trains to Jerusalem had been cancelled because of the state of the line.
   d. Dafna is finding her shoes.
   e. Fred and Susan are finally leaving.
   f. The old man is dying.

Although Examples (5a) and (5b) are slightly marked (but could be improved under the proper pragmatic reading), the remaining examples (see e.g., (5c–f)) clearly refute any claim that progressive aspect cannot appear in combination with achievements. This observation, however, does not mean that progressive aspect in combination with achievements (e.g., [− stages]) and other [+ stages]-predicates such as activities or accomplishments are identical in meaning. Rothstein (2004: §2.3.2) lists five ways in which progressive achievements differ significantly from progressive accomplishments:

Point 1: As noted in (5) above, only some progressive achievements are possible. (Note also that the 'acceptable' ones (cf. (5c–f)) have a 'slow-motion' reading, which is not possible with accomplishments).

Point 2: Temporal modification in the future progressive is different for achievements and accomplishments. Compare (6) and (7) (Rothstein 2004: 43; (21)–(22)):

(6) Accomplishments:
   a. We are eating dinner in half an hour.
   b. I am writing a book in six months.

(7) Achievements:
   a. The plane is landing in half an hour.
   b. We are reaching Tel Aviv Central in five minutes.

The accomplishments in (6) are naturally interpreted as providing information about: (a) when the activities of eating or writing will take place, or (b) "asserting that the whole eventuality will occur within the stated time (e.g., in half an hour or in six

---

5. Data in this section is taken directly from Rothstein (2004: Chapter 2) unless otherwise stated.

months)" (Rothstein 2004:43). On the other hand, the achievements in (7) have a different reading; namely, the temporal modifiers identify when the telic change of state will take place.

Point 3: There are no 'stops along the way' with achievements (Rothstein 2004:43–4; (23)–(24)).

(8) a. Mary is running to the Netherlands. In fact she is running to Amsterdam.
    b. Mary is arriving in the Netherlands. In fact she is arriving in Amsterdam.

(9) a. She is halfway through walking to the station.
    b. #She is halfway through arriving at the station.

Although both (8a) and (8b) are grammatical, they have different implications. "The contrast in grammaticality between Examples (9a) and (9b) clearly demonstrate the inability of the telic change of state associated with the event of arriving, which cannot occur in stages. In conjunction with Point 2 above, temporal modifiers that co-occur with achievements in the (present) progressive can only modify when the telic change of state will occur, but cannot internally modify the achievement" (paraphrased from Rothstein 2004:55).

Point 4: Achievements are very odd in the perfect progressive (Rothstein 2004:44; (26)).

(10) a. She has been cooking dinner (for half an hour).
     b. #Fred and Susan have been leaving.
     c. ?Fred and Susan have been leaving for an hour.

Point 5: With achievements, the activity and the telic point can be modified independently without any difficulty. This, however, is not the case for accomplishments (although Example (11d) suggests that it is possible under a specific reading) (Rothstein 2004:44; (27)).

(11) a. John was dying for a long time, but he actually died pretty quickly.
     b. It was very turbulent while the plane was landing, but we (actually) landed smoothly.
     c. #Mary was writing a book slowly, but she actually wrote it quickly.
     d. At one point, Mary was writing her book very slowly, but when it came down to it, she actually wrote it quickly.

Taken together, as argued by Rothstein (2004), there are clear distinctions between progressive constructions with achievements [− stages] and activities and accomplishments [+ stages]. As we shall see in our data and analysis in Sections 4 and 5, PD speakers recognize this distinction and license different structures for achievements and states that appear in the progressive.

2.2 States in the progressive

In addition to achievements, the other class of eventualities that Rothstein (2004) classifies as [– stages] are states. In this section and the ones that follow, we introduce and elaborate on the dilemma that states present for not only Rothstein's (2004) binary featural classification of eventualities, but also how these findings must be accounted for in our analysis of progressive aspect in PD.

First, Dowty (1979/1991: 173–4; (62)) mentions stative verbs that occur in the progressive:

(12) a. The socks are lying under the bed.
      b. Your glass is sitting near the edge of the table.
      c. The long box is standing on end.
      d. One corner of the piano is resting on the bottom step.

These examples (and others that can be constructed with verbs like *sit, stand, lie, perch, sprawl*, etc.) are paradoxical in connection with most standard claims about the progressive in that they (a) do not involve a volitional subject, and (b) no definite or indefinite change of state is entailed. Furthermore, as noted by Ross (1972) and Dowty (1979/1991), these examples are strange, since they fail 'do-tests' (cf. Ross 1972) (from Dowty 1979/1991: 174; (62')):

(13) a. *What socks did was lie under the bed.
      b. *The glass is sitting near the edge, and the pitcher is doing so too.
      c. *The box is standing on end, which I thought it might do.
      d. *The piano did what the crate had done; rest on the bottom step.

Dowty (1979/1991; §3.8.2) offers the following possible explanations as to why progressive aspect can appear with certain stative eventualities. First, predicates such as *sit, stand, lie*, etc. primarily denote positions of the human body. Some 'volitional' adjectives and predicate nominates (i.e., *be polite, be a hero*) can be argued to signal intentionality. Perhaps in these situations we are dealing with an either/or situation with volitional control or change of state/position. Second, as initially proposed by Taylor (1977), the truth conditions assigned to statives also involve an interval (e.g., *The book is on the table is only true when the book is not in motion or as long is it remains on the table*). Third, Carlson (1977) notes that the 'classic' statives that cannot appear in the progressive (e.g., *know, love, like, believe, hate*, etc.) all turn out to be predicates over objects, not predicates over stages. Carlson proposes a distinction between object-level and kind-level predicates from stage-level predicates. As a result of these hypotheses, Dowty (1979/1991: 184) proposes the following sub-distinctions of stative verbs:

Table 1. Sub-classes of stative eventualities.

	Non-agentive	Agentive
States	*be asleep, be in the garden* (stage-level); *love, know* (object level)	possibly *be polite, be a hero* (possibly an activity?)
	Interval statives: *sit, stand, lie*	Interval statives: *sit, stand, lie* (with a human subject)

Building on these discussions, Maienborn (2003, 2005) concludes that there are two different kinds of states: (1) 'pseudo-stative' verbs (verbs of position and a group containing *sleep, wait, glow* and *stick*, among others), and (2) 'Kimian states' (e.g., including copular constructions and various stative verbs such as *weigh, know,* and *resemble*.) A Kimian state (see Kim 1969, 1976) does not denote an event; it refers to a property being instantiated at a particular time. These contrast with traditional Davidsonian statives that are traditionally argued to contain an event argument. Importantly, these findings suggest that there are sub-distinctions to be found within the class of stative eventualities. From a syntax-semantics interface perspective, as suggested tacitly by Maienborn (2003, 2005) and more explicitly by Rothmayr (2009), stative eventualities cannot be treated as a unified, homogenous class, with these sub-variants of contrasting underlying structures. It will become immediately clear how these internal distinctions within stative eventualities play a fundamental role in our analysis in allowing us to hone in on the key distinctions between English and PD progressive aspect with regard to their (in)ability to co-occur with states.

3. Semantics and syntax of progressive aspect constructions

After establishing the distinction in meaning between progressive aspect in achievement vs. accomplishment and activity predicates and explicating that stative eventualities do not form a natural homogenous class, we are now in a position to discuss the semantic and syntactic properties of progressive aspect constructions. In this paper, we assume a 'first phase' interpretation of the clausal structure of the traditional verb phrase (VP) that is tied to event semantics found in Ramchand (2008):[6]

(14)   [AspP PROG [Init(iator)P α   [Proc(ess)P β   [Res(ult)P γ]]]

Following the structure in (14), the progressive operator (PROG) interacts with the verbal $\sqrt{\text{ROOT}}$ β (which indicates if a particular $\sqrt{\text{root}}$ is specified with a [+ stages]

---

[6]. Hale and Keyser (2005), in contrast to Ramchand (2008), argue that argument structure and event semantics are distinct from one another. Since such claims are orthogonal to our analysis, we will not pursue them further at this point.

feature).⁷ Although we basically agree with the main tenets of Ramchand's approach of amalgamating argument structure and event semantics, we know that her current approach is somewhat incomplete since it neglects the relevant sub-distinctions of stative √roots discussed above.

Higginbotham (2009:139; (47), following Landman 1992) interprets this PROG-head/operator to express a relation between events e and properties of events.

(15) a. John is eating chow mein.
      b. [∃e≈u] Prog(e, ∧λe' eat(John, chow mein, e'))

Following Landman (1992), the abstraction is over the ordered pair of process and telos (Higginbotham 2009:140; (48)).

(16) a. John is crossing the street.
      b. [∃e≈u] Prog(e, ∧λ(e',e'') cross(John, the street, (e',e'')))⁸

Higginbotham (2009:154; (104)) also points out an interesting fact regarding the structural (syntactic) development of the English progressive; namely, the English progressive was originally a nominal construction with a gerundive object, as in (17):

(17) John is at [PRO crossing the street]

Such constructions are still common in English dialects that allow a-prefixing:

(18) He kept on a-laughing all through the movie.⁹

In both (17) and (18), the *(a)t* preposition/particle has its own position for events *e* and licenses the complement phrase as an argument. In agreement with Higginbotham, let us assume that the complement is identical to Landman's proposal: Prog(e, ∧λ(e',e'')). The preposition/particle *at* expresses a relation between events *e* and the properties of events P. Although the interpretation remains the same, modern English witnessed a grammatical reduction of the structure (17). As we shall see in §4.1.1, the structure in (17) is quite similar to the German Progressive in non-standard speech and the PD-construction that we investigate in detail here.

---

7. As a point of clarification, the notion of √ROOT can be understood as a variable for lexical elements that appear in combination with other grammatical information (e.g., tense, aspect, agreement, etc.) when licensed by a given grammar.

8. Higginbotham (2009:140) correctly points out that this interpretation solves the problem of defining what constitutes a 'continuation' of an event. A continuation of an event e such that Prog(e, ∧λ(e',e'')) is an event e''' such that e is an initial segment of e'''.

9. In some dialects such as Appalachian English, *a*-prefixing is also phonologically conditioned; polysyllabic verbs with stress on the second syllable (e.g., *discover) are ungrammatical. See e.g., Higginbotham (2009: §8.11) for similar arguments.

4. Progressive aspect in German, dialectal continental German, and Pennsylvania Dutch

In this section, we illustrate the differences in progressive aspect as found in German, dialectal continental German, and PD.

4.1 (Standard) German

Simply put, there are not comparable English-like progressive forms in German. Semantically approximate progressive forms appear with partitive constructions, adverbials and infinitive-nominalizations (cf. Königs 1995: 153, Bartsch 1995: 142).[10] For example, adverbs such as *gerade, dabei, nun, allmählich, noch, denn, wirklich, tatsächlich, doch* (expressing the temporality associated with the imperfective in certain contexts) are most common:

(19) a. *Thomas singt gerade.*
Thomas sings at the moment
'Thomas is singing at the moment.'
b. *Thomas singt jetzt.*
Thomas sings now
'Thomas is singing right now.'
c. *Thomas singt noch.*
Thomas sings still
'Thomas is still singing.'

Königs (1995: 153–4) notes a few instances where the verb form is changed, as opposed to inserting adverbials (although this is clearly not as productive):

(20) a. *Diese Sorte ist am Aussterben.*
This species is on out.dying
'This species is dying out.'
b. *Ich bin beim Schreiben.*
I am at writing
'I am writing.'

---

10. Van Pottelberge's (2004, 2007) research of periphrastic progressive constructions in Germanic languages makes an important point about cross-linguistic comparisons. He makes the distinction that these adverbial constructions do not actually qualify as progressives. His research further substantiates our main point; namely, that the German progressive is not as fully grammaticalized as English progressive. Additionally, he argues that one of the most recent developments found in this domain (the occurrence of progressive aspect with passive voice structures in Pennsylvania Dutch) is likely not due to contact with English. He also finds that the *am*-periphrasis in Pennsylvania Dutch has been reanalyzed as a verbal infinitive and particle, similar to what is also found Afrikaans and Zürich German.

c. *Die Straße ist im Bau.*
   The street is in building
   'The street is being built/under construction'
d. *Wir haben das schon andiskutiert.*
   We have that already discussed
   'We've been discussing that.'

In sum, as illustrated by Examples (20a–c) the progressive is formed with the copula verb *be* + PREP *an, in* and *bei* and a nominalized form of the verb. In (20d) the prefix *an* has a 'beginning the event' reading (i.e., 'we have already begun discussing X').[11]

4.2 Dialectal (continental) German

Non-standard, dialectal (continental) variants of German exhibit a higher lexical generalization of the am-construction similar to (20a–c) above.[12]

(21) a. *Er ist sein Zimmer am aufräumen.*
       He is his room at.the PART(up).clearing
       'He's tidying up his room.'
   b. **Er ist am sein Zimmer aufräumen.*
   c. **Er ist sein Zimmer auf am räumen.*

According to Stiebels and Wunderlich (1994: 927), (21a) is possible, whereas (21b) and (21c) are not (i.e., the *am*-construction is only grammatical when *am* immediately proceeds the verb).[13] Van Pottelberge (2004, 2007) notes the broad variability in dialectal use of the *am* construction. He concludes, however that this construction is not integrated into any progressive paradigm, as it can be readily replaced by non-progressive forms.

4.3 Pennsylvania Dutch

In an early study, Reed (1947) made several claims about the appearance of progressive aspect in PD. Reed claims that progressives are preferential in certain contexts and used only to express duration in relative aspect. Narrowing the usage of forms, PD progressives may not (according to Reed) occur in the following situations:

---

11. See also the most recent work by Behrens, Flecken and Carroll (2013) on the comparisons of progressives in Dutch, Norwegian, and German.

12. Andersson (1989: 105) claims that the German spoken in the Ruhr area may be the dialect most open to grammaticalization of this form, but he maintains that "the *am*-periphrasis has neither spread over the whole system of verbal form categories, nor has it developed an obligatory use or a high text frequency as is the case with the progressive in English."

13. A word of caution needs to be exercised here; Stiebels and Wunderlich (1994) look exclusively at Ripuarian and Bavarian dialects to reach these conclusions.

a. When the object is qualified with a determiner,
b. When the object is a personal pronoun,
c. With a prepositional phrase (predominantly used with verbs like *wuhne* 'reside,' *bleiwe* 'stay,' and *sitze* 'sit,' and
d. With stative verbs such as *gleiche* 'like' and *verschteh* 'understand'

According to Reed, the following constructions should be (or, at the very least, once were) ungrammatical:

(22) a. *Er is es Buch am lese.*
       He is the book on reading
       Intended: 'He is reading the book.'
   b. *Er is ihn am suche.*
       He is him on searching
       Intended: 'He's looking for him.'
   c. *Er is in de Stadt am wuhne.*
       He is in the city   on living
       Intended: 'He is living in the city.'
   d. *Er is sei Tee am gleiche.*
       He is his tea on liking
       Intended: 'He likes his tea.'

Huffines (1986) notes that the PD progressive is present in both 'fluent' and 'semi-speaker' speech. Furthermore, she provides evidence that contradicts Reed's 'restrictions'; first, progressives can occur with qualified prepositions:

(23) *Er is am Gleeder ins Klasset henke.*[14]
     He is on clothing in closet hang
     'He is hanging clothing in the closet.'

Secondly, progressive forms may be used with stative verbs (particularly 'psychological states'):

(24) *Er is am wunnere, wie er die Ebbel vum Baam   griege kann.*
     he is on wondering how he the apples from the tree get   can
     'He is wondering, how he can get the apples from the tree.'

---

14. In this example, we acknowledge a contrast with continental German dialect examples above (cf. 21a,b) where a bare indefinite plural *Gleeder* 'clothing' can appear after the preposition *am*. From our preliminary data, only bare indefinite plural nouns could appear in this position; however, we acknowledge that any hypotheses developed here must be more rigorously tested with more data. Since this finding does not play a significant role in the topic at hand, we leave this for future research.

In addition to these findings which refute Reed's restrictions, Huffines notes two innovations with the PD progressive forms: First, the movement of the object NP to a medial position between the PREP *am* and the substantive infinitive occurs 50% of the time in her data when the object NP is preceded by an adjective or a possessive. Second, the phonetic realization of *am*, which neutralizes the initial vowel and velarizes the following nasal, producing [əŋ].

Although Huffines refutes (many of) Reed's restrictions, she herself is not restrictive enough in delivering a detailed description of new-found 'restriction' in the distribution of the progressive in PD. Burridge states that certain stative verbs (e.g., *welle* 'want') can also occur in the progressive in PD (1992:212):

(25) a. *Ich bin am wotte   fer sell.*
       I   am on wanting for that
       ? 'I'm wanting that.'
    b. *Ich bin am Sache besser versteh.*
       I   am on things better understanding
       ? 'I'm understanding things better.'

Burridge cites grammaticalization as the process motivating this syntactic innovation for statives, which assigns them a semantically progressive reading. Although the findings of Huffines and Burridge provide insight into the emerging diversity in progressive aspect forms in PD, many puzzles remain unsolved. For example, what sort of restrictions exist with the extension of progressive aspect in PD to statives? Is it more or less restrictive than English? What about achievements, i.e., eventualities that are also [– stages]? Do PD-speakers allow them to appear in the progressive? If so, do they employ the same form? It is with these questions in mind that we undertook and shaped our current investigation.

4.4 Progressive aspect in Big Valley, PA, and Holmes County, OH, Pennsylvania Dutch

For this study, we interviewed 8 native PD-speakers, with four of them coming from Big Valley, Pennsylvania, and four from Holmes County, Ohio. Kishcoquillas 'Big' Valley is located in the Pennsylvania stretches of Appalachia. An historically Amish settlement, the Valley is now home to a dozen different (and non-fellowshipping) Anabaptist groups ranging from sectarian Old Orders to progressive, assimilated Mennonites. As discussed in detail by Brown (2011), three macro-groups exist within these Old Orders, each designated by buggy color. From most conservative, sectarian to more progressive: white, yellow, and black.

Based on the sub-distinctions of stative events introduced in §2.2, we developed a closed questionnaire (see Appendix) to test in which environments progressive aspect could interact with various statives. We tested for the interaction of the following:

a. Different sub-types of stative eventualities (e.g., √STAGE-s and √INDIVIDUAL-s (i.e., Kimian states)),
b. Different sub-types of external arguments (e.g., agent (volitional), agent (non-volitional), experiencer, patient), and
c. the PROG-operator

We conducted both group and individual interviews where consultants were orally presented with data from a closed questionnaire. Researchers read each sentence in PD aloud to the consultants and elicited grammaticality judgments on a Likert scale of 1 (ungrammatical/'I would not use this form' or 'I do not understand this form') to 3 (grammatical/'I would use this construction' or 'This sounds perfectly fine/acceptable to me.'). In instances of ungrammatically, participants were asked to supply a more grammatical rendering of the sentence in question.

4.4.1 *Grammatical acceptability judgments*

Figure 1 below displaces the differences in acceptability amongst of PD-speaking consultants with respect to progressive aspect and its ability to co-occur with different eventualities.

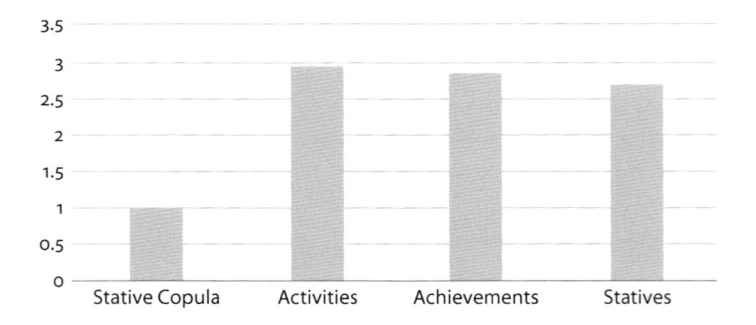

Figure 1. Different eventualities with progressive aspect.

As mentioned above, consultants were orally presented with four types of eventualities (= stative copula, activities, achievements, statives) and were asked to evaluate the likelihood of them using this sentence in their own speech (1–3 Likert Scale; 1 'not likely', 2 'maybe', 3 'definitely'). The acceptability rates in Figure 1 illustrate two interesting findings: First, progressive aspect occurs with statives at almost the same level of acceptability as found with achievements and activity eventualities. Second, and also important, is the clear distinction between 'true' statives and statives that occur with a copula verb, with the latter clearly being judged as ungrammatical by our PD-speaking consultants. These findings based on our pilot study provide further evidence for the reality of portioning statives into sub-classes of predicates. In the section that follows, we provide the sketch of a theoretical analysis that argues for the reanalysis of functional information in the form of atomic units commonly labeled 'features' (Chomsky 1995 et seq.). As we discuss in more detail below, following a recent proposals by

Polinsky (2011) and Putnam and Sánchez (2013), linguistic change in heritage grammar can be interpreted as the reanalysis of systematic elements (again, 'features') where continued activation of the socially-dominant L2 (in this case, English) forces a reanalysis of functional information in the L1 (in this case, PD), which, although still spoken by Old Order Amish, occurs in restricted social domains.

5. Theoretical analysis

Here we model the interaction of stative eventualities and progressive aspect in English and PD. As a general starting point, let us assume that linguistic knowledge can be encapsulated into atomic units known as features. For our immediate purposes, let us further assume (following Chomsky 1995 et seq.) that the follow sets of features comprise the basic sub-classes of features of human grammar:[15]

a. Functional features (FFs),
b. Phonological features (PF features); and,
c. Semantic features

Furthermore, following our brief introduction to the structural properties of progressive aspect and its intersection with (morpho)syntactic structure, we adopt Ramchand's (2008) proposed architecture of a relatively strict union between event semantics and syntactic structure. Under these core assumptions, the variation of progressive aspect structures cross-linguistically boils down to whether or not individual languages permit a PROG-operator to occur with certain aspectual types. If notions such as PROGRESSIVE ASPECT can be classified as an FF, the relationship between FFs and PF-features can vary considerably in their combinatorial properties. For example, in a language where the PROG-operator is morphophonemically realized as an inflected, bound morpheme, a tight connection between the PROG-operator and a structural position can be assumed; however, in a language where a more periphrastic structure is employed, distributed exponency occurs. In accordance with Bonet's (1991) seminal work that suggests that the morphological properties of a language are determined after the successful combination of these feature units with structural notions (commonly referred to as the 'Narrow Syntax' in mainstream generative literature), we also assume that linguistic variation occurs in the mapping of the PROG-operator, PF-features and the structural properties (i.e., syntax) of a language. As such, linguistic variation is understood as variation in exponency and the lexification of combinations of these three units of atomic linguistic knowledge.[16]

---

[15]. See Stroik and Putnam (2013) for a slightly altered version of these fundamental sub-classes of features.

[16]. For detailed discussion of this view of linguistic variation, the reader is referred to Fábregas and Putnam (2013) and (2014).

As a point of departure, we assume that the following three elements constitute the general make up of the input of progressive statives:

a. PROG-operation (cf. (12))
b. √STATIVE-v (i.e., individual-level, stage-level, and Kimian states)
c. An external argument (EA): {x: (non-)volitional agent, patient, experiencer}

In the remainder of this section, we illustrate the difference properties of progressive statives in English and PD along the lines of the system we sketched out above. In addition to a clear, descriptively adequate analysis of these structures we also propose a possible scenario for the expansion of progressive statives in PD within this model. Based on recent work by Putnam and Sánchez (2013) who propose that changes throughout the lifespan of heritage grammar speakers is the result of the reconfiguration and re-assembly of FFs, we advance the claim that a similar process is primarily responsible for the expansion of structures in which progressive aspect (co-occurring with statives) can occur in PD. In this respect, PD is not a heritage grammar *per se* (see our discussion below in Section 6 of this topic), but we simply wish to illustrate that PD can be classified as a contact language. Here we build upon the core proposals of Putnam and Sánchez's (2013) work and provide a straightforward and predictive way in which this expansion has taken place in PD.

5.1.1 *English*

As a starting point, consider the contrast between stage- and individual-level statives and their (in)ability to co-occur with an experiencer external argument:

(26) I am liking my job.
    Input: {PROG-operator, √STAGE-S, EXP-subject}

(27) *I am knowing the answer.
    Input: {PROG-operator, √IND-S, EXP-subject}

The comparison of Examples (26) and (27) illustrates the ungrammaticality of individual-level states being marked with progressive aspect in English. As demonstrated by Example (28) below, stage-level statives and patient external arguments can co-occur with progressive aspect.

(28) The book is sitting on the table.
    Input: {PROG-operator, √STAGE-S, PAT-subject}

In similar fashion, Example (29) shows that stage-level states co-occurring with non-volitional agents are also acceptable in English:

(29) Captain Crunch is sleeping.
    Input: {PROG-operator, √STAGE-S, NVOL-AG-subject}

Stage-level states can also appear with volition agents in English, as evidenced by Example (30):

(30) I am sitting at the table.
Input: {PROG-operator, √STAGE-S, VOL-AG-subject}

The situation with copula verbs (i.e., Kimian statives) and their co-occurrence with statives in the progressive is a little more complicated. To illustrate this point, consider the following data:

(31) He is being polite.
Input: {PROG-operator, √STAGE-S, COPULA, VOL-AG-subject}

(32) *I am being sick.
Input: {PROG-operator, √STAGE-S, COPULA, EXP-subject}

(33) *I am being a man.
Input: {PROG-operator, √IND-S, COPULA, NVOL-AG-subject}

The data in (31), (32), and (33) explicate the fact that the structure of √STATIVE and copular are not identical (contra Ramchand (2008)).[17] This observation is reflected in our constraint inventory, where we posit constraints specifically for stative eventualities and those that also appear with copula verbs. Based on our quick overview of the basic facts of the restrictions of the co-occurrence – and, according to the theoretical desiderata we adopt here, the lexification – of a PROG-operator, √STATIVE-V, and an external argument with varying thematic properties, English bans progressive aspect in copula Kimian statives (cf. (32) and (33) above)) and the lexification of individual-level statives with experiencer subjects in the progressive (cf. (27)). As we see below, PD and English do not radically differ with respect to their lexification properties of these units; however, whereas (27) is ungrammatical in English, similar structures are acceptable in PD. Below we demonstrate how this can be accounted for in the framework we develop in this paper.

5.1.2 Pennsylvania Dutch

The different preferences in the lexification of these features sets in English and PD are quite similar. To illustrate this point, consider the following PD examples:

(34) *Er is in die Stadt am wuhne.*
He is in the town on residing
'He is living/residing in town.'

(35) **Er is en Mann am sei.*
He is a man on being
Intended: 'He is being a man.'

---

[17]. Although we firmly acknowledge that there is a way to provide enough pragmatic content to arrive at grammatical readings of (32) and (33), it would involve a reading that is somewhat counterfactual. We will focus on lexical semantic properties of lexical items in this paper.

(36) *Er is grank am sei.
　　　He is sick　on being
　　　Intended: 'He is being sick.'

(37) Ich bin selli Sach(e) am wisse.
　　　I　am such things on　knowing
　　　'I am knowing such things.'

As in English, both sentences that appear with copula verbs; namely, Examples (35) and (36), are ungrammatical. This indicates that in both English and PD, Kimian statives cannot co-occur (i.e., be lexified) with progressive aspect. However, in contrast to what we observe in English, individual-level states with an experiencer external argument can co-occur in PD (cf. (37)), which, as we noted above in the previous section in our overview of English stative progressives, is not possible (cf. (27)). This represents the key contrast between English and PD with regard to stative eventualities and their (in)ability to co-occur with progressive aspect. Here we witness an expansion in the domain of possible structures/lexifications in PD where statives can occur in progressive aspect; namely, the input {PROG-operator, √IND-S, EXP-subject} represents an acceptable unit of atomic features that can be lexified (i.e., connected with the morphophonemic properties of PD).

Before closing our investigation on the connection between states and progressive aspect, it appears that PD is currently undergoing a shift where stage-level states appearing with patient external arguments (with an input of {PROG-operator, √STAGE-S, PAT-subject}) result in marked structures:

(38) ??'S　Buch is am　　Tisch am sitze.
　　　The book is on the table on　sitting
　　　'The book is sitting on the table.'

As a result of this possible shift currently underway in the PD-grammar, it is unclear whether stage-level statives co-occurring with patient external arguments will become fully grammaticalized in PD. Two points are in order here before moving to the next section: First, the combination of the lexification of these formal features (i.e., their connection with PF-features) can and should be best understood as a gradient process where acceptability (but not grammaticality) is affected. Therefore, variance and gradience in linguistic structure is the norm rather than the exception here. Second, given that the English equivalent of (38) is acceptable in English (cf. (28)), it is fair to postulate that this featural combination could result in a (more) acceptable lexified structure in PD in the future, especially in light of growing contact with monolingual English speakers on the part of L1-PD speakers.

5.1.2.1 √STATIVES vs. √ACHIEVEMENTS. A final word is in order here regarding the difference between √STATIVES and √ACHIEVEMENTS and their ability to coincide with progressive aspect in PD. As reflected in the grammaticality judgments elicited in this study (Figure 1), both √STATIVES and √ACHIEVEMENTS can appear with progressive aspect quite frequently. Our PD consultants did, however, show a very strong preference for constructing √STATIVES and √ACHIEVEMENTS with different syntactic structures. To illustrate this point, consider the following examples:

(38) √ACHIEVEMENT
Er is es Glas draa am breche.
He is the glass almost P break
'He is about to break the glass.'

(39) √STATIVE
Die Leit sin *(draa) am glawwe.
The people are almost P believe
'The people are believing.'

In PD, √ACHIEVEMENTS occur predominantly in combination with the temporal adverbial modifier *draa* (German *gerade* 'just now, currently'), whereas the appearance of *draa* in connection with √STATIVES is virtually unattested.[18] Based on these findings, we arrive at the following generalizations:

a. The PD-grammar recognizes the distinction between √STATIVES and √ACHIEVEMENTS.
b. The classification of a √V as [– stages] does not prevent it from appearing in combination with progressive aspect.

6. Hyperextension

In our analysis of progressive aspect in connection with [– stages]-predicates in PD, we exposed the fact that the fundamental difference between English and PD can be reduced to the crucial difference between whether or not the PROG-operator can occur with experiencer subjects and an individual-level stative, which is not possible in English but appears to be possible in PD. With regard to the syntax-semantics interface, recent research claims that the most permeable parts of a grammar in contact situations are those at interfaces (e.g., discourse-pragmatic and semantic), which are readily grammatical in both languages (cf. Sánchez' (2003, 2004) Convergence Hypothesis). Sorace (2006: 116) clarifies the sharp difference between NARROW versus INTERFACE syntax:

Non-interpretable features that are internal to the computational syntax proper and drive syntactic derivations are categorical in native grammars; are acquired successfully by adult L2 learners; and are retained in the initial stages of individual attrition. Interpretable features that 'exploit' syntactic options and belong to the interface

---

18. In the data produced by informants to 'correct' our elicitations, only one counterexample has the temporal adverbial modifier *draa* with a √STATIVE.

between syntax and other domains, such as the lexicon, discourse, or pragmatics, may present residual optionality in near-native grammars, due to the influence of the native language even at the most advanced competence stage; and are vulnerable to change in individual attrition.

Drawing on similar arguments and observations present in the contact linguistics literature, we show that the PD progressive has converged with English semantics (at least to some extent). However, the mapping is not a simple lexical calque or direct translation from English to PD, which is to be expected in a model of linguistic change that maintains that the reconfiguration of functional features is primarily responsible for the empirical changes we observe here. Burridge's (1992) research elucidates the fact that gradually PD progressives increased until English and PD achieved semantic congruence. The core findings of this study, namely, the fact that PD-speakers can combine [– stages]-predicates with progressive aspect to a greater degree than found in English, is not a novel finding confined to this study. In fact, this phenomenon is widely found in other contact situations, e.g., Hawaiian Creole, where the first appearance of a locative copular-derived *stei* appeared in the 1920s, and now has been extended to cover both progressive aspect and habitual aspect (Roberts 1999: 59). For TMA markings in Principense, Maurer (1997: 422) shows that the present progressive marker *sa* may also be used with stative verbs, which "insist on the presentness of the situation." Varieties of World Englishes and dialectal English show similar hyperextension patterns (data from Gachelin 1997):

(40) a. I am having a cold. (West African English)
 b. Are you wanting anything? (Indian English)
 c. She is having a headache. (Singapore English)
 d. She is knowing her science very well. (East African English)

Crosslinguistically, research has found that the evolution of an aspect system seems to move from progressive to imperfect, by extending the use of the progressive to √STATIVES (e.g., Comrie 1976, Bybee et al. 1994, Ramat 1997). In some respects, the reconfiguration of the PD-grammar in this particular domain simply reflects universal trends, and given that aspect, a grammatical category situated at the syntax-semantics interface involves malleable 'interface features,' it comes as little surprise that changes in this system are underway.

A final question that we must address before moving onto the conclusion concerns the overall stability of the PD-grammar. A valid and interesting question raised to us by Marit Westergaard (p.c.) concerns the possibility of PD being an 'incompletely acquired' language in the sense of Polinsky (1997, 2006, 2008) and Montrul (2002, 2008, 2009). Under this understanding of incomplete acquisition, Montrul (2002, 2008) and Polinsky (2008) find that the late stage acquisition of stative predicate distinctions is the result of faulty aspectual markings in Spanish-English bilinguals and Heritage/American Russian speakers respectively. Although most Amish children come into heavy contact early in their life – either via a formal introduction to English in elementary school or by contact with older siblings who have already begun to acquire English – a key difference between PD-speakers and heritage speakers is the fact that PD continues to thrive as an L1 in conservative sects of the Old Order Amish. Importantly, PD has extended the use of progressive aspect beyond English, but, as we model here, constraints do exist on this newer form. Therefore, the hyperextension of progressive aspect to √STATIVES in PD as well as some World Englishes (cf. (40)) may develop as a result of exposure to English during the critical period of language acquisition, but rather than labeling this as some form of 'incomplete acquisition,' we classify this situation as the result of the convergence of complex – and in some instances typologically contrastive – Principle Linguistic Data (PLD) see Putnam and Sánchez (2013) and references *inter alia*.[19]

PD grammar has not simply copied the English aspectual system in relation to progressive aspect, rather it has constructed its own independent system based on contact with English and the structural representations available to them in PD. We also recognize that there appear to be some typological universals at play here as well (based on the connections with World Englishes and creoles). This, of course, is to be expected in our model of functional feature re-assembly and relexification that has taken place in PD (as well as these other World Englishes and creoles mentioned above). In summary, we concur with the observation that what has taken place – and what likely is still underway – in the PD-grammar is no mere calque of the English aspectual system, but rather the reconfiguration of aspectual information with lexical items and syntactic structure has led to a unique and new aspectual system in current PD.

7. Conclusions and directions for future research

The prime aim of this paper was to gain further insight into (morpho)syntactic and semantic properties of semantic aspect as it is manifest in modern PD. This pilot study shows that PD-speakers in both Big Valley, Pennsylvania, and Holmes County, Ohio, show a hyperextension of progressive aspect in combination with particular combinations of √STATIVES and external arguments not found in (American) English. As discussed in §6, this appears to be an instance of HYPEREXTENSION beyond English usage, but there still exist constraints on the grammaticality of what can be hyperextended.

Concerning future research into the aspectual system of PD and other German-language speech enclaves throughout the world, future research in this domain must take into account tense distinctions along with the aspectual system. Second, as mentioned to us by Dave Embick (p.c.), along with this current shift discussed in this study, it would be interesting to explore how PD-speakers construct habituals of non-statives. Third, as noted by Rothmayr (2009), the appearance of progressive aspect with modals creates a very messy situation. This is based on the fact that the contrasting nature of modal versus lexical verbs; i.e., modal verbs are operators that act on propositions,

---

19. Additionally, substratal influence, especially in the case of World Englishes, as well as access to standard speakers and texts figure into hyperextension in their grammars.

whereas lexical verbs select arguments to form a proposition. Accordingly, it is most likely incorrect to classify modals as √STATIVES (or to associate them with any other Aktionsart-classification for that matter). This finding has a direct impact on the study of progressive aspect in PD, mainly because some of the examples given by Huffines (1986) and Burridge (1992) to illustrate the extension of progressive aspect to 'states' is incorrect. In other words, the fact that (progressive) aspect can appear with modals is itself a mystery and should constitute a separate course of tangential study beyond this current investigation. Fourth, in addition to including tense distinctions into a larger-scale investigation of aspect into PD, the following data (provided to us by Mark Louden, p.c.) seem to indicate that the licensing of progressive aspect interacts also in peculiar ways with voice systems:

(41) a. *Sie sin ihre Septic-tank am ausgebutzt griege.*
They are their septic tank P out-cleaned.$_{PART}$ get
'They are getting their septic tank cleaned out.'
b. *Der Septic-tank is(t) am ausgebutzt wadde.*
The septic tank is P out-cleaned.$_{PART}$ been
'The septic tank has been cleaned out.'

Although the construction in (41a) is found today in non-standard continental German speech patterns (as confirmed by Volker Gast and Ralf Vogel, p.c.), (41b) is not. Once again we have an example of an extension of progressive aspect in a domain unattested in continental German non-standard speech, which is also not possible in English. Lastly, as pointed out to us by Marit Westergaard (p.c.), moving forward research into the aspectual system of PD must move beyond mere structural descriptions and tackle the difficult task of determining exactly what these structures mean. We acknowledge this shortcoming in the current research on this topic, and plan to integrate these issues into our future research on aspect in PD.

Importantly, this paper has not considered the progressive in Pennsylvania Dutch in isolation, but sought to tie its workings into larger issues of contact theory. In so doing, we have avoided the trap of viewing this feature in Pennsylvania Dutch as a 'contamination' from English, but as a creative and dynamic feature that used English as its expansion point. Other contributions in this volume show similar effects to the bilingual syntax and permeability of the grammar. In fact, some of the studies in this volume comment directly on the productive nature of immigrant languages in contact, e.g., Westergaard and Anderssen on Norwegian possessive constructions. We are confident that this pilot study will lead to a deeper understanding of the workings of the bilingual brain and the grammar in contact.

The findings of this pilot study also stand to have a useful effect on the syntax-semantic literature on aspect as well. First, agreeing with Rothmayr (2009), it is hard to maintain the long-standing perception that √STATIVES are a unified class and function as the building blocks of (all) other predicates. Their structure is clearly more complex than is commonly assumed (contra Ramchand 2008, who argues that their structure is 'simple' and similar to copula verbs). In this respect, a more fine-graded treatment of the interaction between duration and √STATIVES is sorely needed alongside a more detailed analysis of the structure(s) of √STATIVES. Lastly, and in connection with the previous point, Rothstein's (2004) distinctions (e.g., [± telic], [± stages]) for classes of eventualities may require (some) revision to account for the sub-class distinctions of √STATIVES.

Appendix

Jake is am grank sei. / Jake is being sick.
Jake is en Mann am sei. / Jake is being a man.
Ruth is iwwer die Schtrooss am laafe. / Ruth is walking across the street.
Die Maem is der Balloon am verbuste. / Mom is popping the balloon.
Die Mannsleit sin der Scheier am baue. / The men are building the barn.
Ich bin am Sache besser versteh. / I am understanding things better.
Sie sin die Leit am glaawe. / They are believing the people.
Dihr seid es Buch am finne. / You are finding the book.
Die Eldre waare am daheem bleiwe. / The parents were staying at home.
Sam is die Katie am liewe. / Sam is loving Katie.
Sam is es Glas am breche. / Sam is breaking the glass.
Mary is am tschumpe. / Mary is jumping.
Ich bin selli Sach am wisse. / I am knowing that thing.
Ich bin am wotte fer sell. / I am wanting that.
John is am Gleeder ins Klaaset henke. / John is hanging the clothes in the closet.
Katie is ihr Tee am gleiche. / Katie is liking her tea.
Mir sin es Schpiel am gwinne. / We are winning the game.
Sam is sie am suche. / Sam is looking for her.
Mary un John sin in Lengeschder am wuhne nau. / Mary and John are living in Lancaster now.

References

Andersson, Sven-Gunnar. 1989. "On the Generalization of Progressive Constructions: 'Ich bin (das Buch) am Lesen' – Status and Usage in Three Varieties in German." In *Proceedings of the Second Scandinavian Symposium on Aspectology*, ed. by Lars-Gunnar Larsson, 95–106. Uppsala, Sweden: Almqvist & Wiksell.
Bartsch, Renate. 1995. *Situations, Tense and Aspect: Dynamic Discourse Ontology and the Semantic Flexibility of Temporal System in German and English*. Berlin: Mouton de Gruyter. DOI: 10.1515/9783110814606
Behrens, Bergliot, Monique Flecken and Mary Carroll. 2013. "Progressive Attraction: On the Use and Grammaticalization of Progressive Aspect in Dutch, Norwegian, and German." *Journal of Germanic Linguistics* 25(2): 95–136. DOI: 10.1017/S1470542713000020
Bonet, Eulalia. 1991. *Morphology After Syntax: Pronominal Clitics in Romance*. Cambridge, MA: MIT dissertation.

Brown, Joshua R. 2011. *Religious Identity and Language Shift Among Amish-Mennonites in Kishacoquillas Valley, Pennsylvania*. University Park, PA: Pennsylvania State University dissertation.

Burridge, Kate. 1992. "Creating Grammar: Examples from Pennsylvania German, Ontario." In *Diachronic Studies on the Languages of the Anabaptists*, ed. by Kate Burridge and Werner Enninger, 199–241. Bochum: Brockmeyer.

Bybee, Joan, Revere Perkins and William Pagliuca. 1994. *The Evolution of Grammar: Tense, Aspect and Modality in the Languages of the World*. Chicago: The University of Chicago Press.

Carlson, Gregory. 1977. *Reference to Kinds in English*. Amherst, MA: University of Massachusetts-Amherst dissertation.

Chomsky, Noam. 1995. *The Minimalist Program*. Cambridge, MA: MIT Press.

Comrie, Bernard. 1976. *Aspect*. Cambridge: Cambridge University Press.

Dowty, David. 1979/1991. *Word Meaning and Montague Grammar: The Semantics of Verbs and Times in Generative Semantics and in Montague's PTQ*. Dordrecht: Kluwer. DOI: 10.1007/978-94-009-9473-7

Fábregas, Antonio and Michael Putnam. 2013. "Parasitic Semantics (or Why Swedish Can't Lexicalize Middle Voice Constructions)." *Proceedings of the Penn Linguistics Colloquium* 36 19(1): 51–58.

Fábregas, Antonio and Michael Putnam. 2014. "The Emergence of Middle Voice Structures With and Without Agents." *The Linguistic Review* 31(2): 193–240. DOI: 10.1515/tlr-2014-0002

Fuller, Janet. 1996. "When Cultural Maintenance Means Linguistic Convergence: Pennsylvania German Evidence for the Matrix Language Turnover Hypothesis." *Language in Society* 25: 493–514. DOI: 10.1017/S0047404500020790

Gachelin, Jean-Marc. 1997. "The Progressive and Habitual Aspects in Non-Standard Englishes." In *Englishes Around the World: Studies in Honour of Manfred Gorlach*, vol. 1, ed. by Edgar W. Schneider, 33–46. Amsterdam: John Benjamins. DOI: 10.1075/veaw.g18.07gac

Hale, Ken and Jay Keyser. 2005. "Aspect and the Syntax of Argument Structure." In *The Syntax of Aspect*, ed. by Nomi Erteschik-Shir and Tova Rapport, 11–42. Oxford: Oxford University Press. DOI: 10.1093/acprof:oso/9780199280445.003.0002

Higginbotham, James. 2009. *Tense, Aspect, and Indexicality*. Oxford: Oxford University Press. DOI: 10.1093/acprof:oso/9780199239313.001.0001

Howell, Robert. 1993. "German Immigration and the Development of Regional Variants of American English: Using Contact Theory to Discover our Roots." In *The German Language in America*, ed. by Joseph Salmons, 190–212. Madison, WI: Max Kade Institute.

Huffines, M. Lois. 1986. "The Function of Aspect in Pennsylvania German and the Impact of English." *Yearbook for German – American Studies* 21: 137–154.

Kim, Jaegwon. 1969. "Events and Their Descriptions: Some Considerations." In *Essays in Honor of Carl G. Hempel*, ed. by Nicholas Rescher, 198–215. Dordrecht: Reidel. DOI: 10.1007/978-94-017-1466-2_10

Kim, Jaegwon. 1976. "Events as Property Exemplifications." In *Proceedings of the Winnipeg Conference on Human Action*, ed. by Myles Brand and Douglas Walton, 159–177. Dordrecht: Reidel.

Königs, Karin. 1995. "Zur Übersetzung der Verlaufsform ins Deutsche." *Lebende Sprache* 4: 153–158.

Landman, Fred. 1992. "The Progressive." *Natural Language Semantics* 1: 1–32. DOI: 10.1007/BF02342615

Louden, Mark. 1988. *Bilingualism and Syntactic Change in Pennsylvania German*. Ithaca, NY: Cornell University dissertation.
Maienborn, Claudia. 2003. *Die logische Form von Kopula-Sätzen*. Berlin: Akademie-Verlag. DOI: 10.1524/9783050082271
Maienborn, Claudia. 2005. "On the Limits of the Davidsonian Approach: The Case of Copula Sentences." *Theoretical Linguistics* 31(3): 275–313.
Maurer, Philippe. 1997. "Tense-Aspect-Mood in Principense." In *The structure and Status of Pidgins and Creoles: Including Selected Papers from the Meetings of the Society for Pidgin and Creole Linguistics*, ed. by Arthur K. Spears and Donald Winford, 415–435. Amsterdam: John Benjamins. DOI: 10.1075/cll.19.23mau
Montrul, Silvina. 2002. "Incomplete Acquisition and Attrition of Spanish Tense/Aspect Distinctions in Adult Bilinguals." *Bilingualism: Language and Cognition* 5: 39–68. DOI: 10.1017/S1366728902000135
Montrul, Silvina. 2008. *Incomplete Acquisition in Bilingualism: Re-examining the Age Factor*. Amsterdam: John Benjamins. DOI: 10.1075/sibil.39
Montrul, Silvina. 2009. "Incomplete Acquisition of Tense-Aspect and Mood in Spanish Heritage Speakers." *International Journal of Bilingualism* 13(3): 239–269. DOI: 10.1177/1367006909339816
Polinsky, Maria. 1997. "American Russian: Language Loss Meets Language Acquisition." In *Annual Workshop on Formal Approaches to Slavic 19 Linguistics: The Cornell Meeting (1995)*, ed. by Wayles Browne, Ewa Dornsich, Natasha Kondrashova and Draga Zec, 370–406. Ann Arbor, MI: Michigan Slavic Publishers.
Polinsky, Maria. 2006. "Incomplete Acquisition: American Russian." *Journal of Slavic Linguistics* 14: 191–262.
Polinsky, Maria. 2008. "Without Aspect." In *Case and Grammatical Relations*, ed. by Greville G. Corbett and Michael P. Noonan, 263–282. Amsterdam: John Benjamins. DOI: 10.1075/tsl.81.13pol
Polinsky, Maria. 2011. "Reanalysis in Adult Heritage Language." *Studies in Second Language Acquisition* 33: 305–328. DOI: 10.1017/S027226311000077X
Putnam, Michael and Liliana Sánchez. 2013. "What So Incomplete About Incomplete Acquisition? A Prolegomenon to Modeling Heritage Grammars." *Linguistic Approaches to Bilingualism* 3(4): 478–508. DOI: 10.1075/lab.3.4.04put
Ramat, Anna Giacalone. 1997. "Progressive Periphrases, Markedness, and Second Language Data." In *Language and its Ecology: Essays in Memory of Einar Haugen*, ed. by Stig Eliasson and Ernst Hakon Jahr, 261–286. Berlin: Mouton de Gruyter.
Ramchand, Gillian Catriona. 2008. *Verb Meaning and the Lexicon: A First-Phase Syntax*. Cambridge: Cambridge University Press. DOI: 10.1017/CBO9780511486319
Reed, Carroll. 1947. "The Question of Aspect in Pennsylvania German." *The Germanic Review* 22: 5–12.
Roberts, Sarah Julianne. 1999. "The TMA System of Hawaiian Creole and Diffusion." In *Creole Genesis, Attitudes, and Discourse: Studies Celebrating Charlene J. Sato*, ed. by John R. Rickford and Suzanne Romaine, 45–70. Amsterdam: John Benjamins. DOI: 10.1075/cll.20.08rob
Ross, John Robert. 1972. "Act." In *Semantics of Natural Language*, ed. by David Davidson and Gilbert Herman, 76–120. Dordrecht: Reidel.
Rothmayr, Antonia. 2009. *The Structure of Stative Verbs*. Amsterdam: John Benjamins. DOI: 10.1075/la.143

Rothstein, Susan. 2004. *Structuring Events*. Malden, MA: Blackwell. DOI: 10.1002/9780470759127

Sánchez, Liliana. 2003. *Quechua-Spanish Bilingualism: Interference and Convergence in Functional Categories*. Amsterdam: John Benjamins. DOI: 10.1075/lald.35

Sánchez, Liliana. 2004. "Functional Convergence in the Tense, Evidentiality and Aspectual Systems of Quechua Spanish Bilinguals." *Bilingualism: Language and Cognition* 7(2): 147–162. DOI: 10.1017/S136672890400149X

Silva-Corvalán, Carmen. 1993. "On the Permeability of Grammars: Evidence from Spanish and English Contact." In *Linguistic Perspectives on the Romance Languages*, ed. by William J. Ashby, Marianne Mithun and Giorgio Perissinotto, 19–43. Amsterdam: John Benjamins. DOI: 10.1075/cilt.103.08sil

Silva-Corvalán, Carmen. 1994/2000. *Language Contact and Change*. Oxford: Clarendon Press.

Smith, Carlota. 1991. *The Parameter of Aspect*. Dordrecht: Kluwer. DOI: 10.1007/978-94-015-7911-7

Sorace, Antonella. 2006. "Gradedness and Optionality in Mature and Developing Grammars." In *Gradience in Grammar: Generative Perspective*, ed. by Gisbert Fanselow, Caroline Féry, Ralf Vogel and Matthais Schlesewsky, 106–124. Oxford: Oxford University Press. DOI: 10.1093/acprof:oso/9780199274796.003.0006

Stiebels, Barbara and Dieter Wunderlich. 1994. "Morphology Feeds Syntax: The Case of Particle Verbs." *Linguistics* 32(6): 913–968. DOI: 10.1515/ling.1994.32.6.913

Stroik, Thomas and Michael Putnam. 2013. *The Structural Design of Language*. Cambridge: Cambridge University Press. DOI: 10.1017/CBO9781139542272

Taylor, Barry. 1977. "Tense and Continuity." *Linguistics and Philosophy* 1(2): 199–220.

Toribio, Almeida Jacqueline. 2004. "Convergence as an Optimization Strategy in Bilingual Speech: Evidence from Code-Switching." *Bilingualism: Language and Cognition* 7(2): 165–173. DOI: 10.1017/S1366728904001476

Van Pottelberge, Jeroen. 2004. *Der am-Progressive: Struktur und parallele Entwicklung in den kontinentalwestgermanischen Sprachen*. Tübingen: Gunter Narr.

Van Pottelberge, Jeroen. 2007. "Defining Grammatical Constructions as a Linguistic Sign: The Case of Periphrastic Progressives in the Germanic Languages." *Folia Linguistica* 41: 99–134.

Vendler, Zeno. 1957. "Verbs and Times." *The Philosophical Review* 66(2): 143–160. DOI: 10.2307/2182371

Vendler, Zeno. 1967. *Linguistics in Philosophy*. Ithaca, NY: Cornell University Press.

Hybrid verb forms in American Norwegian and the analysis of the syntactic relation between the verb and its tense

Tor A. Åfarli
Norwegian University of Science and Technology

English verbs that are nonce borrowed into American Norwegian regularly show Norwegian tense inflection. In this article, I use data of such hybrid verb forms as a starting-point for an investigation of the general theoretical analysis of the morpho-syntactic relation between a verb and its tense affix. I argue that the hybrid verb forms in American Norwegian should be taken as evidence that it is *not* the case that verbs (and inflected words generally) are fully listed with inflectional features in the lexicon and subsequently checked for their inflectional features in the syntax (as suggested in recent minimalist analyses). Instead, I argue that what is contained in the lexicon are the bare verbal items, and that tense morphology is syntactically *assigned* to the item during the derivation.

Keywords: American Norwegian, borrowing, code-switching, language mixing, tense, verb movement

1. Introduction

American Norwegian comprises varieties of the Norwegian language that have been and still are used by Norwegian immigrants to the USA and their descendants from the first half of the 19th century up to today (Haugen 1953, Hjelde 1992, Johannessen and Laake 2011). American Norwegian varieties are often characterized by a quite high degree of mixture from English. A striking property of the English words used in American Norwegian is that these words receive Norwegian inflection even though the stem is borrowed from English. This is illustrated by the verb in bold in (1) (from Haugen 1953: 503).

(1) Å e å   n Eijil helt på å   **hunta**   frosk ute.
and I and he Eijil kept on and hunted frogs outside
'And I and Eijil were busy hunting frogs outside.'

Here the verb stem, *hunt*, is clearly English (the corresponding Norwegian stem would be *jakt-*), while the tense inflection is clearly Norwegian, *-a* being a past tense suffix belonging to the main class of Norwegian weak verbs (thus the Norwegian verb form corresponding to 'hunted' is *jakta*).

In this article, I discuss hybrid verb forms of this type. I investigate what such verb forms may tell us about the relation between the verb stem and the tense suffix in general, and in particular I want to investigate what it can tell us about the proper syntactic analysis of the tense – stem relation in generative grammar. I hope to show that the hybrid verb forms are theoretically interesting, because they support a particular analysis of the relationship between tense and its verbal stem, and of how the verb stem acquires its tense inflection.

The article is organized as follows. In Section 2, I discuss the notion of single word loanwords versus single word code-switching. It is important for my analysis that the hybrid verb forms do not involve just established loanwords, i.e., words that have been borrowed from English and integrated into Norwegian, but that they are rather some type of unintegrated spontaneously borrowed items, i.e., that they are really *hybrid* forms in a sense to be made more precise. In Section 3, I present more data showing hybrid verb forms in American Norwegian. This section, then, provides the empirical basis for the following theoretical discussion. In Section 4, I discuss some theoretical points of departure for the analysis to come, and in Section 5 I discuss some mechanisms that have been proposed in the literature concerning the relation between the verb and its tense inflection and how the verb acquires its tense affix. Section 6 presents my analysis of the tense – verb relation, and show how the theoretical problems posed by the hybrid verb forms are solved given my analysis. Section 7 concludes the article.

2. Why the hybrid verb forms are really hybrid

If verb forms like *hunta* 'hunted' in (1) were established as part of the American Norwegian mental lexicon, they would reasonably be categorized as established loanwords, and it would not be surprising that they get Norwegian tense inflection, like other Norwegian verb stems do. In that case, they would not be hybrid verb forms in the sense under discussion here. So what is a hybrid verb form? I understand a hybrid verb form to be a spontaneously created verb form consisting of elements from (at least) two different languages. Thus, a hybrid verb form is not an established loanword or a single word borrowed form that has become a member of the host language; it is rather a single word code-switched form that is spontaneously borrowed.

There is a long-lasting discussion in code-switching theory about how or to what extent it is possible to tell if a given form is an established loan or a spontaneously borrowed form, e.g., Pfaff (1979), Poplack (2004). Spontaneously borrowed forms are also called 'nonce borrowing'; these are forms that are borrowed *ad hoc* by a speaker in a given situation, and they are not typically used by other speakers of the speech community in similar situations. Established loans, on the other hand, are used by many speakers in the community and may be quite common. It is also usually assumed that spontaneous borrowing presupposes that the speaker is bilingual, at least to some extent, whereas established loanwords are also used by monolingual speakers. Spontaneous borrowing therefore typically takes place in situations of language contact, like the American Norwegian setting.

From the discussion above, it follows that if verb forms in American Norwegian, like *hunta* 'hunted' in (1), are to be counted as hybrid verb forms, they must be spontaneously borrowed or code-switched forms. I take that to mean, among other things, that they are not assigned to a particular inflectional tense class in the established lexicon of (American) Norwegian, but that they are rather assigned tense *ad hoc* when they are 'nonce borrowed' into American Norwegian grammatical structure. The following is a probable kind of procedure for this type of 'nonce borrowing.' Over time the Norwegian mental lexicon internalized by the American Norwegian language users is weakened, and simultaneously they build an ever growing English mental lexicon, which is used when they talk English (they are bilinguals). In situations when they fail to retrieve a Norwegian word for what they want to say (because of lexical attrition or problems with lexical access), or when they simply want to spice up their Norwegian, they pick an English word from their parallel English lexicon and integrate it into the Norwegian structure. Thus, an English verb is 'nonce borrowed' into Norwegian and is assigned tense in the Norwegian syntactic structure, in an *ad hoc* way.

The principled distinction between established loanwords and spontaneously 'nonce borrowed' words is reasonably clear, and can be described as a question of whether the word is drawn from the domestic mental lexicon (established loan), or from the foreign mental lexicon (nonce borrowing). In a given instance, on the other hand, it is often difficult to decide whether a given extraneous form is an established loan or a spontaneously borrowed form (e.g., Eide and Hjelde, this volume). Important criteria have to do with frequency, stability, and diffusion in a speech community. For instance, the more frequently the form is used, the more likely it is an established loan.

Because of the practical indeterminacy in distinguishing between established forms and spontaneously borrowed forms, I cannot guarantee that the examples given below were actually spontaneously borrowed in the particular instance given. Such a determination would at least require a careful investigation of the linguistic situation when the data were collected and the context of utterance of each particular example, which is next to impossible since the data were collected years ago. Still, I believe it is reasonable to assume (i) that spontaneously borrowed and therefore genuinely hybrid verb forms exist in American Norwegian in principle, and (ii) that the mixed forms given were spontaneously borrowed when they first were used in American Norwegian, even though some may have become established loans later. This last point is emphasized in Myers-Scotton (1993: 174), where it is pointed out that words that are included as established loans in a language typically started out as spontaneously borrowed words. Spontaneous borrowing is the gateway through which established loanwords come into a language, according to Myers-Scotton. I therefore assume that all the mixing examples that I use are in principle possible examples of spontaneously borrowed forms, and therefore possible examples of genuinely hybrid verb forms in American Norwegian, and I refer to them as such in the remainder of this article.

3. Data

I now look at more data that exemplify hybrid verb forms in American Norwegian. In (2) I show data that are taken from Haugen (1953: 556 ff.). The English stem that is borrowed is given first, followed by an American Norwegian utterance where this stem is used with Norwegian tense inflection (the relevant inflectional category is given in square brackets).

(2) a. Break: *dei **brek-te** opp prærien.* [past]
 'they broke up the prairie.'
 b. Care: *E tenkte ikkje du **kær-a** så mykje.* [past]
 'I didn't think you cared so much.'
 c. Change: *Han **kjeinj-a** main sin.* [past]
 'He changed his mind.'
 d. Feed: *Dei kan du **fid-a** upp sjøl.* [infinitive]
 'Those you can feed up yourself.'
 e. Feel: *...je **fil-er** likså gått såm da je var to å tjugu år.* [present]
 '...I feels as good as like I was 22 years old.'
 f. Fine: *So **fain-a** eg dai ain dalar kvar.* [past]
 'So I fined them a dollar each.'
 g. Harvest: *sådde å ikkje **harvist-a**.* [past]
 'sowed and not harvested.'
 h. Keep: *De er mange såm **kipp-er** Decorah-Posten.* [present]
 'There are many who keep the Decorah Post.'
 i. Leave: *...frå dei **liv-a** heimen å te dei kåm te kjerka.* [past]
 '...from when they left home and until they came to church.'
 j. Make: *Vi **mæk-ar** goe peing.* [present]
 'We make good money.'
 k. Play: *så **plei-de** dom geimer.* [past]
 'then they played games.'
 l. Reap: *så **ripp-a** dai de.* [past]
 'then they reaped them.'
 m. Run: *såm **rønn-er** farmen.* [present]
 'who runs the farm.'
 n. Settle: *her **sætl-a** e ne å her he e vore.* [past]
 'here I settled down and here I have been.'
 o. Teach: *han **titsj-a** ve Luther [College].* [past]
 'he taught at Luther College.'
 p. Travel: *han måtte **travl-e** omtrent to å tredve mil.* [infinitive]
 'he had to travel about 32 miles.'

Here are some similar examples from Hjelde (1992) (picked from "Alfabetisk liste over lån i amerika-trøndsk," in *op. cit.*: 99ff.).

(3) a. Beg: *begg-a.* [past]
'begged.'
b. Break: ...*de brækk-a stavanj...* [past]
'...they broke their sticks...'
c. Call: ...*vess du kall-a op-en fekk du svar...* [past]
'...if you called him up, you would get an answer...'
d. Cause: *kjøtt som kås-e kænser.* [present]
'meat that causes cancer.'
e. Claim: *kleim-e.* [present]; *kleim-a.* [past]
'claims.' 'claimed.'
f. Collect: *dæm kollækt-a skatt.* [past]
'they collected tax.'
g. Dust: *(ho) døst-a støv.* [past]
'she dusted.'
h. Hunt: *de e moro å hønt-e.* [infinitive]
'it is fun to hunt.'
i. Keep: *ein som kip-e boksa si på.* [present]
'one who keeps his trousers on.'
j. Move: *vi mov-a frå minesota.* [past]
'we moved from Minnesota.'

Neither Haugen (1953) nor Hjelde (1992) have found hybrid verb forms in American Norwegian where the verbal stem is Norwegian and the tense affix is English, or where the verbal stem is English and the tense affix is English as well. What they in fact found is ordinary Norwegian stems with Norwegian tense inflection, naturally enough, since American Norwegian is a variety of Norwegian, and besides that, they also found several instances of English stems with Norwegian tense inflection, as we have already seen in (1)–(3).

In other words, what is found in American Norwegian are the patterns in (4a) or (4b), whereas the patterns in (4c) and (4d) are never found. A proviso is in order here, since the pattern in (4d) may of course be found in a larger chunk when a whole English phrase is code-switched into American Norwegian, a case that I ignore here.

(4) a. stem$_{NO}$-tense$_{NO}$
b. stem$_{ENG}$-tense$_{NO}$
c. *stem$_{NO}$-tense$_{ENG}$
d. *stem$_{ENG}$-tense$_{ENG}$

The pattern in (4) is very robust, and at the outset that is quite surprising, since the speakers in question must be assumed to have parallel lexicons for both Norwegian and English (they are bilingual, as mentioned), and therefore one should expect that they could borrow fully inflected verb forms from English, like in (4d), but that doesn't happen.

On the other hand, the pattern in (4) is fully in tune with what is found in corresponding language mixing or code-switching situations around the globe. (I use the term 'code-switching' both for spontaneous borrowing of bigger phrases and spontaneous borrowing of single words/stems.) Myers-Scotton (1993, 2002) claims that there is necessarily an asymmetry between the two languages involved in code-switching, where one language defines the grammatical frame or matrix – the *Matrix Language* – whereas the other – the *Embedded Language* – is a source for borrowing of lexical stems that are inserted into the grammar frame that the Matrix Language makes available. According to Myers-Scotton, the inflectional affixes as a rule come from the Matrix Language, and they are therefore part of the grammar frame. In American Norwegian, Norwegian is the Matrix Language, whereas English is the Embedded Language, and the pattern shown in (4) is as expected on Myers-Scotton's theory.

4. Theoretical assumptions

I now clarify some theoretical points of departure for my analysis. First of all, I assume that ordinary finite clauses have a minimal structure consisting of CP, TP, and VP, as explained in standard textbooks of generative syntax. This basic structure is shown in (5).

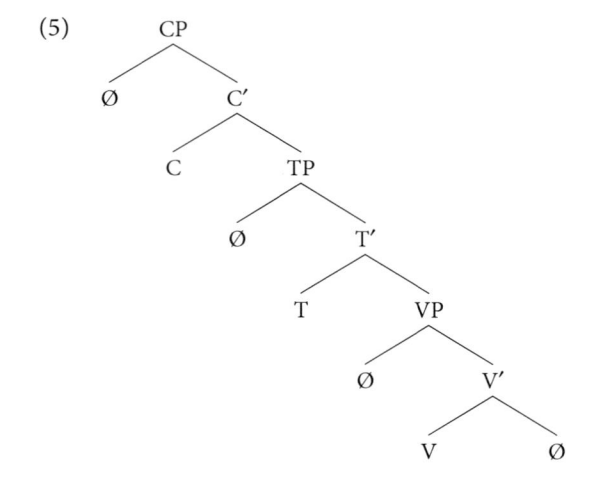

(5)
```
            CP
           /  \
          Ø    C'
              /  \
             C    TP
                 /  \
                Ø    T'
                    /  \
                   T    VP
                       /  \
                      Ø    V'
                          /  \
                         V    Ø
```

Tense is generated under T, and the main verb is generated under V, and T c-commands V. I assume, as is standard in generative grammar, that the verb 'receives' tense through a special relationship between V and its c-commanding T. It is the precise nature of this 'special relationship' that is the topic of this article.

Generally, I take it that hybrid verb forms like those in (2) and (3) indicate that the relation between the verbal stem and its tense inflection is not as tight as one might be inclined to believe, and I proceed on the hypothesis that these hybrid verb forms actually support the generative thesis that the tense inflection is generated independently of the stem that it ultimately becomes a part of (Lasnik 2000). The analysis I defend in Section 6 is founded on this basic assumption, and to the extent that the analysis is successful it constitutes support for the basic assumption.

I make two non-trivial assumptions. First, I assume that the analysis of hybrid verb forms as in (2) and (3) does not require any special mechanisms that are not relevant for the analysis of ordinary monolingual verb forms. In other words, my analysis is a so-called 'Null Theory'. This implies that the analysis of hybrid verb forms can give important insights into the general UG mechanisms that regulate the relationship between a verbal stem and its tense inflection. Actually, as I show, the hybrid verb forms turn out to be a testing ground for any analysis of the relationship between the verb and its tense inflection.

The second important assumption I make is that there is only one mechanism in UG that takes care of the relationship between a verbal stem and its tense inflection. In other words, I will *not* assume that UG allows, e.g., both syntactic V-to-T movement and syntactic T-to-V movement (Affix Hopping). I believe that this is a proper assumption to a restrictive and minimalist analysis.

Towards the end of Section 3, I referred to Myers-Scotton (1993, 2002) and the idea that the Matrix Language provides the grammar frame and the inflectional morphology, whereas the Embedded Language occasionally provides lexical items that are inserted into these frames. I adopt a similar point of departure for my analysis, but this is not unproblematic in a principles and parameters approach (which I am following), where the formation of clause structure is usually assumed to be derivational in that elements from the lexicon are successively taken as input by the operation *Merge* to build larger structures. Such an approach excludes a model where grammar frames are generated first, followed by insertion into those frames by lexical items. Still, there exist models that must be characterized as principles and parameters type models, and where a notion of a grammar template or frame is crucial, like so-called neo-constructional models, which are defended in e.g., Van Hout (1996), Borer (2005), Åfarli (2007), Brøseth (2007), Ramchand (2008), Lohndal (2012), Marantz (2012), and Nygård (2013), cf. also the generator component of Brown and Putnam (this volume). These neo-constructional models agree, broadly speaking, with Myers-Scotton's assumption that structures are generated independently of the lexical items, which are inserted into these structures later, assuming Late Lexical Insertion, but unlike Myers-Scotton they seek to integrate this assumption into an articulated principles and parameters approach to grammar.

I cannot provide a detailed examination of neo-constructional theories, but simply assume it is possible to integrate a frame and late insertion analysis and a generative principles and parameters analysis into one unified and consistent model of grammar. The minimal assumption I want to make explicit here is that the functional structure of the clause (say, the C-projection and the T-projection) and open lexical proto-projections (say, a V-projection) are generated in the Matrix Language as a grammar frame, whereas Late Lexical Insertion inserts lexical stems into the open lexical positions of the proto-projections. Therefore, in American Norwegian, the T-projection and tense will always belong to the Matrix Language, which is Norwegian, whereas it is possible to insert verbal stems from the parallel English lexicon into the verbal proto-projections. In that way, hybrid verb forms like those illustrated in (2) and (3) are generated. I now turn to the generation of such forms.

5. The syntactic relation between T and V: Some (im)possible analyses

We are now in a position to take a closer look at the concrete syntactic mechanisms that relate T and V, resulting in the tense inflection ending up as an integrated morphological part of the verb. I take as my point of departure the two ways for syntactically relating T and V discussed in Chomsky (1995: 195) (my emphasis):

> The main verb typically 'picks up' the features T and Agr […], adjoining to an inflectional element to form [V I]. There are two ways to interpret the process, for a lexical element a. *One is to take a to be a bare, uninflected form; PF rules are then designed to interpret the abstract complex [a I] as a single inflected phonological word. The other approach is to take a to have inflectional features in the lexicon as an intrinsic property (in the spirit of lexicalist phonology); these features are then checked against the inflectional element I in the complex [a I].*

I now investigate these two possibilities in turn, and since I am dealing with American Norwegian, I ignore Agr and just concentrate on the relationship between T and V. Recall that both ways for relating T and V cannot be right, given the parsimonious assumption that UG permits only one mechanism, mentioned in the previous section.

The first possibility, i.e., "to take a to be a bare, uninflected form; PF rules are then designed to interpret the abstract complex [a I] as a single inflected phonological word," seems at the outset quite promising as an analysis of hybrid verb forms in American Norwegian. One could simply assume that the English stem, after being inserted in the V position, moves to T where it "picks up" the Norwegian tense inflection, thus creating the hybrid form.

However, such a straightforward movement analysis runs into a well-known problem when applied to tensed verbs in English. Consider the main clause in (6a), which has a structure like the one shown in (6b).

(6) a. He always claimed these things.
    b. He T [$_{VP}$ always [$_{VP}$ claimed these things]]

According to Pollock (1989), a sentence adverbial (SA) like *always* is left-adjoined to VP in English, cf. *I doubt [that he will always make such claims]*, where the complementizer is positioned in C, the modal auxiliary in T, the main verb in V, and where the SA accordingly must be left-adjoined to VP.

If the SA *always* is left-adjoined to VP in a main clause like the one in (6) as well, which Pollock assumes, the linear position of the SA shows that the main verb cannot have moved out of VP, at least not before Spell-Out, i.e., before the structure is fed into PF (Phonetic Form). Still, the verb has tense inflection. That in fact means that the verb cannot have acquired its tense inflection by V-to-T movement. In other words, English data like the example in (6) show that the tensed verb cannot have acquired its tense inflection by simple V-to-T movement, showing that Chomsky's first possibility cannot be right. Holmberg and Platzack (1995: 49–50) find a corresponding problem in the analysis of embedded clauses in Mainland Scandinavian, a problem that I will not pursue here. Since Chomsky's first mechanism is excluded for English, and possibly also for Mainland Scandinavian, it follows that it cannot be assumed as a possible UG mechanism.

A possible alternative analysis would be to assume syntactic Affix Hopping, i.e., syntactic T-to-V movement downward in the structure. That is the mechanism that Pollock (1989) suggests as a solution to the problem presented by English data like (6). However, I reject such an analysis because it violates a basic principle on movement, namely that the constituent that moves must c-command the position that it moves from. That principle implies that all syntactic movement is upward. There is overwhelming empirical evidence that that assumption is correct. It would amount to a brute stipulation to assume that the analysis of the T – V relation should constitute an exception to this general principle.

A third solution that one could think of is that a 'phonological' version of T-to-V movement (Affix Hopping) takes place in PF, where the c-command restriction (or other syntactic restrictions) is not operative (since PF is not a component in narrow syntax). However, if that were the case, it would be necessary that there is a corresponding invisible LF V-to-T movement in narrow syntax in order to check that the structural restrictions on the T – V relation are actually fulfilled. Technically, this is a possible analysis, but I will still reject it, since it is not parsimonious enough. The analysis is too complex to be credible in a minimalist type analysis, since it involves an operation in one component (PF) that must be checked in another component (LF).

My conclusion from the above is that Chomsky's first take on the T – V relation (i.e., V-to-T movement where the verb as a bare uninflected form picks up tense in T) is not workable. I will now try the other way that Chomsky suggests, namely "to take a to have inflectional features in the lexicon as an intrinsic property (in the spirit of lexicalist phonology); these features are then checked against the inflectional element I in the complex [a I]" (Chomsky 1995: 195).

This second approach assumes that the inflected form of the verb is already created in the lexicon before it is inserted into syntax, and therefore that it is subsequently inserted into the syntax in its fully tensed form. In order to prohibit arbitrary insertion of tensed forms, a given tensed form that is inserted into syntax must be checked to ensure that it occurs in a structurally correct position, i.e., that it is in a structurally appropriate position in relation to T. This check can be accomplished by movement of V to T, observing standard restrictions on head movement. This movement may in principle take place either in visible syntax (before Spell-Out) or in invisible syntax (after Spell-Out), i.e., in LF. What is relevant for the English problem presented by (6) is the second option, i.e., invisible V-to-T movement in LF, since the verb has obviously not moved out of VP in (6) (in the visible syntax), as discussed above.

Assuming invisible V-to-T movement in LF, the mechanism Agree checks if the ready-made tense inflection (feature) on the verb is identical to the tense feature of T. If it is, the tensed form of the verb is licensed, and if it is not, the tensed form is not licensed and the structure is deemed ungrammatical. This analysis is schematically shown in (7). Note that the structure shown here is the structure before the putative LF movement of V+aff to T has taken place.

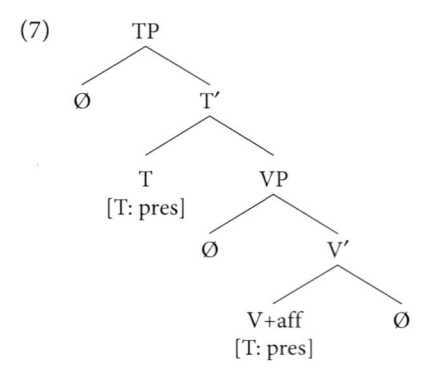

(7)
```
        TP
       /  \
      Ø    T'
          /  \
         T    VP
      [T: pres] / \
               Ø   V'
                  / \
              V+aff  Ø
            [T: pres]
```

This analysis solves the English problem in (6) because the verb now has tense inflection as a lexical property, i.e., at the *in situ* point where it is inserted in the syntax. In other words, the verb has tense before Spell-Out to PF, and therefore it is the tensed form of the verb that is pronounced. Subsequently, invisible V-to-T movement in LF will ensure that the tensed form is licensed (or not), as explained above.

Even though this analysis solves the English problem in (6), as we have seen, the hybrid verb forms in American Norwegian now present a problem. The problem is simply how to ensure that an English verb stem must receive Norwegian tense inflection. If the verb has "inflectional features in the lexicon as an intrinsic property," as suggested by Chomsky (1995: 195), it is in fact very difficult to see how verbs borrowed into American Norwegian from the English parallel lexicon can fail to have English tense inflection, contrary to fact, cf. (4d). In other words, Chomsky's second mechanism seems to make the wrong predictions in the hybrid cases.

Actually, there is a way that this conclusion can be avoided, while maintaining Chomsky's second mechanism, but the cost is high. It is possible to envisage a system where tense affixes are generated freely in the lexicon, e.g., that an English or Norwegian verb stem can be generated in the lexicon with tense inflection taken from any language. So, in the case of American Norwegian hybrid verb forms, how is it possible to ensure that among the maybe fifty or hundred possible tense inflections (possibly belonging to different languages) that a given speaker has in his repertoire, it will turn out that the American Norwegian speaker will select a Norwegian tense inflection to put on a borrowed English verb?

In fact, that can be ensured by adopting a morphological feature which tells what the Matrix Language is in the given instance, in addition to the usual morphological features for tense, etc. In American Norwegian, T belongs to the matrix frame, which is Norwegian. We can therefore assume that T, in addition to the tense feature, also contains a feature <Norwegian>. At the point where the inflected form is LF-moved to T to be checked, only verb forms with features that agree with the corresponding features in T will be licensed. Thus, only English forms with a Norwegian affix, and therefore with the feature <Norwegian> as the highest (and therefore visible) feature, will be able to agree with the corresponding language feature in T. This ensures that the verb ends up as a hybrid form with a Norwegian tense inflection. This analysis is sketched in (8).

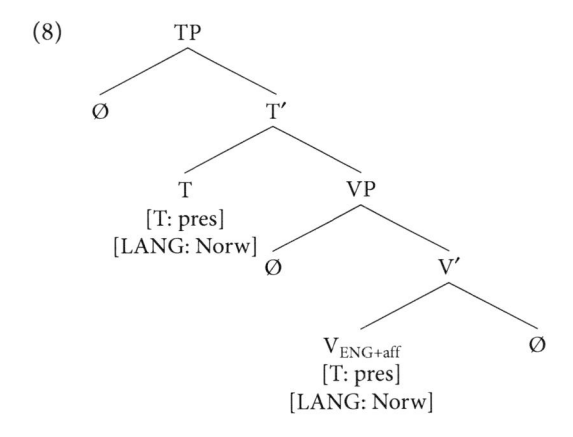

(8)
```
            TP
           /  \
          Ø    T'
              /  \
             T    VP
         [T: pres]  / \
        [LANG: Norw] Ø  V'
                       / \
                  V_{ENG+aff}  Ø
                   [T: pres]
                  [LANG: Norw]
```

If both the tense inflection and the stem are English in a structure like (8), the agreement will fail and the clause will be ungrammatical. This analysis in terms of language features has as a general prediction that a Norwegian grammar frame (i.e., when Norwegian is the Matrix Language) will only license Norwegian inflection on the verb, irrespective of the language of the (borrowed) verb stem. The pattern shown in (4) indicates that this prediction is correct.

Before we take a look at the cost of this analysis, I want to mention briefly another technical possibility for relating T and V. Instead of invisible LF-movement of the verb to T, like I suggested above, one might assume a probe – goal analysis where T is a probe that seeks the verb as its goal (Chomsky 2001). Such an analysis does not assume invisible V-to-T movement, but it still requires that the probe (T) and the goal (V) have matching language features to ensure that the tense inflection of the verb will belong to the same language as the Matrix Language.

What is the cost of adopting an analysis that makes use of language features? First, observe that an analysis in terms of language features manages to 'get the job done.' However, a language feature like <Norwegian> or <English> is not the type of feature that one would expect to be part of the specification of a morphological feature matrix associated with a syntactic structure. The reason is simply that a language feature is not really a morphological feature, but rather a tag for a sociopolitical property. It is the type of 'feature' that one would not expect to be handled by the syntactic checking mechanisms. I therefore assume that language features do not exist in the sense of features that can be checked by the morphological checking mechanisms of language.

To conclude, Chomsky's second take on the T – V relation apparently does not explain the properties of the hybrid verb forms in American Norwegian, and therefore it must be rejected as an analysis of the T – V relation in general, i.e., in UG. Thus, both possibilities proposed by Chomsky (beginning of Section 5) have been rejected as possible candidates for a general UG-based analysis of the T – V relation. What I do in the next section is propose a third type of analysis that, I argue, is able to handle both the hybrid verb forms in American Norwegian as well as the English problem illustrated in (6). The analysis that I'm going to propose relies on root theory and valuation of features.

6. The syntactic relation between T and V: My analysis

I start from an analysis that assumes that a lexeme is a category-neutral root without any inherent morphological features (e.g., Marantz 1997, 2012, Pylkkänen 2008). I refer to this type of analysis as a root analysis. A direct motivation for such an analysis is the existence of a large set of words that can be used as both nouns and verbs. An indication of this word class flexibility is given in (9).

(9) a. noun: (eit) **bad** – verb: ikkje **bad** her.
'a bath.' 'don't take a bath here.'
b. noun: (ein) **mann** – verb: **mann** deg opp!
'a man.' 'pull yourself together.'
c. noun: (ei) **sol** – verb: **sol** deg!
'a sun.' 'sun yourself.'
d. noun: (ein) **buss** – verb: **buss** dei til byen.
'a bus.' 'bus them to town.'
e. noun: (mykje) **mjølk** – verb: **mjølk** denne kua!
'much milk.' 'milk this cow.'
f. noun: (eit) **skriv** – verb: **skriv** brevet straks!
'a note.' 'write the letter at once.'
g. noun: (eit) **telt** – verb: ikkje **telt** her!
'a tent.' 'don't pitch your tent here.

According to the root analysis, word class category and the morphological features of a word are syntactically assigned by the root being syntactically related to the relevant functional categories. Thus, a root becomes a noun by being syntactically related to a nominal functional head (call it *n*), and a root becomes a verb by being syntactically related to a verbal functional head (call it *v*). Pylkkänen (2008: 103) describes the operation that takes place thus: "I will assume that what enters the syntax are category-neutral roots and category-defining functional heads, v (deriving verbs), n (deriving nouns), a (deriving adjectives), and so forth." According to a root analysis, the noun *bad* 'bath' and the verb *bad* 'take a bath' in (9a) are the same element at the lexical root level, but this root is turned into noun by being syntactically related to the functional head n, and to a verb by being related to the functional head v. The relevant structures are sketched in (10) where *R* is used to designate the category-neutral root.

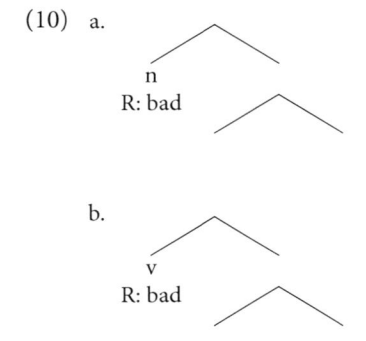

(10) a.

n
R: bad

b.

v
R: bad

The functional heads n and v are in turn syntactically related to higher functional heads which specify the morphological features (inflectional features) that are relevant for the respective word class categories. Both the categorial heads (n, v, …) and the higher functional heads (D, T, …) belong to the grammar matrix or frame of the Matrix Language. Therefore, these heads will always be Norwegian in American Norwegian, i.e., they will contain the properties and features that are relevant for Norwegian.

I use the probe – goal mechanism in my analysis, and furthermore assume valuation of features in a system that operates with valued and unvalued features. For instance, I assume that an inherently valued tense feature under T will value an unvalued tense feature under the categorical functional head v. Note that both T and v are independently motivated categories that belong to the Matrix Language, i.e., Norwegian in the case of American Norwegian. Therefore, tense inflection will always be Norwegian in American Norwegian. On the other hand, a root can in principle be picked from any language, that is from any of the mental lexicons (or lexicon fragments) that the speaker knows. Thus, in the English – Norwegian hybrid verb forms, the root is borrowed from English.

The main point in this analysis is that the generation of the tense inflection is divorced from the generation of the root, and that these two elements are syntactically integrated during the derivation. The analysis is sketched in (11).

(11)   TP
                   / \
                  ∅   T'
                      / \
                T_NORW   vP
                [T: pres] / \
                         ∅   v'
                             / \
                       v_NORW   ∅
                       [T: u]   R: root_ENG
                       (aff)

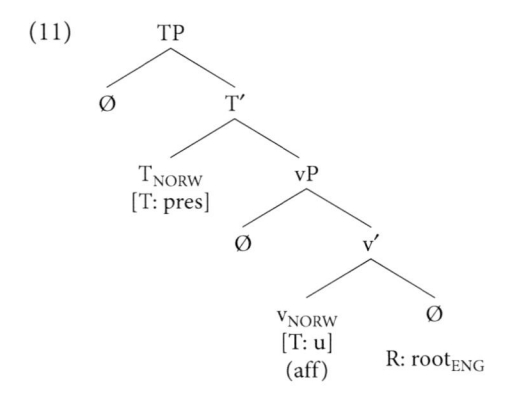

By definition, a root does not contain an inflectional affix, so it is impossible for a root borrowed from English into American Norwegian to get English inflectional morphology. Similarly, it is impossible (in American Norwegian) for a Norwegian root to get English inflectional morphology. Therefore, this analysis predicts that the empirical patterns (4c) and (4d) above are excluded, while (4a) and (4b) are correctly predicted to exist.

How will this analysis make designated language features irrelevant? The functional frame will always belong to the Matrix Language, so for instance T and v only accommodate Norwegian properties and features, and will therefore only permit Norwegian inflectional properties. On the other hand, roots can be borrowed from other languages freely, e.g., from English, and such loans come into the Matrix Language in a prototypical form that is determined in the language that they are borrowed from. Therefore, there is no need for language features on individual lexical items, simply because the language is defined for the whole Matrix Language frame in its entirety, and correspondingly for a whole mental lexicon (or lexicon fragment) in its entirety. Since individual roots or affixes do not need designated language features, such features cannot exist, following minimalist principles.

My analysis permits a root to be borrowed from any mental lexicon (or lexicon fragment) that the speaker may happen to know. It also opens the possibility that new roots may be created spontaneously, thus explaining the existence of so-called 'new words' or nonsense words. My analysis therefore readily predicts the great lexical creativity and flexibility that is in fact encountered in everyday use of language.

How does the analysis proposed above solve the English problem discussed in Section 5 in connection with (6)? Pollock (1989) assumes that sentence adverbials are typically left-adjoined to VP in English, which corresponds to left-adjunction to vP in the structure that I have suggested. The relevant part of the structure of the English example in (6a) is therefore as given in (12).

(12)
```
           TP
          /  \
         Ø    T'
             /  \
            T    vP
         [T: past]
               /  \
              SA   vP
                  /  \
                 Ø    v'
                     /  \
                    v    Ø
                  [T: u]
                   (aff)    R: root
```

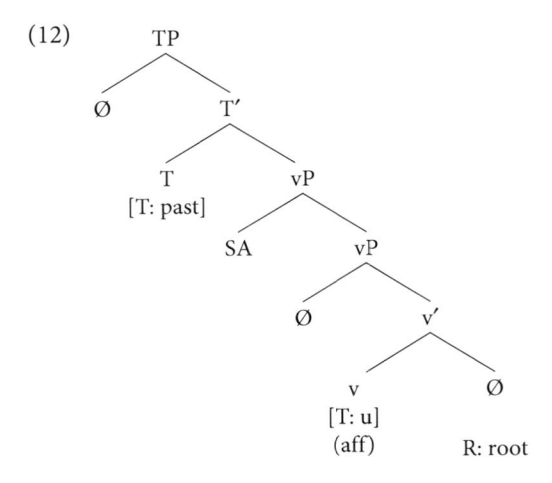

Here the sentence adverbial (SA) is adjoined to vP, as mentioned, and the inherently valued tense feature under T values the unvalued tense feature under v. The root is associated with v and becomes a verb with tense inflection. The adjoined sentence adverbial does not block the valuation process, following standard assumptions. The analysis of the English problem is therefore straightforward on the proposed analysis.

7. Conclusion

If the full tensed verb form is generated in the lexicon, as assumed in Chomsky's second take, there is absolutely no reason to expect that the tense inflection should belong to a language that is different from the language that the verb stem belongs to. On the contrary, one should in fact expect that the stem and inflection belong to the same language, since such a putative generation would take place within one mental lexicon. Hybrid verb forms are therefore clearly unexpected on the assumption that the fully inflected verb form is assembled in the lexicon.

In other words, the existence of the American Norwegian hybrid verb forms discussed here constitutes strong support for the following conclusions: (a) that fully inflected verb forms are not created in the lexicon, and therefore (b) that tense is assigned in the syntax, so that a verb acquires its tense inflection during the syntactic derivation.

Also, I conclude that language features, understood as morphological features that are checked/valued by the mechanisms of narrow syntax, are not required and therefore prohibited in syntax. Thus, any analysis that must assume such features should be discarded, cf. Section 5.

My analysis correctly predicts the empirical patterns given in (4). These patterns are non-trivial and very interesting, not least since they are so clear. Specifically, they show that, hybrid-wise, not any combination of stem and inflection is permitted. My analysis correctly predicts the combinations that are actually found. At the same time, it predicts that extensive borrowing and creation of verb forms take place as a natural part of our everyday use of language, a welcome result given what is in fact encountered in the casual language use.

References

Åfarli, Tor A. 2007. "Do Verbs have Argument Structure?" In *Argument Structure*, ed. by Eric Reuland, Tanmoy Bhattacharya and Giorgos Spathas, 1–16. Amsterdam: Benjamins. DOI: 10.1075/la.108.04afa

Borer, Hagit. 2005. *Structuring Sense*. Vol. I and II. Oxford: Oxford University Press. DOI: 10.1093/acprof:oso/9780199263929.001.0001

Brøseth, Heidi. 2007. *A Neo-Constructional Approach to Computer-Oriented Talk*. Trondheim, Norway: NTNU dissertation.

Chomsky, Noam. 1995. *The Minimalist Program*. Cambridge, MA: MIT Press.

Chomsky, Noam. 2001. "Derivation by Phase." In *Ken Hale. A Life in Language*, ed. by Michael Kenstowicz, 1–52. Cambridge, MA: MIT Press.

Haugen, Einar. 1953. *The Norwegian Language in America: A Study in Bilingual Behavior*. Vol. I and II. Philadelphia: University of Pennsylvania Press.

Hjelde, Arnstein. 1992. *Trøndsk talemål i Amerika*. Trondheim: Tapir forlag.

Holmberg, Anders and Christer Platzack. 1995. *The Role of Inflection in Scandinavian Syntax*. Oxford: Oxford University Press.

Johannessen, Janne B. and Signe Laake. 2011. "Den amerikansk-norske dialekten i Midtvesten." In *Studier i dialektologi och språksociologi. Föredrag vid Nionde nordiska dialektologkonferensen i Uppsala 18–20 augusti 2010. Acta Academiae Regiae Gustavi Adolphi 116*, ed. by Lars-Erik Edlund, Lennart Elmevik and Maj Reinhammar, 177–186. Uppsala: Kungl. Gustav Adolfs Akademien för svensk folkkultur.

Lasnik, Howard. 2000. *Syntactic Structures Revisited. Contemporary Lectures on Classic Transformational Theory*. Cambridge, MA: MIT Press.

Lohndal, Terje. 2012. *Without Specifiers*. College Park, MD: University of Maryland dissertation.

Marantz, Alec. 1997. "No Escape from Syntax: Don't Try Morphological Analysis in the Privacy of Your Own Lexicon." *University of Pennsylvania Working Papers in Linguistics* 4(2): 201–225.

Marantz, Alec. 2012. "Verbal Argument Structure: Events and Participants." *Lingua* 130: 152–168. DOI: 10.1016/j.lingua.2012.10.012

Myers-Scotton, Carol. 1993. *Duelling Languages: Grammatical Structure in Codeswitching*. Oxford: Oxford University Press.

Myers-Scotton, Carol. 2002. *Contact Linguistics: Bilingual Encounters and Grammatical Outcomes*. Oxford: Oxford University Press.

Nygård. Mari. 2013. *Situational Ellipses in Spontaneous Spoken Norwegian: Clausal Architecture and Licensing Conditions*. Trondheim, Norway: NTNU dissertation.

Pfaff, Carol W. 1979. "Constraints on Language Mixing: Intrasentential Code-Switching and Borrowing in Spanish/English." *Language* 55: 291–318. DOI: 10.2307/412586

Pollock, Jean-Yves. 1989. "Verb Movement, UG, and the Structure of IP." *Linguistic Inquiry* 20: 365–424.

Poplack, Shana. 2004. "Code-Switching." In *Soziolinguistik. An International Handbook of the Science of Language* (2nd edn.), ed. by Ulrich Ammon, Norbert Dittmar, Klaus J. Mattheier and Peter Trudgill, 589–596. Berlin: Walter de Gruyter.

Pylkkänen, Liina. 2008. *Introducing Argument*. Cambridge, MA: MIT Press. DOI: 10.7551/mitpress/9780262162548.001.0001

Ramchand, Gillian. 2008. *Verb Meaning and the Lexicon: A First-Phase Syntax*. Cambridge: Cambridge University Press. DOI: 10.1017/CBO9780511486319

Van Hout, Angeliek. 1996. *Event Semantics and Verb Frame Alternations*. Tilburg, Netherlands: Tilburg University dissertation [TILDIL Dissertation Series].

Discourse markers in the narratives of New York Hasidim
More V2 attrition

Zelda Kahan Newman
Lehman College, City University of New York

This paper examines the discourse markers found in the Yiddish narratives of nine Hasidic New York men. It finds one new discourse marker: a grammaticalized use of the word "*shoyn*". Separated intonationally from the two sentences it connects, this new discourse marker helps speakers avoid the subject-verb inversion that marks discoursal continuity in Yiddish. As such, it reinforces a tendency in this community to avoid V2 within a clause and between clauses.

Keywords: discourse markers, V2, grammaticalization

1. Introduction

The informants of this study, the Hasidic speakers of Yiddish in NY, pride themselves on their insularity. They live in a closely-knit community which enforces strict gender division; they adhere to a strict dress code and they maintain their own patterns of religious observance. Because they keep social ties with non-Hasidic Jews as well as non-Jews to a minimum, and are wary of outsiders, their dialect of Yiddish is largely unknown outside their own community.

Assouline (2010: 1–22) and (2014: 163–188) has studied the grammar of Haredi Jerusalemite Yiddish, and the Hebrew sources of Yiddish sermons of ultra-orthodox women, but the former speakers are ideologically as well as geographically different from the informants of this study, and the latter study examines prepared texts, not natural speech. Abugov has studied Yiddish noun plural formation among the children in Kiryat Sanz in Israel, (2014: 9–38), but once again, the informants in Abugov's studies belong to a different group and are exposed to different contact languages than the informants of this study.

Apart from me, only Krogh (2012: 483–506) has studied the language of this community. However, he has not looked at discourse phenomena. What's more, both his work and my own done hitherto have relied on printed texts. And a written language is necessarily different from its spoken counterpart. This paper examines discourse markers in the spoken narratives of nine Hasidic males. I have put recordings as well as phonetic transcriptions of these narratives online in the hope that other researchers will turn to them to study other aspects of the grammar (or phonology) of this community.[1]

2. Dialects of Yiddish

Before the Holocaust, when Europe had millions of native Yiddish speakers, linguists divided the dialects of European Yiddish into three major groups: Northeast Yiddish, Central Yiddish and Southeast Yiddish. These divisions paired geographical areas of Europe with phonological patterns of Yiddish speakers. By the early 21st century, when this study was conducted, the only native Yiddish speakers who were part of a vibrant and growing community were the speakers known as Hasidim. (See also Benor, this volume.) Although these speakers for the most part no longer live in Europe, their vowel patterns still conform to those of their European forebears and these patterns determine their dialect assignment. Some of these Hasidim speak what linguists traditionally called the Northeast dialect, but they are in a minority. The overwhelming majority of New York Hasidim are speakers of what has been called Central Yiddish. But this assignment is based only on their vowel system. This paper deals not with phonology, but with one facet of grammar: the use of Discourse Markers.

3. V2 on three levels

Like all Germanic languages, Yiddish grammar is subject to V2. This rule states that in a declarative sentence, the inflected verb must be in the second position of the main clause. And how can one tell when the second position is to be filled? From a formal syntactic perspective, Weerman (1992: 48) argues that "only one constituent appears in the first position." Proponents of function as an explanatory theory for grammar will say, as Zaretski did, that the first position has been filled when one of the questions who, what, when, where, why, or how, has been addressed (Zaretski 1926: 155–169). Practically speaking, the two approaches are not all that different: each of Zaretski's functional categories is itself one and only one sentence constituent. When that constituent/functional category has been given, the following element of the sentence has to be the inflected verb. In Yiddish, apart from Zarestsky, this rule has been discussed by U. Weinreich (1970: 330–331), Mark (1970: 379–381), Waletzky (1980: 237–315), Kahan Newman (1982: 111–129), Katz (1987: 224–241), Jacobs et al. (1994: 409–411), and Jacobs (2005: 223–226, 262). All of these studies examine the workings of V2 on the sentence level.

---

1. To hear the narratives and see a transcription, go to: www.talkbank.org.

In Yiddish, V2 also operates on the inter-clausal level. This opportunistic use of V2 effectively says: Consider all I have said in the first clause as a topic; what I am telling you now in the following clause is the comment on this topic. Thus, simply by inverting the subject and inflected verb of the second clause, the speaker indicates that the second clause is a subsequence or a consequence of the first clause. For more of this rule on the clausal level, see Taube (2013: 37–46). For example, one can say either:

(1) *Az er kumt arayn, geyt zi aroys*
   As he comes in, goes she out.
   'As soon as he enters, she leaves'

or one can say

(2) *Er kumt arayn, geyt zi aroys,*
   He comes in, goes she out
   'When he enters, she leaves'

The very fact that the second clause begins with an inflected verb is itself an indication of subsequence or consequence; that is why sentence (1) and sentence (2) share a meaning. The adverbial that appears in the sentence-initial position of sentence (1) is, in effect, redundant.

This inversion of subject and inflected verb to indicate subsequence and consequence can extend beyond the clausal level. Calling this phenomenon "consecutive word order," U. Weinreich (1970: 331) gave the following example:

(3) *mayn tate iz geshtorbn, bin ikh geblibn aleyn,*
   My father is(infl vb) died, be(inf vb) I remain alone,
   'My father died, so I remained alone,

   hob ikh ungehoybn tsu arbetn
   have(inf vb) I begun to work
   so I began to work'

Weinreich's example is one of a concatenated, long sentence. Essentially, what he was speaking of is a discoursal phenomenon. In a Yiddish discourse, one need not connect sentential units with adverbs or discourse markers; one can simply rely on subject-verb inversion. The presence of a sentence-initial inflected verb is itself an indication that what follows is a subsequence or consequence of the preceding narrative. This, then, is the third level of V2 in Yiddish, the discoursal level, which this study deals with.

4. The contact situation: English and Yiddish

In English, once the subject of a declarative sentence has been given, the verb must follow; in Yiddish, once the first 'position' has been filled, the inflected verb must follow. Since this sentence-initial position is reserved for a topic in Yiddish, we could reformulate our observation by saying that English is a subject-first language, while Yiddish is a topic-first language. When an element that is not the subject of the sentence is moved to sentence-initial position, linguists say it is topicalized. Along with Prince (1981), Jacobs pointed out (2005: 224): "Topicalization is extremely common in Yiddish, occurring with direct objects, indirect objects, adverbials- thus, almost any constituent fronts to [sentence] initial position, with V-2 [inflected verb in second position] reasserting itself." A well-known passage in the story *Motl Peysi Dem Khazns* (Motl, Peysi the Cantor's Son) by Sholem Rabinovich, known to his readers by the pseudonym of Sholem Aleichem (1944: 34), has the nine year old hero-narrator of the story say with obvious glee:

(4) In   kheyder gey ikh nit; lernen   lern ikh nit;
     In(to) school go I not; to-learn learn I   not,
     '[As for school), I don't go, [as for leaning], I don't learn,

   davenen daven ikh nit; zingen, zing ikh nit; poter   fun altsding.
   to-pray, pray I   not; to-sing, sing I   not; exempt from everything
   [as for praying], I don't pray, [as for singing], I don't sing, I don't have to do anything'

Here we have not only a topicalized sentence-initial prepositional phrase, we also have 3 topicalized verbs (to learn, to pray, to sing). This is a form of topicalization unknown to English. Yet English does have a more limited topicalization operation. Compare the following sentences, the first in English, the second in Yiddish:

(5) a. Him I like, her I don't like.
     b. *Im   glaykh ikh yo; ir   glaykh ikh nisht*
        Him like   I   yes, her   like   I   not
        'I like him, but I don't like her'

As these sentences show, while English, like Yiddish, allows fronting of a non-subject to sentence-initial position, unlike Yiddish, it does not require that the very next element be an inflected verb.

An English Discourse Marker (henceforth DM), placed in sentence-initial position, is no different from other sentence-initial elements; it does not trigger subject-verb inversion. A Yiddish DM, on the other hand, may trigger subject-verb inversion, but it need not do so. In "The Discoursal *iz* of Yiddish" (Kahan Newman 1988), I pointed out that the non-copular *iz* of Yiddish can be used for discourse purposes. This use, which corresponds to Uriel Weinreich's (1968: 34) gloss for *iz*: "so, then, consequently, well, (on resuming a story)," essentially makes *iz* into a DM.[2] The speaker who uses *iz* has lots of wiggle room. (S)he can use *iz* three different ways: the first use,

---

2. Growing up among Central and Southeast Yiddish speakers, I never heard *iz* used as a DM. Even as a child, I knew that when a speaker used *iz* this way, (s)he was not a member of our (Central and Southeastern Yiddish speaking) family.

as an element that does not occupy a place (and as such can even team up sentence-initially with a second DM to make one non-place-holding unit), the second use, as an element that does occupy the first place, and is therefore followed by an inflected verb, or the third use, between sentence-initial material and the inflected verb, where it reinforces the sense that the topic position has indeed been completely filled. An example of the first use (where *iz* joins another DM sentence-initially, and the two together do not occupy a place) is the following sentence:

(6) *Iz, heyst es,   fraytik farn tunkl vern*
So, it's called, Friday before dark becoming
    0   1
'And so, Friday before sundown,

bin ikh ungekumen kayn Yerusholayim
was I   arrived   in   Jerusalem.
        2
I arrived in Jerusalem'

Here the 2 DMs together are assigned place number '0' because they do not occupy a place; it is the time adverbial that follows them that occupies first place, and it triggers the appearance of the inflected verb. Now for an example of the second use, in which the sentence-initial *iz* does trigger the inflected verb. In the following passage taken from a novel by Peretz Markish (1966: 124), two characters are discussing the chances of an armed resistance to the Germans who have occupied their city. Tadeush, one of the men, points out that an entire division of potential soldiers is behind bars. His friend replies:

(7) *Iz darf men efenen dem pavyak, Tadeush*
So, must one open   the jail,   Tadeush
'In that case, Tadeush, we'll have to open the jail'

In sentence (7) *iz* clearly links the sentence it is in with the preceding narrative, and so is immediately followed by the inflected verb. In the third use of *iz* given above, *iz* is placed between the material that occupies the first place of the sentence and the inflected verb of the sentence. In this case, *iz* reinforces the notion that one sentence unit (the topic) has already been filled. Here is an example of this use:

(8) *Mit frishe luft, mit muzik un mit tents   iz*
With fresh air with music and with dance topic
'With fresh air, music and dance,

kon men zey   makhn gezinter
can one them make   healthier
we can make them healthier'

5. Research questions

The analysis of the discoursal *iz* presented above was based on texts purporting to represent NE Yiddish. A natural question that arose in the present study was whether any of the speakers, most of them Central Yiddish speakers, would use the DM *iz*, and if it were used, whether it would be used with inversion, or without inversion. And if it were used with inversion, would it work alone or would it follow other sentence-initial material to reinforce the fact that the topic had indeed been given? Aware as we are that Yiddish can indicate discoursal connectedness with discourse markers (with or without inversion), or with inversion alone, which option is used by these speakers? If the community does have a preference, is the dominant language (one that has its own discourse marking choices) a factor in this community's choice of options?

6. Method

I was contacted by one of the regular attendees of a group called Chulent and asked to speak on a topic relating to Yiddish. Chulent is the name of a group of young men and women, who then gathered regularly on Thursday nights at the Millenary synagogue in Manhattan to listen to music, occasionally listen to a lecture, eat, drink, and mix socially. In Jewish law, Friday begins on Thursday night, and on Friday traditional Jews prepare a dish for the Sabbath (Yiddish *shabes*) known as *chulent*. Because *chulent* was regularly served at the Millenary synagogue on Thursday nights, the meeting itself was dubbed Chulent.

I agreed to speak at Chulent about research I did on an Old Yiddish poem. That was how I informally met some of the young men who regularly showed up there. Once these young men got to know me, they readily agreed to be my informants. I made it clear that whatever they told me about their individual/personal issues was between us. In my research, I discuss their language only. In some cases, they told me which Hasidic group they belonged to; in other cases, they didn't. I didn't press them for personal information. I know from the information that they volunteered that three of the nine informants were brought up in the *Satmar* community, one is from the *Tseylemer* Hasidic community, a close relative to the *Satmar*, and one is a descendant of the Chernobyl (or *Skver*) dynasty.

As a rule, it is difficult, if not impossible, for a female to get male informants in this community. The strict gender division that is the rule for this community does not allow men to speak with women on a one-on-one basis. However, the young men who showed up at Chulent were different. Although they were born into the Hasidic community, their loyalty to the community was wavering. Some still dressed as Hasidic young men are expected to dress; others had already abandoned the community dress code. Some of the young men who attended did so unbeknownst to their families. All who attend Chulent are different from the rest of the insular Hasidic world and open to the outside world.

The informants of this paper are nine young men between the ages of 20–40 who were brought up in Hasidic households and speak Yiddish natively. Having gotten written permission from each of them to put their narratives online, I sat with them in a quiet area and said: "Tell me a story – any story you want." They then launched into a narrative. Some gave me a ready-made anecdote and spoke without hesitation; some retold family stories which had known content but no pre-determined form; some spoke of things that happened to them; still others simply made up a story as they went along.

Table 1. DMs and inversion (+) or (−).

	iz	shoyn	al kol punim/ a punim	bekitser/ akitser	anyway	so	you know
Informant #1	2 (+) 2 (−)	1 (−)					
Informant #2		3 (−)	2 (−)				
Informant #3		3 (−)					
Informant #4		1 (−)					
Informant #5						6 (−)	1 (+) 1 (−)
Informant #6					1 (+) 1 (−)		
Informant #7				3 (+) 3 (−)			
Informant #8							
Informant #9		1 (−)				16 (−)	9 (−)

Table 2. Summary.

Number of DMs + inversion (vb- subj)	7
Number of DMs − inversion (subj- vb)	49
Total number of DMs	56

7. Discussion of the data

7.1 English DMs

Three out of the seven DM tokens in this study are English: *anyway*, *so* and *you know*. For eight of the nine informants, these tend to behave exactly the way a DM behaves in English: they do not 'occupy a place' and consequently, are not followed by subject-verb inversion. Examples of this are: So, *yeder ot zikh genimen lakhn dortn*, So everyone began laughing there, So *ikh el dir geybm di check*, So I will give you the check, Anyway, *kho nisht gehat kan kar demolts*, Anyway I didn't have a car then, Anyway… *ikh zetst mekh arop in khzey nukh alts i shtil*, Anyway, I sit myself down and see all is quiet.

As we will see below, the Yiddish of New York Hasidim can, and does, borrow an English word-order pattern without ever using English at all. But when it does use English DMs, the sentences containing them tend to follow English word-order. Specifically, the English DM is followed by the (Yiddish) subject of the sentence, which is then followed by the (Yiddish) inflected verb. Thus, once the speaker has chosen an English DM, we get the following schema:

English DM	Yiddish Subject	Yiddish verb
1	2	3

Matras (2000: 514) claimed that by preserving the word order of the language from which the discourse marker originates, speakers "simplify their choices." Later, Matras (2009: 155) came up with the following generalization: "The rules of linear ordering which apply in the donor language will accompany grammatical elements borrowed from that language." It is important to be precise here. What we found is consistent with Matras' generalization (not a hard and fast rule) that sentences that begin with English DMs mostly have English word order.

One cannot help noticing the great divergence between informant #9 and the rest of the informants in this corpus. While the others occasionally use English DMs, his narrative is peppered with them. In addition, unlike the other narratives we elicited, his narrative has many examples of code-switching. This might be due to the great divide between him and the other informants. While the other eight young men are second generation native New Yorkers, this young man is a 6th generation native New Yorker: his family arrived in the New World at the turn of the 20th century. Nevertheless, when he does use English DMs, he uses them with Yiddish word order. In his narrative, all 25 of the English DMs 'take up a place' in the sentence, and so are followed by inversion of the (Yiddish) subject and the (Yiddish) inflected verb.

The need to speak of generalizations rather than rules is underscored by another one of our findings. Of the 11 occurrences of English DMs used by our first eight informants, ten are not followed by the inflected verb, but one time the DM *you know* is unexpectedly followed by the inflected verb. Here, then, is a reminder of the need to steer clear of linguistic rules that brook no exception.

Yet another expected finding that emerges from our data is that when there is any borrowing from English (and not all our informants did in fact borrow from English), it tends to be DMs. This has been noted by Brody (1987: 507–532) for Spanish in Mayan languages, by Salmons (1990: 453–480) for English in German-American dialects, and by Maschler (1994: 279–313; 2000: 529–561) for English in Hebrew.

Matras (1998) attributes this "borrowability" to what he calls "pragmatic detachability." DMs, as he sees it, are often not perceived by speakers as genuine borrowing. Unlike content morphemes (which are noted by speaker and hearer alike), these DMs have a pragmatic role in conversation, and hence are discounted by both speaker and hearer. Consequently, they are natural candidates for borrowing. Another one of our expected findings, then, is that English DMs account for nearly half of the DM types in the narratives of these Yiddish speakers.

7.2 The North-east DM *iz*

As we noted earlier, although most Hasidim are CY Yiddish speakers, not all are. Surprisingly, one of the young men at Chulent is a native speaker of the Northeast dialect of Yiddish. This is immediately apparent from the pattern of his vowels. Whereas the other (CY Yiddish) speakers say *zimer* for 'summer,' he says *zumer*. His (NE) *mishpokhe* 'family' is their *mishpukhe*, and while he says *heym* for 'home,' they say *haym*. I did not ask him which of the North-eastern Hasidic groups his family belongs to, and he did not volunteer this information. Aside from his use of NE Yiddish vowels, what sets him apart from the other informants is his use of *iz* as a DM.

As we saw earlier, from everything that is known about *iz*, the speaker who uses it sentence-initially, has the option to allow it a place, and so have it followed by the inflected verb, or not allow it a place, and so have it followed by the subject of the sentence. Our data follows this pattern exactly: of this speaker's 4 uses of *iz*, two are followed by the inflected verb, and two are followed by the subject of the sentence. Here are his four sentences:

(9) *Letste zumer   iz-   bin   ikh geveyn in der heym*
    Last summer is (topic) was (ifl. vb.) I   been   in the house
    'Last summer, I was at home'

On the second occasion when this informant uses *iz*, he again places it between the sentence-initial material and the inflected verb, and so highlights the fact that the topic has been given:

(10) *Kh'gehat a -mayn bester khaver, mayn bester fraynt iz -*
     I had a-   my   best friend, my   best friend **topic**
     'I had a friend, a best friend,-[so]'

     hob   ikh im   geshikt a nakhrikht…
     have (inf vb.) I to-him sent   a message'
     'I sent him a message'

Both sentences (9) and (10) follow the third usage discussed earlier, where the topic-marker *iz* is followed by the inflected verb of the sentence.

However, there are two occurrences in the same narrative when the same speaker uses this *iz* without inverting subject and verb:

(11) *Iz s'kumt   dray   azeyger in der fri*
     So it-comes three o'clock in the morning…
     'So at three in the morning …'

The [s] of *s'kumt* in sentence (11) is the vestigial part of the dummy subject *es/it*. The *iz* in sentence (11) does not 'occupy a place.' Like sentence adverbials, this element is simply ignored by the putative 'place counter.' Accordingly, the next element in the sentence is the (dummy) subject of the sentence. In this informant's fourth use of *iz*, we find two independent clauses, connected by *iz*. In his case, *iz* clearly has the meaning of 'and so,' and once again, there is no subject-verb inversion:

(12) kh'hob gevolt   er zol   geyn oyvn   shlofn,   iz
     I-have wanted he should go upstairs to-sleep   **is**
     'I wanted him to go upstairs to sleep, ***and so***

   kh'hob im geshribn   in a nakhrikht   az…
   I-have to-him written in a message   that…
   I wrote him in a message that…'

Sentences (11) and (12) follow the first usage of *iz* discussed earlier: they use an *iz* that does not 'occupy a place' and so is followed by the subject of the sentence. This speaker, too, follows an expected pattern.

7.3   Central Yiddish DMs: Yiddish compared to English

Among the CY speakers at Chulent, we found three Yiddish DMs: (1) *al kol punim* and *a punim* 'in any case,' (2) *bekitser* and/or *akitser* 'in short,' and (3) *shoyn* 'already.' This last DM exhibits unexpected properties, and so will be discussed in the upcoming section. Not surprisingly, one of the speakers who uses the Yiddish DM *akitser* uses it three times followed by inversion and three times not followed by inversion. Similarly, one of the speakers uses the English DM a*nyway*, sometimes with inversion and sometimes without, and one speaker uses *you know*, sometimes with inversion and sometimes without. This is another one of the expected findings in this study. The fact that both English and Yiddish DMs used by one and the same speaker are occasionally followed by inversion and occasionally not followed by inversion may indicate a phenomenon in flux. Alternatively, it may be that at any one time, the speaker has the option to accord a DM the weight of occupying a place, thereby indicating that (s)he has completed the topic, or alternatively, using the DM as a place marker, a low-on-content element that simply indicates (s)he plans to continue the narrative, but has not yet organized the coming material.

7.4   The innovative DM: Shoyn

The most common Yiddish DM encountered in the narratives of these young men, *shoyn*, was found nine times in the speech of six different informants. It is *shoyn* that is the innovative DM of this corpus. Schematically, the discourses with *shoyn* in them look like this:

Proposition X	*shoyn*	Proposition Y
1	2	3

In each of the cases, the two propositions on either side of *shoyn* are full sentences that end with a sentence-final tonal drop in voice. This is one way that *shoyn* differs from the other DMs in this corpus: all the other DMS are intonationally integrated into the sentences they are found in. *Shoyn*, on the other hand, is left intonationally outside of the sentences it connects. For all that *shoyn* is accorded a sentence-intonation all its own and is not itself a part of either of the sentences it connects, it nevertheless does participate in the semantics of the discourse. Let us examine each of the nine occurrences of this *shoyn* to see exactly how it functions.

7.4.1   As an indicator of a change in illocutionary force

Of all the uses of *shoyn* in this corpus, this first is the most intuitive. After all, the dictionary definition that U. Weinreich gives of *shoyn* in its use within the verbal phrase is "already," and *un shoyn* means "and that's all" (1968: 397). Thus, when used in this corpus before a question, or after it, in anticipation of an answer, or as an answer, *shoyn* can be seen as reinforcing the expected change in the nature of the discourse that has just given and/or the nature of the discourse that will follow:

(13)   *er hot arosgeshlankt fin bes medresh.*
He has   slunk-out from study-hall.
'He slunk out of the study hall.

Shoyn. *Vi gayt men*
Shoyn. Where goes one
[**And now the question**]. Where does a Jew go

a me ken nisht gayn   in bes medresh,   a yid, vi gayt men?
if one cannot go   in[to] (the) study-hall, a Jew, where goes one
if he cannot go to the study-hall, where does he go?'

In sentence (13) the DM *shoyn* lets us know we have finished with a declarative sentence and are about to get an interrogative sentence. The very next sentence in this narrative affords us another look at this same use: *shoyn* that signals a change in the illocutionary force of a sentence in the discourse. Immediately after the question above, we get this second *shoyn*:

(14)   *A yid, vi gayt a yid?*   **Shoyn.**   *Er gayt*
A Jew, where goes a Jew?   **Shoyn.**   He goes
'And as for a Jew, where does he go? [**My answer**] He goes

in   gast hoz…
in(to a) guest house
to a guest-house'

As in sentence (13), the *shoyn* of sentence (14) is at the border of two different kinds of sentences: a question and its answer. This DM, then, simply reinforces what the hearer knows in any case: that the narrative has switched to a sentence with a new illocutionary force.

7.4.2 As an indicator of a counterfactual

In this corpus there is only one case of *shoyn* used with a rising tone. Because the following sentence begins with a lowered tone, it is my understanding that the rise-fall created by these two tones is meant to do what the rise-fall tonal combination in Yiddish generally does: indicate a counterfactual situation (Kahan Newman 2000: 314–316, 328–330).[3] This is borne out, I believe by the sense of the discourse in question. Before we give this third example, we need to give a bit of the context of the narrative. The grandmother of the speaker wandered all over the globe during WWII and has finally arrived in New York. She has her family with her, and she intends to enter the subway with them. However, as it happens, she enters the subway car, but they do not; she realizes as the doors close, that she has left them behind. And here the narrative is: "*Reboyne shel oylem d'host mekh gefirt of di gantse velt, in du vel ikh farloyren vern?!*" 'Lord of the Universe, you led me all over the world, and **here** will I get lost?!' And here the narrator continues:

(15) *Iz zi   ungekimen of di   golden   medine.*   **Shoyn**
      Is she arrived   in the golden land.   **Shoyn**
      'So she arrived in the Golden Land.   **Despite what you'd think,**

   Zi   iz arof of di   nekste treyn...
   She is up-on the next train...
   she got on the next train'

The narrative interpreted: She was in the Golden Land [the US in general, NY in particular]. You might think all was well, but it was not. (All this given by *shoyn*.) She got on the next train.... .

7.4.3 To mean 'and so'

Of all the uses of *shoyn* in this corpus, this use is the one least tied to the dictionary entry for *shoyn*. According to the dictionary, *shoyn* means 'already/finally' and it conveys a sense of finality in its standard use as a modal within the verb phrase. However, as a DM in this corpus, *shoyn* definitely conveys a sense of continuity. In 6 of 9 occurrences, *shoyn* is best translated as 'and so':

(16) *S'kumt   dray azeyger in der fri.*   **Shoyn.** *Mayn tate   geyt shoyn shlofn.*
      It comes 3   o'clock in the morning.   **Shoyn.** My   father goes finally to sleep.
      'Three AM arrives, **and so** my father finally goes to sleep'

---

3. For the intonation pattern for counterfactuals in spoken Yiddish, as opposed to texts, see 314–16 and 328–330. Since this is the only case of the DM *shoyn* used in this way, I am ready to admit that more evidence is needed before this case is made for certain. I would hope that future researchers will be on the look-out for this rising-toned *shoyn* so that we can be certain if there is indeed a pattern here.

(17) in 'vayisuyi':   me furt vayter. **Shoyn.**
"And 'they traveled' [Biblical Hebrew]": one travels on. **Shoyn.**
'And [as it says in the Bible:] 'they traveled.' One travels on. **And so,**

Kayn probleym nisht.
No   problem not.
there was no problem'

(18) *Gayt nisht dorekh kmat a mes les vus a   shadkhn*
Goes not   by   almost a 24 hour period [during] which a matchmaker
'Hardly a day goes by without a matchmaker

zol   mir nisht upshteln in   veln   matsi'a zan   a shidekh. **Shoyn**
should me   not   stop   and want to   offer a match. **Shoyn.**
stopping me and wanting to offer me a match. **And so,**

Ikn bin shoyn   tsigevoynt tse dem
I   am already used   to that
I am used to it'

(19) *Kh'hob zay   genik   in bore park.* **Shoyn.** *Ikh hob   probirt dus beste zikh*
I have them enough in Boro Park. **Shoyn.** I   have tried   the best reflexive to
'I have enough [matchmakers] in Boro Park. **And so**, I did the best I could

arosdrayen fin   ir.
slip out   from her
to get out from under her [grip]'

(20) *Zi   vil   zikh   trefn   mit mir, di parsishe shadkhnte.* **Shoyn.**
She wants (reflex.) to meet with me, the Persian matchmaker. **Shoyn**
'She, the Persian matchmaker, wants to meet up with me. **And so,**

Kh'hob zikh   getrofn mit ir
I have reflexive met   with her
I met up with her'

Our last example needs a bit of comment before it is given. Of all the narratives in this corpus, the one in which this example is found is the most coherent and least interrupted. The speaker clearly had this story ready-made. He never hesitated in his delivery, and the structure he uses is as good as it would be had the narrative been written instead of spoken. The story consists of eighteen clauses, and the DM *shoyn* is found smack in the middle: between the ninth and the tenth clause. The speaker introduces the main character of his story, one *badkhn* 'a joker' in the first sentence. After this character is introduced, every major development in the narrative is signaled by inversion. Put differently, this speaker conveys subsequence and consequence in this narrative by inverting the subject and its inflected verb fourteen (!) times in a narrative that lasts fourteen lines. Midway in this narrative we find *shoyn*:

(21) Ot er gevolt bigln mitn bigl-azn. **Shoyn.**
Have he wanted to iron with the iron. **Shoyn.**
'So he wanted to iron [his shirt] with the iron. **And so,**

Er ot gehaltn di bigl-azn in di hent
He has held the iron in his hands
he held the iron in his hands...'

The DM *shoyn* is innovative in yet another way. The other DMs, Yiddish and English alike, are sometimes followed by inversion and sometimes not followed by inversion. Unlike them, *shoyn* is **never** followed by inversion. Indeed, the very reason *shoyn* is kept intonationally aloof from the two sentences it connects, I contend, is so that the sentence that follows it can have subject-verb word order, in line with the preferred word-order pattern of English.

We noted earlier that the cohesive tie suggested by *shoyn* is merely suggested by the speaker. Its exact meaning needs to be inferred by the hearer. This is precisely what Blakemore noted (1989:232) when she said "even when two sentences are related by a cohesive [Discourse Marker] tie, hearers have to go beyond the linguistic resources in order to recover an interpretation."

Looking at the check-list that Jucker and Ziv (1998:3) reviewed for pragmatic markers, we see that some of the features they mention are shared by all the DMs in our data, but in some cases, *shoyn* is a clear exception to the general rule.

7.4.3.1 *Phonological and lexical features.* Markers are short and phonologically reduced. While we found this in some of the Yiddish DMs (Recall *apunim* for *al kol punim* and *akitser* for *be-kitser*), we did not find this to be true for the relatively new DM: *shoyn*. Nevertheless, phonological reduction may be expected in time. Markers form a separate tonal group. Here the innovation in our data is exceptional among known DMs in that *shoyn* not only forms a separate tonal group; it also exists in total tonal isolation from the sentences it supposedly connects. Markers are marginal, and hence difficult to place in traditional word classes. This is certainly true of *shoyn*. While it is ordinarily a modal, in its use as a DM, it is most certainly not a modal.

7.4.3.2 *Syntactic features.* Markers are, according to this understanding, restricted to sentence-initial position. While they are generally either outside sentence structures or only loosely attached to sentence structure, they are tonally a part of some sentence. Here is where *shoyn* is truly unique. *Shoyn* stands alone tonally and is simply detached from sentences it connects. Markers are optional. Indeed this is the case in our corpus.

7.4.3.3 *Semantic features.* Markers have little or no propositional meaning. This is especially true of the innovative *shoyn* found in our corpus. Markers are multifunctional. Moreover, they operate on several linguistic levels simultaneously.

7.4.3.4 *Sociolinguistic and stylistic features.* Markers are a feature of oral, rather than written discourse. This is why there is no mention of *shoyn* in the linguistic literature. Those who study the written texts of this community simply have not encountered *shoyn*; it is simply not found in written discourse. Markers appear with high frequency. Interestingly, of all the DMs in our corpus, it is the innovative one, *shoyn*, that is most common among our informants. Markers are stylistically stigmatized. This explains why the innovative DM in our corpus, *shoyn*, has not appeared in a written corpus. Markers are often gender specific. This community is known for its gender strict separation; the language patterns of men may well not be the same as those of women. A follow-up to this study would be the examination of DMs among Hasidic women. That remains to be done.

8. Conclusions and explanations

One of the research questions we posed was whether these speakers combine their DMs with inversion. A second question we posed was whether the contact language of the community in any way affects the way this community uses DMs. Finally, we asked whether this community relies at all on inversion alone to convey discourse connectedness. We are now in a position to answer all these questions. The answer to our first question is that while both the English and the standard Yiddish DMs are used both with and without inversion, the new DM that has emerged among these speakers, *shoyn*, is placed where it is in the discourse so that it obviates the need for inversion. The answer to our second question is that it is indeed the nature of English word order that is at work here: once *shoyn* is used, the Yiddish sentence that follows can and does have its subject (not its topic) trigger the inflected verb.

What has happened to *shoyn*, I contend, is that it has undergone grammaticalization. A grammaticalized element is one that has undergone semantic bleaching and is no longer a part of the syntactic category that it belongs to in its standard usage. As such, the non-copular DM *iz* is also a grammaticalized element. As a grammaticalized element, *iz* does not mean '(s)he is,' and it is not part of the verb phrase. Similarly, when grammaticalized, *shoyn* does not mean 'already' and it is not part of the sentence's verb phrase.

Of the four parameters of grammaticalization listed by Heine and Kuteva (2005: 15), three apply to the NE DM *iz* as well as to the CY DM *shoyn*:

a. Extension: The copular *iz* that means '(s)he is' in Standard Yiddish comes to mean 'and so,' while the modal *shoyn*, whose standard meaning is 'already/finally,' is generally also reinterpreted to mean 'and so' when it occurs between two sentences of a discourse.
b. Desemanticization: Also called 'semantic bleaching,' this parameter suggests there is a loss of conventional meaning. Clearly, this is what has happened to both *iz* and *shoyn*. As DMs, they no longer have the meaning(s) they had when they appeared within a verb-phrase. Indeed, like its NE counterpart *iz*, the DM *shoyn* is almost devoid of meaning.

c. Decategorialization: When the DMs *iz* and *shoyn* occur in a discourse, they are not members of the verb-phrase, and it is not subject to the constraints of elements in a verb phrase.

The fourth parameter, phonetic erosion, did not occur with *iz* and has not (yet) occurred with *shoyn*. If indeed, this is the sort of contact-induced grammaticalized element that Heine and Kuteva speak of, a reasonable prediction is that, in time, this *shoyn* will become phonetically reduced.

But unlike its NE counterpart *iz*, the grammaticalized DM *shoyn* is contact-induced: it is the contact language, English, that is responsible for the quirk of this DM. Most DMs are found in the sentence-initial position of an utterance. At the very least, they participate in the intonational structure of the sentence they are in. But in the narratives of these young men, *shoyn* is **not** a part of any sentence at all; it stands between 2 sentences and is a part of neither of them. *Shoyn* stays within its own sentence boundary, it seems, so that the following sentence can have English, rather than Standard Yiddish, word order.

Heine and Kuteva suggest (2005:61) that "it is the word-order arrangement that is present in the model language [the pragmatically dominant language: here English- ZKN] that bilingual speakers of the replica language [the native, but less practical language- Yiddish – ZKN] tend to select, thereby narrowing down the range of syntactic options open to them." Clearly, the Hasidic young men in our study have narrowed their word-order options by using the innovative DM, *shoyn*.

Heine and Kuteva suggested (2005:97) that the creation of what they call "text markers" (our DMs) is an area "that has not been studied in great detail." They went on to say (ibid) that "there are a few findings that suggest the way texts, in particular narrative texts, are organized, is determined, to some extent, by grammaticalization. Paradigm cases concern markers of boundaries, in particular, the beginning and the end of a text, significant units within the text, such as paragraphs and topic change, but also of continuity of narrative discourse. There is a not uncommon pattern whereby transparent expressions such as clausal propositions are grammaticalized to markers of text organization." This study, then, constitutes one more example of the grammaticalization of a modal particle and its transformation into a marker of textual organization.

8.1 V2 attrition on all three fronts

The final, seemingly ancillary, research question was whether inversion alone is used to convey the notion of consequence or subsequence on the discourse level in this corpus. The answer to this question, it turns out, brings us back to the beginning of this paper. I noted that according to the rules of Standard Yiddish, V2 applies on three levels: on the sentence level within one clause, inter-clausally and within a discourse. The data of this study has shown that in order to align their Yiddish with their English, these speakers choose a DM that will allow them to avoid V2 on the discourse level. But this tendency to be more like English and avoid subject-verb inversion after the topic has been given is taking place on more than one front in this community. Some of the other evidence for this shift can be found in the data of this corpus.

Recall that in Standard Yiddish, sentence-initial time adverbials, locative adverbials and sentence adverbials occupy the first place of a sentence. Since this place is the place accorded to a topic in Yiddish, according to the rule of Standard Yiddish, these sentence-initial elements must be followed by the inflected verb of the sentence. However, the speakers of this corpus do not always invert subject and verb after adverbials. What follows is the data on non-inversion after adverbials in this corpus:

Table 3. Non inversion.

	After a time adverbial	After a locative adverbial	After a sentence adverbial
Informant #1	1		
Informant #2	1		
Informant #3	3	1	
Informant #4	–		
Informant #5	1		1
Informant #6	1		
Informant #7	–		
Informant #8	–		
Informant #9	1	2	1

Table 3 shows us that this group is slowly moving away from V2 within a clause. More commonly after a time adverbial, less commonly after a locative adverbial and still less commonly after a sentence adverbial, there simply is no inversion, despite what the Standard rule predicts.

We have data from the Satmar Hasidic community, albeit from women and girls, and not from young men, of non-inversion across clausal boundaries within the same sentence.[4] As it happens, we did not encounter this sort of cross-clausal non-inversion in the present corpus. Nevertheless, it is worth our while to consider the data obtained from interviews conducted among the Satmar women and their daughters. They, too, speak Hasidic Yiddish, and they, too, are subjected to the pressures of the English that surrounds them.

The following data were obtained when the informants were shown two photos. The first was of a young girl exiting her house while her younger brother (whose pants were wet) entered it, and the second showed the two children exiting the house together. The informants were asked to complete a half-sentence begun by the researcher. In the first case, they were asked to complete the half-sentence: *Az er geyt*

---

4. This is data from an unpublished study that I did 8 years ago.

arayn, _____ 'When he goes inside, _____.' In the second case, they were asked to complete the half-sentence, *Ven er kimt aroys*, _____ 'When he comes out, _____.' It was of no consequence to the researcher which verb they chose; what mattered was whether they chose an inflected verb or a subject noun to complete their half-sentence.

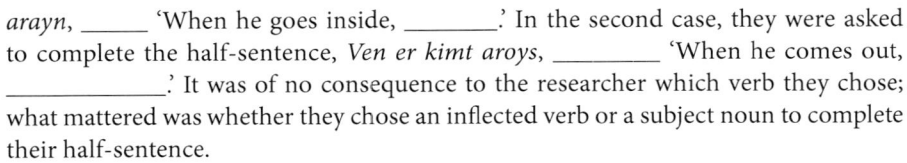

Standard Yiddish demands that the second clause of such sentences begin with an inflected verb. In these cases, the first, dependent, clause, serves as the topic, so to speak, of the second, independent clause. Accordingly, that second clause needs to begin with an inflected verb. As we see in Table 4, the younger Yiddish speakers are moving away from Standard Yiddish and conforming more to the Standard English norm.[5]

Table 4. Inter-clausal non-inversion.

	Satmar mothers	Satmar daughters
Clausal Consequence ([az])	1/11	4/10
Clausal Subsequence ([ven])	1/11	5/10

By now we have seen non-inversion in Hasidic New York Yiddish within a clause (Table 3, based on findings in the present corpus) and inter-clausally within one sentence (Table 4, based on the speech of Hasidic women and their daughters). Our findings for the use of *shoyn*, used as a DM, have shown that non-inversion between sentences of a discourse also occurs in this population. The use of *shoyn* forestalls this option:

Table 5. Only inversion for subsequence and/or consequence.

Informant #1	4 times
Informant #2	14 times
Informant #3	4 times
Informant #4	5 times
Informant #5	19 times
Informant #6	7 times
Informant #7	5 times
Informant #8	6 times
Informant #9	6 times

Table 5 shows the frequency with which inversion alone is used sentence-initially in the present corpus. On the discourse level, this inversion is an option, not a rule-bound requirement. Nevertheless, we note that two of the nine informants (informant #2 and informant #5) account for more than half (33/50) of the cases of inversion

---

5. One of the mothers was also a daughter. This explains the apparent discrepancy in informant numbers.

found in this corpus; seven of the remaining informants use inversion infrequently. What we have, then, is not a rule, but it is a trend: most of these speakers steer away from using inversion alone to convey subsequence and/or consequence in a discourse.

In all three cases, then, within a clause, across clauses but within one sentence, and between sentences within a discourse, Yiddish, because of its topic-first nature, either demands or allows for inversion. In all of these three cases, English, a subject-first language, does not have inversion. Hasidic New York Yiddish, subjected as it is to the pressures of English, is moving away from the Yiddish norm, and towards the English norm. To be sure, this is a slow process, but the indications of syntactic change and the increasing conformity of this community to English norms are evident.

References

Abugov, Netta and Dorit Ravid. 2014. "Noun Plurals in Israeli Hasidic Yiddish: A Psycholinguistic Perspective." In *Yiddish Language Structures*, ed. by Marion Aptroot and Bjorn Hansen. Berlin: De Gruyter Mouton.

Assouline, Dalit. 2010. "The Emergence of Two First Person Plural Pronouns in Haredi Jerusalemite Yiddish." *Journal of Germanic Linguistics* 22(1): 1–22. DOI: 10.1017/S1470542709990183

Assouline, Dalit. 2014. "Veiling Knowledge: Hebrew Sources in the Yiddish Sermons of Ultra-Orthodox Women." *International Journal of the Sociology of Language* 226: 163–188.

Benor, Sarah Bunin. This volume. "How *synagogues* Became *shuls*: The Boomerang Effect in Yiddish-Influenced English."

Blakemore, Diane. 1989. "Denial and Contrast: A Relevance Theoretic Analysis of *but*." *Linguistics and Philosophy* 12: 15–37. DOI: 10.1007/BF00627397

Brody, Jill. 1987. "Particles Borrowed from Spanish as Discourse Markers in Mayan Languages." *Anthropological Linguistics* 29(4): 507–521.

Fuller, Janet. 2006. "The Principle of Pragmatic Detachability in Borrowing: English-Origin Discourse Markers in Pennsylvania German." *Linguistics* 39(2): 351–369.

Heine, Bernd and Tania Kuteva. 2005. *Language Contact and Grammatical Change*. New York: Cambridge University Press. DOI: 10.1017/CBO9780511614132

Jacobs, Neil, Ellen Prince and Johan van der Auwera. 1994. "Yiddish." In *The Germanic Languages*, ed. by Ekkehard König and Johan van der Auwera, 409–411. New York: Routledge.

Jacobs, Neil. 2005. *Yiddish*. New York: Cambridge University Press.

Jucker, Andreas and Yael Ziv. 1998. *Discourse Markers: Descriptions and Theory*. Amsterdam: John Benjamins. DOI: 10.1075/pbns.57

Kahan Newman, Zelda. 1982. *An Annotation of Aizik Zaretski's Praktishe Yidishe Gramatik*. Ann Arbor, MI: University of Michigan dissertation.

Kahan Newman, Zelda. 1988. "The Discoursal *iz* of Yiddish." In *The Prague School and Its Legacy*, ed. by Tobin Yishai. Amsterdam: John Benjamins. DOI: 10.1075/llsee.27.09kah

Kahan Newman, Zelda. 2000. "The Jewish Sound of Speech: Talmudic Chant, Yiddish Intonation and the Origins of Early Ashkenaz." *Jewish Quarterly Review* 90: 293–336. DOI: 10.2307/1454758

Katz, Dovid. 1987. *Grammar of the Yiddish Language*. London: Duckworth.

Krogh, Steffen. 2012. "How Satmarish is Haredi Satmar Yiddish?" In *Yiddish Studies Today*, ed. by Marion Aptroot, Efrat Gal-Ed, Roland Gruschka and Simon Neuberg, 483–506. Düsseldorf: Düsseldorf University Press.

Mark, Yudel. 1970. *Gramatik fun der Yidisher Klal Shprakh*. New York: Alveltlikher Yidisher Kultur Kongres.

Markish, Peretz. 1966. *Trot fun Doyres*. Moscow: Sovyetski Pisatyel.

Maschler, Yael. 1994. "Metalanguaging and Discourse Markers in Bilingual Conversation." *Language in Society* 23(3): 325–366. DOI: 10.1017/S0047404500018017

Maschler, Yael. 2000. "Discourse Markers in Hebrew English Bilingual Conversation Twelve Years Later." *International Journal of Bilingualism* 4(4): 529–61. DOI: 10.1177/13670069000040040801

Matras, Yaron. 1998. "Utterance Modifiers and Universals of Grammatical Borrowing." *Linguistics* 36(2): 281–331. DOI: 10.1515/ling.1998.36.2.281

Matras, Yaron. 2000. "Fusion and the Cognitive Basis for Bilingual Discourse Markers." *International Journal of Bilingualism* 4(4): 505–528. DOI: 10.1177/13670069000040040701

Matras, Yaron. 2009. *Language Contact*. New York: Cambridge University Press. DOI: 10.1017/CBO9780511809873

Prince, Ellen. 1981. "Topicalization, Focus-Movement, and Yiddish-Movement: A Pragmatic Differentiation." *Proceedings of the Seventh Annual Meeting of the Berkeley Linguistics Society (BLS 7)*: 249–264.

Rabinovich, Sholem. 1944. *Motl Peysi dem Khazns*. New York: Hebrew Publishing Company.

Salmons, Joseph. 1900. "Bilingual Discourse Marking: Code Switching, Borrowing, and Convergence in some German-American Dialects." *Linguistics* 28: 453–480.

Taube, Moshe. 2013. "Kemo-Subordinatsye in Yidish: Narative az- zatsn. [Pseudo-Subordination in Yiddish: Narrative Az-Clauses]." In *Studies in Ashkenazi Culture, Women's History, and the Languages of the Jews*, ed. by Israel Bartal, Galit Hasan-Rokem, Ada Rapoport-Albert, Claudia Rosenzweig, Vicky Shifriss and Erika Timm, 37–46. Jerusalem: Hebrew University Press.

Waletzky, Joshua. 1980. "Topicalization in Yiddish." In *The Field of Yiddish: Studies in Language, Folklore and Literature*. 4th collection, ed. by Marvin Herzog, Barbara Kirshenblatt-Gimblett, Dan Miron and Ruth Wisse, 237–315. Philadelphia: Institute for the Study of Human Issues.

Weerman, Fred. 1992. *The V2 Conspiracy: A Synchronic and a Diachronic Analysis of Verbal Positions in Germanic Languages*. Berlin: De Gruyter Mouton.

Weinreich, Uriel. 1968. *Modern English-Yiddish Yiddish-English Dictionary*. New York: McGraw Hill.

Weinreich, Uriel. 1970. *College Yiddish*. Sixth Printing. New York: YIVO Institute for Jewish Research.

Zaretski, Aizik. 1926. *Praktishe Yidishe Gramatik*. Moscow: Shul un Bukh.

PART IV

Lexical change

Maintaining a multilingual repertoire
Lexical change in American Norwegian

Lucas Annear and Kristin Speth
University of Wisconsin–Madison

This paper examines change in the lexicon of American Norwegian by investigating phonemic, semantic and lexical transfer from American English into the heritage Norwegian of the American Midwest. We observe these types of transfer when the semantic structure, phonemic structure, or both, are transferred from English to the heritage variety. Drawing on Matras' (2009) insight that languages converge as a result of the need to simplify the selection procedure, we expect lexical transfer (involving both semantic and phonemic structure) to be the most abundant of these three phenomena as it provides more convergence (simplification). Our findings support this hypothesis and corroborate those of Haugen (1953), showing that lexical transfer is the most common route of convergence in American Norwegian.

Keywords: lexical transfer, semantic transfer, phonemic transfer, heritage language, American Norwegian, multilingual repertoire

1. Introduction

This paper examines how the lexicon of the heritage Norwegian as spoken in America (hereafter 'American Norwegian') has been changed as a result of contact with local American English.[1] As early as the 1850s, it was noted that Norwegian immigrants to America spoke a sort of Americanized Norwegian: "The language of the Norwegians over there [America] is famous. They make haste to mix it with English, and the more they can mix the language, the better" (cited in Haugen 1953: 54). This paper picks up the trail of 'Americanized' Norwegian sixty years after Haugen's writing, while

---

1. We use the definition of "heritage language" given by Rothman (2009: 156): "A language qualifies as a *heritage language* if it is a language spoken at home or otherwise readily available to young children, and crucially this language is not a dominant language of the larger (national) society."

taking into account more recent work on the lexicon, such as Hjelde (1992) and Johannessen and Laake (2012, forthcoming). Through an examination of Norwegian spoken by 16 heritage speakers in the American Midwest, we test a claim inferred from Matras (2009): that languages in contact will create as much overlap in their respective lexicons as possible, as a means of coping with the need to maintain a multilingual repertoire. We hypothesize that because lexical transfer (often called 'borrowing') entails the most overlap (both phonemic and semantic), it will be the preferred method of creating overlap. We quantify the occurrence of various language contact phenomena (i.e., coping strategies) with data from heritage speakers of American Norwegian, and see that our theory holds – Norwegian in America has undergone changes favoring full overlap in lexical structure over partial overlap. That is, change is most often in favor of lexical transfer (wholesale borrowing of phonemic and semantic structures) over either phonemic or semantic transfer alone. This preference is most likely due to language acquisition in a bilingual area with no stark cultural differences. While our findings cannot be generalized to other contact situations, our results help explain ever-present language contact phenomena and speakers' language coping strategies.

Part 2 of this paper outlines and defines the language contact phenomena discussed and how these coping strategies vary in terms of amount of overlap they create. Part 3 provides the theoretical background which motivates our test and in which we frame our argument. Part 4 tests this claim using data from American heritage speakers of Norwegian. Results are discussed in Part 5, and concluding thoughts in Part 6.

2. Background

This paper discusses the results of language contact, a situation in which the outcomes are very much dependent on social factors. So, rather than discuss contact phenomena in a vacuum, we take Sankoff's advice about situating "any discussion of the results of language contact within a sociohistorical perspective that considers the historical forces that have led to language contact" (2001:640). Therefore, in addition to background literature and the language contact theory that forms our point of departure, we also provide background on the types of language contact phenomena found in various language contact situations. We go on to describe the social situation of Norwegian in America and of our speakers.

2.1 Theoretical background

The vast majority of language contact phenomena have in common that they create similarity between two or more languages.[2] This fact underpins much of the scholarship on language contact. Romaine writes that "convergence, interference, and borrowing all have as their linguistic outcome an increase in the similarity between two or more linguistic systems" (1995:75). Beniak, Mougeon and Valois describe convergence as the gradual elimination of non-congruent forms in languages in contact (1984:73, cited in Romaine 1995). Similarly, Matras writes that "borrowing is viewed as a form of levelling of structures across the multilingual repertoire, with the outcome that a single structure is employed, irrespective of interaction context and so irrespective of choice of 'language'" (2009:7).[3]

Matras (2009:151) suggests cognitive motivation for the structural borrowing that creates similarity between languages where there previously was either less or none. This motivation is based on evidence that there is a selection process for choosing context-appropriate forms from a speaker's multilingual repertoire, a process that begins during language acquisition and continues on throughout a speaker's lifetime (2009:16). Regarding this cognitive motivation Matras writes:

> ...the bilingual speaker faces the challenge of maintaining control over the language processing mechanism that enables selection of context-appropriate structures within the repertoire and inhibition of those that are not appropriate. There is pressure on the bilingual to simplify the selection procedure by reducing the degree of separation between the two subsets of the repertoire, allowing the two 'languages' to converge. (2009:151)

Given this pressure to simplify the selection procedure, we can infer that to ease the cognitive processes surrounding the selection procedure, speakers will to some extent match their lexicon to that of the contact language, creating structural overlap. The extent to which this overlap is manifested in languages in contact, however, is largely dependent on the social situation.

2.2 Social influence on language contact phenomena

Sankoff writes, "Broadly speaking, two major social processes have given rise to contact situations of interest to linguistics: conquest and immigration" (2001:642). Our focus with American Norwegian is on the latter, which, according to Sankoff, "has

---

[2]. This overlap is of course counteracted by the need to maintain a distinction between the contact languages, therefore studies of language contact are never as straightforward as "Language A becomes Language B."

[3]. For discussion on non-lexical, semantic convergence, see Brown and Putnam (this volume) on contact-induced extension of the progressive aspect in Pennsylvania Dutch.

usually resulted in rapid linguistic assimilation", and "has often led to borrowing into the immigrant languages" (2001: 642). Language contact as a result of immigration often results in what Matras describes as a situation of dominance and diglossia. Matras attributes the pressure to borrow to the "unidirectionality of bilingualism", where "[m]embers of the weaker group are obliged to maintain tight control over their selection of word forms whilst communicating in the dominant or majority language" (2009: 59). He contrasts this with "lax" control over selection of lexical items "when communicating with fellow speakers of the smaller language" nearly all of whom are bilingual (2009: 59).

Situations of dominance and diglossia, typified by borrowing, are contrasted with situations of linguistic stability, where both social groups and their languages are on equal footing. In such cases of linguistic equilibrium, results of language contact are often seen through the gradual convergence of structures, rather than the transfer of overt lexical items (Matras 2009: 58).

The ancestors of our speakers immigrated to the United States from Norway as long as three or four generations ago, and as recently as second generation settling near or in the rural communities where most of our speakers still live. Though according to Haugen (1953: 23) Norwegian immigration began in 1825, the earliest date that our informants gave for ancestors coming over was 1840. For the communities surveyed, most immigration took place from 1850 though the 1890s, with 1880 through the 1890s being the peak of Norwegian immigration to America. However, immigration certainly did not stop after that time, as at least one speaker from each area reported to have ancestors who immigrated after 1900 and as late as 1922.

Common to all of these waves of immigration, from early on, is the unique brand of Norwegian that was developed due to contact with English. Haugen cites several Norwegians who visited America in the 1850s and observed, "Such Norwegian as they talk here! It is so mixed with English phrases that I was quite annoyed when I first arrived" (1953: 54). Such quotes, including the quote in this paper's Introduction, indicate a lack of social constraints regarding use of American English or of Norwegian that is seen as somehow Americanized. Haugen also makes it clear that loanwords from English frequently went unrecognized by the speakers of those words, and that children acquiring both languages were often unsure in what contexts certain vocabulary items were to be used (1953: 62). Both Haugen (1953: 71, 1956: 99) and Matras (2009) emphasize the contextual (i.e., cultural and social) nature of bilingual language acquisition. For Matras, linguistic socialization is what determines how the repertoire is divided into subsets (i.e., languages) based on what forms are used in what contexts.

In the case of our speakers of American Norwegian, they are all members of the 'terminal' generation of speakers. They were learning Norwegian at a time when English was rapidly taking over areas that had previously been the domain of Norwegian, such as church and family life. If the incorporation of English forms was facilitated by an overlap of contexts in which Norwegian and English were used early on, this overlap was only increased later. The need to speak in Norwegian on topics that were more American culturally (e.g., government and politics, farming, business, machinery and technology, etc.) led to the transfer of many word-forms and shifts in meaning in others. We focus here on three types of linguistic transfer that result from contact with English and the overlap of contexts.

3. Three types of transfer

That the lexicon of American Norwegian has been affected by English to a large degree (even to the extent of affecting modality and the "supposed to" construction, see Eide and Hjelde this volume) is not surprising given that languages in contact tend to become more similar, even more so in a bilingual setting (Matras 2009, Romaine 1995). Clyne (2003: 76–78) identifies many types of transfer that occur in situations of language contact. In this paper we focus only on those types of transfer pertaining to a lexical word: semantic transfer, phonemic transfer and lexical transfer. We use these terms as defined by Clyne (2003). Table 1 shows the possible ways that these types of transfer interact, and helps explain why we discuss three types of transfer in this paper.

Table 1. Transfer according to contact phenomena, as considered in this paper.[4]

Phenomena	Phonemic structure	Semantic structure
Lexical transfer	X	X
Semantic transfer	(*)	X
Phonemic transfer	*X	*
Loan-shifting (sem. transf.)	*	X
Loan-translation (sem. transf.)		X
Phonemic transfer (undocumented)	X	

Semantic transfer is the transfer of semantic structure (that is, meaning) from one language to another. Semantic transfer is often divided into loan-translation (sometimes called "calquing") and loan-shifting. In **loan-translation**, often used in compound words, the semantic structure is transferred via word-for-word translation from one language into another. In other words, native words retain their original meanings and combine in new ways to express an idea from the model language. For example, *laksørret* in American Norwegian (literally 'salmon+trout') is a loan-translation of 'salmon-trout,' one of the various American English words for steelhead, an anadromous type of rainbow trout. Haugen (1956: 48) gives the Spanish example of *casa de corte* 'court house,' where the idea of a 'court house' has been loaned into Spanish, but is expressed using pre-existing Spanish lexical items. **Loan-shifting**, on the other hand, applies a new meaning to a native word that has the same phonological shape as a word in the model language. Haugen (1956: 52) gives the example: *Du må stikke til det* 'you've gotta

---

4. Italicized items are the terms we use throughout the paper. An "X" indicates what is transferred, and "*" indicates pre-existing overlap with the contact language (i.e., American English).

stick to it.' The verb *stikke* means 'to stick/stab with a pointed object' just like it can in English. However, the idiomatic usage of *stikke* meaning 'to be persistent' in this particular phrase is not part of the original Norwegian meaning; *stikke* has been used only because of the similarity in sound to the English model. Because both loan-shifts and loan-translations use an existing native word or words to express a new, foreign, concept that has been transferred from the model language, we use the term 'semantic transfer' to cover both phenomena. Table 1 above shows how loan-shifts and loan-translations both involve semantic transfer but differ based on pre-existing overlap in phonemic structure.

Phonemic transfer is the process by which part of the phonemic structure of the word is transferred. Phonemic transfer in our data is most commonly found in what Clyne (2003: 80) refers to as "compromise forms," in which the pronunciation of two lexical items that have similar sound and meaning converges. For example, the English word *what* is similar in sound and identical in meaning to the dialectal Norwegian *å* (a form of 'what') and in fact one of the heritage speakers of Norwegian used the form *wå* (< *w[hat]* + *å*). This type of phonemic transfer in compromise forms seems to be dependent on pre-existing semantic overlap as well as the pre-existing phonological overlap usual in phonemic transfer (see Table 1). We have not found in the literature or in our own data any instance of the entire phonemic structure of a word being transferred without the accompaniment of the semantic structure.

Lexical transfer includes transfer of both the phonemic and semantic structure of a lexical item from one language into another, where there was previously no similar structure (see Table 1). An example from American Norwegian is use of the word *råd* for the surface that cars drive on. This type of transfer, where the concept for something, in this case 'road,' is borrowed along with its foreign signifier (i.e., the English word 'road'), is often referred to as a 'borrowing,' 'lexical borrowing,' 'loan' or 'loan-word;' we use the term 'lexical transfer' for the sake of transparency and consistency.

In sum, Norwegian speakers in the American Midwest utilized three strategies that narrowed the difference between Norwegian and English: (1) when two words had existing phonemic overlap, the meanings often became more similar (semantic transfer); (2) when two words shared similar meaning and a degree of phonemic overlap, the pronunciation often converged (phonemic transfer); and (3) when a word existed in English but not in Norwegian, the English word could be used in Norwegian while retaining English meaning and phonemic structure (lexical transfer). Differentiating between these types of transfer is not always straightforward. Haugen noted difficulties in the word *pæl* in American Norwegian (1956: 62). In Norwegian this word has the meaning of '½ pint,' but in American Norwegian has the same meaning as English 'pail.' Haugen wrote that if it is indeed the same Norwegian word, with a new meaning applied, then it is a loan-shift (just like *stikke*). But because the pronunciation is also different in American Norwegian, it is also possible that it is a case of lexical transfer and has nothing to do with the native word *pæl*. In Part 5 we look at specific words from our data set that posed difficulties.

4. Methods

The following data comes from over 90 minutes of recorded interviews and conversations conducted in Norwegian with 16 speakers from Wisconsin, Minnesota, and Iowa in the winter and summer of 2010. Data from four of the speakers comes from the *Corpus of American Norwegian Speech* (CANS).[5] These speakers are fluent in both American English and the form of Norwegian they learned as children. By considering only fluent speakers, we avoid having our data skewed by 'errors' or lack of confidence, which might lead to unnatural speech.

Our data consists of lexical items, either single-words or compounds, in which we identified all or part of the structure as transferred from American English. We selected only lexical items that were treated as Norwegian by the speaker, based on either phonological and/or morphological evidence. We do not consider here instances of multiple-transference, where an entire phrase from English was used during a Norwegian exchange. Nor do we include items that were immediately corrected (i.e., mistakes).

Due to the difficulty inherent in distinguishing code-switching, nonce-borrowing, and borrowing amongst bilingual speakers, we count as lexical transfers all instances of single-word items from American English that are treated as Norwegian by the speaker. In a multilingual repertoire, the entire repertoire is available at all times, and forms are selected based on their context-appropriateness, regardless of which "language" they are typically associated with (Matras 2009: 308). Not only are all lexical items available regardless of interaction context, but all aspects of the grammar, phonology, syntax, morphology, etc., are available, so that speakers have not only the ability to select a word from one language and use it in the context of another language, but they also have the ability to either integrate or not integrate a word into other aspects of the grammar. For instance, social pressures might induce a speaker to pronounce words of one language with an accent meant to sound funny or educated.[6] There is no evidence that there were social inhibitions against integrating loans into American Norwegian (as noted previously in the quotes Haugen collected). Thus we include as lexical transfers all English lexical items that were treated as Norwegian in the speech context, while those that were clearly used as English (i.e., code-switches) were excluded.

---

5. Speakers blair_WI_01gm, blair_WI_02gm, decorah_IA_01gm, and decorah_IA_02gm. Data available at http://www.tekstlab.uio.no/nota/NorAmDiaSyn/index.html (Johannessen and Laake 2010).

6. Oswalt points out that in Kashaya, only lexical transfers from Spanish are integrated phonologically, while those transferred from English are not, since all who speak Kashaya speak English, while few speak Spanish (1985: 528). In other words, they are aware that the words are English and, for social reasons, do not integrate these words. Even though frequency of these items would support interpreting them as instances of lexical transfer, many researchers do not consider them to be such (Oswalt 1985: 528).

Once we had identified lexical items by transfer type, we sorted occurrences into spreadsheets, as in Figure 1. Occurrences were labeled by: transfer type (e.g., "ST" in Figure 1 indicates "semantic transfer"); classification as either function or content words (F.W. and C.W. in column two); classification as noun, verb, or adjective (includes adverbs); and by lemma. The rightmost column shows the occurrence in context. Not shown are speaker identification and location.

transfer type	F.W.(1). or C.W.(2)	noun(1), verb(2), adj(3)	token		context
ST	2		2	call	Og eh, vi stopp in der, og *kalt*'n på telefon...
ST	2		1	cousin	det e to tå *kosine* mine her
ST	2		1	cousin	Så e hadde nå ei *kosin* så leve ut i Oregon
ST	2		1	dollar	den trippen den ti kosta han seksti *daLa*.
ST	2		1	dollar	Du fekk ti *daLar* for ei ku kanskje
ST	2		2	go	kå'n k'ai *gå* fra der.
ST	2		2	go	Je kunne *gå* ganske mange plasser men Bergen det var for mye åt me.
ST	2		2	go	Oh ja, vi brukte *går* julebukk kver-, kver Christmastid.
ST	2		1	grade	Så hadde hu meg i andren blad- *grad*.
ST	2		1	grade	så når jeg kom til skolen, uh, i første *grad*

Figure 1. Screen shot of spreadsheet.

5. Results and discussion

Out of approximately one and one half hours of recordings, consisting of introductions, family history, farming, etc., we identified 233 instances of words in which all or part of the structure – phonemic or semantic – had been transferred from American English. Many of these instances were repeats of the same item, and the total number of individual lexical items identified was 125.

Most items were relatively easily placed into one of the three categories described above: lexical transfer, semantic transfer, and phonemic transfer. Instances of lexical transfer were typically the most easily identified category, and they were also the most frequent of the three. These transfers were 86% content words (64% of which were nouns) and 14% function words (prepositions, interjections, discourse markers, etc.).

Table 2. Total number of occurrences by transfer type.

Transfer type	Occurrence	Percentage
Lexical transfer	154	66%
Semantic transfer	51	22%
Phonemic transfer	6	3%
Ambiguous	22	9%

Semantic transfer enjoyed high frequency in terms of total number of instances (Table 2), but this number is bumped down significantly when the data is organized in terms of number of different lemmas attested (see Table 3).

Table 3. Total number of lemmas by transfer type.

Transfer type	Lemmas	Percentage
Lexical transfer	87	70%
Semantic transfer	19	15%
Phonemic transfer	6	5%
Ambiguous	13	10%

In both ways of organizing the data, lexical transfer was the most common form of transfer in our data, and in terms of lemmas, was more frequent than semantic or phonemic transfer, indicating greater diversity of lexical transfers, with a more constrained set of semantic transfers and phonemic transfers.

5.1 Lexical transfer

Lexical transfer comprised the largest amount of our data. Instances of lexical transfer in our data can be seen in Table 4 below.

Table 4. Lemmas undergoing lexical transfer. 154 total occurrences, 87 lemmas.

Lemma	#	Lemma	#	Lemma	#	Lemma	#	Lemma	#
a	1	acre	2	advertising	1	amish	1	and	6
army	1	at	1	auction	5	aunt	2	baby-combine	1
barn	1	Bergenism	1	boxcar	1	break(v)	1	bundle	1
bundle-wagon	2	candy	1	car	2	care(n)	3	care(v)	1
cent	1	chopper	1	college	3	college prof.	1	cord	1
country	2	crop	1	cultivator	1	dust	1	easier	1
English	2	farm(adj)	2	farm(n)	8	farm(v)	5	farmer	1
farming	1	field	2	figure(n)	1	figure out	1	fill(v)	1
fjord	1	flu	1	fourth	1	gee	1	graduate-school	1
guide(n)	4	harvest(v)	1	lake	1	lumbercamps	1	Norway	2
now	1	PhD	1	pioneer	1	plenty	1	probably	2
raise	3	rent	6	research	1	right	1	script	1
show	1	silage	1	silo	2	single-row	1	soybean	1
spend	1	stable	1	stack	1	store	1	straight-combine	1
stuff	3	suppose	1	swather	2	teacher	2	then	1
tour-guide	1	tractor	8	train	2	trip	2	valley	1
visit(v)	4	vote(v)	1	well	1	what	1	when	1
with	1	woman	1						

While many of these lexical transfers require little discussion, as they are quite plainly transfers from English that did not exist previously in Norwegian, some items do need explaining. Perhaps the most obvious of these is the word *fjord*. This has been included as an instance of lexical transfer due to its distinctly foreign treatment morphologically. The speaker, speaking of a trip that he had made to Norway, said, "…*og vi reiste gjennom alle fjordsa*". It is the use of the English plural marker -*s*, in combination with the Norwegian definite marker -*a* to indicate 'the fjords,' as opposed to *fjordene*, *fjordan*, or something of the like. Haugen notes that importing the English plural marker -*s* "becomes such a common thing that the N[orwegian] suffixed article may be added to it, producing a hybrid inflexion -*s* + -*a* 'the,' e.g., *kisa* 'the keys'" (1953: 398). We follow Haugen in treating this instance as an importation of the plural -*s* suffix along with an English noun. Had there been no such distinct morphological indications, *fjord* would have, of course, been treated as its native homonym. An additional item that has been pointed out to us by an outside reviewer is dialectal form [treən] *train*, in Norway, which might indicate that *train* in the above table is an instance of semantic transfer. However, given its pronunciation in our data as either 'monophthongally' with a high, front offglide as [treʲn], or diphthongally as [traɪn], we have included it here as an instance of lexical transfer. Finally, though the tractor was introduced to Norway in the early 1900s, we follow Haugen (1953) and Hjelde (1992) in considering it a case of lexical transfer.

5.2 Semantic transfer

Table 5. Lemmas undergoing semantic transfer. 51 total occurrences, 19 lemmas.

Lemma	#	Lemma	#	Lemma	#	Lemma	#
anymore*	4	around	1	right*	1	call	1
corn	2	cousin	3	dollar	3	go	3
grade	2	hard	2	high school	3	live	17
mile	1	place	2	small	2	tell	1
to	1	well	1	way	1		

While lexical transfer entails the transfer of phonological and semantic structures, instances of semantic transfer in our data were most often cases where the phonemic shape of the word corresponded with the phonemes in a related English word. For instance, Norwegian *leve* 'to live' is easily identified by speakers as similar to English *live*. The entire semantic structure however, does not correspond to English. While English *live* can mean to reside (e.g., 'I live on the home farm'), the equivalent native construction in most Norwegian dialects is the verb *å bo*. American Norwegian, however, has transferred the meaning of 'to reside' from English and uses *leve* for both meanings of 'to live' and 'to reside.'

Figure 2. Distribution of *levde* (light color) and *livde* (dark color) in Norway. Mapped using the Nordic Dialect Corpus (Johannessen et al. 2009).

The past tense form of *leve* 'to live,' was attested on multiple occasions as *livd* and *livde* by one Minnesota community of speakers we interviewed. Though this pronunciation would appear to be a case of phonemic transfer due to influence from English, it is in fact an attested form in Norway (see Figure 2), and its range includes the Nordfjord area, where a significant number of the informants from that Minnesota community have family origins. Thus what might appear to be a unique form due to contact between Norwegian and English is in fact probably a result of dialect contact, perhaps further propagated locally by existence of the form in English. It should be noted that our classification of the verb *leve* based on this data is different from that of Johannessen and Laake (2012, and forthcoming), who found that the English verb *live* had been borrowed and taken over the Norwegian equivalent *å bo* or *å leve*.

Similar to the transfer of meaning in *leve*, there is already phonemic overlap in *grad*, even though the meanings in Norwegian *grad* and English *grade* are different. While in American English *grade* is most often used for classes in school (e.g., 2nd, 3rd, 4th grade), in modern Norwegian it most often has the meaning 'degree,' as in 'to a greater degree' as well as 'fifteen degrees Celsius.' In American Norwegian, however, the English meaning of *grade* (as in a class grade) has been transferred to *grad*. Semantic transfer then results in the same meaning in both English and Norwegian.

There are two exceptions (marked with asterisks in Table 5) in our data where instances of semantic transfer did not already contain some phonemic overlap. These instances are *beint* and *noe mer*. *Beint* is used regularly in American Norwegian as 'straight' or 'directly' in phrases like, 'he went right/straight/directly to school,' etc. The use of *beint* in this case was in the phrase "*beint nå*" 'right now' (CANS, blair_WI_02gm), as what Haugen would classify as a loan-translation. The same is the case with *noe mer* to have the adverbial meaning of English 'anymore.' When asked if he could still read Norwegian, one of our informants responded: "*Itt' noe mer*" 'not anymore.' Note that the fact that *beint* and *noe mer* are exceptions and not the rule underscores our thesis that, barring social factors restricting the overt transfer of lexical forms, transfers that result in more structural overlap will be more abundant than those that do not.

5.3 Phonemic transfer

Table 6. Lemmas undergoing phonemic transfer. 6 total occurrences, 6 lemmas.

Lemma	#	Lemma	#	Lemma	#	Lemma	#
are	1	find	1	generation	1	university	1
was	1	what[7]	1				

Phonemic transfer was the most difficult category to pin down. The difficulty in deciding exactly what constitutes phonemic transfer is as follows: if an existing word in Norwegian resembles the English equivalent, and furthermore, those words have the same semantics and similar phonemic shape, then according to our hypothesis there is motivation to lessen the distance between these two forms, resulting in convergence – in this case phonemic. However, if this phonemic convergence is total (i.e., the end result is total overlap in phonemic shape between the languages), then it is unclear whether or not lexical transfer or phonemic transfer has taken place (remember lexical transfer entails transfer of phonemic shape as well). Thus we include no data under the category of phonemic transfer in which there is total overlap of the phonological shape of a word. These ambiguous examples are given below. What we have included are instances of increased overlap where some overlap already existed. For instance [v] was at times replaced by [w] in copulatives, e.g., *var* > *war* 'was.' Phonemic transfer is not limited to high-frequency items such as *var*. *University* was attested as [junɪvɛɹsɪ'tetɛɹ], with the initial glide transferred from English. Thus the only positive identification of instances of phonemic transfer is where there has been only partial phonemic transfer, resulting in more, but not total overlap.

[7.] The instance of *what* classified here as PT and pronounced [wå], is distinct from the instance of *what* as classified under lexical transfer and pronounced [wʌt].

5.4 Ambiguous cases

Table 7. Lemmas in which it is unclear whether *lexical transfer* or *phonemic transfer* has taken place. 22 total occurrences, 13 lemmas.

Lemma	#	Lemma	#	Lemma	#	Lemma	#
coffee	2	family	5	February	1	hay	1
history	1	home	1	more	1	museum	2
said	1	to	1	we	2	no	3
yes	1						

The cases listed in Table 7 represent lexical items that are similar in phonological shape, both in Norwegian and English. In our data, they have converged towards English in all cases. For example, *kaffe/kaffi* is pronounced [kåffi] in our data. Were we to analyze this as *phonemic transfer*, either /a/ > /å/ and /ə/ > /i/ (if *kaffe* > *kåffi*), or just /a/ > /å/ (if *kaffi* > *kåffi*). While we are inclined to categorize some of these (e.g., *to, no, yes*) under lexical transfer, and some (e.g., *coffee, family, history, more, we*) under phonemic transfer, we are not with confidence able to do so without a more refined test.

5.5 Exceptional cases

It has been pointed out to us that there are a few cases where, based on our hypothesis (and the general trends of language contact), unexpected changes have occurred. These cases are the noun *portrett* and verb *travla* (both discussed in Johannessen and Laake 2012, forthcoming, and mentioned in Hjelde 1992: 118, 126, and the latter in Haugen 1953: 602). *Portrett* 'portrait' exists with similar meaning in both Norwegian and English, but in American Norwegian the meaning has shifted from a painting or photograph of especially the upper body and face, to refer generally to any picture. According to our hypothesis this change is unexpected because it is a change that does not provide more overlap, but rather less. The meaning of *portrait/portrett* in each respective language overlapped previously, but in American Norwegian obtained an almost entirely new meaning. *Travla* is a similar though slightly different case. It is not entirely clear whether or not it is a transfer from English, or if it was an existing word in Norwegian that shifted meaning and gained popularity after leaving Norway. Regardless, with the meaning of 'to walk/go about on foot,' *travla* clearly does not have the same meaning(s) as English 'travel,' nor, according to Johannessen and Laake (forthcoming) does it have the same meaning as it does in Norway. These two items present a problem since despite their similarity in semantics and phonemic shape, there has been no convergence of any sort in American Norwegian, and in the case of *portrett* we see actual divergence.

Despite the problems presented by *portrett* and *travla*, our hypothesis otherwise holds true. That more overlap would be preferred over partial overlap was underscored by the fact that in 89% of the lemmas classified as semantic transfer there was preexisting phonemic overlap (as in the case of *leve*, the exception being the extended meanings of *beint* and *noe mer* in Table 5). In the same way, phonemic transfer always occurred in cases where there was preexisting semantic overlap and partial phonemic overlap.

Our observations supplement an observation by Haugen (1953:95) regarding transferred English terminology for harvesting in American Norwegian. He notes that of 32 words in Norwegian connected with harvesting, American Norwegian had retained only 17 of these. Of these existing 17 words, two changed meaning to align with the English meaning, and two were already nearly identical to the English equivalent. To round out the vocabulary, another 13 words were transferred from English. In the end there were 30 words associated with the harvest, meaning that "the cultural shift was actually complete, for the E[nglish] and Am[erican] N[orwegian] vocabulary structure in this area was now identical, with a one-to-one correspondence between them" (Haugen 1953:95).

There are two further points worth commenting on regarding our data and Haugen's. Haugen (1953:406) notes the following percentages of total loans per word class, reasoning that there are more nouns and verbs borrowed than any other class of words, because nouns and verbs are more abundant in the lexicon:

Nouns – 75.5; Verbs – 18.4; Adj – 3.4; Adv./Prep – 1.2; Interj. – 1.4

Our data shows relatively similar results when borrowings per word-class are a percentage of the total number of lexical items transferred (see Table 8 below). One thing to note immediately is how much lower the percentage of nouns is in our data.

Table 8. Data per word class for number of lemmas borrowed.

	Nouns	Verbs	Adj/Adv	Function words
lemmas per lexical transfer	64%	16%	7%	13%
instances per lexical transfer	62%	18%	5%	14%
lemmas for all transfer types	58%	18%	10%	14%
instances for all transfer types	55%	23%	8%	14%

Looking at the middle row labeled "instances per lexical transfer," the one key difference to be seen comparing our data to Haugen's is that there is a much larger percentage of function words in our data (13–14%) depending on how the data is organized).

This number is much higher than the 2.6% given by Haugen, even if Adv./Prep. and Interj. are combined. This may be an area of the American Norwegian lexicon that has undergone change over the course of the last century. Furthermore, this finding corroborates Brown and Putnam's findings (this volume) regarding the vulnerability of the grammar to discourse-pragmatic changes (in their case at the morphosyntactic level with the extension of progressive aspect in Pennsylvania Dutch stative constructions).

6. Conclusions

In this paper we have tested a claim inferred from Matras (2009), that the more overlap that is created through borrowing, the better, since this will provide more ease on cognitive processes surrounding the selection of context-appropriate forms, one of the motivations Matras gives for borrowing (2009: 151). To test this claim we used data gathered from speakers of American Norwegian in Minnesota, Iowa, and Wisconsin. Based on social factors, we hypothesized that lexical transfer from English to Norwegian should occur with more frequency than semantic or phonemic transfer because lexical transfer entails more overlap (and thus more ease on cognitive processes), while semantic and phonemic transfer entail only partial overlap.

If Matras' theory did not hold, we would expect American Norwegian to either remain utterly distinct from American English or to have undergone changes such that American Norwegian would lose similarities already shared with American English (as happened with the semantic changes of *portrett*). Haugen, as we saw earlier, noted the Americanization of Norwegian in the United States. Our own hypothesis, that more overlap is better overlap, is also confirmed by our data. Lexical transfer occurred more frequently than both semantic transfer and phonemic transfer, an outcome we attribute to a combination of social and cognitive factors, as outlined above. In further support of our hypothesis, the instances of semantic transfer and phonemic transfer in our data show that semantic transfer and phonemic transfer tend to have the same cumulative effect as lexical transfer by itself: complete or nearly complete overlap in phonemic and semantic structure.

Thus if we consider the final results of lexical transfer, semantic transfer and phonemic transfer, they are essentially the same: overlap in both semantic and phonological structure. Lexical transfer does this in one fell swoop by transferring everything from English. Phonemic transfer and semantic transfer provide even more overlap for structures that already have some.

References

Beniak, Édouard, Raymond Mougeon and Daniel Valois. 1984. "Sociolinguistic Evidence of a Possible Case of Syntactic Convergence in Ontarian French." *Journal of the Atlantic Provinces Linguistic Association* 6–7(Spring): 73–88.

Clyne, Michael. 2003. *Dynamics of Language Contact*. Cambridge: Cambridge University Press. DOI: 10.1017/CBO9780511606526

Haugen, Einar. 1953. *The Norwegian Language in America: A Study in Bilingual Behavior*. 2nd Edition. Bloomington, IN: Indiana University Press.

Haugen, Einar. 1956. *Bilingualism in the Americas: A Bibliography and Research Guide*. (Publications of the American Dialect Society 26). Tuscaloosa, AL: University of Alabama Press.

Hjelde, Arnstein. 1992. *Trøndsk talemål i Amerika*. Tapir: Trondheim.

Johannessen, Janne Bondi and Signe Laake. 2010. *Corpus of American Norwegian Speech*. http://www.tekstlab.uio.no/nota/NorAmDiaSyn/index.html

Johannessen, Janne Bondi and Signe Laake. 2012. "Østnorsk som norsk fellesdialekt i Midtvesten." *Norsk lingvistisk tidsskrift* 30(2): 365–380.

Johannessen, Janne Bondi and Signe Laake. Forthcoming. "Eastern Norwegian as a Common Norwegian Dialect in the American Midwest." *Journal of Language Contact*.

Johannessen, Janne Bondi, Joel Priestley, Kristin Hagen, Tor Anders Åfarli and Øystein Alexander Vangsnes. 2009. "The Nordic Dialect Corpus – An Advanced Research Tool." In *Proceedings of the 17th Nordic Conference of Computational Linguistics NODALIDA 2009*. NEALT Proceedings Series 4, ed. by Kristiina Jokinen and Eckhard Bick, 73–80. Tartu: Tartu University Library (electronic publication).

Matras, Yaron. 2009. *Language Contact*. Cambridge: Cambridge University Press. DOI: 10.1017/CBO9780511809873

Oswalt, Robert L. 1985. "The Infiltration of English into Indian." *International Journal of American Linguistics* 51(4): 527–529. DOI: 10.1086/465959

Romaine, Suzanne. 1995. *Bilingualism*. 2nd Edition. Blackwell: Cambridge, USA.

Rothman, Jason. 2009. "Understanding the Nature and Outcomes of Early Bilingualism: Romance Languages as Heritage Languages." *International Journal of Bilingualism* 13(2): 155–163. DOI: 10.1177/1367006909339814

Sankoff, Gillian. 2001. "Linguistic Outcomes of Language Contact." In *Handbook of Sociolinguistics*, ed. by Jack Chambers, Peter Trudgill and Natalie Schilling-Estes, 638–668. Cambridge, USA: Blackwell.

How synagogues became *shuls*
The boomerang effect in Yiddish-influenced English, 1895–2010

Sarah Bunin Benor
Hebrew Union College

This paper introduces the "boomerang effect," the resurgence of substrate features that were previously on the wane. Among American Jews, Yiddish loanwords have waned and waxed over the past century, and in the domains of religion and popular culture, we currently see increased use of certain loanwords, including *shul* ('synagogue'), *leyn* ('chant Torah'), *daven* ('pray'), and *chutzpah* ('gall'). This paper offers evidence for this trend using data from a survey about language use, a corpus study of the American Jewish press from 1895 to the present, and analysis of media oriented toward young Jewish adults. These findings are discussed in light of changes in American society and in the Jewish community, as well as the notion of the "third-generation return."

Keywords: Yiddish, lexicon, loanwords, ethnicity, boomerang effect, substrate effect, substratal influence, American Jews, survey, newspaper, Jewish English

1. Introduction

When a minority group shifts to the majority language within a generation or two, what happens to their original language? Does it continue to exert substratal influence on the new language as used by group members? In this paper, I offer evidence that American Jews continue to use lexical elements of their main ancestral language, Yiddish, even several generations after the major wave of Yiddish-speaking immigration (1880–1920) and even when the speakers have little or no proficiency in spoken Yiddish. While some loanwords from Yiddish are on the decline, others are increasing in use.

Data in this paper come from three sources:

a. a survey about language and identity among contemporary Jews, in which correlations between age and the use of specific loanwords give us a sense of change in apparent time;

b. a corpus study of two American Jewish newspapers from 1895 to the present, in which we see shifts in the use of certain Yiddish loanwords;
c. a synchronic, qualitative analysis of the use of Yiddish loanwords in contemporary media oriented toward young Jewish adults, including a website, a magazine, a book, a film, and a political organization.

First I give background information about Yiddish and about the theoretical approach toward substrate effects, then I present each of the data sources and its findings, and finally I discuss the results in relation to broader trends within American society and the Jewish community.

1.1 Yiddish

Like all the languages analyzed in this volume, Yiddish is a Germanic language, but one with significant influences at all levels from Slavic languages and – mostly in lexicon – from Hebrew, Aramaic, and Jewish varieties of medieval French and Italian. Although its history is subject to academic debate (see, e.g., Weinreich [1973] 2008, Katz 1987, Wexler 2002, Beider 2013), most scholars agree that Jews began speaking a Germanic language in what is now Germany around the start of the second millennium, and when they moved eastward to Slavic lands, they maintained their Germanic language and incorporated many influences from Slavic languages. By the 19th century, Yiddish was well established as the spoken language of millions of Jews in Eastern Europe. Over the next century, the vast majority of Yiddish speakers shifted to local languages, immigrated to the United States, Israel, and elsewhere, or were killed in the Holocaust.

Of the millions of Yiddish speakers who immigrated to the United States in the late 19th and early 20th centuries, most shifted to English within a generation or two. The most recent United States Census Bureau report, from the 2007 American Community Survey, found that 158,991 people in the United States speak Yiddish at home; most of them are also proficient in English (Shin and Kominsky 2010: 6–7). Many contemporary Yiddish speakers are elderly Holocaust survivors, although their numbers are decreasing due to their advancing age. A large and growing percentage of contemporary Yiddish speakers are Haredi (Ultra-Orthodox) Jews, especially Hasidim in the New York area (see Kahan Newman, this volume). They tend to have high birth rates (Cohen et al. 2012) and continuing ideological attachment to Yiddish (Isaacs 1999, Fader 2009). In addition, there are a few dozen young non-Orthodox Jews who feel a strong ideological attachment to Yiddish and decide to raise their children speaking Yiddish (Chernikoff 2008). Because of the continued intergenerational transmission of Yiddish in some Hasidic communities, we cannot say that Yiddish is endangered. On the other hand, outside of Hasidic communities, Yiddish use is dwindling and, as Avineri (2012) points out, most American Jews experience and discuss Yiddish as an endangered language.

Although Yiddish use is in decline, researchers have shown that "postvernacular" use of Yiddish is on the rise (Shandler 2006, Avineri 2012, Soldat-Jaffe 2012). Shandler defines postvernacularity as people privileging the symbolic understanding of a language over its communicative use. In the case of Yiddish, he writes, "the language's primary level of signification – that is, its instrumental value as a vehicle for communicating information, opinions, feelings, ideas – is narrowing in scope. At the same time its secondary or meta-level of signification – the symbolic value invested in the language apart from the semantic value of any given utterance in it – is expanding" (Shandler 2006: 4). There has been an increase in the number of Yiddish festivals and material cultural products, such as t-shirts and refrigerator magnets, and most of the people who engage with these products cannot speak or even understand full Yiddish sentences. Another way that individuals engage with Yiddish in a postvernacular way is through the use of Yiddish loanwords within English, the focus of this paper. While several other chapters in this volume focus on the integration of English loanwords into immigrant languages (e.g., Ehresmann and Bousquette; Eide and Hjelde; and Annear and Speth), this chapter focuses on Yiddish loanwords in the English spoken (mostly) by descendants of Yiddish speakers.

1.2 The boomerang effect

Descendants of Yiddish speakers are not the only group to exhibit a resurgence of substrate effects that had appeared to be on the wane. Researchers have found this pattern in a Cajun community in Louisiana (Dubois and Horvath 2000) and in an Indian and Pakistani immigrant community in London (Sharma 2011a, 2011b). I refer to this phenomenon as the "boomerang effect" because of the curvilinear pattern seen in graphs of these substrate influences:

a. A group closest to the ancestral language uses some substratal features.
b. The next generation uses fewer of these features, often to distinguish themselves from their parents.
c. A subsequent generation expresses interest in their heritage language and uses some of the substratal features more than their parents.

One factor behind the resurgence of substrate effects in these groups may be increasing consciousness about and pride in ethnic and/or regional distinctiveness and perhaps some enregisterment, the process of linguistic features becoming associated with particular groups (Johnstone et al. 2002, Agha 2003, Johnstone 2009; see also Benor 2010). This paper offers evidence for the boomerang effect among American Jews, as well as discussion of the factors behind it.

2. Findings

2.1 Survey

One way to investigate the correlation between age and loanword use is through a written questionnaire asking respondents whether they use specific words. While self-reports do not necessarily reflect actual language use, and therefore should be treated with some caution, the advantage is that such a method allows us to reach a much larger population than we would with observation/recording of individuals' speech.

In 2008 I conducted an Internet-based survey with sociologist Steven M. Cohen (Benor and Cohen 2011, Benor 2011). The survey asked respondents whether they know and use dozens of Hebrew and Yiddish words (e.g., *shpiel* 'pitch,' *shul* 'synagogue,' *leyn* 'chant Torah,' *chutzpah* 'gall,' *maven* 'expert,' *yofi* 'nice') and other linguistic features (e.g., various New York regionalisms and Yiddish constructions like "she has what to say"), as well as about language proficiency and demographic traits such as age, religious observance, and family immigration history. We invited subscribers to various Jewish and linguistics email lists, as well as about 600 personal contacts, to respond to the survey and forward the invitation to their Jewish and non-Jewish friends. Over 40,000 people responded, including the sample used in this paper: 25,179 people who grew up and now live in the United States, currently identify as Jewish, and report that they spoke only English in the home growing up.

Similar to random samples of American Jews (e.g., Kotler-Berkowitz et al. 2003), the survey sample we obtained is diverse according to age, region, denomination, Jewish educational background, and percentage of friends who are Jewish. Our sample over-represents women and those who are religiously engaged. We cannot make assumptions about the general American Jewish population based on this non-random sample (e.g., 20% of American Jews use word X), but we can conduct analysis of sub-groups within the sample (e.g., reported use of word X correlates with frequency of synagogue attendance). In this paper I focus on a small subset of the survey data, including Yiddish proficiency, nine Yiddish words and constructions, age, and a variable I call "generation from immigration," based on how many of the respondent's four grandparents were born in the United States.

Before getting into details of Yiddish loanword usage, let us look at respondents' self-reports of Yiddish language knowledge (Table 1). Knowing at least some Yiddish correlates strongly with age. Given that the sample includes only people who grew up speaking English in the home, it is not surprising that few respondents in all age groups report proficiency in Yiddish.

Table 1. Yiddish language knowledge, correlated with age.

Age	18–24	25–34	35–44	45–54	55–64	65–74	75+
N (approx)[1]	1,160	2,857	2,779	5,228	7,550	4,490	1,731
% who report at least "some" Yiddish	15.8	15.1	18.6	29.8	38.1	50.4	63
% who report Yiddish proficiency	1.1	1.3	0.9	1.3	1.3	2.9	7.4

Some might question the use of age as an independent variable in this case, given that Jews in the US are descended from people who immigrated from various places and in various periods, not just from Eastern Europe between 1880 and 1920. If we

---

1. These Ns apply to all age tables in this paper (although each question had slightly different numbers of respondents, the numbers were very close).

look at "generation from immigration" (number of grandparents born in the US) among descendants of Yiddish-speaking immigrants, we see a similar trend (Table 2). Because both age and generation correlate with Yiddish knowledge, and because they are strongly correlated with each other, the regression analyses reported below are based on a scale combining age and generation.

Table 2. Percent of descendants of Yiddish-speaking immigrants who report knowing at least some Yiddish, correlated with number of grandparents born in US.

# of grandparents born in US	4	3	2	1	0
% who report at least "some" Yiddish knowledge	16	19	25	31	49

Tables 1 and 2 indicate that Yiddish is in decline: most of the younger respondents and those with more American-born grandparents have little or no knowledge of Yiddish. This is corroborated by anecdotal evidence about children of immigrants preferring English over Yiddish. For example, a second-generation survey respondent wrote in an open-ended question about language, "As with many people of my generation (boomers), my parents kept Yiddish as a 'secret language' when they did not want us to know what they were talking about." Among those who did speak Yiddish in the home, many expected their children to respond in English. Another survey respondent wrote, "I understood everything my grandparents said to me, as we lived with them, but they wanted me to speak back in English: '*Red tzu mir in ainglish.*' ['Speak to me in English.] Therefore I don't speak Yiddish well, but *ich farshtait* [sic. 'I understand']." English was seen as a means of integrating culturally and economically into American society, and most children of Yiddish-speaking immigrants did not value Yiddish maintenance. Therefore, it is to be expected that Yiddish proficiency is low several generations after the mass wave of immigration.

The survey asked respondents whether they use specific Yiddish-origin loanwords within English. Given the decreasing Yiddish proficiency, one might expect that Yiddish loanwords would also be decreasing. As Table 3 indicates, this is the case for several Yiddish words, including *naches* ('pride') and *maven* ('expert'); younger survey respondents are less likely to report using these (and several other words). However, as Table 4 indicates, some Yiddish words are actually increasing; younger respondents are more likely to report using *shul* ('synagogue'), "staying *by* us" ('at our house'), and several other Yiddish-influenced words and constructions.

Table 3. Declining use: % in each age group who report using specific Yiddish words in English.

Age	18–24	25–34	35–44	45–54	55–64	65–74	75+
naches ('pride')	43	50	59	72	79	82	84
maven ('expert')	33	48	61	75	84	88	89
macher ('big shot')	31	47	56	71	77	80	79
heimish ('cozy, home-like')	20	33	45	60	68	76	78

Table 4. Increasing use: % in each age group who report
using specific Yiddish words and constructions in English.

Age	18–24	25–34	35–44	45–54	55–64	65–74	75+
shul ('synagogue')	64	64	60	59	52	44	43
good Shabbos (Sabbath greeting, vs. Israeli Hebrew *Shabbat shalom*)	50	49	44	42	40	36	32
leyn ('chant Torah')	30	29	26	27	24	16	8
drash ('sermon')	28	28	25	24	19	15	9
by us (vs. 'at our house'; cf. Yid. *bay undz*)	30	29	26	27	24	16	8

The main factor behind this surprising finding is religiosity. The Yiddish loanwords and constructions in Table 4 are all used predominantly in religious contexts. Even the phrase "by us" is often used in discussions of Sabbath meal plans, as in, "Are you eating by us next Shabbos?" (*Shabbos* is the Ashkenazi Hebrew variant of 'Sabbath' used by many Orthodox Jews, compared to Israeli Hebrew-influenced *Shabbat*, used by many non-Orthodox Jews). The increasing use of these words and phrases in the younger generations relates to the growing importance of religious activities among many younger American Jews. Although a large percentage of Jews, especially children of one Jewish and one non-Jewish parent, are disengaging from religious life, we also see the opposite trend: young Jews re-embracing the religion and culture of their ancestors. This involves not only the use of Yiddish (and Hebrew) words but also increased observance of Jewish religious practices. This is certainly the case for *baʿalei teshuva*, non-Orthodox Jews who become Orthodox (Benor 2012a), but it can also be seen among Reform, Conservative, and other Jews who have intensified their religious engagement.

While we see religious intensification in all age groups, it is particularly pronounced among Jews under 35. Perhaps the age correlations in Table 4 are merely remnants of greater religiosity among younger survey respondents. To check for this, as well as to tease apart other factors, I conducted logistic regression analyses on each word, using several independent variables: a scale combining age and generation ("age+gen"), Sabbath observance, synagogue attendance, Orthodox identity, percent of friends who are Jewish, Yiddish ancestry, having lived in New York, time spent in Israel, and Aramaic knowledge. I found that age+gen has an independent effect on all of them, although it is always weaker than Orthodox identity, Sabbath observance, and some of the other variables related to religiosity (see details in Benor 2011). Even though religiosity plays an important role in American Jews' use of certain Yiddish words, age and generation from immigration are also significant factors. This suggests that the words in Table 4 are increasing in use over time.

2.2 Corpus study

In synchronic research on sociolinguistic variation, we can never be sure that patterns according to age represent changes in progress. It might be the case that individuals change their language as they age (age grading). To supplement the synchronic survey data, I turn to historical data from written Jewish English. First, I selected the word *shul*, which is increasing according to the survey data, and I analyzed its use in articles published by the Jewish Telegraphic Agency (JTA). JTA is a New York-based English-language news service with reporters around the world. It provides content for over 100 Jewish newspapers, mostly in the United States. The entire corpus of articles published by JTA from 1923 to 2008 is available online, and it includes a quarter of a million articles.

Because an increase in the use of a loanword might represent an increase in discourse about its referent, it is useful to include non-loan equivalents in the quantitative analysis. Therefore, I searched the JTA corpus for tokens of *synagogue*, *temple*, and *shul*, including the alternate spellings *schul*, *schule*, *shool*, and *shule*. I eliminated any tokens that were names (e.g., Samuel L. Schul), as well as tokens that referred to schools (the word means both 'synagogue' and 'school' in Yiddish). The search function in this database yields results according to article, so an article containing, for example, seven tokens is registered the same way as an article containing only one token. Using these results, I calculated the occurrence of *shul* and its alternate spellings as a percentage of all of the possible words (*shul*, *synagogue*, and *temple*) for each year. As Figure 1 indicates, the use of *shul* increased dramatically in the 1980s. Clearly the findings of the survey are evidence of a change in progress, rather than age grading.

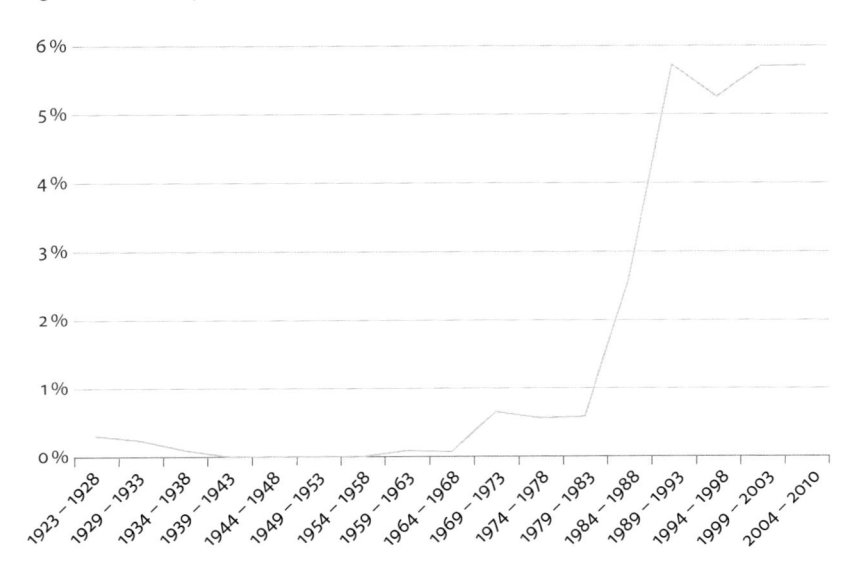

Figure 1. Articles with *shul* as a percentage of total articles with *synagogue*, *temple*, or *shul*, per year, averaged across 5-year periods in JTA corpus.

As *shul* increased in the 1980s, it also acquired a relatively standard spelling. Over the entire period of the study, there are 558 tokens of *shul* and 28 tokens of all of the other spellings combined (*schul*, etc.). All but two of the tokens of alternative spellings occur between 1923 and 1935, and the two that occur in recent years refer to specific synagogues in Australia and France: the Roscoe Street Shule and La Schule.

Even though the use of *shul* has increased significantly, *synagogue* and *temple* are still much more common. For example, in 2005, there were 456 articles with *synagogue*, 151 with *temple*, and 54 with *shul*.

The trend for *shul* is not just about numbers increasing over time; it is also about changing use. In the early years, the word was used mostly in quoted speech, as in a 1930 article: "The non-religious element hotly contest this claim. 'It's these schul people that are to blame,' they say." Many of these tokens are marked as foreign with quotes or italics, as in 1928: "the poor Jew who tried to get into a 'schul' on Yom Kippur without a ticket." There are also a few tokens that are not in quoted speech and are not marked as foreign, as in a 1933 historical article about Shearith Israel, referred to several times as the "Spanish and Portuguese Synagogue":

> Prayers, ceremonials, chants, memorials as well as a living memory of the long-dead who once met in council to devise ways and means of establishing a schul, the first in North America, for the early Jews who settled in Manhattan, lend Shearith Israel dignity and solemnity that are absent from other similarly great institutions.

It is possible that, by using a Yiddish word, this writer was indicating his Ashkenazi roots in contrast to the Sephardi Jews he was writing about.

The word *shul* does not appear at all in the JTA corpus in the 1940s and '50s, a time when Jews in America were generally integrating into American society and working their way up the socioeconomic ladder by entering lucrative professions and moving to the suburbs. In the 1960s and '70s it occurs mostly in the names of historic synagogues, as in "the famous old 'Rashi Shul'" (1961) and "the historic Blue Hill Avenue Shul" (1966), and in quoted speech. Interestingly, it even occurs in a quote from a US-trained rabbi in Iran: "In my shul every Sabbath evening we have more than a thousand people" (1979). This rabbi is not descended from Yiddish speakers but likely learned this word when he attended rabbinical school in the US. There are also a few tokens of *shul* outside of quoted speech.

From the mid-1980s to the present, *shul* has seen broader use. It is still used in the names of historic synagogues and in quoted speech, but it is also used as an alternative way to say synagogue or temple shortly after one of those words has already been used. This 1987 headline is an example: "Vandalism of Synagogue Was Racist, Shul's Lawyer Tells Supreme Court." Sometimes *shul* is used first, as in this headline from 2006: "Extreme Shul Makeover Bringing the Shul to the People: an out of Synagogue Experience." In addition, *shul* is used in reference to Orthodox synagogues, as in 2004: "In a First, Orthodox Shul Hires Woman to Rule on Certain Jewish Legal Issues." It is possible that some writers understood *shul* to refer to Orthodox synagogues and *synagogue/temple* to non-Orthodox ones (see Kaufman 1999). Especially in the 1990s and 2000s we also see more general uses, such as a rabbi "who admits sneaking the Macarena into his shul's Simchat Torah celebration" (1997) and "Gay Shul's Siddur Features Prayer for 'Unexpected Intimacy'" (2008).

Shul is not the only Yiddish word that has increased in use in recent years. I also searched the JTA corpus for tokens of *daven*, a Yiddish word for 'pray' that stems from a Hebrew word meaning 'whisper.' I selected this word because the survey data does not indicate that it is increasing in the younger generations. Even so, based on anecdotal evidence, I expected to find that this word was used more in recent decades than in the early part of the 20th century. Indeed, that is the case. In the JTA corpus, *daven* is much less common than *shul* overall, and its increase happened a bit later. There are no articles with *daven* from 1923 through 1970. There are two in the 1970s, one in the 1980s, four in the 1990s, and 16 in the 2000s. (Because the word *daven* is so rare, analyzing it in relation to *pray* would not be helpful.) Most of the tokens of *daven* are in quoted speech, and several are translated as "pray." Based on the lower incidence of *daven* than *shul* in JTA, and the fact that it is used mostly in quoted speech, it seems that *daven* is considered more appropriate for spoken than written registers. Even so, it is possible that, like *shul*, *daven* will continue to expand in numbers and into new contexts.

We see a similar trend with the word *chutzpah* ('nerve, gall'). I selected this word to determine if the increase in Yiddish words can also be seen outside of the religious domain. In the survey data, age+gen has a significant independent effect on the use of *chutzpah* in its negative sense (as in "Can you believe that guy's chutzpah?"): younger Jews are *less* likely to use it than older Jews. Even so, the use of this word has also increased in the JTA corpus over the last few decades, as Figure 2 indicates. This analysis is based on raw numbers of articles with the word *chutzpah*, as no comparable English equivalent exists.

As the analysis of *chutzpah* indicates, it is not only words in the religious domain that are increasing in the Jewish press; it is also words that have become common in general American English. According to my survey data, many non-Jews report using the word *chutzpah*, especially in its positive sense (as in "I really admire that guy's chutzpah"). It has been used in the general American press, even in southern newspapers (Bernstein forthcoming), and Oprah Winfrey gave out the "Chutzpah Award" for a few years. A search on Google's Ngram viewer (which includes Jewish-audience books among its large corpus of English-language books) finds that *chutzpah* was very rare before the 1960s and then increased steadily from the mid-1960s to 2005. It is unclear whether the spread beyond Jewish communities influenced or was influenced by the spread within Jewish communities – probably a bit of both.

The data from the JTA corpus demonstrate that several Yiddish words have increased in the past few decades in a national written venue. To check whether we see the same trends at a local level, I analyzed the use of a few Yiddish words in a second corpus, the Pittsburgh Jewish newspaper, known from 1895 to 1966 as the *Jewish Criterion* and from 1967 to the present as the *Jewish Chronicle*. While I might have selected any city's Jewish newspaper, I selected Pittsburgh's because its back issues

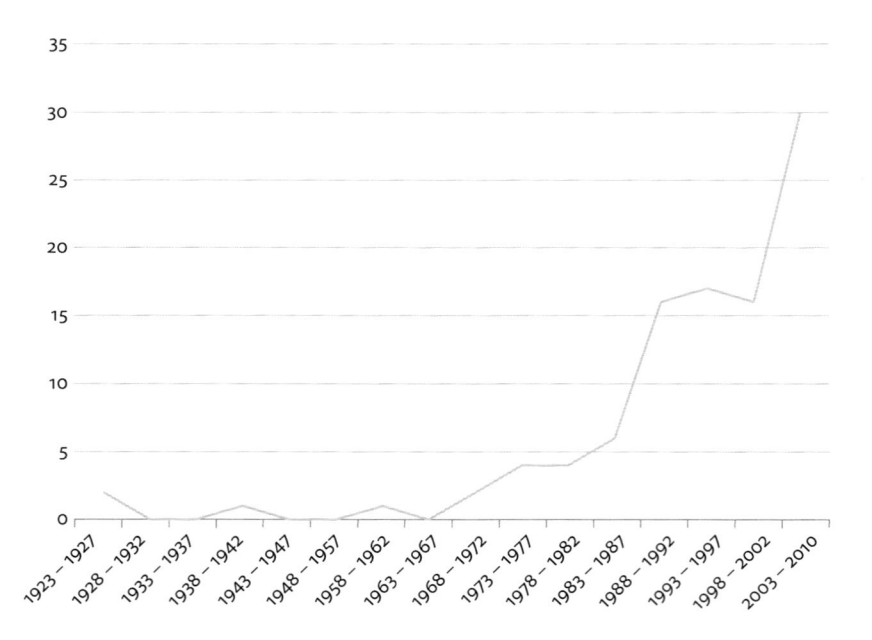

Figure 2. Average # of articles with *chutzpah* per year in JTA corpus.

are available online in a searchable format. Like other eastern and midwestern cities, Pittsburgh was a destination for thousands of Jewish immigrants, mostly from Russia and Poland, around the turn of the 20th century, in addition to a sizeable German-Jewish population that had arrived a few decades earlier (Taylor 1943).

As Figure 3 indicates, the incidence of *shul* increased significantly in the 1980s, like in the JTA corpus. At the same time, we also see a difference: *shul* was used more in the earlier decades in the Pittsburgh corpus than in the JTA corpus. (The search function in the Pittsburgh Jewish newspaper corpus yields results per issue rather than per article, so an analysis of *shul* as a percentage of *synagogue*, etc., is not feasible, and the percentages in Figure 1 and Figure 3 are not directly comparable.) Several of the tokens of *shul* in the Pittsburgh data are from quoted speech within articles, reminding us that the word *shul* was not completely absent from American Jewish speech in the 1920s through 1980s. Perhaps it was seen as part of a more informal register, less appropriate for print journalism than for spoken conversations. In addition, because Pittsburgh has a sizeable Orthodox population (12.6% of 45,000 Jews total, according to Schoor 1984), it is possible that the use of *shul* was greater there than it was in cities with smaller Orthodox populations. Some of the uses of *shul* do refer to Orthodox congregations, such as a 1949 use of *shul* referring to the Orthodox Shaare Torah.

To sum up the corpus study, it is clear that the use of *shul* and a few other Yiddish words increased significantly in the Jewish American press – both on national and local levels – in the 1980s and 1990s. This is especially true for Yiddish words in the religious domain (*shul*, *daven*) but we also see this trend in the non-religious word

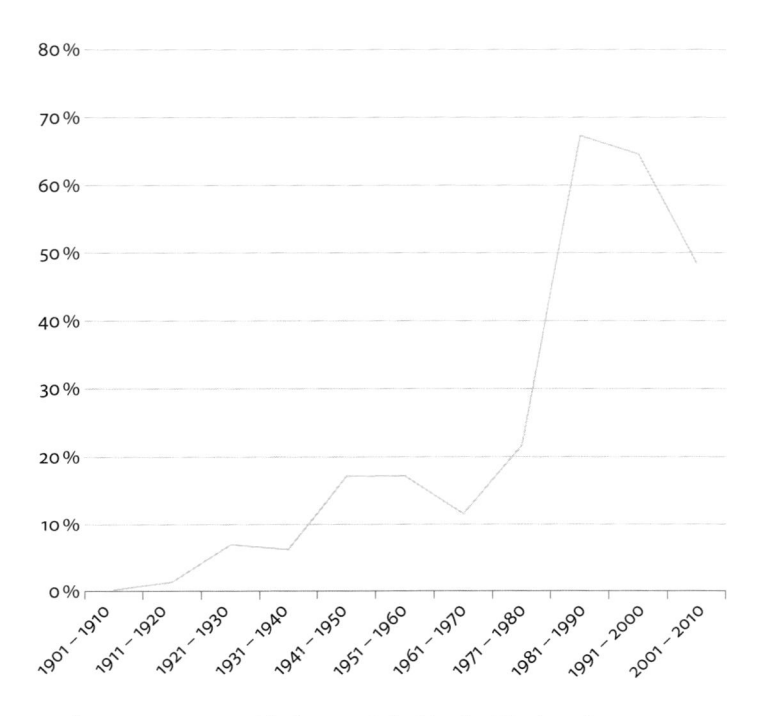

Figure 3. % of issues per year with the word *shul* in the Pittsburgh corpus.

chutzpah. As the next section explains, it is not just the mainstream Jewish press that features an increase in Yiddish words; it is also cultural venues geared toward young Jewish adults.

2.3 Media geared toward young Jewish adults

In 2010, a few Jews in their 20s and 30s created a website geared toward new parents. It included information on Jewish birth ceremonies, Jewish baby names, family-oriented Jewish traditions, and raising children in interfaith families. They considered several names for the website – and even consulted with me as a linguist with expertise about Jewish English. They wanted something that was recognizably Jewish but would not scare off people with little Jewish education. Ultimately they settled on a name that includes a Yiddish word: "Kveller.com: A Jewish Twist on Parenting." Why would a site geared toward young Jewish parents highlight a Yiddish word, *kvell* ('feel or express pride'), which is associated with grandparents pinching their grandchildren's cheeks? I would argue that the reason is the recent change in the social meaning of many Yiddish loanwords: they have acquired associations with young, hip, ironic, urban Jewishness, a quality sometimes lightheartedly referred to as "Heebster," a combination of "Heeb" and "hipster."

We see this trend in several Heebster-oriented cultural venues (see discussion in Benor 2012b, from which parts of the following discussion have been adapted). The original Heebster organ, Heeb Magazine, published from 2002–2010 and now available online, included several sections with Yiddish names: "The Whole *Megillah*" ('long, engrossing story or description,' lit. 'scroll'), "*Nosh* Pit" ('snack,' based on "mosh pit," a section about food), and "Urban *Kvetch*" ('complaint,' likely based on the New York delivery service "UrbanFetch"). One image, from an article about the need for a Jewish Disney princess, not only uses a Yiddish phrase ("oy vey" – 'oh no') but also presents it in faux-Hebrew lettering (Figure 4). As Shandler explains, the rendering of English letters in a form that looks like Hebrew letters "marks the words as distinctively Jewish while integrating them into a more widely familiar communicative code. The use of these fonts thus resembles 'kosher-style' cuisine, preserving manner while altering, even subverting, substance" (Shandler 2006: 156).

Figure 4. Image from Heeb Magazine (http://heebmagazine.com/disneys-next-princess-whens-our-turn/39117).

Another example of Heebster Yiddish comes from the 2003 movie *The Hebrew Hammer*, a satire of "blaxploitation" films. The young Jewish characters use Yiddish loanwords like *shlep* ('carry') and *bubbele* ('sweetie') and Yiddish-influenced constructions like "eat by us," "you may have what to brag about," and "you want I should talk dirty to you?" They also tap into the association between Jews and the [x] sound, using [x] in place of /h/, /k/, and /r/: "The 'xood,'" "Xebrew," "Xadillac," and "xemove" (remove). By using exaggerated Yiddishisms, this film offers a satirical, entertaining take on American Jewish culture, directed especially toward young, urban Jews with Yiddish-speaking ancestry.

We see a similar (over)use of Yiddish-influenced English in Lisa Alcalay Klug's 2008 *Cool Jew: The Ultimate Guide for Every Member of the Tribe*. This humorous book presents Jewish ethnicity, culture, and religion as cool by combining informative text with top ten lists, diagrams, and hip hop imagery. *Cool Jew* includes Yiddish loanwords from the religious domain, such as *shul*, *frum* ('religious'), and *shlogn kapores* ('expiation of sins through swinging chickens over one's head'), as well as loanwords outside of the religious domain, such as *gornisht* ('nothing'), *shmear* ('spread'), and *yiddishe kopf* ('Jewish head'). This book even features a chapter titled "Heebster Spoken Here" and a recurring sidebar called "FYI: For the Yiddish Impaired."

Even though materials like these are produced by and for young Jews, their creators also recognize the ideological connection between Yiddish and grandparents. One organization taps into this connection to convince young Jews to call their "bubbes" ('grandmas') and "zeydes" ('grandpas') in swing states like Florida and Ohio and convince them to vote for Democrats in presidential elections. The organization now known as the Jewish Council for Education and Research publicized these efforts in the 2004, 2008, and 2012 elections using different names: "Operation *Bubbe*," "The Great *Schlep*" ('long journey'), and "Call Your *Zeyde*." All three of these Internet-based campaigns used Yiddish words, not only in their titles but also in their publicity materials. The most recent one, a video parody of Carly Rae Jepsen's "Call Me Maybe," portrayed a young woman calling her bubbe and zeyde and convincing them to vote for Barack Obama, using several Yiddish words. The young woman says, "So *nu* ('so?'), how's West Palm Beach?" Her bubbe says "*keppie*" ('head') and "Why don't you be a *mensch* ('good person') and vote Obama?" Her zeyde has a Yiddish accent ("vell, vell") and says, "*sheyna punim*" ('pretty face'), "*shanda*" ('scandal'), and "The president does have a *heimishe neshama*" ('warm, familiar soul'). Clearly the creators of this video understand that members of their target audience, young Jewish adults, associate Yiddish words and pronunciations with their grandparents. But they also recognize the infusion of these words in Jewish youth culture.

This brief description of the use of Yiddish loanwords in media geared toward young Jewish adults parallels the findings from the survey and corpus studies. Although Yiddish is associated with elderly Jews, it has also come to be associated with "cool Jews" in their 20s and 30s. "Heebster" culture uses select Yiddish loanwords for ironic and comic effect, drawing from both the religious and secular spheres and showing young Jews' ambivalent orientation toward their Jewish roots and the communal structures that engage their parents (see Cohen and Kelman 2005 on irony in Jewish youth events). In other words, postvernacular Yiddish indexes not only nostalgia and connection to the immigrant generation but also a young Jewish hipness.

3. Discussion and conclusion

The data presented in this paper point to dual trends in the use of a Germanic language in America, a century after this language was introduced to this country on a large scale. Vernacular Yiddish is in decline, and postvernacular Yiddish is on the rise. While some Yiddish loanwords are used mostly by older Jews, others are used more by younger Jews. The trend we might expect several generations after the mass wave of Yiddish-speaking immigration – decline in Yiddish-influenced English – is taking place with some loanwords. But the opposite trend is taking place with others, especially words in the religious domain and an ironic use of others.

This can be seen as an example of the boomerang effect in ethnic language use, in which descendants of people who shifted away from a language come to embrace elements of it. Why are the great-grandchildren of immigrants embracing their ancestral language, albeit in postvernacular ways? There are a few factors. First, Jews today feel increasingly comfortable displaying their distinctness in full view of their non-Jewish neighbors, colleagues, friends, and spouses. This was not the case in the mid-20th century, when the children of immigrants worked hard to distance themselves from their parents' embarrassing accents and other cultural practices. The trend toward ethnic pride and multiculturalism that began in late-1960s America had a large impact on Jews' pride in their distinctness. In addition, this can be seen as an instance of Hansen's (1938) theory of the "third-generation return": "What the son wishes to forget the grandson wishes to remember." Although some scholars have criticized this theory as not being supported by data (e.g., Gans 1979, Lyman 1995, Kaufman 2012), it seems to be valid in this and other cases of the boomerang effect. Of course the grandchildren do not fully reclaim the language and culture of their (immigrant) grandparents. The postvernacular nature of this "return" is akin to Gans's (1979) notion of "symbolic ethnicity." Even so, it is clear from the data presented in this paper that Hansen's theory points to something real: some young Jews today are expressing interest in elements of Yiddish culture that their parents and grandparents eschewed.

Another factor in the contemporary interest in Yiddish and use of Yiddish loanwords is the expanding "salad bar" of Jewish expression (Horowitz 2003): Jews today have an increasing array of options for religious, cultural, political, and social engagement with other Jews. Postvernacular Yiddish is just one of these options; others include synagogue attendance, advocacy work for Israel or for economic justice in American cities, the local food movement, and Ladino folk music. Different Jews embrace different options, and some participate in multiple ones. Engagement with Yiddish allows some young Jews to align themselves with certain individuals and to distinguish themselves from others.

Also contributing to the increase in Yiddish loanwords is the renaissance in Jewish religious observance. While many young Jews today (especially children of mixed marriages) are distancing themselves from the religiosity of their ancestors, some are (re-)embracing it, voluntarily taking on the strictures of Orthodox religious observance. Partly because vernacular Yiddish is still used in some Orthodox communities, the ideological connection between Yiddish words and Orthodoxy remains strong. When Jews embrace Orthodoxy they also adopt many of the Yiddish-origin features Orthodox Jews commonly use within English (Benor 2012a). Some of these features spread to non-Orthodox communities through overlapping social networks. We might hypothesize the spread of Yiddish-origin features in the religious domain as follows: Yiddish-speaking Haredi Jews interact with Haredi Jews who do not speak Yiddish, who interact with Modern Orthodox Jews, who interact with non-Orthodox Jews. Through these interactions, Yiddish words and constructions spread, as less religious Jews look to more religious Jews as a model to emulate.

Note that this paper focuses on loanword use among American Jews, of which only about 10% are Orthodox (although this percentage is growing due to high birth rates). The survey respondents did include Orthodox Jews, and the Jewish press analyzed reaches a partly Orthodox audience. Even so, an analysis focusing only on Orthodox groups would find much more Yiddish influence, as well as an increasing use of specific features, like "staying by us" (Benor 2012a).

While the data presented here are about Yiddish, and some of the details are unique to Jews as an ethno-religious community, much of the analysis is applicable to other ethnic groups in America, including those that speak other Germanic languages. The current historical moment in the United States is conducive to the symbolic return to the language of one's ancestors, whether they assimilated to English following immigration or colonial conquest. In contrast to the first half of the twentieth century, many people today express personal connection to their ethnic distinctiveness and its linguistic manifestation. Shandler's (2006) notion of postvernacularity sheds light on how people relate to a minority language when a large percentage of its speakers have shifted to the dominant language. The methods used in this study to investigate the trajectories of postvernacular Yiddish – survey, corpus study, and cultural analysis – might be useful in research on other languages and groups. The boomerang effect certainly does not apply in every situation of language shift. But in some cases, focusing on the curvilinear pattern of language use gives us a better understanding of the connection between language and ethnic identity.

References

Agha, Asif. 2003. "The Social Life of a Cultural Value." *Language and Communication* 23: 231–73. DOI: 10.1016/S0271-5309(03)00012-0

Annear, Lucas and Kristin Speth. This volume. "Maintaining a Multilingual Repertoire: Lexical Change in American Norwegian."

Avineri, Netta. 2012. *Heritage Language Socialization Practices in Secular Yiddish Educational Contexts: The Creation of a Metalinguistic Community*. Los Angeles, California: University of California Los Angeles dissertation.

Beider, Alexander. 2013. "Reapplying the Language Tree Model to the History of Yiddish." *Journal of Jewish Languages* 1(1): 77–121. DOI: 10.1163/22134638-12340003

Benor, Sarah Bunin. 2010. "Ethnolinguistic Repertoire: Shifting the Analytic Focus in Language and Ethnicity." *Journal of Sociolinguistics* 14(2): 159–183. DOI: 10.1111/j.1467-9841.2010.00440.x

Benor, Sarah Bunin. 2011. "Jewish Languages in the Age of the Internet: An Introduction." *Language and Communication. Special issue on "Jewish Languages in the Age of the Internet"* 31(2): 95–98.

Benor, Sarah Bunin. 2012a. *Becoming Frum: How Newcomers Learn the Language and Culture of Orthodox Judaism*. New Brunswick: Rutgers University Press.

Benor, Sarah Bunin. 2012b. "Echoes of Yiddish in the Speech of Twenty-First-Century American Jews." In *Choosing Yiddish: Studies on Yiddish Literature, Culture, and History*, ed. by Lara Rabinovitch, Shiri Goren and Hannah Pressman, 319–337. Detroit: Wayne State University Press.

Benor, Sarah Bunin and Steven M. Cohen. 2011. "Talking Jewish: The 'Ethnic English' of American Jews." In *Ethnicity and Beyond: Theories and Dilemmas of Jewish Group Demarcation. Studies in Contemporary Jewry*, vol. 25, ed. by Eli Lederhendler, 62–78. Oxford: Oxford University Press.

Bernstein, Cynthia. Forthcoming. "Lexical Features of Jewish English in the Southern United States." In *Language Variety in the South III: Historical and Contemporary Perspectives*, ed. by Michael Picone and Catherine Davies. Tuscaloosa: The University of Alabama Press.

Chernikoff, Helen. 2008. "Yiddish Revival Creates Rift with Hebrew Speakers." *Reuters*, November 3, 2008. http://www.reuters.com/article/2008/11/03/us-yiddish-revival-idUSTRE4A213V20081103.

Cohen, Steven M. and Ari Y. Kelman. 2005. *Cultural Events and Jewish Identities: Young Adult Jews in New York*. New York: National Foundation for Jewish Culture. http://www.bjpa.org/Publications/details.cfm?PublicationID=2911.

Cohen, Steven M., Jacob B. Ukeles and Ron Miller. 2012. *Jewish Community Study of New York: 2011: Comprehensive Report*. UJA-Federation of New York. http://www.ujafedny.org/get/196904/.

Dubois, Sylvie and Barbara Horvath. 2000. "When the Music Changes, You Change Too: Gender and Language Change in Cajun English." *Language Variation and Change* 11: 287–313.

Ehresmann, Todd and Joshua Bousquette. This volume. "Phonological Non-Integration of Lexical Borrowings in Wisconsin West Frisian."

Eide, Kristin Melum and Arnstein Hjelde. This volume. "Borrowing Modal Elements into American Norwegian: The Case of *suppose(d)*."

Fader, Ayala. 2009. *Mitzvah Girls: Bringing Up the Next Generation of Hasidic Jews in Brooklyn*. Princeton: Princeton University Press.

Gans, Herbert J. 1979. "Symbolic Ethnicity: The Future of Ethnic Groups and Cultures in America." *Ethnic and Racial Studies* 2(1): 1–20. DOI: 10.1080/01419870.1979.9993248

Hansen, Marcus. 1938. *The Problem of the Third Generation Immigrant*. (Augustana Historical Society Publications 8). Rock Island, IL: Augustana Historical Society.

Horowitz, Bethamie. 2003. *Connections and Journeys: Assessing Critical Opportunities for Enhancing Jewish Identity*. Revised version. New York: UJA Federation. http://databank.bjpa.org/Studies/details.cfm?StudyID=539.

Isaacs, Miriam. 1999. "Haredi, Haymish and Frim: Yiddish Vitality and Language Choice in a Transnational, Multilingual Community." *International Journal of the Sociology of Language* 138: 9–30.

Johnstone, Barbara. 2009. "Pittsburghese Shirts: Commodification and the Enregisterment of an Urban Dialect." *American Speech* 84(2): 157–175. DOI: 10.1215/00031283-2009-013

Johnstone, Barbara, Neeta Bhasin and Denise Wittkofski. 2002. "'Dahntahn' Pittsburgh: Monophthongal /aw/ and Representations of Localness in Southwestern Pennsylvania." *American Speech* 77(2): 148–176. DOI: 10.1215/00031283-77-2-148

Kahan Newman, Zelda. This volume. "Discourse Markers in the Narratives of New York Hasidim: More V2 Attrition."

Katz, Dovid (ed). 1987. *Origins of the Yiddish Language*. Oxford: Pergamon Press.

Kaufman, David. 1999. *Shul with a Pool: The "Synagogue-Center" in American Jewish History*. Waltham: Brandeis University Press.

Kaufman, David. 2012. *Jewhooing the Sixties: American Celebrity and Jewish Identity*. Waltham: Brandeis University Press.

Kotler-Berkowitz, Laurence, Steven M. Cohen, Jonathon Ament, Vivian Klaff, Frank Mott and Danyelle Peckerman-Neuman. 2003. *The National Jewish Population Survey 2000–01: Strength, Challenge and Diversity in the American Jewish Population*. New York: United Jewish Communities.

Lyman, Stanford M. 1995. *Color, Culture, Civilization: Race and Minority Issues in American Society*. Urbana: University of Illinois Press.

Schoor, Ann G. 1984. *Survey of Greater Pittsburgh's Jewish Population, 1984*. Pittsburgh: United Jewish Federation of Pittsburgh. http://jewishdatabank.org/Studies/details.cfm?StudyID=366.

Shandler, Jeffrey. 2006. *Adventures in Yiddishland: Postvernacular Language and Culture*. Berkeley: University of California Press.

Sharma, Devyani. 2011a. "Return of the Native: Hindi in British English." In *Chutnefying English: The Phenomenon of Hinglish*, ed. by Rita Kothari and Rupert Snell, 1–21. New Delhi, India: Penguin.

Sharma, Devyani. 2011b. "Style Repertoire and Social Change in British Asian English." *Journal of Sociolinguistics* 15(4): 464–492. DOI: 10.1111/j.1467-9841.2011.00503.x

Shin, Hyon B. and Robert A. Kominski. 2010. "Language Use in the United States: 2007." *American Community Survey Reports*. U.S. Census Bureau. http://www.census.gov/hhes/socdemo/language/data/acs/ACS-12.pdf.

Soldat-Jaffe, Tatjana. 2012. *Twenty-First Century Yiddishism*. Brighton: Sussex Academic Press.

Taylor, Maurice. 1943. "A Sample Study of the Jewish Population of Pittsburgh, 1938." In *Jewish Population Studies* (Jewish Social Studies Publications 3), ed. by Sophia M. Robinson, 81–108. New York: Conference on Jewish Relations. http://www.jewishdatabank.org/Archive/Jewish_Population_Studies_1943_Robinson__Multiple_Studies_Included.pdf.

Weinreich, Max. (1973) 2008. *History of the Yiddish Language*. New Haven: Yale University Press.

Wexler, Paul. 2002. *Two-Tiered Relexification in Yiddish: Jews, Sorbs, Khazars, and the Kiev-Polessian Dialect*. Berlin: Mouton de Gruyter. DOI: 10.1515/9783110898736

Phonological non-integration of lexical borrowings in Wisconsin West Frisian

Todd Ehresmann and Joshua Bousquette
University of Wisconsin–Madison / University of Georgia

Working with heritage speakers of West Frisian living in Wisconsin, the following chapter examines the frequency of use of English lexical items in spoken Wisconsin West Frisian and the phonological (non-)integration of these lexemes. The data show a comparatively low frequency of borrowing compared to other heritage communities, with a corresponding lack of phonological integration. We categorize the consultants as 'coordinate bilinguals,' who have simultaneous on-line access to lexical items from both language-specific lexicons. Consultants' balanced bilingualism minimizes the cross-linguistic transfer of both lexical items and phonology while accessing lexical items from either lexicon. This coordinate bilingualism account is supported by the sociolinguistic evidence of a context-dependent diglossia – parallel to the Dutch-Frisian diglossia in the Netherlands – in which both English and West Frisian were restricted to specific domains. It is argued here that social context, as well as the multiple-lexicon coordinate bilingualism model, can best account for these data.

Keywords: bilingualism, heritage language, West Frisian, code switching, phonological integration, lexicon

1. Introduction[1]

Building on previous research on incorporation of loanwords[2] in North American heritage[3] communities, this chapter examines a West Frisian community of first and second generation speakers for evidence of phonological incorporation of English (L2) lexemes into speakers' West Frisian (L1). Dealing with a hitherto unstudied heritage language community with regard to loan incorporation, this study of Wisconsin West Frisian introduces the time-depth of settlement (measured in generations removed from Europe) as a variable, while remaining a historical and social parallel to other heritage communities in the Upper Midwest that experienced similar periods of bilingualism and subsequent, near-complete language shift to English monolingualism, including German (Lucht 2007, Wilkerson and Salmons 2008, 2012, Frey 2013), Norwegian (Haugen 1950, 1953, Hjelde 1996, Johannessen and Laake forthcoming, Annear and Speth this volume), and Swedish (Cederström 2014, Larsson et al. this volume).

Data drawn from fieldwork conducted in 2008 and 2009 with first and second generation speakers suggest that inter-sentential code switches incorporating English lexemes into spoken West Frisian is minimal, with a relatively low number of English tokens, and virtually no examples of structural integration. These results are consistent with Matras' (2009) model of code switching among bilinguals, as opposed to loan incorporation, in which lexemes are structurally integrated into the matrix language.

We argue that the low frequency of code switching and phonological incorporation of loans exhibited by bilingual consultants in this data set results from the balanced bilingualism of the consultants, and the context-specific patterns of language acquisition and use in the community. Balanced bilingualism among first and second generation speakers allows speakers to control language mode, and to minimize the influence of English while speaking West Frisian, resulting in a low frequency of code switching. Balanced bilingualism among individuals parallels context- and situation-specific use of language in the community, with sociolinguistic evidence detailing a language diglossia inherited from European Frisian communities in the Netherlands and perpetuated in the Upper Midwest. West Frisian immigrants replaced Dutch with English as the language of communication for commerce, education and inter-community interactions, but retained West Frisian in familial and social contexts

---

1. We would like to thank Joe Salmons, Janne Bondi Johannessen, Lucas Annear and Kristin Speth for comments and discussions, as well as the audience members at the Second Workshop on Immigrant Languages in America and our anonymous reviewers. Usual disclaimers apply. We also thank our consultants for their time and hospitality.

2. We use 'loan' or 'loanword' in a neutral sense with respect to phonological integration, as compared to integrated 'borrowing' and non-integrated 'code switching.'

3. We define a heritage language as one that is acquired as an L1 in a natural setting, typically in the home or in the community (cf. Rothman 2009).

post-immigration, particularly in instances where multiple factors intersected, e.g., in agrarian labor (Bousquette 2010). The context-specific language acquisition and use among balanced bilinguals is here argued to result in a state of 'coordinate' bilingualism, in which lexical items are drawn from language-specific lexical inventories, which reflect language-specific phonology (Weinreich 1953, Ervin and Osgood 1954, Hamers and Blanc 2000). Instances of code switching, though rare, therefore reflect language-specific phonological patterns; source-language phonology is maintained in 32 of 33 total instances of inter-sentential code switches, resulting in a clear lack of phonological integration of code switches. We conclude that coordinate bilingualism resulted from the shallow time-depth of settlement and recent immigration and context-specific use of language, and that this coordinate bilingualism accounts for the lack of phonological integration of English lexical items into Wisconsin West Frisian.

This chapter begins with a profile of the consultants and method of data collection in §2, followed by a historical profile of language use in the community in §3. Previous literature on bilingualism is discussed in §4, focusing on the interaction between multiple language-specific grammars and lexicons. Data are presented in §5, followed by an analysis and discussion of the findings in §6, and concluding remarks in §7.

2. Consultants, methods

2.1 Data set and speaker profile

Interviews were conducted in 2008 and 2009 with 9 consultants, of which data from four consultants are considered in greater detail here.[4] As of 1910, the community of Randolph Township consisted of 680 individuals, with 387 (57%) of them being proficient speakers of West Frisian. The highest concentration of proficient speakers (and ethnic Frisians) was concentrated in Randolph Center, which was incorporated as Friesland, WI, in 1946 (Bousquette and Ehresmann 2010: 260–262). The population of Friesland at time of interview was 303, of which only a handful (ca. less than two dozen by the consultants' estimation) were proficient speakers.

The data set consists of two first generation and two second generation speakers. Parents of second generation speakers emigrated to Wisconsin during the early 20th century, while first generation immigrants came to the United States (and eventually Wisconsin) after the end of WWII (see Table 1). All speakers are proficient English-Frisian bilinguals with some degree of Dutch proficiency from pre-immigration education, or from the influence of the Dutch Reform church and bible; and were in their late 70's or early 80's at time of interview.

---

4. Recordings are now housed at the Max Kade Institute Sound Archive at the University of Wisconsin–Madison.

Table 1. Wisconsin Frisian speaker profiles.

Speaker	Gender	Generation	Year of emigration[5]	Age at emigration
1	M	1st	1947	16
2	F	1st	1948	~15
3	M	2nd	~1908	n/a
4	F	2nd	1920	n/a

All speakers were previously acquainted with one another, being classmates, coworkers or neighbors in a small, rural community. Speakers 2 and 4 are cousins, but did not meet each other until speaker 2 emigrated to Wisconsin at age 15. Topics of conversation included discussions about Wisconsin and the home country in Friesland Province, The Netherlands, in addition to present-day topics. Researcher-directed conversation touched on the differences between Friesland Province and Friesland, WI, as well as aspects of daily life, especially pertaining to language use. Consultants either grew up on farms or worked as farmers themselves, so farm terminology (and technological terminology in general) comprised a good amount of their conversation, and provided a good deal of tokens. Consultants report that while West Frisian was widely spoken in the community when they were younger, present-day use of the language is now limited to social gatherings among the remaining speakers in the community; West Frisian is maintained in the community by personal relationships between individuals, rather than through institutional support.

All data was recorded and analyzed using the open source acoustic software Praat (Boersma and Weenink 2012). Recordings were combed for the use of single English tokens during interactions in West Frisian, taken from running speech in both individual interviews and group conversation. These tokens were then analyzed to discern whether they maintained English phonological patterns, or were incorporated into the West Frisian phonological system. In previous work on this community, Ehresmann and Bousquette (2011) found that speakers exhibited both Frisian-like 'glottal tension' and English-like 'glottal width' systems of marking voicing distinction in consonants (cf. Avery and Idsardi 2001, Iverson and Salmons 1995, 2003, 2007). Consistent with the findings of Simon and Leuschner (2010) and Simon (2011), the use of this 'mixed' phonological system rules out stops as viable indicators of phonological incorporation. This study therefore focuses on other typological differences in the phonological systems of the languages, including the realization of /r/ and /g/, particularly in rare instances of recasting, where semantic equivalents (or cognates) are presented as near minimal pairs.

---

5. For second generation Wisconsin-Frisians, the year of emigration of the parents is given.

2.2 Method

In order to categorize the English tokens found in the Frisian data, we follow Annear and Speth (this volume), which in turn builds on the work of Clyne (2003) and Matras (2009). We categorize English tokens among Wisconsin West Frisian speakers based on three primary diagnostics: the speaker's (bilingual) proficiency, the regularity of use of the token; and whether or not the token is structurally integrated (here measured as phonological incorporation). Ranging from non-incorporated borrowings – or code switches – to complete syntactic and phonological incorporation of the lexical item, Matras' continuum (Figure 1; cf. Matras 2009: 111) measures the degree of integration of a given token based on three separate criteria: Matras argues that non-integrated code switching is infrequently employed by bilingual speakers, while integrated borrowing is expected to occur regularly among monolinguals. Given the degree of bilingualism in the present data set, regularly occurring, phonologically integrated tokens reflect borrowing, while isolated and non-integrated tokens reflect code switching behavior.

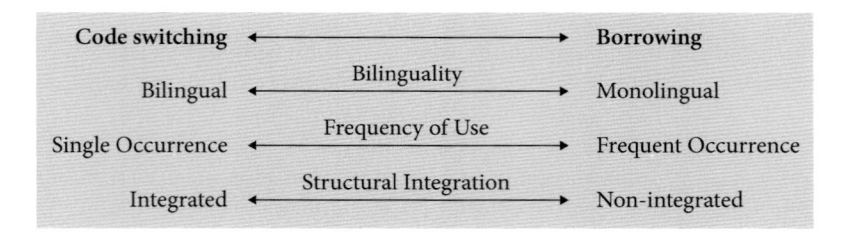

Code switching	←————————————→	**Borrowing**
Bilingual	←——— Bilinguality ———→	Monolingual
Single Occurrence	←——— Frequency of Use ———→	Frequent Occurrence
Integrated	←——— Structural Integration ———→	Non-integrated

Figure 1. Continuum of code switching and borrowing.

Annear and Speth (this volume) follow Myers-Scotton (1993: 163) and Matras (2009: 110–113) in categorizing code switches in terms of 'core' versus 'cultural.' Lexemes termed 'core' are those for which an equivalent exists in both the donor (embedded) and recipient (matrix) language. Bilingual speakers who have access to core lexemes in both languages may access either language-specific lexicon, but will do so infrequently, and without integrating the core lexeme into the matrix language (in this case, West Frisian). In contrast, 'cultural' lexemes are those for which there is no equivalent between the two languages, and therefore cultural lexemes are often borrowed, meaning they are structurally integrated into the matrix language, and may even (eventually) be integrated into the lexicon of the matrix language. Cultural lexemes are typically borrowed to fill semantic gaps such as technology (e.g., German *das iPhone, der Wii*), cultural notions with specific or untranslatable meanings (e.g., *Zeitgeist, Schadenfreude, der Shitstorm*), or new lexical items not present in the recipient language, such as lexemes for flora, fauna, food and drink (e.g., *coffee* in English and other languages, originally from Arabic, borrowed with the introduction of the plant and beverage).

In a similarly categorical analysis, Annear and Speth (this volume) follow Haugen (1956) in analyzing different types of 'transfer', in which the phonemic structure, semantic structure, or both are incorporated into American Norwegian. They find that speakers employed cultural borrowings to fill semantic gaps, such as the incorporation of English *barn* for the sort of region-specific storage facility (which causes ambiguity with the inherited term for 'child'). However, they also found that English borrowings replaced existing, more specific, core European Norwegian terms. One such example is borrowing of English *road* as American Norwegian *råd*, exhibiting both semantic and phonemic transfer – or in our terminology, a phonologically incorporated, core borrowing.

We arrange our analysis here in much the same way, designating tokens as being shared, 'core' elements of each language-specific lexicon, versus 'cultural' elements that were not present in European Frisian at the time of emigration of the consultants (or their parents). The difference between core and cultural is therefore a measure of whether these West Frisian speakers have access to a semantic equivalent in their heritage variety (core), or whether they draw on – or incorporate – an English lexeme to express the same semantic role. Technological innovations not present at time of immigration are therefore considered cultural terminology because they were not present in the variety brought over with immigrants, despite how central such things as tractors and combines might have been to Midwestern farmers.[6,7]

Secondly, we determine to what degree the borrowed English token has been incorporated phonologically into Frisian. Considered here are the differences between West Frisian and English in the realization of /r/ and /g/, which are clearly defined and distinct in both languages, as well as in this heritage variety (Sipma 1913, Tiersma 1985). Analysis of the varied realizations of both phonemes in borrowed tokens is considered in the analysis of recasts.

3. Community profile of language use

As touched on briefly in §2.1, a primarily diglossic situation existed in Randolph and Friesland, WI, in the early 20th century. West Frisian and English were the primary languages used in the community, and each language was used exclusively in a given social domain. West Frisian was used in the immediate community between family members and on the farm; English was used when communicating outside of the immediate community, or with non-proficient Frisian speakers.

---

6. This is a departure from Clyne (2003), who argues that language-specific (cultural) terms may be 'core' in the sense of being centrally important to the daily life or identity of the individual.

7. Galema reports that mechanized farming like threshing was known to immigrant Frisian farmers living in Iowa in 1889, while the technology remained unknown in Friesland Province at the time (1996: 201).

Due in large part to recent immigration, the predominant ethnic group and spoken language of Randolph Township in the early 20th century was West Frisian; 37% of the Township was first or second generation Frisian, with local concentrations exceeding 75% in the town center (Bousquette and Ehresmann 2010: 260).

Regarding language proficiency, 57% of the community was 'likely proficient' in the language in 1910, meaning that they were either an attested native speaker of Frisian, or lived in a household with at least one non-English-proficient family member. Perhaps more telling is the fact that 105 individuals in a community of 680 – more than 15% of the population – reported an inability to speak English on the 1910 census, reporting instead proficiency in Frisian.[8] These Frisian speakers were able to function socially and economically in the community due to the presence of proficient – and even monolingual – speakers of West Frisian in high profile positions central to the community. Even as late as 1930, the town postmaster, two pastors, a livestock dealer, a produce dealer, a cattle dealer, a farm equipment dealer, a retail/merchant business owner and a number of salesmen and skilled craftsmen reported proficiency in Frisian[9] (Bousquette 2010). It is therefore reasonable to assume that a monolingual Frisian farmer could conduct most or all of his business in the community using only Frisian. Interviews conducted in 2008 and 2009 confirm that West Frisian was spoken regularly on the farm, and in fact, many consultants describe their own language as being "rough," "slang," or "barn-Frisian" because they learned it and spoke it while working on the farm. Frisian was additionally spoken not only on the farms, but also in the community, and even had such inertia that there is anecdotal evidence of other immigrants learning Frisian rather than English (Bousquette and Ehresmann 2010: 263–264):

> *De meestn die tot skoale gingen dan...'r wienen meer Friezen dan Dutsers. Dat he sei ... dat he de eerste dei dat he na de skoale gyng. Da kaam he thuus en sei it z'n mam...ik moat it Fries lere oos ben ik net meer ien bij de oaren wan' de oaren prate altyd Fries.*
>
> 'The most that went to school then...there were more Frisians than Germans. He saw that ... on the first day that he went to school. Then he came home and said it to his mom...I have to learn Frisian or else I won't fit in with the others because the others always speak Frisian.'

---

8. Similarly high concentrations of monolingual speakers are also attested in 1910 for WI-German communities of Hustisford (24% monolingual, Wilkerson and Salmons 2012) and New Holstein, WI (28%, Frey 2013).

9. The 1930 US Census reports these speakers as uniformly "Dutch" from "Holland," though the same individuals were reported as separately "Frisian" or "Dutch" in 1910. Assuming a continuation of the relative concentrations of each group from 1910, those reported as "Dutch" in 1930 can be reasonably assumed to be roughly 90% Frisian and 10% Dutch.

Other consultants attested to the use of Frisian on the playground at school, even though English was legislated as the official language of instruction in Wisconsin, and older students frequently translated English instructions for younger students, and children of recent immigrants.

4. Modeling bilingual processing in a heritage community

Adopting a basic generative model, we assume that syntactic and phonological features are cohesively bundled in (or as) lexical items (Chomsky 1965). We expand this framework to account for multiple, language-specific grammars (and lexicons). Recent work on code switching (Grosjean 2008, Koostra et al. 2010) has argued for just such an interaction between different language-specific lexicons, with inter-sentential code switching being the result. In fact, a growing body of research has argued that these language-specific grammars (and lexicons) are not at all privative, but rather may involve not just online lexical transfer (i.e., code switching), but also the borrowing of productive morphological forms (Kolmer 2012) or syntactic structures (Bousquette et al. 2013) under heavy and prolonged contact situations. A working definition of how this sort of bilingual transfer occurs at the lexical level is provided by Grosjean (2008: 63–64):

> Bilinguals who are highly dominant in one language may simply not be able to control language mode in the same way as less dominant or balanced bilinguals. Although they may deactivate their stronger language in a monolingual environment that requires only the weaker language, it will simply not be developed enough or active enough to allow them to stay in a monolingual mode. Future research will have to investigate the underlying mechanisms that make a stronger language "seep through" despite the fact that it has been deactivated.

While this notion of 'dominance' and cross-linguistic 'seeping' certainly invokes notions of incomplete acquisition and attrition in heritage communities (Anderssen and Westergaard this volume, cf. Menn (1989), Sasse (1992: 61) and Lipski (2009) for a nuanced view of 'forgetters' and 'rusty' speakers, respectively), the present study builds on Bousquette et al. (forthcoming) in defining the dominant language in terms of "frequency of activation of the language-specific grammar" (2); a shift in dominance so defined may shift the directionality of code switching or borrowing, or affect the frequency of the same. To that definition, we may add a socio-linguistic component, that the dominant language is context-specific, dependent on the social situation, location, conversational topic, or the individuals present (as noted in §2.1).[10] In addition to Grosjean's assertion that balanced bilinguals can better control language mode and limit 'seeping' of lexical items, a context-determined dominance of West Frisian could further reduce the frequency of English code switches.

---

10. We thank an anonymous reviewer for the reminder that code switching varies based on setting.

Turning our attention towards a synchronic analysis, coordinate bilingualism (Weinreich 1953, Ervin and Osgood 1954, Lambert and Crosby 1958) provides a model of language acquisition and use consistent with the notion of multiple language- and context-specific grammars. This definition differentiates coordinate bilinguals drawing lexemes from two different languages – from 'compound' bilinguals having "one conceptual representation common to both languages" (Hamers and Blanc 2000: 163). The distinction between a compound and coordinate bilingual is outlined as being a matter of acquisition (Hamers and Blanc 2000: 27, emphasis added):

> [A compound bilingual] individual who learned both languages as a child in the same context is more likely to have a single cognitive representation for two translation equivalents, whereas **one who learned an L2 in a context different from that of his L1** will probably have a coordinate organization, that is, he will have separate representations for two translation equivalents.

The prediction is therefore that simultaneous bilinguals – that is, children who acquire two different languages as children and become equally proficient in both – are more likely to be compound bilinguals. However, simultaneous bilinguals who acquire two languages in different contexts – as well as sequential bilinguals who acquire native-like proficiency in a second language only after first language acquisition – will have two separate, language-specific lexical representations of equivalent semantic tokens from both the L1 and L2. This is illustrated graphically in Figure 2 below using West Frisian and English cognates *bruorren* and *brothers*.

Compound bilingual

L1 'bruorren'
         \
          single   → bruorren/brothers
          concept
         /
L2 'brothers'

Coordinate bilingual

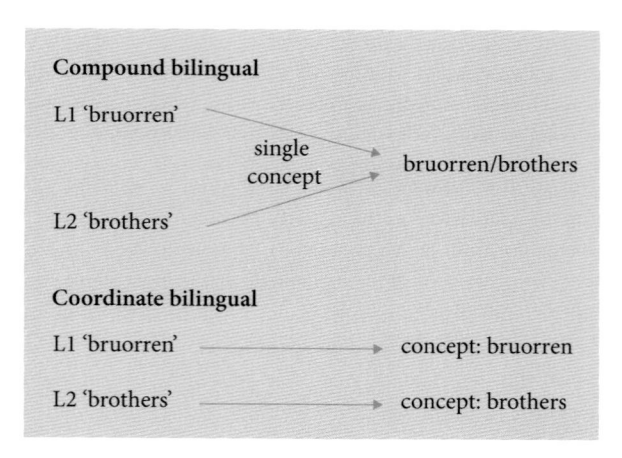

L1 'bruorren' ─────────→ concept: bruorren

L2 'brothers' ─────────→ concept: brothers

Figure 2. Compound and coordinated bilingualism.[11]

Working within the framework outlined here, the baseline hypothesis is that our first and second generation consultants are balanced bilinguals, and are therefore able to

---

11. This has been modified from Hamers and Blanc (2000).

control language mode; inter-sentential code switching should also be infrequent. Based on the pattern of context-specific acquisition and language use of West Frisian vis-à-vis English in Randolph and Friesland, WI, consultants should pattern as coordinate bilinguals. Therefore, cultural borrowings for which there is no equivalent in the L1 should be code switched or accessed independently, from the L2 Lexicon, without being phonologically incorporated into the L1. Core terminology should be less frequently code switched than cultural terminology among balanced bilinguals, since balanced bilinguals would be expected to control language mode and access the equivalent L1 lexeme. As with cultural code switches, core code switches are not expected to be phonologically integrated, since they are similarly drawn from the L2 lexicon among coordinate bilinguals.

5. Data

5.1 Number, type and frequency of English tokens

The data retrieved from the four speakers over three hours of recordings reveals a surprisingly small number of English tokens given the amount of material, as compared to interviews of similar length with speakers of other heritage varieties spoken in the Upper Midwest (Annear and Speth this volume). Consultants occasionally switched entirely to English, especially when pragmatically appropriate or necessary, e.g., when the phone rang or when a non-proficient speaker entered the room, but specifically inter-sentential switching was rare. In all, 33 English tokens were found, 16 of which were cultural tokens and 17 of which consisted of core vocabulary. Tokens appearing as part of a compound or phrase are given in parentheses (see Table 2 below).

Table 2. Examples of core and cultural[12] tokens in WI-Frisian.

Cultural	Core
automobile (automobile trouble)[13]	anything
bombs	barn (barn-Frisian)
combines	bicycle
dollar	brothers
gay parade	canal

12. A reviewer points out that some technological tokens treated here as 'cultural' may be 'core' vocabulary for post-WWII immigrants, including specifically bombs and planes. There may be individual variation, but categorical organization e.g., '20th century technological innovations' may be more accurate.

13. The phrase *automobile trouble* includes both a cultural borrowing in *automobile* as well as a core borrowing of *trouble*. Other compounds include only single borrowed elements.

Table 2. (*continued*)

Cultural	Core
hearing aid	decorate
Iowa	enough (enough tiid)
Korea	exciting
millionaire	granddaughter
Mount Vernon	quite (ik lees quite vaak)
planes	midnight
siding	potatoes
thrift store	religion
tractors	slang
Turkey	summer
Washington	trouble (automobile trouble)
	ya know

Many of the cultural tokens were from expected semantic categories, including technology (*tractor, combine, automobile*), place names (*Iowa, Washington*), and lexemes specific to American life (*thrift store, dollar*). Counted among the core tokens were familial relations (*brother, granddaughter*), time expressions (*midnight, summer*), discourse or modal particles (*quite, ya know*), as well as some more common lexemes (*potatoes, religion*).

The tokens showed little evidence of morphological or phonological integration. In fact, in only one example, *automobile trouble*, do we find any apparent evidence of phonological incorporation of the English token. In the spectrogram below, we observe the Frisian [ɾ] in *trouble* rather than the expected English [ɹ]. The flapping of the /r/ is visible in the slight bump in F2, F3 and F4, across the third to fifth formant markers in the highlighted section.

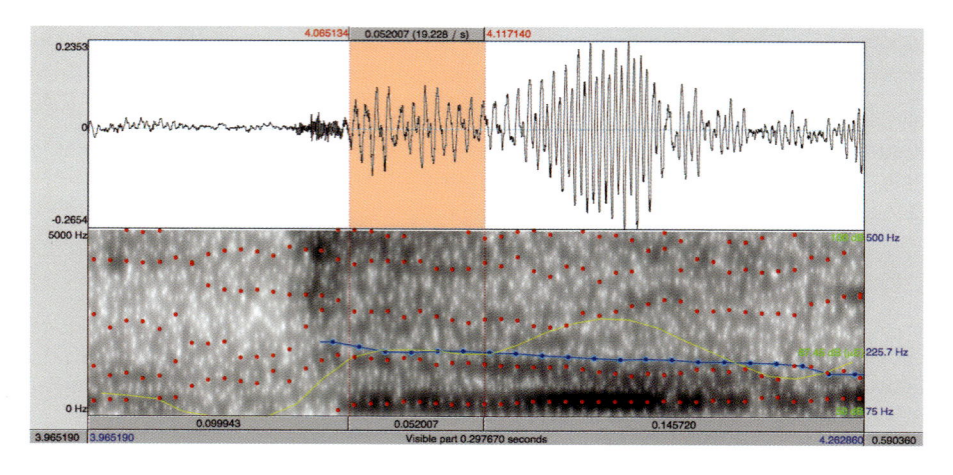

Figure 3. *automobile trouble* with [ɾ] (Speaker 4).

An alternate analysis interprets the phoneme as a trilled /r/.[14] Based on what appears to be multiple high and low points in especially the F2 and F3 values, this may be plausible. However, the quality of the recording does not permit identification of single versus multiple closures, which would differentiate the flapped /r/ from the trilled /r/. Both the flap and the trill may be variants of the same West Frisian phonological representation (cf. Harbert 2007: 54), which maintains the typological distinction with English retroflex or approximant /r/.

By contrast, in the token *hearing aid*, and in all other tokens containing the /r/ phoneme, we can clearly see the retroflex [ɻ] typical of English rather than the Frisian flap, marked by the rising F3 and F4 formant values at the end of the articulation of the approximant in the transition into the following vowel (see Figure 4, highlighted section).

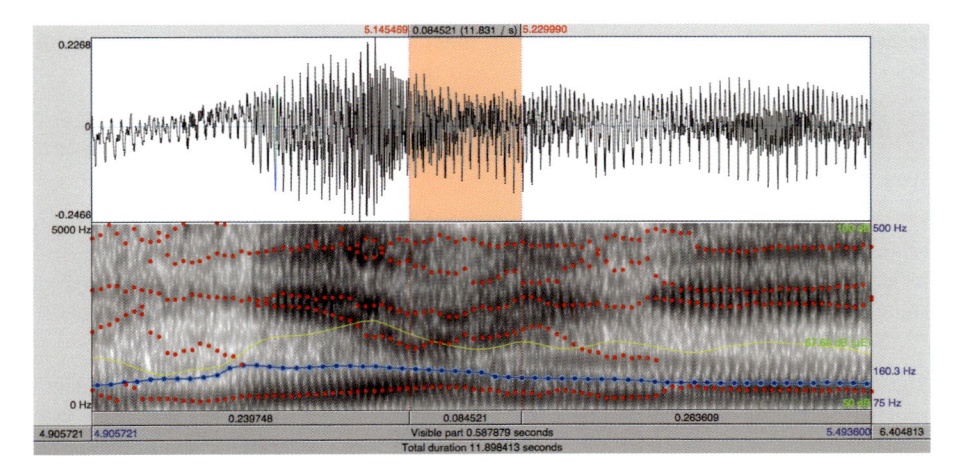

Figure 4. *hearing aid* with /ɻ/ (Speaker 2).

The articulation of /r/ is not related to phonological or phonetic environment, because while *trouble* is phonologically incorporated, *tractors* is not. There is also no emerging pattern of integration based on semantic category: if considered a cultural, technological token by association with *automobile*, then *(automobile) trouble* shows phonological incorporation, but the same does not hold true for other cultural terms, including *tractor*, and *hearing aid*. Similarly, if *trouble* is taken as a core lexeme with a West Frisian equivalent, then there is no explanation as to why another abstract concept like *religion* is not incorporated. The phonological incorporation of this single token is not related to semantic category, and phonological incorporation occurs neither robustly nor systematically.

---

14. We thank an anonymous reviewer for this point.

In comparing first and second generation WI-Frisians, no clear pattern emerges regarding either frequency of loan use, or regarding lexical category: unincorporated place names were used by speaker 1 (*Washington, Mount Vernon*) as well as by speaker 4 (*Korea, Iowa, Turkey*); cultural borrowings were used by speaker 2 (*siding, thrift store*) as well as by speaker 4 (*dollar*); and all four speakers employed core loans from English – speaker 1 (*brothers*), speaker 2 (*granddaughter*), speaker 3 (*enough, quite*) and speaker 4 (*potatoes, religion*). Only speaker 4, who is Wisconsin-born, produced a phonologically-incorporated token (*automobile trouble*).

Perhaps the most interesting phenomena present in the data were 'recast' tokens, words first uttered in English, but with the Frisian equivalent immediately following. Of the thirty-two English tokens identified, four were recasts. Though they cannot be considered borrowings,[15] they are notable for two reasons: first, the nature of the recast tokens are interesting in that they represent particularly basic vocabulary; second, recasts do not fill a semantic gap, as both tokens are clearly available to speakers. A brief look at examples of recast tokens reveals this fact:

Table 3. Recast tokens in WI-West Frisian.

West Frisian	English
kanaal	canal
bruorren	brothers
religie	religion
ierappel	potato

These examples provide insight as to how bilinguals draw on their respective language-specific phonologies. In all of the above examples, speakers access the language-specific L1 and L2 phonologies for each token. For example, in the spectrograms below, we see the *religion* uttered by speaker 2 – a female first generation speaker – first in English, then in Frisian. The highlighted section depicts the affricate /dz/ in the first graphic, while the second shows the voiceless velar fricative typical of the Frisian cognate *religie*.

The first portion of the affricate, similar to a /d/, is visible in the drop in the F2 and F3 values, and the interruption of voicing (shown by the blue bar and aperiodic frequencies) during the closure. The onset of the second half of the affricate – similar to a /z/ – is visible in the presence of voicing, marked again by the blue bar and the return to a periodic frequency in the highlighted section.

---

15. Recast tokens do not reflect borrowing in that by nature they are not filling a semantic gap in the lexicon, or replacing a native item in the lexicon.

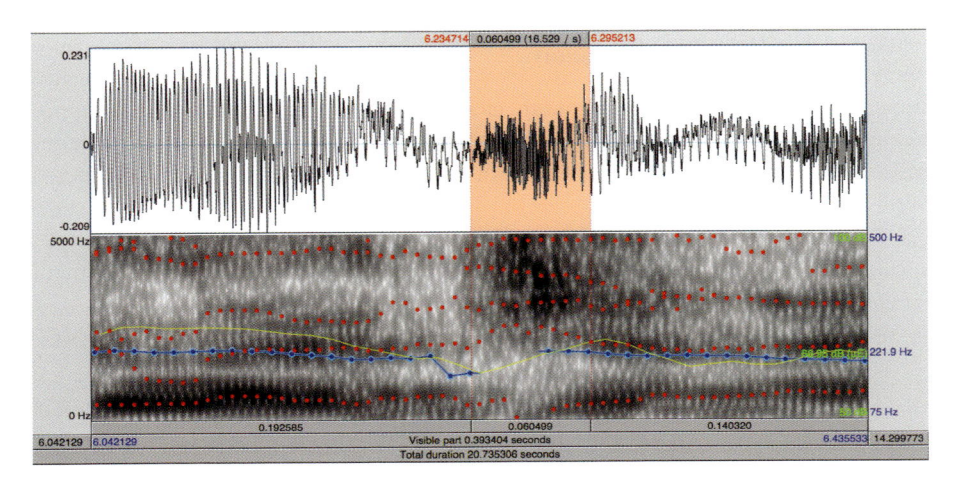

Figure 5. *religion* with /dz/ (Speaker 2).

Contrasting the exhibited English phonology in the previous example is the West Frisian token below (Figure 6). Rather than the two-part affricate visible in Figure 5, this example shows a uniform, voiceless fricative. There is no discernible dip in the formant values to denote any stop or change in quality, and there is no discernible periodicity to denote voicing.

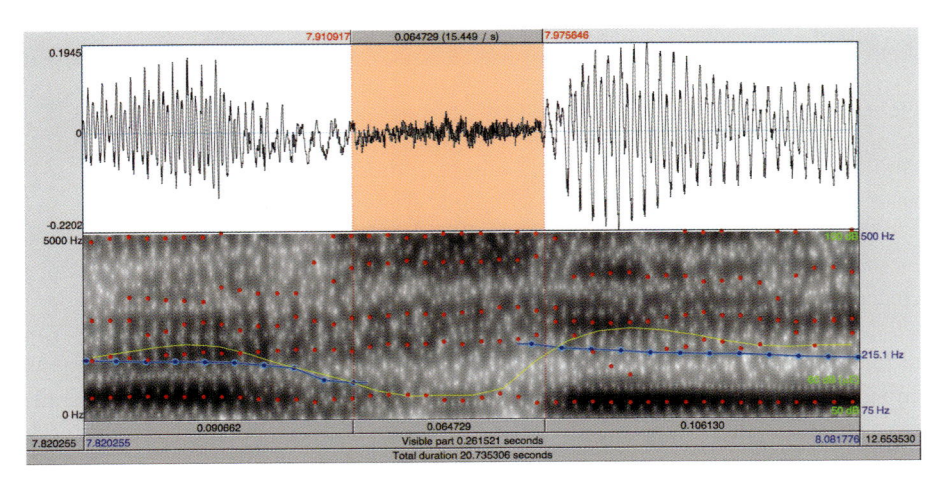

Figure 6. *religie* with /x/ (Speaker 2).

This particular recast shows that the speaker is not only providing two competing language-specific lexical items for the same referent, but also shows that the speaker employs language-specific phonemes in the realization of those lexemes. Furthermore, the phonemes differentiating the two tokens are also language-specific: in the English token, speaker 2 uses an English affricate, as is in 'barge,' which is not an available phoneme in West Frisian. In contrast, the West Frisian token realizes the /g/ as a voiceless fricative, consistent with Dutch pronunciation of *religie*, or as in *goed* 'good.' This phoneme is not available in the English phonemic inventory, and therefore clearly delineates the phonetic realization of the English token from that of the (Dutch-influenced) West Frisian token.[16]

Recasts were also attested for second generation speakers. In this second example, speaker 3 first utters *brothers* with a distinctly English voiced retroflex approximant /r/ (Figure 7).

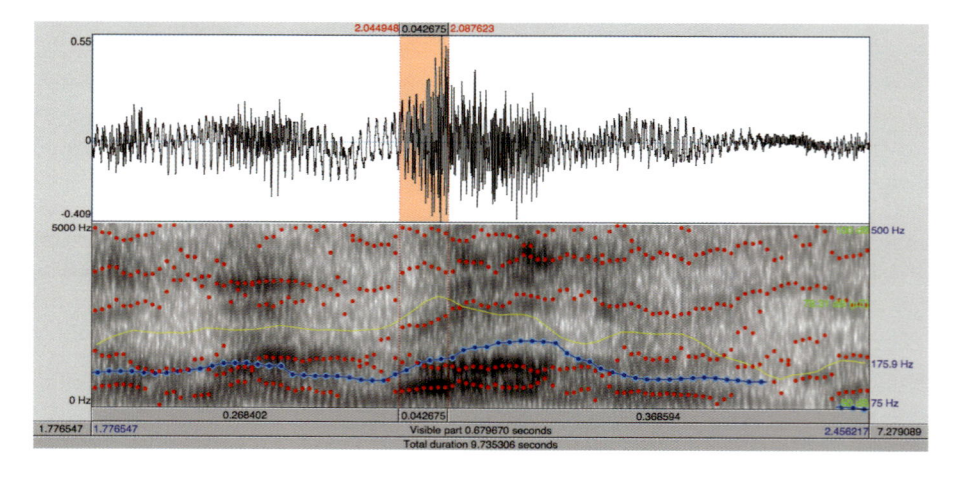

Figure 7. *brothers* with [ɹ] (Speaker 3).

Similar to the *hearing aid* example in Figure 4, the English-like realization of /r/ is visible in the rising F3 value in the highlighted section.

By contrast, in the spectrogram of the Frisian recast token immediately following, *bruorren*, one can clearly see the different wave form of the highlighted /r/ showing a voiced alveolar trill/flap expected in Frisian.

Much like the *automobile trouble* example in Figure 3, the flap is visible in the dip in formant values – especially the F3 value – denoting a change in quality before the anticipation and eventual onset of the diphthong. As in the previous *religion* example from speaker 2, this example from speaker 3 shows a recast of two cognates, with each lexeme reflecting a language-specific phonological system.

---

16. A reviewer noted that this phoneme and lexical item could be a borrowing from Dutch. Given that Dutch was the language of religion in the community (cf. §2.1) this is a plausible explanation.

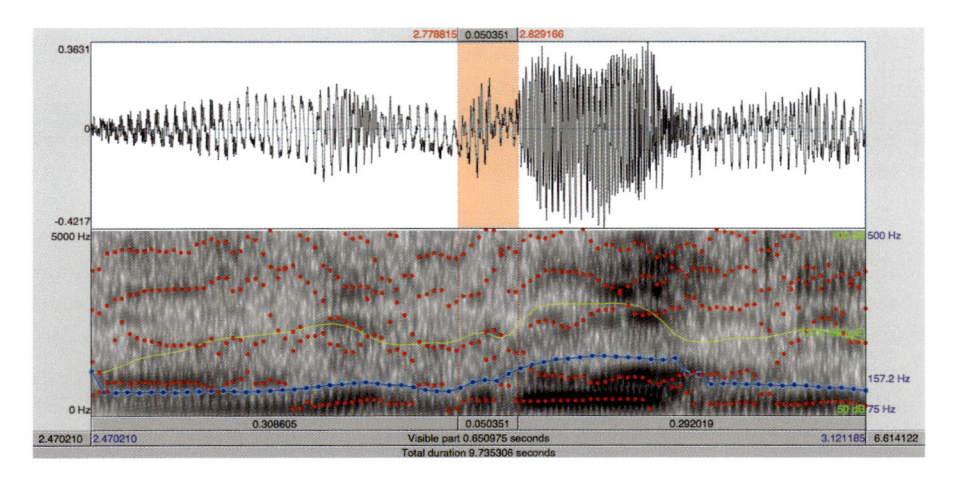

Figure 8. *bruorren* with /r/ (Speaker 3).

6. Analysis and discussion

These data provide a number of interesting points for discussion. First, the presence of a comparably low raw number of L2 tokens over the course of more than three hours of group conversation (33) is noteworthy. This stands in stark contrast to studies on Norwegian-Americans, including Annear and Speth (this volume), who find a total of 74 individual lexical items in just one hour of conversation. In calculating average frequency of English tokens in running speech, Annear and Speth's 12 consultants each employ roughly 6 English lexemes per hour. The rate of occurrence doubles if repetitions of the same lexemes are included (134 occurrences). The four West Frisian consultants considered here, however, average between 2 and 3 English lexemes per hour, with only a handful being used more than once (*barn, siding, ya know*). With a low rate of occurrence of English tokens even in comparison with other heritage communities, these West Frisian speakers pattern after Matras's (2009) expected bilingual speaker, who infrequently uses non-incorporated L2 lexemes in the L1. Our second generation consultants – being raised in Frisian-speaking households – were indeed bilingual. As evidenced by interviews conducted in 2008 and 2009 (and verified by 1910 and 1930 census data), immediately local social, administrative and commercial institutions were Frisian, though extra-community ties such as public education were English. Bilingualism was common, necessary, and context-specific.

For speakers who were raised in the Netherlands and emigrated as teenagers or young adults, the same pattern of context-specific language use holds true: West Frisian was the language of the home and on the farm, whereas Dutch was the language of instruction in school, in church, and in populated urban areas, such as the market in the nearby town of Dokkum. This bilingual characteristic was a parallel diglossic situation to that in Wisconsin; Frisian immigrants were able to supplant Dutch with

English for limited extra-communal interactions, while maintaining Frisian as their L1 in their most local interactions (Bousquette and Ehresmann 2010).

Regarding phonological incorporation, code switching data in this study are consistent with Matras' (2009) predictions for bilingual speakers, with English lexemes in spoken Frisian being infrequent and phonologically non-incorporated. This pattern holds for all four consultants in the data set, regardless of gender or whether the consultant was first or second generation. The same consistency in the data set holds when comparing core versus cultural classes: both first and second generation speakers code switch with both cultural and core classes, and 32 of 33 tokens maintain source language (English) phonology. However, while non-integrated core code switches do provide support for a coordinate bilingualism analysis, the remaining question is why non-integrated code switches occur at all. One explanation may relate to the issue of language dominance, where increased frequency of activation of especially a socially-dominant L2 (like English) seeps into the L1. This need not happen wholesale, however, and controlling language mode may be more difficult for certain elements. Koostra et al. (2010), in a study on Dutch-English bilinguals, did find that code switching increased in frequency when both languages aligned syntactically. Such an argument is consistent with Muysken (2000:11), who assumes that a necessary degree of similarity between the grammars of two languages is required to facilitate intra-sentential code switching. This is likely the case with *ya know* and *quite*, which as discourse elements occur in largely the same syntactic environment in both West Frisian and English. Such syntactic alignment of both languages minimalizes the processing cost associated with activating both language-specific grammars simultaneously.

Context may also play a role in facilitating code switches. For instance, interactions with a *granddaughter* likely occur in English, since West Frisian in Wisconsin is a moribund variety not spoken by the successive generations. Such associations may trigger an English language mode, rather than the code switch reflecting a difficulty in controlling language mode. In effect, topic or context may prime individuals for specific language modes, activating one context- and language-specific lexicon over the other. Similar processes may also account for the additional half-dozen non-integrated core lexemes; however, the total number of occurrences (not including the recasts) is so small for 4 speakers over two separate fieldwork sessions that further analysis would border on conjecture.

Turning to the issue of integration, the lack of phonological integration of the vast majority of English tokens can also be attributed to speakers' coordinate bilingualism. Consistent with the English-Frisian diglossia evident from both interview and census data, consultants' access to separate, language-specific lexicons results also in language-specific phonology for English lexemes while speaking West Frisian, under the assumption that phonological features are encoded on lexical items (Chomsky 1965, 1995). Cultural borrowings fit this pattern cleanly in that speakers may access English lexemes directly in order to fill a semantic gap, without having to incorporate the lexeme into their West Frisian lexicon. In fact, none of the cultural borrowings exhibit phonological incorporation, supporting the argument that these lexical items are coming directly from the English lexicon.

Analyzing the data in a coordinate bilingualism framework, core lexical items pattern differently than cultural lexical items in two meaningful ways. First, the four recast tokens – all of which were core lexical items – all maintained language-specific phonology. *Canal, brothers, religion* and *potato* maintained English phonological patterns, while the realization of equivalent *kanaal, bruorren, religie* and *ierappel* was consistent with West Frisian (or possibly Dutch) phonology, providing evidence that these lexical items were accessed from separate, language-specific lexicons during even rapid, conversational speech. Interaction between two simultaneously active language-specific lexicons is evident in the accessing of semantically equivalent lexical items that maintain language-specific phonology.

The second point in which core lexical items pattern differently than cultural items derives from the fact that core items – unlike cultural items – do not fill a semantic gap in the matrix language lexicon. Incorporating an English lexical item into the Frisian lexicon is redundant – and unmotivated – when there is already a Frisian equivalent. This is most clearly illustrated by the minimal pair *ierapple / potato* in the recast tokens, because it shows two semantically equivalent lexemes that are not historical cognates. Therefore, while non-integrated cultural code switches attest to simultaneous accessibility of two language-specific lexicons, non-integrated core code switches attest to the presence of two simultaneously accessible lexemes in different language-specific lexicons. This is particularly clear in recast tokens.

In light of the above analysis, we modify the generative model of a single lexicon to allow for multiple language-specific lexicons, consistent with recent work on the interaction between language-specific grammars (Koonstra et al. 2010, Bousquette et al. 2013, forthcoming). The Minimalist Program explanation of code switching assumes a single lexicon, and assumes the incorporation of the borrowed token into the single lexicon of an individual speaker, complete with all of the phonological, syntactic and morphological characteristics encoded. However, such approaches cannot account for the data presented here, treating phonologically unincorporated code switches or borrowings as incompletely or incorrectly acquired, and characteristic of less proficient or monolingual speakers (cf. Calabrese and Wetzels 2009). An alternative approach, the Matrix Language Frame Model (MLFM), would treat West Frisian as the 'matrix language' that provides the frame, and English as the 'embedded language' that "will contribute only content morphemes which are set into a basically ML structure" (Bentahila 1995: 135–136). However, this framework does not appropriately account for the almost exception-less (32/33 tokens) maintenance of EL phonology across code switches, nor can it account for the complete lack of morphological transfer between ML and EL in code switches. The MLFM cannot account for why *brothers* shows the English plural marking *-s* while the recast token *bruorren* exhibits West Frisian plural morphology; MLFM would predict both to have a basic ML morphology, similar to the productivity of the English *-s* plural marker in American Norwegian noted by Haugen (1953: 398). Most importantly, neither the Minimalist nor MLFM model has a viable rubric for diagnosing incorporated versus non-incorporated lexemes. Coordinate bilingualism provides a model that is applicable to these data, and that portrays phonological non-incorporation of code switches as a predictable and viable – though rare – occurrence in the speech of proficient heritage speakers.

7. Conclusion

These Wisconsin West Frisian data are particularly valuable as a study of a community with a relatively shallow time depth of bilingualism, which contrasts with related studies on heritage communities in the Upper Midwest with 3rd, 4th or even 5th generation speakers. As a contemporary community to those American Norwegian communities studied in this volume, this West Frisian enclave patterns very differently with respect to code switching, reflecting a balanced English-Frisian bilingualism. Following our coordinate bilingualism analysis of the data, the linguistic diglossia in the community accounts for the lack of phonological integration of even infrequent code switches, such that the sociolinguistic situation derives the psycholinguistic. This community in its relatively late settlement (early 20th century) and shallow time depth shows a rapid transition from a functioning bilingual community to a uniformly monolingual English community – in most cases within one generation – thus shortening the period of active bilingualism among speakers in the community. This, combined with the lack of dedicated, incorporated Frisian-language institutions (cf. Bousquette and Ehresmann 2010, Frey 2013) meant that there were no domains where Frisian language use could continue (e.g., church, school, or media). This ended the short period of active bilingualism in the community, with the shift from bilingualism to English monolingualism nearly complete, save for the remaining speakers of this moribund variety. Current data from this last generation of proficient speakers, however, sheds light on both the influence of a linguistic diglossia on language processing, as well as on the interaction of two language-specific grammars in a bilingual community of first and second generation speakers.

References

Anderssen, Merete and Marit Westergaard. This volume. "Word Order Variation in Norwegian Possessive Constructions: Bilingual Acquisition and Attrition."
Annear, Lucas and Kristin Speth. This volume. "Maintaining a Multilingual Repertoire: The Lexicon of American Norwegian."
Avery, Peter and William J. Idsardi. 2001. "Laryngeal Dimensions, Completion and Enhancement." In *Distinctive Feature Theory*, ed. by T. Alan Hall, 40–71. Berlin: Mouton de Gruyter.
Bentahila, Abdelali. 1995. "Review of *Dueling Languages: Grammatical Structure in Codeswitching* by Carol Myers-Scotton." *Language* 71: 135–140. DOI: 10.2307/415966

Boersma, Paul and David Weenink. 2012. *Praat 5.3.34*. http://www.fon.hum.uva.nl/praat/
Bousquette, Joshua. 2010. "Undifferentiated Agrarian Division of Labor as Horizontal Structure: A Warren-Based Approach to Immigrant Language Maintenance in Friesland and Randolph Twp., WI." Manuscript.
Bousquette, Joshua and Todd Ehresmann. 2010. "West Frisian in Wisconsin: A Historical Profile of Immigrant Language Use in Randolph Township." *It Beaken* 72(1): 247–278.
Bousquette, Joshua, Benjamin Frey, Nick Henry, Daniel Nützel, Michael Putnam, Joseph Salmons and Alyson Sewell. 2013. "How Deep is Your Syntax – Filler-Gap Dependencies in Heritage Language Grammar." *University of Pennsylvania Working Papers in Linguistics* 19(1): 19–30.
Bousquette, Joshua, Michael Putnam, Joseph Salmons, Benjamin Frey and Daniel Nützel. "Multilingual Gramars, Dominance and Optimalization." In *Advances in OT syntax and semantics*, ed. by Géraldine Legendre, Michael Putnam and Erin Zaroukian, 326–370. Oxford: Oxford University Press.
Calabrese, Andrea and W. Leo Wetzels. 2009. "Loan Phonology: Issues and Controversies." In *Loan Phonology* (Current Issues in Linguistic Theory 307), ed. by Andrea Calabrese and W. Leo Wetzels, 1–10. Amsterdam: John Benjamins. DOI: 10.1075/cilt.307.01cal
Cederström, B. Marcus. 2014. "Swedish Space in Upper Midwestern Churches." *American Studies in Scandinavia*, 44(1): 29–47.
Chomsky, Noam. 1965. *Aspects of the Theory of Syntax*. Cambridge, MA: MIT University Press.
Chomsky, Noam. 1995. *The Minimalist Program*. Cambridge, MA: MIT Press.
Clyne, Michael. 2003. *Dynamics of Language Contact*. Cambridge: Cambridge University Press. DOI: 10.1017/CBO9780511606526
Ehresmann, Todd and Joshua Bousquette. 2011. "Laryngeal Distinction in Wisconsin West Frisian: Phonetic and Phonological Evidence from Wisconsin Frisian." Manuscript.
Ervin, Susan M. and Charles E. Osgood. 1954. "Second Language Learning and Bilingualism." *Journal of Abnormal and Social Psychology* 58: 139–145.
Frey, Benjamin. 2013. *Toward a General Theory of Language Shift: A Case Study in Wisconsin German and North Carolina Cherokee*. Madison, WI: University of Wisconsin-Madison dissertation.
Galema, Annemieke. 1996. *Frisians to America 1880–1914: With the Baggage of the Fatherland*. Groningen: REGIO-Projekt Uitgevers.
Grosjean, François. 2008. *Studying Bilinguals*. Oxford: Oxford University Press.
Hamers, Josiane F. and Michel Blanc. 2000. *Biliguality and Bilingualism*. Cambridge, UK: Cambridge University Press. DOI: 10.1017/CBO9780511605796
Harbert, Wayne. 2007. *The Germanic Languages* (Cambridge Language Surveys). Cambridge, UK: Cambridge University Press.
Haugen, Einar. 1950. "The Analysis of Linguistic Borrowing." *Language* 26: 210–231. DOI: 10.2307/410058
Haugen, Einar. 1953. *The Norwegian Language in America: A Study in Bilingual Behavior*. Philadelphia: University of Pennsylvania Press.
Haugen, Einar. 1956. *Bilingualism in the Americas: A Bibliography and Research Guide*. (Publications of the American Dialect Society 26). Tuscaloosa, AL: University of Alabama Press.
Hjelde, Arnstein. 1996. "Some Phonological Changes in a Norwegian Dialect in America." In *Language Contact Across the North Atlantic*, ed. by Per Sture Ureland and Iain Clarkson, 283–295. Tübingen: Max Niemeyer Verlag.

Iverson, Gregory K. and Joseph Salmons. 1995. "Aspiration and Laryngeal Representation in Germanic." *Phonology* 12: 369–96. DOI: 10.1017/S0952675700002566

Iverson, Gregory K. and Joseph Salmons. 2003. "Laryngeal Enhancement in Early Germanic." *Phonology* 20: 43–72. DOI: 10.1017/S0952675703004469

Iverson, Gregory K. and Joseph Salmons. 2007. "Domains and Directionality in the Evolution of German Final Fortition." *Phonology* 24: 1–25. DOI: 10.1017/S0952675707001133

Johannessen, Janne Bondi and Signe Laake. Forthcoming. "Eastern Norwegian as a Common Norwegian Dialect in the American Midwest." *Journal of Language Contact*.

Kolmer, Agnes. 2012. *Pronomen und Pronominalklitika in Cimbro: Untersuchungen zum grammatischen Wandel einer deutschen Minderheitensprache in romanischer Umgebung* (ZDL Beihefte 150). Stuttgart: Franz Steiner Verlag.

Koostra Gerrit, Janet van Hell and Ton Dijkstra. 2010. "Syntactic Alignment and Shared Word Order in Code-Switched Sentence Production: Evidence from Bilingual Monologue and Dialogue." *Journal of Memory and Language* 63(2): 210–231. DOI: 10.1016/j.jml.2010.03.006

Lambert, J. Havelka and Cynthia Crosby. 1958. "The Influence of Language-Acquisition Contexts on Bilingualism." *Journal of Abnormal and Social Psychology* 56: 239–244. DOI: 10.1037/h0040216

Larsson, Ida, Sofia Tingsell and Maia Andréasson. This Volume. "Variation and Change in American Swedish."

Lipski, John. 2009. "'Fluent Dysfluency' as a Case of Congruent Lexicalization: A Special Case of Radical Code-Mixing." *Journal of Language Contact* 2: 1–39. DOI: 10.1163/000000009792497742

Lucht, Felecia. 2007. *Language Variation in a German-American Community: A Diachronic Study of the Spectrum of Language Use in Lebanon County*. Madison, WI: University of Wisconsin-Madison dissertation.

Matras, Yaron. 2009. *Language Contact* (Cambridge Textbooks in Linguistics). Cambridge, UK: Cambridge University Press. DOI: 10.1017/CBO9780511809873

Menn, Lise. 1989. "Some People Who Don't Talk Right: Universal and Particular in Child Language, Aphasia, and Language Obsolescence." In *Investigating Obsolescence: Studies in Language Contraction and Death* (Studies in the Social and Cultural Foundations of Language 7), ed. by Nancy Dorian, 335–345. Cambridge, UK: Cambridge University Press. DOI: 10.1017/CBO9780511620997.026

Muysken, Pieter. 2000. *Bilingual Speech: A Typology of Code-Mixing*. Cambridge, UK: Cambridge University Press.

Myers-Scotton, Carol. 1993. *Dueling Languages: Grammatical Structures in Codeswitching*. Oxford: Clarendon Press.

Rothman, Jason. 2009. "Understanding the Nature and Outcomes of Early Bilingualism: Romance Languages as Heritage Languages." *International Journal of Bilingualism* 13(2): 155–163. DOI: 10.1177/1367006909339814

Sasse, Hans-Jürgen. 1992. "Language Decay and Contact-Induced Change." In *Language Death: Factual and Theoretical Explorations with Special Reference to East Africa*, ed. by Matthias Brenzinger, 59–80. The Hague: Mouton de Gruyter.

Simon, Ellen. 2011. "Laryngeal Stop Systems in Contact: Connecting Present-Day Acquisition Findings and Historical Contact Hypotheses." *Diachronica* 28(2): 225–254. DOI: 10.1075/dia.28.2.03sim

Simon, Ellen and Torsten Leuschner. 2010. "Laryngeal Systems in Dutch, English and German: A Contrastive Phonological Study on Second and Third Language Acquisition." *Journal of Germanic Linguistics* 22(4): 403–424. DOI: 10.1017/S1470542710000127

Sipma, Pieter. 1913. *Phonology and Grammar of Modern West Frisian, With Phonetic Texts and Glossary*. London and New York: Oxford University Press.

Tiersma, Pieter Meyes. 1985. *Frisian Reference Grammar*. Ljouwert: Fryske Akademie.

Weinreich, Uriel. 1953. *Languages in Contact. Findings and Problems*. New York: Publications of the Linguistic Circle of New York 1.

Wilkerson, Miranda and Joseph Salmons. 2008. "'Good Old Immigrants of Yesteryear' Who Didn't Learn English: Germans in Wisconsin." *American Speech* 83(3): 259–283. DOI: 10.1215/00031283-2008-020

Wilkerson, Miranda and Joseph Salmons. 2012. "Linguistic Marginalities: Becoming American Without Learning English." *Journal of Transnational American Studies* 4(2), acgcc_jtas_7115. http://www.escholarship.org/uc/item/5vn092kk.

Borrowing modal elements into American Norwegian
The case of *suppose(d)*

Kristin Melum Eide and Arnstein Hjelde
Norwegian University of Science and Technology / Østfold University College

In a corpus of more than 120 hours of recorded American Norwegian speech we find the word *spost*, which looks like a non-Norwegian item. This word appears to be in normal use, although Norwegian Americans deny using it. Apparently this is the modal structure 'be supposed to' / 'I suppose' being borrowed from English into American Norwegian. In this article we examine how these structures are used in American Norwegian, and how they are modified and incorporated into the language. Furthermore we look at the various meanings such constructions have and potential models for it in Norwegian. This study contributes to the literature on borrowing of modal expressions in contact. According to Matras and Sakel (2007), borrowing of verb-related categories, such as modality, is rarely discussed in the literature, although in reality it is quite frequent. Judging by how often modal expressions are borrowed from one language to another, modality itself stands out as category which is prone to borrowing. We also discuss how the use of *spost* in some instances can be interpreted as a discourse marker, and if it is only the item that is borrowed, or also the grammatical pattern associated with it.

Keywords: borrowing, epistemic modality, evidential modality, deontic modality, convergence, matter replication, pattern replication, bilingual mind

1. Introduction

Much of the previous research on the Norwegian language in America has focused on different aspects of English lexical material, which, to a greater or lesser degree, has been incorporated into the American-Norwegian language. The borrowing process itself, and also how these words have been incorporated into the Norwegian language system, has been in focus of many such studies, including those of the pioneers Flaten and Flom in the early 1900s (Flaten 1900–04, Flom 1900–04, 1903, 1912, 1926,

1929, 1931). The scholar who has done the most in this area is without doubt Einar Haugen. But even if he states that "(t)he heart of our definition of borrowing is then the attempted reproduction in one language of patterns previously found in another" (Haugen 1950: 212) – which should include different kinds of transfer, it is clear in *The Norwegian Language in America* (Haugen 1953), as well as in later works, that his focus is on various aspects of lexical borrowings. Also others in recent times who have worked with language contact and borrowing in American Norwegian (Annear and Speth this volume, Johansen 1970, Hjelde 1992, 1996a, 1996b, Johannessen and Laake 2011, 2012) and in American Frisian (Ehresmann and Bousquette this volume) have focused on aspects of lexical borrowing, while structural features in grammar and word order hardly are touched upon. However, this heavy focus on loanwords is not only a defining characteristic of the study of American Norwegian but a more general tendency. Matras and Sakel (2007) point out such deficiencies in language contact research and Sakel (2007: 44) says that the literature on borrowing hardly has focused on grammatical features; borrowing of typically verb-related features, such as tense, aspect and modality, are rarely discussed.[1]

We to some extent follow the tradition of research in American Norwegian by studying elements of the vocabulary, but this time through a detailed study of one word, the English word *suppose(d)* as used in American Norwegian dialects.

[spuːst] in its various forms is clearly an element of the modal domain. As such it can be seen as a function word, perhaps also as a discourse marker. Through an investigation of this word, we also hope to be able to shed some light on the process of borrowing of function words and functional expressions. We discuss to what extent this word can be said to be an integrated part of the American Norwegian vocabulary, we investigate its attested uses, and especially focus on modal meanings associated with *suppose(d)*.

We base this chapter on three different datasets collected over the last 25 years. The oldest of these is from 1987, documenting the *Inntrøndsk* dialect in Minnesota, North and South Dakota (Hjelde 1992). This material consists of approximately 40 hours of audio recordings of some 30 informants. Furthermore, we use material collected in Coon Valley and Westby, Wisconsin, in 1992 and 1996. This consists of 80 hours of recorded speech and documents the language of around 60 informants, most born in America with roots in the Gudbrandsdalen area in Norway. Both these collections contain a mix of interviews with the informants and conversations between multiple informants or between the informant(s) and field worker. The third set of data are observations and records done when participating in the fieldwork organized by the NorAmDiaSyn project in autumn 2010 and spring 2011. This material consists of video recordings made in some of the old Norwegian-American settlements in Minnesota, Iowa and Wisconsin. However, only small portions of these recordings are so far transcribed or analyzed in any systematic way.

---

1. As exceptions Matras and Sakel refer to some of their own earlier work, e.g., Matras (2002). We also mention Kahan Newman (this volume).

Before proceeding, we give some relevant examples of how *suppose(d)* may be used in American Norwegian:[2]

(1) Å så va de så rart, Arnstein, du va itj [spʊst] te å ji dæm nå
And then it was so strange, Arnstein, you were not [spʊst] to to give them any
'And it was very strange, Arnstein, you weren't supposed to give them any

mat, dæm ha me littegrainj. ...
food they had with a little ...
food, they brought a little, ...

men æ ga dæm mat æ, du va itj [spʊst] te 'e.
but I gave them food I, you were not [spʊst] to that
but I gave them food, I did, you were not supposed to.'
(Lac Qui Parle, MN 1987)

(2) No fer ti'n så gifte døm se med ka som helst, no.
Now for time.DEF.DAT then marry they REFL with anything now
'Nowadays, they will marry anything.

Men mi, mi va'kje [spʊːst] tå gjera det mi, veit du.
But we, we weren't [spʊːst] to to do that we, you know
But we, we weren't supposed to do that.'
(Harmony, MN 2010)

(3) Men æ [spoʊs] dæm ha bæd vinjtjra alj åver.
But I [spoʊs] they had bad winters all over.
'But I suppose they had bad winters all over.'
(Powers Lake, ND 1987)

(4) Å derre e [spoʊsa] å vårrå eit tre som va planjtja på heimplass'n
And there.DEF is [spoʊsa] to be a tree that was planted on homeplace.DEF
'And that is supposed to be a tree that was planted on the home farm

henjnjes Johanna B. som levd væstpå hen.
her Johanna B. who lived west.on here
of Johanna B. who lived here in the west.'
(Lac Qui Parle, MN 1987)

(5) Han e [spʊːst] te å vara rikti go, han.
He is [spʊːst] to to be right good he
'He is supposed to be quite good, he is.'
(Coon Valley, WI 1992)

2. Degree of integration

We turn now to some of the grammatical properties associated with American Norwegian *spost* in its various forms, but first discuss whether this word can be said to be an integrated part of the American Norwegian vocabulary, and if so, to what

---

2. We employ a simplified phonetic transcription, where *lj, tj, dj, nj* mark palatalized consonants. Our transcription does not generally distinguish between the many *l* sounds, so the apical *l*, the laminal *l* and the retroflex flap are all represented simply by *l*.

extent (Hjelde 2001). In the tradition of Shana Poplack, loanwords are often understood as words from the L2 system, transferred and incorporated into the L1 system. In this way loanwords may differ dramatically from codeswitching, which amounts to switching between two (or more) distinct language codes or systems, and such a switch can be within sentences or between sentences. Thus loanwords imply a change in the linguistic system of the recipient language, meaning that it is related to competence (cf. Myers-Scotton 1990: 85). Codeswitching, on the other hand, does not involve any such change in codes; it is related to performance, not competence. But despite the fact that loanwords and single-word codeswitching theoretically are two very different phenomena, they can also be very difficult, not to say impossible, to distinguish in a material consisting of spontaneous speech. In this article, we will nevertheless argue that [spʊːst] has the status of a loanword in American Norwegian.

There are at least two things that may weigh against the assumption that [spʊːst] is a part of the vocabulary of American Norwegian. First of all, it is not mentioned by Haugen (1953) as a loanword, which we might expect if it was in common use at that time. But it was never Haugen's intention to list every loanword he found. He documented altogether well over 3,000 loanwords, and as can be expected, he did not comment on all of them (1953: 556). The word list presented in *The Norwegian Language in America* only contains the most frequent words (documented at least 15 times in his material) or words with "special feature of interest," amounting to just over 10% of the total material he found. However, we also know that the American Norwegian language has changed since Haugen studied it, so even though Haugen did not document the use of this word, it might well be that [spʊːst] entered the language more recently.

Another issue in interpreting [spʊːst] as a loanword is that Norwegian-Americans themselves deny using it when speaking in Norwegian. During the fieldwork in 2011, several informants were asked directly about the use of [spʊːst], and all rejected it as a part of American Norwegian language, saying that this word belongs to English, not Norwegian. But one may well question the reliability of self-reporting and acceptability tests when working in a labile multilingual environment. Both Labov (1966) and Trudgill (1972) found large discrepancies between what people believe they say and what they actually do say. Poplack and Sankoff also warn against the use of acceptability tests when working with multilinguals:

> Acceptability is notoriously misleading, especially in contexts where the recipient language is socially inferior to the donor. Even in cases where neither language is stigmatized, Hasselmo documents for Swedish-English bilingualism cases where items were identified as being of English origin, yet showed low translatability, but high acceptability.　　　　　　　　　　　　　　　　　　　　　　　　(1984: 104)

Lesley Milroy (1987: 186) also noted that in a bilingual society one can often find the idea of 'pure' language as an ideal, and this is probably also the case in many Norwegian-American communities. It is not uncommon to encounter people who regret that they cannot speak Norwegian like people do in Norway. Many have also been in Norway and found that the variety spoken there is different from their own, and they are also very aware of what is 'real Norwegian' and what is not in their vernacular. And in an interview situation, many will try to use words like *bil*, *veg* and *elv* instead of [kaːr] 'car', [roːd] 'road' and [ˈrøveɾ] 'river'. To what extent they manage to do so, is another matter. As an example, one informant from 1992 tried to avoid the use of loanword [lɛik] 'lake', which is the common word used in American Norwegian. Obviously he did not know what the 'proper' Norwegian term for this was, so he introduced the word [mjøːs] – derived from Mjøsa, a lake not far away from where his ancestors came from.

It has been argued that the frequency of a word in average speech can be used as an indicator of the extent to which the word is a part of the vocabulary (e.g., Poplack and Sankoff 1984, Myers-Scotton 1990). Even if we have to take such features as word class and domain into consideration, it is reasonable to acknowledge that a word which is used by many language users in the community and is frequent in speech has become an integrated part of the vocabulary. On the other hand, frequency is not a reliable indicator for identifying loanwords. Poplack et al. (1988) used a corpus of over two million words in which some 2000 loanwords were identified. But despite the fact that this corpus was very large, she found that one thousand of these loanwords were documented only once, and as few as 5% of these were documented in the speech of more than two informants (Poplack et al. 1988: 57–58). In our material we find 23 examples of [spuːst] in different varieties used by 16 different informants. The use of this word is attested in four different communities in three states: Coon Valley and Westby, Wisconsin (1992), Powers Lake, North Dakota (1987), Lac Qui Parle (1987) and Harmony (2010) in Minnesota. Hence [spuːst] is comparatively quite common in our material, although we will not use frequency as the sole grounds for classifying it as a loanword.

3. Linguistic integration

Phonetic integration is seen by many authors as a strong indication that the word is a loan, and not a code-switch (Halmari 1993, 1997). In American Norwegian, we find the stem of the word *suppose(d)* realized in different ways showing different degrees of phonetic integration. In this study we use the realization of the root vowel /o/, which in American English (AmE) usually is diphthongized to [oʊ], as a hallmark to determine to what degree this word shows phonetic integration into American Norwegian. Haugen writes that this American English vowel is often realized in three different ways in American Norwegian loanwords: as Norwegian [o]: [roːd] 'road' and [stoːv] 'stove,' as Norwegian [ʊ]: [kʊːt] 'coat' and [gruːv] 'grove' and Norwegian [ʉ], [ˈgʉfər] 'gopher.' These three ways of substituting this AmE vowel are also found forty years later in the Norwegian *Inntrøndsk* dialect in America (Hjelde 1992: 56–57). Haugen further mentioned that especially younger informants with Eastern Norwegian backgrounds tended not to substitute this phoneme at all, they rendered it as [oʊ] (Haugen 1953: 427). In our material we find *suppose* realized with either [ʊ] or [oʊ], as [spuːs] or [spoʊs]. But the realization with [ʊ] is clearly the most common one, close to three-quarters of all examples feature this 'Norwegian' monophthong. Particularly in the past participle we find the pronunciation with the monophthong [spʊ(ː)st], while the present tense normally is realized without such vowel substitution, as [spoʊs]. These forms also reveal that *suppose* only partially is adapted to the Norwegian quantity system since participial [spʊːst] is most often realized with an 'over-long' syllable with long vowel followed by two consonants, [spʊːst], a syllable structure avoided in most Norwegian dialects. On the other hand, we also find several examples following 'Norwegian' rules, with a short vowel, [spʊst].

From our material it is difficult to assess to what degree *suppose* is integrated into the Norwegian morphological system as we do not have evidence for the complete paradigm; we only have *suppose* documented in present tense (*æ* [spoʊs] 'I suppose') and the past participle (*Han e* [spʊːst] *te å vara riktig god, han* 'He is supposed to be really good, (he)'). Only for one of the informants do we find evidence for the use of both present tense and past participle, which makes it impossible to reconstruct the idiolectal system of inflection for *suppose*. This one informant has [spoʊs] in the present tense and [spʊ(ː)st] in the participle, a distribution that may be regulated by the quantity as we find the diphthong before a single consonant, while we have a realization with monophthong before a consonant cluster. Haugen points out that the most common categorization of borrowed verbs is weak verbs, especially so-called *a*-verbs, such as *hepna* 'happen' and *kåvra* 'cover' (Haugen 1953: 455). The same is also found in the *Inntrøndsk* dialect in America, where almost all of these verbs fall into this class of weak verbs (Hjelde 1992: 94–96). *Suppose* does not follow this pattern since we only find it as [spoʊs] and [spʊːs] in present tense, without a formative, as expected for the first class of weak verbs. This of course can indicate a lack of integration, i.e., that *suppose* is a code-switch. But at the same time we do find several verbs in Norwegian with this form in the present tense, particularly verbs like *slåss* 'fight' and *lates* 'pretend' in *Inntrøndsk* dialects rendered as [ʃles] and [læs] in the present tense. In past participles we find forms like [spoʊːst], [spʊst], [spʊːst] and [²spʊːsa], where [spʊːst] is the most common. The example [²spʊːsa] shows that the verb can be categorized as a weak *a*-verb, although we lack documentation of the present tense for this speaker. The other three variants may well be interpreted as lack of morphological integration. But here it is also possible to interpret these forms as integrated since the formative -*t* is also used in Norwegian to mark past participles of weak verbs. Haugen (1953: 455–456) points out that although most verbs in American Norwegian are classified in the 1st class of weak verbs, there are also several examples of borrowed verbs which fall into the other verb classes. Obviously it is a problem to this analysis that we do not find any examples of the present tense consistent with such an interpretation.

When it comes to syntactic use of *suppose*, we see two different models on which the use can be based in American English. One is related to the use in the present tense, where the syntactic structure [æ spoʊs] corresponds to English *I suppose*. Here we find nothing to indicate particular syntactic integration, but nothing that would point in the opposite direction either. More interesting are the different types found in association with the participles. It is reasonable to assume the American English construction *be supposed to* serves as a model for the use of *suppose* in American Norwegian. An indicator of syntactic integration will be the use of particles following the participle. If the structure of the American English is copied, we should expect to find American-English *to* copied and realized as either [tə] *til* or infinitive marker [o]. On the other hand, if this borrowing is syntactically integrated, we should expect that the American English particle *to* will be replaced by Norwegian [tə o] *til å*. In our material we find three variants:

(6) a. [²spoʊsa o] / [spoːst o]   (2 occurrences)
    b. [spoʊst tə]   (1 occurrence)
    c. [spʊ(ː)st tə o]   (16 occurrences)

Variants with only infinitive marker [o] can be seen as a plain copy of the American pattern *supposed to*. [spoʊst tə] is however ambiguous. We can see this as copying as well, resulting in the Norwegian preposition [tə] *til*. But we should be aware that even in some Norwegian-Norwegian dialects we do in fact find [tə] used as an infinitive marker, especially where standard Norwegian has *til å*, but also in the position where we would not otherwise find the preposition *til* (Faarlund 2003: 74–75). The most frequent construction in our material is preposition + infinitive marker, and this can hardly be explained as anything else than a syntactic integration of *suppose*.

To sum up, we have tried to show that although there are certain arguments supporting the idea that *suppose* is not an integrated part of the American-Norwegian vocabulary, there are many arguments pointing the opposite way, and we find it prudent to consider *suppose* an integrated part of the American Norwegian language.

4. Borrowing of functional words and grammatical features

As mentioned in the introduction, most studies of American Norwegian focused on borrowing, integration and the use of lexical loanwords. Borrowing of functional expressions and grammatical structures has traditionally attained less interest among scholars, and this neglect is typical, not only for the literature on American Norwegian, but for the linguistic literature on borrowing and language contact more generally. Sakel (2007: 44) for example claims that "[l]ittle attention has been granted in the literature to borrowing of features belonging to the domain of verbs …; reports on the borrowing of T(ense), M(odality), A(spect) markers are quite rare".

One explanation for this lack of interest could be that such borrowings of functional expressions (a category including both modal verbs and discourse markers) are very rare, and as such not found worthy of a discussion in the literature. Haugen (1956: 67) argues for example that functional words are rarely borrowed from one language to another: "function words, which only occur as parts of utterances, are seldom borrowed." However, this assertion is not supported by more recent research (e.g., Östman 1981, Salmons 1990, Matras and Sakel 2007, Boas and Weilbacher 2007,

Matras 2009, 2011). Instead, these studies claim that functional expressions are quite frequently borrowed, and Matras and Sakel (2007) report on a larger study, including some thirty languages, in which they found transfer of functional words from one language to another in all of the contact situations and in all of the languages studied.[3] And Sakel (2007:24) argues that "function words are borrowed easily and relatively early on in contact situations."

Matras (2011:216) presents a 'borrowing hierarchy' specifically for the different types of functional expressions, where categories universally prone to borrowability end up high in the hierarchy. Matras claims that discourse markers (including 'tags' like *I mean, right, I suppose*, etc.) top this hierarchy. According to this hierarchy, discourse markers are among the functional expressions found to be most easily borrowed in language contact situations. The fact that specifically discourse markers are easily borrowed is also confirmed by other researchers. Boas and Weilbacher (2007) cite two decades of research on the borrowing of discourse markers, like *well* and *you know* from English to bilingual communities in the United States (including German dialects in America). An early work on the topic is Salmons (1990), who investigates how typical German discourse markers (*ja, mal, wohl* and *weisst du*) gradually are replaced by an English set of discourse markers.

Much of the research in this area relates, positively or more critically, to Matras' (1998) hypothesis of a hierarchy of pragmatic separateness: Items that are primarily used for verbal gestures, as to organize the exchange of turns in communication, have little lexical content and can easily be perceived as separate from the content of that statement. *Eller hva* 'or what' and *ikke sant* 'right,' are examples of such discourse markers with the function to organize exchange of turns, and we may say that they are oriented towards the listener, for him/her to respond or to take the initiative in the conversation. Other types of discourse markers, more speaker-oriented ones, are used to express to what extent the speaker is confident about the truth of what the proposition expresses (Östman 1981, Boas and Weilbacher 2007). Examples of such markers are *antar jeg* 'I guess,' *har jeg hørt* 'I've heard,' etc. According to Matras (1998), such items are easily borrowed from one language and into another.

There exist many similarities between the latter type, speaker-oriented discourse markers, and speaker-oriented types of modality. Both speaker-oriented modality and speaker-oriented discourse markers deal with how the speaker relates to the statement. Some scholars consider these two to be almost equal; this is especially the case for speaker-oriented discourse markers and what is known as epistemic modality (see Section 6). Coates (2003:331) writes:

---

3. It is quite difficult to report the actual number of contact situations in this collection of languages since the compilation contains "languages with a single contemporary contact language as well as those spoken in either a multilingual setting or a linguistic area" (Matras and Sakel 2007:10). Thus this is a matter of how to count.

> In everyday spoken interaction, epistemic modality is used to convey the speaker's attitude to the proposition, not to convey some objective truth. … Epistemic modality encompasses a wide range of linguistic forms, from the modal auxiliaries … and modal adverbs such as *perhaps, possibly* and *probably*, to discourse markers such as *I mean, I think* and *well*. Such words and phrases are sometimes referred to as 'hedges' [and…] have the effect of damping down the force of what is said [.]

According to this, there is a considerable overlap between some types of discourse markers and some types of modality, particularly speaker-oriented modality like epistemic modality:

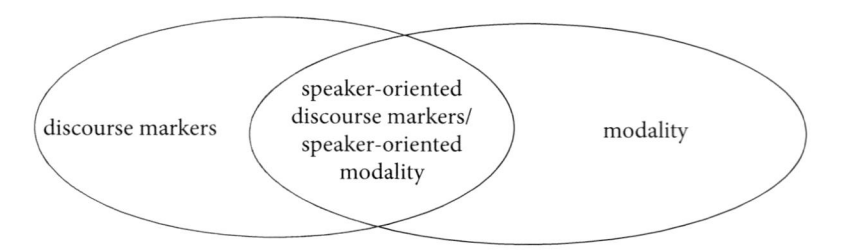

Figure 1.

Boas and Weilbacher (2007: 34–35) claim that the speaker-oriented discourse markers employ one of the most crucial functions of discourse markers, namely "[t]o mitigate the speaker's responsibility for the subject matter of an utterance." This is quite reminiscent of the classic definition of epistemic modality as we find it in Palmer (2001: 8): "[W]ith epistemic modality speakers express their judgments about the factual status of the proposition".

Assuming that speaker-oriented discourse markers and speaker-oriented modality belong to the same type of category, pragmatically, functionally and even semantically, it may not be surprising that modality markers are often borrowed from one language to another. In line with Matras' greater linguistic project, Matras and Sakel (2007) also establish so-called borrowing hierarchies, where they try to make generalizations about which grammatical markers are most easily borrowed. As mentioned, different types of discourse markers rank high on this hierarchy, but modality is also at the top of the list over grammatical categories particularly prone to borrowing (Matras 2007: 45):

> This picture lends itself to an interpretation in terms of the hierarchy [below], which depicts the likelihood of the respective categories to be affected by contact: modality > aspect/aktionsart > future tense > (other tenses).

Thus no grammatical categories are more or equally susceptible to borrowing in a language contact situation compared to modality. Especially when we look at the kind of borrowing Matras labels 'matter replication,' modality stands out as the most frequent (2007: 46):

Modality shows the most widespread contact phenomena, especially as regards matter replication. Almost half of the sample languages show matter replication of modality markers ....

Just as there are different types of discourse markers, there are also many different types of modality. The term 'modality' often appears as an umbrella term for various types of grammatical categories in which some can be said to be speaker-oriented (as epistemic modality, see above), agent-oriented or subject-oriented. The latter type of modality relates to a kind of relationship between the subject and the situation described by the predicate, e.g., deontic modality, describing the types and degrees of a (social) commitment, like *should*, *must*; or permission, like *could*. Another important type is dynamic modality, describing the ability, willingness or desire of an intentional agent[4] (*could*, *would*), see Palmer (1986, 2001). Matras (2007: 45) suggests the following hierarchy for the different types of modality and their likelihood of being borrowed:[5]

Obligation > necessity > possibility > ability > desire

Both 'necessity' and 'possibility' can include both epistemic, deontic and dynamic modality. If we use the modal verb *kunne* 'could' as an example, it has 'possibility' as its basic reading, as in *Mari kan spille piano* 'Mari can play the piano.' In addition to this basic reading, this sentence also has a potential epistemic reading ('I think that Mari is playing the piano now'), a deontic reading ('I allow for Mari to play the piano') and a dynamic reading ('One of Mari's skills is that she knows how to play the piano'). We can find similar examples for the basic reading 'necessity.' In the utterance *Jon må kaste opp* 'Jon must throw up,' the modal verb *må* 'must' has one reading implying that the speaker has a strong presumption that Jon is throwing up as we speak (epistemic reading). Another reading is that the speaker urges Jon to throw up (deontic reading), and a third reading is where the necessity is perceived by Jon himself (dynamic reading). There is no reason to believe that 'necessity' and 'possibility' in Matras' hierarchy should relate to only one particular type of modality. The null hypothesis should be rather that both epistemic and deontic necessity, as well as epistemic and deontic possibility are encompassed by this hierarchy.

In short, discourse markers and expressions of modality are both types of functional expressions. Among the verb-related grammatical markers in the domains of tense, aspect and modality, Matras' studies have shown that modality is the category

---

4. Dynamic modality encoding ability also tolerates a non-intentional agent, e.g., *Denne nøkkelen kunne åpne alle dører* 'This key could open any door.'

5. "The hierarchy proceeds from the most intensive external force, to the most participant-internal dimension. It is identical to the hierarchy identified by Elšík and Matras (2006) for the borrowing of modality markers in Romani dialects: necessity > ability > (inability) > volition. The more abstract theme in this hierarchy might be described as the degree of 'speaker control,' low speaker control correlating with high borrowability" (Matras 2007: 45).

most easily borrowed from one language to another. If we look solely at the borrowing hierarchy over other types of functional expressions, we find that discourse markers are borrowed at a very early stage (Matras 2011:216). There is also a clear pragmatic and functional overlap between speaker-oriented types of modality and speaker-oriented types of discourse markers (Coates 2003:331). As the term indicates, the speaker-oriented types concern the speaker's attitude to what is said, especially when it concerns the speaker's judgment of the probability, reliability or credibility of a proposition. According to Coates such expressions are used with a pragmatic purpose, which is to modify the strength of the statement or to make it less categorical. And according Matras (1998, 2009, 2011) these kinds of elements, with a function quite independent of the propositional content of the statement, are the most prone to borrowing in a language contact situation.

5. On matter replication and pattern replication

In many of Matras' works a fundamental difference is invoked between two basic types of borrowing: matter replication and pattern replication (e.g., Matras and Sakel 2007:4). In matter replication (MAT) the element itself is what is borrowed; in pattern replication (PAT) the pattern (e.g., syntactic pattern or concept) belonging to a certain word or element is what is borrowed. Sakel (2007:14) describes the two notions as follows:

> We speak of MAT-borrowing when morphological material and its phonological shape from one language is replicated in another language. PAT describes the case where only the patterns of the other language are replicated, e.g., the organization, distribution and mapping of grammatical or semantic meaning, while the form itself is not borrowed.

To illustrate pattern replication as we understand it we provide the example of reflexive omission in modern Norwegian. In recent years the keen observer will have had the opportunity to note that Norwegian verbs that used to require reflexive objects (i.e., inherently reflexive verbs; Busterud 2006, 2014) now seem to be laxing this requirement such that the reflexive particle is no longer an obligatory element of the construction. Verbs of this type are *relatere (seg) til* 'relate to,' *tiltrekke (seg)* 'attract,' *restituere (seg)* 'restitute,' *sosialisere (seg)* 'socialize' and many others. Note that the verb itself is not what is borrowed at this stage, because the verb has existed in Norwegian for hundreds of years. Instead the argument structure of the verb is changing, from obligatorily overtly expressing the reflexive object to omitting this object. The very likely suspect for the source of this changing argument structure is interference from English. As you can observe in the translations of these verbs, the reflexive particle is non-obligatory in English, and for modern Norwegians who relate (!) to English on a daily basis, adopting the English argument pattern for these verbs seems a likely thing to do (Sunde 2013). In our view, this is a very clear example of pattern replication, PAT.

We find a comparable trend for the inherently reflexive verbs in Norwegian spoken in America. Especially frequent in our data is the complex verb *gifte seg* 'marry,' as in the following examples from Coon Valley and Westby (also Johannessen and Laake 2012, their example 9c) which loses its reflexive particle as well as its accompanying preposition *med* 'with.' Thus, the Norwegian source construction is *jifte seg med* 'marry REFL with,' where both particles have to give way to the simpler structural pattern seemingly borrowed from the English corresponding verb *marry*.

(7) a. *E jifta norsker*
 I married Norwegian
 'I married a Norwegian'
 (cp. E jifta *meg* med en norsker)
 b. *A Gina jifta'n Ole.*⁶
 she Gina married him Ole
 'Gina married Ole.'
 (cp. Gina jifta *seg* med Ole)
 c. *Du måtte itte jifte katolikker, da veit'u!*
 you must not marry catholic then you know
 'You couldn't marry a Catholic in those days, you know.'
 (cp. Du måtte itte jifte *deg* med...)

Note also that the reflexive is not always omitted, and we also find examples where the reflexive does appear with the inherently reflexive verbs, as in another example of the verb *gifte seg* 'marry.'

 d. *Dom jifte seg ein dag og divorsa nækste*⁷
 they married REFL one day and divorced next
 'They married one day and got divorced the next day.'

We find similar tendencies with many inherently reflexive verbs in American Norwegian, cf. the verbs *skynte seg* 'hurry,' *forandre seg* 'change' and *bosette seg* 'settle':

 e. *Vi skunna – å fekk hestan inn i balin att*
 We hurried and got the horses in the barn again
 'We acted quickly and got the horses back into the barn.'
 (cp. Vi skunna *oss*)
 f. *Det har forandra – my*
 it has changed – a-lot
 'It has changed a lot.'
 (cp. Det har forandra *seg*)

---

6. The particles *a* and *n* are preproprial articles. They are obligatory with first names and some kinship terms in many Norwegian dialects.

7. This verb *divorsa* is obviously also borrowed from English, the corresponding Norwegian verb is *skille seg* 'separate themselves.' *Nækste* is clearly also influenced from English; the corresponding Norwegian word would be *næste*.

g. *Så bosatte dom – iblant tyske folk*
   then settled they – among German people
   'Then they settled among German people.'
   (cp. Så bosatte dom *seg*)

In our opinion these examples constitute clear illustrations of pattern replication. According to Matras (2007: 45) when we study borrowing of modality markers, pattern replication (PAT) is not as frequent as matter replication (MAT) (cf. above). We should note however that borrowing of solely the element without borrowing one single aspect of its pattern is rarely attested in language contact literature. Especially the function of a given element is frequently borrowed along with the element itself, cf. Sakel (2007: 14, 26). As mentioned above, 'mapping of grammatical or semantic meaning' as well as 'distribution' are other important aspects of pattern replication when borrowing an element from one language to another (Sakel 2007: 14).

> In many cases of MAT-borrowing, also the function of the borrowed element is taken over, that is MAT and PAT are combined. MAT-borrowing without any PAT … is very rare and mainly occurs in the lexicon; i.e., usually MAT is taken over with at least part of its original PAT. (2007: 26)

6. Modality in Norwegian and English

Norwegian and English are closely related, and it comes as no big surprise that they share a lot of features in the domain of modality (cf. Eide 2005). One of these common denominators, also a common feature for Germanic languages in general, is that many markers of modality have two distinct readings: one so-called root reading (term due to Hofmann 1976), e.g., a deontic (or dynamic) reading, and one epistemic or evidential reading, the latter illustrated in (8b) and (8c) below.[8]

The deontic reading signifies that some state-of-affairs is desired, mandatory or allowed, whereas the epistemic reading encodes the speaker's evaluation of the likelihood of a given proposition. In many languages, not only Germanic ones, we find exactly these two readings in what looks like one and the same linguistic expression. This is true for modal verbs, like the Norwegian *skulle* 'be supposed to' in (8a), but also other modal constructions, like the English *be supposed to* and the Norwegian *være nødt til* 'be obliged to' in (8b) and (8c). Note especially that the two readings we find with *skulle* and *be supposed to* are exactly parallel, deontic (specifically 'intention') and evidential (specifically 'hear-say').

---

8. In this paper we only consider evidential readings as a special case of epistemic the reading, although they are in fact quite different in nature. *Epistemic* usually implies a pure truth evaluation of a proposition, whereas *evidential* regards the speaker's source of information (Palmer 2001). For our purposes, the relevant evidential reading is the 'hear-say' reading, implying that the speaker has their information from a third party, i.e., he is referring a claim made by someone else, cf. Eide (2005).

(8) a. *Døra skal være stengt.*
door.DEF shall be closed

   I. There exists an intention that the door is (kept) closed (deontic reading)
   II. There exists a claim that the door is now closed (evidential reading)

b. The door is supposed to be closed.

   I. There exists an intention that the door is (kept) closed (deontic reading)
   II. There exists a claim that the door is now closed (evidential reading)

c. *Døra er nødt til å være stengt.*
door.DEF is needed to be closed

   I. It is necessary that the door is (kept) closed (deontic reading)
   II. I am almost certain that the door is now closed (evidential reading)

There are thus major similarities between the possible readings of modal verbs in Norwegian and English ('mapping from grammatical or semantic meaning') and even the inventory of modals for the most part overlaps in the two languages. There are indeed cognates in the two languages with a similar meaning and function, but there are also significant differences especially regarding the distribution of modals in Norwegian versus English. Modals have very different restrictions in the two languages regarding their possible forms, and thus also very different distribution. English employs only finite forms of modals, and for instance infinitival and past participial modals are non-occurring and ungrammatical (**to can, *have could; *to must, *have must*). This contrasts strongly with the Norwegian modals with their full paradigm of finite and non-finite forms, including the infinitive and the past participle (*å kunne* 'to can.INF,' *har kunnet* 'have could.PERF'; *å måtte* 'to must.INF,' *har måttet* 'have must. PERF'). The fact that English modals lack non-finite forms effectively blocks the possibility of stacking English modals, whereas Norwegian modals are perfectly happy appearing in a sequence of two or more modals (*Marit skal kunne spille piano* 'Marit is supposed to be able to play the piano'). In these cases the leftmost modal typically receives an epistemic or evidential reading, but this is not an absolute rule; we also find occurrences of two epistemic modals (*Dette vil kunne bli et problem* 'This will possibly be a problem') or two deontic modals in a row (*Folk burde måtte ta en test før de går ut med deg* 'People ought to have to take a test before dating you').

7. The use of suppose(d)/[spoʊs], [spuːst] in American Norwegian

In a language contact situation, like the one once found in 'Norwegian America' where most people are practicing bilinguals, the language user typically will try to unify the two language systems, as any language user will search for convergence, according to Matras (2009: 151, 237):

> [T]here is pressure on the bilingual to simplify the selection procedure by reducing the degree of separation between the two subsets of the repertoire [. W]e might view the replication of patterns as a kind of compromise strategy that … reduce[s] the load on the selection … mechanism by allowing patterns to converge, thus maximizing the efficiency of speech production in a bilingual situation.

The notion 'replication of patterns' is used in a variety of meanings throughout the language contact literature, and we have already quoted Haugen (1950: 212) who does indeed talk about "reproduction of patterns" from a source language to a borrowing language, whereas his research primarily is concerned with lexical borrowings. In his terminology it thus suffices to borrow the element itself to fulfill the definition of 'replication of patterns.' We adopt instead the line of Matras and Sakel who try to differentiate borrowing of matter versus borrowing of patterns (even though matter replication rarely exists without any aspect of pattern replication according to Sakel 2007: 26). Taking Matras and Sakel's view as our point of departure, we have identified three aspects of pattern replication as especially relevant to our study: distribution, mapping of grammatical or semantic meaning, and function. We discuss these in turn.

First, it seems evident that the bilingual situation in American Norwegian communities has not lead to systematic pattern replication of the distribution of English modals from the source language English into American Norwegian. If this were the case, we would expect that Norwegian non-finite forms of modals cease to appear in the bilingual's Norwegian speech, replicating the system employing solely finite modals, as in English. However, non-finite forms of modals certainly occur in our material (cf. (9a)), and in Haugen's material from the 1940s we also find attested various types non-finite forms of modals (cf. (9b)).

(9) a. …prøvde på *å sku* finnje'n da veit du.
 …tried on to shall.INF find'him then you know
 '…they were trying to find him, you know.'

 b. Vi kvinnfolka i bygda vår *ha måtta* liggje
 we women-folk in village.DEF have must.PERF lie.PERF
 'Us women in our village have had to get down

 på hann å kne å skura golv.
 on hand and knee and scrubbed floor.DEF
 on hands and knees and scrub the floors.'

We thus do not find systematic (or at least wholesale) borrowing of the distributional pattern of modals from English into Norwegian, hence the tendency to reduce "the degree of separation between the two subsets of the repertoire" (cf. quote above) has not resulted in such rather dramatic outcomes. Moreover, simply borrowing one modal marker ([spuːst], [spoʊs]) from English into Norwegian might not be likely to trigger systematic syntactic changes of this scale.

Regarding the distribution of the borrowed element [spuːst], [spoʊs] it resembles the distributional patterns of *suppose(d)* in the source language, allowing us to assume that not only the element *supposed* [spuːst], [spoʊs] is borrowed, but also the distribution that goes with it. We need to make one important note regarding this distribution. In one of the two uses of this modal marker we find the present form and the syntactic structure [æ spoʊs] which corresponds closely to the English structure *I suppose*, and in this use there is no obvious difference between the application of this element in American Norwegian and the English source construction (cf. Section 3 above). Admittedly only 4 out of our 23 occurrences of this modal marker show this use, hence it is impossible of course to draw very clear conclusions.

(10) a. *Men æ [spoʊs] dæm ha bæd vinjtjra alj åver.*
but I suppose they had bad winters all over
'But I suppose they had bad winters all over.'

b. *Men æ [spoʊs] hain va vel ut i kailla,*
But I suppose he was well out in cold.DEF
'But I suppose he was out in the cold,

... arbeitt tå sæ da veit du.
...worked it off REFL then you know
...He worked it off, you know.'

c. *Æ tru kanskje dæm mått betal littegranj, fer når dæm*
I believe they must pay little-bit because when they
'I think maybe they had to pay a small amount, because when they

pekka ut nå lannj så mått dæm gå te Mainot å sain opp paper.
drew up some land then must they go to Mainot and sign up paper.
drew up land they had to go to Minot to sign up a paper.

Så æ [spoʊs] dæm mått betal littegranj.
So I suppose they must pay little-bit
So I suppose they had to pay a small amount.'

d. A: *Men Nårge tru æ fekk elæktrisitin tidlear ennj*
But Norway believe I got electricity.DEF earlier than
'But Norway, I think, got the electricity earlier than

hen i Amerika.
here in America
here in America.'

O: *Ja, æ [spoʊs], ja.*
yes I suppose yes
'Yes, I suppose so, yes.'

In these examples, [spoʊs] is evidently used as a discourse marker (more on this below). In such cases [spoʊs] is an active verb in the present tense (corresponding to

I suppose) and the distribution seems to be simply transferred from source language into recipient language.

In the remainder of the occurrences, 19 in number, we find variants of [spʊːst] used as a past participial passive. As mentioned in Section 3, there exists some variation regarding the syntactic frame of these participles, but still there are only 3 out of 19 instances where the 'English' frame accompanies the participle, with only one particle after the verb (like in the English construction *supposed to*). 16 of the 19 instances display instead the 'Norwegian' structure, patterning with *være nødt til å* 'be obliged to,' employing both the infinitival marker *å* and the preceding preposition *til* 'to' after the participle; cf. (6) above, repeated here as (11).

(11) a. [²spoʊsa o] /[spuːst o] (2 occurrences)
     b. [spoʊst tə] (1 occurrence)
     c. [spu(ː)st tə o] (16 occurrences)

Looking solely on this participial use one may very well ask whether all aspects of the distributional patterns carry over from source language to recipient language since the particles following the participle occur as expected from the Norwegian pattern, not from the pattern found in the source language.

In 'mapping of grammatical or semantic meaning' on the other hand the present tense use of the marker evidently displays the meaning 'I suppose so,' quite identical in American Norwegian and English. Even here, however, there are clearly Norwegian models to support this type of construction, like *æ tru* 'I believe,' *æ meine* 'I mean,' *æ antar* 'I presume' and many others, e.g., Example (10c). The readings and nuances of the participial use are clearly also parallel in American Norwegian and English; one deontic reading (of intention) and one evidential (hear-say) reading, cf. (8) above, and the adjacent discussion.

Sometimes it is clearly very difficult to distinguish whether a deontic or epistemic/evidential reading is intended (or relevant); many utterances and contexts allow for both readings. This vagueness or polysemy is acknowledged to be quite typical for modal expressions of the relevant type. Thus we find examples of such ambiguity in (12a, b), where it seems hard to determine whether we have an epistemic or evidential reading ('no one has ever told me that you are from Trondheim') or an obligation, i.e., deontic reading ('you are not allowed to (pretend that you) come from Trondheim').

(12) a. *Du må itj bynn å snakk tronjæmmer hen no,*
        you must not begin to speak Trondheimer here now
        'You mustn't start speaking like someone from Trondheim now;

        du e itj [spʊst] *te å vårrå tronjæmmer!*
        you are not supposed to to be Trondheimer
        You're not supposed to be from Trondheim.'

    b. *Dom e* [spʊst] *te å væra der, mongsan.*
        they are supposed to be there, Hmongs.DEF
        'The Hmongs (i.e., Chinese) are supposed to live there.'

In about half of our occurrences of [spʊːst] the deontic reading is what seems more natural.⁹

(13) a. *Vi va [spʊːst] te å lær engelskt, da veit'u.*
we were supposed to to learn English then know you
'We were supposed to learn English, you know.'

b. *Vi va [spʊːst] te å kåmmå opp hær, da veit'u.*
we were supposed to to come up here then know you
'We were supposed to ascend here, you know.'

c. *...dom e itj [spʊːst] te å vara råf hell da veit'u.*
...they are not supposed to be rough either then know you
'...They are not supposed to be rough either, you know.'

d. *Dom e [spʊːst] te å ta vækeisjn så ofte, da ma.*
they are supposed to take vacation so often then you-know
'They are supposed to take vacation so often, you know.'

e. *Hå e vi [spʊːst] te å laga på nå da?*
what are we supposed to make on now then
'What are we supposed to talk about now?'

The epistemic/evidential reading appears with roughly the same frequency. This is the more natural reading in half of the instances of [spʊːst] in our material.

(14) a. *Det va [səpʊːst] te å vara messom beste sigartobakken som va.*
it was supposed to to be sort-of best sigar-tobacco that was
'It was supposed to be about the best sigar tobacco there was.'

b. *De' ska [spʊːst] te å vara bære mjølk det, greid ei, da ma.*
it shall supposed to to be better milk that, grade A, then you-know
'That is supposed to be better milk, grade A, you know.'

c. *Å, vi e nu [spʊːst] å vårrå så fri vi, men ...*
oh we are now supposed to be so free we but ...
'Oh, we are supposed to be so free, we are, but...

æ kannj no itj sjå de helljer.
I can now not see that either
I can't really see it.'

d. *Sulphur Acid, veit'u, nei de' [spʊːs] te å vara deindjær.*
Sulphuric acid, know you, no that supposed to to be danger
'Sulphuric acid, you know, that's supposed to be dangerous.'

---

9. In writing 'about half' we capture the fact that different readers might have found the other (epistemic or evidential) reading just as natural, even if we discussed every single example before deciding on a specific reading seemingly more natural in that specific context. Again, modal expressions are notoriously vague, and in some cases the speaker will exploit this fact more or less intentionally to underdetermine the utterance.

e. *Wæll, kjøtt e [spʊst] te å vårrå hælsi, kjæm du ihau farin min,*
Well meat is supposed to to be healthy, come you in-head dad.DEF my
'Well, meat is supposed to be so healthy, remember my dad;

kjæm du ihau kor my hain åt kjøtt?
come you in-head how much he ate meat
remember how much he ate meat?

In all these examples we find *supposed*/[spʊːst] as a perfect participle, and nearly always following the copula (but note the exception in (14b) where the participle follows the modal *ska* 'shall') just as the pattern predicts both in English and in the Norwegian model construction *være nødt til å* 'be obliged to.'

Since *supposed to* has an epistemic/evidential reading and a deontic reading in English (cf. the example in (8b) above) and since [spʊːst] displays exactly these readings in American Norwegian, it seems tempting to claim that this is a definite instance of pattern replication. However, this is in effect not as unequivocal as it might seem. Recall from Section 6, and particularly the discussion pertaining to the examples in (8), that English and Norwegian are exactly the same in this regard; in fact the modals in all the Germanic languages (and certain other modal expressions) are capable of both an epistemic/evidential and a deontic reading. Even though Norwegian does not have an element exactly corresponding to [spʊːst] regarding semantic aspects and syntactic distribution (since [spʊːst], unlike the real modal verbs, obligatorily appears with the copula) we still find a modal *skulle* 'shall' providing exactly the same combination of readings, i.e., evidential and deontic. In this case it is possible to argue that the language user seeks to minimize the differences between the language systems (Matras 2009: 151, 237) resulting in the same readings for [spʊːst] and *skulle*. However, it is not unambiguous that this is due to adjusting [spʊːst] to an existing Norwegian model, the modal *skulle*, or whether this ensues from importing the pattern belonging to *supposed to* in the source language.

The discussion of the distribution of [spoʊs] and [spʊːst] thus does not give unequivocal answers to whether or not this is pattern replication, and neither does the discussion of nuances of meaning. Finally, we investigate the third aspect of pattern replication on our list. In our data three functions clearly stand out.

(15) a. [spʊːst] as a marker of deontic modality
b. [spʊːst] as a marker of epistemic/evidential modality
c. [spoʊs] as a discourse marker

The function as a marker of deontic and epistemic/evidential modality is performed by the perfect participle [spʊːst], as discussed above. The purpose of the element in these cases is to encode that there exists an intention about the occurrence of a specific state of affairs, which is often interpreted as an obligation or a social commitment (cf. examples in (13) above; cf. also Sections 4 and 6); in the epistemic/evidential case the purpose is to express an assumption or an evaluation of a proposition based on third party information, i.e., hear-say (cf. the examples in (14) and Sections 4 and 6).

As mentioned above, only four of our attested instances show the use of [spoʊs] as a discourse marker, shown in (10) above and repeated here for convenience as (16):

(16) a. *Men æ [spoʊs] dæm ha bæd vinjtjra alj åver.*
  but I suppose they had bad winters all over
  'But I suppose they had bad winters all over.'

 b. *Men æ [spoʊs] hain va vel ut i kailla,*
  But I suppose he was well out in cold.DEF
  'But I suppose he was out in the cold,

  … arbeitt tå sæ da veit du.
  …worked it off REFL then you know
  …He worked it off, you know.'

 c. *Æ tru kanskje dæm mått betal littegranj, fer når dæm*
  I believe they must pay little-bit because when they
  'I think maybe they had to pay a small amount, because when they

  pekka ut nå lannj så mått dæm gå te Mainot å sain opp paper.
  drew up some land then must they go to Mainot and sign up paper.
  drew up land they had to go to Minot to sign up a paper.

  Så æ [spoʊs] dæm mått betal littegranj.
  So I suppose they must pay little-bit
  So I suppose they had to pay a small amount.'

 d. A: *Men Nårge tru æ fekk elæktrisitin tidlear ennj*
  But Norway believe I got electricity.DEF earlier than
  'But Norway, I think, got the electricity earlier than

  hen i Amerika.
  here in America
  here in America.'

  O: *Ja, æ [spoʊs], ja.*
  yes I suppose yes
  'Yes, I suppose so, yes.'

Observe that this use strongly resembles other types of discourse markers as described and discussed in Section 4 above, like *you know, I think, I mean,* and many others. It seems quite clear that the speaker employs [spoʊs] to encode that he is not quite certain of the truth value of the proposition asserted, but he presumes it is true, or at least is willing to admit it might be true. This aligns with the quote from Coates above, that discourse markers of this type are used to take some of the force out of the assertion. It also seems evident that this semantically and functionally corresponds to the epistemic/evidential reading of [spoːst], easily interpreted as the passive variant of [spoʊs]; 'it is claimed/assumed/held that p' versus 'I claim/assume/hold that p.'

Let us look more closely at the example in (16c). This example is very interesting in revealing that the speaker uses *æ spous* quite identically to *æ tru* 'I believe.' Fuller (2001:362) points out that discourse markers like English *you know* and German *weisst du* appear in the same discourse contexts, and given that such markers have quite a similar distribution, it is not surprising, according to Salmons (1990), that many bilinguals vacillate between these two. We might ascribe the same properties to bilinguals vacillating between *æ spous* and *æ tru,* since the speaker seems to be using these two interchangeably (although the material is of course much too limited to say anything about relative frequency and the like).

Example (16d) also shows quite clearly that *æ spous* can be used as a prototypical discourse marker, where the speaker acknowledges that he is willing to accept what the interlocutor is claiming in the previous utterance. This comes close to what Boas and Weilbacher (2007: 34–35) claim to be one of the most crucial tasks of discourse markers: "To mitigate the speaker's responsibility for the subject matter of an utterance."

As a discourse marker, as a marker of epistemic modality, and as a marker of deontic modality the functions of [spuːst]/[spoʊs] seemingly correspond exactly to those of English *suppose(d)*. Hence it is a plausible interpretation of the facts that not only the element *suppose(d),* but even the function of this element has been borrowed from English into American Norwegian; in effect, this is a matter replication as well as pattern replication. One possible objection to this analysis would be that one might imagine a scenario where [spuːst] and [spoʊs] were borrowed from English into American Norwegian as two totally separate lexemes with no internal connection to each other in the mental grammar of the user, where both lexemes have adjusted to Norwegian without carrying on the source language pattern. Obviously it would be very hard to rule out this possibility given that we have very few attested examples, i.e., in reality too few to allow us detect any sort of pattern, and especially since almost none of our informants display examples of both uses, i.e., [spuːst] and [spoʊs]. We however remind the reader that according to Sakel (2007: 14, 26); the most common type of borrowing involves a combination of matter replication and pattern replication, and that "MAT-borrowing without any PAT ... is very rare ...; i.e., usually MAT is taken over with at least part of its original PAT" (cf. quotes above).

Finally, exactly this element *suppose(d)* seems to be high on a scale of borrowability, even in other contact situations where English is the donor language. It is also borrowed from English into Pennsylvania German, according to Burridge (2007:183):

(17) Ich bin supposed fer kumme.
 I am supposed for come
 'I will come.'

Burridge lists *suppose(d)* as one of the linguistic elements from English regularly employed to express future in Pennsylvania German.[10]

---

10. For an interesting discussion and a diachronic overview of the path travelled by *be supposed to* in its development into 'a semi-modal' in modern English, cf. Noël and van der Auwera (2009).

8. Summing up

The linguistic element [spʊːst]/[spoʊs] seems to be well integrated into the American Norwegian lexicon, it is quite widespread, and phonetically it is relatively well adapted to the Norwegian phonological system. Admittedly, this holds to a greater extent for the participle [*spʊːst*] and perhaps somewhat less for the present form [spoʊs], where the English diphthong is maintained, and even with the participle is may be a bit unexpected to find an overlong syllable instead of a reduced vowel.[11] This is not unprecedented in the Norwegian system, however. Morphologically, it is very hard to decide which system rules the ground, since there is convergence between the English and the Norwegian systems in the relevant respects. Syntactically the relevant construction has models in both Norwegian and English, and especially the construction *være nødt til å* 'be obliged to' emerges as a very plausible Norwegian model. We have discussed whether this is solely matter replication or whether we find pattern replication too, and we discussed aspects of pattern replication that seem relevant; distribution, meaning (i.e., 'mapping of grammatical or semantic meaning'), and function. The distribution of these elements is similar to that of the source language English but also the recipient language Norwegian, except that [spʊːst] mostly occurs with particles (preposition + infinitival marker) according to the Norwegian pattern. 'Mapping of grammatical or semantic meaning' gives no clear cut answers either, since there is substantial overlap between the system of modals in English and Norwegian as regards readings and use. What does point to an aspect of pattern replication however is the fact that the three functions displayed by [spʊːst]/[spoʊs] in American Norwegian exactly corresponds to the three functions of this element in the source language English; as a marker of evidential/epistemic modality, as a marker of deontic modality, and as a discourse marker. But even here one might object that this does not necessarily reveal a systematic relation between [spʊːst] and [spoʊs], and that these elements are instead borrowed as independent lexemes. Thus it is difficult to determine whether this is pattern replication or adaptation of borrowed elements into the models of the recipient language. Following Matras' (2009) hypothesis that the language user seeks convergence between the different systems available to him, the source of the pattern may not be as important: What is important is that the language user seeks and attains convergence.

Suppose(d) is evidently high on the borrowability scale in contact situations, quite expectedly, given that the word form itself, i.e., the given linguistic element, is borrowed into other contact varieties as well (cf. data from Pennsylvania German in (17) above), but also given the fact that modals expressing obligation and commitment (and other types of necessity) are among the highest ranking element types on Matras' borrowability hierarchies (2007: 45). Furthermore, modality in and by itself ranks high on the list of elements frequently borrowed from one language to another, and is

---

11. It is not unusual that borrowed words in American Norwegian are realized with an 'overlong' syllable, like e.g., [læːst] 'last,' [vʌːɹst] 'worst' and [²ɹæːntʃɔɹan] 'the ranchers.'

borrowed more easily than, e.g., aspect and tense elements. Discourse markers are also high-ranking elements on the same lists, and *suppose(d)* is employed even in this particular function.

References

Annear, Lucas and Kristin Speth. This volume. "Maintaining a Multilingual Repertoire: Lexical Change in American Norwegian."

Boas, Hans C. and Hunter Weilbacher. 2007. "How Universal is the Pragmatic Detachability Scale? Evidence from Texas German Discourse Markers." In *Texas Linguistics Society 9: Morphosyntax of Underrepresented Languages*, ed. by Frederick Hoyt, Nikki Seifert, Alexandra Teodorescu and Jessica White, 33–58. Stanford, CA: CSLI Publications.

Burridge, Kate. 2007. "Language Contact in Pennsylvania German." In *Grammars in Contact. A Cross-Linguistic Typology*, ed. by Alexandra Y. Aikhenvald and R. M. W. Dixon, 179–200. Oxford: Oxford University Press.

Busterud, Guro. 2006. *Anaforer i norsk som andrespråk* [Anaphors in Norwegian as a second language]. Trondheim, Norway: Norwegian University of Science and Technology MA thesis.

Busterud, Guro. 2014. *Anaforiske bindingskonstruksjoner i norsk som andrespråk* [Anaphoric binding constructions in Norwegian as a second language]. Trondheim, Norway: Norwegian University of Science and Technology dissertation.

Coates, Jennifer. 2003. "The Role of Epistemic Modality in Women's Talk." In *Modality in Contemporary English*, ed. by Roberta Facchinetti, Manfred G. Krug and Frank Robert Palmer, 331–348. Berlin: Mouton De Gruyter.

Ehresmann, Todd and Joshua Bousquette. This volume. "Phonological Non-Integration of Lexical Borrowings in Wisconsin West Frisian."

Eide, Kristin Melum. 2005. *Norwegian Modals*. (Studies in Generative Grammar 74). Berlin: Mouton De Gruyter.

Elšík, Viktor and Yaron Matras. 2006. *Markedness and Language Change: The Romani Sample*. Berlin: Mouton De Gruyter.

Faarlund, Jan Terje. 2003. "Reanalyse og grammatikalisering i norske infinitivskonstruksjonar." In *Språk i endring: Indre norsk språkhistorie*, ed. by Jan Terje Faarlund, 57–79. Oslo: Novus.

Flaten, Nils. 1900–04. "Notes on the American-Norwegian with Vocabulary." *Dialect Notes* 2: 115–126.

Flom, George T. 1900–04. "English Elements in Norse Dialects of Utica, Wisconsin." *Dialect Notes* 2: 257–268.

Flom, George T. 1903. "The Gender of Norse Loan-Nouns in Norse Dialects in America." *The Journal of English and Germanic Philology* 5: 1–31.

Flom, George T. 1912. "Det norske sprogs bruk og utvikling i Amerika." *Nordmands-Forbundet* 4: 233–250.

Flom, George T. 1926. "English Loanwords in American Norwegian. As spoken in the Koshkonong Settlement, Wisconsin." *American Speech* 1: 541–558. DOI: 10.2307/452150

Flom, George T. 1929. "On the Phonology of English Loanwords in the Norwegian Dialects of Koshkonong in Wisconsin." *Arkiv for Nordisk Filologi – Tilläggsband till bd.* XL: 178–189.

Flom, George T. 1931. "Um det norske målet i Amerika." *Norsk aarbok*: 113–124.

Fuller, Janet M. 2001. "The Principle of Pragmatic Detachability in Borrowing: English-Origin Discourse Markers in Pennsylvania German." *Linguistics* 39: 351–369. DOI: 10.1515/ling.2001.014

Halmari, Helena. 1993. "Structural Relations and Finnish-English Code Switching." *Linguistics* 31: 1043–1068. DOI: 10.1515/ling.1993.31.6.1043

Halmari, Helena. 1997. *Government and Codeswitching: Explaining American Finnish*. (Studies in Bilingualism Series 12). Amsterdam: John Benjamins. DOI: 10.1075/sibil.12

Haugen, Einar. 1950. "The Analysis of Linguistic Borrowing." *Language* 26: 210–231. DOI: 10.2307/410058

Haugen, Einar. 1953. *The Norwegian Language in America*. Philadelphia: University of Pennsylvania Press.

Haugen, Einar. 1956. *Bilingualism in the Americas: A Bibliography and Research Guide*. (Publications of the American Dialect Society 26). Tuscaloosa, AL: University Alabama Press.

Hjelde, Arnstein. 1992. *Trøndsk talemål i Amerika*. Trondheim: Tapir.

Hjelde, Arnstein. 1996a. "The Gender of English Nouns Used in American Norwegian." In *Language Contact Across the North Atlantic*, ed. by P. Sture Ureland and Iain Clarkson, 297–312. Tübingen: Max Niemeyer Verlag.

Hjelde, Arnstein. 1996b. "Some Phonological Changes in a Norwegian Dialect in America." In *Language Contact Across the North Atlantic*, ed. by P. Sture Ureland and Iain Clarkson, 283–295. Tübingen: Max Niemeyer Verlag.

Hjelde, Arnstein. 2001. "A bilingual community and research problems: The Coon Prairie settlement and problems of distinguishing language contact phenomena in the speech of Norwegian-Americans." In *Global Eurolinguistics – European Languages in North America – Migration, Maintenance and Death*, ed. by P. Sture Ureland, 209–229. Tübingen: Max Niemeyer Verlag.

Hofmann, T. Ronald. 1976. "Past Tense Replacement in the Modal System." In *Syntax and Semantics*, vol. 7, ed. by J. McCawley, 86–100. New York: Academic Press.

Johannessen, Janne Bondi and Signe Laake. 2011. "Den amerikansk-norske dialekten i Midtvesten." In *Studier i dialektologi och sociolingvistik. Föredrag vid Nionde nordiska dialektologkonferensen i Uppsala 18–20 augusti 2010. Acta Academiae Regiae Gustavi Adolphi 116*, ed. by Lars-Erik Edlund, Lennart Elmevik and Maj Reinhammar, 177–186. Uppsala: Kungl. Gustav Adolfs Akademien för svensk folkkultur.

Johannessen, Janne Bondi and Signe Laake. 2012. "Østnorsk som norsk fellesdialekt i Midtvesten." *Norsk Lingvistisk Tidsskrift* 30(2): 365–380.

Johansen, Kjell. 1970. "Some Observations on Norwegian in Bosque County, Texas." In *Texas Studies in Bilingualism: Spanish, French, German, Czech, Polish, Sorbian, and Norwegian in the Southwest, With a Concluding Chapter on Code-Switching and Modes of Speaking in American Swedish*, ed. by Glenn G. Gilbert, 170–178. Berlin: Walter de Gruyter.

Kahan Newman, Zelda. This volume. "Discourse Markers in the Narratives of New York Hasidim: More V2 Attrition."

Labov, William. 1966. *The Social Stratification of English in New York City*. Washington, D.C.: Center for Applied Linguistics.

Matras, Yaron. 1998. "Utterance Modifiers and Universals of Grammatical Borrowing." *Linguistics* 36: 281–331. DOI: 10.1515/ling.1998.36.2.281

Matras, Yaron. 2002. *Romani: A Linguistic Introduction*. Cambridge: Cambridge University Press. DOI: 10.1017/CBO9780511486791

Matras, Yaron. 2007. "The Borrowability of Structural Categories." In *Grammatical Borrowing in Cross-Linguistic Perspective* (Empirical Approaches To Language Typology 38), ed. by Yaron Matras and Jeanette Sakel, 31–74. Berlin / New York: Mouton de Gruyter.

Matras, Yaron. 2009. *Language Contact*. Cambridge: Cambridge University Press. DOI: 10.1017/CBO9780511809873

Matras, Yaron. 2011. "Universals of structural borrowing." In *Linguistic Universals and Language Variation*, ed. by Peter Siemund, 200–229. Berlin: Mouton de Gruyter.

Matras, Yaron and Jeanette Sakel. 2007. "Introduction." In *Grammatical Borrowing in Cross-Linguistic Perspective* (Empirical Approaches To Language Typology 38), ed. by Yaron Matras and Jeanette Sakel, 1–14. Berlin / New York: Mouton de Gruyter.

Milroy, Lesley. 1987. *Observing and Analyzing Natural Languages. A Critical Account of Sociolinguistic Method*. (Language in Society 12). Oxford: Blackwell.

Myers-Scotton, Carol. 1990. "*Code-Switching* and Borrowing: Interpersonal and Macrolevel Meaning." In *Codeswitching as a Worldwide Phenomenon*, ed. by Rodolfo Jacobson, 85–105. New York: Peter Lang.

Noël, Dirk and Johan van der Auwera. 2009. "Revisiting *be supposed to* from a diachronic constructionist perspective." *English Studies* 90(5): 599—623.

Östman, Jan-Ola. 1981. *You Know: A Discourse Functional Approach*. Amsterdam: Benjamins. DOI: 10.1075/pb.ii.7

Palmer, Frank R. 1986. *Mood and Modality*. Cambridge: Cambridge University press.

Palmer, Frank R. 2001. *Mood and Modality*. 2nd edition. Cambridge: Cambridge University Press. DOI: 10.1017/CBO9781139167178

Poplack, Shana and David Sankoff. 1984. "Borrowing: The Synchrony of Integration." *Linguistics* 22: 99–135. DOI: 10.1515/ling.1984.22.1.99

Poplack, Shana, David Sankoff and Christopher Miller. 1988. "The Social Correlates and Linguistic Processes of Lexical Borrowing and Assimilation." *Linguistics* 26: 47–104. DOI: 10.1515/ling.1988.26.1.47

Sakel, Jeanette. 2007. "Types of Loan: Matter and Pattern." In *Grammatical Borrowing in Cross-Linguistic Perspective* (Empirical Approaches To Language Typology 38), ed. by Yaron Matras and Jeanette Sakel, 15–29. Berlin, New York: Mouton de Gruyter.

Salmons, Joseph. 1990. "Bilingual Discourse Marking: Code Switching, Borrowing, and Convergence in Some German-American Dialects." *Linguistics* 28: 453–480. DOI: 10.1515/ling.1990.28.3.453

Sunde, Anne Mette. 2013. *Bortfall av obligatoriske refleksiver i norsk* [Omission of obligatory reflexives in Norwegian]. Trondheim, Norway: Norwegian University of Science and Technology MA thesis.

Trudgill, Peter. 1972. "*Sex* and *Covert Prestige*: Linguistic Change in the Urban British English of Norwich." *Language in Society* 1: 179–195. DOI: 10.1017/S0047404500000488

PART V

Variation and real-time change

Changes in a Norwegian dialect in America

Arnstein Hjelde
Østfold University College

In this article I investigate dialect variation in the old Norwegian settlement around Coon Valley and Westby in Vernon County, Wisconsin, with a focus on how the Norwegian dialects spoken here have changed over time. The language in this community is well documented; the oldest recordings are from 1931, the most recent ones were done in 2014. By comparing such recordings from different times, I point to some tendencies of how different Norwegian speech varieties have changed in the settlement towards the formation of a koiné.

Keywords: koiné, koinéization, Norwegian dialects, heritage language, language change, change in morphology, change in phonology

1. Background

Almost all research on the Norwegian language in America during the 20th century focused on changes due to the intense contact with English. And most scholars, from Flaten (1900–04) and Flom (1900–04, 1903, 1912, 1926, 1929, 1931) around 1900, Haugen (1956, [1953] 1969) and Oftedal (1949a, 1949b) in the mid-1900s to myself (Hjelde 1992, 1996a, 1996b) at the end of the century focused on different aspects of the vocabulary, especially how English lexical items have been introduced into Norwegian. During the last years we have seen renewed interest in the study of the America-Norwegian language, and new aspects are investigated, as seen in this volume's studies by Allen and Salmons, Golden and Lanza, Johannessen, and Westergaard and Anderssen. But at the same time, this volume's contributions by Annear and Speth, Johannessen and Laake, and Åfarli make it very evident that vocabulary is still attracting interest from scholars. Up till now, nothing has been done on how different Norwegian dialects have changed over time due to contact with other dialects from Norway. There are reasons to believe that this process has not followed the same paths in all Norwegian-American communities: Some settlements were established by people from a rather small area in Norway and where everybody spoke the same dialect when they settled. Others were populated by people from different places in Norway, speaking a greater range of dialects. It is fair to assume that in the first case, the dialects did not change much except for changes due to contact with English. On the other hand, in communities where different dialects met, we should expect to find that dialect contact over time results in the formation of a 'new' dialect, a koiné.

2. Coon Valley and Westby

Coon Valley and Westby are small towns in Vernon County in the southwestern part of Wisconsin. This is in the core Norwegian settlement area founded in the mid-1800s (Qualey 1938), and Norwegian influence in this area is still quite strong. The 2000 US Census (US Census Bureau 2000) shows that in Wisconsin there is an area from Vernon County in the south and up towards Polk County and Barron County in the north, where more than one out of every five inhabitants claims Norwegian ancestry. In Trempealeau County, 40% claim to have Norwegian background, while in Vernon County 36% make a similar claim. These are the two counties in Wisconsin with the highest ratio of Norwegian-American population, and where they make up the largest ethnic group. According to the 2000 census (US Census Bureau 2000), these were also the two counties in Wisconsin with the highest density of Norwegian speakers. In Trempealeau County there were 410 such speakers, 3.8% of all Norwegian-Americans in this county, while in Vernon County there were 480, 5.1% of the Norwegian-Americans. It has to be said that the 2000 Census statistics are based on samples and are only estimates. But still this is the only information available, and at least suggests something about the number of speakers.

The Norwegian settlement around Coon Valley and Westby dates back to 1848, the same year Wisconsin was founded as a state. The sociologist P.A. Munch, who studied this settlement in the 1940s, pointed out that the geographical borders of the settlement to a great extent were defined as early as the 1870s; after this point growth in population took place within these borders and did not result in any geographical expansion (Munch 1954:114). This growth within limited borders also resulted in a pressure on other ethnic groups to leave: "the tendency having been to get rid of foreign elements within the area of the settlement itself rather than expanding into new areas" (Munch 1949:782). Furthermore, he describes this Norwegian community as socially and economically self-sufficient, and not under any control by 'Yankees' or Anglo-Americans. In this way, the community could, at least to some extent, isolate itself from the mainstream society. Munch also writes (1954:784):

> This community is very hard to break into, as is felt strongly by everyone who has tried it. There is a strong loyalty to the community and a correspondingly strong social pressure against any deviation from the accepted local pattern. What foreign elements have come in have either been assimilated completely to the cultural pattern of the community or they have been isolated socially until they preferred to leave.

Munch (1954) also comments on what he calls *gossip circles*, or social networks, as we probably would call them today, and he points out that these mostly consisted of people with a Norwegian ethnic background. And such a strategy, where ethnicity to a great extent regulates social interactions, is also important for explaining why the Norwegian language has been retained for such a long time in this community.

Haugen describes Coon as a settlement heavily dominated by people from Gudbrandsdalen, and he includes Biri as a part of Lower Gudbrandsdalen (Haugen [1953] 1969:610–611). This Gudbrandsdalen dominance has been quite strong since this settlement was founded, but at the same time it is also a fact that immigrants from other parts of Norway settled here as well. Today it is very difficult to conduct a survey on from where in Norway the people living here have their background. Quite a few lack detailed information on where their ancestors came from, who have never been to Norway and who do not have contact with family there. In order to get a better picture of the background of this settlement, I have looked at the birthplace of the first immigrants. Coon Valley Church and Coon Prairie Church each published books to celebrate the congregations' fiftieth anniversaries (Holand 1927, 1928). Here we find short biographies of the first 551 male pioneers and church members who settled, i.e., the first generation male immigrants who came to America between 1839 and 1877. It is not unproblematic to use this data in order to gain information on from where the Norwegian-Americans in this area today have their background, but still I think that this will give at least an indication of what dialect background people here should be expected to have.

40% came from Gudbrandsdalen, especially from the municipalities in the lower part of the valley, such as Fron, Øyer and Gausdal. In addition 15% came from Biri. Furthermore, there were quite a few from Telemark (9%), Hurdal (5%), as well as the Sogn, Lista and Flekkefjord area (5% each). There also seems to be some difference between the Coon Valley and Coon Prairie area. Whereas Coon Prairie had many from Biri (17%), there were many from Nord-Fron (19%) and Øyer (16%) in Coon Valley. This corresponds to some degree to Einar Haugen's observation on dialect use in this settlement: He found that the prevailing dialect in most of this settlement was from Lower Gudbrandsdalen; but in the area northeast of Coon Valley, known as Timber Coulee (Skogdalen), he found many speaking a more northern Gudbrandsdal variety, especially from Fron (Haugen 1953:611). And information from Holand (1928), paired with Plat books, indicates that immigrants from Fron showed a strong tendency to settle in the Timber Coulee area. However, today it is not possible to detect any such local geographical variation, especially since many of the Norwegian speakers today are retired people who have left the farms and moved into town.

3. The material

The Norwegian language around Coon Valley and Westby is well documented thanks to sound recordings done by Seip and Selmer in 1931, by Haugen in 1942, Kruse in 1986, myself in 1992, 1996 and 2010 and video recordings by the NorAmDiaSyn project every year from 2010 to 2015. The first recordings of Norwegian-Americans done for the purpose of linguistic studies were conducted in 1931 by the two Norwegian professors Didrik Arup Seip and Ernst W. Selmer, who spent the fall term in the Midwest, doing fieldwork with the aim of studying Norwegian dialects in the States. According to their fieldnotes, they also spent some time in the Coon area. Most of their recordings have been lost, and as far as I have been able to determine, only two from this area survive. The technical quality of this material is not very good and the recordings are very short (about 3 minutes for each); thus I have not relied on them in this study. The recordings by Einar Haugen are in a much better state; he was in this area during the fall of 1942. Altogether he had 31 informants from this area when he worked on *The Norwegian Language in America*, of which he recorded 26. The oldest recorded speaker was born in 1849 (93 years old), the youngest in 1911 (31 years), the average age was 67 years. Eight were born in Norway, the rest in the States. Some of these recordings are rather short, lasting only two minutes while the longest is 55 minutes. Altogether he did six hours of recordings in this area. In addition he also did some recordings of people who were not classified as informants. Parts of this material were also transcribed by Haugen and his assistant Magne Oftedal, and the recordings and transcriptions are now available from the Text Laboratory on the Internet.[1]

In 1992 I spent three months in Wisconsin, doing fieldwork in this area. During this period I recorded approximately 80 hours of some 60 Norwegian-Americans born between 1905 and 1932. The oldest one emigrated as a young boy together with his parents, while the others were born in the Midwest.

In 2010 I had the opportunity to take part in fieldwork organized by the NorAmDiaSyn project, and after this organized fieldwork was done, I returned to the Coon area to do more recordings on my own. This time I was especially looking for 'young' speakers, i.e., people born after 1940, a category of informants I had not encountered during the 1990s.

In this article I use these three sets of recordings. Altogether this material covers speakers born between 1849 and 1961, a time warp of more than 100 years and several generations. And by comparing the language documented in these recordings I also hope to be able to find out the direction in which the dialects have evolved over these years. The local people often refer to in their Norwegian vernacular as "Coon Valley norsk" or "Westby norsk," and my aim will also be to see if this refers to a consistent language norm, a koiné which has evolved when speakers with different dialect

---

1. http://www.tekstlab.uio.no/nota/NorDiaSyn/dialektlyd.html

background have met. It is possible that such a process was well on its way in the 1940s as Haugen comments that "[t]he prevailing dialect is that of Lower Gudbrandsdalen, especially Biri; this is often referred to as 'Westby Norwegian'" (Haugen 1953:610).

4. An America-Norwegian koiné?

Kerswill and Trudgill (2005:196) have pointed out two archetypal situations where a koiné is formed. One involves immigration to unpopulated areas, illustrated by the colonialization of New Zealand. The other concerns the development of urban communities within a limited geographical area, where the emergence of the Norwegian industrial communities Høyanger, Odda and Tyssedal are used as typical examples. And even if the situation in Coon is different from New Zealand, as well as Høyanger, Odda and Tyssedal, we find several features in both these scenarios, relevant for Coon. First of all, emigrating to America represented a break with their places of origin in Norway; thus dialect norms and dialect change back in the Old World would not be a norm for the language spoken on the prairie. At the same time the isolation from Norway was not total, and for a long time newcomers arrived speaking unmodified Norwegian, and it is reasonable to assume that this slowed the koinéization process. Secondly, Coon can also resemble the development of new industrial communities in the sense that people with different dialects settled down here. And even if the dialects from Biri and the lower Gudbrandsdalen area dominated, they were definitely not the only varieties spoken here.

In addition to dialectal variation and contact, it is also important to remember that this was a ground for intensive contact between Norwegian and English. Over time, this proved to have a dramatic effect on the Norwegian language in America, partly because Norwegian changed as a result of this contact, but mostly because the outcome of this contact was a language shift: today Norwegian is about to disappear on the prairie. When the speakers themselves are asked to characterize "Westby norsk" and "Coon Valley norsk," they point at all the borrowed lexical elements used. But at the same time, English has obviously not always been in such a dominating position; at a micro level, Norwegian was also quite dominating in this settlement at least until World War II, at one time even people with German and Irish background had to speak Norwegian in order to function in this community. Evidence for this is found in Haugen's recorded material from Coon Valley, where one of the speakers of Norwegian (10C14)[2] had a German background and thus grew up with German as his first language.

Trudgill et al. (2000) describe the typical koinéization process in three stages, where each stage might correspond to one generation. The first stage, dominated by first generation immigrants, is characterized by dialectal variation with some

---

2. The informant code used by Haugen (1953).

rudimentary tendencies towards leveling. The second stage, dominated by second generation inhabitants, typically demonstrates extreme variability and further leveling. The last stage, involving the third and subsequent generation immigrants, is characterized by consolidation, dialectal leveling and the emergence of a rather unified language norm. The three different sets of recorded materials used in this study, might at least to some degree, correspond to these three stages. In the recordings from 1942 we find quite a few first generation immigrants, even if the immigration to Coon had been going on for over 90 years when these recordings were made. The informants recorded in the 1990s were with one exception born in America, and they might represent stage two in this model. The informants recorded in 2010–12 might represent the last stage, many of them were born after 1940 and were third or fourth generation Americans.

5. The language varieties

If we assume that the recordings done by Haugen document the actual language variation found in Coon in the early 1940s, we can classify the spoken varieties into three main types: East Norwegian, especially Gudbrandsdal dialects, West Norwegian dialects, and normalized speech, where the East Norwegian variety is most frequent. And in the rest of this article, I will focus on how these three types evolved over the years.

5.1 West Norwegian dialects

In Haugen's material from 1942 we find several informants speaking a West Norwegian dialect, among them a couple from Eresdalen in Romsdalen (informant 11R1 and 11R2). The wife talks about how hard it was in every way to adjust to life in this new country. The language was also a problem, but she does not mention problems with English. What she complains about is the communication with people from Gudbrandsdalen; they did not understand some words she used, and they made fun of her. The consequence was that she had to adjust to the Gudbrandsdalen dialect, and then they understood her. Most features in the dialect of these two speakers do no doubt belong to the Romsdal dialect, but with some accommodations towards the east Norwegian dialects of Gudbrandsdalen.

This tendency to accommodate not only affects vocabulary. We also find the same on the morphological and phonological levels. And while lexical accommodation can be explained as a strategy to facilitate understanding, this is hardly the motivation for the phonological and morphological changes. One feature used to identify dialect areas in Norway, is endings in disyllabic infinitives. While all such infinitives in the Romsdal dialect end in *-e*, the East Norwegian dialects have a system of different endings, *-e* or *-a*, so-called *kløyvd infinitiv* 'divided infinitive,' and in the speech of these two informants from Romsdal, we find tendencies towards such an eastern Norwegian system, like [foˈ¹tæʈʲə] 'tell,' but [²jæːra] 'do' and [²vaːra] or [²væːrə] 'be,' and it is hard to believe that the *-e* infinitive endings in the Romsdalen dialect should cause any communicative problems. But in the Coon context, the system with only *e*-infinitives could be felt as marked, and as such it was replaced by a system with *kløyvd infinitiv* 'divided infinitives.' Furthermore, none of these two informants use the traditional personal pronoun form from Romsdal, which is [iː] 'I.' Instead we find [jeː] and [eː]. The form [iː] has a limited distribution in Norwegian dialects, found in two areas in Norway, including parts of Romsdalen. That the pronoun [iː] is regarded as marked is maybe not too strange since it stands out from the East Norwegian forms [jeː] and [eː], and more so considering how frequent personal pronouns are in speech. Eresfjorden, where these two informants come from, is furthermore a border area for the [iː] isogloss, the neighboring communities have [eː], and we should perhaps expect that this form would be the selected substitute. And [eː] is used by them, but we also find the form [jeː], probably because this was the most frequent form found in this settlement at that time. Furthermore, we find that the Romsdal negation particle [²içə] often is substituted by [²itə] or [²icə], but these three are obviously competing forms in the vernacular of these two.

Fifty years later, when I did fieldwork in Coon in 1992, I did not come across any speakers of a West Norwegian vernacular, and I did not come into contact with anybody living in this area with a West Norwegian background either. At that time the identity of the community was solely linked to Gudbrandsdalen, and people with a west Norwegian background, the so-called Sognings and Flekkefjordings, were in general associated with the neighboring town Viroqua and its surroundings, which traditionally was a West Norwegian settlement.

Western dialects in Coon were probably associated with the first generation immigrants, and my assumption is that later generations took up the Gudbrandsdalen dialect which they learned from their peers, or they became monolingual English speakers. Since in the 1990s West Norwegian dialects were no longer found in Coon, or even in the traditional West Norwegian communities in Vernon County like Viroqua, there are now very few people left who speak these dialects.

5.2 Normalized speech

In the Haugen material from 1942 we do find quite a few examples of people trying to moderate their speech towards the written Dano-Norwegian standard. Today it is of course difficult to know if the recordings really reflect the way these people normally spoke, or if the informants have several registers, and that the formal atmosphere associated with a professor and his recording equipment also triggers a more formal register of speech. Field notes made by Magne Oftedal when he assisted Haugen in 1948 reveal that it was not uncommon for informants to change their speech towards the written standard during the recording sessions. And as can be expected, the use of normalized speech is especially found among educated people and urban dwellers. One of these represented in the recorded material is the minister of the Coon Prairie church. He prepared a written manuscript for the recording session, from which he read. It is somewhat puzzling that Haugen afterwards chose to spend time transcribing this recording. One of the other informants, 11C2, was raised in Coon Valley, but she was a trained nurse and lived in La Crosse at the time these recordings were done. Even though she says at the beginning of the interview that she is going to speak the traditional Coon Valley dialect, she is not able to live up to that intention fully. Thus we find dialectal forms like the pronoun [jeː], the negation particle [ite], palatal consonants, *kløyvd* infinitive 'divided infinitives' and tendencies towards the use of the dative case. However, we also find many examples of more 'bookish' forms like [²ike] *ikke* 'not,' [¹vʊdan] *hvordan* 'how,' [¹tiːd-n] *tiden* 'time,' [eːn gaŋ] *en gang* 'once,' [miːn fa¹miːliə] *min familie* 'my family'. Her brother, on the other hand, who was a farmer in Coon Valley, does not show any such tendencies.

The fact that informants were able to normalize their speech towards the written Norwegian standard shows that they were familiar with this variant. It is reasonable to believe that such knowledge was quite widespread in this community in the 1940s. Newspapers and books were still printed in Dano-Norwegian, most people were confirmed in Norwegian and had training in reading Norwegian through the so-called 'summer school' or 'religious school,' offered by the church for a few weeks during the summer. In Coon Valley and Westby, Norwegian was also used in church on a regular basis even after World War II, so the congregation would have been quite familiar with this spoken variety. It can also be mentioned that the cinema in Westby showed Norwegian movies without dubbing from the 1940s and well into the 1960s, thus this was another arena where people would be exposed to a spoken standard of Norwegian.

But the situation changed dramatically for this spoken variety during the next decades: When I did fieldwork in this area in 1992, I only found two individuals who spoke a standard-like variety of Norwegian, and both had strong ties to Norway or Norwegian written culture, more than to the local Norwegian-American community. One had a background as a teacher, while the other was very interested in contemporary Norwegian literature. But even if there were not many who spoke this variety of Norwegian, most of the informants were familiar with it as many of them were confirmed in Norwegian and had been to the Norwegian 'summer school.' And as late as the 1990s, the church offered services in Norwegian a couple of times a year.

In 2010 I encountered only one speaker using a standardized variety of Norwegian, and this was one of the two I found during the 1990s who still was alive. Today the written standard cannot serve as a norm for a spoken *lingua franca*, simply because very few Norwegian-Americans are familiar with written Norwegian (cf. Johannessen and Laake 2012). Very few can read Norwegian, and it is not heard in church anymore. And it is interesting to note that the situation here is very different from what has happened in the American Swedish communities, where the dialects have vanished and what can be found today is in general standardized Swedish (Larsson et al. this volume).

However, it is likely that this standardized speech will be the last to survive in America. Some of those growing up as monolingual English speakers, but with an interest for their ethnic background, might compensate the lack of Norwegian learning at home by studying Norwegian at the university. But such individuals will use Norwegian to keep contact with their background across the Atlantic, not to be a part of any traditional Norwegian-American speech community.

5.3 East Norwegian dialects

Most of Haugen's informants from 1942 had dialect backgrounds from the lower part of Gudbrandsdalen, including Biri; however, they did not all speak the same. We find phonological and morphological variation which for the most part correlates with the variation in dialect features found in the Gudbrandsdalen area between Biri in the south and Fron to the north. We can reasonably assume that much of this variation relates to where in the Gudbrandsdalen area they have their roots, but we also find individual variation which indicates instability or even change in the language system. We can for example see this variation in the competing personal pronoun forms [eː] and [jeː] for 1st person singular. Traditionally, [eː] is found from Gausdal and Øyer and northwards, while [jeː] is found south of this area. Informants from Fron seem to be the only ones consistently using [eː] as the sole pronominal form, for the others it is hard to find any consistent pattern. Some individuals vacillate between the use of [jeː] and [eː], and this is especially common among those born in America. The only 1st person plural pronoun found is [viː], even if the northern part of Gudbrandsdalen, from Fron, has [ʊs]. However, this latter form is obviously marked and avoided. As can be expected, the only negation particle found is [²itə]. This is in accordance with the areas of distribution for this particle in Norway, the area around Lake Mjøsa and north up to Nord-Fron.

Palatalization of dental consonants in stressed syllables is a dialect feature that we find in the speech of most speakers of East Norwegian dialects in Coon, like in [²haʎiŋ₁daːɽ] *Hallingdal*, [laɲ] *land*, [stʉɲ] *stund* 'while' and [²kaʎə] *kalle* 'call'. This palatalization is in some dialects quite weak, and can also be realized as so-called 'palatal segmentation,' a process where the palatalization has resulted in a segment [i] instead of a palatal consonant, like [²æⁱlə] *alle* 'all', [²pæⁱno] *panner* 'pans' and [bjøⁱn] *bjørn* 'bear'. In northern parts of Gudbrandsdalen we also expect palatalization of dental consonants in unstressed syllables, but we do not find much evidence for this in the Haugen material: only one of the informants has this feature, as in [²kaːraɲ] *karane* 'the men,' and this man was born in Fron. But palatalization of dental consonants in unstressed syllables seems to be regarded marked and thus avoided by the second generation immigrants. On the other hand, other dialect features typical of the northern part of Gudbrandsdalen seem to be more robust, as with short root syllables in words with vowel balance, as in [²jɛra] *gjera* 'do' and [²moɽo] *mala* 'grind,' and also the 'European u' ([u]) is still quite frequent, like in [²uksər] *oksar* 'oxen,' [²uɲə] *unge* 'young,' and [²sumə] *somme* 'some.'

In morphology we also find several examples of variation. This is the case for past tense of the 1st class of weak verbs, the so-called 'a-verbs.' In Gudbrandsdalen dialects, we expect to find the past tense suffix -*a*, while in Biri and around Lake Mjøsa, we find -*e ([-ə])*. In Coon this pattern is partly intact in the sense that people with a Gudbrandsdalen background in general apply the -*a* formative, while people from Biri in general apply the -*e ([-ə])*. However, people from the area around Mjøsa show instability, and the same speaker may use both [²fiskə] and [²fiska] *fiska* 'fished'. For one consultant the distribution of these two endings seems to be ruled by the origin of the verb, borrowed elements are assigned -*a*, while Norwegian ones get -*e*. She talks about [²kastə] *kasta* 'threw' and [²rɛknə] *rekna* 'counted,' but [²çuːsa] 'chose' and [²saɪsa] 'sized,' but the material is too limited to draw decisive conclusions. We also find other speakers who clearly do not follow this distribution, like [²fiska]/[²fiskə] *fiska* 'fished', [²stʊpa] *stoppa* 'stopped', [²hʊntə] 'hunted' and [²kɛtʃə] 'catched.' The only explanation I can see for this variation is a general instability in the system.

In this context it is also relevant to look at the use of -*r* to mark present tense of weak verbs and also as a marker of plural indefinite form of nouns. It has to be said that the Haugen material does not show many present tense verbs, mostly because the speakers are invited to talk about the 'old days.' The dialects of Fron and Ringebu do not have the -*r* formative in present tense of weak verbs, nor in plural indefinite form of nouns, while in Biri, -*r* is found in both these types. In the geographical area in between, -*r* is present for nouns, but not for verbs. In the Haugen material we find that the distribution is unchanged for nouns, those with a background from Fron do not have this formative, while all the others have kept it. When it comes to the present tense of weak verbs, the picture is less clear. We find it in the speech of all coming from Biri, but we can also find that it has spread to others as well. I find it reasonable to look at this as the result of some kind of dialect leveling.

We also find use of dative in nouns in these recordings, but it is also obvious that the use of dative case is on its way out. Only the first generation immigrants seem to have this system intact. Examples of dative forms are also found in the speech of others, but its use is no longer consistent.

In general it is fair to say that in the 1940s we cannot talk about "Westby norsk" and "Coon Valley norsk" as a narrow, coherent norm without any dialect variation. What we find is phonological and morphological variation, but within clear limits. This variation is only partly determined by the dialectal background of the speaker, and we also find individual variation which is the result of competing norms in a rather labile linguistic environment.

In the 1990s the different East Norwegian dialects have still not merged into a consistent koiné, in fact the recordings done at that time document more dialectal variation than what is found in Haugen's material from the 1940s, and we find several dialectal features that are not found in Haugen's recordings. An example of this is the system of personal pronouns. Like in 1942 we find [jeː] and [eː] used for 1st person singular form, both are commonly used, and even the same speaker can use these two different forms. Most speakers use the personal pronoun [viː] in 1st person plural, but now we also find a handful informants using [os] as the subject form, in accordance with dialects from the upper part of Gudbrandsdalen. The fact that such forms are documented in 1992, but not in 1942, does of course not mean that this is a new development in Coon. The recorded material collected in 1992 is more than ten times as big as the one from 1942, thus we can expect that it documents language variation to a higher degree. A similar increase in the variation is found for the negation particle. As in the 1940s, [²itə] is still the most frequent form, but in addition we also find realizations with palatal fricative [²içə] or palatal plosive [²icə]. It is not surprising to find forms with palatal fricative [²içə], since this corresponds to the upper Gudbrandsdalen dialect. But the form with palatal plosive [²icə] is hard to explain, as it does not belong to any dialect in this part of Norway. It is a typical feature in some dialects from Østerdalen, but hardly any immigrants came to Coon from this area. The only explanation I have is that it is the result of a neutralization strategy, based on the two forms [²itə] and [²içə], where the plosive realization of [t] is combined with the palatal realization of [ç], resulting in [c].

When it comes to syllable structure in words with vowel balance, we find a few examples of realization with short root syllable, like [²komo] *koma* 'come' and [²jɛra] *gjera* 'do,' but most speakers do now have a realization with long syllable. The so-called 'European u' is still quite common, like in [huːs] *hus* 'house' and [²uksə] *okse* 'oxen.' As in the 1940s, palatalization of dental consonants in stressed syllables is common, like in [laɲ] *land* 'land,' [¹syɲ₁daːn] *søndagen* 'the Sunday,' [²kafi₁kaɲa] *kaffikanna* 'the coffee pot,' [²aʎri] *aldri* 'never,' [²kvɛʎan] *kveldane* 'the evenings,' [rʉɲc] *rundt* 'around,' [rɛɟ] *redd* 'scared' and [²skøɟə] *skodde* 'fog.' And similarly, some of the speakers do also have such palatalization in unstressed syllables, like [²skʉrɨɲ] *skolen* 'the school,' [²bɾɔfɨɲ] 'the bluffs,' [²nɔʃkəraɲ] *norskarane* 'the Norwegians' and [²ʊŋaɲ] *ungane* 'the children.' However, this is an area of individual variation, and the same speaker can vary between forms with and without such palatalization, like in [²çæʈ[aɲ] *kjertlane* 'the glands', but [²hɛstan] *hestane* 'the horses.'

Plural indefinite forms of nouns are marked with -r by most speakers, even if we also find examples without this ending, like in [²hɛstər] *hestar* 'horses' and [²tiːər] *tider* 'times' but [²hɛstə] *hestar* 'horses' and [²kʉːə] *kuer* 'cows.' Here we might also have individual variation and the same speaker can produce plural forms both with and without -r.

In present tense of weak verbs, -r is not commonly used, even if it can be found. Examples: [²pɾaɲcə] *plantar* 'plant,' [²snakə] *snakkar* 'talk' and [²brʉːkə] *bruker* 'use' but also [²arbeiər] *arbeider* 'work.' And the past tense of weak verbs of first declination, the so-called *a*-verbs, does in most cases employ -*a* as the formative. However, we can also find a few instances where -*e* ([-ə]) is used. Examples: [²snaka] *snakka* 'talked,' [²tryska] *trøska* 'threshed,' but [²pɾantə] *planta* 'planted' and [²hʉntə] 'hunted.'

It is obvious that the dative case was in decline during the 1990s, as it was fifty years earlier. Very few have dative at all in their dialect, and those who have it, do not use it consistently. Examples of dative use in the material is [ɛ va dən ²yŋstə tɔ ²jɛntʊm] *eg var den yngste av jentene* 'I was the youngest of girls.DEF.DAT' and [²høːna mə ²ccʉkɾɨɲʊm] *høna med kjuklingane* 'hen.DEF with chickens.DEF.DAT).' The collapse of the dative system is not only found in American Norwegian, it is also common in many dialects in Norway, thus this is a process that very well might have started in Norway and continued in the New World. This development is however not a general phenomenon affecting all Norwegian dialects in America. In the Trønder communities visited in the 1980s as well as during the last years, it was possible to find speakers with a rather intact dative system (Hjelde 1992). But while these Trønder speakers came from communities with roots in only one small area of Norway and where all spoke a rather consistent dialect where dative was morphologically marked in only one way, the population in Coon comes from a larger area where dative can be marked by several formatives. And I find it reasonable to assume that the fact that dative could be formed in several different ways in the different Norwegian dialects originally represented in Coon has led to instability and finally the collapse of dative marking of nouns.

The recordings done in Coon during the last years confirm that still today there is a lot of dialectal variation in the speech of those with an East Norwegian (especially Gudbrandsdal) background. And in general, the situation today is quite similar to what it was during the 1990s. Most of the variation documented at that time is still heard today. But if we look at the speakers from 2010–11, this is not a surprise; the NorAmDiaSyn project has many of the same informants as I had in 1992, or they come from the same age group and social networks as informants I had back then. Thus, the conclusion of this article could be that 160 years of inter-dialectal contact has not resulted in the formation of a koiné in Coon, and the Norwegian language will disappear before such a process is completed. This is not unique for this particular community, as the same is reported from German-speaking communities in the Midwest (Seifert 1993: 323–324).

But if we look at the youngest speakers, i.e., those born between 1940 and 1961, a rather different picture emerges. These were all together 13 informants (12 men and 1 woman), and most had similar backgrounds to the informants in the 1940s and 1990s, being closely associated to farming in one way or another. In this group we find a rather coherent language without much variation.

One of the few dialectal features where we can find variation in this group of 'young' speakers, is the personal pronoun, 1st person singular form, where most use [eː], but where we also find [jeː]. It is somewhat surprising that [eː] has become the most frequent form among this age group, as [jeː] was more frequent in the recordings done in the 40s and 90s, and I am not able to give any good explanation for this. All have [viː] as the personal pronoun in plural and [²itə] as the negation particle. Furthermore we find palatalization of dental consonants in stressed syllables, but we do not find such palatalization in unstressed positions. Examples: [haɲ] *han* 'he,' [brɛɲc] *brent* 'burned' and [skrɛʎ] *skrell* 'crash.' However, the realization of these palatal consonants is rather weak. The system of kløyvd infinitiv 'divided infinitive' is still intact, like in [²taːɽa] *tala* 'talk,' [²jæːra] *gjera* 'do' but [²snakə] *snakke* 'talk' and [²drɛkə] *drikke* 'drink.' We do not find infinitives with a short root syllable, and also the 'European u' is quite rare among members of this age group.

Plural indefinite forms of nouns are marked with -r, resulting in forms like [²tʊmər] *tommer* 'inches,' [²kʉːər] *kyr* 'cows,' [²goŋər] *gonger* 'times' and [²viːkʉr] *veker* 'weeks.' But -r is not used in the present tense of weak verbs, as in [²reisə] *reiser* 'travel,' [²cçøːrə] *køyrer* 'drive' and [trʉː] *trur* 'believe.' In past tense of 1st class of weak verbs, we only find the formative -a, not -e, as in [²skrata] *skratta* 'laughed,' [²mjoɽka] *mjølka* 'milked' and [²laːga] *laga* 'made.' All this is in accordance with tendencies seen in 1992, when these forms were most frequent. The dative case, well on its way out in the 90s, is now totally gone. And since we hardly find any variation in this age group, it is reasonable to argue that a koiné has evolved among these speakers in Coon.

6. Conclusion

The literature often posits that the formation of a koiné normally is done in three generations; Kerswill (2002: 670) states that "(k)oineization ... typically takes two or three generations to complete, though it is achievable within one." In Coon we find that process is not yet completed, but among the youngest speakers, i.e., those born in the 1940s or later, we can argue that such a norm is established. It is remarkable how long this process has taken. It is more than 160 years since Norwegians started to settle in this area, and for a century the language was handed down to new generations. It is difficult to say why this process has taken so long, but one important factor here is that the immigration from Norway into this area lasted for many years, and that the continuous inflow of new immigrants slowed down this process.

It is also worth noting that the Norwegian-Americans themselves are not aware of the dialectal variation found in this area. Hardy any of the informants in 1990s or the 2010s reflected on this variation, instead claiming that everybody in Coon spoke the same Norwegian dialect. Furthermore, there is no reason to believe that there were any differences in social status related to the various dialectal variants. And since the variation found was not noticed by the Norwegian speakers and status was not relevant, there was probably no strong social driving force facilitating the formation of a koiné.

Another factor which might have slowed this process, is what Ibarra (1976: 245) and Munch (1954: 197) call "clannish(ness)." Munch and Ibarra emphasize the strong family ties found among Norwegian-Americans in this community and social activities are to a high degree directed towards the family. This loyalty towards roots and family might also have linguistic consequences, in the sense that the family was an important agent for the choice of linguistic norms, more important than peer groups. An argument for such an interpretation is that we find among Haugen's recordings an informant talking a dialect very similar to the dialect of the 'young' speakers of today. This man, 10C14, did not have a Norwegian background. He grew up with German as his first language and learned Norwegian from his Norwegian friends and classmates when he started at school. He was in his late 40s when the recordings were done, and at that time he claimed to speak Norwegian better than German. The point here is that his own family has not influenced his Norwegian dialect, and it is fair to assume that he does not attach special attitudes to different Norwegian dialectal variants. As he learned Norwegian from his peers, it is also reasonable to assume that his language reflects the most frequent forms heard in his surroundings.

He has acquired the system of divided infinitives. We do find palatalization of dental consonants in stressed syllables, but not in unstressed ([køɲ] *korn* 'corn,' but [²moron], not [²moroɲ] *morgon* 'morning'), a system similar to what we find in Gudbrandsdalen south of Fron. We find *-r* as a marker of plural indefinite form of nouns, [²hæstər] *hestar* 'horses,' [²kʉːər] *kyr* 'cows,' but *-r* is not used to mark present tense of weak verbs, [²kɛʎə] *kalle* 'call,' a distribution which we traditionally find in Gausdal, Øyer and Fåberg, but not Biri. He does not use *-n* to mark plural definite forms of nouns [²ʊŋa] *ungane* 'the kids,' as found in the area from Fåberg and southwards. He has the [eː] as personal pronoun singular, which we find north from Øyer and Gausdal, while the plural form is [viː], which we find southwards from Øyer and Gausdal. Most phonological and morphological features in this informant's dialect corresponds with the dialect as we find it in the area around Øyer and Gausdal, an area which geographically, as well as dialectally is in the middle between the two 'extremes' represented in Coon, Fron and Biri.

When Norwegians in the same age group as this informant did not acquire the same variety, it might be because of their loyalty to family and the dialect spoken at home. But even if the formation of a koiné took a long time in Coon, we can clearly recognize the two first stages outlined by Trudgill and Kerswill in the recordings from the 1940s and 1990s, and we also see the third and final step in the speech of the youngest Norwegian speakers today.

References

Åfarli, Tor A. This volume. "Hybrid Verb Forms in American Norwegian and the Analysis of the Syntactic Relation Between the Verb and its Tense."
Allen, Brent and Joseph Salmons. This volume. "Heritage Language Obstruent Phonetics and Phonology: American Norwegian and Norwegian-American English."
Annear, Lucas and Kristin Speth. This volume. "Maintaining a Multilingual Repertoire: Lexical Change in American Norwegian."
Flaten, Nils. 1900–04. "Notes on the American-Norwegian with Vocabulary. *Dialect Notes* 2: 115–126.
Flom, George. T. 1900–04. "English Elements in Norse Dialects of Utica, Wisconsin." *Dialect Notes* 2: 257–268.
Flom, George T. 1903. "The Gender of Norse Loan-Nouns in Norse Dialects in America." *The Journal of English and Germanic Philology* 5: 1–31.
Flom, George T. 1912. "Det norske sprogs bruk og utvikling i Amerika." *Nordmands- Forbundet* 4: 233–250.
Flom, George T. 1926. "English Loanwords in American Norwegian. As spoken in the Koshkonong Settlement, Wisconsin." *American Speech* 1: 541–558. DOI: 10.2307/452150

Flom, George T. 1929. "On the Phonology of English Loanwords in the Norwegian Dialects of Koshkonong in Wisconsin." *Arkiv for Nordisk Filologi – Tilläggsband til bd.* XL: 178–189.

Flom, George T. 1931. "Um det norske målet i Amerika." *Norsk aarbok*: 113–124.

Golden, Anne and Elizabeth Lanza. This volume. "Coon Valley Norwegians Meet Norwegians from Norway: Language, Culture and Identity Among Heritage Language Speakers in the U.S."

Haugen, Einar. 1956. *Bilingualism in the Americas: A Bibliography and Research Guide*. (Publications of the American Dialect Society 26). Tuscaloosa, AL: University Alabama Press.

Haugen, Einar. (1953) 1969. *The Norwegian Language in America*. Bloomington / London: Indiana University Press.

Hjelde, Arnstein. 1992. *Trøndsk talemål i Amerika*. Trondheim: Tapir.

Hjelde, Arnstein. 1996a. "The Gender of English Nouns Used in American Norwegian." In *Language Contact Across the North Atlantic*, ed. by P. Sture Ureland and Iain Clarkson, 297–312. Tübingen: Max Niemeyer.

Hjelde, Arnstein. 1996b. "Some Phonological Changes in a Norwegian Dialect in America." In *Language Contact Across the North Atlantic*, ed. by P. Sture Ureland and Iain Clarkson, 283–295. Tübingen: Max Niemeyer.

Holand, Hjalmar R. 1927. *Coon Prairie: en historisk beretning om den Norske evangeliske lutherske menighet paa Coon Prairie. Skrevet i anledning av dens 75-aarsfest i 1927*. Minneapolis: Augsburg Publishing House.

Holand, Hjalmar R. 1928. *Coon Valley: en historisk beretning om de norske menigheter i Coon Valley, skrevet i anledning av kaldets 75-aarsfest i 1928*. Minneapolis: Augsburg Publishing House.

Hjelde, Arnstein. 2012. ""Folkan mine, dæm bære snakka norsk" – norsk i Wisconsin frå 1940-talet og fram til i dag." *Norsk Lingvistisk Tidsskrift* 30(2): 183–203.

Ibarra, Robert A. 1976. *Ethnicity Genuine and Spurious – A Study of a Norwegian Community in Rural Wisconsin*. Madison, WI: University of Wisconsin-Madison dissertation.

Johannessen, Janne Bondi. This volume. "Attrition in an American Norwegian Heritage Language Speaker."

Johannessen, Janne Bondi and Signe Laake. 2012. "To myter om det norske språket i Amerika: Er det gammeldags? Nærmer det seg en bokmålsstandard?" *Norsk Lingvistisk Tidsskrift* 30(2): 204–228.

Johannessen, Janne Bondi and Signe Laake. This volume. "On Two Myths of the Norwegian Language in America: Is it Old-Fashioned? Is it Approaching the Written Bokmål Standard?"

Kartsamling for leksikografi, http://www.edd.uio.no/perl/search/search.cgi?appid=2108;tabid =2338&lang=NNO (Accessed February 12, 2011) [A collection of detailed dialect maps from Norway.]

Kerswill, Paul. 2002. "Koineization and Accommodation." In *The Handbook of Language Variation and Change*, ed. by J. K. Chambers, Peter Trudgill and Natalie Schilling-Estes, 669–702. Blackwell: Oxford.

Kerswill, Paul and Peter Trudgill. 2005. "The Birth of New Dialects." In *Dialect Change: Convergence and Divergence in European Languages*, ed. by Peter Auer, Frans Hinskens and Paul Kerswill, 196–220. Cambridge: Cambridge University Press. DOI: 10.1017/CBO9780511486623.009

Larsson, Ida, Sofia Tingsell and Maia Andréasson. This Volume. "Variation and Change in American Swedish."

Munch, Peter A. 1949. "Social Adjustment Among Wisconsin Norwegians." *American Sociological Review* 14(6): 780–787. DOI: 10.2307/2086680

Munch, Peter A. 1954. "Segregation and Assimilation of Norwegian Settlements in Wisconsin." *Norwegian-American Studies and Records* 18: 102–140.

Oftedal, Magne. 1949a. "Norsk talemål i Amerika." *Syn og segn* 55: 195–203.

Oftedal, Magne. 1949b. "The Vowel System of a Norwegian Dialect in Wisconsin." *Language* 25: 261–267. DOI: 10.2307/410087

Qualey, Carlton Chester. 1938. *Norwegian Settlement in the United States.* Northfield: NAHA.

Seifert, Lester W. J. 1993. "The Development and Survival of the German Language in Pennsylvania and Wisconsin. In *The German Language in American, 1683–1991*, ed. by Joseph C. Salmons, 322–337. Madison: Max Kade Institute for German-American Studies.

Synopsisen, http://www.edd.uio.no/perl/search/search.cgi?appid=145&tabid=2165 (Accessed February 12, 2011) [A collection of detailed information on pronunciation and morphology from each Norwegian county (*kommune*).]

Trudgill, Peter J., Elizabeth Gordon, Gillian Lewis and Margaret Maclagan. 2000. "Determinism in New-Dialect Formation and the Genesis of New Zealand English." *Journal of Linguistics* 36: 299–318. DOI: 10.1017/S0022226700008161

US Census Bureau. 2000. US Census, Special Tabulation 224.

Westergaard, Marit and Merete Anderssen. This volume. "Word Order Variation in Norwegian Possessive Constructions: Bilingual Acquisition and Attrition."

On two myths of the Norwegian language in America
Is it old-fashioned? Is it approaching the written Bokmål standard?

Janne Bondi Johannessen and Signe Laake
University of Oslo

The article discusses two claims about Heritage Norwegian in the American Midwest. One is that the Norwegian-speaking descendants of Norwegian immigrants speak an 'archaic' form of Norwegian. The other is that their language approaches the written Norwegian Bokmål standard, i.e., has moved away from the dialects spoken by original immigrants. Evidence from the lexicon and grammar help answer the questions in the title. The answer to the first question is partly positive, depending on what aspects of language are focussed on, while the answer to the second one is negative.

Keywords: Heritage Norwegian, Bokmål, vocabulary, grammar, comparisons with European Norwegian

1. Introduction[1]

In this paper, we examine the two claims about the Norwegian heritage language in America presented in the title: that it is archaic, and that it has developed towards

---

[1]. We would like to thank Jan Terje Faarlund, Klaus Johan Myrvoll and Joseph Salmons for excellent comments on previous written versions of this paper. We would also like to thank participants at the seminars where we have presented material that has led to this paper, in Decorah (Iowa, USA), Gottskär (Sweden), Fefor, UiO and UiT (Norway). Specifically we would like to thank Oddrun Grønvik, Arnstein Hjelde, Mark Louden, and Mike Putnam for good questions and comments. Finally we want to mention our fantastic informants, who are indispensible for our work.

The work was partly supported by the Research Council of Norway through its Centres of Excellence funding scheme, project number 223265, and through its funding of the project NorAmDiaSyn, project number 218878, under the BILATGRUNN/FRIHUM scheme.

the written language standard Bokmål.[2] We draw data from four informants in the Midwest, selected because their grandparents all came from the same Norwegian dialect area. We will compare the language of these four informants with that of four Norwegian dialect speakers from the same area (Gausdal, Gudbrandsdalen). This way we can determine if one of the language varieties appears more archaic in its words and grammar than the other. Furthermore, we also do a three-way comparison of American Norwegian, European (dialect) Norwegian and Bokmål. This will allow us to determine whether American Norwegian is more standardized or Bokmål-like than the equivalent dialect in Norway.

Both questions are interesting from a general linguistic perspective: While it is often claimed that heritage languages are archaic, what exactly is it about them that causes this attitude amongst the general public? The idea that a heritage language develops in the direction of a standard is possibly less widespread among the public, but the claim is made several times in Haugen's seminal *The Norwegian Language in America* (1953).

2. Is the Norwegian language in America archaic?

Many of those European Norwegians who have Norwegian American relatives, report that their language is "just like listening to grandma." We examine to what extent the heritage variety is archaic, and in that case, which aspects of the language that may be considered old. We will study morphology and lexicon – and in the latter category, both function words and lexical words.

2.1 Data material: Informants

We compare two groups, one American and one Norwegian, with the same dialect background in Norway. The assumption is that if a phenomenon (grammatical or lexical) is found in American Norwegian but not in European Norwegian, then it is an old phenomenon (of course unless it is a loan from English or in other ways first emerged in the USA).

We chose four informants from the fieldwork done in March 2010 (see Johannessen and Laake 2011, 2012, forthcoming) – from Westby, WI, and Sunburg, MN: Archie, Eunice, Florence and Howard. Their grandparents or great grandparents emigrated from the southern part of the valley of Gudbrandsdalen in Eastern Norway. Not all of them know the background of all of their ancestors. We have detected a certain prestige in having roots in Gudbrandsdalen. Furthermore, it is a very long valley, so many

---

2. Bokmål is one of two written standards for the Norwegian language. See Section 3.

may generalize their background to it out of convenience. Nevertheless, our findings support reports about this background with dialect features of their speech. Three of our speakers have never been to Norway, and the fourth only for two short visits. None of them read Norwegian well or have had much contact with Norwegians from Norway. They are all in their eighties, born between 1922 and 1930. Their language will be compared with that of a group of Norwegians from Gausdal, Gudbrandsdalen. This place is represented in the Nordic Dialect Corpus (Johannessen et al. 2009). Here we also find four informants, all of whom are younger than our four Americans; two males under 30 and two females over 50 years.[3]

At the time of writing, the American Norwegian recordings are available as untranscribed video files. It has therefore been necessary to listen to the recordings (about three hours altogether; we have chosen footage in which informants are talking to each other and not to one of us), and make accurate notes. In the Norwegian dialect corpus, however, all the recordings are transcribed and grammatically annotated so that it has been easy to use this as control material. The process has been to first go carefully through the American Norwegian material, and afterwards check the various phenomena in the Nordic Dialect Corpus, using targeted searches.

When we write 'America' and 'American Norwegians' in this article, we mean more specifically the informants we have chosen, but we think the conclusions can be generalized to most of the Midwest, because we have shown elsewhere (Johannessen and Laake 2011, 2012, forthcoming) that the Norwegian language of the Midwest has so much in common that it should be regarded as one linguistic variety. When we write 'Norway' and 'Norwegians,' we mean Gausdal and the people there.

2.2 Investigation of pronouns

We begin by looking at the pronominal system in both Norwegian varieties. Most pronouns are frequent, providing a good basis for comparison. Example (1) suggests that there are no major differences between the two varieties.

(1) a. Nå ringe *romm* ti meg frå Minneapolis
now phone they to me from Minneapolis
'Now they phone me from Minneapolis.' (Archie, Westby, WI)

b. så stirre *rømm* bare dumt på deg
then stare they only stupidly on you
'Then they just stare stupidly at you.' (Gausdal_05um)

---

3. The Norwegian informants are anonymous, but the informant codes reveal some information. They consist of the place name (Gausdal) followed by codes for gender and age: uk=young woman, um=young man, gk=old woman, gm=old man.

Table 1. Pronouns in America and Norway.

	America		Norway	
	subject	object	subject	object
1.PERS.SG.	/e/ /i/	/me/	/e/	/me/
2.PERS.SG.	/dʉ/, /rʉ/⁴		/dʉ/, /rʉ/	/de/, /re/
3.PERS.SG.	/hæin/, /han/, /n/	**/hanom/**, /han/, /n/	/hæin/, /han/, /n/	/han/, /n/
	/hu/	/hu/	/hu/	/hu/
	/de/, /dæ/, /re/	/de/, /dæ/, /re/	/dæ/, /de/, /re/	/dæ/, /de/, /re/, /di/, /ri/
1.PERS.PL.	/vi/	/ʉs/	/vi/	/øs/
2.PERS.PL.	/di/, /ri/	/døk/, /røk/⁵	**/døk/, /røk/**	/døk/, /røk/
3.PERS.PL.	/dem/, /dum/, /døm/, /rem/, /rum/	/dum/, /røm/, /dem/, /rum/	/døm/, /røm/	/døm/, /røm/
Others	/inan/, /noga/, /no:go/, /noka/, /noen/, /hor/, **/sʉme/**		/inan/, /no:go /, /hor/	

There is variation in the use of pronouns both in America and in Norway, and mostly the same variants are found in both places,⁶ save for a few minor differences (shown in bold in the table above, and in the examples below):

In America we find *hanom*, which in Norwegian can be both dative and accusative:⁷

(2) *e tala på det åt <u>hanom</u>*
     I spoke on it to him
     'I talked about it to him.'   (Archie, Westby, WI)

---

4. Some may think that /r/-initial pronouns are only the result of phonological rules – that they appear after a vowel (see Lie 1984: 4). We do not agree with this assumption. For arguments, see Johannessen (2012).

5. 2. PERS.PL. object in America has been added from later fieldwork.

6. Klaus Johan Myrvoll, based on Skjekkeland (1997) and others, has made us aware that /i/ (1.PERS.SG.) and /ʉs/ (1.PERS.PL.) are unexpected because the former is found only in the very north part of Gudbrandsdalen, while the latter is found only in the western part of Gudbrandsdalen (in the valleys of Hallingdal and Valdres). He also points out that *hanom* is not typical of Gudbrandsdalen, where one would expect a rounded vowel in the first syllable, and that the contrast *di – døkk* has not been found in Gudbrandsdalen since the 1880s (supported by Storm 1920: 67). These facts suggest that the Norwegian Americans do not speak a 'pure' Norwegian dialect, but that their variety contains features from other dialects, a feature of koinéization. See Section 3.

7. Jan Terje Faarlund (p.c.) informs us that *hanom* /hænom/ can also be used as an accusative form in East Norwegian dialects.

But it is the only form we find that can be dative, so we will not generalize from this one occurrence. On the other hand, we find many examples of *di* and *ri* 'it' in Gudbrandsdal. This is a dative form that we do not find in America, see (3).

(3) jæu ra   en jer   se   nå   ått <u>di</u>
    yes then one makes oneself now to   it
    'Oh, yes, one does have some thought on it.'   (Gausdal_05um)

In America, we find a difference between subject and object forms in the 2.PERS.PL., with a contrast between /di/ and /døk/. This distinction is on its way out in Norway, where /døk/ or /røk/ have taken over completely. We see an example of *di* in American Norwegian in (4):

(4) hå   va   re <u>di</u> gjorde during recess?
    what was it you   did   during recess
    'What did you do during recess?'   (Eunice, Sunburg, MN)

Finally, the pronoun *summe* 'some' is different in the two Norwegian varieties. We return to this term in Section 2.4.

In the case of pronouns, there are, then, a couple of cases where American Norwegian is more archaic, maintaining the distinction between the two forms of 2.PERS.PL., and the pronoun *summe*. With the exception of these two (plus the *hanom* form), there is much more that unites than divides the two language varieties with respect to pronouns.

2.3 Morphology

2.3.1 Dative

Dative was a case category in Old Norse. It has been disappearing from European Norwegian for several hundred years, but there is still a belt that runs across southern Norway that has retained the dative (Eyþórsson et al. 2012). Vestad (2002: 17) writes about the Gausdal dialect that the use of dative is stable among most adults, but he believes that it is on its way out in the younger generation. Dative is triggered by certain prepositions, but also by some verbs and adjectives. It can only be found in words that express definiteness, such as pronouns and definite nouns.

We see that throughout Table 2, the America column is empty (we have left out the one example of *hanom* from Section 2.2), while the column from Gausdal is filled with dative forms. Dative in Gausdal is clearly a category that is still alive, as the examples show, and there were many more hits in the corpus to choose from. Since dative is an ancient category, the comparison shows Gausdal in Norway as the more archaic variety, while American Norwegian is far more innovative. It should be noted that case, and perhaps especially dative, is a category that is often lost in language contact situations, see for example Putnam (2003), Boas (2009) for the loss of dative case in varieties of American German. On the other hand, dative has been disappearing from

Table 2. Dative in America and Norway.

	America	Norway (all four Gausdal informants)
Pronouns	–	*de e nå mye på grunn tå **di*** 'it is because of **that**'
Nouns SG FEM	–	*behøve da itte utu **byggd'n** her* 'don't need to get out of **the village** here'
Nouns SG MASC	–	*menn denna ræsjtubben ifrå borrtpå **garda*** 'but this little road from over at **the farm**'
Nouns PL MASC	–	*e sennte ut en lapp åt **sjueneklassingom*** 'I sent out a note to **the seventh-graders**'
Nouns PL NEUT	–	*litt føranndringer på **sysstemom*** 'some changes in **the system**'
Preproprial article FEM	–	*vi jekk åt **n** Anna* 'we walked to ART Anna'

Norwegian dialects since the 1300s, and this fact about American Norwegian might as easily be an adaption to other dialects and part of a koniéization process.

2.3.2 Two infinitival suffixes

Many dialects in the eastern part of Norway, including our Gudbrandsdalen dialect (Vestad 2002:22), have two infinitival suffixes (rather than one, as in the Bokmål standard). This is an old system, developed from a distinction in Old Norse, where infinitives that in Old Norse had a long root syllable and a short final syllable now have an infinitive ending in *-e*, while infinitives with a short root syllable now end in *-a*. In America we find this infinitive system, but we also find it in Gausdal. See (5) and (6) for *-e* and *-a*, respectively.

(5) a. *kanskje e må prøve n*
    maybe I must try it
    'Maybe I must try it.' (Eunice, Sunburg)

b. *e skal kjøpe meg en slik Fiat*
    I shall buy myself a such Fiat
    'I'll buy myself that kind of Fiat.' (Gausdal_05um)

(6) a. *atte rom kunne ikkje komma heimat*
    that they could not come home
    'That they couldn't come home again.' (Eunice, Sunburg)

b. *kjem te å fløtta*
    come to to move
    'Will be going to move.' (Gausdal_05um)

There are many similar examples in the recordings. In Table 3, we present some additional verbs.

Table 3. The infinitive system with two suffixes in America and Norway.

	America (Eunice)	**Norway (young people from Gausdal)**
Infinitives in -*e*	*besøke* 'visit,' *prate* 'talk,' *prøve* 'try,' *tenkje* 'think,' *travle* 'walk,' *åpne* 'open'	*hæille* 'hold,' *kjøpe* 'buy,' *knote* 'speak impure dialect,' *skjønne* 'understand,' *tene* 'earn'
Infinitives in -*a*	*baka* 'bake,' *eta* 'eat,' *gjøra* 'do,' *hugsa* 'remember,' *komma* 'come,' *tørja* 'dare,' *væra* 'be'	*fløtta* 'move,' *gjæra* 'do,' *komma* 'come,' *laga* 'make,' *veta* 'know,' *væra* 'be,' *laga* 'make'

We have only used examples from Eunice here, but this infinitive system is equally present in the other three informants, as well as in those from Gausdal. There is, then, no difference in the two groups, and it is not possible to say that one group uses a more archaic variant.

2.3.3 Inflection of finite verbs

In the Gausdal dialect, weak (regular) verbs have a present tense form ending in -*e* or -*a* (and thus not -*er* or -*ar*), while the preterit of these verbs is -*te*, -*de* or -*a*. In the present and preterit tenses of strong verbs there is umlaut and no suffix (Vestad 2002:21–22, Papazian and Helleland 2005: §3.3.2). Vestad (2002:20–21) writes that the past participle ends in -*e* and not -*i* (unless there is an -*i* in the stem), which is otherwise common in eastern Norway. In (7) and Table 4 we see examples of weak verbs in the present and preterit, and the examples clearly show that the language varieties are the same with regard to weak verb inflection.

(7) a. <u>Bruke</u> dokk kjøttkaker borti der?
    use you meat.cakes over there
    'Do you use meat cakes over there [i.e., in Norway]?' (Florence, Westby)
  b. De e mange som <u>bruke</u> varmekabler
    it is many who use heating.cables
    'There are many who use heating cables.' (Gausdal_01um)

Table 4. Weak verbs in America and Norway.

	America	**Norway**
Weak verbs, present tense	*bruke* 'uses,' *kjøpe* 'buys,' *koke* 'cooks,' *stoppe* 'stops,' *tenkje* 'thinks'	*bruke* 'uses,' *heite* 'is called,' *kjenne* 'knows,' *kjøre* 'drives,' *klare* 'manages,' *tenkje* 'thinks'
Weak verbs, preterit tense	*brukte* 'used,' *døe* 'died,' *glømte* 'forgot,' *hugsa* 'remembered,' *hørde* 'heard,' *kjøfte* 'bought,' *kvilte* 'rested,' *likte* 'liked,' *pleide* 'used to,' *prata* 'talked,' *rende* 'ran,' *snakka* 'talked,' *snudde* 'turned,' *spurde* 'asked,' *tala* 'talked,' *travla* 'walked,' *trudde* 'thought'	*brukte* 'used,' *kjøfte* 'bought,' *kjørde* 'drove,' *hørde* 'heard,' *likte* 'liked,' *passa* 'suited,' *snakka* 'talked,' *spurde* 'asked,' *stirra, trudde, tænkte*

In (8) and Table 5 we present examples of strong verbs in the present tense, past tense and past participle.

(8) a. om dem <u>kjøm</u> te ...
if they come to
'if they are going to...' (Eunice, Sunburg)
b. <u>kjem</u> te å fløtta
come to to move
'going to move' (Gausdal_05um)

Table 5. Strong verbs in America and Norway.

	America	Norway
Strong verbs, present tense	et 'eats,' feng[8] 'gets,' kjæm 'comes,' kjøm 'comes,' ligg 'lies,' te 'takes,' veit 'knows'	hæng 'hangs,' kjæm 'comes,' ligg 'lies,' lyt 'must,' te 'takes,' tek 'takes,' tæk 'takes,' veit 'knows'
Strong verbs, preterit tense	flaug 'flew,' fækk 'got,' ga 'gave,' gjekk 'walked,' jaug 'lied,' satt 'sat,' såg 'saw,' to 'took,' vart 'became,' vog 'weighed'	fækk 'got,' ga 'gave,' gjekk 'walked,' laut 'had to,' låg 'lay,' satt 'sat,' såg 'saw,' tok 'took,' vart 'became'
Strong verbs, pres. part.	vøri 'been'	drivi 'done,' vore 'been,' vorti 'become'

Both Norwegian varieties have the system of weak and strong verbs. We have some examples of past participle -i. This does not seem to follow the system Vestad mentioned, but it is found in both America and Norway. There are some minor differences between the verb inflection in America and Norway, but both conform to descriptions in the dialect literature. There is thus no reason to regard one system as more archaic than the other.

2.4 Function words

We have compared the morphology of American Norwegian and Gudbrandsdal Norwegian, and there is little (apart from the dative) that distinguishes the two variants. But as we looked at the pronoun system in 2.2, we found a few minor differences. It is thus possible that if we move away from the morphological to the lexical domain, there may be larger differences. In Table 6 we present a list of function words we have found amongst the Norwegian Americans and amongst those from Gausdal. We have put in bold print those words that we will discuss in more detail below. The standard orthographical form is presented in the third column, with their English equivalent in inverted commas.

---

8. The form *feng* does not exist in Norway and we think it emerged on analogy with the pres. part. *fenge*, after the pattern *gjeng – gjenge* 'walk, walked.'

Table 6. Some function words in America and Norway.

America	Norway	Equivalent in written Norwegian and gloss
båe	–	både 'both'
da ma	da ma	skjønner du 'you see'
fyri	fyri	før 'before'
hell	hell	heller 'neither'
horr	horr	hver 'each'
inte	–	ikke 'not'
itte	itte	ikke 'not'
messom	messom	liksom 'just like'
mykji	mye	mye 'much'
summe	–	noen 'some'
ur	–	av 'of'
visst	visst	hvis 'if'
ein og tjuge	tjuge	tjueen 'twenty one'
æller	æller or ældri	aldri 'never'
æu	æu	og 'too'
åt	åt	til 'to'

The bolded words are candidates for archaisms. While pronouns and verb morphology are frequent and thus likely to be found in almost any text, individual words, even function words, are more dependent on the text type, contents and the choices of the speaker. To counteract this, we will increase the geographical search area if we get negative results amongst Gausdal informants.

båe (*både*) 'both': While this term does not appear in the Gausdal recordings, there are many examples in the other recordings of the county of Oppland, for example in Vang, Skjåk and Lom, and east of Gausdal, in Hedmark. In Gausdal we have found no examples of the standard *både* either. We assume, therefore, that this word represents an accidental gap in the material, and that *båe* is also used in Gausdal.[9]

inte (*ikke*) 'not': We have found examples of this negation form in the border areas next to Sweden, namely Aremark, Fredrikstad, Rømskog, Råde and Trysil, but not in Gausdal or the rest of the Oppland County. We thus assume that *inte* in the Midwest is borrowed from another dialect, or from Swedish.

mykji (*mye*) 'much': The pronunciation *mykji* /²myçi/ was not found in Gausdal, but there are some hits in the corpus further west; in Valdres and Hallingdal. In Gausdal, however, there are numerous examples of the standard *mye* /²my:e/. East of Gausdal, in Hedmark, there are no examples of *mykji*. We assume that the isogloss for *mykji* runs west of Gausdal, and that the Norwegian American variant is borrowed from

---

9. Klaus Johan Myrvoll informs us that according to Jenshus (1986: 79), *båe* is found in Fron in Gudbrandsdalen, which supports our assumption of an accidental gap.

western dialects.[10] A corpus search for various realisations of *mye* gives us the picture in Figure 1 (showing southern Norway), where the dark markers indicate the fricative pronunciation (*mykji*), and the light show variants with only vowels. We see that Gausdal, located just southeast of the word *Norway* on the map, is clearly in the area without the fricative.

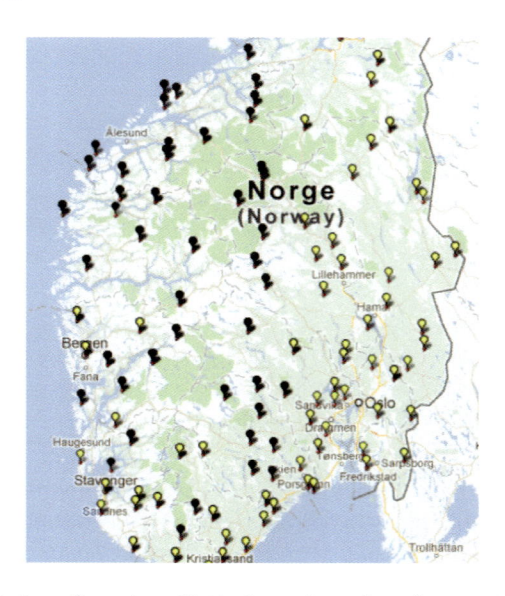

Figure 1. Pronunciation of *mye* 'much': Dark markers show forms with fricative, *mykji* /²myçi/; light markers show those without, *mye* /²my:e/.

summe (*noen*) 'some': We have not found this word in Gausdal, but it occurs elsewhere in the county in the Nordic Dialect Corpus. Of the 33 hits in the county 28 are from the part of the corpus containing old recordings from the Oslo Dialect Archive, which are 40–50 years older than the rest of the recordings. The five informants that are not from the Dialect Archive recordings are all in the 'old' age group. When almost all the hits are from the Dialect Archive part of the corpus, this indicates a phenomenon that is not frequent in the modern language. Informants in the older material have a total of 255,000 words in the corpus, which is negligible compared with the modern material of 1,874,000 words. The modern part is therefore more than seven

---

10. We have actually checked whether *mykji* exists amongst old people in Gausdal. We phoned the now recently deceased, 85 year old Ruth Grimstad, who according to both herself and others spoke old-fashioned, pure Gausdal dialect. During that conversation she never used any other pronunciation than *mye*, even when we tried to trigger the fricative form. We asked for example *Var det mykji snø i år* 'Was there much snow this year?' and she answered *Ja, veldig mye* 'Yes, very much.'

times larger than the old part. If the word *summe* was equally common in the modern language, we would expect seven times more occurrences of it in the modern part of the corpus. But since there are more occurrences in the older part, we conclude that *summe* is old-fashioned and it follows that this also is true for American Norwegian. (Grammatically, *summe* is interesting, see Sandøy 1996).

ur (*av*) 'of': There are no examples of *ur* from Gausdal in the Nordic Dialect Corpus. Only one person uses this word in the whole corpus, in the old Dialect Archive part of the corpus, in a recording of a man from the valley of Østerdalen. It might be tempting to think that this word is borrowed into American Norwegian from another dialect, but Vestad (2002:98) gives a caption that reads: *Svatsum held på å ta ei rype "utur snørun"* 'Svatsum is taking a grouse *out* of the snare' [quotation marks in original]. And indeed we find some more examples by searching for *tur* as well. Most are from the Swedish border, but Bardu in North Norway (with its immigrant population from Østerdalen) and the area of Hadeland in the central parts of East Norway are represented. Again, the examples are either from the old Dialect Archive recordings or from old informants in the Nordic Dialect Corpus. We can then conclude that *ur* is an archaic feature of American Norwegian.

We have looked at 16 function words. Of these, 11 were used by the Gausdal informants in the Nordic Dialect Corpus. Five function words found in America were not found in Gausdal. Two are certain archaisms: *summe* and *ur*. We conclude this based on the fact that while we have found examples of these words in the areas around Gausdal, they were only in the older recordings or amongst older informants. That we did not find *båe* is probably an accidental gap in the material, while we believe that *inte* and *mykji* have been borrowed from other Norwegian dialects in America.

2.5 Lexical words

To determine whether American Norwegian is old-fashioned when it comes to lexical words, we selected some words we thought might be candidates for this. They are shown in Table 7. Again, we have highlighted in bold the words that only exist in America, without equivalents in the recordings from Gausdal.

With function words, we noted a methodological problem that a particular word we were looking for could just happen not to be represented in the corpus. We had to investigate thoroughly and look at other dialects to try to determine in each case what the lack of an equivalent would mean. In the case of lexical words, this becomes more of a problem, as we cannot expect informants in the two investigated areas to speak about the same topics, and hence use the same lexical items. Here, too, we must extend the basis for comparison as needed. Table 7 gives some words from American Norwegian that we believe are typically dialectical, and potentially archaic. We have bolded those words that we have not found amongst the informants from Gausdal, and examine these below.

Table 7. Lexical words in America and Norway.

America	Norway	Gloss
beint (fram)	–	'straight'
bøte	–	'repair'
flaug	*flaug*	'ran'
færdug	*ferdig*	'finished'
fælt adv	–	'very'
gamlaste	*gamler*	'oldest'
gæli	*gæli*	'wrong'
heimat	*heimat*	'home again'
koma i hau	*koma i hau*	'remember'
kropp	*kropp*	'person'
krøtter	–	'cattle'
li på	–	'pass' (about time)
rumpe	–	'tail'
stutt	*stutt*	'short'

beint 'straight': We have not found this word in Gausdal, and only two cases in the rest of Oppland. There are 25 hits in total in all of Norway, but only four amongst young informants, and as many as eight from the Dialect Archive recordings. The alternative word *rett* 'straight' gave 41 hits in the Oppland county, and three in Gausdal. Together this suggests that *beint* may be on its way out, and that American Norwegian thus may be old-fashioned here.

fælt 'very': There are no results for this word, used as an adverbial negative polarity item followed by an adjective in Gausdal, but there are six hits in Oppland County, and three from the Dialect Archive recordings. Conversly, we have searched for the alternative, by searching for *ikke* 'not' followed by *veldig* 'very' and then an adjective. This yielded 14 hits in Oppland, and almost all informants were young, 12 of 14. There is no doubt that for the word *fælt*, American Norwegian is archaic.

li på 'pass' (about time): There are only two hits of the verb *li på* in Oppland, and both are from the Dialect Archive of old recordings. Again American Norwegian is old-fashioned.

rumpe 'tail': There are a total of six relevant hits (those meaning 'tail') throughout the Nordic Dialect Corpus, and four of them are from Dialect Archive, while the other two are from an old man. It may seem that this, too, is somewhat archaic. However, we find only four relevant hits with the alternative *hale* with the same meaning from all over Norway, so the basis of comparison is too small to draw a firm conclusion.

krøtter 'cattle': There are nine matches for this word in Oppland, by one young and six old informants, plus two from the Dialect Archive. There are 32 hits for the alternative *ku/kyr*, amongst these six in Gausdal. It thus appears that the latter is more modern, unless there are significant meaning differences that we do not see. It is most likely, however, that *krøtter* is old-fashioned, which means that American Norwegian is, too. *Krøtter* can strictly speaking have a meaning that is broader than that *ku/kyr* because sheep can also be used with this term. However, we know that our informants have only meant *cattle* 'cows,' so the question is not relevant.

bøte 'repair': In Oppland there is only one hit in the corpus, from the old Dialect Archive, while there are three hits for the alternative *reparere* (two young and one old). There is a possibility that there is a meaning difference for the different hits (*bøte* applies to for example fishing nets, while *reparere* applies to cars, tractors and furniture). If we look at the whole of Norway, the picture is clear: *bøte* occurs only five times (two from the Dialect Archive, two by old informants and one by a young informant). There are a total of 27 hits for *reparere*, and from all groups of informants, but only three from the Dialect Archive. It seems reasonable to conclude that the *bøte* is archaic, and that American Norwegian is, too.

It looks like American Norwegian is more old-fashioned than Norwegian (represented by the Gausdal dialect) at the lexical level. We had selected 14 words that we thought likely candidates for archaisms. Of those, eight were also used by the people in Gudbrandsdalen (in Gausdal), while six words were not. Five of these seem to be on their way out, when we take into account the age of those who use it elsewhere in Oppland and Norway, and the date of recording, and the comparison with words that could be regarded as alternatives. The archaic words are: *beint, fælt, li på, krøtter, bøte*. One of them, *rumpe* 'tail,' is harder to determine. We have many hits in the oldest sources (the Dialect Archive recordings and old informants), but we have only few for the alternative *hale*. When there are so many hits from the Dialect Archive, this may be because the people recorded generally talked more about animals than the new informants. So for the word *rumpe*, we cannot draw a conclusion. But otherwise, on the basis of the lexical words we have investigated, we conclude that American Norwegian is more archaic than the Norwegian spoken in Gudbrandsdalen.

As noted in Section 2.1, at the lexical level, there are great similarities amongst Norwegian Americans across the whole Midwest (see Johannessen and Laake 2011, 2012, forthcoming), when it comes to loan words and new meanings of old words. Since we have seen that morphology and lexicon contain material from more than one dialect, we see this as a sign of koniéization in American Norwegian.

2.6 Conclusion on whether American Norwegian is archaic

All in all, we can conclude that American Norwegian is not more old-fashioned when it comes to pronouns and morphology. Although we have seen a case of a pronominal contrast in the 2.PERS.PL. in American Norwegian not found in Gudbrandsdalen, the latter still has a fully functional dative system not found in America. At this point Gausdal Norwegian appears more archaic. When it comes to vocabulary, the situation is somewhat different. Many of the function words and lexical words used by our four informants in the Midwest, are no longer used amongst young people in Norway; we often find them in use only amongst the oldest informants in the Nordic Dialect Corpus and in the old recordings of the Dialect Archive. It thus appears that the first myth, that American Norwegian is archaic, may be true, but first and foremost when it comes to vocabulary. The grammar is more or less the same.

When it comes to pronouns and function words, we saw some examples of variation that suggest that American Norwegian has elements from more than one Norwegian dialect area. We also saw that the dative is gone. This suggests that the language of Norwegian Americans has undergone an incomplete koniéization process (see also Annear and Speth, Hjelde, Smits and van Marle, all in this volume).

3. Has the Norwegian language in America approached Bokmål?

3.1 Einar Haugen on the development of American Norwegian

The Norwegian Language in America (1953) by Einar Haugen, professor at the University of Wisconsin, Madison, and later at Harvard University, is a significant and insightful book on the Norwegian language in America in the 1940s; it has also had great influence on research on American immigrant languages in general. Here he argues that "the dialects in the Midwest could be characterized as a 'gradual elimination of conspicuous forms," and that "many speakers have departed from their native speech in the general direction of the BL [book language] without of course attaining the norms of the latter" (1953: 352). About linguistic change, he says that it is "nearly always moving from a less to a more widely-used form, which is often that of urban DN [Dano-Norwegian]" (1953: 353). He says about the language that children learnt: "they adopted as their own that dialect which was most generally used in the community, which often meant the dialect that was most close to DN [Dano-Norwegian]" (1953: 350).

Before we pursue this question, we must clarify what Haugen meant by Book Language and Dano-Norwegian. He was well versed in the history of written languages. His doctoral thesis was about Ivar Aasen's Nynorsk written standard, and he wrote extensively on language planning and written language standards, especially in the comprehensive *Language Conflict and Language Planning: The Case of Modern Norwegian* from 1966. Even if he used different terms, both Book Language and Dano-Norwegian, he was not necessarily referring to two different things. Over the years, both Nynorsk and Bokmål been called by different names. Haugen (1966: 19) talks about *Danish Norwegian* and puts *Riksmål* in parentheses. Later (36ff.) he discusses the written language that contrasted with the *Landsmål*, and explains that several terms were used before 1899: *det alminnelige Bogsprog* (the Common Book Language*)*, Norwegian-Danish and Danish-Norwegian, until it was called *Riksmål*.

Before 1899 the term *Rigsmaal* was used for the general book language, which did not show marked dialect traits (Haugen 1966:38). In 1928, the Norwegian Ministry of Church and Education, KUD, decided that *det alminnelige Bogsprog* should now be called *Bokmål* (Haugen 1966:90). It seems reasonable that Haugen with his terms *Dano-Norwegian* and *Book Language* referred to *Riksmål* as a rather general term, a Danish-Norwegian book language without general dialect, as he himself describes the early use of this word. We are then talking about a fairly conservative, Danish-influenced language, significantly more so than the current Bokmål. For this paper we choose to use the current Bokmål as a standard of comparison because we know it best, and because there are good reference works. Since current Bokmål has more dialect features than the old Riksmål, any language that has moved in the direction of the latter, should even more so have moved towards the former. If Haugen is right in his assertion, then, American Norwegian should at least have moved towards Bokmål, which is more Norwegian than Riksmål was at the beginning of the century. We use the word Bokmål in the rest of this paper, and take that to include Bokmål, Riksmål, Book Language, and Dano-Norwegian.

Let us now examine Haugen's claim. We assume that if American Norwegian has moved towards Bokmål, then it will be at least as Bokmål-like as the Gausdal dialect, and possibly more. We choose a number of features for further investigation: pronouns, verb inflection, function words (other than pronouns), lexical words, and some syntactic phenomena, like preproprial articles, possessives, and word order in constituent questions.

3.2 Pronouns

Building on Section 2, we compare pronouns with both Gausdal dialect and Bokmål:

Table 8. Nominative pronouns in America and Norway.

	America	Norway	Bokmål	Bokmål standard pronunciation
1.PERS.SG	/e/, /i/	/e/	jeg	/jæi/
2.PERS.SG	/dʉ/, /rʉ/	/dʉ/, /rʉ/	du	/dʉ/
3.PERS.SG.MASC	/hæin/, /han/, /n/	/hæin/, /han/, n/	han	/han/
3.PERS.SG.FEM	/hu/	/hu/	hun	/hʉn/
3.PERS.SG.NEUT	/de/, /dæ/, /re/	/dæ/, /de/, /re/	det	/de/
1.PERS.PL	/vi/	/vi/	vi	/vi/
2.PERS.PL	/di/, /ri/	/døk/,/røk/	dere	/de:re/
3.PERS.PL	/dem/, /dum/, /døm/, /rem/, /rum/	/døm/, /røm/	de	/di/

In general the two spoken languages pattern together, and Bokmål stands alone with its own forms. There is therefore no change in the direction of Bokmål Norwegian in America on this point.

3.3 Verb inflection

We have already seen that American Norwegian has an infinitive system with two alternative suffixes. This is a feature found in East Norway, but not in Danish. It was accepted as an alternate form in Bokmål in 1938, and removed again in 2005. It was clearly not part of the Bokmål that Haugen's informants had been exposed to at school, given that these recordings were done with adult speakers in the 1930s and 1940s. The infinitive system in American Norwegian, with two suffixes, is thus something that exists in spite of rather than because of Bokmål.

Consider now the inflection of finite verbs, as introduced in Section 2.

Table 9. Inflection of finite verbs, present and past tense, weak and strong conjugations.

America	Norway	Bokmål	Bokmål standard pronunciation
/²çø:pe/ 'buys'	/²çø:re/ 'drives'	kjøper, kjører	/²çø:per/, /²çø:rer/
/²spu:de/ 'asked'	/²spu:de/ 'asked'	spurte	/²spʉ:ʈe/
/¹haft/ 'had'	/¹haft/ 'had'	hatt	/¹hat/
/¹çæm/ 'comes'	/¹çæm/ 'comes'	kommer	/¹komer/
/¹¹ljæʉg/ 'lied'	/¹læʉt/ 'ought'	jugde, måtte	/²jʉgde/, /²måte/
/²vø:ri/	/²vo:re/	vært	/¹væʈ/

The table shows that American Norwegian and Gausdal Norwegian hardly differ from each other at any point, while both are clearly different from Norwegian Bokmål with respect to whether a verb belongs to the weak or strong class (seen in the past tense by the presence of a past tense dental suffix or umlaut, respectively), and also with respect to the nature of the various suffixes (presence or absence of -r in the present tense in the weak conjugation class, voiced or unvoiced dental suffix in the past tense etc.). Nothing in the verb inflections approaches Bokmål.

3.4 Function words

Having looked at grammatical phenomena, we now turn to the lexicon. We begin with function words, and reproduce the table from Section 2, Table 6, this time with Bokmål forms as well.

Table 10. Function words in America, Norway and in Bokmål.

America	Norway	Bokmål	Bokmål standard pronunciation
/²boːe/ 'both'	–	begge	/²bege/
/¹da ma/ discourse particle	/da ma/	–	–
/²fyːri/ 'before'	/²fyːri/	før	/¹føːr/
/¹heľ/ 'either'	/¹heľ/	heller	/¹heler/
/¹hor/ 'each'	/¹hor/	hver	/¹væːr/
/²inte/ 'not'	–	ikke	/²ike/
/²ite/ 'not'	/²ite/	ikke	/²ike/
/²mesom/ 'about'	/²mesom/	liksom	/²liksom/
/²myçi/ 'much'	/²myːe/	mye	/²myːe/
/²sʉme/ 'some'	–	noen	–
/¹ʉːtʉr/ 'out of'	–	ut av	/¹uːtav/
/¹vist/ 'if'	/¹vist/	hvis	/¹vis/
/²çʉːge/ '20'	/²çʉːge/	tjue	/²çʉːe /
/²æʎer/ 'never'	/²æʎer/, /²ældri/	aldri	/²aldri/

Here too, American Norwegian does not resemble Bokmål more than the Gausdal Norwegian does. Indeed, the two spoken varieties have something in common, while Bokmål is the odd one out. So there is no movement towards Bokmål here.

3.5 Lexical words

Here we investigate the lexical words first explored in Section 2. When we compare the lexical words in American Norwegian with the Gausdal dialect and Bokmål, we cannot ask what is allowed in the Bokmål standard. The Bokmål of today has a great many words which are typically Norwegian, and often found in the dialects. So if we are to compare, it must be to investigate whether the actual use of our particular words is found in all three sources, and to what extent. In Table 11 we have put a percent sign in the Bokmål column to indicate the words used in American and Gausdal Norwegian that can also be used in Bokmål. We have also added the more common expression for comparison, as we will show below. To study the actual use of these words in Bokmål, we used the large Lexicographical Bokmål Corpus (LBC). This corpus contains over 40 million words from many different sources, including novels, which are in principle more close to speech (and hence possibly to dialects) than scientific reports or newspapers. In this corpus, we have looked for a number of the American Norwegian words we found earlier. The number for each hit is given in parenthesis.

Table 11. Lexical words in America, Norway and Bokmål.

America	Norway	Bokmål
/¹bæint ¹fram/ 'straight ahead'	/¹ret ¹fram/	beint fram (0), rett fram (338)
/²bø:te/ 'repair'	–	bøte (%), reparere
/¹flæʉg/ 'ran'	–	flaug (%), løp
/²fæɖʉg/ 'finished'	/²fæɖi/	ferdig
/¹fæ: ʈ/ ADV 'very'	–	fælt (%), så
/²gamʂaste/ 'oldest'	/²gamʂer/	eldste
/²gæ:ʂi/ 'wrong'	/²gæ:ʂi/	galt
/¹hæimat/ ADV 'home'	/¹hæimat/	heim (253), hjem (20,737)
/²koma i hæʉ/ 'rememember'	/²koma i hæʉ/	komme i hug (2), huske (8899)
/¹krop/ 'person'	/¹krop/	kropp (%), person
/¹krøter/ 'cattle'	–	krøtter (10), ku (951)
/²læi po:/ 'as time went by'	–	lei på (%), det hadde gått en stund

This comparison is slightly more difficult than the previous ones, given that some of the American words have more than one meaning. If we do a search in the corpus and get thousands of hits, the task of calculating how many we have found with the desired meaning would be too time-consuming. For example, for the verb *flaug* (past tense of *fly*) we are only looking for the meaning 'run,' but the corpus contains nearly 12,000 examples, most of which probably mean 'move in the air.' For such examples of homonymy we cannot determine how many are used with the intended meaning.

Our findings are startling clear. We first go through the words or expressions that have a single meaning, which we are able to compare properly. *Beint fram* 'straight ahead' is commonly used in American and Gausdal Norwegian. In the LBC this expression has no hits, while the alternative *rett fram* has 338. We then looked at word *heim* 'home,' which has 253 hits in the LBC, as against 20,737 for the alternative *hjem*. *Komme i hug* 'remember' has only 2 hits, while the alternative *huske* has 8,899. The last of the words we have been able to count is *krøtter* 'cattle' has 10, while *ku* has 951. There is thus a massive discrepancy between the typically American Norwegian lexical word or expression and the Bokmål one.

Next, consider those words that we cannot count. *Bøte* is polysemous in Bokmål between 'repair some concrete thing' and 'repair some abstract damage.' This word is used frequently in Bokmål in the latter meaning, but not in the former. We present the overall numbers, but the reader should keep this fact in mind. *Bøte* gives 449 hits, and *reparere* 1,096, showing the infrequency for the former. We mentioned *flaug* above, and we choose to do a search in spite of the homonymy problem. We get only 11 hits for *flaug* in all meanings, and 4,539 for the alternative *løp* (specified as a verb, to avoid hits for the homonymous noun). *Færdug, gamlaste* and *gæli* cannot be used as search expressions, since they have non-standard morphological suffixes. The negative polarity adverb *fælt* 'very,' used in phrases like *itte fælt langt* 'not very far,' with *fælt* being unstressed, is used in Bokmål in its original meaning 'bad,' and so it will be very hard to search in a way that will distinguish these meanings. In addition the alternative *så* can be used both as a negative polarity item *ikke så langt* 'not very far,' but also as an ordinary adverb meaning 'that,' as in *ikke så langt* 'not that far' with a different stress pattern (with stress on the adverb *så*). A count would therefore need for every hit to be investigated either by audio (impossible in a written text corpus) or by studying the surrounding text in each case. This is totally impossible. The adverb *så* with all its meanings has 238,597, i.e., nearly quarter of a million hits in the LBC, and these will not be investigated here. The word *kropp* meaning 'person' is relatively rare in Bokmål. However, the word itself is frequent given its meaning 'body.' A count is not feasible for this reason. The expression *lei på* 'time went by' is impossible to compare with anything else, given that there are so many alternatives, including a variety of alternative words like *timer* 'hours,' *dager* 'days,' *uker* 'weeks,' *måneder* 'months,' *år* 'years,' *en stund* 'a while,' etc.

Haugen does not mention the Nynorsk written language standard, but since our Norwegian Americans have a heritage background from some of the areas in Norway in which Nynorsk was used in the schools, we find it natural to compare the American Norwegian with this standard, too. Nynorsk was created by the great grammarian Ivar Aasen as a written standard based on the Norwegian dialects rather than on Danish (Aasen 1864). The council of Eastern Gausdal introduced Nynorsk into all schools already in 1908, which was 30 years earlier than other villages in central and southern Gudbrandsdalen (Holthe 2011:6).

It is immediately clear that when we do searches in the Oslo Corpus of Tagged Norwegian Texts, the Nynorsk part, we find greater correlation between the American Norwegian language and this written standard. We get, for example, 80 hits for *beint fram*, and 24 hits for *rett fram*. Compared with the Bokmål corpus the difference is enormous, recall that the ratio there was 0:338. Another example is *bøte*, which gives 43 hits, while *reparere* only gives 28. In Bokmål the latter had more than double the hits of the former.

The lexical words we have chosen for this section, originally selected as candidates for being archaic, are clearly not close to the Bokmål standard. Instead, they are, with a few exceptions, very close to the equivalent language variant at home, in Gausdal, Gudbrandsdalen. They are closer to the Nynorsk standard, which is not surprising, since Nynorsk is based on the Norwegian dialects. But this standard was not the one Haugen had in mind, and American Norwegian cannot be said to have approached Bokmål.

3.6 Syntax

Johannessen and Laake (2011, 2012) show some typical syntactic constructions in American Norwegian. We present some of them here, to compare with Bokmål.

3.6.1 Preproprial articles

Preproprial articles can be found in dialects across great parts of Norway (see Torp 1973, Håberg 2010). Gausdal is one of the areas where this article is used, and so is our American Norwegian. Consider some examples in (9):

(9) a. n Hans og n Anton
he Hans and he Anton
'Hans and Anton' (Archie)
b. ho Lina Bakkom
she Lina Bakkom
'Lina Bakkom' (Florence)
c. ho Jane
she Jane
'Jane' (Eunice)
d. ho Susan Galstad
she Susan Galstad
'Susan Galstad' (Howard)

Preproprial articles are not part of the Bokmål standard, and normally not in Nynorsk either.

3.6.2 Possessives

In many dialects a version of the preproprial article is used to express possession. They are common in American Norwegian:

(10) a. mor hennes Karen
mother her Karen
'Karen's mother' (Archie)
b. syster hass Ray
sister his Ray
'Ray's sister' (Florence)
c. innkjøringa hass Howard
drive his Howard
'Howard's drive' (Archie)

This construction, too, is not used in the written language. So this has not been an approach toward Bokmål.

3.6.3 Word order in constituent questions

Many Norwegian dialects have a special word order in constituent questions. They can have the verb as the third constituent (V3) rather than the second (V2), which is normally required in Norwegian main clauses (see Nordgård 1988, Rognes 2011, Westergaard and Vangsnes 2005, Åfarli 1986). We also find the word order in American Norwegian:

(11) a. *Hå   ru   kalla herring på norsk?*
       what you call herring in Norwegian
       'What do you call herring in Norwegian?'   (Florence)
    b. *Håkke som va   president da?*
       who   that was president then
       'Who was president then?'   (Florence)

This word order is not used in Bokmål, so there is no change toward it here.

3.7 Conclusion on whether American Norwegian has moved toward Bokmål

In this section we have looked at pronouns, verb inflection, other function words, lexical words and syntax in American Norwegian, Gausdal Norwegian and Bokmål. At no point is American Norwegian closer to Bokmål than to the Gausdal dialect. Indeed, both are far from Bokmål. But in Section 2, where we investigated whether American Norwegian is old-fashioned, we actually found that it is more innovative than the Gausdal dialect in that it does not have dative, a fact probably caused by the language or dialect contact situation There is nothing else that justifies Haugen's claim.

One could ask whether our method is optimal. A possible scenario is that both American Norwegian and Gausdal Norwegian have approached the Bokmål standard. If that were the case, Haugen's claim would not be wrong, just incomplete, since he did not mention Norwegian in Norway at the same time. In order to leave out this possibility, we would have to find samples of very old Gausdal Norwegian, which is not feasible for the purposes of this paper. However, if they really had developed in such a way, independent of each other, we should have expected that they would have approached Bokmål in different ways, but as we have seen so far, American Norwegian and Gausdal Norwegian are very similar to each other. We therefore leave out this scenario.

We should ask why Haugen made this claim. There are several possibilities. First, he met many educated people who were well acquainted with the Norwegian written language. It is likely that their language, more than that of farmers and workers, was closer to Bokmål. It is possible that Haugen met a disproportionate number of wealthy, educated people, given that he needed electricity for the recordings, something not everybody might have been able to offer. Second, his observation may have been colored by his own view on standardization. He grew up with the dialect that originated in Oppdal, Norway, but gradually changed his own Norwegian towards Riksmål (Bokmål) (Haugen 1966: unpaginated p. 2 in the preface). Maybe it influenced his view on the language of others, as well. A third possibility is that some of Haugen's informants actually knew two varieties of Norwegian; one standardized Bokmål, and one dialect. In this case it could be that these people exposed the standard Bokmål when talking to the distinguished professor, while they spoke the dialect at home and with each other. Many of Haugen's informants were actually 1st generation immigrants, and had themselves immigrated to America. These may have had a better grasp of the Bokmål standard than those who were born in America.

By and large, there is very little reason to think that Norwegian Americans should change their language in the direction of Bokmål. Over the years, few have had Norwegian education, and most have only heard spoken Bokmål in the occasional church service or (in the early years of immigration) by a school teacher at the country school. Very few of the speakers we have met have attended Norwegian country schools in America; these had been closed down many years before, and seemingly had little impact on the language. There had been Norwegian-language newspapers, but this language was far from anybody's spoken vernacular, and it is unlikely that they should be influenced by a written source. Most of the Norwegian Americans we have met on our travels have clearly not been exposed to Bokmål. To this we add that the authors of the paper have had to change our dialect in our meetings with the Norwegian Americans. Our dialect from Oslo, which is very well-known to any person in Norway independent of geographical background and close to the written Bokmål standard, was like a foreign language to our informants. Question words like *hvordan, hva,* og *når* 'how, what, and when' were not understood, and it was only when we changed to *håssen, åssen, hå, å, å tid* (dialectal form of the same question words) that our informants could understand us. This tells us that their speech is far removed from Bokmål standard.[11]

It is interesting that Hjelde (this volume) also discusses the possibility of normalization in American Norwegian. He says that while in the 1940s there were people who had an idea of a language standard via newspapers, church, school and first generation immigrants, this idea slowly disappeared since there were fewer who could read Norwegian or who heard it in church. We have further shown that there is nothing in American Norwegian that seems to be influenced by Bokmål. So to the extent that there used to be people who knew this standard, their influence has been limited. The Norwegian situation is therefore very different from the Swedish one, in which the spoken language has been undergoing normalization, and the dialect variation has been disappearing, for several hundred years before the emigration to America even started (see Larsson et al. this volume).

4. Conclusion

In this paper we have discussed to myths of American Norwegian. One is the popular idea that it is an old-fashioned variety. The other, expressed by the great linguist Einar Haugen, is that it is standardized in the direction of Bokmål. To evaluate these claims, we have studied different aspects of the language: the pronominal system, inflection patterns, function words and lexical words, and syntax, and we have compared these

---

11. But there are arguments that there has been a change towards a common eastern Norwegian language variety. This variety has little in common with Bokmål, but has a lot in common with the dialects in the valleys and villages north of Oslo. (See Johannessen and Laake 2011, 2012, forthcoming.)

with the language of modern Gausdal (Gudbrandsdalen, Norway), which is the area from which the people investigated in this study originate. We have also compared the same language with Bokmål.

The results are quite clear. The American Norwegian language is not archaic from the point of view of grammar. The dative system has disappeared, which makes American Norwegian rather modern, but there is some variation in the area of function words, suggesting a koniéization process. On the other hand, looking at the vocabulary, we have shown that it is fair to say that it is more archaic than that in Gausdal Norwegian. There are, however, also great lexical similarities amongst American Norwegians across the whole Midwest (see Johannessen and Laake 2011, 2012, forthcoming), which supports the koinéization hypothesis. The American Norwegian language has not been standardized in the direction of Bokmål. It lacks dative, but this is most likely caused by other factors. In all other linguistic areas, American Norwegian and Gausdal Norwegian are on the same side of the dividing line, while Bokmål is on the other.

References

Aasen, Ivar. 1864. *Norsk grammatik*. Oslo: Cammermeyers Forlag.
Åfarli, Tor Anders. 1986. "Absence of V2 Effects in a Dialect of Norwegian." In *Scandinavian Syntax*, ed. by Östen Dahl and Anders Holmberg, 8–20. Stockholm: University of Stockholm, Institute of Linguistics.
Annear, Lucas and Kristin Speth. This volume. "Maintaining a Multilingual Repertoire: The Lexicon of American Norwegian."
Boas, Hans C. 2009. "Case Loss in Texas German: The Influence of Semantic and Pragmatic Factors." In *The Role of Semantic, Pragmatic and Discourse Factors in the Development of Case*, ed. by Jóhanna Barðdal and Shobhana Chelliah, 347–373. Amsterdam/ Philadelphia: John Benjamins Publishing Company. DOI: 10.1075/slcs.108.18boa
Eyþórsson, Þórhallur, Janne Bondi Johannessen, Signe Laake and Tor A. Åfarli. 2012. "Dative Case in Icelandic, Faroese and Norwegian: Preservation and Non-Preservation." *Nordic Journal of Linguistics* 35(3): 219–249. DOI: 10.1017/S0332586513000036
Håberg, Live. 2010. *Den preproprielle artikkelen i norsk. Ei undersøking av namneartiklar i Kvæfjord, Gausdal og Voss*. Oslo, Norway: University of Oslo MA thesis.
Haugen, Einar. 1953. *The Norwegian Language in America*. Philadelphia: University of Pennsylvania Press.
Haugen, Einar. 1966. *Language Conflict and Language Planning. The Case of Modern Norwegian*. Cambridge, MA: Harvard University Press. DOI: 10.4159/harvard.9780674498709
Hjelde, Arnstein. This volume. "Changes in a Norwegian Dialect in America."
Holthe, Ane. 2011. *Nynorsk i motvind: Skolemålsutviklingen i Gausdal etter 1950*. Oslo, Norway: University of Oslo MA thesis.
Jenshus, Gunnar. 1986. *Fronsmålet*. Vinstra: Fron historielag.
Johannessen, Janne Bondi. 2012. "Har ru bursdag? Da ska re feires! Om isoglossene for r-initielle funksjonsord." In *Fra holtijar til holting – språkhistoriske og språksosiologiske artikler til Arne Torp på 70-årsdagen*, ed. by Unn Røyneland and Hans Olav Enger, 183–195. Oslo: Novus forlag.

Johannessen, Janne Bondi, Joel Priestley, Kristin Hagen, Tor Anders Åfarli and Øystein Alexander Vangsnes. 2009. "The Nordic Dialect Corpus – An Advanced Research Tool." In *Proceedings of the 17th Nordic Conference of Computational Linguistics NODALIDA 2009.* NEALT Proceedings Series 4, ed. by Kristiina Jokinen and Eckhard Bick, 73–80. Tartu: Tartu University Library (electronic publication).

Johannessen, Janne Bondi and Signe Laake. 2012. "Østnorsk som fellesdialekt i Midtvesten." *Norsk Lingvistisk Tidsskrift* 30(2): 365–380.

Johannessen, Janne Bondi and Signe Laake. 2011. "Den amerikansk-norske dialekten i Midtvesten." In *Studier i dialektologi och sociolingvistik. Föredrag vid Nionde nordiska dialektologkonferensen i Uppsala 18–20 augusti 2010. Acta Academiae Regiae Gustavi Adolphi 116,* ed. by Lars-Erik Edlund, Lennart Elmevik and Maj Reinhammar, 177–186. Uppsala: Kungl. Gustav Adolfs Akademien för svensk folkkultur.

Johannessen, Janne Bondi and Signe Laake. Forthcoming. "Eastern Norwegian as a Common Norwegian Dialect in the American Midwest." *Journal of Language Contact.*

Larsson, Ida, Sofia Tingsell and Maia Andreasson. This volume. "Variation and Change in American Swedish."

Lie, Svein. 1984. "Noen abstraksjonsproblemer i fonologien." *Norskrift* 42: 1–11.

Nordgård, Torbjørn. 1988. "Omkring ordstilling i hv-spørsmål i norske dialekter." *Skriftserie fra Institutt for fonetikk og lingvistikk* 33(A): 26–37.

Papazian, Erik and Botolv Helleland. 2005. *Norsk Talemål.* Kristiansand: Høyskoleforlaget.

Putnam, Michael. 2003. "The Prepositional Case in German-American Dialects." *Focus on German Studies* 10: 207–224. http://drc.libraries.uc.edu/handle/2374.UC/1968

Rognes, Stig. 2011. *V2, V3, V4 (and maybe even more). The Syntax of Questions in the Rogaland Dialects of Norwegian.* Oslo, Norway: University of Oslo MA thesis.

Sandøy, Helge. 1996. "Somme – eit semantisk skilje i norske dialektar." *Nordica Bergensia* 9(96): 90–102.

Skjekkeland, Martin. 1997. *Dei norske dialektane – Tradisjonelle særdrag i jamføring med skriftmåla.* Kristiansand: Høyskoleforlaget.

Smits, Caroline and Jaap van Marle. This volume. "On the Decrease of Language Norms in a Disintegrating Language."

Storm, Johan. 1920. *Ordlister over lyd- og formlæren i norske bygdemaal; udgivne ved Olai Skulerud.* Kristiania: Dybwad (commission).

Torp, Arne. 1973. "Om genitivsomskrivninger og -s-genitiv i norsk." *Maal og Minne* 3–4: 125–150.

Vestad, Jon Peder. 2002. *Gausdalsmålet.* Gausdal: Gausdal dialekt- og mållag.

Westergaard, Marit Richardsen and Øystein Alexander Vangsnes. 2005. "Wh-Questions, V2, and the Left Periphery of Three Norwegian Dialect Types." *Journal of Comparative Germanic Linguistics* 8: 117–158. DOI: 10.1007/s10828-004-0292-1

URLs

Lexicographical Bokmål Corpus: http://www.hf.uio.no/iln/tjenester/kunnskap/samlinger/bokmal/veiledningkorpus/index.html

Nordic Dialect Corpus: http://www.tekstlab.uio.no/nota/scandiasyn/index.html

Oslo Corpus of Tagged Norwegian Texts, the Nynorsk Part: http://www.tekstlab.uio.no/norsk/korpus/nynorsk/netscape/treord/oktntn.shtml

Coon Valley Norwegians meet Norwegians from Norway
Language, culture and identity among heritage language speakers in the U.S.

Anne Golden and Elizabeth Lanza
University of Oslo

> *What I talk is kind of a Nor-Coon Valley Norwegian.*
> Sylvia (82)

This article focuses on linguistic and cultural identity constructions in interactions between members of the last generation of a former heritage language speaking community and speakers from the homeland of their ancestors. The data come from fieldwork involving narratives of personal experience in a Norwegian heritage community in the U.S. that is currently undergoing a language shift. Results revealed that speakers negotiated various identities through their categorization strategies and positioning towards their heritage language and culture. Language is still esteemed as a marker of cultural identity; however, emphasis on cultural artifacts and traditions for accentuating ethnic identity in the U.S. is also made by those whose fluency in the heritage language was faltering. Narratives of personal experience provide a privileged site for investigating issues of language, culture and identity among heritage language speakers.

Keywords: identity constructions, Norwegian heritage community, language shift, language maintenance, narratives, language choice

1. Introduction[1]

In this article we present a study of identity constructions in interactions in which members of the last generation of a former heritage language speaking community meet speakers from the home country of their ancestors. We address the question as to how these speakers present themselves in interaction and how they negotiate their

---

[1]. This work was partly supported by the Research Council of Norway through its Centres of Excellence funding scheme, project number 223265.

identities with their conversational partners – the way they present their languages and cultures, English and Norwegian; how they learned the languages; how they evaluate them and use them; and their evaluation of their own and others' ways of speaking Norwegian.

The data stem from fieldwork in a Norwegian heritage community in the state of Wisconsin in the U.S. that is currently undergoing a language shift. Speakers of the last generation that acquired Norwegian during childhood are in their eighties and have maintained the language to various degrees. The study of Norwegian in diaspora provides an interesting arena for investigating the inherent relationship between language and culture in a community that has maintained the language across several generations despite the ambient melting pot ideology prevalent in the U.S. Although the community is currently undergoing an inevitable language shift, a strong Norwegian identity is still constructed and negotiated especially among the elderly generation not only through language but also through other semiotic resources. Studies in Norway have revealed that Norwegians perceive their language as a core value of culture and identity (cf. Skjåk and Bøyum 1995), and we may ask whether language is perceived to be of equal importance in this community as well, as expressed in interactions with Norwegians from Norway (cf. Mills 2004, Lanza and Svendsen 2007). Based on data from Australia, Smolicz (1981) claimed that language is perceived as vital to the maintenance of the core values of certain cultures, communities, and religions; moreover, it may be seen as a critical feature in regards to individuals' multiple identities – language as a semiotic signal. This was indeed the finding of the Norwegian study (Skjåk and Bøyum 1995); however, in a language shift situation, a broader view of identity needs to be addressed. Moreover, a closer look at how individuals actually negotiate their identities locally in interaction deserves further attention in the study of language shift. How do speakers of the last generation of Norwegian speakers construct linguistic and cultural identities in conversations with speakers from the homeland of their ancestors?

In the following, we first present a short historical background for the community under study. Thereafter, we discuss our data collection techniques and the theoretical framework we employed for addressing our research questions. Our analysis focuses on four speakers for whom we present conversational interactions in which identity issues are highlighted. We also investigate how our role as researchers affects the data we collect and the conclusions we reach concerning language maintenance and shift, an issue that is not always addressed in such studies. In conclusion, we discuss our results in light of work on other heritage language communities and consider the implications our results have for the study of heritage communities in general.

2. Background: The Norwegian language in the U.S.

Coon Valley is situated in western Wisconsin, near the city of La Crosse, not far from the border to Minnesota. It is part of the Coon Prairie settlement along with the town of Westby, at one time an almost exclusively Norwegian community (Hjelde 2000). In 1950, 95% of the population of Westby had a Norwegian background (Munch 1954). According to the U.S. Census of 1990, still 60% of the 4165 inhabitants in the Coon Valley and Westby area maintained that they had a Norwegian background. 562 respondents said they used "Scandinavian" at home – and in this area, this means Norwegian, which represents 22% of all the Norwegian Americans there. This was a high percentage as the other Norwegian American communities in the U.S. hardly passed the rate of 10% Norwegian users (Hjelde 2000).

The Coon Prairie settlement is relatively old with the first Norwegians having arrived in 1849 from the southern part of the state, particularly Koshkonong. They settled first on the prairie around Westby, then around Coon Valley. Their Norwegian heritage was primarily from the area of Gudbrandsdalen, in particular the southern part, and the area around Lake Mjøsa (Hjelde 2000), about 100 km north of Oslo, the capital of Norway.

The reason for the strong Norwegian language maintenance in this particular area was explained by the sociologist P. A. Munch (1954) as being the result of the ethnic strategy used in building up the settlement, an 'intensive' rather than an 'extensive' strategy. An intensive strategy is characterized by the ethnic group's gathering in a clearly defined area in which this group is dominant, thus resulting in less contact with the surroundings, with other ethnic groups and other languages. In the Coon Prairie settlement, where Munch did his research, this was the case, and Norwegian was the primary language of the settlement. Another ethnic strategy is what Munch (1954) called the 'extensive strategy.' In this case the settlement underwent strong expansion into neighboring areas at the same time as people with different ethnic backgrounds were settling in the core area of the settlement. This would lead to a greater need to use English (Hjelde 2000).

Another factor for the long-lasting maintenance of Norwegian is the rather homogenous Norwegian background of the settlers – they mainly came from Gudbrandsdalen with its distinct dialect – resulting in little dialectal variation. The church was probably a third factor – there were strong bonds between Norwegians and the Lutheran Evangelical Church while the other dominating ethnic groups in the district were Roman Catholic (Hjelde 2000). Religion has proved to be a strong factor supporting language and culture maintenance (cf. Joseph 2004, Omoniyi and Fishman 2006, Lanza and Svendsen 2007). According to sociologist Ibarra (1976: 220), in 83% of the marriages in the three largest churches in Coon Prairie between 1873 and 1975, both the bride and the bridegroom were of Norwegian extraction.

The Norwegian community managed to maintain the language across several generations. In a study of German immigration to Wisconsin, Wilkerson and Salmons (2008: 260) note that:

> the basic picture is one of considerable German-only monolingualism [….] The full range of evidence shows that into the twentieth century, many immigrants, their children, and sometimes their grandchildren remained functionally monolingual many decades after immigration into their communities had ceased.

This situation is contrary to the myth stating that the old immigrants to the U.S. became bilingual almost immediately after arriving. There is no reason to believe that the Norwegian immigrant population was different from the German in the beginning of the twentieth century.

Times have changed, however, and as Hjelde (2000) points out, 70% of those speaking Norwegian according to the U.S. Census in 1990 were born before 1926. The youngest person Hjelde met on his field trip in recent years that could understand Norwegian was born in 1972, indicating that Norwegian had been in daily use in her childhood.

The pioneering work on the Norwegian language in America by Einar Haugen (1953) was to a great extent based on interviews and audio recordings from Wisconsin (and the eastern part of Iowa and Minnesota) and several of his interviewees were in fact from Coon Prairie. One of Haugen's important studies was devoted to the particular vocabulary that had developed in the American variety of Norwegian as a result of language contact, called loan words or borrowings. In his well-known two-volume work *The Norwegian Language in America,* Haugen (1953) categorizes and explains the emergence, functions and development of the variety of new vocabulary in the community's American Norwegian as an answer to the speakers' particular needs. This line of research is still vital and Haugen's work has been influential in this regard. Indeed Haugen's study of the Norwegian language in the U.S. is a hallmark study in the field of bilingualism.

3. Data collection

The data on which the analysis in this chapter is based stem from field work done in Wisconsin in 2010, a trip prepared by the project *Norwegian American Dialect Syntax* (NorAmDiaSyn).[2] The authors of this article joined this research group and collected parallel data. While the focus in the NorAmDiaSyn is on the variety of Norwegian spoken by Norwegian descendants – their Norwegian dialect – our focus and interest are on the actual language users as we explore issues of identity and ideology, dimensions important to language maintenance. We collected the data in a type of focus group setting, in which a focus group conversation involves "carefully planned discussions designed to obtain perceptions on a defined area of interest in a permissive, non-threatening environment" (Krueger 1994:6). Our focus group conversations were

---

2. http://www.tekstlab.uio.no/nota/NorAmDiaSyn/english/index.html

informally organized with three to four researchers from Norway at a time talking to local participants from Coon Valley, who were waiting to be video-recorded by the interviewers from the NorAmDiaSyn group. Our talk was centered on topics related to language, schooling, and visits to and from Norway, in which we encouraged the participants to tell stories. In our analysis, we also draw on the video-recorded dialogues carried out by the NorAmDiaSyn group.

In this particular study, the data are mainly from one focus group conversation, marked FG in the text examples (see Example (1) below at the end of the transcription), which was carried out at the home of two elderly brothers we refer to as the Bakke brothers. Furthermore, some data from five video-recorded NorAmDiaSyn conversations at the same location are brought into the analysis. These are marked NorAmDiaSyn with different numbers indicating the participants. The focus group discussion was conducted around the kitchen table while the authors of this article (Anne and Eliz in the transcripts) were present throughout the talk, guiding the conversation, first with the two whom we have given the names Sylvia and John, and then with the two speakers we named Eric and Arnold as they were waiting to be called in for video-taping by the NorAmDiaSyn group in turns. Other Norwegian researchers (named Inga, Leif, Arne and Jorun) joined in the conversation intermittently. In the interactions the speakers never oriented to the second author's U.S. background as she presented herself as a Norwegian researcher. The data were transcribed by linguistically trained students who entered the data into a database. The transcription conventions employed are listed in the appendix.

In order to give an idea of the participation of the speakers in the interactions, and hence the extent of our data that form the basis for the interactional analysis, we have counted the turns of each participant in the focus group conversation, as noted in Table 1. We define the turn at talk as the time during which the speaker has the floor, including minimal responses such as *yes/yeah* and *ja* 'yes'. Although equating turns at talk with interactional participation can be problematized, such an overview can nonetheless indicate the extent to which the different participants engaged in the interactions. Table 1 presents an overview of the two groups' turns at talk in the interactions.

Table 1. Speakers' turns at talk in the main database.

Speaker	Individual turns	Group turns
Norwegians from Norway		1516
Coon Valley Norwegians		1293
Sylvia	611	
John	383	
Eric	181	
Arnold	118	
Total		2809

The Coon Valley Norwegians participated eagerly in the conversations, as we see in Table 1, although some were more talkative than others. A further look at their language choice in their contributions to the conversations and at the topics of talk can provide insight into their identity constructions as they interact with Norwegians from Norway. The elicitation of narratives about their upbringing and their current life provided an appropriate context for investigating issues of heritage language and culture maintenance. Before we examine language choice in the interactions, we now turn to the theoretical perspectives we draw upon in our analysis of language, culture and identity among these heritage speakers.

4. Theoretical perspectives: Why narratives?

Narrative-based research has expanded in recent years and proven to be fruitful in identity studies (cf. De Fina and Georgakopoulou 2012). Narratives have both a cognitive and social function. Brockmeier and Carbaugh (2001:1) point out "the importance of narrative as an expressive embodiment of our experience, as a mode of communication, and as a form for understanding the world and ultimately ourselves". Narratives are "important in people's lives because it is through these forms of knowledge that our lives hang together" (Lantolf and Thorne 2006:138). Narratives "provide a window to the study of identity" (Golden and Lanza 2012:28–29), as speakers employ narratives to construct social and cultural identities. One and the same event can be perceived very differently by various speakers, and one and the same speaker can narrate the same event differently depending upon context. Hence in narration the speaker creates a story world to tell about the event in such a way that the speaker's stance to the events is revealed (cf. Brockmeier and Carbaugh 2001). Through the study of various linguistic resources (for example, lexical choice, indirect speech, pronouns, metaphors), we may study how this story world is created, and how the narrator both constructs and negotiates various identities in that story world. Narratives serve a dual function in research: as an object of study in itself and as a fruitful device for eliciting language use as people get involved in speaking about themselves.

Sociolinguistic approaches to the study of narrative have been influenced by the work of Labov (cf. Labov and Waletsky 1967, Labov 1972) in which an emphasis is on a closed temporal order in discourse with a focus on narrative monologues, the so-called 'big stories' or canonical form of narratives. More current approaches to the study of narrative examine 'small stories,' or non-canonical forms of narratives – narrative fragments (Georgakopoulou 2007), short statements about actions. A so-called 'dimensional' approach to the study of narrative proposed already by Ochs and Capps (2001) covers the span between the 'big' and 'small' stories in which a continuum of possibilities is outlined for five different dimensions of narratives: tellership, tellability, embeddedness, linearity and moral stance. For example, there are dimensions to tellership, or who tells the story, spanning from the monologue to the co-construction of narratives by several speakers. In other words – there are many different types of narrative, from the smallest 'snippets of talk' to the longer story of one's life. Such an approach to the study of narrative allows the analysis of possibilities at various points on the continuum and hence allows for a more in-depth study of emergent identities in interaction. Small stories are also called 'narratives-in-interaction' (Georgakopoulou 2007), and this term underpins the idea that these stories are not merely isolated fragments in the interaction, but that they are inherently part of the activity or performance.

Identity construction in narrative has also been studied through a closer look at the categorization strategies a narrator employs, as "self-identities are ... often built on the basis of opposition or contrast with others" (De Fina 2003: 139) in the story world the speaker creates in narration. In this regard, we may ask what kind of categories are used for self and other descriptions and which ones are the most salient as the speakers engage in talk about their heritage. Moreover, as narratives are often built around actions, we may investigate what kinds of actions and reactions (and implicitly what kinds of values and norms) are associated with those categories. Hence narratives provide us with a means to investigate ideologies about language and culture.

5. Identity as a social construction

The approach to identity, or rather identities, we take is a post-modern one in which identities are perceived as negotiated and emergent in interpersonal communication (cf. Bucholtz and Hall 2005). We view identity:

> ... as performed rather than as prior to language, as dynamic rather than fixed, as culturally and historically located, as constructed in interaction with other people and institutional structures, as continuously remade, and as contradictory and situational.... Thus the practice of narration involves the 'doing' of identity, and because we can tell different stories we can construct different versions of self.
> (Benwell and Stokoe 2006: 138)

This approach is in reaction to an essentialist view of identity, which dictates who we are and what we do. Such a view conceives of identity as static while through the post-modern approach, identities are viewed as dynamic and changing as an interaction unfolds, as intertwined in the performance of the narrative.

The notion of 'agency' has proved fruitful in the analysis of identity construction in interaction (De Fina 2003, De Fina et al. 2006, Lanza 2012). Agency is understood as "the socioculturally mediated capacity to act" (Ahearn 2001: 109). Identity is indeed "a process always embedded in social practices," as highlighted by De Fina, Schiffrin, and Bamberg (2006: 2), who further stress "the centrality of processes of indexicality in the creation, performance, and attribution of identities" (De Fina et al. 2006: 3). In other words, the individual can use various linguistic resources that index or point to particular identities s/he wishes to construct and with a particular degree of agency in the narratives.

The role of power and power relations should not be underemphasized in this process. Agency and power are indeed interconnected, for agency is a major basis for claiming power (Al Zidjaly 2009: 177). Hence through the use of various linguistic resources, the speaker can negotiate identities in interaction that have more or less empowered or diminished agency (Golden and Lanza 2012, Lanza 2012). By describing past events, a narrator can reinforce or even create a more active, assertive self – or a more passive and victimized person – and hence different degrees of agency. And these selves may react to each other in various story worlds (cf. Pavlenko and Blackledge 2004). When telling their stories, narrators often "*enact* a characteristic type of self, and through such performances they may in part become that type of self" (Wortham 2000: 158). The past events described in narratives must not be confused with so called 'objective facts': "stories, unlike propositional accounts, are not exclusively hemmed in by the demands of *verifiability*" (Bruner 2010: 45). A story of a past event told to a group of people one day might differ from the 'same' story told by the same narrator another day. The 'here and now' is different from the 'there and then' (cf. Bruner 2001).

A concept that is drawn upon in numerous studies of narratives and identity is positioning (cf. Harré and van Langenhove 1999). In interaction, the narrators will position themselves, that is, they will present different entities in different ways, the figures in their stories as well as themselves. As noted above, narrators do so by describing or categorizing an individual as a particular type of person or by representing themselves as particular sorts of people (engaging in particular activities and relating to others in characteristic ways). De Fina et al. (2006: 8) claim "Positioning provides a central theoretical construct and valuable tool for studying identity." It is important to point out that positioning is grounded in the interaction and not assumed beforehand by pre-existing structures.

We now turn to the data to investigate how the Coon Valley speakers negotiate their identities through their categorization and positioning towards their heritage language and culture.

6. Interactions in Coon Valley

The entire interview in the focus group conversations may be seen as an overarching narrative (Reissman 1993) or autobiography since the participants tell and co-construct their identities not only as descendants of Norwegian immigrants to the U.S. but also in other roles. In the following, we illustrate these various identity constructions in the data. Initially, we address the issue of language choice.

6.1 Language choice

Language choice can be indexical of various identities the speaker attempts to negotiate in interaction. The choice of which language to use in a bilingual setting, however, is also influenced by language competence or language preference, which in turn may be related to language competence. Language competence and language preference may give rise to language negotiation sequences. In the documentation of heritage languages, the researcher invariably attempts to elicit that language in data collection. In this regard, the reflexivity of the researchers' role – not only how they elicit talk, but also how they affect the talk they elicit – is important to consider. When Sylvia describes her way of speaking Norwegian, she positions herself as a somewhat different Norwegian speaker and is reluctant to use her variety, but the Norwegian researchers quickly assure her of the value of her way of speaking. In the following example, we see how the Norwegian researchers encourage Sylvia to use her Norwegian, despite her reluctance initially in line 1 in which she speaks English. A language negotiation sequence ensues in which the Norwegian researchers maintain their use of Norwegian and encourage Sylvia's use of Norwegian. However, Sylvia does not switch in Example (1) except for short remarks like *ja* 'yes' and *så* 'so.'[3]

(1) 1 Sylvia: **But you understand English, so I can talk English.** @ (.)
     2 Anne: *Å nei, vi må høre at du snakker eh norsk.*
          'Oh no, we have to hear you speak eh Norwegian.'
     3 Eliz: @
     4 Sylvia: *Ja.*
          'Yes.'
     5 Leif: *Du snakker, du* [*kan snakke begge deler.*]
          'You speak, you [can speak both (languages).]'
     6 Sylvia: [But eh, I-]
          I [I talk # what] I talk is kind of a Nor-Coon Valley Norwegian.
     7 Eliz: [*Du kan blande*] *så mye du vil.*
          '[You can mix] as much as you want.'
     8 Anne: *Ja, men –*
          Yes, but –
     9 Eliz: *Ja, men det er det vi er interesserte i* [*å høre om.*]
          'That is what we are interested   [in hearing.]'
    10 Anne: [*Vi er*] *interesserte i Coon Valley Norwegian.*
                                      '[We are] interested in Coon Valley Norwegian.'
    11 Sylvia: **Because of my my father talked to me in Norwegian all the time (.) and so that I would answer him in half English and half Norwegian.**

---

3. See transcription conventions in the Appendix.

12 Leif: Mm #
              [Men det] er det er akkurat den norsken vi har lyst at du skal
                                                                    [snakke.]
              '[But that] that is exactly the Norwegian we want you to [speak.]'
13 Sylvia: [Så]   [@]
              '[So]'
14 Leif: Og den er god, den. Den er # det er god norsk, det.
              'And it is good. It is # it is good Norwegian.'   (FG 1: 32–2: 04)

Initially, Sylvia attempts to negotiate English as the language choice of interaction. However, one researcher emphasizes that they want to hear her speak Norwegian (l. 2) while another states that she can use both Norwegian and English (l. 5). Sylvia overlaps (l. 6) with Leif before he states that she can also use English; she hesitates before indicating her variety of Norwegian. The use of the discourse marker *but* indexes a denial of expectation that she speak Norwegian. She refers to her individual variety of Norwegian as a "kind of a Nor-Coon Valley Norwegian" (l. 6). She indexes herself as not being competent in the language as she used both English and Norwegian in speaking to her father in growing up. Implicit in her response is an ideology of low esteem attributed to her variety of Norwegian. In line 11 she states that she spoke half in English and half in Norwegian, implying that the variety she speaks is a mixed one. Indeed in line 7, the researcher had encouraged her to mix. Leif emphasizes that *det er akkurat den norsken vi har lyst at du skal snakke* 'that is exactly the Norwegian we want you to speak' (l. 12), thus positioning Sylvia as a perfect Coon Valley speaker. In line 14, Leif assures her of the value of her Norwegian. In Example (1) we see the attempted co-construction of Sylvia's identity as a Coon Valley speaker and the researchers negotiate their identities as researchers and even teachers, who are in the position to evaluate Sylvia's Norwegian.

In a similar example, Sylvia explicitly states her negative self-evaluation of her spoken language skills (lines 1 and 6 in Example (2)), this time in Norwegian. Despite this, the researchers continue to ascribe her personal agency in her language skills as we see in Jorun's reply in line 2, that she can in fact speak the language despite her indicating the contrary. The researchers attempt to empower her as an accomplished speaker of the language throughout the interaction. In Example (2) we witness the co-construction of Sylvia's personal agency as a heritage language speaker.

(2) 1 Sylvia: Ja, **but** je- jeg jeg er ikke så fælt til god å snakke norsk.
                 'Yes, **but** I–I I am not so bad to good at speaking Norwegian.'
     2 Jorun: <u>Jo</u>, det er du, jeg har jo hørt deg masse, jeg.
                 '<u>Yes</u> you are, I have heard you a lot.'
     3 Sylvia: Ja, men …
                 'Yes, but…'
     4 Jorun: Du snakker bra nok for meg!
                 'You speak well enough for me!'

5   Inga: # *Ja, men du satt jo, vi vi snakka mye norsk, du snakka jo så bra som bare det.* # *Ja.*
'# Yes, but you were sitting, we we talked a lot of Norwegian, you spoke really so well. #Yes.'

6   Sylvia: *It # eh nokså dårlig.*
'It # eh quite poor.'

7   Inga: *Nei.*
'No.'

8   Jorun: *Nei, men det var faktisk noe jeg kunne ha sagt i stad, jeg glemte å si det.*
'No, but that was in fact something I could have said a while ago. I forgot to say it.'
{Unintelligible background conversation.}
Men det er at det- det er dere som er ekspertene her. # *Dere er jo eksperter på deres eh Coon Valley-norsk.*
'But it is that- that you are experts here. # You are experts of your eh Coon Valley Norwegian.'

9   Sylvia: *Ja.*
'Yes.'

10 Jorun: *Den kan jo ikke vi.*
'That one we don't know.'

11 Sylvia: *Ja.*
'Yes.'

12 Jorun: *Så vi veit jo ikke det.*   # [*Vi hører jo bare at dere snakker bra.*]
'So we don't know that. # [We only hear that you are speaking well.]'

13 Sylvia: [*Du du kan snak- snakke mere.*]
                                         '[You you can spe- speak more.]'

14 John: *Ja,* **I don't...**
'Yes, **I don't...**'

15 Jorun: *Ja ja,*   [*begge to.*]
'Yes yes, [both of you.]'

16 Inga: [*Men*] *du veit det er ikke det er ikke spørsmål om å snakke godt eller ikke godt.* (.) *Jorun vil høre hvordan dere* [*snakker norsk i Coon Valley*] =
'[But] you know that it is not a question about speaking well or not well. (.) Jorun wants to hear how you [speak Norwegian in Coon Valley]' =

17 Jorun: [*Ja, ja, ja.*]
                                                                        '[Yes, yes, yes.]'

18 Inga: = *så dere skal snakke akkurat sånn som dere gjør her.*
= 'so you're going to speak exactly the way you do it here.'

> 19 Jorun: Ja, [og] jeg hører jo at det er bra òg.
> 'Yes, [and] I hear that it is good too.'
> 20 Inga: [Og det] det er det det er. # Det er bra. # Det er det som er bra.
> '[and it] it is what it is. # It is good. # That is what is good.'
> (FG 1:18:42–1:19:36)

Al Zidjaly (2009: 196) emphasizes the importance of "conceptualizing agency as collaborative and interactive". This exchange in Example (2) clearly illustrates how agency is co-constructed and ratified through the researchers' positive encouragement. While Sylvia complains about her Norwegian not being good, the others reject this claim. Jorun, moreover, says Sylvia is among "the experts" (l. 8), attributing to Sylvia a high degree of agency.

6.2   Sylvia: "I don't know how to say all that in Norwegian"

We have noted Sylvia's way of excusing her choice of English in interaction, through her explicitly saying so as demonstrated in both Examples (1) and (2). And turning to John (l. 13) in Example (2), she says *Du kan snak- snakke mer* 'You can spe- speak more.' But we also find that she repeatedly asks *How do you say that?*, meaning 'How do you say that in Norwegian.' Moreover, she also often shifts to English even when the language of conversation has been successfully negotiated to Norwegian. In the end, she actually exclaims: *I'm all talked out*, not only referring to things to talk about, but also to her apparent struggle to construct utterances in Norwegian. These examples illustrate her negotiation of an identity as an insecure Norwegian speaker, as she excuses herself towards the interlocutors from Norway. In the conversation, Sylvia employs metaphors that reveal her conceptualization of language as an entity that you possess more or less of ('you can talk more'), an entity with varying quality ('it's not very good', 'it's kind of bad') and an entity that has its limits ('I'm all talked out'). Metaphor is here defined in line with Conceptual Metaphor Theory as presented by Lakoff and Johnson (1980) and further developed by Lakoff (1993), Gibbs (1994), Lakoff and Johnson (1999), and Kövecses (2002). In this framework, metaphor is seen as a mapping between two domains, a source domain and a target domain. It is a way of conceiving of one thing in terms of another. As Kövecses (2006: 130) points out, "The connections between the two are set up either because the two domains display some generic structural similarity or because they are correlated in our experience." The primary function of metaphors is understanding: complex or abstract phenomena – like languages – are seen as things that are well known – like objects – and as such, may be dealt with and reflected upon.

> Understanding our experiences in terms of objects and substances allows us to pick out parts of our experience and treat them as discrete entities or substances of a uniform kind. Once we can identify our experiences as entities or substances, we can refer to them, categorize them, group them, and quantify them – and, by this means, reason about them.   (Lakoff and Johnson 1980: 25)

Metaphors are also employed in identity constructions (cf. Golden and Lanza 2013). By presenting her Norwegian language as an object of poor quality and as almost vanished, Sylvia negotiates an identity of a low proficient Norwegian language speaker. However, in spite of her reluctance to speaking Norwegian, Sylvia speaks for longer stretches and uses a direct communication strategy of asking for help, indicating her willingness to construct a Norwegian identity in talk. The topic of conversation is inevitably focused on the Norwegian language in the U.S. as the researchers are on fieldwork to investigate the phenomenon. Nonetheless Sylvia speaks often about modern Norway as opposed to the Norwegian community of her youth, as some of the speakers do. Her initiatives almost consistently touch upon topics associating her with Norway. Hence this choice also indexes her attempts at negotiating a Norwegian heritage identity. Furthermore, Sylvia showed letters to the researchers (and asked for help in translating them), old tickets and pictures. Later she insisted on our visiting her home where she had many Norwegian cultural artifacts on display. Moreover, she encouraged her husband Arnold to tell stories involving people they refer to as "Norwegians." She also often refers to herself doing (what she perceives as) Norwegian activities such as baking for Christmas: *Jeg baker alt norsk* 'I bake all Norwegian things.' Her maintaining of Norwegian traditions is an asset that she flaunts. One of the researchers even commented upon this and Sylvia reveals an implicit obligation to her heritage to do so in her reply, as we see in Example (3).

(3) 1 Inga: *Jeg trur dere nesten er flinkere til å holde på de gamle norske juletradisjonene enn vi er i Norge.*
                 'I think you (PL.) are almost better at keeping the old Norwegian Christmas traditions than we are in Norway.'
     2 Sylvia: *Vi må gjøre det.*
                 'We have to do it.'   (FG 58:48–58:53)

Sylvia is positioned by Arnold, her husband, as being a 'bone fide' Norwegian. She is the one that has been most often to Norway and has the most Norwegian relatives. Hence he co-constructs her Norwegian identity with her. We assisted her in reading a book she had bought in Norway during an extended family reunion. In the book she learned that her grandfather in fact had had a child before marriage to her grandmother. This excited her as it implied she had more relatives in Norway and implicitly had a further claim to a Norwegian identity. Her Norwegianness is constructed through her relations to Norwegians in Norway, and having more Norwegian relatives seems to make her more Norwegian. Hence other semiotic resources are also construed as part of heritage identity construction (see 6.3 below).

(4) 1 Sylvia: **I want you to translate something for me. # I'm wondering # eh about this book.**
                 Jeg var på Solørlag-stevne. # Og jeg kjøpte denne boka. # Og inni her s- #ehm #

'I was at the Solørlag reunion. And I bought this book. And inside here s- #ehm #'
now I was wondering # did my grandpa have a child before he got married?
2 Others: @ (.)
3 Eliz: **The secret comes out.**
4 Inga: *Du # det var svært vanlig # det hadde oldefaren min også. @ # Så det var helt – det var ganske vanlig.*
'Well # that was very common # my great-grandfather also had one (child). @ # So it was completely – it was quite common.'
5 Sylvia: **I'm trying to figure that out.**
6 Jorun: **Who is your grandfather?**
7 Sylvia: **Paul.**
8 Inga: **Paul.**
9 Sylvia: *Ja.*
'Yes'
10 Inga: *Han hadde ei datter som var født ehm #*
'He had a daughter that was born ehm.'
he he had a daughter born in 1887.
11 Sylvia: **Yeah, I see (.) he married Grandma in 1900, I think.**
12 Jorun: **OK, yes.**
13 Sylvia: **So.**
14 Jorun: **That's right, yes.**
15 Sylvia: **So I might have a lot of other relatives I don't even know about?**
16 Anne: [*Det er*] *sant.*
'[That's] true.'
17 Jorun: [**Yes.**]
18 Leif: @
19 Anne: *Du må reise til Norge igjen.*
'You have to travel back to Norway.'
20 Sylvia: *Ja!*
'Yes!'   (FG 27:25–28:27)

In Example (4) we see how Sylvia's Norwegian identity is reassured with the others in the conversation as she discovers she has more relatives than she previously realized.

6.3 Other semiotic resources in identity construction

Identity construction also occurs through non-verbal behavior and the use of cultural artifacts. Norskedalen (http://norskedalen.org/) is a Nature and Heritage Center in Coon Valley that was founded in 1977 and has activities all year long. Sylvia clearly made a point of her involvement in the center stating "Arnold and I were along from the very beginning." When we later visited her home, we found it highly decorated with pictures and hand-sewn tapestries on the walls with inscriptions, most of which had something to do with Norway. For example, at the door there was a welcome sign (*Velkommen*) and outside there was a Norwegian mailbox. Pictures of Vikings, trolls and Norwegian landscape scenes donned the walls inside her home.

Hence despite her seeming reluctance to use her variety of Norwegian and her implicit ideology toward that variety as having low esteem in comparison with present-day Norwegian from Norway, Sylvia attempts to construct a Norwegian identity, of which she is proud. In interaction with the Norwegian researchers, she co-constructs this identity with them, also through her narratives of her youth but particularly through her involvement nowadays in extended family reunions in Norway. Her pride in her Norwegian heritage, however, is most demonstrable through her adherence to Norwegian Christmas traditions and her cultural artifacts that decorate her home. In Section 9 below, we return to the use of other cultural artifacts in identity construction. We now turn to the other Coon Valley Norwegians in the focus group.

6.4   John and Eric: Hard-working Norwegians

A common motif among the Coon Valley Norwegians we spoke to was that of a hard-working individual. Stories of childhood attested to the challenging times these people were confronted with in the Midwest. John and Eric are brothers ('the Bakke brothers') who have held together throughout their lives. Both men present themselves as hard-working, frugal men who enjoyed being self-sufficient. However, farming had its price; in particular John's health was affected. In Example (5), we see how the conversation takes place entirely in Norwegian, including Sylvia's participation, until line 16 when John inserts an English word into his utterance. John's switch triggers Sylvia's switch to English in line 18. Throughout the focus group discussion, John spoke mostly Norwegian. John, however, renegotiates language choice in the conversation by switching back to Norwegian in line 21, although his minimal response in line 19 is Norwegian. In line 23 John repeats in English what he has said in Norwegian and then continues in English. Repetition for emphasis by code-switching is a common discourse strategy in multilingual encounters (Auer 1998). John's repetition in line 23 serves to underscore the hard time he had had, and this is confirmed in line 25.

(5) 1   Inga: *Å, dere hadde mjølkekyr?*
             'Oh, you had dairy cows?'
     2   John: *Ja.*
             'Yes.'
     3   Inga: *Ja, akkurat.*
             'Yes, exactly.'
     4   John: *Vi selde ut de to i 2002.*
             'We sold out the two in 2002.'
     5   Inga: *Jaha # akkurat.*
             'Oh yeah # exactly.'

6	John:	*Men vi heldt att fem @*
		'But we held onto five @'
7	Sylvia:	*Og vi avla tobakk.*
		'And we cultivated tobacco.'
8	John:	*Og så tobakk.*
		'And then tobacco.'
9	Sylvia:	*Vi ha- vi hadde mye tobakk her.*
		'We ha- we had a lot of tobacco here.'
10	Inga:	*Åja, så dere hadde t- eh -*
		'Oh yeah, so you had t- eh'
11	John:	*Nei, det var mye # å gjøre # tre æker.*
		'No, there was a lot # to do # three acres.'
12	Inga:	*Med tobakk? Ja.*
		'With the tobacco? Yes.'
13	Anne:	*Ja.*
		'Yes.'
14	Inga:	*Men var det vanlig å dyrke tobakk eh # her i Wisconsin?*
		'But was it common to cultivate tobacco eh # here in Wisconsin?'
15	Sylvia:	*Det var lortete arbeid*
		'It was dirty work'
16	John:	*og drevet på med å @ # **exercise** @*
		'and used to @ # **exercise** @'
17	Inga:	*Jaha.*
		'Oh yeah.'
18	Sylvia:	**But it was a good cash crop.**
19	John:	*Ja.*
		'Yes.'
20	Inga:	*Jaha?*
		'Oh yeah?'
21	John:	*Nok åt skatten.*
		'Enough for taxes.'
22	Inga:	[*Akkurat.*]
		'[Exactly.]'
23	John:	[**Ta- taxes.**] @
24	Inga:	*Ja # ja # ja. # Så, ja vel.*
		'Yes # yes # yes. # So, ok.'
25	John:	**I've done too much hard work.** @ (FG: 33:42–34:34)

The Bakke brothers are positioned by Sylvia as capable, not only of farming, but also of preserving and using products from the animals, the fields and the garden in the kitchen. Their activities go beyond normal cooking, they even churn butter. Their rationale for this was their eagerness to be self-sufficient. John remembers when he had to buy milk in Example (6).

(6) 1 Inga: *Så du kan kinne?*
'So you can churn butter?'
2 John: *Ja, jeg bruker # elektrikk.*
'Yes, I use # electric.'
3 Inga: *Å, du bruker, jaha.*
'Oh, you use, yeah.'
4 Anne: *Ja.*
'Yes.'
5 Eliz: **Wow.**
6 John: *Du, den går fort.*
'Hey, it goes fast.'
7 Eliz: *Eget smør, det er ikke så verst.* @
'Your own butter, that's not bad. @'
8 Anne: *Så du kjøper ikke smør i* =
'So you don't buy butter in' =
9 John: [*Jeg har ikke kjøpt*] *sia et heilt år.*
'[I haven't bought] since a year ago.'
10 Anne: =[**eh in the store?**]
11 Inga: *Nehei.*
'Really?'
12 Eliz: **Wow.** @
13 Anne: *Ikke me- ikke mjølk og ikke smør og*
'Not mi- not milk and not butter and'
14 John: *Vi kjøpte mjølk når kua var tørr i januar.*
'We bought milk when the cow was dry in January.'
15 Eliz: [@]
16 Ing: [*Ja*]
'[Yes]'
17 John: @
18 Anne: *Og ikke epler og ikke # ikke brød, og*
'And not apples and not # not bread, and'
19 John: *Men vi må kjøpe egg.*
'But we have to buy eggs.' (FG 41:27–41:58)

John presents himself as being particularly faithful to his work and duty from childhood on. After school he and his brother would go straight to the cow shed (*når vi kom att så var det å gå beint borti fjøset*). The one time he missed his milking was, he said, when he was appointed to jury duty (Example (7), l. 12, 14). Talking about work, he often connected it with health problems: his health was affected by hardship. In his interactions, he persistently used Norwegian, not only when addressed but also when initiating an interaction. Examples (7) and (8) illustrate this. Note that in Example (7), the English insertions are of cultural borrowings (l. 6, 14).

(7) 1 Inga: *Hadde dere andre dyr? # Hadde dere andre dyr # på eh -*
'Did you have any other animals? # Did you have any other animals # on eh -'

2 John: *Jeg hadde høner mange år sia, men* =
'I had hens many years ago, but' =

3 Inga: *Ja, akkurat, ja.*
'Yes, exactly, yes.'

4 John: = *81 slutta vi.*
= '81 we stopped.'

5 Inga: *Jaha # ja, ja. # Ja.*
'Ok # yes, yes. # Yes.'

6 John: *Etter vi solgte, så kjøpte vi # vi hadde att fem ## kuer. (.) Så # kjøpte kalver borti # **sales barn** og # avla dem opp.*
'After we sold, then we bought # we had left 5 ## cows. (.) Then # bought calves over at the # **sales barn** and # bred them.'

7 Inga: *Jaha.*
'Ok.'

8 John: *Solgte de att.*
'Sold them back.'

9 Inga: *Akkurat # ja, ja # ja. Var det kanskje lettere å drive med enn mjølkekyr?*
'Right # yes, yes # yes. Was it maybe easier to work with than with dairy cows?'

10 John: *Kneet mitt vart # jeg mjølka # i 47 år.*
'My knee became # I milked # for 47 years.'

11 Inga: *Jaha # ja.*
'Well # yes.'

12 John: *Så missa jeg éi mjølking på 47 år.*
'So I missed one milking in 47 years.'

13 Inga: *Ja, det var # det var bra.*
'Yes, that was # that was good.'

14 John: *Og det var **jury duty**.*
'And that was **jury duty**.' (FG 37:22–37:58)

(8) 1 Jorun: *Så du har vært hjemme # heime og vært her, du.*
'So you have been at home # at home and been her.'

2 John: *Ja.*
'Yes.'

3 Eliz: *[Stelt huset, ja.]*
'[Took care of the house, yeah]'

4 Jorun: *[Ja, passa]* =
'[Yes, looked after]' =

5 John: *Ja, passa på # passa på farmen.*
'Yes, looked after # looked after the farm.'

	6	Anne:	Mm.
	7	Jorun:	[Ja]
			'[Yes]'
	8	Eliz:	[Hm]
	9	Jorun:	Men det er trivelig.
			'But that's nice.'
	10	John:	Jeg har gjort så mye hardt arbeid. @
			'I have done so much hard work. @'
	11	Inga:	Ja, ja. # Du har [jobba hardt.]
			'Yes, yes # You have [worked hard.]'
	12	John:	[Jeg kan ikke] kan ikke løfte opp hånda heller.
			'[I can't] lift up my hand either.'

(FG 44:15–44:34)

Hence the Coon Valley speakers negotiate identities of hard workers, identities that actually intertwine with the traditional conception of the Norwegian immigrants that migrated to the Midwest in the US, as described by Lovoll (2006).

6.5   The old school and community in Coon Valley

Earlier experiences with the Norwegian language are important, for example, attendance at school. Attitudes towards Norwegian and the use of Norwegian in school and elsewhere in the community are important aspects of identity formation. Sylvia talks about the old Norwegian community, but as she grew up talking both English and Norwegian (in Westby) and received her religious confirmation in an English-language ritual, most narratives about Norwegian in the schools are from the Bakke brothers who grew up at a farm in Coon Valley. John says that in their school most of the children were Norwegian-speaking, and that he learned more English after he quit school. They spoke Norwegian outside the classroom, but were supposed to talk English in class. There seemed to be variation in how the individual teachers reacted to Norwegian being spoken in class. Eric said it was 'dangerous' as they would be punished (l. 4). Such a remark reflects his personal perception of the situation, as constructed in his story world.

(9)	1	Inga:	Ja. # Men lærerinna ville vel at dere skulle snakke engelsk =
			'Yes. # But the teacher wanted you to speak English I guess' =
	2	Eric:	Ja, i [klass- i klassa], så.
			'Yes, in the [class- in the class], so.'
	3	Inga:	= [inne? I klassa?]
			= '[inside? In the class?]'
	4	Eric:	Var farlig det å snakke [engelsk] inne ## eller norsk inne.
			'Was risky to speak [English] inside. ## or Norwegian inside.'
	5	Inga:	[@]

	6	Anne:	*Var det farlig?*
			'Was it risky?'
	7	Eric:	*Å det var-, da måtte en sit- sitte att etter skolen* =
			'Oh it was-, then you had to sit- stay back after class' =
	8	Inga:	*Da @*
			'So @'
	9	Eric:	= *lenge.*
			= 'a long time.' (FG 1:38:50–1:39:05)

Such attitudes among some of the teachers surely contributed to negative attitudes towards the heritage language. Both Eric and John say that they could not speak English when they started school, and that they were both set back one year. This was common, they say. They went to school for eight years. The teachers' attitudes are, however, not always revealed as negative. Sylvia and John recalled a boy who answered back to the teacher, saying, according to Sylvia *Jeg kan ikke forstå alt det tull som du skriver på der* 'I cannot understand all that nonsense you are writing there,' referring to English. The teacher, who understood Norwegian, just laughed. Hence the positioning of a strict teacher at school could be the recall of how hard learning the new language in school was for a child who only spoke Norwegian at home as well as the frustrations the country boys felt by being set back a year. As pointed out by Wilkerson and Salmons (2008), monolingual immigrants were common into the 20th century.

Arnold grew up in another district and he spoke English when he started school. All three men – Eric, John and Arnold – had a Norwegian Lutheran confirmation, and the priest gave them religious instruction in Norwegian. As noted above, religion is closely connected with language maintenance in immigrant communities. In Examples (10) and (11), Eric expresses the difficulties he experienced in his initiation into English.

(10)	1	Jorun:	*Når tid # e lærte du engelsk?*
			'When # was it that you learned English?'
	2	Eric:	*var var da jeg begynte på skolen da jeg var en seks år ## jeg visste ikke forskjell på # "ja" og "nei" vet du på engelsk # e når jeg begynte.*
			'was was when I began at school when I was 6 years old ## I didn't know the difference between # "yes" and "no" you know in English # e when I started'
			(NorAmDiaSyn 03)
(11)	1	Anne:	*Kan du huske det hvor vanskelig det var da du begynte på skolen?*
			'Can you remember it how difficult it was when you started school?'
	2	Eric:	[*Det var vanskelig*] *eh* =
			'[It was difficult] eh' =
	3	Anne:	[*Kan du huske?*]
			'[Can you remember?]'

	4	Eric:	*var i andre klasse ## hun satte meg bak att fra tredje* =
			'was in second grade ## she sat me back from third' =
	5	Anne:	[*Ja.*]
			'[Yes.]'
	6	Eric:	= [*til andre*] =
			= '[to second]' =
	7	Arnold:	[*andre*] *klasse.*
			'[second] grade.' (FG 1:38:03–1:38:18)

Sylvia confirmed the tradition of intermarriage in the Norwegian community in Coon Valley (cf. marriage statistics by Ibarra 1976, noted above) and even mentioned the Church's involvement in keeping the community Norwegian. Sylvia resorts back to English in lines 4, 6 and 8 in Example (12).

(12)	1	Arne:	*da dere var unge # var det viktig å gifte seg med norske?*
			'when you were young # was it important to get married to Norwegians?'
	2	Sylvia:	*å ja*
			'oh yes'
	3	Arne:	*ja?*
			'yes?'
	4	Sylvia:	*ja # em #* **how shall I say the minister encouraged it**
			'yes'
	5	Arne:	[*jaha*] *# det gjorde han ja?*
			'[yeah] # that he did yes?'
	6	Sylvia:	[@] **don't leave @ you know # and eh they encouraged # if you sold your place # to sell it to a Norwegian**
	7	Arne:	*jaha # det òg ja?*
			'yeah # that too yes?'
	8	Sylvia:	[*ja*] **# but now that's gone sort of**
			'[yes]'
	9	Arne:	[*ja*]
			'[yes]' (NorAmDiaSyn 01–02)

Gender differences have often been invoked in studies of language maintenance and shift (cf. Mukherjee 2003). According to Eric, though, there was no prestige in talking Norwegian: "Norwegian goes with the dirty and the untidy… the boys". The girls wanted to be refined (*fine* in Norwegian) thus revealing a traditional attitude towards women and female behavior. However, just this wish to aspire socially is explained by Eric as one of the main reasons for the decrease in Norwegian use by women. Another is the elder generation's passing away.

(13)	1	Eric:	*Det var eh jenten- # jentene som eh # slutta # å snakke norsk, visst.*
			'It was eh the girl- # the girls who eh # quit # talking Norwegian, certainly.'

> 2 Inga: *Det var det?*
> 'It was?'
> 3 Eliz: *Åh.*
> 'Oh.'
> 4 Eric: *Det var # eh forskjell # guttene # var ikke så nøye om de var lortete og* =
> 'There was # eh a difference # the boys # were not so fussed if they were dirty and' =
> 5 Inga: @
> 6 Anne: *Nei.*
> 'No.'
> 7 Eric: = *og bustete hår, og # men jentene ville være fine* =
> = 'and tousled hair, and # but the girls wanted to be refined' =
> 8 Inga: *Jaha?*
> 'OK'
> 9 Eric: = *å snakke norsk, det var ikke riktig fint* =
> = 'to talk Norwegian, that wasn't really refined' =
> 10 Inga: *Å nei, det var ikke det, så de ville*
> 'Oh no, not that, so they wanted'
> 11 Eric: = *var ikke fint nok.*
> = 'were not good enough.'
> 12 Anne: *Nei.*
> 'No'
> 13 Inga: *Nei.*
> 'No'
> 14 Eric: *Så en brukte engelsk, da.*
> 'So one used English then.' (FG 1:40:23–1:40:49)

In Example (13) we witness a direct attestation of the impact of attitudes to language maintenance and how that interacted with the gender variable.

6.6 Identities as elderly people

All of the participants in the interactions negotiate many identities, among them, an identity as elderly people with several family members, friends and neighbors all having passed away. They connect this to their lack of Norwegian practice and hence what they see as inaccuracy in speaking 'good' Norwegian.

> (14) 1 Arnold: *De ble borte foreldra, og kusiner og onkler, så blir det # veit # eh mindre og mindre ut av det norske* [*språket.*]
> 'They passed away parents, and cousins and uncles, so there is # know # less and less of the Norwegian [language.]'
> 2 Anne: [Mm.]
> 3 Inga: [Mm.]

4   Eric: *Jeg minker på det.* (.)
             'I decrease in it.' (.)
5   Arnold: *Det minker på.* @
             'It decreases @'
6   Anne: [*Ja*] # *ja.*
             '[Yes] # yes.'
7   Inga: [Mm.]
8   Eric: *Ja, nå sist # denne uka, de gravde nå # eh om torsdagen ho* **Paula**.
             'Yes, just recently # this week, they buried now # eh on Thursday **Paula**.'
9   Arnold: **Paula**.
10 Eric: *Hun var med i klassen vår.*
             'She was in our class.'   (FG 1:39:07–1:39:36)

The Coon Valley heritage speakers' conversation often touches upon comparisons between 'now' and 'before,' not only concerning language, but also health – John needs a cane now so he feels that he does not get much done. 'Before' he would work; he would feel his strength and speed, and would speak Norwegian more often. 'Now' is described more or less as the opposite, a matter of going to funerals. The demise of family members and friends is equated with the demise of the Norwegian language in Coon Valley.

7. Identity as Norwegians and Americans

We investigated the narratives in which Norway or Norwegians are a theme – where the Coon Valley Norwegians identify themselves with Norway. This is of course the most natural topic in this setting since the researchers were visiting to collect data on Norwegian. All of the participants emphasized when Norwegians were present in different events in the story worlds they created, as when Sylvia in talking about her grandfather going to war adds: "And eh (.) there were mainly (.) Norwegians." She also mentioned Norwegians when talking about Christmas and bringing cakes to the elderly residing in nursing homes: "there (.) are many Norwegians who live there." Norway and Norwegians were highly topicalized.

The Coon Valley participants were also positioned as Norwegians by the researchers present as well as by the other participants. When John asked how we – the research team – found him and Eric, Eliz positions them in line 2 as 'real' Norwegians (and Anne chimes in in line 3) because many had indicated they were the best ones to speak to. John confirms this appraisal in line 5. Sylvia agrees, notably in English (l. 7). John maintains Norwegian in the conversation in line 9, pointing out that he has been in many newspapers. Sylvia points out that he is famous in line 15 to which he distances himself yet at the same time appreciates the compliment, indicating a certain amount of pride in the fact that he has gained attention as a Norwegian.

(15) 1 Anne: = *Men jeg vet at det var flere som hadde nevnt deg og Eric, "dere må opp og snakke med med John og Eric".*
= 'But I know that there are several (people) who had mentioned you and Eric, "you all have to go up and talk with John and Eric".'
2 Eliz: *Ekte nordmenn.*
'Real Norwegians.'
3 Anne: *Ekte nordmenn.*
'Real Norwegians.'
4 Sylvia: *Ja.*
'Yes.'
5 John: *Ja, [det er vi.]*
'Yes, [that we are.]'
6 Anne: *[Det var mang-]* =
'[There were man-]' =
7 Sylvia: **That's for sure.**
8 Anne: = *flere som hadde sagt fra ulike-*
= 'several who had said (that) from various-'
9 John: *Vært i så mange aviser, så.*
'Been in so many newspapers, so.'
10 Sylvia: *Ja.*
'Yes.'
11 John: *Trur sju-åtte paper.*
'Believe seven-eight papers.'
12 Sylvia: **[I think so.]**
13 John: *[@]*
14 Anne: *Har du det?*
'Have you?'
15 Sylvia: **You're famous, you're famous.**
16 John: *Uff, ja. @*
'Uff, yes @' (FG 1:07:49–1:08:10)

As Blommaert (2005: 205) points out, "in order for an identity to be established, it has to be *recognized* by others." In Example (15) it seems like the ascribed identity (how people see us, as 'real' Norwegians) and the assumed identity (how we see ourselves, as 'famous' Norwegians) to a certain extent coalesce. Being known as a Norwegian, however, is also demanding, as John points out in Example (16).

(16) 1 John: *Det var en som var ifra # La Crosse-revyen* =
'Once there was someone from # the La Crosse journal' =
2 Inga: *Akkurat.*
'Right.'
3 John: = *Han var femten ganger* =
= 'He was fifteen times' =

	4	Inga:	*Jaha?*
			'Yeah?'
	5	John:	= *og tok bilde* =
			= 'and took pictures' =
	6	Inga:	[*Ja, akkurat.*]
			'[Yes, right.]'
	7	John:	[*Jeg ble så lei.*]
			'[I got so tired.]'
	8	Sylvia:	[@]
	9	Anne:	[*Ja, jeg skjønner.*]
			'[Yes, I understand.]'
	10	John:	*Kunne nesten ikke snu seg før* =
			'Couldn't turn around before' =
	11	Anne:	*Nei, han tok* [*bilder hele tida*]?
			'No, he took [pictures all the time]?'
	12	John:	= [*jeg ble sku-*] *ble skutt.*
			= '[I got sho-] got shot.'
	13	Eliz:	[*Ja.*] @
	14	Sylvia:	[@]
	15	John:	@ <XXX> *han var.*
			'@ <XXX> he was.'
	16	Inga:	*Ja # så da syns du det ble litt for mye?*
			'Yes # so then you think it got to be too much?'
	17	John:	*Ja, det va # litt for mye.* @
			'Yes, it was # a little too much. @' (FG 1:09:08–1:09:33)

Interestingly, John and Eric did not yearn to return to the fatherland, Norway, despite their linguistic and cultural maintenance. Eric went once, John never did. In Example (17), he recounts his experience.

(17)	1	Anne:	*Ja, kan du fortelle hvordan det var å være i Norge?*
			'Yes, can you tell how it was to be in Norway?'
	2	Eric:	*Å eh …*
			'Oh eh…'
	3	Eliz:	*Når var du?*
			'When were you?'
	4	Eric:	*Jeg var da fornøyd med # etter tre dager, så kunne jeg reist hjem att.*
			'I was satisfied with # after three days, so I could have traveled back home.'
	5	Anne:	*Er det sant?*
			'Really?'
	6	Eric:	*Ja.* @
			'Yes. @'

	7	Anne:	*Ja.*
			'Yes.'
	8	Eric:	*Jeg syntes jeg har sett eh hva # jeg ville se. # Jeg ville se vikingbåten.* =
			'I think I have seen eh what # I wanted to see. # I wanted to see the Viking ship.' =
	9	Anne:	*Ja.*
			'Yes.'
	10	Eric:	= *Det var første tingen jeg ville vite av.*
			= 'That was the first thing I wanted to know about.'
	11	Anne:	*Ja.*
			'Yes.'
	12	Eric:	*Etter jeg så den, så da var jeg ferdig.*
			'After I saw it, then I was finished.'
	13	Anne:	*Ja.*
			'Yes.'
	14	Inga:	*Jaha?*
			'Yeah?'
	15	Eric:	*Ja.*
			'Yes.'
	16	Anne:	*Men traff du noen eh slektninger?*
			'But did you meet any eh relatives?'
	17	Eric:	*Å ja.*
			'Oh, yes.'
	18	Anne:	*Ja # likt-, men var det morsomt å snakke med dem, eller?*
			'Yes # did (you) like-, but was it interesting to talk to them, or what?'
	19	Eric:	*De hadde ikke svært mye å snakke om, syns jeg det.*
			'They didn't have too much to talk about, I think.'
			(FG 1:20:37–1:21:11)

In Example (17) we see that Eric's goal in going to Norway was merely to visit the Viking ships, cultural artifacts. Once the mission was accomplished, he was ready to return home. Moreover, he did not really socialize with his relatives, finding them rather quiet. For Eric Norway was not paradise, and he did not like the forests, as they seemed threatening, as noted in Example (18).

(18)	1	Anne:	*Me- # hadde du hørt # syns du Norge var annerledes enn det du trodde? # Det du hadde hørt fortellinger om?*
			'Bu- # had you heard # do you think Norway was different from what you thought? # What you had heard stories about?'
	2	Eric:	*Jeg visste ikke at det var så mye skog som det.*
			'I didn't know that there was so much forest as there is.'
	3	Anne:	*Nei?*
			'No?'
	4	Eliz:	*Åja.*
			'Oh yes.'

5	Anne:	*Var skog,* [*mere skog.*]	
		'Was forest, [more forest.]'	
6	Eric:	[*Det var mye*] *mer skog enn jeg trudde det var.* (.)	
		'[There was much] more forest than I thought there was.' (.)	
7	Anne:	[*Ja.*]	
		'[Yes.]'	
8	Inga:	[*Ja.*] *Ja.*	
		'[Yes.] Yes.'	
9	Eric:	*Jeg kunne blitt borte på fem minutter.*	
		'I could get lost in five minutes.'	
10	Inga:	@	
11	Eric:	*De kjørte på sideveg- # snudde av vegen og # og kjørte inn i skogen =*	
		'They drove on a side road- # turned around # and drove into the forest'=	
12	Anne:	*Ja.*	
		'Yes.'	
13	Eric:	= *Jeg ikke kunne =*	
		= 'I couldn't' =	
14	Anne:	*Nei.*	
		'No.'	
15	Eric:	= *funnet vegen ut att.*	
		= 'find the way out again.'	(FG 1:22:41–1:23:09)

Arnold, on the other hand, emphasizes that he was well acquainted with Norwegian customs; he relates this to his father, indicating the importance of his family in his life. Even though his father died when Arnold was young (that is the explanation for why Arnold started to speak English at an early age), he must have introduced Arnold to Norwegian customs, as he was not surprised when he went to Norway. According to Arnold, his father was born at Tretten – he felt that was important even if his father had left Norway in 1916, only 16 years old.

(19) 1 Anne: *Syns du Norge var eh # annerledes enn du tenkte på forhånd? ## Var det # forskjellig fra # du trodde?*
'Do you think Norway was eh # different from what you thought beforehand? ## Was it # different from # you thought?'
2 Inga: *Var eh # var Norge slik som eh du hadde hørt deg fortalt om?*
'Was eh # was Norway like eh what you had heard told about?'
3 Arnold: <XXX>, *var vel det meste, ja.*
'<XXX>, was that for the most part, yes.'
4 Anne: *Ja, så du ble ikke overrasket? # Var ingen eh #* **surprise***?*
'Yes, so you were not surprised? # was no eh # **surprise**?'
5 Arnold: **No.** (.)
6 Inga: @
7 Anne: @

8   Arnold: *Far min var født på Tretten, han, veit du så.*
        'My father was born in Tretten, ya know.'
9   Anne: *Ja, men hadde han fortalt* [*mye om*] ...
        'Yes, but had he told you [much about]...'
10 Arnold: [*Ja, jeg vet*] *jeg vet # vi visste nokså mye om det før* =
        '[Yes, I know] I know # we knew quite a lot about it before' =
11 Anne: *Ja.*
        'Yes.'
12 Arnold: = *før vi reiste.*
        = 'before we left.'
13 Inga: *Og det var slik som han hadde fortalt?*
        'And it was the way he had told you?'
14 Arnold: *Ja.*
        'Yes.'   (FG 1:29:01–1:29:18)

Interestingly, the researcher Anne inserts an English word in line 4, a translation of what she has just said in Norwegian. And Arnold then responds in English in line 5. However, he renegotiates Norwegian as the language of interaction in line 8.

In connection with the video-recorded NorAmDiaSyn conversations, the principal investigator followed a protocol including a questionnaire with one of the questions requiring the respondent to answer if she/he were Norwegian or American. Implicit in this type of question is an essentialist conception of identity, that is, that one has one or the other identity (see Section 5 above). This conception is in contrast with the understanding that we espouse in our analysis in which the participants' negotiation of various identities is traced in interaction – the speakers constructed both Norwegian and American identities. Nonetheless such a pointed question revealed interesting responses, as we see below.

(20) 1 Jorun: [..] *er du norsk eller amerikansk?*
        '[..] are you Norwegian or American?'
     2 Sylvia: *norsk*
        'Norwegian'
     3 Jorun: *du er norsk?*
        'You are Norwegian?'
     4 Sylvia: *ja @*
        'Yes @'   (NorAmDiaSyn 01–04)

In line 3, Jorun appears surprised at Sylvia's response that she is Norwegian. This is surely since Sylvia repeatedly switched over to English. Interestingly, Sylvia reconfirms her response in line 4 finishing off with a chuckle, implying that she understands Jorun's surprise.

(21) 1 Jorun: *er du norsk eller amerikansk?*
'Are you Norwegian or American?'
2 Arnold: *norsk eh*
'Norwegian eh'
3 Jorun: *eh kan jeg spørre deg også Eric er er du norsk eller amerikansk?*
'eh can I ask you too Eric are are you Norwegian or American?'
4 Eric: *jeg er # amerikaner # norsk-amerikaner # norsk* **American**
'I am # an American # Norwegian American # Norwegian **American**'
5 Jorun: *ja # ja nei men det er bra svar det # ja # nei men da*
'yes # yes no but that is a good answer # yes # no but then'
6 Eric: *jeg har norsk # norsk blod men # men jeg bor i Amerika* (.)
'I have Norwegian # Norwegian blood # but I live in America' (.)
7 Arnold: *men man prøver å holde seg på n- # norsk så mye som en kan da veit du*
'but we try to stick to N- # Norwegian as much as we can you know' (NorAmDiaSyn 02–03)

Sylvia, who often tried to negotiate language choice in the conversations over to English and hesitated in speaking Norwegian, assuredly acclaims a Norwegian identity, as we see in Example (20). Eric, who attempts to stick to Norwegian, points out that he indeed is both Norwegian and American – Norwegian American. Quite poignantly, he ascribes to himself a Norwegian – American identity in which he uses both languages, as we see in line 4.

8. Multilayered positioning work

We have many identities and in interactions, various identities can be constructed depending on various interactional goals and contexts. The four participants from Coon Valley in the interactions we have analyzed speak from different positions and construct various identities in their narratives – as an elderly person, as a farmer/factory worker, as a brother /wife/ relative, as an American in Coon Valley (and Norway), a Norwegian in Coon Valley, a heritage language maintainer (2nd–3rd generation), a polite host, a humorous person – to name but a few. Their competence and ease in using their variety of Norwegian vary.

Language negotiation is indeed an important feature of a multilingual context (cf. Auer 1998). To study the relationship between cultural identity and language preference (which may be related to linguistic competence), we have analyzed in more detail the extent of the Coon Valley speakers' language use in the focus group conversations. We have compared the four individuals' actual language use in the conversations, including switches into English, the use of English loan words, or the use of English initiated by some of the researchers. We have measured the proportion of turns in

Norwegian for the four speakers in relation to their total number of turns involving discernible elements of English or Norwegian. Turns with the particular Coon Valley /American English vocabulary (established loan words from English into their Norwegian like *fence, rubber, barn, travle*) are coded as Norwegian, but turns with various English elements (insertions of English words not integrated into Coon Valley Norwegian, tags as well as full English turns) are counted as English. Turns with only names, sounds (*hmh, oi*), laughter, and so forth, are considered 'undefinable' and are not counted. Table 2 presents an overview of the four speakers' use of the two languages in the conversations.

Table 2. Speakers' turns at talk in English and Norwegian in the focus group conversations.

Speaker	Sylvia	John	Eric	Arnold
Norwegian	227 (40.8%)	262 (80%)	168 (98.2%)	98 (89.1%)
English	330 (59.2%)	66 (20%)	3 (1.8%)	12 (10.9%)
Total Norwegian & English turns	557	328	171	110
Undefinable turns	54	55	10	8
Total turns	611	383	181	118

In Table 2 we see that the three men had a greater use of Norwegian in their turns than did Sylvia, who had slightly more turns in English. Note that percentages are of turns at talk that are definable as Norwegian or English.

As for the use of English, what is of particular interest is the speaker's use of English in the conversation in response to the use of English in a preceding turn by another person in the interaction (researchers or other participants). In other words, we investigate to what extent the four speakers in focus **initiate** a language negotiation sequence by switching to English or whether they **maintain** English as the language of interaction used by the prior speaker. Table 3 presents the results of this inquiry.

Table 3. Speakers' turns at talk in English in the focus group conversation: Self-initiated or other-initiated.

Speaker	Sylvia	John	Eric	Arnold
English initiated by self	274 (83%)	29 (42%)	3 (100%)	11 (91,7%)
English initiated by others	56 (17%)	37 (58%)	0	1
Total English turns	330	66	3	12

Table 3 indicates that Sylvia not only had more turns with English, she initiated switches to English more often, thus renegotiating language choice in the interaction.

We see that Eric and Sylvia are at different ends of the continuum, with Eric hardly ever switching into English, and Sylvia doing so very frequently. Arnold and John are in the middle and it seems like John also switches into English at times. However, a closer analysis of the speakers' turns reveals that most of John's English turns are a result of other people talking to him in English. In other words, English is initiated by the others. Sylvia, with her frequent switches into English, is present in the conversation with John. Hence, John initiates English more seldom than Arnold although in general John has more Norwegian turns than Arnold.

As we did not measure each participant's linguistic proficiency in Norwegian, we portray the actual language choice as language preference; this is particularly evident in the case of Sylvia. However, it appears clear from the interactions that these preferences reflect the individual's present proficiency in the language or at least the individual's ability to access that knowledge. In this comparison of the speakers, we suggest a scale, from Sylvia on the one end to Eric on the other, indicating their preference for Norwegian, which implicitly indicates their proficiency in the language.

Sylvia	Arnold	John	Eric

Less preference (proficiency)   Most preference (proficiency)

We have also taken heed of how the speakers actually spoke, their differences in comprehending different dialects used by the Norwegian researchers, their awareness of dialects as well as their own comments on their language competence and use. Our evaluation of their fluency is supported by this consideration. An example is how John uses some English words, probably frequent in the Coon Valley or American variety of Norwegian, where Eric uses the expected Norwegian word, e.g., John: *sh- sh- shute døra att døra* ('sh- sh- **shut** the door') (NorAmDiaSyn-data 03-04) as opposed to Eric: *stenge* ('close'), and John: *var* **square** *#* **square** *(.) spiker før den tida* ('were **square** # **square** (.) nails before that time'), as opposed to Eric's utterance: *det er firkanta spiker* ('they are square nails') (NorAmDiaSyn-data 03-04).

Interestingly, Sylvia who uses Norwegian much less in the conversations is the one who stresses her Norwegian identity the most, along with her husband Arnold. Also she refers to other semiotic resources for underscoring this identity as through her many Norwegian artifacts and her maintenance of cultural traditions. The Bakke brothers, on the other hand, did not display such cultural artifacts in their home and they were the ones who used Norwegian the most. However, they had kept Norwegian newspapers and letters, and Eric wrote regularly to a Norwegian relative who had visited them in Coon Valley quite a few years before.

Nonetheless we have to stress that there are other factors rendering Sylvia (or the others) so involved in Norwegian and Norway. Sylvia expresses greater interest in decorating her house and she was more involved in various activities in the community, for example, visiting elderly people in the nursing home. Moreover, both she and her husband were involved in Norwegian heritage activities: this was part of their family activities, doing things together as a couple. The two brothers have spoken Norwegian to each other all their life. Hence gender may also be a factor, and the family situation as well, and last, but not least – these are all elderly people – and hence they like to talk about the old days. And these old days involve aspects of their Norwegian heritage.

9. Discussion and conclusion

The complexity of ethnic identity and the relative importance of language as a marker of ethnic identity are discussed in other heritage language studies. King (2001) provides an insightful account of indigenous communities in South America where the heritage language is threatened. A comparative perspective is applied in King's study of two indigenous yet mostly Spanish-speaking communities in the Ecuadorian highlands whose heritage language is Quechua with the Ecuadorian varieties referred to as Quichua. While the heritage language is the same, each community accorded different values to the language. In the urbanized community, which also comprised non-indigenous arenas, and where the distinction between indigenous and non-indigenous has faded away, Quichua was highly esteemed as a marker of ethnic identity, despite its infrequent use in the community. Indeed it was considered "an indexical sign of ethnic membership" (King 2001: 190). According to the other community, which was rural agro-pastoral, the Quichua language did not have this same value. The defining characteristic of indigenous persons for this community was "that they worked in the countryside with animals; did not mind getting dirty; and regularly traveled long distances by foot" (King 2001: 190). Hence it was their rural lifestyle that was the primary marker of ethnicity, and not the language.

Our analysis focuses on identity construction in the narratives of four speakers in Coon Valley, where we examine the interplay among language, culture and identity through various interactional examples. We investigate the specific interactions these speakers were engaged in – conversations between them and the Norwegian researchers. In other contexts the same speakers may construct other and perhaps different identities. Among these Coon Valley Norwegians, we experienced a situation that appeared to be in a mid-position in comparison with the Quichua communities in Ecuador. Language was highly esteemed as a marker of ethnic identity; indeed there was pride in the fact that the elderly still maintained the language. For those, however, whose fluency in the language was faltering, more emphasis was placed on cultural artifacts and cultural traditions for accentuating ethnic Norwegian identity in the US. In other words, these objects and traditions are allocated socio-cultural meanings by the Coon Valley Norwegians in their identity construction.

Lane (2009) observed a similar phenomenon in her investigation of language shift and identity construction in two Finnish-speaking communities: one in Canada and the other in northern Norway. Although both communities are undergoing language shift and displayed similar objects in their homes, these objects carried overt symbolic value only in the Canadian community, which is geographically much further away from Finland. More ethnographic work in Norwegian-speaking communities in the U.S. will be needed to investigate the relationship between language shift and identity construction.

Other factors are also involved in identity construction among the last users of a heritage language in the community, and these may be individual. De Bot and Schrauf (2009) relate language shift to the so-called MOM framework (Means, Opportunity and Motivation) in referring to individual speakers. As they note (de Bot and Schrauf 2009: 11):

> Elderly bilinguals may show language decline, but again it needs to be established whether such shifts are caused by a decline in linguistic and cognitive *means*, a decline in *opportunities* to use languages in a meaningful way, or a decline in the *motivation* to communicate and use the language.

Regarding the four elderly people from Coon Valley, it seems like the opportunity to use the language is the most important explanation for them; their means are varying but their motivation is still strong. This was clearly demonstrated when Eric took the initiative to ask the researchers what they had learned from their data collection experience, implying that the Norwegians from Norway 'you' (in plural, *dere*) do have things to learn from the Coon Norwegian 'us' (*oss*). Displaying a high degree of agency, he asked the researchers for an evaluation of the Coon Valley Norwegians' participation in the project:

(22) 1 Eric: *Har dere lært noe enda*
 'Have you learned anything yet'
 2 Inga: Hm?
 3 Eric: *Har dere lært noe enda?*
 'Have you learned anything yet?'
 4 Inga: *Ja, [vi har lært] mye, ja.*
 'Yes, [we have learned] a lot, yes.'
 5 Anne: [*Vi har lært mye, vi.*]
 '[We have learned a lot.]'
 6 Eric: *Er dere fornøyde med # oss?*
 'Are you satisfied with # us?' (FG 1:20:07)

The answer is truly that through the interactions with the Coon Valley Norwegians, the Norwegians from Norway did indeed learn a lot about heritage language situations and there is still much more to be discovered. Moreover, they were very satisfied. Coon Valley is a captivating community for investigating issues concerning language, culture and identity among heritage language speakers. And narratives of personal experience provide a privileged site for investigating these issues.

Appendix: Transcription conventions

-	self-interruption
@	laughter
@@@	marked laughter
#	short pause
##	longer pause
\<XXX\>	unclear
[]	overlapping speech
__	stress
(.)	smaller segments left out
=	latching
Bold	English word/utterance
Norwegian	Norwegian utterances
'English'	English translation of Norwegian utterances are given in single quotation marks

References

Ahearn, Laura M. 2001. "Language and Agency." *Annual Review of Anthropology* 30: 109–137. DOI: 10.1146/annurev.anthro.30.1.109

Al Zidjaly, Najma. 2009. "Agency as an Interactive Achievement." *Language in Society* 38: 177–200. DOI: 10.1017/S0047404509090320

Auer, Peter (ed). 1998. *Code-Switching in Conversation*. London: Routledge.

Benwell, Bethan and Elizabeth Stokoe. 2006. *Discourse and Identity*. Edinburgh: Edinburgh University Press.

Blommaert, Jan. 2005. *Discourse: A Critical Introduction*. Cambridge: Cambridge University Press. DOI: 10.1017/CBO9780511610295

Brockmeir, Jens and Donald A. Carbaugh (eds). 2001. *Narrative and Identity. Studies in Autobiography, Self and Culture*. Amsterdam: John Benjamins. DOI: 10.1075/sin.1

Bruner, Jerome. 2001. "Self-Making and World-Making." In *Narrative and Identity. Studies in Autobiography, Self and Culture*, ed. by Jens Brockmeir and Donald A. Carbaugh, 25–37. Amsterdam: John Benjamins. DOI: 10.1075/sin.1.03bru

Bruner, Jerome. 2010. "Narrative, Culture and Mind." In *Telling Stories. Language, Narrative and Social Life*, ed. by Deborah Schiffrin, Anna De Fina and Anastassia Nylund, 45–49. Washington, DC: Georgetown University Press.

Bucholtz, Mary and Kira Hall. 2005. "Identity and Interaction: A Sociocultural Linguistic Approach." *Discourse Studies* 7(4/5): 585–614. DOI: 10.1177/1461445605054407

De Bot, Kees and Robert W. Schrauf (eds). 2009. *Language Development Over the Lifespan*. New York: Routledge.

De Fina, Anna. 2003. *Identity in Narrative. A Study of Immigrant Discourse*. Amsterdam: John Benjamins. DOI: 10.1075/sin.3

De Fina, Anna and Alexandra Georgakopoulou. 2012. *Analyzing Narrative. Discourse and Sociolinguistic Perspectives*. Cambridge: Cambridge University Press.

De Fina, Anna, Deborah Schiffrin and Michael G. W. Bamberg. 2006. *Discourse and Identity*. Cambridge: Cambridge University Press. DOI: 10.1017/CBO9780511584459

Georgakopoulou, Alexandra. 2007. *Small Stories, Interaction and Identity*. Amsterdam: John Benjamins. DOI: 10.1075/sin.8

Gibbs, Raymond W. 1994. *The Poetics of Mind: Figurative Thought, Language and Understanding*. Cambridge: Cambridge University Press.

Golden, Anne and Elizabeth Lanza. 2012. "Narratives on Literacy: Adult Migrants' Identity Construction in Interaction." In *Literacy Practices in Transition. Perspectives from the Nordic Countries*, ed. by Anne Pitkänen and Lars Holm, 27–53. Bristol: Multilingual Matters.

Golden, Anne and Elizabeth Lanza. 2013. "Metaphors of Culture: Identity Construction in Migrants' Narrative Discourse." *Intercultural Pragmatics. Special issue on "Metaphor and Culture: A Relationship at a Crossroads"* 10(2): 295–314.

Harré, Rom and Luk van Langenhove (eds). 1999. *Positioning Theory*. Oxford: Blackwell.

Haugen, Einar. 1953. *The Norwegian Language in America: A Study of Bilingual Behavior*. Bloomington: Indiana University Press.

Hjelde, Arnstein. 2000. *The Norwegian Language in America*. http://nabo.nb.no/trip?_b=EMITEKST&urn=%22URN:NBN:no-nb_emidata_1186%22

Ibarra, Robert A. 1976. *Ethnicity Genuine and Spurious: A Study of a Norwegian Community in Rural Wisconsin."* Madison, WI: University of Wisconsin-Madison dissertation.

Joseph, John E. 2004. *Language and Identity. National, Ethnic, Religious*. New York: Palgrave Macmillan.

King, Kendall. 2001. *Language Revitalization Processes and Prospects*. Bristol: Multilingual Matters.

Kövecses, Zoltan. 2002. *Metaphor. A Practical Introduction*. Oxford: Oxford University Press.

Kövecses, Zoltan. 2006. *Language, Mind, and Culture. A Practical Introduction*. Oxford University Press.

Krueger, Richard A. 1994. *Focus Groups: A Practical Guide for Applied Research*. Thousand Oaks: Sage.

Labov, William. 1972. *Language in the Inner City*. Philadelphia: University of Pennsylvania Press.

Labov, William and Joshua Waletsky. 1967. "Narrative Analysis." In *Essays on the Verbal and Visual Arts*, ed. by June Helm, 12–44. Seattle: University of Washington Press. Reprinted in *Narrative and Life History* 7: 1–38.

Lakoff, George. 1993. "Contemporary Theory of Metaphor." In *Metaphor and Thought*. 2nd edition, ed. by Andrew Ortony, 202–251. Cambridge: Cambridge University Press. DOI: 10.1017/CBO9781139173865.013

Lakoff, George and Mark Johnson. 1980. *Metaphors We Live By*. Chicago: University of Chicago Press.

Lakoff, George and Mark Johnson. 1999. *Philosophy in the Flesh*. New York: Basic Books.

Lane, Pia. 2009. "Identities in Action: A Nexus Analysis of Identity Construction and Language Shift." *Visual Communication* 8(4): 449–468. DOI: 10.1177/1470357209343360

Lantolf, James P. and Steven L. Thorne. 2006. *Sociocultural Theory and the Genesis of Second Language Development*. Oxford: Oxford University Press.

Lanza, Eilzabeth. 2012. "Empowering a Migrant Identity: Agency in Narratives of a Work Experience in Norway." *Sociolinguistic Studies. Special issue on "Agency and Power in Multilingual Practices"* 6(2): 285–307.

Lanza, Elizabeth and Bente A. Svendsen. 2007. "Tell Me Who Your Friends Are and I Might Be Able to Tell You What Language(s) You Speak: Social Network Analysis, Multilingualism, and Identity." *International Journal of Bilingualism* 11(3): 275–300. DOI: 10.1177/13670069070110030201

Lovoll, Odd S. 2006. *Norwegians on the Prairie. Ethnicity and the Development of the Country Town*. St. Paul: Minnesota Historical Society Press.

Mills, Jean. 2004. "Mothers and Mother Tongue: Perspectives on Self-Construction by Mothers of Pakistani Heritage." In *Negotiation of Identities in Multilingual Contexts*, ed. by Aneta Pavlenko and Adrian Blackledge, 161–191. Bristol: Multilingual Matters.

Mukherjee, Dipika. 2003. "Role of Women in Language Maintenance and Language Shift: Focus on the Bengali Community in Malaysia." *International Journal of the Sociology of Language* 161: 103–120.

Munch, Peter A. 1954. "Segregation and Assimilation of Norwegian Settlements in Wisconsin." In *Norwegian-American Studies and Records* 18: 102–140. http://www.naha.stolaf.edu/pubs/nas/volume18new/preface.htm

Ochs, Elinor and Lisa Capps. 2001. *Living Narrative: Creating Lives in Everyday Storytelling*. Cambridge MA: Harvard University Press.

Omoniyi, Tope and Joshua Fishman. 2006. *Explorations in the Sociology of Language and Religion*. Amsterdam: Benjamins. DOI: 10.1075/dapsac.20

Pavlenko, Aneta and Adrian Blackledge. 2004. *Negotiation of Identities in Multilingual Contexts*. Multilingual Matters.

Riessman, Catherine K. 1993. *Narrative Analysis*. Newbury Park: Sage.

Skjåk, Knut K. and Bjug Bøyum. 1995. *Intervjuundersøking om nasjonal identitet* [Interview investigation of national identity]. NSD Rapporter, Nr. 103. Bergen: Norsk samfunnsvitenskapelig datatjeneste.

Smolicz, Jerzy J. 1981. "Core Values and Cultural Identity." *Ethnic and Racial Studies* 4(1): 75–90. DOI: 10.1080/01419870.1981.9993325

Wilkerson, Miranda E. and Joseph Salmons. 2008. "'Good Old Immigrants of Yesteryear' Who Didn't Learn English: Germans in Wisconsin." *American Speech* 83(3): 259–283. DOI: 10.1215/00031283-2008-020

Wortham, Stanton. 2000. "Interactional Positioning and Narrative Self-Construction." *Narrative Inquiry* 10(1): 157–184. DOI: 10.1075/ni.10.1.11wor

Variation and change in American Swedish

Ida Larsson*, Sofia Tingsell** and Maia Andréasson**
*University of Oslo / **The University of Gothenburg

This chapter surveys variation and change in Swedish spoken in America. We compare data from a corpus of American Swedish collected in Minnesota 2011 with material collected in the 1960s. Linguistic change in American Swedish can partly be accounted for in terms of koinéization. Marked dialect features seem to have disappeared quickly from American Swedish, but we can also observe dialect mixing and simplifications in, e.g., the pronominal system. At the same time, Swedish has been lost in the public domain, and there is considerable variation between speakers even with the same dialect background. It can also be noted that some speakers (even those that have Swedish as a first language) now have linguistic features that are otherwise typical of second language learners. We attribute this to the loss of Swedish-speaking communities, but view it as features of language learning rather than attrition. The paper concludes that it is mainly in the lexicon that American Swedish stands out. This variety of Swedish has its roots in a *koiné* situation of speakers of different Swedish dialects living together, but also includes language-contact traits from English.

Keywords: American Swedish, heritage language, koinéization, dialect leveling, language contact, bilingual acquisition, attrition

1. Introduction

From the late 1800s to the early 1900s, as many as 1.3 million Swedes left their homeland to find a new life in America. People from all parts of Sweden emigrated, although different areas and social groups were represented to a varying extent in different periods, e.g., Hasselmo (1974: 12). This means that a large proportion of the world's Swedish speakers actually lived in America at that time. Even today many Swedes emigrate to the United States. Despite this, we do not know much about the Swedish spoken in America during the great emigration, nor do we know much about contemporary American Swedish.

In the 1960s, a large body of American Swedish material was collected, over 300 hours of recorded speech, and based on this material a few studies were published (see

Hedblom, 1963, 1970, 1978, 1982). However, with the exception of Hasselmo (1974), few major linguistic studies of Swedish language in America have been published (but see Karstadt 2003, a longitudinal study on linguistic variation and identity). The project 'Swedish in America' is investigating Swedish language in the U.S. today and to what extent today's American Swedish differs from the Swedish spoken in the U.S. 50 years ago. In June 2011, we made our first field trip to Minnesota to collect new material. We can now study linguistic change in American Swedish in real time (cf. Bailey 2002, Sundgren 2002, and Hjelde this volume).

In this chapter, we give an overview of the new material and from our initial observations outline what seems to be central aspects of the development of American Swedish, and discuss the processes involved. We do not give quantitative data or detailed analyses of specific linguistic phenomena (but see Larsson and Johannessen 2015a, 2015b, for a study of embedded word order and Tingsell 2013 on reflexives).

In Section 2, we present our consultants and methods of data collection. Sections 3, 4 and 5 focus on factors that bear on linguistic variation and change in American Swedish, and which in some way relate to contact between linguistic systems. First, Section 3 considers factors related to variation within Swedish, dialect features in American Swedish, and koinéization. Section 4 gives a short overview of features that are due to contact between Swedish and English. In Section 5, we discuss individual variation relating to acquisition and attrition in different settings, and consider factors that relate to the multilingual situation. Section 6 gives a summary and conclusion.

2. Data collection

Recordings made by Folke Hedblom and Torsten Ordéus in the 1960s consist of interviews of varying length (and varying degrees of formality) with 1st–4th generation speakers of Swedish, with family from almost all areas of Sweden. Many of the consultants are first generation immigrants who emigrated from Sweden as children or young adults. Others are descendants of Swedes who emigrated during the 19th or early 20th century, and many of them grew up with Swedish as the only first language (L1).[1] Some of the consultants clearly have English as the strongest language, but Hedblom was particularly interested in Swedish dialects, and not in heritage language, second language (L2) acquisition or language attrition, and this is reflected in different ways in the material.

---

1. We use the term 'first language' to refer to a native language acquired naturalistically in a home(-like) setting, from birth. The term 'second language' here includes languages that are not acquired from birth, but which might have been acquired naturalistically and partly in a home(-like) setting. We use the term 'heritage language' for a first language which is not the dominant language in the society.

The main purpose of the 2011 Minnesota fieldwork was to document Swedish spoken in the United States today, and make it possible to investigate change in American Swedish since the 1960s. We made recordings with different groups of speakers to get an overview of the speech community and enable comparison between different types of speakers, and we used several methodologies in the data collection. In this section, we give a short overview of this new material (see also Andréasson et al. 2013).

2.1 Interviews, questionnaires and elicitation

During fieldwork, we collected four different types of linguistic material: a relatively free conversation (interview) between the consultant and a researcher, a guided conversation where the consultant speaks on the basis of a series of pictures, an oral questionnaire where grammaticality judgments were elicited, and finally a written survey on the consultant's (linguistic) background.[2] The methods were intended to capture different linguistic abilities, from free speech to grammar skills and intuitions.

In the interviews, which constitute the largest part of the material, the consultants talk freely about topics of their own choice; the interviewer spoke as little as possible. The subjects mostly cover topics like personal immigration history, childhood and memories, and language use. The background survey provides us with opportunities to put the consultants' linguistic practice in a larger context and to relate it to the multilingual situation. The background survey also addresses underlying factors that enable sociolinguistic and dialectological studies.

2.2 Consultants

Many early Swedish Americans lived in areas where Swedish was used both in schools and in church up until the 1920s, both in the cities and the countryside (cf. Hedblom 1963: 115). In these linguistic enclaves, Swedish newspapers were published and read, and people could to a large extent get around in their everyday lives speaking mainly Swedish. Even today there are descendants of the many Swedes who emigrated in the late 19th or early 20th century who speak Swedish, and who have Swedish as their only L1. Some tell us that they did not learn English until they started school. However, these speakers are now typically over 80 years old, and the old emigrant Swedish variety must now largely be described as dying (as noted already by Hasselmo 1974). Descendants of the fourth generation immigrants seem to acquire Swedish at home only very rarely. One of the purposes of the data collection was to document this early American Swedish before it has completely disappeared.

At the same time, it was important to include other types of speakers of American Swedish in the investigation, in order to get a clearer view of the American Swedish

---

2. Not all speakers were able to provide grammaticality judgments (due to age, etc.).

speech community, and to allow for comparison (e.g., to isolate factors determining the linguistic competence of the speakers; see Section 5 and cf. Larsson and Johannessen 2015a, b and Tingsell 2013). The material therefore includes both more recent immigrants (and their descendants), and consultants who have learned and do speak Swedish, but not as (their only) first language.

Altogether 45 consultants were interviewed and recorded. Most were second-generation (23) or third-generation (18) immigrants. Four of the third-generation immigrants spoke very little or no Swedish. Four speakers were first-generation immigrants; two had immigrated as adults and two had arrived with their parents, as children. 12 state that Swedish was either the only or the most common language in their homes during their childhood, and 16 give English as their stronger home language. Today, English is by all measures the stronger language for all American-born speakers, and these speakers generally report that they only speak Swedish once or twice a week, or less often. With few exceptions, they do not read or write Swedish.

All in all, 37 speakers had parents or grandparents that emigrated from Sweden before 1930, or were themselves first generation immigrants that arrived earlier. 8 speakers were descendants of emigrants that left Sweden after 1930, and two were first generation immigrants that emigrated after 1930. The language situation for more recent Swedish Americans was of course very different from the situation for the many early immigrants. The group of speakers that are descendants of people that emigrated during the later part of the 20th century, or who emigrated themselves during the second half of the 20th century, typically had learned English in school in Sweden, and they therefore knew some English already on arrival in America. Moreover, they generally did not settle in Swedish enclaves, or continue to attend Swedish church, etc. Their children have grown up in an English-speaking community, and this obviously has had consequences for parents' as well as children's use of Swedish in their homes. At the same time, these speakers have new means of communicating with other Swedish speakers. Many of them are active in Swedish heritage societies and travel to Sweden from time to time.

In the following, we consider some of the factors that have played a role in the development of American Swedish, investigating both how American Swedish differs from Standard Swedish, and how present-day American Swedish differs from the older American Swedish described, e.g., by Hedblom and Hasselmo.[3] Here, we focus on descendants of people who emigrated in the period between 1850–1930. In the next section, we consider the dialect situation in America.

---

3. The term 'Standard Swedish' is used to refer to the standard as spoken in Sweden, and the term 'Standard American Swedish' refers to the variety spoken in America. The former and the latter are clearly not standards in precisely the same sense. Standard American Swedish has, for instance, never been taught in schools, and it is not a written language.

3. Dialects in American Swedish

During the mass-emigration around 1850–1930, many of the emigrants chose to settle in the same area as family members or others from the same home district. However, emigration generally led to contact among people from different dialect areas, and the children of those first immigrants came to grow up in heterogeneous Swedish-speaking communities. Hedblom (1992: 8, our translation) talks about "a violent rearrangement of the geography of the traditional dialects." Neighbors could speak widely different dialects and even have a hard time understanding each other's Swedish. Hedblom reports that some of his consultants had adopted (or had tried to adopt) a new dialect (1963: 148). Against this background, one could expect that dialects were leveled and that a koiné gradually developed. By koiné we mean a new variety is "a result of contact between speakers of mutually intelligible varieties of that language" and which "occurs in new settlements to which people, for whatever reason, have migrated from different parts of a single language area" (Kerswill 2002: 669).

In this section, we compare the use of dialect features in the recordings from the 1960s with speakers in the new material. We focus on speakers that are descendants from areas in Northern Sweden (cf. Hedblom 1978 on the dialect spoken in Hälsingland), and speakers with Swedish as their L1. Section 3.1 gives a background to the dialectal variation in Sweden at the time of emigration. Section 3.2 and 3.3 discusses the use of dialect features in the 1960s and today. Finally, Section 3.4 is concerned with dialect leveling and language contact more generally.

3.1 Linguistic variation in Sweden in the 19th century

Spoken Standard Swedish is a rather recent phenomenon. In the 19th century, there was considerable geographical and social variation in Swedish. As noted, American Swedish immigrants from different areas of Sweden sometimes had a hard time understanding each other. At the same time, already in the 17th century, there seem to have been tendencies towards a spoken language in Sweden that was not specific to certain geographical areas.

In a discussion of Swedish from the 18th century, Sven Hof (born 1703) distinguishes three different speech styles: "the speech of the common man" with a pronunciation that separates the speaker from "honest people," "common speech," used in daily life, and "public speech," used in speaking to a large group of people (Hof 1753: §117 f.). The good 'common speech' includes pronunciations like *allri* for written *aldrig* 'never'; the reading pronunciation [aldrig] is common in Present-Day Swedish. At the same time, Hof dislikes dialect forms like *fräga* [fræːga] for *fråga* [frɔːga] 'question,' or *stolana* for *stolarna* 'the chairs.' The common speech variety is not dialect, nor does it involve reading pronunciation, and it is not simply the language of the Bible ('Book Swedish' in the terminology of Widmark 2000). Widmark (2000) points out that it should be treated as a sociolect, rather than a dialect or standard language in the modern sense. In the 17th–18th centuries, it is more than anything the language spoken by educated people and nobility. Like Hof, Samuel Columbus (born 1642) locates 'the best language' in a rather large area with Stockholm and Uppsala as the center (e.g., Larsson 2004).

A distinction between speech styles similar to Hof's is still made in descriptions from the end of the 19th and beginning of the 20th centuries (e.g., Lyttkens and Wulff 1889, Noreen 1903 and the discussion in Widmark 2000). For instance, Noreen (1903) distinguished the following spoken forms: *hafver han tagit det* 'has he taken it' in public speech versus *ha(r) han tagi(t) de(t)* in private society and *ha n tatt* (or *taji, teje*) *e(t)* in less educated private society (1903: 30). We thus note considerable differences between stylistic levels, and variation within a given style. As in the 17th and 18th centuries, the 'common speech' is connected to education and status, and dialect features seem to have been associated with lower status and with the peasantry.

Through the reformation and the translation of the Bible (in 1541), the Swedish language gained a stronger position in church. In Laurentius Petri's church ordinance (1571), it is said that during the morning song children should read three paragraphs, chosen so that the content is suitable 'for the people.' During the evening song, children heard the catechism, read in Swedish. Records from the parish catechetical meeting suggest that the Swedish population was to a large extent able to read as early as the 17th century. School attendance (for six years) was made compulsory in Sweden in 1882, and it is likely that at least some work was done in order to make pupils adopt a standard-like pronunciation.

In the 19th century, many Swedish speakers in other words had access to a (regional) standard or Book Swedish, through school and church. At least to some extent, they had a linguistic repertoire that let them switch between varieties or styles depending on situation. This is obviously true also for some of the Swedes that emigrated to America at the time. However, the large groups of farmers and workers without higher education who emigrated during the second part of the 19th century and beginning of the 20th century most likely spoke dialect, i.e., had a linguistic system which differed from the standard language in systematic ways and which could be geographically located. At the same time, these speakers presumably had some awareness of the lower status of dialects, and they had some (passive) knowledge of official or standard language. We can further assume that they had had more contact with Book Swedish (through written texts and the church) than with the spoken language of the nobility.

The dialects themselves were obviously not completely unaffected by the development of the standard. By the end of 19th century, migration within Sweden also has some linguistic effects. In the American Swedish recordings made in the 1960s, Mrs. Backlund, born 1891 in Ragunda (Jämtland, Northern Sweden), tells Hedblom about linguistic changes that arose when they built the local power plant and people moved there from other parts of Sweden; see (1).[4] Mrs. Backlund states in her discussion

---

4. Hedblom's recordings are referred to by the tape number that the recording has in the archive of the Institute of Language and Folklore in Uppsala All proper names that refer to new recordings have been anonymized, but Hedblom's consultants have not.

with Hedblom that people started speaking "better". Still today, dialect speakers in the area refer to the regional standard as "speaking more properly" or "speaking better." In Northern Sweden, the standard language had the strongest influence in the towns along the coast, and in places where power plants or lumber industries were developed.

(1) *de medförde ju att de kåm fålk ifrån alla håh-* (.)
    that led.to   PART that there came people from all pla-
    'This lead to (a situation where) people came from

   olika landskap i Sverje (.) *så de blev*
   different regions in Sweden so it became
   different regions in Sweden and it [i.e., the language] became

   uppblandat å dåm tala mera fint såm man säjer
   mixed   and they spoke more nicely as you say
   mixed, and they spoke better, so to speak.'

                                               Mrs. Backlund
   born 1891 in Ragunda, Jämtland
   Recorded by Hedblom, AM90B

Some American Swedes did not emigrate directly from the home community but first spent time in a Swedish city, working in the growing industries (cf. Hedblom 1992, who uses the term 'secondary immigration').

For our purposes, it is important to distinguish in principle between changes within a single variety – or the grammatical system of individuals – and alternations between one variety (or speech style in the sense of Hof and Noreen) and another (e.g., between dialect and standard).[5] In the American Swedish context, we can note changes within the language of individual speakers which cannot simply be understood as a switch from one stable or invariant variety to another, but rather involves the development of a new variety. This American Swedish variety largely seems to develop out of the dialects, in a situation of extensive dialect contact, but it is clearly also affected by English (as we will see further in Section 4 below), and it is probably not completely independent of (speakers attitudes towards) the development of a spoken standard in Sweden. We return to this complexity in Section 3.4 below.

3.2 Dialects in earlier American Swedish

As noted above, the Swedish dialects were at the time of emigration associated with low status and the lower social classes, both in Sweden and Swedish America (cf.

---

5. We are well aware that it is hardly possible to give a principled definition of the term 'variety' (e.g., Fraurud and Boyd 2011). At the same time, the term is clearly useful to discuss the language of a group of individuals who communicate with each other, and whose language therefore share some characteristics, and distinguishes them from other groups. We obviously do not mean to say that a variety is ever completely homogeneous or stable.

Hedblom 1992: 8, 12).⁶ Hedblom (1992: 23) observes that his American Swedish consultants prefer the Swedish varieties spoken in the central parts of Sweden (around Stockholm and Uppsala), just like Columbus and Hof did some centuries earlier. Our consultants sometimes mention that older relatives were teased for speaking dialect. To avoid linguistic class marking, early American Swedes often switched to English as soon as they could (Hasselmo 1974: 75 ff.).

One of our consultants explains that her grandmother wanted her to learn "proper Swedish" and not the peasant variety that she herself knew. Hedblom (1963) notes that, contrary to his expectations, only a minority of his consultants speak 'traditional' dialect. Instead, the majority have a leveled and standard-like (or bookish) language, with influence from English. For instance, during the interview with Hedblom, Mrs. Backlund in Example (1) above has a regionally colored standard-like language, often with reading pronunciation (cf. Example (4) below). It is, however, not self-evident that she speaks the same way with Folke Hedblom as she would, e.g., with her children. On the contrary, Mrs. Backlund's repertoire allows her to speak both dialect and 'more properly' (see further below). Also other speakers in the recordings from the 1960s admit that they speak dialect at home, but are reluctant to do so during the interview, even though Hedblom tries to persuade them. Hedblom himself speaks Standard Swedish with northern elements. As a university professor, he has considerable theoretical knowledge of the dialects and has a northern dialect in his own repertoire. (See Nilsson 2011 for a discussion of how dialect speakers adapt their language in discourse.)

However, a minority of the speakers in the recordings from the 1960s speak dialect even during the interview. Mrs. Hansson from Resele (Ångermanland, Northern Sweden) is one of these, see (2) below. She emigrated to Mora, Minnesota, as a child, at the very beginning of the 20th century.

(2) MrsH: *så döppe dåm å   (.) um vartanne (.) hele natta tycke*
so dipped they and   by turns   all night think
'So they dipped in turns. All the night, I think

ja dåm va   juppe [(.)] å   jorde ljuse   (.) å =
I they were up   and made the.candles   and
they were up, to make the candles and'

INT: [a]
ah
'Ah'

---

6. In this respect, the conditions for the development of American Swedish is slightly different from those for, e.g., American Norwegian (cf. Johannessen and Laake this volume). In Norwegian, dialects are not in the same way associated with social status, and for a long time Danish was used as the written language in Norway.

MrsH: = inge(n)   fick   gå å   öppne döra   (dåm had börte)
         no.one   could   go and   open the.door   they had away
         'no one was allowed to open the door [...]

för   då   vart'e   bögn   på ljuse
because then   became.it   bends   on the.candle
because then, the candles would come out curved.'   Mrs. Hansson
                                                        born 1893 in Resele, Ångermanland
                                                        Recorded by Hedblom, 113B_m

Mrs. Hansson's language has many of the features we expect in the dialect of Ångermanland (e.g., Dahlstedt and Ågren 1980). In Hansson's vowel system, we can note [oː] or [ɔ] for Standard Swedish [aː] or [a] in [boːna] 'the children' and [kɔlt] 'cold'.[7] Moreover, Hansson has [i] for standard [e], e.g., in [himː] 'home'. The retroflex [d] in the standard corresponds to a cacuminal *l*, e.g., in [kaɽe] 'to card'. Vowels are reduced or lost, e.g., in the suffixal definite article, as in *båtn* 'the boat' for standard *båten,* or *tin* 'the time' for standard *tiden.* The sentence negation is reduced from *inte* to *itt* or *int.* Also vowel length sometimes differs from Standard Swedish. Mrs. Hansson says [døːra] 'the door' for standard [dœrːən] in (4). According to the historical dictionary SAOB (1893–), this form is 'highly dialectal'. Unlike Standard Swedish, Mrs. Hansson also shows examples of vowel balance. In the verbal inflection, infinitives with an old long root syllable end in -*e*, whereas old short syllabic roots form infinitives with an -*a: fiske* 'to fish,' *styre* 'to rule, control,' *stärne* 'to stop' but *täla* 'speak' and *vära* 'be'. In Standard Swedish, infinitives always take -*a.*

In Mrs. Hansson's noun inflection, we can observe definite plurals in -*en* as in *getten* 'the goats' (standard *getterna*) and *nätten* 'the nights' (standard *nätterna*). Definite singular forms of feminine nouns end in -*a*, as in *döra* 'the door' or *natta* 'the night' in the example above. Feminine and masculine pronouns are used also to refer to inanimates. Standard Swedish has not preserved feminine and masculine as separate genders, and has a specific common gender pronoun (*den*) for inanimates. Hansson does, on the other hand, not make a morphological distinction between nominative and accusative case of pronouns. She has [døm] or [dem] for the standard variant [dɔm] both in subject and object position; see (3). In the feminine, the form *a* is used for standard *hon* 'she' or *henne* 'her,' and *n* is used in the masculine for *han* 'he' or *honom* 'him'. To Noreen (1903), the forms *a* and *n* belong in the 'less educated private discourse.'

---

7. In Old Swedish (c. 1200–1526), the syllable system is simplified and the vowel system changes considerably (e.g., Widmark 1998 on the Swedish Great Vowel Shift). Different areas are affected in different ways, and at partly different times, and the vowel systems vary considerably between dialects.

(3) MrsH: *båna   er besynnerlig ja kan en- aller   minnes- s att je*
children are strange   I can   never remember that I
'Children are funny, I can never remember that I

fö- je förstog   va   såm eh (.) eh va   såm sa-e va
un- I understood what that eh   eh what that said what
un-… I did understand what was said, what

dem jole fast   int ja kunne täla
they did although not I   could speak
they did, even though I couldn't speak.'

INT: *(ja) så*
                                              yes so
                                              'Yes so'

MrsH: *ja kan ja kan (alle) minnes   va nån ti   såm int*
I can I can   never remember was any time that not
'I can never remember that there was any time

såm int ja visste va   såm gick försegick
that not I knew what that went went.on
that I did not know what was going on.'   Mrs. Hansson
                                   born 1893 in Resele, Ångermanland
                                   Recorded by Hedblom, 113B_m

In syntax, Hansson places the negation before a weak subject pronoun, e.g., a 'high' negation, illustrated two times in Example (3) (see Johannessen and Garbacz 2011 for discussion), which is not consistent with the Swedish standard. In the lexicon, we find dialectal forms like *bögn* 'bends,' and the copula *varda* 'become' for standard *bli* (see Lundqvist 2014 for an overview of *varda* and *bli* in contemporary Scandinavian dialects). In other words, Mrs. Hansson's language is dialectal throughout, in phonology, morphology, syntax and lexicon.

In the older American Swedish recordings, there are speakers with the same or a very similar dialectal background as Mrs. Hansson, who lack all or almost all of the mentioned dialect features. Mrs. Friesendahl from Näsåker in Ångermanland says [baɳ] 'children' not the dialectal [boːn], [hemː] 'home' not [himː], *nätterna* 'the nights' not *nätten*, *inte* 'not' not *itt* or *int*, i.e., she uses the Standard Swedish forms. In some cases, she even has reading pronunciations like [laːdugoːdaɳa] for standard [lagoːdaɳa] 'the barns' and [soːdana] for standard [sɔna] 'such.' The dialect word for 'barn' is *föjs* (from *fä-hus* 'cattle-house'), and it is mentioned by Hedblom during the interview. Generally, Mrs. Friesendahl does not use dialectal lexical forms, and she lacks dialectal features like vowel balance. However, her language is not completely without regional features. For instance, she uses the pronoun *han* 'he' to refer to masculine inanimates like the road or the village, and the possessive form is *hanses* not *hans* as in Standard Swedish. Friesendahl also often has non-agreeing predicative adjectives, as in (4). This is typical of many northern dialects and of the Northern Regional Standard.[8]

(4) *första året   vi   var gift*
    first the.year we were married
    'the first year we were married'

                                                                                 Mrs. Friesendahl
                                          born 1878 in Näsåker, Ångermanland
                                              Recorded by Hedblom, Am117A_m

As illustrated by the examples from Mrs. Hansson and Mrs. Friesendahl, the old recordings include speakers with dialect features on all linguistic levels as well as speakers who have a leveled language with only few regional elements. In other words, we find the entire span of variation that we expect in speakers that emigrated from Sweden around the turn of the 19th century, given the observations in Lyttkens and Wulff (1889) and Noreen (1903). However, as noted, the standard or 'common speech' was hardly fully established among the Swedish peasantry. In America, the situation is different: we find dialect speakers, but, like Hedblom, we can observe a rather rapid leveling of dialects among the majority of speakers and the establishment of a new common variety (which however contains both intra- and inter-individual variation). Although Mrs. Friesendahl does not speak in dialect, her language is in several ways distinct from Standard Swedish (cf. Section 4). Hasselmo (1974) talks about an 'American Swedish norm.'

3.3 Dialect features in present-day American Swedish

In the new recordings, there is also considerable variation between speakers. This variation can however not easily be understood in terms of a span from highly dialectal speakers to regional standard, Book Swedish or what can be referred to as Standard American Swedish. On the contrary, neither of the extremes can be found in the new material. Most of our consultants have a language with some regional flavor, with more or fewer dialectal traits, but what dialectal features are present varies. One speaker can have dialect features that are missing in another speaker with the same background (who in turn can have features that are missing in the language of the former). In this section, we look more closely at two speakers, Gerald and Albert, who are descendants from Ångermanland (and Medelpad) in Northern Sweden, just like Mrs. Hansson and Mrs. Friesendahl. Both Gerald and Albert have Swedish as their L1, and for Albert, it is his only L1. Gerald is born in Mora, Minnesota, where Mrs. Hansson was recorded almost 50 years earlier.

---

8. Absence of agreement can sometimes also be a consequence of language contact and attrition. In this context it is, however, clearly dialectal, since Mrs. Friesendahl's morphology does not show any other signs of attrition or influence from English morphology.

From prosody alone, it is immediately clear that Gerald's family comes from Northern Sweden. In phonology and morphology, there are features that place his speech in or around Ångermanland. In Example (5) below, we note dialectal present tense forms of verbs without an ending: *behöv* 'need' for standard *behöv-er*, and also the infinitival -s form *känns* 'feel' for standard *kännas* has a regional flavor of Northern Swedish. Moreover, Gerald uses the pronominal from *ne* 'it' for Standard Swedish *den* (common gender) or *det* (neuter), and this form can be found in Ångermanland. Dialectal features like these do not occur in the standard-like language, e.g., of Mrs. Friesendahl, but are part of the dialect.

(5) du behöv inte betala mej för   ja ÅCKSÅ kåm från
you need not pay me because I also come from
'You don't need to pay me, because I also come from

Sverje å ja hade ne mycke SVÅRT att börje bli
Sweden and I had it very hard to start become
Sweden and I had a very hard time when I started to become

dåktor här i Amerika (.) så att nu vet ja att hur du
doctor here in America so that now know I that how you
a doctor here in America, so now I know how things are for you.

har ne så du fö- du behöv inte känns att du måst betala mej
have.it so you fo- you need not feel that you must pay me
So you don't need to feel that you have to pay me.'   Gerald, born 1926
parents from Skorped, Ångermanland

At the same time, many of the features found in Mrs. Hansson's dialect are clearly missing in Gerald's. Gerald sometimes has the standard form *inte* 'not,' sometimes the regional *int*, but the form *itt* is missing. Pronunciations like [boːn] 'child' are also missing; Gerald uses the standard form [baːɲ]. We can note vowel reduction as in *börje* 'to begin' for standard *börja* in the example above (line 2), but no systematic vowel balance. The pronominal forms *a* 'she/her' and *n* 'he/him' are missing. In the example above, he has the copula *bli* 'become' and not *varda* like Mrs. Hansson. On the whole, Gerald's vocabulary seems to contain very few (if any) dialect-specific words.

In other words, we note both leveling and simplification in Gerald's language, as compared to the more conservative dialect spoken by Mrs. Hansson. At the same time, Gerald's language is distinct both from Standard Swedish and the standard-like American Swedish spoken by Mrs. Friesendahl, and contains dialectal or marked features that are missing in the language of speakers like Mrs. Friesendahl in the old recordings.

Albert has preserved the dialect to a higher extent than Gerald; see (6) where he talks about someone from southern Sweden who is hard to understand.

(6) A: de va så hårt- hård å förstå'n
it was so hard hard to understand.him
'It was so hard to understand him.'

INT: *ja*
yes
'Yes'
A: *hja*
h-yes
'h-Yes'
INT: *de e annorlunda*
it is different
'It's different.'
A: *ja* (.) *hanne-* (.) *han levde omtrent tjugu mil*
yes he- he lived about twenty miles
'Yes, he lived about twenty miles
från K--- här
from K --- here
from K---'
INT: *ja*
yes
'Yes'
A: *å när han ble äldre så flytte'n in till*
and when he became older so moved.he
'and when he got older, he moved into
stan här (.) *å när ja tjöre påstn så kåm en*
town here and when I drive the.mail so came one
town here. And when I was delivering the post, he came
fram (.) *å skulle prata mej- mä mej*
forward and would talk me with me
up to me and tried to speak to me'
INT: *ja*
yes
'Yes'
A: *å han var så hör- hård ti att förstå* *hehehe*
and he was so hear- hard to to understand *laughter*
'and he was so hard to understand (LAUGHTER).
ja vante- ja vante (*varn en*)
I wasn't I wasn't (used him)
I wasn't used to him.'
INT: *ja*
yes
'Yes' Albert
born 1921, parents from Matfors,
Medelpad and Hoting, Ångermanland.

In Albert's language, we find several dialectal features that we know from Mrs. Hansson. With respect to phonology, he has forms like [duːter] for [dɔtːer] 'daughter' and a retroflex *n* in [vaːɳ] 'used to' for standard [vaːn], which are highly dialectal. In the pronominal system we find forms like *a* for 'she/her' and *n* for 'he/him.' Albert's language can, however, hardly be considered dialectal at all linguistic levels, like Mrs. Hansson's. Just like Gerald, Albert says [baːɳ] 'child' and [hemː] 'home,' and the copula is *bli* 'become.' His lexicon shows few dialectal elements. For instance, Albert says *potatis* 'potato' and not *pära*, which is common in Northern Swedish dialects, and *prata* 'talk' not *tala* or *täla* 'talk' like Mrs. Hansson. In the example above, we also note the word *omtrent* 'around' which most likely is from Norwegian; it is not part of the (dialectal) vocabulary in Sweden. Albert also at some point says *akkurat* 'precisely,' which is also Norwegian; the Swedish word would be *precis*. During the interview, Albert says that there were many Norwegians in the area when he grew up and that nobody speaks "pure Swedish anymore."

Compared to the dialect speakers in the recordings from the 1960s, both Gerald and Albert are more leveled, and we can also note both dialect mixing (or language mixing) and simplifications in their linguistic systems. Compared to the standard-like speakers in the older material, on the other hand, our consultants seem to speak more dialect, if anything. On the whole, it seems as if the public or official American Swedish has disappeared in the course of the last 50 years. Descendants of speakers like Mrs. Backlund, Mrs. Hansson and Mrs. Friesendahl do not read and write Swedish, and they can hardly be said to live in Swedish-speaking communities. In other words, Swedish has lost more or less its entire public domain (for discussion of some further implications of this domain loss, see Section 5), but survived as a home language, and the home variety tends to be dialect. During the interview, Mrs. Backlund lets Hedblom know that she speaks dialect with her children, and that "that seems easier for them." Speakers like Gerald and Albert, who belong to the same generation as Mrs. Backlund's children, do not alternate between different varieties of Swedish (e.g., dialect and Standard America Swedish) depending on situation. They only have one Swedish variety in their repertoire, a leveled American Swedish (with some marked dialectal features), and they alternate between this variety and English.

3.4 Dialect leveling and language contact

While the most standard-like American Swedish has largely disappeared since Hedblom and Ordéus made their recordings in the 1960s, we can, as we saw above, note dialect leveling, mixing and simplifications also in Present-Day American Swedish. Hedblom (1992) states that the 'traditional' dialects do not survive in America for more than three generations, at least not outside the linguistically most homogeneous areas. It can also be noted that already second generation American Swedes have a weaker conception of the linguistic norm – they can no longer identify 'the best Swedish.'

The tendencies towards standardization, and the linguistic attitudes that the immigrants brought with them from their home country, are likely to have affected the direction that the development of American Swedish took. At the same time, it seems clear that the linguistic situation in the immigrant communities accelerated the change. In Sweden at the time, the linguistic situation can be described in terms of variation between varieties (e.g., public language and dialect) among certain speakers. In America, we can in a different way note a rapid leveling of the dialects (i.e., change within a variety).

The American Swedish described by Hedblom and Hasselmo can to a large extent be understood in terms of koinéization (cf. Kerswill 2002, Johannessen and Laake this volume, Hjelde this volume on Norwegian, and Boas 2009, Nützel and Salmons 2011 on German). As noted, Hedblom observes that a minority of his consultants speak dialect, and Hasselmo uses the term 'American Swedish norm.' When people from different dialect areas migrate and come to settle in the same community, they tend to adapt to one another. As far as we can see, American Swedes avoid dialect-specific vocabulary. The also use elements from different dialects or languages, and in some cases a dialect-specific word can instead be established as part of the standard (see Section 4).

According to Kerswill (2002), mixing and leveling (i.e., loss of marked or unusual features) are typical for koinéization. In the development of a koiné, we also expect simplifications in the system, like the loss of gender distinctions and vowel balance in the language of Gerald. In the new recordings, we further note more variation both within and across speakers, as compared with earlier generations.

The development of American Swedish since the 1960s can, however, not be construed fully in terms of continuous koinéization. Rather, the loss of Swedish in the public domain seems to have led to a reintroduction of dialect features into American Swedish (perhaps again followed by leveling), but on an individual level. As we will see further below, speakers like Gerald and Albert integrate features from the old standard-like American Swedish into their language, as well as features from the dialect that their parents or grandparents brought with them.

The situation is however more complex, since it is hardly possible to completely distinguish the processes that depend on dialect contact from those that are tied to contact between Swedish and English. On the contrary, the noted variation, leveling and simplification can also to some extent be explained by bilingualism and contact with English, just like the loss of the standard-like and public American Swedish is a consequence of the weaker position of Swedish, both in the American society and in the individual. We can observe direct influence of English in the language of both Gerald and Albert. In Example (5), Gerald places an adverbial before the finite verb, as in English: he says *jag också kom från Sverige* 'I also came from Sweden' which would be judged ungrammatical by native speakers in Sweden (see Section 4.3 and 5). Albert says that the speaker from southern Sweden was *hård te förstå* 'hard to understand,' not like most Swedes' *svår att förstå* 'difficult to understand.' The influence of English seems stronger in Gerald than in Albert, and it is not only lexical but has also affected word order. It is also possible that the simplifications in the pronominal systems, or the absence of overt present tense morphology, are consequences of the bilingualism of the speakers. It is well known that, e.g., morphological gender is sensitive, both in second language acquisition and in attrition (see Section 5, and, e.g., Håkansson 1995 and Schmid 2002).

Even if some of the features of Present-Day American Swedish clearly are a consequence of dialect contact and dialect mixing, we hardly expect complete koinéization in American Swedish, since Swedish is reduced to a language used primarily between family members (if at all). Instead, the development seems to involve a gradual switch to English. In the following section, we look at some contact features in American Swedish observed in the recordings from the 1960s and our new material. We try to isolate some features that may be seen as specific to American Swedish, and features that the early immigrants seem to have shared, independent of their geographical origin in Sweden.

4. Contact features in American Swedish

In the previous section, we argued that the development of American Swedish can to some degree be understood in terms of koinéization. Koinéization is generally understood as the development of a new variety through contact between mutually intelligible varieties of a language (dialects). However, we have also seen evidence of the more complex situation of American Swedish, since also contact with English and bilingualism clearly has influenced the development. In this section, we consider features that might be viewed as an established part of American Swedish spoken by early immigrants and their descendants, and which in other words are not only idiosyncratic features of the language use of individual speakers in a contact situation. We return to questions of bilingualism, acquisition and attrition in Section 5.

It is obviously often difficult to determine whether features from English should be seen as direct borrowing by the individual speaker, or not. However, in many cases lexical and syntactic traits that occur systematically, and not only in individual speakers, can be viewed not as direct transfer or borrowing, i.e., not as an ongoing process, but as involving "a kind of language change whereby a new, intermediate, system is created by a bilingual from elements of both languages. The resulting system is distinct from either as spoken by monolinguals" (Ameel et al. 2009: 271, cf. also Pavlenko 1999). It is the features that are part of this system that we focus on here. The discussion will necessarily be kept brief, and phonological and morphological features are left aside.[9] Sections 4.1–4.2 discuss lexical and functional vocabulary, and Section 4.3 briefly comments on syntactic features of American Swedish. Section 4.4 concludes the section and briefly discusses what is left of the variety among the (somewhat) younger American Swedish speakers.

---

9. Hasselmo (1974) discusses also phonological features of American Swedish.

4.1 The lexicon

The establishment (and loss) of an American Swedish variety in the speech community can first and foremost be observed in the lexicon. The lexicon is obviously also the area where we most easily can observe conventionalization, and the area that is most easily affected by transfer.

American Swedish is typically characterized by lexical borrowing from English. This has been observed in previous studies (in particular Hasselmo 1974), and American Swedish is in this respect similar to, e.g., American Icelandic (see Arnbjörnsdottír 2006: 53) and American Norwegian (see Haugen 1969 [1953], cf. Johannessen and Laake 2012). For instance, American Swedish speakers use the forms *buildingarna* 'the buildings' for Sw. *byggnaderna* and *putta* 'put' for Sw. *sätta* (examples from recording of Anders Källman born 1881, AM79). In examples like these, an English root is combined with regular Swedish inflection (see Åfarli this volume). This type of transfer seems rather more common in old recordings than in the present-day, where inflection is also typically transferred (i.e., it is a question of code-switching rather than lexical borrowing; cf. Section 5). However, this remains to be investigated in detail. At the level of the individual, it clearly matters how Swedish was acquired, and which language is the strongest (see Section 5).

As noted in previous studies, borrowed forms are sometimes established as part of the American Swedish lexicon. When Konrad (born 1933 in Minnesota, 2nd gen., L1-Swedish) says *visita mej* 'visited me' for Sw. *besökte mej* he most likely uses the only word for 'visit' he knows, and the form he learnt as a child. In a conversation in Karlstad, Minnesota, between Lilian (born 1929) and Elaine (born 1920), two second and third generation speakers with Swedish as their first language, Elaine cannot remember the word for English *walk* and Lilian therefore supplies *travla*; see Example (7). The Standard Swedish word for *travla* is *gå* (cf. American Norwegian which also has the word *travla* 'walk,' discussed in Johannessen and Laake 2012 and forthcoming, and Section 4.4).

(7) E: *vi vi vi eh # walked #*
    we we we eh   walked
    'We walked'

L: *travla*
   travla
   'walked'

E: *vi travla med barnen   från andra plasser nära oss*
   we travla with the.children from other places near us
   'We walked with the children from other places near us'
                                            Lilian, 2nd gen., born 1929
                                            Elaine, 3rd gen., born 1920

In American Swedish, the meaning of the word *gå* has converged with English *go* (cf. Annear and Speth this volume and, e.g., Clyne 2003 and Ameel et al. 2009 for a discussion of convergence). With few exceptions, the speakers in the recordings we have examined say that they *går till Sverige* 'go to Sweden,' where Standard Swedish would use *åka* 'go,' *fara* 'go' or *resa* 'travel' when the transportation is not by foot.

Although some of the borrowed words and semantic convergence, e.g., of *gå* with English *go* can be viewed as part of the older American Swedish variety, it is a natural development in a contact situation. Many of the features of American Swedish are of this type. Another similar example is the adverb *just* which in Standard Swedish has a temporal meaning 'just now,' but is used with the meaning 'only' (Sw. *bara*) by many of the speakers (including Mrs. Friesendahl), both in the new and old recordings. Very similar examples can be found also in Heritage Icelandic (Arnbjörnsdottír 2006), German (Boas 2009) and Norwegian (Annear and Speth this volume).

That words like *visita* or *travla* (and *gå* meaning 'go') are established in American Swedish perhaps becomes particularly clear when American Swedes come in contact with Standard Swedish. One speaker, Shirley (born 1941 in Minnesota, 2nd gen.) comments explicitly on the American Swedish vocabulary. When she was around 20 years old and returned from her first trip to Sweden, she tried to teach her parents (first generation immigrants) that the Swedish word for English *stove* is not *stov* but *spis*, and that the sidewalk is not called *sidewalken* but *trottoaren*. She says that her parents "wouldn't learn," but Shirley herself does not say *stov* or *sidewalken* but uses the Standard Swedish words. She does in other words not fully speak the old American Swedish variety (see further below).

The observed lexical changes are, as noted, partly an automatic consequence of contact with English. However, they can also be explained by the rapidly changing society and the growing industrialization at the time of the settlement. As pointed out by Hedblom (1974: 54), the Swedish word *spis* 'stove' generally meant 'fireplace' for the early emigrants. When they first encountered an iron stove, they called it something else, namely *stov*. As we have seen, also the koiné situation has clearly affected the development of the American Swedish lexicon. Dialect-specific words that were not understood by all speakers are avoided, and exchanged with a different Swedish word or a word borrowed from English.

4.2   Function words

Semantic convergence can be observed also in the use of function verbs and prepositions, as for instance in time adverbials (again, as in Icelandic, German and Norwegian). This holds even for first generation Swedish Americans. In Example (8), Mrs. Hansson uses the preposition *för* 'for' with the complement *många år* 'many years.' Standard Swedish has the preposition *i* 'in' in durative adverbials. Similar examples are attested also for several speakers in the new recordings; one example is given in (9).

(8) *pappa hade gikt för många år   innan han dog*
    father had gout for many years before he died
    'Father had gout for many years before he died.'   Mrs. Hansson, 1st gen.
                                                        born 1893 in Resele, Ångermanland
                                                        Recorded by Folke Hedblom, 113B_m

(9) *ja var där för lite granna*
    I was there for little bit
    'I was there for a little while.'   Edward, 2nd gen., born 1921c.

In Standard Swedish, the complement of *arg* is a prepositional phrase with *på* 'on.' In American Swedish, the complement preposition used is instead often *med* 'with' in convergence with the English expression *angry with*, see (10).

(10) *och va   va   min far   va arg   med va det att*
     and what what my   father was angry with was that that
     'What my father was angry with, was that

     farfar   när   han söp   [...]
     grandfather when he   drank
     my grandfather, when he drank, [...]'   Konrad, 2nd gen., born 1933

Also when it comes to location adverbs, American Swedish contrasts with Standard Swedish, and looks more similar to English. One example is the use of the adverbs *här* 'her' and *där* 'there.' In English, *here* and *there* include a meaning of general proximity and distance relative to the speaker, as well as a more specific meaning of direction towards or away from the speaker. Standard Swedish *här* 'here' and *där* 'there' have a narrower meaning, and are used only to express general proximity/distance, while other adverbs, *hit* 'hither' and *dit* 'thither,' are used to express directionality. The distinction between locative and directional adverbs seems to have been partly lost in American Swedish:

(11) *dem kom just här – till den här trakten*
     they came right here   to this here neighborhood
     'They came right here to this neighborhood'   Theodor, 3rd gen., born 1922

Also with respect to relative adverbs American Swedish converges with English. Almost all Hasselmo's (1974) consultants accept sentences like (12), with the proximal *where*. Standard Swedish has the distal locative *där* 'there.'

(12) *det var stan   var   han var född*
     it was the.town where he was born
     'It was the town where he was born.'

Examples corresponding to (12) are not uncommon in the recordings, as in (13).

(13) så han hade plats var   han kunn leva
     so he had place where he could live
     'So he had a place where he could live'   Vaughn, 3rd gen., born 1930
                                                                L1-Swedish

4.3 Syntactic constructions

It is well known that syntax is less readily affected by contact than lexicon and morphology, and this is also noted by Hedblom (1974) (e.g., Argyri and Sorace 2007, Sorace and Serratice 2009 and references cited there for discussion of syntactic transfer). Nevertheless, both Hedblom and Hasselmo (1974) show that there are constructions where English constructions has influenced American Swedish. One such example is VP-ellipsis. Hedblom (1974: 39) provides the example in (14) below.

(14) Så han jeck te Maple Hill skolan; dom allihop gjorde, tänker jag
     so he went to Maple Hill school;   they all   did   think I
     'So, he went to Maple Hill school; they all did, I think.'

Here, the object pronoun *det* is missing in the clause *dom allihop gjorde* 'they all did.' This is grammatical in English, but not in Standard Swedish, nor in the speaker's home dialect, according to Hedblom (1974). Standard Swedish requires a VP-anaphor *det* 'it' with the pro-verb *göra* 'do.'

Also the use of passive forms appears to be affected by English (cf. Hasselmo 1974, and Putnam and Salmons 2013 on loss of passives in American German). American Swedish has eventive passives with *vara* 'be' + participle; see (15) where Standard Swedish would have a morphological passive (or possibly a periphrastic passive with *bli* 'become'). In Standard Swedish, *vara* is only used in stative passives (e.g., Engdahl 2006 on Swedish passives).

(15) De var byggd här så vi   kunde ha   en präst ifrån Sverje
     it was built here so we could have a pastor from Sweden
     'It was built here so that we could have a pastor from Sweden'
                                                    Vaughn, 3rd gen., born 1930

In (14) above, a quantifier intervenes between the subject and the finite verb, as in the English translation. Standard Swedish has a verb second (V2) requirement, and the quantifier must therefore follow the verb, if the subject is sentence-initial. As we will see in Section 5, V2 has however not been systematically lost in American Swedish, but is still often the rule (cf. Eide and Hjelde 2015 for Norwegian). Note for instance that there is a case of subject-verb inversion in (14) (*tänker jag* 'think I'). Hasselmo's (1974) consultants generally judge sentences with V2-violations as ungrammatical. With respect to word order, there seem to be little reason to distinguish the American Swedish variety from Standard Swedish. Instead, variation depends on incomplete acquisition, or attrition in the individual (see Larsson and Johannessen forthcoming a, forthcoming b for embedded word order). We return to this in Section 5 below.

4.4 Intermediate summary

In this section, we have seen examples of features that distinguish American Swedish from Standard Swedish that are a consequence of contact with English. In many cases it is not possible to distinguish established features from spontaneous direct transfer. However, particularly in the lexicon we can find evidence of a different kind of contact, namely between different speakers of American Swedish, where also features transferred from English become part of the American Swedish koiné. Similar developments can be noted for other immigrant groups (e.g., Johannessen and Laake 2012, forthcoming).

In other words, both types of contact discussed (contact between dialects and contact between Swedish and English) are factors in the development of American Swedish, and they are clearly interrelated. As noted in Section 3, Swedes who spoke a dialect with low status often switched to English, and dialect words that were not shared by the entire community were sometimes replaced by an English word. It is in fact not always immediately clear which factor is at play. As pointed out by Johannessen and Laake (2012 and forthcoming), the verb *travla* (cognate with English *travel*, from French) exists in Norwegian dialects. It also occurs in dialects in Sweden (e.g., in Södermanland and Uppland, according to Rietz 1962), where it means 'tread and trample down' or 'wade in snow or sand.' That this word was established as part of American Swedish, with a slightly modified meaning, is in other words not necessarily due to transfer from English, although the fact that *gå* 'walk' has converged with English *go*, and the fact that English has a word *travel*, probably has had some influence.

In comparing old and new recordings, we have noted that the standard-like American Swedish has largely disappeared since the 1960s, and that the variation between speakers is not of the same kind as 50 years ago. In the discussion of the lexicon, we also saw that the particular American Swedish vocabulary is to some degree disappearing. Speakers like Shirley do not, as noted, use words like *travla* or *stov*. We have suggested that these changes relate to the fact that Swedish has lost the public domain, and that present-day American Swedish speakers have more varied and more limited input (and output) of Swedish. This clearly affects the language of these speakers in other ways than through direct transfer. In the next section we turn to the role of bilingualism at the level of the individual.

5. Bilingualism at an individual level

We have seen that both the old and the new recordings contain features that distinguish American Swedish from Standard Swedish, both structurally and lexically, and these features are shared by many of the American Swedish speakers. There are examples of lexical transfer and semantic convergence, deviations from Standard Swedish in the use of prepositions and adverbs, but also what can seem to be more sporadic examples of V2-violations. Clearly not all features are an established part of an American Swedish variety at the level of the speech community. We have observed considerable variation between speakers, with respect to dialect features, English influence as well as features that can perhaps rather be understood as a consequence of the specific contexts of language acquisition and use for the heritage speakers. In this section we turn to the fact that all of our consultants are to a considerable degree bilingual and that some of the variation and distinctive traits of their linguistic production may actually be due to this. In this section, we address the fact that, on an individual level, bilingualism affects language in more ways than through transfer (and the role of transfer for the grammars of bilingual speakers is in fact debated, Odlin 1989, Larsson and Johannessen 2015b and references there). Here, we focus on questions of incomplete acquisition and language attrition in heritage language speakers.

5.1 Sources of impact on American Swedish

As the Swedish language communities in America are getting smaller and more and more scarce, Swedish is reduced to a language spoken primarily within the family. Since normative resources such as newspapers and social events are absent, and since Swedish is no longer used in church, we expect contemporary American Swedish to be more diverse than it was in the old enclaves. Today's Swedish speakers can also, to some extent, be more influenced by Standard Swedish through the Internet and contacts with relatives in Sweden, although this holds only for a small minority of our consultants. In Section 3 above, we suggested that this new linguistic situation – the loss of the public domain – explains the fact that speakers like Gerald and Albert have more dialect features than standard-like speakers in the old recordings. We also noted that Gerald sometimes deviates from the Standard Swedish V2-rule. The question then is to what extent V2-violations are actually deviations (non-target-like), and what, in that case, the origin for the deviation is.

It is known that most heritage language speakers share some features with L1-speakers and some with L2-speakers (Montrul 2010: 11). Typical of L1 acquisition is that it has taken place in a naturalistic setting at the earliest possible age of onset (from birth). Many of the American Swedish speakers' backgrounds leave no reason to believe otherwise than that this is how they started to acquire Swedish. At the same time, deviations from standard grammatical structures are typical for both heritage speakers and L2-speakers. L2-acquistion of V2 in Swedish is much discussed (e.g., Ganuza 2008), and it has been noted that it is so typical of L2-speakers and interlanguage speakers (Selinker 1972) that it has gained an almost symbolic migrant-language status in Sweden (Källström 2011).

We noted in Section 4.3 above that Hasselmo's consultants generally judged examples with V2-violations as ungrammatical, and that V2-violations are hardly a systematic characteristic shared by a majority of American Swedes in the recorded material. Rather than being part of American Swedish, the V2-violations could thus be a typical L2-speaker feature, or a consequence of incomplete acquisition. Normally, we would perhaps expect only L2-speakers to show signs of incomplete acquisition, but under some circumstances, when the learner receives limited (and conflicting) input, it is possible even for L1-speakers to acquire an incomplete linguistic system (and then, normally acquire a complete system of another language, in this case generally English). Montrul (2008, 2010) argues that even early bilinguals can show signs of incomplete acquisition, if language input is reduced before the "closure of the critical period" (2010: 20). Larsson and Johannessen (2015a, b) argues that embedded word order is incompletely acquired by American Scandinavian heritage speakers.

Most of our American Swedish L1 speakers have had somewhat reduced Swedish input even before beginning school, and after early childhood the input is restricted further. The American Swedish heritage speakers have for instance not been schooled in Swedish; and attending school (in English) is the most prominent activity of their youth, before they the start their own families, often with non-Swedish speaking spouses and children. The question is whether the lack of formal Swedish instruction in school will reduce the input of speakers that grew up in Swedish enclaves enough to even affect a certain domain (such as the academic one). As noted, many families in the Swedish enclaves read Swedish newspapers and attended church in Swedish, circumstances that might be enough to make up for the lack of formal training of a more 'official' or cognitively more demanding (compare Cummins' (2000) BICS- and CALP-distinction) proficiency of Swedish. In this way, the Swedish-speaking community differs from most of the other heritage language speakers that arrived in the USA and lived in ethnic and linguistic enclaves at about the same time as our consultants grew up. The Swedish migrants were all literate from a very early point in the migration history (cf. Section 3.1). Reading even complicated matters, political and religious texts etc., was in other words possible for the Swedish migrants, a fact that often rendered them a reputation in the USA of being well educated, which facilitated the process of getting employed in the new country. Literacy in a heritage language has also been shown to have impact on the production of some grammatical structures in other languages (Rothman 2007). The effects of reduced input and the role of literacy clearly varies between different linguistic domains, and even between different linguistic tasks (e.g., Montrul et al. 2008).

Another (interrelated) possibility is that what might be considered part of American Swedish or a result of incomplete acquisition may rather result from language attrition. Speakers such as Gerald may at one point have acquired Swedish fully, but at a later state started to lose some of its features, hence the V2-violations.

However, attrition is generally not assumed to affect core grammar (Lubinska 2011, Montrul 2008), and Hedblom's observation that American Swedish syntax is more resistant to English influence than the lexicon may in fact reflect this. The first signs of language attrition are normally instead a lack of accessibility, and lexical retrieval delays – a speaker has to look for words. On the other hand, Seliger and Vago (1991) claim that attrition can also affect grammatical features of a language, usually in terms of simplifications, and then V2-violations could be such a simplification. Seliger and Vago (1991) distinguish two different kinds of attrition: external, that has to do with the influence of the L2 on the L1, and internal, that has to do with typologically marked structures of the L1. In the case of V2-violations, both external and internal attrition could affect the word order of Swedish in America, since English is not a consistent V2-language, and since V2 is typologically marked. Hence, we cannot completely overlook the effects of possible attrition, even when considering grammatical properties in the linguistic production of our consultants. As argued by Larsson and Johannessen (2015b), V2-violations are in fact typical of speakers who show other signs of attrition (lexical retrieval delays, morphological reductions) and who have not used their L1 Scandinavian regularly for many years (cf. Eide and Hjelde 2015, for a similar view).

To recapitulate, differences between American Swedish and Standard Swedish can be explained in many ways. They could be an inherent part of an American Swedish variety, but they could also be due to incomplete L1-acquisition or to attrition of the L1. It is also possible that a language that has been forgotten can be reacquired by the adult speaker, and then for that reason look like an L2. To further complicate matters, we do not know exactly what input the speakers have been subjected to. When trying to pin down what may be traits originating in American Swedish (which, of course, itself is a result of language contact), linguistic clues are clearly not enough. By combining them with sociolinguistic variables, however, the various explanations are easier to tease out. In the following, we therefore look in more detail at linguistic production of two speakers: Edward and Shirley, with partly different sociolinguistic backgrounds.

5.2 Edward and Shirley: Acquisition or attrition?

Edward was born in Mora, Minnesota, in 1921 to two Swedish-born parents. He has Swedish as his L1, and learned English at the age of six, when starting school. Edward says that, apart from school, he lived in an entirely Swedish-speaking community (enclave). His family and friends always spoke Swedish, and activities outside the home (shopping and church-going, etc.) were also in Swedish. The family had access to Swedish newspapers.

Shirley was born in the Minneapolis area in 1941 to two Swedish-born parents. Her L1 is Swedish, but English was spoken in her home as well, and could be considered her second L1. Swedish seems to have been first and foremost a family language. Activities outside the home took place in English, and this was sometimes even the case within the family, especially since one of Shirley's sisters found it difficult to speak English only in school. English was spoken more and more frequently in the family in order to help the children accommodate to that language.

Generally, Shirley deviates from Standard Swedish more often than Edward. She produces V2-violations, agreement violations and gender violations. For instance, she says *många född i Sverige* 'many born in Sweden' with the participle *född* in singular (common gender) and not the Standard plural *födda*. She also says *en program* 'a program' with the common gender indefinite article *en*; in Standard Swedish *program* is neuter (*ett program*). Shirley also shows more codeswitching than speakers like Edward, an example is given in (16).

(16) S: *ja   ja   va   i   skolan ja*
             yeah, yeah, was in school yeah
             'Yeah, (I) was in school, yeah,

             skulle   vara   (.)   köks   (°skol°)   lärarinna?
             should be   kitchen school teacher
             (I) was supposed to be a home economics teacher.'
     INT: ah
     S: *home economoics teacher heter   de här*
             home economics teacher is.called it   here
             'That's what they call it here.'
     INT: ha
     S: *å   de va   mestan sying- sying?*
             and it was mostly sewing sewing
             'And it was mostly sewing,

             inte så mycke koking   (.)   kokning
             not so much cooking   cooking
             and not that much cooking.'   Shirley, 2nd gen., born 1941

Here, Shirley uses English words in an otherwise Swedish context (*home economics teacher heter de här* 'home economics teacher it is called here'). She also has grammatical codeswitching, and uses English suffixes with Swedish roots (*kok-ing, sy-ing*). When talking about her career, Shirley has obvious difficulties in finding Swedish words and switches completely to English, but she switches back to Swedish when leaving this particular topic. It seems, then, that Shirley has some domain loss (or she has not acquired Swedish for all domains); topics that are related to contexts outside of everyday language and family language, are not easily accessible to her in Swedish.

Edward, who used Swedish in a wider variety of settings during his upbringing, shows no sign of a domain loss. He speaks readily about any subject in Swedish, even about his career and adulthood. Moreover, he does not produce any V2-violations, gender violations or congruency violations. However, Edward does use some English words and semantic convergence (see Example (9) above). These deviations from Standard Swedish can be accounted for in terms of the difference between Standard

Swedish and the American Swedish variety that Edward presumably acquired as a child, and they are not signs of incomplete acquisition or attrition. Judging from our knowledge of Edward's background, we have no reason to doubt that he has at one point fully acquired Swedish (with some possible exceptions, see Larsson and Johannessen 2015a, b).

The same patterns as Edward's can be found in other older speakers who have grown up in other Swedish-speaking enclaves, as we saw in Section 4. As noted, Albert, born in a Swedish enclave in 1921 to two Swedish-speaking parents, has both dialect features and features that are most likely due to contact. As we have also seen, it is not always easy to separate the two kinds of influence, and it is possible that they are interrelated. When Albert says *de va ingen te prate me* 'there was no one to talk with,' the structure differs from Standard Swedish in two ways. First, in Standard Swedish, the verb *va(r)* 'was' is less common in existential sentences of this kind than the verb *finnas* 'to exist, to be present.' Second, in Standard Swedish the infinitival marker is *att* and not *te* (a dialect form of the standard preposition *till* 'to'). Both deviations could originate in language contact, since English uses the copula *be* in existential sentences, and since the preposition *te/till* corresponds to English *to*. However, both deviations are also present in non-standard varieties of Swedish: some dialects use *vara* 'be' more in presentation sentences, and many dialects introduce infinitives with *te/till* (see Hagren 2008).

It is in other words often impossible to distinguish effects of language contact from effects of dialectal contact in the individual cases, and the two can reinforce each other. In any case, we can conclude from the material that existential sentences have the verb *vara* 'be' and *te/till* in the American Swedish of speakers born in Swedish-speaking enclaves in the 1920s or before that. By combining linguistic factors with sociolinguistic factors, we can in other words identify an American Swedish variety, used by speakers like Edward and Albert, but hardly by Shirley. At the same time, there is, as we saw in Section 3 above, considerable variation also among speakers like Albert and Edward. As we have seen, this is largely due to the fact that American Swedish has been reduced to a family language. Speakers like Edward and Albert do generally not speak Swedish to each other, but use their stronger language, English.

6. Conclusion

We have compared present-day American Swedish (in recordings from 2011) with Swedish spoken in America 50 years ago (in recordings from the 1960s), and with Standard Swedish. We have observed several different sources for the particularities of American Swedish, and they are intertwined in rather complex ways, reinforcing each other. One is the dialects, and the mixture of dialects in Swedish America: some dialect features are retained (or reintroduced) by individual speakers, but, e.g., dialectal vocabulary has been lost. We have also noted reading pronunciations, which most likely originate from the Book Swedish of the Church and religious congregations. We argued that the tendencies towards a spoken standard in Sweden ('the common speech') affected the direction of the development, directly or indirectly. Attitudes surely influenced which dialect features were lost. Changes like that from dialectal *pära* to standard *potatis* 'potato' are expected: *potatis* was the word used in 'the common speech,' and speakers from southern Sweden would not necessarily have recognized the northern dialectal form.

A second source is English, and the bilingualism of the heritage speakers. We have given examples of lexical and grammatical transfer from English and suggested that in some cases, the transferred forms have become part of American Swedish. On the other hand, transfer and convergence are natural processes in contact situations, and the features of American Swedish often have direct parallels, e.g., in American Icelandic, American German and American Norwegian.

We have also noted changes in American Swedish since the 1960s. In the older recordings, we observed variation between dialect speakers and speakers of a more standard-like variety. In the new recordings, we find no evidence for alternations between varieties. Instead, there is more inter- and intra-individual variation, and we suggested that this is due to the fact that Swedish has lost the public domain. The effects of bilingualism are different, and somewhat younger speakers in the recordings rather behave like L2-speakers. Clearly, language acquisition and language attrition, the social status of the Swedish language in the community, as well as patterns of communication, must be taken into account. Some instances of leveling and simplification in the linguistic system can be attributed to incomplete language acquisition or attrition (rather than koinéization). The comparison between two speakers, one typical of the inhabitants of Swedish enclaves in Minnesota, and one typical of a somewhat later, urban bilingual family, shows that the importance of continuous and diverse input and output of the heritage language is important in order for the individual to acquire and maintain a native-like Standard Swedish proficiency. It also shows that the American-Swedish is disappearing, and that it is no longer fully acquired by children.

References

Ameel, Eef, Barbara C. Malt, Gert Storms and Fons Van Assche. 2009. "Semantic Convergence in the Bilingual Lexicon." *Journal of Memory and Language* 60(2): 270–290.

Andréasson, Maia, Ida Larsson, Benjamin Lyngfelt, Jenny Nilsson and Sofia Tingsell. 2013. "I jakt på amerikasvenskan". In *Svenskans beskrivning 32*, ed. by Björn Bihl, Jessica Eriksson, Peter Andersson and Lena Lötmarker, 83–93. Karlstad: Karlstads universitet.

Argyri, Efrosyni and Antonella Sorace. 2007. "Crosslinguistic Influence and Language Dominance in Older Bilingual Children." *Bilingualism: Language and Cognition* 10(1): 79–99.

Arnbjörnsdottír, Birna. 2006. *North American Icelandic. The Life of a Language*. Manitoba: The University of Manitoba Press.

Bailey, Guy. 2002. "Real and Apparent Time." In *The Handbook of Language Variation and Change*, ed. by J. K. Chambers, Peter Trudgill and Natalie Schilling-Estes, 312–332. Malden, MA: Blackwell Publishing.

Boas, Hans. 2009. *The Life and Death of Texas German*. Durham, NC: American Dialect Society.

Clyne, Michael G. 2003. *Dynamics of Language Contact: English and Immigrant Languages*. Cambridge: Cambridge University Press.

Columbus, Samuel. *En swensk ordeskötsel*, ed. by Sylvia Boström, 1963. Uppsala: Almqvist and Wiksell.

Cummins, Jim. 2000. *Language, Power and Pedagogy. Bilingual Children in the Crossfire*. Clevedon, UK: Multilingual matters.

Dahlstedt, Karl-Hampus and Per-Uno Ågren. 1980. *Övre Norrlands bygdemål : berättelser på bygdemål med förklaringar och en dialektöversikt*. Umeå: Vetenskapliga biblioteket i Umeå.

Eide, Kristin Melum and Arnstein Hjelde. 2015. "V2 and Morphological Paradigms in Norwegian Varieties Spoken in the American Midwest." In *Heritage Languages in the Americas: Theoretical Perspectives and Empirical Findings*, ed. by Richard Page and Michael Putnam.

Engdahl, Elisabet. 2006. "Semantic and Syntactic Patterns in Swedish Passives." In *Demoting the Agent*, ed. by Benjamin Lyngfelt and Torgrim Solstad, 21–45. Amsterdam: John Benjamins. DOI: 10.1075/la.96.04eng

Fraurud, Kari and Sally Boyd. 2011. "The Native-Non-Native Speaker Distinction and the Diversity of Linguistic Profiles of Young People in Multilingual Urban Contexts in Sweden." In *Young Urban Swedish. Variation and Change in Multilingual Settings*, ed. by Roger Källström and Inger Lindberg, 67–88. Gothenburg: Department of Swedish language.

Ganuza, Natalia. 2008. *Syntactic Variation in the Swedish of Adolescents in Multilingual Urban Settings. Subject-Verb Order in Declaratives, Questions and Subordinate Clauses*. Stockholm, Sweden: Stockholm University dissertation.

Hagren, Kristina. 2008. *Hur märks infinitiven? Infinitivkonstruktioner i svenska dialekter med fokus på infinitivmärket*. Uppsala: Uppsala Universitet.

Håkansson, Gisela. 1995. "Syntax and Morphology in Language Attrition. A Study of Five Bilingual Expatriate Swedes." *International Journal of Applied Linguistics* 5: 153–171.

Hasselmo, Nils. 1974. *Amerikasvenska. En bok om språkutvecklingen i Svensk-Amerika*. (Skrifter utgivna av Svenska språknämnden 51). Stockholm: Esselte studium.

Haugen, Einar. (1953) 1969. *The Norwegian Language in America: A Study in Bilingual Behavior*. Philadelphia: University of Pennsylvania Press.

Hedblom, Folke. 1963. "Om svenska folkmål i Amerika. Från Landsmåls- och Folkminnesarkivets bandinspelningsexpedition 1962." *Svenska landsmål och svenskt folkliv 1962*.

Hedblom, Folke. 1970. "Amerikasvenska texter i fonogram. 1. Hälsingland. Bergsjömål. Utskrift och kommentar." *Svenska landsmål och svenskt folkliv 1969* 92: 1–52.

Hedblom, Folke. 1974. "Svenska dialekter i Amerika. Några erfarenheter och problem." *Kungl. Humanistiska Vetenskaps-Samfundet i Uppsala. Årsbok 1973–1974*.

Hedblom, Folke. 1978. "Hälsingemål i Amerika." *Svenska landsmål och svenskt folkliv 1977*.

Hedblom, Folke. 1982. "Swedish Dialects in the Midwest: Notes from Field Research." *Svenska landsmål och svenskt folkliv 1981*.

Hedblom, Folke. 1992. "Dialekt och språknorm i Svensk-Amerika. Värderingar och attityder från 1960-talet." *Svenska landsmål och svenskt folkliv 1992*.

Hof, Sven. 1753. *Swänska språkets rätta skrivsätt*, ed. by Mats Thelander. Uppsala Universitet: Institutionen för nordiska språk.

Johannessen, Janne Bondi and Piotr Garbacz. 2011. "Fältarbete med Nordic Dialect Corpus." In *Studier i dialektologi och språksociologi. Föredrag vid Nionde nordiska dialektologkonferensen i Uppsala 18–20 augusti 2010, Acta Academiae Regiae Gustavi Adolphi 116*, ed. Lars-Erik Edlund, Lennart Elmevik, and Maj Reinhammar, 169–176. Uppsala: Swedish Science Press.

Johannessen, Janne Bondi and Signe Laake. 2012. "Østnorsk som norsk fellesdialekt i Midtvesten." *Norsk Lingvistisk tidsskrift* 30(2): 365–380.

Johannessen, Janne Bondi and Signe Laake. Forthcoming. "Eastern Norwegian as a Common Norwegian Dialect in the American Midwest." *Journal of Language Contact*.

Källström, Roger. 2011. "Multiethnic Language in Reviews of the Novel *Ett öga rött*." In *Young Urban Swedish. Variation and Change in Multilingual Settings*, ed. by Roger Källström and Inger Lindberg, 125–148. Gothenburg: Department of Swedish.

Karstadt, Angela. 2003. *Tracking Swedish-American English. A Longitudinal Study of Linguistic Variation and Identity*. [Studia multiethnica Upsaliensia 16]. Uppsala: Acta Universitatis Upsaliensis.

Kerswill, Paul. 2002. "Koineization and Accommodation." In *The Handbook of Language Variation and Change*, ed. by J. K. Chambers, Peter Trudgill and Natalie Schilling-Estes, 669–702. Oxford: Blackwell Publishers.

Larsson, Ida. 2004. *Språk i förändring. Adjektivändelserna -a och -e från fornsvenska till nysvenska*. [MISS 49]. Göteborg: Institutionen för svenska språket.

Larsson, Ida and Janne Bondi Johannessen. 2015a. "Embedded Word Order in Heritage Scandinavian." In *New Trends in Nordic and General Linguistics*, ed. by Martin Hilpert, Janet Duke, Christine Mertzlufft, Jan-Ola Östman and Michael Rießler, 239–269. Berlin: Linguae et Litterae, Mouton de Gruyter.

Larsson, Ida and Janne Bondi Johannessen. 2015b. "Incomplete Acquisition and Verb Placement in Heritage Scandinavian." In *Moribund Germanic Heritage Languages in North America: Theoretical Perspectives and Empirical Findings*, ed. by Richard Page and Michael Putnam. Leiden, Netherlands: Brill.

Lubinska, Dorota. 2011. *Förstaspråksattrition hos vuxna: exemplet polsktalande i Sverige*. Stockholm: Center for Research on Bilingualism.

Lundquist, Björn. 2013. "*Bliva* and *varda*." In *The Nordic Atlas of Linguistic Structures Journal Online* 1: 270–269. http://www.tekstlab.uio.no/nals

Lyttkens, Ivar Adolf and Fredrik Wulff. 1889. *Svensk uttalsordbok*. Lund: Gleerup.

Montrul, Silvina. 2008. *Incomplete Acquisition in Bilingualism: Re-examining the Age Factor*. Amsterdam/Philadelphia: John Benjamins. DOI: 10.1075/sibil.39

Montrul, Silvina. 2010. "Current Issues in Heritage Language Acquisition." *Annual Review of Applied Linguistics* 30: 3–23. DOI: 10.1017/S0267190510000103

Montrul, Silvina, Rebecca Foote and Silvia Perpinán. 2008. "Gender Agreement in Adult Second Language Learners and Spanish Heritage Speakers: The Effect of Age and Context of Acquisition." *Language Learning* 58(3): 503–553. DOI: 10.1111/j.1467-9922.2008.00449.x

Nilsson, Jenny. 2011. "Dialektal anpassning i interaktion." In *Interaktionell dialektologi*, ed. by Gustav Bockgård and Jenny Nilsson, 223–250. Uppsala: Institutet för språk och folkminnen.

Noreen, Adolf. 1903. *Vårt språk: nysvensk grammatik i utförlig framställning*. Band I. Lund: Gleerup.

Nützel, Daniel and Joseph Salmons. 2011. "Language Contact and New Dialect Formation: Evidence from German in North America." *Language and Linguistics Compass* 5(10): 705–717. DOI: 10.1111/j.1749-818X.2011.00308.x

Odlin, Terence. 1989. *Cross-Linguistic Influence in Language Learning*. Cambridge: Cambridge University Press. DOI: 10.1017/CBO9781139524537

Pavlenko, Aneta. 1999. "New Approaches to Concepts in Bilingual Memory." *Bilingualism: Language and Cognition* 2(3): 209–230. DOI: 10.1017/S1366728999000322

Petri, Laurentius. 1571. *The Swenska Kyrkeordningen*. Stockholm.

Putnam, Michael and Joseph Salmons. 2013. "Losing Their (Passive) Voice: Syntactic Neutralization in Heritage German." *Linguistic Approaches to Bilingualism* 3(2): 233–252. DOI: 10.1075/lab.3.2.05put

Rietz, Johan Ernst. 1962. *Svenskt dialektlexikon. Ordbok öfver svenska allmogespråket*. Lund: C. W. K. Gleerups förlag.

Rothman, Jason. 2007. "Heritage Speaker Competence Differences, Language Change, and Input Type: Inflected Infinitives in Heritage Brazilian Portuguese." *International Journal of Bilingualism* 11: 359–389. DOI: 10.1177/13670069070110040201

SAOB = Svenska Akademiens ordbok över svenska språket, 1893–.

Schmid, Monika S. 2002. *First Language Attrition, Use and Maintenance. The Case of German Jews in Anglophone Countries*. Amsterdam: John Benjamins. DOI: 10.1075/sibil.24

Seliger, Herbert W. and Robert Vago. 1991. "The Study of First Language Attrition: An Overview." In *First Language Attrition*, ed. by Herbert W. Seliger and Robert Vago, 3–15. New York: Cambridge University Press. DOI: 10.1017/CBO9780511620720.001

Selinker, Larry. 1972. "Interlanguage." *International Review of Applied Linguistics* 10: 209–241. DOI: 10.1515/iral.1972.10.1-4.209

Sorace, Antonella and Ludovica Serratrice. 2009. "Internal and External Interfaces in Bilingual Language Development: Beyond Structural Overlap." *International Journal of Bilingualism* 13(2): 195–210. DOI: 10.1177/1367006909339810

Sundgren, Eva. 2002. *Återbesök i Eskilstuna: en undersökning av morfologisk variation och förändring i nutida talspråk*. Uppsala: Uppsala Universitet.

Tingsell, Sofia. 2013. "Reflexive Binding in Heritage Language Speakers of Swedish in the USA." Manuscript.

Widmark, Gun. 1998. *Stora vokaldansen: om kvantitativa och kvalitativa förändringar i fornsvenskans vokalsystem*. Uppsala: Gustav Adolfs akad.

Widmark, Gun. 2000. "Boksvenska och talsvenska. Om språkarter i nysvenskt talspråk." In *Boksvenska och talsvenska. Ett urval uppsatser samlade till författarens 80-årsdag 31 juli 2000*, ed. by Gun Widmark, 19–56. Uppsala: Institutionen för nordiska språk. [Reprinted from *Språk and stil* N.F. 1991, 1: 157–198.]

On the decrease of language norms in a disintegrating language

Caroline Smits and Jaap van Marle
Open University of the Netherlands

This paper deals with the issue of norm awareness in decaying American Dutch, the language of the ethnic Dutch in the American Midwest. It is investigated to what extent inflectional 'mistakes' are recognized. This investigation was carried out by means of an acceptability test. These findings are then compared with data from free conversation. Although this paper focuses on the decrease of language norms in the first place, it also contributes to a better understanding of heritage languages in their final stage, i.e., when they are on the verge of extinction.

Keywords: American Dutch, norm awareness, inflectional 'mistakes', reflection versus production, storage/irregularity, spontaneous purism

1. Introduction[1]

In the second half of the 19th and the beginning of the 20th century a relatively large number of Dutch speakers migrated to the United States, particularly to the Midwest (Lucas 1955, Van Hinte 1985). The majority of these immigrants were orthodox Calvinists, a fact which has been of crucial importance to the maintenance as well as the development of Dutch in the New World (Van Marle and Smits 1996). For many of these immigrants – and their descendants – Dutch was the language of communication, at least within the family, until the first half of the 20th century. However, as soon as the immigrants settled in the United States they came in contact with socially dominant English as well, especially through school. For many decades, then, there has been a bilingual situation, particularly in the isolated rural areas. At first, Dutch was the mother tongue and the linguistically dominant language, whereas in later years English became more and more prominent. However, particularly during and after the second World War the number of domains in which Dutch was spoken decreased

---

1. We have profited from the comments of two anonymous reviewers.

rapidly. From that time on, for most Dutch Americans, even in the more isolated rural areas, socially dominant English also became linguistically dominant.

When the interviews that this paper is based on were made (1989), Dutch was no longer in regular use and on the verge of extinction. Even so, in those days there were still quite a few Dutch Americans left who had maintained their ethnic language. Not surprisingly, both in terms of knowledge and proficiency, the differences among these speakers are considerable. Some of them still spoke their ethnic language fluently, whereas others were clear semi-speakers in the sense of Dorian (1981). In the remainder of this paper, we refer to the language spoken by these Americans of Dutch descent as American Dutch (AD).[2]

Clearly, the term 'American Dutch' requires clarification. By American Dutch we understand the standard-like variety of Dutch that was used in the U.S. As noted in Van Marle (2014), in relation to the Second Immigration[3] to the U.S., two types of Dutch should be distinguished: 'standard-like' American Dutch and American Dialectal Dutch.[4] Standard-like American Dutch was particularly prominent in Iowa but it can also be found in Michigan and Wisconsin among educated speakers. In contrast to Iowa, in Michigan and Wisconsin American Dialectal Dutch is dominant.[5] This difference between Iowa on the one hand and Michigan and Wisconsin on the other relates to the fact that the majority of the immigrants in Iowa came from the western parts of the Netherlands, whereas the majority of the immigrants in Michigan and Wisconsin came from the eastern and southern parts of the Netherlands. As discussed in Van Marle (2014), the preference of standard-like American Dutch involves the conscious choice of the Dutch Americans in Iowa – particularly Pella – to imitate the developments in the Netherlands where in the second half of the 19th century a

---

2. These interviews form part of a corpus of American Dutch that was collected by the authors of the present paper between 1989 and 2001 (Van Marle 2001b). In this paper we will concentrate on AD as it was recorded in Iowa in the spring and summer of 1989. This 1989 corpus consists of interviews with several second, third, and fourth generation immigrants, and immigrants of mixed (second, third, and fourth) generation. The major part of the 1989 corpus consists of (i) free conversation and (ii) a translation test in which English sentences had to be translated into Dutch. In addition, a number of informants also participated in (iii) a so-called 'acceptability test.' In both the translation test and the acceptability test, focus was on the American Dutch inflectional system (of both noun, adjective and verb). In this paper on norm awareness in AD, we will particularly be concerned with the results of the acceptability test. However, we will also use data from free conversation for comparison.

3. The variety of Dutch related to the First Immigration is often referred to as 'Leeg Duits' (= Low Dutch) or Jersey Dutch. See Van Marle (2001a) for an overview.

4. The third type, 'mixed Yankee Dutch' spoken in the big cities of Michigan, is irrelevant in this connection. See Van Marle (2008, 2010).

5. See Van Marle (2005) for Michigan, and Van Marle (2012a) for Wisconsin.

spoken standard language gradually developed.⁶ The net result of the developments referred to above is that in Iowa – and among educated speakers in Michigan and Wisconsin as well – a standard-like variety developed which lacked clear dialect features. This was already observed by the first serious scholars of American Dutch – Jo Daan and Henk Heikens (see fn. 9) – who complained about the 'non-dialectal' – and 'standard-like' – character of the variety of Dutch that they encountered in Pella, Iowa.⁷ Clearly, this rise of American Dutch in Iowa resulted in the loss of the original dialects and Frisian.⁸

As far as the linguistic aspects of AD are concerned, it may not come as a surprise that this language is different from Standard Dutch (SD), i.e., the language presently spoken in the Netherlands. Present-day AD, being socially as well as linguistically the non-dominant language, exhibits the effects of both language contact (as a result of interference from English) and language attrition (either after acquisition has been completed or due to incomplete, i.e., interrupted, acquisition). Consequently, AD displays all kinds of deviations from SD, whereas, of course, it also consists of forms which are completely in line with SD. In relation to the part of the grammar that we focus on in this paper, i.e., inflection, these deviations are the result of processes such as: (i) the transfer of both inflectional elements and structure from English, (ii) the reduction of distinctions encoded in the Dutch inflectional system, e.g., by way of using uninflected instead of inflected forms, and (iii) the creation of new forms leading to either regularization (i.e., a decrease of irregularity) or deregularization (i.e., an increase of irregularity). Note that these processes may interact and that, consequently, it is often difficult, or even impossible, to determine the strength of each individual force (Van Marle and Smits 1996 and, particularly, Smits 1996).

Furthermore, AD is not a 'newly crystallized' language (Weinreich 1953: 69–70) as, for instance, Afrikaans is, the Dutch daughter language spoken in Southern Africa. That is, AD has not developed into a new stable system, but is instead in a process of disintegration. Consequently, at least as far as inflection is concerned, AD displays a striking degree of variation. As an illustration of this, consider the following example which is drawn from the translation test (see fn. 2). As a translation of 'they worked,' we not only came across the regular preterite *ze werkten* (stem *werk* + regular preterite suffix *-te* + plural ending *-n*) which is also the form used in SD, but all sorts of other

---

6. Such a shift to the standard variety has also been reported for other immigrant communities, cf. Smits (1996: 18–19) for further discussion.

7. See Van Marle (2014) for a general discussion of the rise of AD in Iowa. For a detailed and principled discussion of the alleged occurrence of dialect features in American Dutch, see also Van Marle and Smits (2002) and Smits (2002). Note, finally, that we have never claimed that in American Dutch no remnants of the original dialects can be found. The problem is, however, that, on a closer look, most examples of potential dialect features still present in American Dutch are little convincing.

8. See Van Marle (2012b) for Frisian, as well as Ehresmann and Bousquette (this volume).

forms as well. For instance, *ze hebben gewerkt* (present perfect), *ze werk-en* (present plural?/ infinitive?), *ze werk-t* (present 3rd person singular?/ transferred English preterite *-ed* [t]?), and *ze werk* (verb stem?/ English-based present tense form?). Note, also, that variation does not only occur between speakers, but also within the language of one and the same speaker. One of our informants, for instance, gave the following three translations which he all considered to be correct Dutch renderings of 'they worked': *ze werkt, ze hebben gewerkt* and *ze werkten* (which is the form used in SD).

Given this large-scale variation in AD inflection, the following questions arise in relation to 'norm awareness' in AD:

I. Are the grammatical norms which hold for SD still recognized in AD, and if so, to what extent? Or, put differently, can you make a mistake in AD?
II. Are there any differences between the results of the acceptability test and free conversation regarding the extent to which speakers of AD cling to the SD norms?
III. Are there any differences between speakers with regard to the extent to which norms are still recognized?
IV. Is the existence of norms equally strong/weak in all parts of the inflectional system? To put it differently, are there differences between the inflectional system of the noun, the adjective and the verb in relation to the extent to which SD norms are preserved?
V. Are there indications for the rise of new norms in AD, i.e., norms which are different from SD?

We investigate these questions regarding the existence of norms in AD, as noted, mainly by means of an analysis of data from an acceptability test (fn. 2). In discussing some of these questions, however, these data will be compared with those from free conversation.

The remainder of this paper is structured as follows. In Section 2, a description will be given of how the data under discussion were collected. In Section 3, the above raised questions regarding the existence of norms in AD will be investigated (except for question 5, discussed in Section 4). In Section 4, finally, we discuss the general conclusions which can be drawn from the results found in Section 3.

2. The data

In the acceptability test, 14 informants were given sentences containing inflectional forms deviating from SD. Since all sentences come from an older corpus of American Dutch, all are actually attested in AD.[9] From a SD point of view, these deviations are

---

9. This corpus was collected by J. Daan and H. Heikens in 1966. It consists of free conversation only. See Smits (1996) for further discussion of both the corpus from 1966 and the one from 1989.

quite dramatic and relate to the pluralization of nouns, the conjugation of verbs (both in the present tense and in the preterite), as well as the declension of adjectives. In order to get an idea of the nature of the deviations presented to the informants, consider the following examples:

(1) Nouns
    a. *mijn twee **broer** die waren naar Racine gegaan*
       'my two brothers had gone to Racine'
       (singular form *broer* instead of SD plural ***broer-s***)
    b. *ze moesten altijd de kinderen Hollandse **vrages** leren*
       'they always had to teach the children Dutch questions'
       (pluralization by means of *-es* instead of SD plural ***vrag-en***)

(2) Verbs present tense
    a. *hij **dragen** altijd witte handschoenen*
       'he always wears white gloves'
       (plural form?/infinitive? instead of SD 3rd person singular ***draag-t***)
    b. *dat **doet** ik vaak*
       'I do that often'
       (3rd person singular instead of SD 1st person singular ***doe***)

(3) Verbs preterite
    a. *toen wij **trouw***
       'when we married'
       (verb stem?/English-based present tense form? instead of SD regular preterite plural ***trouw-de-n***)
    b. *ik liep zo hard dat ik **val***
       'I ran so quickly that I fell'
       (present tense form instead of SD irregular preterite singular ***viel***)

(4) Adjectives
    a. *het was maar een **kleine** boertje*
       'he was just a small farmer'
       (declined form of the adjective instead of SD undeclined ***klein***)
    b. *en dan over een **ander** brug*
       'and then across an other bridge'
       (undeclined form of the adjective instead of SD declined ***ander-e***)

All sentences were presented on tape, i.e., in spoken form. In this way, an average of 25 sentences were presented to each informant. In sum, 345 sentences were judged. The recorded sentences were played to the informants and they had to judge each sentence as either correct or incorrect immediately after presentation. In case the informant judged a sentence as incorrect, it was checked whether this judgment actually concerned the inflectional form in question. If a sentence was judged as incorrect on the basis of considerations other than deviations in inflection – such as considerations relating to lexical or semantic properties of the sentences in question – it was concluded that the informant considered the inflectional form to be correct.[10]

Finally, as pointed out in Section 1, these data are compared with data from free conversation. These latter data stem from the 1989 corpus as well (fn. 2). During these conversations, topics were discussed such as how Dutch was acquired, the domains in which Dutch was used, and the attitudes towards Dutch ethnicity. Obviously, these conversations had a much more informal character than the acceptability test (see 3.2.). From the conversations all inflectional forms were extracted, i.e., both forms that are in line with SD and forms deviating from SD.

3. Norms in AD

In this section the first four questions that were raised in the introduction will be elaborated upon. As was pointed out above, question V will be discussed in Section 4.

3.1 Question (I): Are the grammatical norms which hold for SD still recognized in AD?

This question will be tested with the acceptability test. Consider Table 1 on the rejection of forms deviating from SD in the acceptability test:

Table 1 shows that the percentage of recognized – i.e., rejected – deviant inflectional forms is remarkably low. Out of the 75 nominal plurals which deviate from SD, only 17 were recognized, i.e., 22.7%. As far as the prototypical, regular verbs with an infinitive in *-en* are concerned (cf. *zwemm-en* 'to swim'), only 15.3% of the deviating present tense forms were recognized as such. The non-prototypical, irregular verbs with an infinitive in *-n* (e.g., *gaa-n* 'to go') do relatively well: 25% were recognized as

---

10. The question arises how reliable these answers are. Are 'naive' language users capable of distinguishing 'incorrect,' 'deviant,' 'ungrammatical' forms at all, or do they simply accept any form presented to them? In our view, there is no straightforward answer to this question, in that this issue highly depends on the types of forms that these naive speakers have to judge. There seems to be much difference between e.g., the evaluation of subtle word order issues or 'gross inflectional errors.' The latter type of deviations are treated in this paper. The forms in question are similar to *they walks, she see, he go'ed* (instead of *they walk, she sees* and *he went*) in English. Since inflection in general exhibits little variation (Section 3.1), one may take the line that these inflectional errors will generally not go unnoticed. In addition, in Section 4 it will become clear that most speakers of AD do not simply accept all forms presented to them. In short, the reliability of acceptability tests no doubt represents a serious issue. However, in relation to the forms focused on in this paper, the risk of using this type of test seems acceptable.

Table 1. Rejection of inflectional forms deviating from Standard Dutch in the acceptability test.

	total	rejected	% rejected forms
nouns	75	17	22.7
present tense verbs in -en	85	13	15.3
present tense verbs in -n	32	8	25
regular preterite verbs	13	1	7.7
irregular preterite verbs	75	21	28
adjectives	65	0	0

deviant from SD.[11] As far as the preterite is concerned, we see the following picture: deviations in the case of verbs with a regular preterite in SD were recognized in only 7.7% of all cases, whereas irregular preterites score relatively high: 28% were recognized as deviating from SD. The behavior of adjectives, finally, is especially remarkable, since the number of recognized deviations is nil. That is, all 65 'incorrectly' declined adjectives presented were accepted. This is tantamount to saying that the SD norm for the declension of adjectives is completely lost in AD.

On the basis of the above it can be concluded that by far the majority of the inflectional forms that deviate from SD are accepted by our informants. This holds for both nouns, verbs, and adjectives. Except for the irregular preterites whose rejection scores rank somewhat higher (28%), the rejection rate of *all* other inflectional forms is 25% or less. In these latter categories *of all deviant inflectional forms 75% or more are not recognized at all*. This is all the more remarkable in light of the fact that inflection is generally considered (one of) the most tightly structured and stable parts of the grammatical system. That is, inflectional rules are considered to be 'compulsory' (in the sense of being dictated by sentence structure). As a consequence, inflectional systems generally display hardly any variation. Actually, in non-disintegrating languages deviant inflectional forms will normally be observed immediately, since they imply a kind of variation which 'healthy' languages are claimed to never exhibit (cf. Carstairs 1987).

3.2 Question (II): Are there any differences between the acceptability test and the free conversations regarding the extent to which the informants in our corpus cling to the SD norms?

This question is taken up by means of comparing the results of the acceptability test with those drawn from free conversation. In this connection we start from the assumption that the informants will reach the SD norm more closely in 'reflection' (i.e., in the

---

11. These irregular verbs in -*n* have as their most salient characteristic that their infinitives are monosyllabic (disregarding derived and compound forms, of course), cf. *gaa-n* 'to go,' *staa-n* 'to stand,' *doe-n* 'to do,' *slaa-n* 'to hit,' *zie-n* 'to see.'

acceptability test) than in actual production (i.e., in conversations). In relation to the latter, the following remarks are due: First, in reflection – at least in non-disintegrating languages – speakers are often well aware of the existing norms, although in actual speech they may not always be able to avoid forms running counter to the norms. It may well be that this is *a fortiori* so for speakers of disintegrating languages. These speakers may find considerable difficulties in the process of on-line speech production, whereas their knowledge of the grammatical system may still be largely intact (Sharwood Smith and Van Buren 1991). Second, the more formal the situation is, the more attention will be paid to speech, and the more careful the speech style will be (Labov 1972).[12] As said, in our view there can be no doubt that the acceptability test represents a more formal situation than free conversation which was highly informal.

On the basis of the above, it may be expected that in reflection more attention will be paid to the norms than in actual production. Consequently, *we start from the idea that our informants will be more able to observe deviations from SD in the acceptability test than to avoid deviations in free conversation*. Now, consider Table 2 on the retention of SD inflection for nouns and verbs in free conversation, and note that adjectival declension will come up for discussion later:[13]

Table 2. Retention of Standard Dutch inflectional forms in free conversation.

	total	SD	% SD
nouns	255	242	95
present tense verbs in -en	879	704	80
present tense verbs in -n	41	25	60.1
regular preterite verbs	72	40	55.5
irregular preterite verbs	333	218	65.5

From Table 2 it follows that in free conversation speakers of AD do much better than expected, particularly much better than in the acceptability test. Different from what we expected, in free conversation the SD norm is reached much more closely than in the acceptability test. This holds for both nouns, present tense verbs and preterite verbs.

It can also be inferred from Table 2 that there are differences between inflectional categories. The SD system of noun pluralization, for instance, is largely preserved in actual production in AD: of a total of 255 plurals, 242 were in line with SD, i.e., 95%.

---

12. Note, that the latter observation relates to phonological rather than grammatical phenomena.

13. The following discussion of inflection in free conversation is based on the data of only 10 of the 14 speakers who participated in the acceptability test. The fact is, that, at the time this paper was written, the conversations of the 4 most proficient speakers of AD (i.e., those speakers whose language conforms to SD most) had not been analyzed yet. However, since the language of these four speakers is most in line with SD, additional data from conversations of these informants would only make the differences between test and conversations more significant (cf. below).

(It should be noted, though, that in conversations the regular plurals are far more prominent than in the acceptability test.) Furthermore, it appears that in free conversation present tense verbs with an infinitive in *-en* are relatively well preserved too, though less so than nominal plurals: 80% of these verb forms conform to SD patterns. In conversations the non-prototypical *-n* verbs are less well preserved, only 60.1% in line with SD. The SD regular system for the formation of the preterite is even more affected in AD: in production only 55.5% of these forms are in line with SD. The SD irregular preterites are somewhat better preserved than their regular counterparts, 65.5% of these forms are like SD.

In short, in free conversation nouns are best preserved, present tense *-en* verbs somewhat less, whereas irregular preterites, present tense *-n* verbs, and regular preterites (in increasing order) appear to be much more dramatically affected. But, whatever the differences between the inflectional systems of nouns, present tense and preterite verbs, most remarkable is the fact that *in actual production inflection is always significantly much more in line with SD than in reflection*. Put differently, in the conversations many speakers of AD succeed in avoiding inflectional forms that deviate from SD quite well. These speakers, however, experience much difficulty in detecting deviant inflectional forms in the acceptability test (i.e., in the speech of others). Clearly, this runs completely counter to our assumption that the informants would conform to the SD norm more closely in reflection than in production.

Let us now turn to the declension of adjectives in free conversation. In order to appreciate the tendencies within the adjectival system in AD, we will have to discuss SD adjectival declension first. In SD the declension of the attributive adjective depends both on gender and number of the noun it modifies and on the preceding determiner. Most varieties of SD have a two-article system: *het* is associated with neutral nouns, while *de* is associated with originally feminine and masculine nouns. Plural nouns always take *de*. In by far the majority of cases attributively used adjectives take a declined form in *-e*. The fact is, that all singular nouns having *de* as article and all plural nouns take a declined adjective irrespective of accompanying determiners and, in the case of plural nouns, irrespective of the gender of the noun they modify. However, when adjectives refer to singular *het* nouns, things are different. These nouns take a declined adjective when the noun is definite, but an undeclined adjective in case the noun is indefinite. This is tantamount to the following: if the noun is singular, neutral and indefinite the adjective takes the undeclined form, in all other cases the declined form of the adjective is used. Now consider Table 3 on adjectival declension in free conversation:

Table 3. Adjectival declension in free conversation.

	total	% undeclined adjectives	% declined adjectives
singular, neutral, indefinite nouns	40	37.5	62.5
all other nouns	146	12.3	87.7

From Table 3 it can be inferred that in AD conversations adjectival declension is different from SD. Actually, the SD system for declension of attributive adjectives has largely been lost. In general, there is a strong tendency in AD to use the declined adjective, even in the context where SD uses the undeclined form, i.e., in the cases with singular, neutral, indefinite nouns (although in that case this tendency is less strong). In AD the preference for declined adjectives is so strong that the stand may even be taken that in this variety of Dutch a new rule is developing which reads: in attributive position adjectives are always declined.[14]

From the results of the acceptability test (cf. Table 1) it is obvious that the SD norm for the declension of adjectives has been lost. Recall, that the number of recognized deviations from SD in that test was nil. That is, all 65 'incorrectly declined' adjectives were judged acceptable. That is, both cases in which a declined adjective instead of an undeclined adjective was used and cases in which an undeclined instead of a declined adjective was used were accepted. The results in Table 1 also show that in reflection there is no evidence for a new system emerging in spontaneous speech. Whereas in production there is an overall preference for declined adjectives in attributive position, from the acceptability test it follows that this preference does not have the status of overt norm. Both declined and undeclined adjectives are judged equally. In a way, this is consistent with our findings on the behavior of nouns and verbs. In all three cases norms are reached more closely in production than in reflection. Note, however, the crucial difference between nouns and verbs on the one hand, and adjectives on the other. In free conversation SD forms are still largely preserved in the case of nouns and verbs. In the case of adjectives this is not so. Instead, a new rule is developing which seems to oust the original system; this new rule, however, is not supported by the acceptability test.

3.3 Question (III): Are there any differences between speakers with regard to the extent to which norms are still recognized?

The answer to this question is no doubt affirmative. See Table 4 below. First, out of the 14 informants who participated in the acceptability test, 7 were *not* capable of detecting *any* deviations at all in any of the sentences presented to them. That is, no less than 50% of our informants considered all deviant inflectional forms – be it deviations regarding the inflection of nouns, adjectives, or verbs – to be correct, i.e., SD, forms. Moreover, the remaining 7 speakers – that is, the speakers who did turn down at least part of the forms presented to them – by no means exhibit an equally strong inclination to reject inflectional forms deviating from SD.

---

14. Van Marle (1995) points out that the trend to generalize the declined adjective can also be found in other varieties of overseas Dutch, such as Surinamese Dutch and East Indian Dutch. In addition, as can be inferred from Table 3, in AD a trend in the opposite direction is present as well: on a much more marginal level, undeclined adjectives are generalized at the cost of declined adjectives.

Table 4. Percentage of rejected forms for each informant participating in the acceptability test.

informant	% rejected forms
1	68%
2	60%
3	54.5%
4	25%
5	24%
6	18.8%
7	16%
8	0%
9	0%
10	0%
11	0%
12	0%
13	0%
14	0%

Table 4 shows that, as far as the 'rejection-inclined' speakers are concerned (i.e., 1–7), there is a rather sharp contrast between speakers 1–3 on the one hand and speakers 4–7 on the other. Whereas the former three speakers detected at least half of the deviating inflectional forms presented to them (between 54.5% and 68%), the latter speakers only detected a quarter or less of the deviations. From these results we conclude that for these 7 rejection-inclined speakers the answer to the above question about the occurrence of individual differences should be affirmative as well. That is, even if informants are inclined to regard some of the inflectional forms presented to them as unacceptable, this inclination is by no means equally strong for all of them.[15]

Finally, the 7 speakers who refrained from rejecting any sentence at all are not necessarily informants who deviate most dramatically from SD in actual speech production. That is to say, among these 7 there are some who proved to be quite capable of producing SD forms in free conversation. Conversely, most of the speakers who did manage to detect deviations from SD in the acceptability test scored relatively high in the production of SD forms. Note, however, that the latter pattern is not without exceptions. At least one informant who did well in the acceptability test scored relatively low on SD forms in conversations. Consequently, these findings indicate that there is not always question of one-to-one relationships between production and reflection.

---

15. These differences do not seem to be related to differences in socio-economic classes. All of our informants were (retired) farmers and shopkeepers.

3.4 Question (IV): Is the existence of norms equally strong/weak in all parts of the inflectional system?

The fourth question will be dealt with by means of a more detailed discussion of the differences in rejection scores between the inflectional systems of nouns, adjectives and verbs. In the light of this issue we will use Table 5 instead of Table 1. As discussed above, 7 out of 14 speakers regarded all test sentences as acceptable, i.e., SD, sentences. Table 5, then, is exclusively based on data from the 7 'rejection-inclined' informants, i.e., the informants who turned down at least some inflectional forms. From this table the differences between the various subsystems in terms of rejection scores become more apparent:

Table 5. Rejection of inflectional forms deviating from Standard Dutch in the acceptability test by the 7 rejection-inclined speakers.

	total	rejected	% rejected forms
nouns	42	17	40.5
present tense verbs in -*en*	47	13	27.7
present tense verbs in -*n*	17	8	47
regular preterite verbs	5	1	20
irregular preterite verbs	35	20	57.1
adjectives	28	0	0

In general, even among the 7 rejection-inclined informants, the rejection score is, in our view, remarkably low. Except for the irregular preterites (with a rejection score of 57.1%), *all* other categories have a rejection score below 50%. Evidently, this means that, with the exception of the irregular preterites, in all categories more than half of the deviant inflectional forms were not recognized whatsoever, not even by the 7 speakers who turned out to be most critical to inflectional deviations from SD.

From Table 5 it also follows that in relation to the acceptability of inflectional deviations the diverse subsystems behave differently. Deviant adjectival forms were never rejected, whereas deviant nominal plurals score relatively high (40.5%). The verb system does not exhibit a uniform pattern: irregular -*n* verbs (present tense forms) and irregular preterites score relatively high (47% and 57.1% respectively), whereas regular present tense and regular preterite forms score remarkably low (27.7% and 20% respectively). Note, though, that these findings are not too surprising in the light of our earlier work on overseas Dutch. Van Marle and Smits (1989, 1993, 1995) and Smits (1993) reached similar conclusions on the basis of an analysis of inflectional forms in conversations in the 1966 corpus and in the translation test in the 1989 corpus, respectively.[16]

---

16. As noted in Section 3.2, there are also differences between the inflectional subsystems in free conversations. Although these differences parallel the differences in the acceptability test to a large extent, the parallelism is far from complete. Consider, for instance, the relationship

The relatively high rejection score of nominal plurals should, in our view, be attributed to the fact that in AD the system of noun pluralization is still largely intact (also: Smits 1996). As can be drawn from both the translation test and free conversation (cf. also Table 2), the SD rules for nominal plurals are relatively well preserved and, consequently, our informants are still quite capable to reject forms deviating from these rules in the acceptability test.

For verbs, things are different. Generally, the verb system is less well preserved than the nominal system. That is, the speakers of American Dutch are less capable of applying the rules of verb conjugation and rejecting verb forms deviating from the rules in the acceptability test. As a result, in the case of verbs it is particularly the verb forms which do not involve application of the actual rule system (i.e., non-prototypical, irregular -*n* verbs and irregular preterites) that have a relatively high score in the acceptability test. Put differently, deviations within the irregular classes are more often noticed than deviations within their regular counterparts. The fact is, of course, that irregular verb forms cannot be predicted by general rule, but that these forms have to be learned by rote. In sum, as far as verbs (both present and preterite) are concerned 'storage' is of more relevance than systematicity. Systematicity, then, does not always lead to a generally high percentage of rejection. Instead, in the case of verbs, and different from nouns, the most prominent factor which appears to bring about rejection is storage, the psycholinguistic counterpart of the linguistic notion of irregularity. This outcome is in complete harmony with Smits (1993).

No doubt, the behavior of adjectives is most remarkable. As we have seen, this is the only inflectional subsystem which – as far as free conversation is concerned – seems to have developed into a new, more or less stable, system. The tendency to generalize the inflected form in attributive position is so strong that it is tempting to assume that a new rule is coming into existence: 'attributively used adjectives are declined in -*e*.' In sharp contrast to this finding, however, are the results from the acceptability test. Not one of our informants rejected any of the attributively used *undeclined* adjectives presented to them.[17]

4. General discussion

Clearly, the crucial issue is that the outcome of the acceptability test contradicts our assumption according to which the SD norm should be obeyed more readily in reflection than in production. As has become clear, in AD the reverse is the case. In

---

between -*en* verbs and -*n* verbs in the present tense: in the acceptability test the -*n* verbs score highest whereas in free conversations it is the -*en* verbs which score highest.

17. The extent to which factors such as absence of meaning distinctions, the – presumably – limited role of storage, and the 'subconscious' character of adjectival declension in general play a part, awaits further study.

production inflectional forms conform more to SD norms than in reflection. In our view, this is mainly due to the fact that free conversation, so to say, gives a distorted picture of the knowledge that the present-day speakers of AD actually have of the overall grammatical system of Dutch. In Smits (2001) a similar conclusion was reached. That paper compared inflection in conversations and translations. This comparison made clear that in this case, too, inflection was more affected in translations than in conversations. That is, there is a clear parallel between the results of the translation test and the acceptability test, as opposed to the results from free conversation. Speakers of AD score considerably better in informal free conversation than in the tests. Like the acceptability test discussed above, then, the translation test reveals that speakers of AD only have a weak control of the inflectional system. AD as it figures in free conversation can best be regarded as a 'strongly reduced' variety of Dutch for which it holds that:

a. In free conversation speakers of AD are free to use rules which they still have a relatively strong control of.
b. Consequently, in free conversation speakers of AD can avoid all rules which are less well mastered, meaning that they can avoid all kinds of difficulties. In addition, many rules have been 'generalized' considerably.
c. In free conversation it is not only the rule system which is reduced but also the lexicon. As a consequence, small classes of non-prototypical forms (such as the irregular *-n* verbs) have become highly marginal. The direct result of this is, that many speakers of AD are only able to apply the most frequent – and 'generalized' – rules to the prototypical cases.
d. Finally, it may well be that many of the forms used in free conversation are drawn straight from memory, meaning that in these cases there is no question of the application of rules at all (also Smits 2001). That is, for many of the present-day speakers of AD it may well be the case that 'disintegrating' AD is to a large extent based on memory, much more so than in the case of 'healthy' languages.

The conversational data, then, do not give an accurate picture of the extent to which speakers of AD still manage to apply the overall grammatical system of Dutch. Instead, in the conversations we are faced with a restricted variety of Dutch which involves only a limited number of (generalized) rules, a restricted lexicon, and which heavily depends on memory. Conversely, in the acceptability test as well as in the translation test the speakers of AD were confronted with Dutch in its 'full range' and were forced to apply their, impoverished, knowledge of the system to a wide variety of forms, most of which do not form part of present-day AD any more. In short, both the translation test and the acceptability test give a similar and more accurate picture of the actual knowledge of the overall grammatical system of Dutch that the present-day speakers of AD still have. As became clear in the above, this knowledge is seriously affected. As a matter of fact, for most speakers of AD it holds that their overall knowledge of Dutch is much more affected than the conversations suggest, since their native variety of Dutch (i.e., American Dutch) is nothing but a highly reduced version of their original ethnic language.

To be clear, our conclusion that AD represents a 'reduced variety' of Dutch is not meant to imply any negative judgment, neither with respect to this language nor with respect to its speakers. Our above remarks are meant to be nothing but an objective characterization of present-day AD vis-à-vis SD. As to our appreciation of the competence and skills of the present-day speakers of AD, rather the reverse is the case, In our view it is quite remarkable how proficient many present-day speakers of AD still are, how much they still know about their ethnic language, and how efficient 'reduced' AD in informal in-group communication still is. However 'reduced,' to many present-day speakers AD is still valuable and functional, while the language skills of many present-day speakers – not infrequently third or even fourth generation Americans – are no doubt impressive.

The results of the acceptability test presented above may bring to light another specific characteristic of the present-day speakers of AD as well. This regards the attitude which these Dutch descendants have towards the language of 'the old country.' The fact is, that speakers of AD have a high esteem of both the Netherlands and the Dutch language. They are proud to be of Dutch descent and of the fact that they have preserved the language and are still able to speak it. As an effect, they are extremely pleased to be confronted with it, even to the extent that they simply do not consider the possibility of rejecting a Dutch sentence. Put differently, many speakers of AD are quite willing to accept all 'Dutch-like' sentences presented to them. Most likely, a precondition to this permissive attitude towards language norms is their impoverished knowledge of the overall grammatical system.

The potential role of the positive attitude towards Dutch also comes up for discussion in relation to the fifth, and final, question raised in the introduction:

4.1 Question (V): Are there indications for the rise of a new norm in AD, i.e., a norm which is different from SD?

It is naturally not simply the case that AD is lacking any norms whatsoever. As became clear above, half of our informants have preserved at least part of the SD norms holding for the inflection of nouns and verbs. In morphology no new overt norms have come into existence, even not in the case of the adjective. However, on the lexical level things appear to be different. In general, our informants appeared to be very keen on the occurrence of English elements in AD, meaning that the use of English vocabulary in AD sentences was strongly criticized, even by speakers who were not 'rejection-inclined' at all.[18] That is, on the lexical level a new norm appears to have come

---

18. Some speakers even exhibit a sort of 'anti-English' attitude when they speak Dutch. One of our informants, for instance, avoided the normal, i.e., English, pronunciation of the place name *Orange City*. Apparently unable to come up with a Dutch rendering of this place name, he preferred the French pronunciation instead. In other cases, present-day speakers of AD still use the old, and strongly 'Dutchified,' pronunciation of English place names when they are speaking Dutch.

into existence. Crucially, this lexical norm is much easier to handle than the more complicated grammatical norms bearing upon the abstract inflectional system. Also interesting about this new norm is, that it indicates that puristic trends may develop spontaneously and need not be the result of the efforts of generations of schoolmasters.

To conclude, our above findings can only fully be appreciated in light of the following two facts. First, present-day AD is a highly reduced language variety which is only a faint reflection of the original ethnic language that the Dutch settlers brought to the New World. Second, the majority of the present-day speakers of AD have an extremely positive attitude towards 'the old country' and the language that is spoken there. The joint effect of these two forces leads to, first, the uncritical acceptance of far too many 'unconventional', though Dutch or Dutch-like, forms. As noted above, this acceptance presupposes a lack of knowledge of the overall grammatical system from the part of the speakers and, second, a remarkably strong tendency to criticize non-Dutch, i.e., English, lexical elements in American Dutch.

References

Carstairs, Andrew. 1987. *Allomorphy in Inflection*. London: Croom Helm.
Dorian, Nancy C. 1981. *Language Death. The Life Cycle of a Scottish Gaelic Dialect*. Philadelphia: University of Pennsylvania Press.
Labov, William. 1972. *Sociolinguistic Patterns*. Philadelphia: University of Pennsylvania Press.
Lucas, Henry S. 1955. *Netherlanders in America. Dutch Immigration to the United States and Canada, 1789–1950*. Ann Arbor: University of Michigan Press.
Sharwood Smith, Michael and Paul van Buren. 1991. "First Language Attrition and the Parameter Setting Model." In *First Language Attrition*, ed. by Herbert W. Seliger and Robert M. Vago, 17–30. Cambridge: Cambridge University Press. DOI: 10.1017/CBO9780511620720.002
Smits, Caroline. 1993. "Resistance to Erosion in American Dutch Inflection." In *Yearbook of Morphology 1993*, ed. by Geert Booij and Jaap van Marle, 155–184. Dordrecht: Kluwer. DOI: 10.1007/978-94-017-3712-8_5
Smits, Caroline. 1996. *Disintegration of Inflection: The Case of Iowa Dutch*. (HIL Dissertations 22). The Hague: Holland Academic Graphics.
Smits, Caroline. 2001. "Iowa Dutch Inflection: Translations Versus Conversations." In *Sociolinguistic and Psycholinguistic Perspectives on Maintenance and Loss of Minority Languages*, ed. by Tom Ammerlaan, Madeleine Hulsen, Heleen Strating, Kutlay Yagmur, 299–318. Münster: Waxmann.
Smits, Caroline. 2002. "On the (Non-)Persistence of Dialect Features in American Dutch (2): The Case of Iowa Dutch." In *Present-Day Dialectology*, ed. by Jan Berns and Jaap van Marle, 243–267. Berlin: Mouton de Gruyter.
Van Hinte, Jacob. 1985. *Netherlanders in America. A Study of Emigration and Settlement in the Nineteenth and Twentieth Centuries in the United States of America*. Edited by Robert P. Swierenga. Grand Rapids: Baker Book House. [Revised and translated version of the Dutch edition of 1928]

Van Marle, Jaap. 1995. "On the Fate of Adjectival Declension in Overseas Dutch (With Some Notes on the History of Dutch)." In *Historical Linguistics 1993*, ed. by Henning Andersen, 283–294. Amsterdam: Benjamins. DOI: 10.1075/cilt.124.23mar

Van Marle, Jaap. 2001a. "American 'Leeg Duits' ('Low Dutch') – A Neglected Language." In *Global Eurolinguistics. European Languages in North America – Migration, Maintenance and Death*, ed. by P. Sture Ureland, 79–101. Tübingen: Niemeyer.

Van Marle, Jaap. 2001b. "The Acculturation of Dutch Immigrants in the USA: A Linguist's View." In *The Dutch Adapting in North America*, ed. by Robert Harms, 18–26. Grand Rapids, MI: Calvin College.

Van Marle, Jaap. 2005. "On the Divergence and Maintenance of Immigrants Languages: Dutch in Michigan." In *Language Diversity in Michigan and Ohio: Towards Two State Linguistic Profiles*, ed. by Brian D. Joseph, Carol G. Preston and Dennis R. Preston, 169–187. Ann Arbor: Caravan.

Van Marle, Jaap. 2008. "Yankee Dutch Literature as a Marker of Acculturation." In *Dutch-American Arts and Letters in Historical Perspective*, ed. by Robert P. Swierenga, Jacob E. Nyenhuis and Nella Kennedy, 61–67. Holland, MI: Van Raalte.

Van Marle, Jaap. 2010. "Yankee Dutch: Later Developments." In *Across Borders. Dutch Migration to North America and Australia*, ed. by Jacob E. Nyenhuis, Suzanne M. Sinke and Robert P. Swierenga, 135–144. Holland, MI: Van Raalte.

Van Marle, Jaap. 2012a. "Dutch Immigrants in Wisconsin: Their Linguistic Heritage." In *Diverse Destinies. Dutch Kolonies in Wisconsin and the East*, ed. by Nella Kennedy, Mary Risseeuw and Robert P. Swierenga, 221–233. Holland, MI: Van Raalte.

Van Marle, Jaap. 2012b. "On the Survival of the Frisian Language in Wisconsin." In *Diverse Destinies. Dutch Kolonies in Wisconsin and the East*, ed. by Nella Kennedy, Mary Risseeuw and Robert P. Swierenga, 235–246. Holland, MI: Van Raalte.

Van Marle, Jaap. 2014. "On the Shift to Standard Dutch in Dutch-American Immigrants Communities." In *Dutch Americans and War: United States and Abroad*, ed. by Robert P. Swierenga, Nella Kennedy and Lisa Zylstra, 351–361. Holland, MI: Van Raalte.

Van Marle, Jaap and Caroline Smits. 1989. "Morphological Erosion in American Dutch." In *Vielfalt der Kontakte*, ed. by Norbert Boretzky, Werner Enninger and Thomas Stolz, 37–65. Bochum: Universitätsverlag Brockmeyer.

Van Marle, Jaap and Caroline Smits. 1993. "The Inflectional Systems of Overseas Dutch." In *Historical Linguistics 1989*, ed. by Henk Aertsen and Robert Jeffers, 313–28. Amsterdam: John Benjamins. DOI: 10.1075/cilt.106.23mar

Van Marle, Jaap and Caroline Smits. 1995. "On the Impact of Language Contact on Inflectional Systems: The Reduction of Verb Inflection in American Dutch and American Frisian." In *Linguistic Change Under Contact Conditions*, ed. by Jacek Fisiak, 179–206. Berlin: Mouton de Gruyter.

Van Marle, Jaap and Caroline Smits. 1996. "American Dutch: General Trends in its Development." In *Language Contact Across the North Atlantic*, ed. by P. Sture Ureland and Ian Clarkson, 427–442. Tübingen: Niemeyer.

Van Marle, Jaap and Caroline Smits. 2002. "On the (Non-)Persistence of Dialect Features in American Dutch (1): General Aspects." In *Present-Day Dialectology*, ed. by Jan Berns and Jaap van Marle, 231–242. Berlin: Mouton de Gruyter. DOI: 10.1515/9783110904765

Weinreich, Uriel. 1953. *Languages in Contact*. The Hague: Mouton.

Index of languages and dialects

A
Afrikaans   6, 144, 391
Alsatian (Texas)   123, 125–126, 128, 130
Arabic   238
Aramaic   14, 218, 222

D
Danish   6, 312–314, 317, 366
Dano-Norwegian   289–290, 312–313
Dutch   3–9, 11–13, 15–17, 42, 44, 47, 70, 79, 99–101, 114, 130, 135, 144–145, 147, 151, 156–157, 203, 215, 234–236, 240, 248–251, 255, 389–396, 398, 400–405
    American Dutch   5, 389–392, 401–402, 404–405
    Yankee Dutch   8, 390, 405

E
English   1–13, 15–17, 21–22, 28–30, 33–38, 41–43, 46–49, 53–54, 56, 58–60, 64–65, 71–80, 82, 84–86, 88–89, 91–93, 97–101, 103–106, 108–115, 117–119, 121, 123–126, 129–130, 135–137, 142–145, 147, 149–158, 160–166, 168–175, 177, 180–181, 184–185, 187, 191–197, 201, 204–223, 225, 227–252, 255–257, 259–263, 266–274, 276–280, 283–284, 287–290, 296–298, 300, 306, 324–326, 331–332, 334, 337, 339, 341–345, 349–353, 356, 358–362, 365–366, 369, 372–387, 389–394, 403–404
    American English   97, 99, 104–105, 109, 112–114, 125, 129, 158, 201, 204–205, 207–208, 211, 215, 225, 260–262, 296, 352, 387
    World Englishes   137, 154–155

F
Finnish   92, 279, 354
French   99–100, 103, 110, 216, 218, 279, 379, 403
    Cajun (French)   219, 232

F
Frisian   3–7, 12–13, 15, 232, 234–253, 255, 257, 278, 391, 405
    West Frisian   3–5, 7, 12–13, 15, 232, 234–243, 245–253, 255, 278

G
German   1–9, 11, 15–17, 69, 100–103, 110, 113–115, 117–121, 123, 125–131, 137, 143–146, 153, 155–159, 185, 196–197, 226, 235, 238, 240, 253–255, 263, 268, 276–280, 287, 294–295, 298, 303, 321–322, 325–326, 373, 376, 378, 385–388
    Standard German   117–118, 120–121, 123, 125–129, 131
    Texas German   117, 119–120, 123, 129–131, 278, 321, 386
    German dialects   1, 8, 11, 15, 123, 263
    Germanic (languages)   1–3, 5–6, 8, 70, 88, 93, 114, 130–131, 144, 157, 159–160, 179, 196–197, 218, 229, 231, 253–255, 268, 274, 278, 296, 322, 387

H
Hawaiian Creole   154, 159
Hebrew   14, 178, 185, 190, 196–197, 217–218, 220, 222, 225, 228, 232

I
Icelandic   3, 5–7, 9–10, 15, 72–93, 321, 375–376, 385
    North American Icelandic   10, 15, 72–75, 77–85, 91–93, 385
    flámæli   89–90
Italian   42, 218

K
Korean   92, 110

L
Low German (Plattdeutsch)   8, 123

M
Mainland Scandinavian   169
Mayan (languages)   185, 196

N
Norwegian   1, 3–7, 10, 14–16, 21–26, 28–30, 33–46, 48–65, 68–71, 73, 78, 92–93, 97–116, 121, 124, 129, 145, 156–157, 161–166, 168, 170–176, 201–207, 210–216, 231–232, 235, 239, 249, 251–254, 256–262, 266–272, 274, 276–280, 283–304, 306–307, 309–327, 330–337, 339, 341–346, 349–358, 366, 372–373, 375–376, 378–379, 385–387
    American Norwegian   3–5, 10, 41, 44, 46, 49, 55–57, 59, 62–65, 69–70, 92, 97–99, 105–107, 124, 129, 161–166, 168, 170–175, 201–207, 210–211, 213–216, 231–232, 239, 251–252, 256–262, 267, 269–272, 274, 276–279, 293, 296–297, 300–301, 303–304, 306, 309–321, 326, 366, 375, 385

Heritage Norwegian 35, 37,
   46, 49, 65, 111, 113, 201, 299
East Norwegian dialects 10,
   34, 288, 291–292, 302
European Norwegian 46,
   49, 64–65, 68, 98, 106,
   112–113, 239, 299–300, 303
West Norwegian dialects
   288–289
Bokmål 39, 44, 70, 297,
   299–300, 304, 312–322
Nynorsk 312, 317–318,
   321–322

P
Pennsylvania German 4, 15–16,
   158–159, 196, 276–279
Pennsylvania Dutch 3–9, 11, 15,
   42, 44, 130, 135, 144–145, 147,
   151, 156, 203, 215
Polish 100, 279
Principense 154, 159

Q
Quechua 160, 354
Quichua 354

R
Romani 265, 278–279
Russian 78–79, 91–92, 110,
   154, 159

S
Slavic (languages) 92, 100,
   159, 218
Somali 100
Spanish 70, 87, 92, 110, 154,
   159–160, 177, 185, 196, 205,
   207, 224, 279, 354, 387
Swedish 3, 5–7, 12, 41–42, 44,
   49–50, 52, 54–55, 70, 73, 89,
   122, 130, 158, 235, 253–254,
   259, 279, 290, 297, 307, 309,
   320, 322, 359–370, 372–388

Book Swedish 363–364,
   369, 385
Standard Swedish 12, 362–
   363, 366–370, 375–380,
   382–385
Northern Swedish 370, 372

Y
Yiddish 3–7, 13–16, 178–181,
   183–187, 189, 191–197, 217–233
Hasidic Yiddish 13–15,
   194, 196
Central Yiddish 14, 179,
   183, 187
Eastern Yiddish 14

Index of names

A
Aasen, I.   312, 317, 321
Abugov, N.   178, 196
Åfarli, T.   4, 44, 115, 161, 167, 176, 216, 283, 296, 318, 321–322, 375
Agha, A.   219, 231
Ågren, P.-U.   367, 386
Ahearn, L.   329, 356
Al Zidjaly, N.   330, 334, 356
Aleichem, Sholem   181
Allen, B.   3, 97–98, 103–105, 113, 121, 129, 283, 296
Ameel, E.   374, 376, 385
Anderssen, M.   3, 21–23, 25–26, 28, 30, 33, 42, 44, 49–50, 52–53, 55, 69, 71, 88, 93, 156, 241, 252, 283, 298
Andersson, S.-G.   73, 145, 157, 385
Andréasson, M.   5, 44, 130, 254, 297, 359, 361, 385
Angantýsson, Á.   89, 91
Annear, L.   4, 49, 69, 97, 101, 113, 124, 129, 201, 219, 231, 235, 238–239, 243, 249, 252, 257, 278, 283, 296, 312, 321, 376
Argyri, E.   378, 385
Arnbjörnsdóttir, B.   3, 7, 10, 15, 72–77, 79–82, 84, 87, 90–91, 93
Assouline, D.   178, 196
Auer, P.   16, 297, 337, 351, 356
Avery, P.   100, 113, 237, 252
Avineri, N.   14–15, 218, 231

B
Bailey, G.   360, 386
Bar-Shalom, E.   81, 91
Barrière, I.   13, 15
Bartsch, R.   144, 157
Beam, R.   11, 15
Beckman, J.   103, 113
Behrens, B.   145, 157

Beider, A.   218, 231
Beijbom, U.   12, 15
Beniak, É.   203, 216
Benmamoun, E.   72–76, 81–82, 86–87, 89, 91
Benor, S.   4, 7, 179, 196, 217, 219–220, 222, 228, 230–232
Bentahila, A.   251–252
Bentzen, K.   28, 33, 44–45, 50, 53–55, 69
Benwell, B.   329, 356
Bernstein, C.   225, 232
Bessason, H.   74–75, 77–78, 80, 92
Bhasin, N.   232
Blackledge, A.   330, 358
Blake, R.   87, 92
Blakemore, D.   191, 196
Blanc, M.   236, 242, 253
Blommaert, J.   346, 356
Boas, H.   117–130, 262–264, 276, 278, 303, 321, 373, 376, 386
Boersma, P.   237, 253
Bohnacker, U.   42, 44
Bonet, E.   149, 157
Borer, H.   167, 176
Born   47, 69
Bothorel-Witz, A.   125, 130
Bousquette, J.   4, 7, 13, 15, 219, 232, 234, 236–237, 240–241, 250–253, 257, 278, 391
Boyd, S.   365, 386
Bøyum, B.   324, 358
Bradley, T.   105, 114
Brister, L.   118, 130
Brockmeir, J.   356
Brody, J.   185, 196
Brøseth, H.   167, 176
Brown, J.   4, 7, 42, 44, 124, 130, 135, 147, 158, 167, 203, 215
Bruner, J.   330, 356
Bucholtz, M.   329, 356

Buffington, A.   11, 15
Burke, D.   48, 69
Burridge, K.   14, 135–136, 147, 154, 156, 158, 276, 278
Busterud, G.   266, 278
Bybee, J.   154, 158

C
Calabrese, A.   251, 253
Capps, L.   328, 358
Carbaugh, D.   328, 356
Cardinaletti, A.   24, 44
Carlson, G.   136, 141, 158
Carstairs, A.   395, 404
Cederström, M.   235, 253
Chen, M.   101, 110–112, 114
Chernikoff, H.   218, 232
Chomsky, N.   148–149, 158, 168–172, 175–176, 241, 250, 253
Clardy, C.   119–121, 124, 130
Clyne, M.   205–206, 216, 238–239, 253, 376, 386
Coates, J.   263, 266, 275, 278
Cohen, S.   218, 220, 229, 232–233
Columbus, S.   364, 366, 386
Comrie, B.   154, 158
Crosby, C.   242, 254
Cummins, J.   381, 386

D
Dahlstedt, K.-H.   367, 386
De Bot, K.   355–356
De Fina, A.   328–330, 356–357
Dijkstra, T.   254
Dorian, N.   254, 390, 404
Dowty, D.   136, 141, 158
Dubois, S.   219, 232

E
Eckman, F.   99, 114
Ehresmann, T.   4, 7, 13, 15, 219, 232, 234, 236–237, 240, 250, 252–253, 257, 278, 391

Eide, K.   4, 49, 69, 163, 205, 219, 232, 256, 268, 278, 378, 382, 386
Eikel, F.   117–121, 124–125, 127–130
Eiríksson, H.   79, 92
Elšik, V.   265, 278
Embick, D.   135, 155
Endresen, R.   105, 114
Engdahl, E.   378, 386
Eyþórsson, Þ.   89, 92, 303, 321

F
Faarlund, J.-T.   15, 24, 31, 44, 52, 69, 262, 278, 299, 302
Fábregas, A.   149, 158
Fader, A.   13, 15, 218, 232
Fader, A.   13, 15, 218, 232
Fairbanks, G.   111, 114
Fishman, J.   2, 6, 13, 15–16, 325, 358
Flaten, N.   256, 278, 283, 296
Flege, J.   100, 114–115
Flom, G.   256, 278, 283, 296–297
Fraurud, K.   365, 386
Freed, B.   81, 92
Frey, B.   9, 11, 15, 17, 235, 240, 252–253
Frey, W.   9, 11, 15, 17, 235, 240, 252–253
Fuller, J.   131, 135, 158, 196, 276, 279

G
Gachelin, J.-M.   154, 158
Galema, A.   12–13, 15, 239, 253
Gans, H.   230, 232
Ganuza, N.   381, 386
Georgakopoulou, A.   328–329, 356–357
Gibbs, R.   334, 357
Gilbert, G.   8, 15, 117–123, 125–126, 128, 130–131, 159, 279
Golden, A.   4, 189, 283, 297, 323, 328, 330, 335, 357
Grosjean, F.   2, 15, 241, 253

H
Håberg, L.   318, 321
Hagen, K.   44, 70, 115, 216, 322

Hagren, K.   384, 386
Håkansson, G.   44, 89, 92, 374, 386
Haldeman, S.   11, 15
Hale, K.   135, 142, 158, 176, 310–311
Hall, K.   113, 252, 329, 356
Halmari, H.   260, 279
Hamers, J.   236, 242, 253
Hansen, M.   196, 230, 232
Harbert, W.   245, 253
Harré, R.   330, 357
Hasselmo, N.   12, 15, 259, 359–362, 366, 369, 373–375, 377–378, 381, 386
Haugen, E.   2, 10, 15, 75, 78, 92, 98–100, 108–109, 114, 159, 161, 164–165, 176, 201, 204–207, 210, 212–216, 235, 239, 252–253, 257, 259–262, 270, 279, 283, 285–292, 295, 297, 300, 312–314, 317, 319–321, 326, 357, 375, 386
Hedblom, F.   360–369, 372–373, 376–378, 382, 386
Heine, B.   192–193, 196
Helleland, B.   115, 305, 322
Higginbotham, J.   143, 158
Hjelde, A.   4, 41, 44, 46, 49, 69, 78, 92, 97–98, 102, 114, 161, 163–165, 176, 202, 205, 210, 213, 216, 219, 232, 235, 253, 256–257, 259–261, 279, 283, 294, 297, 299, 312, 320–321, 325–326, 357, 360, 373, 378, 382, 386
Hof, S.   363–366, 386
Hofmann, R.   268, 279
Holand, H.   285, 297
Holmberg, A.   169, 176, 321
Holthe, A.   317, 321
Honeybone, P.   100, 114
Horowitz, B.   230, 232
Horvath, B.   219, 232
House, A.   17, 92, 111, 114, 130, 297, 404
Howell, R.   14, 99, 114, 137, 158
Huffines, L.   11, 16, 135, 146–147, 156, 158

I
Ibarra, R.   295, 297, 325, 343, 357
Idsardi, W.   100, 113, 237, 252
Isaacs, M.   13, 16, 218, 232
Iverson, G.   97, 99–100, 114, 237, 254

J
Jacobs, N.   14, 16, 179, 181, 196
Jakobson, R.   46–47, 70, 87, 92
Jenshus, G.   307, 321
Johannessen, J.   1, 3–4, 10, 16, 37, 41–42, 44, 46–47, 49, 63, 65, 67–68, 70, 73, 88, 91–92, 97–98, 102–103, 115, 161, 176, 202, 207, 211, 213, 216, 235, 254, 257, 267, 279, 283, 290, 297, 299–302, 311, 317, 320–322, 360, 362, 366, 368, 373, 375, 379–382, 384, 387
Johansen, K.   257, 279
Johnson-Weiner, K.   11, 16
Johnson, M.   11, 16, 334, 357
Johnstone, B.   219, 232
Jónsson, J.   14, 84, 92
Jordan, T.   118, 130
Joseph, J.   325, 357–358
Jucker, A.   191, 196
Julien, M.   23, 34, 44, 52–53, 70

K
Kagan, O.   2, 16
Kahan Newman, Z.   4, 7, 178–179, 181, 189, 196, 218, 232, 257, 279
Källström, R.   381, 386–387
Karstadt, A.   360, 387
Karttunen, F.   81, 92
Katz, D.   14, 16, 179, 196, 218, 232
Kaufman, D.   225, 230, 232
Keijzer, M.   47, 69
Kelman, A.   229, 232
Kerswill, P.   8, 16, 117, 135, 287, 295–297, 363, 373, 387
Keyser, J.   112, 115, 142, 158
Kim, J.   73, 86, 91–92, 142, 158
King, K.   45, 354, 357
Kloss, H.   11, 16, 118, 130
Kochetov, A.   100, 115
Kolmer, A.   241, 254

Index of names

Kominski, R.   17, 233
König, W.   123, 130, 196
Königs, K.   144, 158
Koostra, G.   241, 250, 254
Köpke, B.   47, 71
Kotler-Berkowitz, L.   220, 233
Kövecses, Z.   334, 357
Krabbendam, H.   7, 16
Kristjánsson, J.   9, 16, 74, 92
Kristoffersen, G.   100, 103, 104, 115
Kristoffersen, K.   15, 50, 52, 55, 70
Krogh, S.   178, 197
Krueger, R.   326, 357
Kuteva, T.   192–193, 196

L

Laake, S.   4, 10, 16, 41–42, 44, 49, 63, 70, 97, 161, 176, 202, 207, 211, 213, 216, 235, 254, 257, 267, 279, 283, 290, 297, 299–301, 311, 317, 320–322, 366, 373, 375, 379, 387
Labov, W.   80, 92, 259, 279, 328, 357, 396, 404
Lakoff, G.   334, 357
Lambert, H.   81, 92
Lambert, R.   242, 254
Landman, F.   138, 143, 158
Lane, P.   354, 357
Lantolf, J.   328, 357
Lanza, E.   4, 283, 297, 323–325, 328–330, 335, 357–358
Larsson, I.   5, 7, 41, 44, 47, 65, 67–68, 70, 122, 130, 157, 235, 254, 290, 297, 320, 322, 359–360, 362, 364, 379–382, 384–385, 387
Lasnik, H.   167, 176
Lehiste, I.   111, 115
Leuschner, T.   237, 255
Lie, S.   44, 69, 141–142, 270, 302, 322
Lipski, J.   241, 254
Lødrup, H.   15, 24, 31, 37, 39, 44–45
Lohndal, T.   14, 167, 176
Louden, M.   11, 16, 135, 156, 159, 299
Lovoll, O.   341, 358

Lubinska, D.   382, 387
Lucas, H.   69, 129, 201, 231, 235, 252, 278, 296, 321, 389, 404
Lucht, F.   9, 16, 126–127, 131, 235, 254
Lundquist, B.   15, 368, 387
Lyman, S.   230, 233
Lyttkens, I.   364, 369, 387

M

MacKay, I.   115
Maddieson, I.   124–125, 130
Maienborn, C.   136, 142, 159
Marantz, A.   167, 172, 176
Mark, Y.   16, 135, 156, 159, 179, 197, 299, 357
Markish, Peretz   182, 197
Matras, Y.   185, 197, 201–205, 207, 215–216, 235, 238, 249–250, 254, 256–257, 262–266, 268–270, 274, 277–280
Maurer, P.   154, 159
Menn, L.   83, 241, 254, 304
Miller, R.   232, 280
Mills, J.   324, 358
Milroy, L.   73, 92, 259, 280
Minkova, D.   99, 115
Moen, P.   98–99, 115
Montrul, S.   2, 16, 47, 70, 73–74, 87, 91–92, 154, 159, 380–382, 387
Mougeon, R.   203, 216
Mukherjee, D.   343, 358
Munch, P.   284–285, 295, 298, 325, 358
Muysken, P.   250, 254
Myers-Scotton, C.   163, 166–167, 176, 238, 252, 254, 259–260, 280
Myrvoll, K.   15, 299, 302, 307

N

Nagy, N.   100, 115
Nettle, D.   128, 130
Nicolini, M.   127, 130
Nilsson, J.   366, 385, 387
Nöel, D.   276, 280
Nordgård, T.   318, 322
Noreen, A.   364–365, 367, 369, 387

Nützel, D.   8, 16, 102, 115, 253, 373, 387
Nygård, M.   167, 176

O

Ochs, E.   328, 358
Odlin, T.   380, 388
Oftedal, M.   283, 286, 289, 298
Omoniyi, T.   325, 358
Osgood, C.   236, 242, 253
Östman, J.-O.   70, 262–263, 280, 387
Oswalt, R.   207, 216

P

Pagliuca, W.   158
Palmer, F.   264–265, 268, 278, 280
Papazian, E.   305, 322
Pastorius, Francis Daniel   11
Pavlenko, A.   71, 330, 358, 374, 388
Pavlenko, A.   71, 330, 358, 374, 388
Penn, William   11, 135, 158
Perkins, R.   158
Peterson, G.   111, 115
Petri, L.   131, 364, 388
Pfaff, C.   162, 177
Philipp, M.   125, 130
Pierce, M.   3, 117, 124, 128, 130
Piske, T.   100, 115
Platzack, C.   44, 54–55, 71, 169, 176
Polinsky, M.   2, 16, 47, 71–75, 77–79, 81, 86, 90–92, 149, 154, 159
Pollock, J.-Y.   168–169, 174, 177
Poplack, S.   162, 177, 259–260, 280
Popperwell, R.   103, 115
Priestley, J.   44, 115, 216, 322
Prince, E.   181, 196–197
Purnell, T.   97, 104, 110, 113, 115
Putnam, M.   2, 4, 7, 17, 42, 44, 47, 67, 70–71, 73, 76, 87–88, 91, 93, 124, 130, 135–136, 149–150, 155, 158–160, 167, 203, 215, 253, 299, 303, 322, 378, 386–388
Pylkkänen, L.   172–173, 177

Q
Qualey, C.   284, 298

R
Rabinovich, S.   181, 197
Ramchand, G.   142–143, 149, 151, 156, 159, 167, 177
Ravid, D.   196
Reed, C.   135, 145–147, 159
Richardsen, M.   322
Riessman, C.   358
Rietz, J.   379, 388
Ringen, C.   101, 103, 106–107, 113, 115–116
Roberts, S.   154, 159
Roesch, K.   117, 125–128, 130
Rognes, S.   318, 322
Romaine, S.   128, 130, 159, 203, 205, 216
Ross, J.   141, 159
Rothman, J.   2, 17, 47, 71, 102, 115, 201, 216, 235, 254, 381, 388
Rothmayr, A.   136, 142, 155, 156, 159
Rothstein, S.   136–141, 157, 160

S
Sakel, J.   256–257, 262–264, 266, 268, 270, 276, 280
Salmons, J.   1, 3, 5, 8–9, 16–17, 46, 97–98, 100, 102, 113–115, 117, 121, 123, 125–129, 131, 135, 158, 185, 197, 235, 237, 240, 253–255, 262–263, 276, 280, 283, 296, 298–299, 325, 342, 358, 373, 378, 387–388
Sánchez, L.   71, 93, 135–137, 149–150, 153, 155, 159–160
Sandøy, H.   309, 322
Sankoff, D.   259–260, 280
Sankoff, G.   202–203, 216
Sapon, S.   111, 116
Sasse, H.-J.   241, 254
Schirmunski, V.   123, 131
Schmid, M.   47, 71, 374, 388
Schoor, A.   226, 233
Schrauf, R.   355–356
Seifert, L.   278, 294, 298
Seip, D.   286
Seliger, H.   382, 388, 404

Selinker, L.   381, 388
Selmer, E.   286
Serratrice, L.   388
Shafto, M.   48, 69
Shandler, J.   14, 17, 218–219, 228, 231, 233
Sharma, D.   219, 233
Sharwood Smith, M.   396, 404
Shin, H.   13, 17, 218, 233
Sigurðsson, G.   78, 80, 87, 93
Silva-Corvalán, C.   137, 160
Simley, A.   98–99, 108–109, 115
Simon, E.   99–100, 115, 197, 237, 254–255
Simonsen, H.   50, 52, 55, 70, 113
Sipma, P.   239, 255
Skjåk, K.   307, 324, 358
Skjekkeland, M.   302, 322
Smith, C.   138, 160, 396, 404
Smits, C.   5, 312, 322, 389, 391–392, 400–402, 404–405
Smolicz, J.   324, 358
Solberg, P.   46
Soldat-Jaffe, T.   218, 233
Sorace, A.   42, 45, 153, 160, 378, 385, 388
Speth, K.   4, 49, 69, 97, 101, 124, 129, 201, 219, 231, 235, 238–239, 243, 249, 252, 257, 278, 283, 296, 312, 321, 376
Starke, M.   24, 44
Stefánsson, V.   75, 77, 93
Stevens, K.   109, 112, 115–116
Stiebels, B.   145, 160
Stokoe, E.   329, 356
Storm, J.   302, 322
Stroik, T.   149, 160
Sunde, A.   266, 280
Sundgren, E.   360, 388
Svendsen, B.   324–325, 358
Swierenga, R.   7, 17, 404–405

T
Taraldsen, K.   23, 45
Taranrød, B.   65, 71
Taube, M.   180, 197
Taylor, B.   136, 141
Taylor, M.   226, 233
Thorne, S.   328, 357
Tiersma, P.   239, 255

Tingsell, S.   5, 44, 130, 254, 297, 322, 359–360, 362, 385, 388
Toribio, A.   135, 137, 160
Torp, A.   15, 318, 321–322
Trudgill, P.   8, 16, 125, 128, 131, 177, 216, 259, 280, 287, 296–298, 386–387

U
Ukeles, J.   232

V
Vago, R.   382, 388, 404
Valois, D.   203, 216
Van Buren, P.   396, 404
Van Coetsem, F.   98–99, 102, 116
van der Auwera, J.   196, 276, 280
Van Dommelen, W.   101, 106–107, 115–116
Van Hell, J.   254
Van Hinte, J.   12, 17, 389, 404
Van Hout, A.   167, 177
Van Langenhove, L.   330, 357
Van Marle, J.   5, 7, 17, 312, 322, 389–391, 398, 400, 404–405
Van Pottelberge, J.   144–145, 160
Vangsnes, Ø.   23, 44–45, 115, 216, 318, 322
Vaux, B.   109, 116
Veltman, C.   6, 17
Vendler, Z.   138, 160
Vennemann, T.   124, 131
Vestad, J.   303–306, 309, 322
Viðarsson, H.   84, 93

W
Waggoner, D.   5, 17
Waldmann, C.   54–55, 71
Waletzky, J.   179, 197
Weenink, D.   237, 253
Weerman, F.   179, 197
Weilbacher, H.   130, 262–264, 276, 278
Weinreich, M.   233, 236
Weinreich, U.   2, 179–181, 188, 197, 218, 242, 255, 391, 405

Westergaard, M. 3, 21–22, 28, 44–45, 49–50, 54–55, 71, 73, 88, 93, 135, 154, 156, 241, 252, 283, 298, 318, 322
Wetzels, L. 251, 253
Wexler, K. 42, 45
Wexler, P. 218, 233
Widmark, G. 363–364, 367, 388

Wiesinger, P. 123, 131
Wikström, Å. 50, 55, 71
Wilkerson, M. 5, 17, 235, 240, 255, 325, 342, 358
Wilson, J. 126–127, 131
Winford, D. 99, 116, 159
Wittkofski, D. 232
Wokeck, M. 11, 17
Wortham, S. 330, 358

Wulff, F. 364, 369, 387
Wunderlich, D. 145, 160

Z
Zaretski, A. 179, 196–197
Zaretsky, E. 81, 91
Zimmerman, S. 111, 116
Ziv, Y. 191, 196

Index of subjects

A

acceptability (grammatical) 5, 148, 152, 259, 389–390, 392, 394–403
accessibility 251, 382
acquisition 2–3, 5, 16, 19, 21–22, 26, 28–31, 39–55, 65–73, 75–76, 81, 87–93, 100, 102, 114–115, 122, 154–155, 159, 202–204, 235–236, 241–243, 252, 254–255, 298, 359–360, 374, 379–382, 384–385, 387, 391
adverbs 53, 60–68, 89, 144, 180, 208, 264, 316–317, 376–377, 380
adverbials 46, 61–63, 67–68, 144, 153, 168, 174–175, 180–182, 186, 194, 212, 310, 373, 376
Affix Hopping 167, 169
agency (community) 223, 329–330, 332, 334, 355–357
agreement 51, 55, 59, 70, 81, 143, 171, 369, 383, 387
allophone 99, 119–120
American Community Survey 5–6, 17, 218, 233
American Jews 4, 217–220, 222, 230–232
Amish 11, 147, 149, 154–155, 158, 209
Anabaptists 9, 11, 16, 147, 158
anaphor 86, 378
archaisms 307, 309, 311
aspiration (phonetic) 97, 105, 114, 254
attrition 2–3, 5, 10, 19, 21–22, 37, 39–44, 46–48, 51, 65, 67–68, 71–73, 79, 81–82, 87, 89, 91–93, 102, 122, 153–154, 159, 163, 178, 193, 232, 241, 252, 279, 297–298, 359–360, 369, 374, 379–382, 384–386, 388, 391, 404

B

bilingual mind 256
bilingualism 2, 4, 9, 16–17, 40, 45, 70–71, 75, 91–93, 102, 115, 159–160, 197, 204, 216, 234–236, 238, 242, 249–254, 259, 279, 297, 326, 358, 373–374, 379–380, 385, 387–388
boomerang effect 4, 196, 217, 219, 229–231
borrowing, *see also* nonce borrowing 4, 69, 98–99, 161–163, 166, 176–177, 185, 196–197, 202–204, 206–207, 215, 232, 234–235, 238–239, 241, 243, 246, 248, 253, 256–257, 262–266, 268, 270, 276, 279–280, 374–375
borrowing hierarchy 263, 266
reborrowing 99–100

C

Canada 9–10, 47, 70, 72, 74, 78, 88–89, 123, 354, 404
Catholic 7, 267, 325
census 5–6, 9, 13, 17, 74, 218, 233, 240, 249–250, 284, 298, 325–326
codeswitching 176, 252, 254, 259, 279–280, 383
comparisons 29, 51, 71, 100, 144–145, 299, 345
complexity 3, 21–22, 26, 28, 30, 40–41, 43, 99, 131, 354, 365
compositional definiteness 44, 46–47, 50, 52–53, 55, 58, 65–66, 68–69
consecutive word order 180
contrastive focus 25
conventionalization 375
convergence 4, 16, 44, 69, 124, 130, 135, 137, 153, 155, 158, 160, 197, 201, 203–204, 212–213, 216, 256, 269, 277, 280, 297, 376–377, 380, 383, 385
Convergence Hypothesis 137, 153
Coon Valley 33, 36, 257–258, 260, 267, 283–287, 290, 292, 297, 323, 325, 327–328, 330–333, 336–337, 341, 343, 345, 351–355
corpus 3–4, 25–26, 36, 39–41, 44–45, 49–50, 56–57, 59, 62–65, 69–70, 77, 80, 103, 105, 115, 185, 187–196, 207, 211, 216–218, 223–227, 229, 231, 256, 260, 301, 303, 307–312, 315–317, 322, 359, 387, 390, 392, 394–395, 400
Corpus of American Norwegian Speech 49, 56–57, 59, 62–65, 69–70, 207, 216
cultural artifacts 323, 335, 336, 337, 348, 353, 354

D

dative 42, 69, 82, 84–86, 124–125, 290, 292–295, 302–304, 306, 311–312, 319, 321
definiteness 21, 23–24, 31–34, 40, 42–44, 46–47, 50–53, 55–59, 65–66, 68–69, 303
deontic 256, 265, 268–269, 272–274, 276–277
derivation 161, 173, 175–176
dialect 1–2, 4, 7–8, 10–12, 14–16, 23, 25, 28, 32, 34, 39, 41, 43–44, 48–50, 53, 59, 63, 69–70, 92–93, 98, 101–103, 105, 113–119, 121, 123–125, 129–131, 143, 145–146, 178–179, 185–186, 197, 210–211, 216, 232–233, 253–254, 257, 260–263, 265, 267, 278–280,

283–313, 315, 317–322, 325–326, 353, 359–360, 362–370, 372–374, 376, 378–380, 384–387, 391, 404–405
dialect contact   211, 284, 319, 365, 373–374
diglossia   204, 234–235, 250, 252
discourse marker   178, 181, 185, 191, 256–257, 271, 274–277, 332
domain loss   372, 383
double definiteness   23
duration   97, 106–112, 114–116, 136, 145, 157

E
embedded language   166–167, 251
epistemic   256, 263–265, 268–269, 272–278
ethnicity   217, 228, 230–232, 285, 297, 354, 357–358, 394
evidential   256, 268–269, 272–275, 277

F
finite verbs   53–54, 62, 64, 88–89, 305, 314, 373, 378
fortis   97, 99, 101, 103–112, 116
frequency   3–4, 21–22, 25–26, 28, 30, 38, 40–45, 79, 145, 163, 192, 195, 207–208, 212, 215, 220, 234–235, 241, 243, 246, 249–250, 260, 273, 276
Friesland   12–13, 236–237, 239, 243, 253
function words   208, 214, 257, 262–263, 300, 306–307, 309, 312–315, 319–321, 376

G
grammar   2, 4–5, 8, 15, 24, 35, 40, 42, 44–46, 48–49, 51, 63, 69, 75, 78, 80, 87, 127, 137, 143, 149–150, 152–156, 158, 160, 162, 166–167, 171, 173, 178–179, 196, 207, 215, 241, 253, 255, 257, 276, 278, 299–300, 312, 321, 361, 382, 391
grammaticalization   145, 147, 157, 178, 192–193

Gudbrandsdalen   257, 285, 287–289, 291–293, 296, 300–302, 304, 307, 311, 317, 321, 325

H
Haredi   13, 16, 178, 196–197, 218, 230, 232
Hasidim   13–14, 178–179, 185–186, 218, 232, 279
heritage language   2, 10–11, 15, 44, 46–47, 49, 71–77, 79, 81, 86, 88, 90–93, 97, 102, 113, 129, 159, 201, 219, 231, 234–235, 253, 283, 296–297, 299–300, 323–324, 328, 330, 332, 342, 351, 354–355, 359–360, 380–381, 385, 387–388
heritage community   241, 323–324
Hutterites   9

I
identity constructions   4, 323, 328–330, 335–337, 354–355, 357
immigration   2, 7, 10, 12–13, 16–17, 49, 73–75, 90, 110, 114, 118, 158, 203–204, 217, 220–222, 229, 231, 236, 239–240, 287–288, 295, 320, 325–326, 361, 365, 390, 404
imposition   98–99, 108
incomplete acquisition   2, 16, 46–47, 65, 67–68, 70–71, 81, 88, 91–93, 102, 154–155, 159, 241, 378, 380–381, 384, 387
indefinite determiner   46–47, 51–52, 55, 57, 65–66, 68
infinitives   45, 144, 147, 164–165, 262, 269, 288–290, 294, 296, 304–305, 314, 367, 384, 388, 392–395, 397
inflection   42, 50, 59, 161–162, 164–171, 173, 175–176, 261, 305–306, 313–314, 319–320, 367, 375, 391–398, 402–405
information structure   24, 28, 45
interaction   13, 71, 73, 78, 102, 129, 147, 149, 157, 203, 207, 230, 235–237, 241, 250–252,

264, 285, 323–324, 327–332, 334, 337, 339, 344, 350–357
Interface Hypothesis   42
interview   41, 77–80, 92–93, 101, 122–123, 148, 194, 207, 236–237, 240, 243, 249–250, 257, 260, 290, 326, 330, 358, 360–361, 366, 368, 372, 390
intervocalic voicing   98
Iowa   7–8, 10, 12–13, 207, 215, 239, 244, 246, 257, 299, 326, 390–391, 404

K
kinship terms   34, 36, 38, 41, 43, 267
koiné   4–5, 7, 10, 12, 283–284, 286–287, 292, 294–296, 359, 363, 373, 376, 379
koinéization   283, 287, 302, 321, 359–360, 373–374, 385

L
language attrition   21–22, 37, 39, 41, 43, 46–47, 72, 81, 87, 92, 122, 360, 380–382, 385–386, 388, 391, 404
language change   16, 92, 98, 124–125, 232, 278, 283, 374, 388
language contact   2, 4, 16, 70, 72, 90, 92, 98–100, 114–117, 125, 137, 160, 163, 196–197, 202–205, 213, 216, 253–254, 257, 262–264, 266, 268–270, 278–280, 297, 303, 322, 326, 359, 363, 369, 372, 382, 384, 386–387, 391, 405
language maintenance   16, 118, 128–131, 253, 323–326, 342–344, 358
language preference   331, 351, 353
language shift   3, 7, 9, 11, 15, 17, 91, 128–129, 158, 231, 235, 253, 287, 323–324, 354–355, 357–358
laryngeal contrasts   98, 101, 115
laryngeal features   97, 100
laryngeal phonetics   97, 100, 115
laryngeal phonology   97, 113–114

Index of subjects   417

Laryngeal Realism   100, 104, 114
late lexical insertion   167
lenis   97–98, 106–107, 110–113, 116
lenition   102, 121
leveling (dialect)   8–9, 12, 288, 292, 359, 363, 369–370, 372–373, 385
lexical retrieval   79, 382
lexical transfer   201–202, 205–210, 212–215, 241, 380
lexical words   205, 300, 309–313, 315–317, 319–320
lexicon   3–4, 10, 47, 71–72, 74, 77–79, 124, 129, 131, 154, 159, 161–163, 167–170, 173–177, 201–203, 205, 214–215, 217–218, 234, 238–239, 243, 246, 250–252, 268, 277, 299–300, 311, 314, 321, 359, 368, 372, 375–376, 378–379, 382, 385, 402
literacy   5, 39, 73, 75, 79, 102, 357, 381
loanwords, *see also* borrowing   4, 35, 38, 43, 77–79, 124, 130, 162–163, 204, 206, 217–223, 227–230, 235, 257, 259–260, 262, 278, 296–297
Lutheran   11, 325, 342

M

Manitoba   9, 15, 74, 78–80, 91–93, 385
markedness   117–118, 124, 159, 278
matrix language   158, 166–168, 171, 173–174, 235, 238, 251
matter replication   256, 264–266, 268, 270, 276–277
MAT   64, 258, 266, 268, 276
Mennonites   11, 147, 158
method   50, 92, 111, 183, 202, 220, 236, 238, 280, 319
Midwest   7–8, 10, 12, 16, 38, 49, 70, 97–98, 101–102, 110–113, 115, 201–202, 206, 216, 235, 243, 252, 254, 286, 294, 299–301, 307, 311–312, 321–322, 337, 341, 386–387, 389

Minnesota   10, 12, 33, 38, 98, 101, 108, 115, 165, 207, 211, 215, 257, 260, 325–326, 358–361, 366, 369, 375–376, 382, 385
mixing (dialect)   77, 161, 163, 166, 177, 254, 359, 372–374
modality   158, 205, 256–257, 263–266, 268, 274, 276–278, 280
mood   86, 88, 92, 137, 159, 280
Moravians   11
morphological change   81, 288
morphology   3–4, 10, 35, 40, 42–43, 73, 81–83, 91–92, 157, 160–161, 167, 174, 207, 251, 283, 291, 298, 300, 303, 306–307, 311, 368–370, 374, 378, 386, 403–404
multilingual repertoire   69, 129, 201–203, 207, 231, 252, 278, 296, 321

N

names   57, 78, 82, 135, 223–224, 227–229, 244, 246, 267, 312, 327, 352, 364, 403
narratives   178–180, 182, 184–190, 193, 197, 232, 279, 323, 328–330, 337, 341, 345, 351, 354–358
negation   46–47, 53–55, 63–69, 289–291, 293–294, 307, 367–368
neo-constructional   167, 176
newspaper   8–10, 13, 38–39, 76, 118, 127, 217–218, 223, 225–226, 290, 315, 320, 345–346, 353, 361, 380–382
nonce borrowing   162–163
NorAmDiaSyn   1, 33, 41, 46, 49, 207, 216, 257, 286, 294, 299, 326–327, 342–343, 350–351, 353
Nordic Dialect Corpus   4, 41, 44, 103, 105, 115, 211, 216, 301, 308–310, 312, 322, 387
norms, grammatical   5, 196, 287, 292, 295, 312, 322, 329, 389, 392, 394–396, 398, 400, 402–404
North Dakota   9, 74, 76–77, 79–80, 90–91, 93, 260

noun phrase   46, 51–52, 55–56, 58–60, 62, 65–66, 68
null theory   167

O

order of acquisition   28, 46, 49, 51, 66, 68

P

passive voicing   97, 101, 106–107, 109, 113
pattern replication   256, 266, 268, 270, 274, 276–277
PAT   150, 152, 266, 268, 276
phonemic transfer   201, 205–206, 208–209, 211–215, 239
phonetic enhancement   109, 112, 114
phonological change   89, 95, 114, 253, 279, 297
phonological contrast   109
phonology   3–4, 10, 14, 49, 72, 74, 80–81, 89, 91, 97–100, 103–104, 109, 113–117, 125, 129, 168–169, 179, 207, 234, 236, 247, 250–251, 253–255, 278, 283, 296–297, 368, 370, 372
positioning   5, 323, 330, 332, 342, 351, 357–358
possessive   21–45, 71, 93, 147, 156, 252, 298, 368
prenominal   21–28, 30–33, 35–44, 52
postnominal   21–37, 39–44
prepositional phrase   146, 181, 377
PPs   61, 66
preposition   56, 60, 68, 82, 143, 146, 208, 262, 267, 272, 277, 303, 376–377, 380, 384
preterite   391–393, 395–397, 400–401
privative   100–101, 241
privativity   104
probe – goal   171, 173
pronoun   24, 59, 62, 65, 146, 289–292, 294, 296, 303, 306, 367–368, 378

R

real-time change   4, 281
Reformed   11
regression hypothesis
　37, 46–47, 49, 66, 68, 70, 87
root   82, 142–143, 172–175,
　260, 268, 291, 293–294, 304,
　367, 375

S

second language acquisition,
　see acquisition   5, 40, 71, 92,
　100, 114, 122, 159, 374
semantic bleaching   192
semantic transfer   82, 201–202,
　205–206, 208–211, 214–215
sentence-initial   60, 63, 66,
　180–183, 186, 191, 193–194, 378
sonorant devoicing   97–98,
　100–101, 103–105, 113
sound change   117, 129
South Dakota   10, 257
spread glottis (phonological
　feature)   100–101, 104, 107,
　109
subject-first language   181, 196
subject-verb inversion   4, 178,
　180, 181, 187, 194, 378
subjunctive   81, 86–88, 91
subordinate clauses   28, 46–47,
　50, 53–55, 63–68, 386
substrate   4, 217–219
survey   5–7, 17, 76, 91, 101,
　217–223, 225, 229, 231, 233,
　253, 285, 359, 361
syntax   3–4, 10, 42–44, 70–72,
　74, 81, 88, 91–92, 98, 115, 135,
　142, 149, 153–154, 156–161, 166,
　169–170, 173, 175–177, 207, 253,
　279, 317, 319–322, 326, 368,
　378, 382, 386

T

tense   39, 50, 81–82, 120, 137,
　143, 155–171, 173, 175, 211,
　257, 261, 264–265, 271–272,
　278–279, 291–293, 295–296,
　305–306, 314, 316, 370, 374,
　392–397, 400
tense affix   161–162, 165
tense inflection   161–162,
　164–171, 173, 175
topic-first language   181
topicalization   46–47, 54–55,
　60, 67–68, 181, 197
transfer   38, 79, 82, 84, 86, 91,
　116, 201–202, 204–215, 234,
　239, 241, 251, 257, 263, 374–
　375, 378–380, 385, 391

U

unrounding   83, 120–123, 126,
　128–129

V

V-to-T movement   167, 169–171
V3   46–47, 53–55, 60, 62,
　64–68, 89, 318, 322
variation (linguistic)   4, 7, 16,
　21–22, 28, 32, 38, 40, 43–44, 71,
　73, 75, 77–78, 80, 82, 90, 93,
　105, 113–115, 121, 125, 130, 149,
　223, 232, 243, 252, 254, 272,
　280–281, 283, 285, 287–288,
　291–295, 297–298, 302, 312,
　320–322, 325, 341, 359–360,
　363–364, 369, 373, 378–380,
　384–388, 391–392, 394–395
verb second (V2)   46–47, 378
V2 attrition   178, 193, 232, 279
V2-violations   378, 380–383
verb   4, 37, 46–47, 53–54,
　60–66, 69–70, 81–86, 88–89,
　91, 138, 142, 144–145, 148, 159,
　161–173, 175–182, 184–187,
　189–195, 206, 208, 210–211,
　213, 256–257, 261, 265–267,
　271–272, 292, 296, 305–307,
　310, 313–314, 316, 318–319, 373,
　378–379, 384, 386–387, 390,
　392–393, 397, 400–401, 405
verbal inflection   367
vocabulary   4–5, 204, 214, 243,
　246, 257–260, 262, 278, 283,
　288, 296, 299, 311–312, 321,
　326, 352, 370, 372–374, 376,
　379, 384, 403
voice (phonological feature)
　25, 99–100, 144, 156, 158,
　188, 388
vowels   3, 89–90, 101, 103, 106,
　114, 117–126, 128–130, 186,
　308, 367
VP-ellipsis   378

W

Westby   33, 36, 257, 260, 267,
　283–284, 286–287, 290, 292,
　300–302, 305, 325, 341
Wisconsin   1, 4–5, 7–8, 10,
　12–13, 15–17, 33, 61, 97, 101,
　110, 113, 135, 201, 207, 215,
　232, 234–238, 241, 246,
　249–250, 252–255, 257, 260,
　278, 283–284, 286, 296–298,
　312, 324–326, 338, 357–358,
　390–391, 405
word order   4, 21–24, 27–28,
　30, 34–35, 38–40, 42–47, 50,
　54–55, 60, 62–68, 70–71, 81,
　89, 93, 127, 180, 185, 191–193,
　252, 254, 257, 298, 313, 318–319,
　360, 373, 378–379, 381–382,
　387, 394

Y

YIVO   14–15, 197